Second Course

HOLT
Literature
&Language
Arts

 Mastering the California Standards
Reading · Writing · Listening · Speaking

 HOLT, RINEHART AND WINSTON

A Harcourt Classroom Education Company

Austin • New York • Orlando • Atlanta • San Francisco • Boston • Dallas • Toronto • London

EDITORIAL
Project Directors: Kathleen Daniel, Mescal Evler
Executive Editors: Juliana Koenig, Kristine E. Marshall
Manager of Operations and Planning: Bill Wahlgren
Managing Editors: Marie Price, Mike Topp
Manager of Editorial Services: Abigail Winograd
Senior Product Manager: Don Wulbrecht
Editorial Staff: Jane Archer-Feinstein, Susan Kent Cakars, Mikki Gibson, Annie Hartnett, Sean W. Henry, Julie Barnett Hoover, Tressa Sanders, Errol Smith, Amy Strong, Suzanne Thompson, Michael Zakhar
Copyediting Manager: Michael Neibergall
Copyediting Supervisor: Mary Malone
Copyeditors: Christine Altgelt, Joel Bourgeois, Elizabeth Dickson, Emily Force, Julie A. Hill, Julia Thomas Hu, Barbara Coeyman Hults, Jennifer Kirkland, Millicent Ondras, Dennis Scharnberg
Project Administration: Lori de la Garza, *Editorial Operations Supervisor;* Elizabeth LaManna, *Editorial Finance Manager*
Editorial Support: Renée Benitez, Louise Fernandez, Christine Han, Mark Holland, Ruth Hooker, Bret Isaacs, Marcus Johnson, Laurie Muir, Joie D. Pickett, Margaret Sanchez, Kelly Tankersley, Tom Ver Gow
Editorial Permissions: David Smith, Carrie Jones

Index: Alana Cash

ART, DESIGN, AND PRODUCTION
Director: Athena Blackorby
Senior Design Director: Betty Mintz
Design: Fred Yee, Rich Colicchio, Peter Sawchuk
Design and Electronic Files: Kirchoff/Wohlberg, Inc.; Preface, Inc.
Photo Research: Kirchoff/Wohlberg, Inc.; Omni–Photo Communications, Inc.
Photo Researcher: Richard Benavides, Image Acquisitions
Art Buyer Supervisor: Michelle Rumpf, Image Acquisitions
Production Manager: Catherine Gessner
Production Coordinator: Dolores Keller
Production Assistant: Myles Gorospe

Program Authors

Kylene Beers established the reading pedagogy for Part 1 of *Holt Literature and Language Arts* and wrote the lessons in the Reading Matters section of the book. A former middle-school teacher, Dr. Beers has turned her commitment to helping readers having difficulty into the major focus of her research, writing, speaking, and teaching. A clinical associate professor at the University of Houston, Dr. Beers is also currently the editor of the National Council of Teachers of English journal *Voices from the Middle*. She is the author of *When Kids Can't Read: The Reading Handbook for Teachers Grades 6–12* and co-editor of *Into Focus: Understanding and Creating Middle School Readers*. She has served on the review boards of the *English Journal* and *The Alan Review*. Dr. Beers currently serves on the board of directors of the International Reading Association's Special Interest Group on Adolescent Literature.

Lee Odell helped establish the pedagogical framework for Part 2 of *Holt Literature and Language Arts*. Dr. Odell is Professor of Composition Theory and Research and, since 1996, Director of the Writing Program at Rensselaer Polytechnic Institute. He began his career teaching English in middle and high schools. More recently he has worked with teachers in grades K–12 to establish a program that involves students from all disciplines in writing across the curriculum and for communities outside their classrooms. Dr. Odell's most recent book (with Charles R. Cooper) is *Evaluating Writing: The Role of Teacher's Knowledge About Text, Learning, and Culture*. He is Past Chair of the Conference on College Composition and Communication and of NCTE's Assembly for Research. Dr. Odell is currently working on a college-level writing textbook.

Special Contributors

Flo Ota De Lange and **Sheri Henderson** helped plan and organize the program and played key roles in developing and preparing the informational materials.

Flo Ota De Lange is a former teacher with a thirty-year second career in psychotherapy, during which she studied learning processes in children and adults. These careers have led to her third career, as a writer.

Sheri Henderson brings to the program twenty years of experience as a California middle-school research practitioner and full-time reading and language arts teacher at La Paz Intermediate School in Saddleback Valley Unified School District. She regularly speaks at statewide and national conferences.

Since 1991, DeLangeHenderson LLC has published forty-three titles designed to integrate the teaching of literature with standards requirements and state and national tests.

Writers

John Malcolm Brinnin, author of six volumes of poetry that have received many prizes and awards, was a member of the American Academy and Institute of Arts and Letters. He was a critic of poetry and a biographer of poets and was for a number of years Director of New York's famous Poetry Center. His teaching career, begun at Vassar College, included long terms at the University of Connecticut and Boston University, where he succeeded Robert Lowell as Professor of Creative Writing and Contemporary Letters. Mr. Brinnin wrote *Dylan Thomas in America: An Intimate Journal* and *Sextet: T. S. Eliot & Truman Capote & Others.*

John Leggett is a novelist, biographer, and teacher. He went to the Writer's Workshop at the University of Iowa in the spring of 1969, expecting to work there for a single semester. In 1970, he assumed temporary charge of the program, and for the next seventeen years he was its director. Mr. Leggett's novels include *Wilder Stone, The Gloucester Branch, Who Took the Gold Away?, Gulliver House,* and *Making Believe.* He is also the author of the highly acclaimed biography *Ross and Tom: Two American Tragedies* and of a biography of William Saroyan, *A Daring Young Man.* Mr. Leggett lives in California's Napa Valley.

Joan Burditt is a writer and editor who has a master's degree in education with a specialization in reading. She taught for several years in Texas, where her experience included work in programs for readers having difficulty. Since then she has developed and written instructional materials for middle-school language arts texts.

Madeline Travers Hovland, who taught middle school for several years, is a writer of educational materials. She studied English at Bates College and received a master's degree in education from Harvard University.

Richard Kelso is a writer and editor whose children's books include *Building a Dream: Mary Bethune's School; Walking for Freedom: The Montgomery Bus Boycott; Days of Courage: The Little Rock Story;* and *The Case of the Amistad Mutiny.*

Mara Rockliff is a writer and editor with a degree in American civilization from Brown University. She has written dramatizations of classic stories for middle-school students, collected in a book called *Stories for Performance.* She has also published feature stories in national newspapers and is currently writing a novel for young adults.

Program Consultants

SENIOR PROGRAM CONSULTANT

Carol Jago is the editor of CATE's quarterly journal, *California English.* She teaches English at Santa Monica High School, in Santa Monica, and directs the California Reading and Literature Project at UCLA. She also writes a weekly education column for the *Los Angeles Times.* She is the author of several books, including two in a series on contemporary writers in the classroom: *Alice Walker in the Classroom* and *Nikki Giovanni in the Classroom.* She is also the author of *With Rigor for All: Teaching the Classics to Contemporary Students* and *Beyond Standards: Excellence in the High School English Classroom.*

CONTENT-AREA READING CONSULTANT

Judith L. Irvin served as a reading consultant for the content-area readers for *Holt Literature and Language Arts: The Ancient World; A World in Transition;* and *The United States: Change and Challenge.* Dr. Irvin is a Professor of Education at Florida State University. She writes a column, "What Research Says to the Middle Level Practitioner," for the *Middle School Journal* and serves as the literacy expert for the *Middle Level News,* published by the California League of Middle Schools. Her several books include the companion volumes *Reading and the Middle School Student: Strategies to Enhance Literacy* and *Reading and the High School Student: Strategies to Enhance Literacy* (with Buehl and Klemp).

ADVISORS
Dr. Julie M. T. Chan
Director of Literacy Instruction
Newport-Mesa Unified School District
Costa Mesa, California

Cheri Howell
Reading Specialist
Covina-Valley Unified School District
Covina, California

José M. Ibarra-Tiznado
ELL Program Coordinator
Bassett Unified School District
La Puente, California

Dr. Ronald Klemp
Instructor
California State University, Northridge
Northridge, California

Fern M. Sheldon
K–12 Curriculum and Instruction Specialist
Rowland Unified School District
Rowland Heights, California

CRITICAL REVIEWERS
Josephine M. Hayes
Costa Mesa High School
Costa Mesa, California

Stacy Kim
Rowland Unified School District
Rowland Heights, California

Jennifer Oehrlein
Tewinkle Middle School
Costa Mesa, California

Beverly Sparks
John W. North High School
Riverside, California

FIELD-TEST PARTICIPANTS
Karen G. Armstrong
William Dandy Middle School
Fort Lauderdale, Florida

Joyce Patterson
Stewart Middle School
Tampa, Florida

Christina Scarpaci
South Hills Middle School
Pittsburgh, Pennsylvania

Sean Stromberg
South Hills Middle School
Pittsburgh, Pennsylvania

PART 1   **Mastering the California Standards in Reading**

Chapter

Structures: Patterns of Meaning

Standards Focus

Vocabulary Development 1.1 Analyze idioms, analogies, metaphors, and similes to infer the literal and figurative meanings of phrases.

Vocabulary Development 1.2 Understand the most important points in the history of the English language, and use common word origins to determine the historical influences on English word meanings.

Reading Comprehension (Focus on Informational Materials) 2.2 Analyze text that uses proposition and support patterns.

Literary Response and Analysis 3.2 Evaluate the structural elements of the plot (for example, subplots, parallel episodes, climax), the plot's development, and the way in which conflicts are (or are not) addressed and resolved.

**Mastering
the Standards**

Chapter

Characters: Doing the Right Thing

 Standards Focus

Vocabulary Development 1.2 Understand the most important points in the history of the English language, and use common word origins to determine the historical influences on English word meanings.

Reading Comprehension (Focus on Informational Materials) 2.3 Find similarities and differences between texts in the treatment, scope, or organization of ideas.

Literary Response and Analysis 3.3 Compare and contrast motivations and reactions of literary characters from different historical eras confronting similar situations or conflicts.

**Mastering
the Standards**

Chapter

Being There: Setting

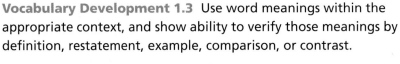

Standards Focus

Vocabulary Development 1.3 Use word meanings within the appropriate context, and show ability to verify those meanings by definition, restatement, example, comparison, or contrast.

Literary Response and Analysis 3.4 Analyze the relevance of the setting (for example, place, time, customs) to the mood, tone, and meaning of the text.

Chapter

4

We Still Believe

 **Standards Focus**

Vocabulary Development 1.3 Use word meanings within the appropriate context, and show ability to verify those meanings by definition, restatement, example, comparison, or contrast.

Literary Response and Analysis 3.5 Identify and analyze recurring themes (for example, good versus evil) across traditional and contemporary works.

Mastering
the Standards

Chapter

Imagine That! Literary Devices

Standards Focus

Vocabulary Development 1.1 Analyze idioms, analogies, metaphors, and similes to infer the literal and figurative meanings of phrases.

Literary Response and Analysis 3.6 Identify significant literary devices (for example, metaphor, symbolism, dialect, irony) that define a writer's style, and use those elements to interpret the work.

Contents   **A11**

Sound and Sense: Forms of Poetry

Chapter

6

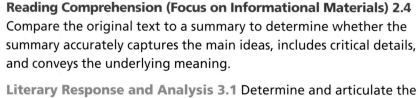

Standards Focus

Reading Comprehension (Focus on Informational Materials) 2.4
Compare the original text to a summary to determine whether the summary accurately captures the main ideas, includes critical details, and conveys the underlying meaning.

Literary Response and Analysis 3.1 Determine and articulate the relationship between the purposes and characteristics of different forms of poetry (for example, ballad, lyric, couplet, epic, elegy, ode, sonnet).

Chapter 7

Literary Criticism: The Person Behind the Text

Standards Focus

Vocabulary Development 1.1 Analyze idioms to infer the literal and figurative meanings of phrases.

Vocabulary Development 1.3 Use word meanings within the appropriate context, and show ability to verify those meanings by definition, restatement, example, comparison, or contrast.

Reading Comprehension (Focus on Informational Materials) 2.7 Evaluate the unity, coherence, logic, internal consistency, and structural patterns of text.

Literary Response and Analysis 3.7 Analyze a work of literature, showing how it reflects the heritage, traditions, attitudes, and beliefs of its author (biographical approach).

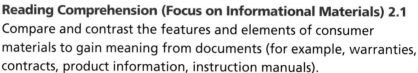

8

Reading for Life
by Sheri Henderson and Flo Ota De Lange

Standards Focus

Reading Comprehension (Focus on Informational Materials) 2.1
Compare and contrast the features and elements of consumer materials to gain meaning from documents (for example, warranties, contracts, product information, instruction manuals).

Reading Comprehension (Focus on Informational Materials) 2.5
Understand and explain the use of a complex mechanical device by following technical directions.

Reading Comprehension (Focus on Informational Materials) 2.6
Use information from a variety of consumer, workplace, and public documents to explain a situation or decision and to solve a problem.

Reading Matters by Kylene Beers 560

PART 2   **Mastering the California Standards in Writing, Listening, and Speaking**

Introduction

 Standards Focus

Writing Strategies 1.0 Students progress through the stages of the writing process.

Writing Strategies 1.1 Create compositions that establish a controlling impression.

Shoe, by Jeff MacNelly, reprinted by permission: Tribune Media Services.

Workshop

3

Technical Documents

Standards Focus

Writing Applications 2.6 Write technical documents.
Listening and Speaking Strategies 1.9 Interpret and evaluate the
various ways in which image makers (for example, illustrators)
communicate information.

Workshop

Research

Standards Focus

Writing Applications 2.3 Write research reports.
Speaking Applications 2.3 Deliver research presentations.

Workshop

Persuasion

Standards Focus

Writing Applications 2.4 Write persuasive compositions.
Speaking Applications 2.4 Deliver persuasive presentations.
Listening and Speaking Strategies 1.9 Interpret and evaluate the various ways in which visual image makers (for example, graphic artists, illustrators, news photographers) communicate information and affect impressions and opinions.

Workshop

6

Writing for Life

Standards Focus

Writing Strategies 2.5 Write documents related to career development, including simple business letters and job applications.

Learning About Paragraphs

Standards Focus

Writing Strategies 1.0 Students write clear, coherent, and focused essays. Essays contain formal introductions, supporting evidence, and conclusions.

Writing Strategies 1.1 Create compositions that establish a controlling impression, have a coherent thesis, and end with a clear and well-supported conclusion.

Writing Strategies 1.2 Establish coherence within paragraphs through effective transitions.

Writing Strategies 1.3 Support theses or conclusions with analogies, paraphrases, quotations, opinions from authorities, comparisons, and similar devices.

Writing Strategies 1.6 Revise writing for appropriate organization, consistent point of view, and transitions between passages and ideas.

Mastering the Standards ▶

Mini-Workshops

Standards Focus

Writing Applications 2.0 Students write narrative, expository, and descriptive essays.
Writing Applications 2.1 Write short stories or narratives.
Writing Applications 2.2 Write responses to literature.
Writing Applications 2.6 Write technical documents.
Listening and Speaking Applications 2.3d Organize and record information on charts, maps, and graphs.

Writing

Media

CALVIN & HOBBES © 1989 Watterson. Distributed by Universal Press Syndicate. Reprinted with permission. All rights reserved.

Resource Center

SKILLS

Literary Response and Analysis Essays

Reading Matters: Strategy Lessons

Literary Skills

SKILLS, STANDARDS, AND FEATURES

 Reading Skills for Literary Texts

 Reading Skills for Informational Texts

 Vocabulary Skills

STANDARDS

Review Standards from Earlier Grades

Vocabulary Development

Reading Comprehension

Literary Response and Analysis

Grade-Level Standards Reviews

Reading Comprehension

Literary Response and Analysis

FEATURES

Grammar Link Mini-Lessons

Focus On

Writing / Critical-Thinking / Language Mini-Lessons

Test Smarts

FICTION

Short Stories

Fables

DRAMA

POETRY

PROFESSIONAL MODELS FOR WRITING

You Can't Soar If You Can't Fly the Plane

by Kylene Beers

He was eighty-five years old when he stood in front of the younger man who was wearing a T-shirt that said "A-One Flyers." He told the flight instructor again, "I'm not leaving until you sign me up for flying lessons." The flight instructor said, "Sir, I just don't understand why, at eighty-five, you want to learn how to fly." The old man crossed his arms and said, "I'll never be able to soar if I can't fly the plane."

The man had a point, a good point: *Wanting* to soar wasn't enough to make the soaring happen. He had to know how to fly the plane if he really wanted to climb the clouds.

Think about the things you want to do—all the ways you want to soar. If you want to soar with your favorite computer games, you've got to know all the rules. If you want to soar with sports, you've got to practice. If you want to soar with your grades, you've got to study.

You Can't Soar If You Can't Read

Perhaps more than anything else in life, reading has the potential for letting you soar. With reading you can learn to do just about any-thing—from building an ark to repairing your zither (or even figuring out what a zither is). With reading you can step back in time, go forward in time, and travel to new lands. With reading you can meet characters who are just like you or as far removed from you as you can possibly imagine. Sometimes books act as mirrors, showing us characters who remind us of ourselves. At other times, books act as windows, showing us characters and situations that take us far beyond ourselves.

Sometimes we need lessons to help us accomplish all the things a skilled reader can do. This textbook is your manual for soaring—it's your pilot's lesson plan for helping you soar as high as you can.

Using the Standards to Set the Standard

This book is designed to help you master the skills you need to be a strong reader *and* writer. The California standards are your tour guide. They will lead you through this book, helping you learn the literacy skills you'll need for this year, for your remaining years in school, and for your life as a member of society.

Everyone who worked on this book—the people who chose the reading selections, the people who wrote the activities, the people who chose the artwork—continually asked themselves, "How do we create a book that not only meets the California standards but also *sets* the standard when it comes to helping students become readers and writers?" We think that as you read through this book, you'll find that we answered that question by providing you with

- interesting selections to read
- powerful models to help you learn to write
- lots of opportunities to practice new skills
- specific information about each standard—so that you will always know what is expected of you
- the kinds of topics and art that middle-schoolers have told us interest them

In this book, then, you'll get practice in all kinds of language skills.

You will read all kinds of material, from ads to odes, from stories to Web pages.

You will learn better ways to talk, listen, and write.

You will understand more, sound better, and be more confident about what you know and understand.

What's in This Book?

Holt Literature and Language Arts has three parts:

- Part 1 covers reading of all types—literature and informational texts.
- Part 2 covers writing, speaking, and listening.
- The last part of the book is a reference section, full of special activities and information you might need as you work through Parts 1 and 2.

Part 1

The chapters in Part 1 begin with an essay that explains the key standards you'll be mastering in the chapter. Then you'll read several literary selections. Following almost every literary selection, you will find some interesting readings, called informational texts. These might be newspaper or magazine articles, Web pages, instructional manuals, interviews, signs, maps, or other documents. All of these informational texts relate to the piece of literature. For example, after the story "In Trouble," about Gary Paulsen's experiences with sled dogs, you'll find an informational article about some of the breeds of dogs used to pull sleds. Along the way you'll find a lot of help in acquiring new words.

Here is a diagram showing how a chapter in Part 1 might look:

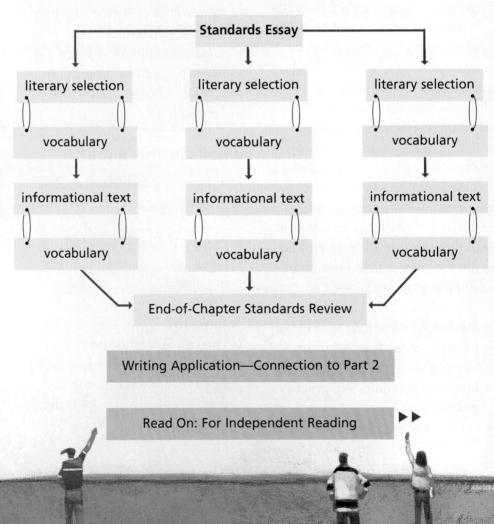

Part 2

Part 2 is a series of big and small workshops that will help you *write.* Here are workshops on writing narratives, essays, research reports, responses to literature—all the writing skills required by the California standards. Part 2 also includes workshops in listening and speaking. All of Part 2 will help you practice the writing, listening, and speaking skills that you are required to master by the end of this school year.

Part 3

Need help with a literary term? Could you use some tips for taking tests? Do you want to find out where to go for help in identifying the main idea of an informational text? Turn to Part 3. Part 3 includes a section called Test Smarts, with tips for test taking. Part 3 includes definitions of literary terms and of reading and informational terms. Part 3 includes a glossary and extensive indexes. Part 3 is your Resource Center.

A Book with a Big Idea

This is a book with a big idea—that you are going to learn a lot about your language.

This book came together because of the efforts of lots of people—writers, editors, artists, teachers, and even students like you.

Now it's time for us to hand the book to you, the reader. We hope you'll use it as a key to lifetime literacy and as a guide to lifetime reading. Enjoy!

 At our Internet site you can discover much more about the stories, poems, and informational materials in this book. You can look at how professional writers work. You can even submit your own writing for publication on an online gallery. As you use *Holt Literature and Language Arts* to master the standards, look for the very best online resources at **go.hrw.com.**

GO TO: go.hrw.com
KEYWORD: HLLA

Mastering the California Standards in Reading

vocabulary

informational materials

literature

Chapters

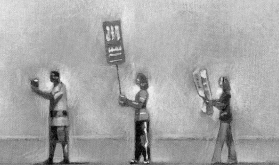

1

Structures
Patterns of Meaning

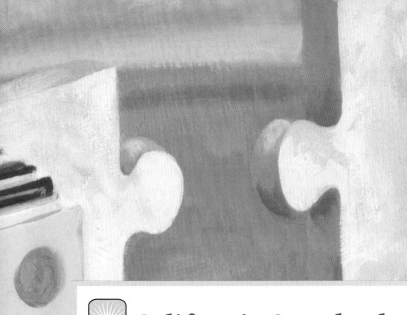

 # California Standards

Here are the Grade 8 standards you will study for mastery in Chapter 1. You will also review a standard from an earlier grade.

Reading

Word Analysis, Fluency, and Systematic Vocabulary Development

1.1 Analyze idioms, analogies, metaphors, and similes to infer the literal and figurative meanings of phrases.

1.2 Understand the most important points in the history of the English language, and use common word origins to determine the historical influences on English word meanings.

Reading Comprehension (Focus on Informational Materials)

2.2 Analyze text that uses proposition and support patterns.

Literary Response and Analysis

3.2 Evaluate the structural elements of the plot (for example, subplots, parallel episodes, climax), the plot's development, and the way in which conflicts are (or are not) addressed and resolved.

Grade 7 Review
3.2 Identify events that advance the plot, and determine how each event foreshadows future action(s).

KEYWORD:
HLLA 8-1

Plot *by* Madeline Travers Hovland

A CHAIN OF EVENTS

Plot is the chain of related events that tells us what happens in a story. When a plot is well mapped out, it hooks us and we say we can't put the story down. The "hook" of the plot, the part that grabs us and keeps us reading, is usually a **conflict,** or problem faced by a character. The conflict might be a struggle with another character or with a force of nature, such as a tornado. We become curious and want to learn how the conflict is **resolved,** in other words, how the story turns out.

Here's an old story you may know:

Let's say three small pink pigs—Rupert, Rosemary, and Desmond—are building cottages when a wolf turns up and watches, his eyes yellow and shifty.

At once this storyteller hooks our curiosity by making us fear that a conflict will start between the pigs and the wolf. The pigs want to live in peace and safety. The wolf wants food.

The wolf says that the pigs are trespassing and should find another site. The pigs protest that they have a permit to build there. It was given to them by a rabbit who had come by earlier. The wolf declares that the permit is no good, swallows it in one gulp, and says that unless the swine are gone by evening, he will blow their cottages off the map.

Now **complications** are developing. We worry that the wolf will wreck the pigs' houses. Also, since the wolf is a carnivore, a meat-eating animal, there is a good chance the pigs will follow their permit down his throat.

Rupert hurries to finish his house with straw. Rosemary finishes hers with wood, and Desmond finishes his with fiberglass and aluminum siding. Then each pink pig goes inside to await developments.

The suspense is at a peak. What will happen to the pigs? The next event marks the **climax** of the story, when the outcome of the conflict is decided.

Just as he promised, the wolf turns up as the sun goes down. He huffs and puffs and blows Rupert's straw house to dust. Next he turns to Rosemary's house, and soon it too is blown to smithereens. But the wolf's deepest huffs and most violent puffs leave Desmond's fiberglass house unshaken.

The last part of a plot is the **resolution.** This is the end of the story, when all loose ends are tied up and we know what happens to the characters. In traditional fairy tales, as you know, villains like the wolf are punished, so that the story ends "happily ever after."

Reading Standard 3.2
Evaluate the structural elements of the plot (for example, subplots, parallel episodes, climax), the plot's development, and the way in which conflicts are (or are not) addressed and resolved.

You may want to decide the resolution of this story yourself. What could possibly happen to the wolf? What could possibly happen to Rupert and Rosemary?

Subplots: Several Stories in One

If you think of movies and TV shows you've seen and of novels you've read, you know that stories often have subplots. **Subplots** are plots that are part of the larger story but are not as important. (The prefix *sub–* means "under" or "less important than.") In *The Diary of Anne Frank* (page 217), the major plot pits the Frank and Van Daan families against the Nazis. A subplot follows the growing attraction between Anne Frank and Peter Van Daan.

Parallel Episodes: Repeated Scenes

If you've read the traditional story of those three pigs, you might remember that the wolf goes to each house and says, "Little pig, little pig, let me come in." The plot repeats, with minor changes, each pig's response to that challenge. These are simple examples of **parallel episodes,** in which the story-teller repeats the main outline of an episode several times.

Map out the plot structure of a story you are familiar with. The story could be from a book or from TV or the movies.

Practice

Map out the plot structure of a story you are familiar with. The story could be from a book or from TV or the movies. Use a graphic like this:

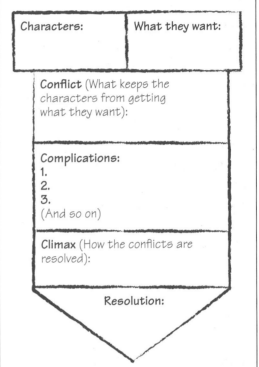

Characters:	What they want:

Conflict (What keeps the characters from getting what they want):

Complications:
1.
2.
3.
(And so on)

Climax (How the conflicts are resolved):

Resolution:

If you can find **subplots** in your story, fill out another chart just like this one.

Peanuts reprinted by permission of United Feature Syndicate, Inc.

Broken Chain

Literary Focus
Conflict

Every story is built around a **plot,** a series of related events. The main ingredient in a plot is a **conflict** of some kind. Usually a conflict starts when a character wants something very badly and takes steps to get it. Along the way, problems develop: Somebody else wants the same thing, the boat capsizes, or a storm causes the electricity to go out. These are examples of **external conflicts:** The character struggles against outside forces. Conflicts can also be **internal:** A character might have to fight shyness, keep a terrible secret, or control fear. In many stories both kinds of conflict exist side by side. In this story, Alfonso has many conflicts. What internal conflict is revealed in the very first line?

Reading Skills
Summarizing a Plot

You can **summarize** most plots by using a strategy called **somebody wanted but so.** Think of "Somebody" as the main character. "Wanted" is what that character wants. "But" means complications develop that make it harder for the character to get what he or she wants. "So" is how it all works out at the end. As you read this story about a boy who wants several things, look for the little open-book signs ( ) alongside the text. Stop at those points to answer the questions about the plot.

Make the Connection
Quickwrite ✏

This story is about a boy's first date. You'll see that his problems are like those many of us face—he worries a lot about how he looks—and everything seems to go wrong. In your journal, describe how you think most thirteen- and fourteen-year-olds feel about themselves.

Vocabulary Development

These are the words you'll be learning as you read this story:

apparent (ə·per′ənt) *adj.:* visible. *Alfonso was proud that the muscles on his stomach were apparent.*

sullen (sul′ən) *adj.:* grumpy; resentful. *Ernie became sullen when the girls didn't show up for the date.*

impulse (im′puls′) *n.:* urge. *Alfonso regretted his impulse to clean his bike chain.*

retrieved (ri·trēvd′) *v.:* got back. *Alfonso retrieved the chain he had thrown away.*

emerged (ē·murjd′) *v.:* came out. *Alfonso emerged from behind the hedge to meet Sandra.*

Broken Chain

Gary Soto

Alfonso sat on the porch trying to push his crooked teeth to where he thought they belonged. He hated the way he looked. Last week he did fifty sit-ups a day, thinking that he would burn those already apparent ripples on his stomach to even deeper ripples, dark ones, so when he went swimming at the canal next summer, girls in cut-offs would notice. And the guys would think he was tough, someone who could take a punch and give it back. He wanted "cuts" like those he had seen on a calendar of an Aztec[1] warrior standing on a pyramid with a woman in his arms. (Even she had cuts he could see beneath her thin dress.) The calendar hung above the cash register at La Plaza. Orsua, the owner, said Alfonso could have the calendar at the end of the year if the waitress, Yolanda, didn't take it first.

---

1. **Aztec:** member of an American Indian people of what is now Mexico.

Vocabulary
apparent (ə·per′ənt) *adj.:* visible; easily seen; obvious.

Alfonso studied the magazine pictures of rock stars for a hairstyle. He liked the way Prince looked—and the bass player from Los Lobos. Alfonso thought he would look cool with his hair razored into a V in the back and streaked purple. But he knew his mother wouldn't go for it. And his father, who was puro Mexicano, would sit in his chair after work, <u>sullen</u> as a toad, and call him "sissy."

Alfonso didn't dare color his hair. But one day he had had it butched on the top, like in the magazines. His father had come home that evening from a softball game, happy that his team had drilled four homers in a thirteen-to-five bashing of Color Tile. He'd swaggered into the living room but had stopped cold when he saw Alfonso and asked, not joking but with real concern, "Did you hurt your head at school? ¿Qué pasó?"[2]

Alfonso had pretended not to hear his father and had gone to his room, where he studied his hair from all angles in the mirror. He liked what he saw until he smiled and realized for the first time that his teeth were crooked, like a pile of wrecked cars. He grew depressed and turned away from the mirror. He sat on his bed and leafed through the rock magazine until he came to the rock star with the butched top. His mouth was closed, but Alfonso was sure his teeth weren't crooked.

> **✎ PLOT**
> 1. Who is the main character? What does he want?

Alfonso didn't want to be the handsomest kid at school, but he was determined to be

better looking than average. The next day he spent his lawn-mowing money on a new shirt and, with a pocketknife, scooped the moons of dirt from under his fingernails.

He spent hours in front of the mirror trying to herd his teeth into place with his thumb. He asked his mother if he could have braces, like Frankie Molina, her god-son, but he asked at the wrong time. She was at the kitchen table licking the envelope to the house payment. She glared up at him. "Do you think money grows on trees?"

His mother clipped coupons from magazines and newspapers, kept a vegetable garden in the summer, and shopped at Penney's and Kmart. Their family ate a lot of frijoles,[3] which was OK because nothing else tasted so good, though one time Alfonso had had Chinese pot stickers[4] and thought they were the next best food in the world.

He didn't ask his mother for braces again, even when she was in a better mood. He decided to fix his teeth by pushing on them with his thumbs. After breakfast that Saturday he went to his room, closed the door quietly, turned the radio on, and pushed for three hours straight.

He pushed for ten minutes, rested for five, and every half hour, during a radio commercial, checked to see if his smile had improved. It hadn't.

Eventually he grew bored and went outside with an old gym sock to wipe down his bike, a ten-speed from Montgomery Ward. His thumbs were tired and wrinkled

---

3. **frijoles** (frē·khô′lās′) *n.:* Spanish for "beans."
4. **pot stickers** *n.:* dumplings.

Vocabulary
sullen (sul′ən) *adj.:* grumpy; resentful.

---

2. **¿Qué pasó?** (kā′ pä·sô′): Spanish for "What happened?"

and pink, the way they got when he stayed in the bathtub too long.

Alfonso's older brother, Ernie, rode up on *his* Montgomery Ward bicycle looking depressed. He parked his bike against the peach tree and sat on the back steps, keeping his head down and stepping on ants that came too close.

Alfonso knew better than to say anything when Ernie looked mad. He turned his bike over, balancing it on the handlebars and seat, and flossed the spokes with the sock. When he was finished, he pressed a knuckle to his teeth until they tingled.

Ernie groaned and said, "Ah, man."

Alfonso waited a few minutes before asking, "What's the matter?" He pretended not to be too interested. He picked up a wad of steel wool and continued cleaning the spokes.

Ernie hesitated, not sure if Alfonso would laugh. But it came out. "Those girls didn't show up. And you better not laugh."

"What girls?"

Then Alfonso remembered his brother bragging about how he and Frostie met two girls from Kings Canyon Junior High last week on Halloween night. They were dressed as Gypsies, the costume for all poor Chicanas[5]—they just had to borrow scarves and gaudy red lipstick from their abuelitas.[6]

Alfonso walked over to his brother. He compared their two bikes: His gleamed like a handful of dimes, while Ernie's looked dirty.

"They said we were supposed to wait at the corner. But they didn't show up. Me and Frostie waited and waited. . . . They were playing games with us."

Alfonso thought that was a pretty dirty trick but sort of funny too. He would have to try that someday.

"Were they cute?" Alfonso asked.

"I guess so."

"Do you think you could recognize them?"

"If they were wearing red lipstick, maybe."

Alfonso sat with his brother in silence, both of them smearing ants with their floppy high tops. Girls could sure act weird, especially the ones you meet on Halloween.

Later that day, Alfonso sat on the porch pressing on his teeth. Press, relax; press, relax. His portable radio was on, but not loud enough to make Mr. Rojas come down the steps and wave his cane at him.

Alfonso's father drove up. Alfonso could tell by the way he sat in his truck, a Datsun with a different-colored front fender, that his team had lost their softball game. Alfonso got off the porch in a hurry because he knew his father would be in a bad mood. He went to the backyard, where he unlocked his bike, sat on it with the kick-stand down, and pressed on his teeth. He punched himself in the stomach, and growled, "Cuts." Then he patted his butch and whispered, "Fresh."

After a while Alfonso pedaled up the street, hands in his pockets, toward Foster's Freeze, where he was chased by a ratlike Chihuahua.[7] At his old school, John Burroughs Elementary, he found a kid hanging upside down on the top of a

---

5. **Chicanas** (chi·kä′nəz): Mexican American girls and women.
6. **abuelitas** (ä′bwä·lē′täs) *n.:* in Spanish, an affectionate term for "grandmothers," like *grandmas* in English.

7. **Chihuahua** (chi·wä′wä): small dog with large, pointed ears.

barbed-wire fence with a girl looking up at him. Alfonso skidded to a stop and helped the kid untangle his pants from the barbed wire. The kid was grateful. He had been afraid he would have to stay up there all night. His sister, who was Alfonso's age, was also grateful. If she had to go home and tell her mother that Frankie was stuck on a fence and couldn't get down, she would get scolded.

"Thanks," she said. "What's your name?"

Alfonso remembered her from his school and noticed that she was kind of cute, with ponytails and straight teeth. "Alfonso. You go to my school, huh?"

"Yeah. I've seen you around. You live nearby?"

"Over on Madison."

"My uncle used to live on that street, but he moved to Stockton."

"Stockton's near Sacramento, isn't it?"

"You been there?"

"No." Alfonso looked down at his shoes. He wanted to say something clever the way people do on TV. But the only thing he could think to say was that the governor lived in Sacramento. As soon as he shared this observation, he winced inside.

Alfonso walked with the girl and the boy as they started for home. They didn't talk much. Every few steps, the girl, whose name was Sandra, would look at him out of the corner of her eye, and Alfonso would look away. He learned that she was in seventh grade, just like him, and that she had a pet terrier named Queenie. Her father was a mechanic at Rudy's Speedy Repair, and her mother was a teacher's aide at Jefferson Elementary.

When they came to the street, Alfonso and Sandra stopped at her corner, but her brother ran home. Alfonso watched him stop in the front yard to talk to a lady he guessed was their mother. She was raking leaves into a pile.

"I live over there," she said, pointing.

Alfonso looked over her shoulder for a long time, trying to muster enough nerve to ask her if she'd like to go bike riding tomorrow.

Shyly, he asked, "You wanna go bike riding?"

"Maybe." She played with a ponytail and crossed one leg in front of the other. "But my bike has a flat."

"I can get my brother's bike. He won't mind."

She thought a moment before she said, "OK. But not tomorrow. I have to go to my aunt's."

"How about after school on Monday?"

"I have to take care of my brother until my mom comes home from work. How 'bout four-thirty?"

"OK," he said. "Four-thirty." Instead of parting immediately, they talked for a while, asking questions like "Who's your favorite group?" "Have you ever been on the Big Dipper at Santa Cruz?" and "Have you ever tasted pot stickers?" But the question-and-answer period ended when Sandra's mother called her home.

📖 **PLOT**

2. What else does Alfonso want?

Alfonso took off as fast as he could on his bike, jumped the curb, and, cool as he could be, raced away with his hands stuffed in his pockets. But when he looked back over his shoulder, the wind raking through his butch, Sandra wasn't even looking. She was already on her lawn, heading for the porch.

That night he took a bath, pampered his hair into place, and did more than his usual set of exercises. In bed, in between the push-and-rest on his teeth, he pestered his brother to let him borrow his bike.

"Come on, Ernie," he whined. "Just for an hour."

"Chale,[8] I might want to use it."

"Come on, man, I'll let you have my trick-or-treat candy."

"What you got?"

"Three baby Milky Ways and some Skittles."

"Who's going to use it?"

Alfonso hesitated, then risked the truth. "I met this girl. She doesn't live too far."

Ernie rolled over on his stomach and stared at the outline of his brother, whose head was resting on his elbow. "*You* got a girlfriend?"

"She ain't my girlfriend, just a girl."

"What does she look like?"

"Like a girl."

"Come on, what does she look like?"

"She's got ponytails and a little brother."

"Ponytails! Those girls who messed with Frostie and me had ponytails. Is she cool?"

"I think so."

Ernie sat up in bed. "I bet you that's her."

Alfonso felt his stomach knot up. "She's going to be my girlfriend, not yours!"

"I'm going to get even with her!"

"You better not touch her," Alfonso

---

8. **chale** (chäʹlä): Spanish slang expression roughly meaning "it's not possible."

snarled, throwing a wadded Kleenex at him. "I'll run you over with my bike."

For the next hour, until their mother threatened them from the living room to be quiet or else, they argued whether it was the same girl who had stood Ernie up. Alfonso said over and over that she was too nice to pull a stunt like that. But Ernie argued that she lived only two blocks from where those girls had told them to wait, that she was in the same grade, and, the clincher, that she had ponytails. Secretly, however, Ernie was jealous that his brother, two years younger than himself, might have found a girlfriend.

PLOT

3. What complication has developed?

Sunday morning, Ernie and Alfonso stayed away from each other, though over breakfast they fought over the last tortilla. Their mother, sewing at the kitchen table, warned them to knock it off. At church they made faces at one another when the priest, Father Jerry, wasn't looking. Ernie punched Alfonso in the arm, and Alfonso, his eyes wide with anger, punched back.

Monday morning they hurried to school on their bikes, neither saying a word, though they rode side by side. In first period, Alfonso worried himself sick. How would he borrow a bike for her? He considered asking his best friend, Raul, for his bike. But Alfonso knew Raul, a paperboy with dollar signs in his eyes, would charge him, and he had less than sixty cents, counting the soda bottles he could cash.

Between history and math, Alfonso saw Sandra and her girlfriend huddling at their lockers. He hurried by without being seen.

During lunch Alfonso hid in metal shop so he wouldn't run into Sandra. What would he

say to her? If he weren't mad at his brother, he could ask Ernie what girls and guys talk about. But he *was* mad, and anyway, Ernie was pitching nickels with his friends.

Alfonso hurried home after school. He did the morning dishes as his mother had asked and raked the leaves. After finishing his chores, he did a hundred sit-ups, pushed on his teeth until they hurt, showered, and combed his hair into a perfect butch. He then stepped out to the patio to clean his bike. On an impulse, he removed the chain to wipe off the gritty oil. But while he was unhooking it from the back sprocket, it snapped. The chain lay in his hand like a dead snake.

PLOT

4. What problem is caused by the broken chain?

Alfonso couldn't believe his luck. Now, not only did he not have an extra bike for Sandra, he had no bike for himself. Frustrated and on the verge of tears, he flung the chain as far as he could. It landed with a hard slap against the back fence and spooked his sleeping cat, Benny. Benny looked around, blinking his soft gray eyes, and went back to sleep.

Alfonso retrieved the chain, which was hopelessly broken. He cursed himself for being stupid, yelled at his bike for being cheap, and slammed the chain onto the cement. The chain snapped in another place and hit him when it popped up, slicing his hand like a snake's fang.

"Ow!" he cried, his mouth immediately going to his hand to suck on the wound.

After a dab of iodine, which only made his cut hurt more, and a lot of thought, he

Vocabulary
impulse (im′puls′) *n.:* urge.
retrieved (ri·trēvd′) *v.:* got back.

went to the bedroom to plead with Ernie, who was changing to his after-school clothes.

"Come on, man, let me use it," Alfonso pleaded. "Please, Ernie, I'll do anything."

Although Ernie could see Alfonso's desperation, he had plans with his friend Raymundo. They were going to catch frogs at the Mayfair canal. He felt sorry for his brother and gave him a stick of gum to make him feel better, but there was nothing he could do. The canal was three miles away, and the frogs were waiting.

Alfonso took the stick of gum, placed it in his shirt pocket, and left the bedroom with his head down. He went outside, slamming the screen door behind him, and sat in the alley behind his house. A sparrow landed in the weeds, and when it tried to come close, Alfonso screamed for it to scram. The sparrow responded with a squeaky chirp and flew away.

At four he decided to get it over with and started walking to Sandra's house, trudging slowly, as if he were waist-deep in water. Shame colored his face. How could he disappoint his first date? She would probably laugh. She might even call him menso.[9]

He stopped at the corner where they were supposed to meet and watched her house.

---

9. **menso** (men′sô) *adj.:* Spanish for "stupid."

But there was no one outside, only a rake leaning against the steps.

Why did he have to take the chain off? he scolded himself. He always messed things up when he tried to take them apart, like the time he tried to repad his baseball mitt. He had unlaced the mitt and filled the pocket with cotton balls. But when he tried to put it back together, he had forgotten how it laced up. Everything became tangled like kite string. When he showed the mess to his mother, who was at the stove cooking dinner, she scolded him but put it back together and didn't tell his father what a dumb thing he had done.

Now he had to face Sandra and say, "I broke my bike, and my stingy brother took off on his."

He waited at the corner a few minutes, hiding behind a hedge for what seemed like forever. Just as he was starting to think about going home, he heard footsteps and knew it was too late. His hands, moist from worry, hung at his sides and a thread of sweat raced down his armpit.

He peeked through the hedge. She was wearing a sweater with a checkerboard pattern. A red purse was slung over her shoulder. He could see her looking for him, standing on tiptoe to see if he was coming around the corner.

What have I done? Alfonso thought. He bit his lip, called himself menso, and pounded his palm against his forehead. Someone slapped the back of his head. He turned around and saw Ernie.

"We got the frogs, Alfonso," he said, holding up a wiggling plastic bag. "I'll show you later."

Ernie looked through the hedge, with one eye closed, at the girl. "She's not the one who messed with Frostie and me," he said finally. "You still wanna borrow my bike?"

Alfonso couldn't believe his luck. What a brother! What a pal! He promised to take Ernie's turn next time it was his turn to do the dishes. Ernie hopped on Raymundo's handlebars and said he would remember that promise. Then he was gone as they took off without looking back.

PLOT
5. How is one of Alfonso's problems resolved?

Free of worry now that his brother had come through, Alfonso emerged from behind the hedge with Ernie's bike, which was mud-splashed but better than nothing. Sandra waved.

"Hi," she said.

"Hi," he said back.

She looked cheerful. Alfonso told her his bike was broken and asked if she wanted to ride with him.

"Sounds good," she said, and jumped on the crossbar.

It took all of Alfonso's strength to steady the bike. He started off slowly, gritting his teeth, because she was heavier than he thought. But once he got going, it got easier. He pedaled smoothly, sometimes with only one hand on the handlebars, as they sped up one street and down another. Whenever he ran over a pothole, which was often, she screamed with delight, and once, when it looked like they were going to crash, she placed her hand over his, and it felt like love.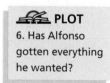

PLOT
6. Has Alfonso gotten everything he wanted?

Vocabulary
emerged (ē·mʉrjd′) v.: came out.

Gary Soto

"Your Lives Are at Work, Too"

Gary Soto (1952–   ) was born and raised in Fresno, California, the setting of many of his stories, poems, and autobiographical pieces. In his writing, Soto tries to re-create the sights and sounds of the Mexican American neighborhood in which he grew up. He advises young writers to "look to your own lives," which is exactly what he does:

> What are your life stories? Can you remember incidents from your childhood? Some of you will say that your lives are boring, that nothing has happened, that everything interesting happens far away. Not so. Your lives are at work, too.

Soto's poem "Oranges" (see page 460) is based on an incident in his life, but "Broken Chain" is more loosely drawn from his experience:

> No, I'm not Alfonso in the story 'Broken Chain.' It's pure fiction, with the wild purpose of stirring in you—the reader—the feeling of one day latching onto a girlfriend or boyfriend. When I was Alfonso's age, I would have loved to have a girlfriend on my handlebars. Instead, I had my little brother, better known as chipped-tooth Jimmy, who often hopped onto my bike and cruised the streets of my hometown, Fresno, California. He was no 'Sandra.' Instead, Jimmy was a heavy problem, because it was my job to take care of him while my parents went off to work.

For Independent Reading

"Broken Chain" comes from *Baseball in April,* a book of short stories about growing up. You'll find "Oranges," along with other poems, in *A Fire in My Hands.*

Literary Response and Analysis

Reading Check

1. To **summarize** the **plot** of "Broken Chain," fill in a chart like this one. You'll probably add two more rows to retell the story.

Somebody	Wanted	But	So
Alfonso	to look better	he couldn't get braces	he tried to push his teeth into place

Then

Alfonso			

Interpretations

2. How does Alfonso feel about not having a bike for his date? Give details from the story that show his feelings.

3. In this story, Alfonso faces both **internal** and **external conflicts.** Describe four of his conflicts. Which do you think is his greatest challenge? Why?

4. Some stories have **subplots,** or minor plots that relate to the main plot. "Broken Chain" really has two plots: one involving Alfonso and the girl and one involving Alfonso and his brother. Which of those plots is the **subplot**? Explain your answer.

5. This story is told from a boy's viewpoint. In your experience, which of Alfonso's feelings are shared by girls?

Evaluation

6. How do Alfonso's feelings compare with the feelings you described in your Quickwrite? Do Alfonso's feelings and behavior seem realistic to you? Explain.

7. "Broken Chain" has also been published under the title "First Love." Which **title** do you think is better? Why?

Writing
Helpful Hints

Identify a problem that Alfonso has in the story (for example, worrying about his appearance or not knowing what to say to Sandra). Pretending you are Alfonso, write a **letter** to an advice column explaining your problem. Then, switch papers with a classmate, and take the role of the columnist. Respond to Alfonso with practical, encouraging advice.

Reading Standard 3.2
Evaluate the structural elements of the plot (for example, subplots, parallel episodes, climax), the plot's development, and the way in which conflicts are (or are not) addressed and resolved.

Vocabulary Development

History of the English Language: Latin Roots

How Did Latin Get in There? When Alfonso worries that Sandra will call him *menso,* he is using the Spanish word for "stupid." If you know that a word is Spanish or comes from a Spanish word, you can be pretty sure it has a Latin root. Why? Because Spanish is a **Romance language.** No, not "romance" with flowers and violins. Romance languages developed from the language spoken by Roman soldiers who, for six hundred years, went about conquering the Western world, or at least most of Europe, North Africa, and the Middle East.

The Roman Armies Spread Latin. The Romans usually won their battles. They spoke Latin, and they made everyone else speak Latin too. Then they kept things peaceful for hundreds of years. In that peaceful time the language they spoke took on regional variations, so that eventually the modern languages of French, Spanish, Portuguese, Italian, and Romanian developed. Thus, when Alfonso speaks Spanish, he is actually speaking a modern version of Latin, as people do when they speak any of the Romance languages.

Latin Comes into English. Alfonso also speaks English, about 60 percent of which can be traced to Latin. However, English isn't a Romance language. Then how did so much Latin get into it? Well, thanks to the Romans and, later, the Roman Catholic Church, Latin got around. Just about every language in the Western world eventually borrowed from it. Latin was also the language of scholars for many centuries. But there was one other event that resulted in the addition of thousands of Latin words to the English language. That was the Norman Conquest of England.

In the year 1066, William the Conqueror, a Norman (from Normandy, in France) who spoke French, invaded England and became king. As a result, French—and, through it, Latin—became a major influence on the development of English.

(continued on next page)

Reading Standard 1.2 Understand the most important points in the history of the English language, and use common word origins to determine the historical influences on English word meanings.

Study the following derivations, or origins, of the words in the Word Bank. (The abbreviation *L* stands for "Latin." *ME* stands for "Middle English.")

apparent L *apparere*, "to appear"

sullen L *solus*, "alone"

impulse L *impellere*, "to drive"

retrieved ME *retreven*, "to find again"

emerged L *e–*, "out" + *mergere*, "to immerse"

> **Word Bank**
> apparent
> sullen
> impulse
> retrieved
> emerged

1. How is the Latin or Middle English meaning reflected in the modern meaning of each English word? (Do any of the derivations puzzle you?)

2. What other English words can you think of that come from *apparere, solus,* and *mergere*?

Grammar Link MINI-LESSON

When to Use Apostrophes

Apostrophes are used for two reasons: to show where letters in a word are missing (*it's* stands for "it is") and, in a noun, to show possession (*Alfonso's teeth*).

- Use an apostrophe in a contraction to show where letters have been left out. (A contraction is a combination of words from which letters have been omitted.)

  It's [it is] **broken.**
  You're [you are] **in trouble.**
  They're [they are] **furious.**
  Who's [who is] **asking the question?**

- Use an apostrophe to form the possessive case of a noun (to show ownership).

  Sandra's hair [the hair of Sandra] **is in ponytails.**
  The boys' bikes [the bikes of the boys] **are broken.**
  A boy's bike [the bike of a boy] **is broken.**

- Do not use an apostrophe to form the plural of a noun.

  The girls never showed up.

- Do not use an apostrophe with the possessive form of a personal pronoun (*yours, hers, his, its, ours, theirs*).

  His bicycle is broken. May I borrow yours?

Write out each of these sentences, and correct any errors you find in the use of apostrophes.

1. Its broken.
2. Its chain is on the ground.
3. Your kidding!
4. You're girlfriend is here.
5. Your always late.
6. Who's bike are you riding?
7. Is the bike your's?
8. The boys took the girls bikes.
9. Her's needs a tuneup.

For more help, see Apostrophes in the *Holt Handbook*, pages 351–356.

Road Warriors, Listen Up: Some Rules for Streetwise Biking

Analyzing Proposition and Support

In this chapter you will be looking at a variety of informational texts. In each text the writer presents a **proposition,** an important idea or opinion, and **supports** the proposition with reasons. Reasons may be statistics, examples, anecdotes, and expert opinions.

In the model below, the writer states his proposition right upfront, in the title. After you've studied the model, read the following informational essay on bike safety. Look for the writer's proposition in the first paragraph, and try to find at least one supporting reason in each paragraph that follows.

Has the writer made a good case?

Kids Should Be Paid for Chores

I strongly believe that kids should be paid for doing chores around the house. Kids all across the country constantly nag their parents for money to go to the movies, buy CDs, go to McDonalds, and do many other things. Many parents complain about kids always asking for money.

Parents constantly complain that kids don't help out around the house enough. Lots of times parents nag kids until they clean up their rooms, put out the trash, cut the lawn, do the dishes, shovel the snow, and do many other chores.

Why can't kids and parents reach a compromise about money and chores? Parents would pay kids who remember to do their chores, without being reminded, a small fee for the work done. Kids would no longer ask for money.

This compromise teaches kids responsibility. They would learn that you don't get anything for doing nothing. When their chores are completed, with no nagging, they'd be paid whatever the parents had agreed to pay them. Kids could spend the money on things they like. They'd learn to save money for the expensive items.

No more nagging kids begging for money. No more nagging parents begging kids to clean up. Both kids and parents would be getting something they want.

—T. J. Wilson
Atlantic Middle School
North Quincy, Massachusetts

The writer states his **proposition** twice—in the title and in the first sentence of the text.

The writer gives **examples** to illustrate the problem.

The writer restates the issue as a question and gives **two reasons** to support his proposition.

The writer elaborates by giving several **more reasons** to support his proposition.

The writer ends with a strong **closing statement** citing the benefits of the recommended course of action.

Reading Standard 2.2
Analyze text that uses proposition and support patterns.

Road Warriors, Listen Up:
Some Rules for Streetwise Biking

When you ride a bike on city streets, you share the road with speeding fire engines, ambulances, and police cars. You see—but can't see around—giant-sized trucks with eighteen wheels instead of your two. Sports cars and SUVs zip in and out of lanes. Everyone's in a hurry, and there you are, with less protection than anyone else in a moving vehicle. Your best defense is your good sense. To ride a bike safely—on highways or byways—you've got to know and follow the rules of the road.

The consequences of not following bike-safety rules can be painful, if not fatal. Every year in the United States there are about eight hundred deaths due to bike accidents. More than half a million people end up in emergency rooms because of bike injuries.

To protect yourself against serious injury, wear a bike helmet whenever you hop on a bike, even for a short ride. A helmet that meets safety standards may seem expensive, but your intact brain is worth the investment. Bike helmets can reduce head injuries by as much as 80 percent.

To ride safely, you need to hear approaching traffic, barking dogs, and shouting drivers. Therefore, you should never ride wearing headphones. Wait to listen to music till you get where you're going. If you carry a cell phone or a pager, pull over to the side of the road before you take or make a call or check your beeper.

Biking safely also means obeying traffic signs and signals. Stop signs and red lights apply to everyone on the road, not just cars. State laws—and common sense—dictate that bicyclists ride on the right side of the road, in the same direction as all other traffic, not against it. When you come to an intersection, wait for the green light before you ride across. Remember that pedestrians always have the right of way, whether they are on the sidewalk or in the street.

Watch out for road hazards. (There are even more obstacles to worry about than cars and trucks and people.) Steer around potholes, bumps, gravel, piles of leaves, and grates covering storm drains. Use hand signals to alert drivers to your intentions. When you're not making a hand signal, be sure to keep both hands on your handlebars.

Biking is excellent practice for driving later on. Safe biking will help prepare you to be a safe driver. Even when you're old enough to drive a car, however, you'll probably still go biking. It's fun. It's an inexpensive way to travel. And it's great exercise. Whatever your age, always remember to follow the rules for streetwise biking. The life you save may be your own!

—Madeline Travers Hovland

Reading Informational Materials

Reading Check

1. What moving vehicle on the road has the least amount of protection?

2. According to the writer, what can happen if you don't follow bike-safety rules?

3. Why should you wear a bike helmet?

4. Who always has the right of way?

5. How does streetwise biking prepare riders for the future?

TestPractice

Road Warriors, Listen Up:
Some Rules for Streetwise Biking

1. Which sentence best states the writer's **proposition,** the main idea of the article?
   - **A** Biking safely means obeying traffic signs and signals.
   - **B** Watch out for road hazards.
   - **C** Biking is excellent practice for driving later on.
   - **D** To ride a bike safely, you've got to know and follow the rules of the road.

2. Which of the following is a statistic used to support the main idea of the article?
   - **F** The consequences of not following bike-safety rules can be painful, if not fatal.
   - **G** Bike helmets can reduce head injuries by as much as 80 percent.
   - **H** When you come to an intersection, wait for the green light before you ride across.
   - **J** Safe biking will help prepare you to be a safe driver.

3. "More than half a million people end up in emergency rooms because of bike injuries." This sentence is an example of a —
   - **A** personal experience
   - **B** proposition
   - **C** supporting detail
   - **D** main idea

4. The overall **purpose** of the article is to —
   - **F** discourage bikers
   - **G** convince readers that bike safety is important
   - **H** explain how to buy a good bike helmet
   - **J** get readers interested in bike riding

5. Another good **title** for this article might be —
   - **A** "Walk, Don't Bike"
   - **B** "My Experiences as a Cyclist"
   - **C** "Bike Now, Drive Later"
   - **D** "Biking Safely: Your Best Defense on Two Wheels"

Reading Standard 2.2 Analyze text that uses proposition and support patterns.

Flowers for Algernon

Literary Focus
Subplots and Parallel Episodes

A long story, like the one that follows, might have a **subplot,** a minor plot that relates in some way to the major story. A long story might also have **parallel episodes,** in which the writer repeats certain elements of the plot. For example, you probably remember all those fairy tales that have three parallel episodes (writers back then seem to have liked the number three). The king might test his three daughters three times to see if they are loyal to him. Goldilocks tries the bears' beds three times to see which one is just right. Watch for both subplots and parallel episodes in "Flowers for Algernon."

Reading Skills
Using Context Clues

Right at the start of "Flowers for Algernon," you'll notice that Charlie has trouble with spelling. To figure out what his misspelled words are meant to be, try sounding out each one. (Charlie usually spells words the way they sound.) If you're still stuck, check the word's context. The context will often give you enough **context clues,** or hints, to help you figure out the word's meaning. For example, on page 23, Charlie writes *faled*. You could figure out that this is his spelling of *failed* by sounding the word out or by looking at the context clue in the sentence just before it: "I had a test today."

Reading Standard 3.2
Evaluate the structural elements of the plot (for example, subplots, parallel episodes).

Make the Connection
Quickwrite ✏

Take a class poll: Would you rather be the most popular person in your school or the smartest person in your school?

On a small piece of paper, write either *S* for "smartest" or *P* for "most popular," and pass your response to a designated vote counter. (Even if you'd like to choose both, for now just choose one.) Tally the responses on the chalkboard. How close was the vote? Discuss what you think your classmates' reasons were for answering as they did.

Now, write a brief response to one of these questions:

- What are the advantages and disadvantages of popularity? of intelligence?

- What sacrifices do people make to fit in?

- What is good or bad about being unusual?

Vocabulary Development

You'll have to know these words as you read "Flowers for Algernon":

misled (mis·led′) *v.:* fooled; led to believe something wrong. *Joe and Frank misled Charlie into thinking they were his friends.*

tangible (tan′jə·bəl) *adj.:* capable of being seen or felt. *An early tangible benefit of Charlie's operation was his improved skill at spelling.*

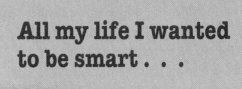

All my life I wanted to be smart . . .

Flowers for Algernon

Daniel Keyes

refute (ri·fyoot´) *v.:* prove wrong using evidence. *Charlie used his research to refute the work of Drs. Nemur and Strauss.*

invariably (in·ver´ē·ə·blē) *adv.:* always. *Charlie's co-workers invariably laughed at his mistakes.*

regression (ri·gresh´ən) *n.:* return to an earlier or less advanced condition. *After his regression the mouse no longer could find his way through the maze.*

verified (ver´ə·fīd´) *v.:* confirmed. *Charlie wanted the results of his research verified by other scientists.*

obscure (əb·skyoor´) *v.:* hide. *Charlie wanted to obscure the fact that he was losing his intelligence.*

deterioration (dē·tir´ē·ə·rā´shən) *n.* used as *adj.:* worsening; decline. *Because of his mental deterioration, Charlie could no longer read German.*

hypothesis (hī·päth´ə·sis) *n.:* theory to be proved. *The doctors' hypothesis was that they could improve intelligence through surgery.*

introspective (in´trə·spek´tiv) *adj.:* looking inward. *Charlie kept an introspective journal of his thoughts and feelings.*

1

progris riport 1—martch 5 1965

Dr. Strauss says I shud rite down what I think and evrey thing that happins to me from now on. I dont know why but he says its importint so they will see if they will use me. I hope they use me. Miss Kinnian says maybe they can make me smart. I want to be smart. My name is Charlie Gordon. I am 37 years old and 2 weeks ago was my brithday. I have nuthing more to rite now so I will close for today.

progris riport 2—martch 6

I had a test today. I think I faled it. and I think that maybe now they wont use me. What happind is a nice young man was in the room and he had some white cards with ink spilled all over them. He sed Charlie what do you see on this card. I was very skared even tho I had my rabits foot[1] in my pockit because when I was a kid I always faled tests in school and I spilled ink to.

I told him I saw a inkblot. He said yes and it made me feel good. I thot that was all but when I got up to go he stopped me. He said now sit down Charlie we are not thru yet. Then I dont remember so good

---

1. **rabits foot:** The hind foot of a rabbit is sometimes used as a good-luck charm.

but he wantid me to say what was in the ink. I dint see nuthing in the ink but he said there was picturs there other pepul saw some picturs. I coudnt see any picturs. I reely tryed to see. I held the card close up and then far away. Then I said if I had my glases I coud see better I usally only ware my glases in the movies or TV but I said they are in the closit in the hall. I got them. Then I said let me see that card agen I bet Ill find it now.

I tryed hard but I still coudnt find the picturs I only saw the ink. I told him maybe I need new glases. He rote somthing down on a paper and I got skared of faling the test. I told him it was a very nice inkblot with littel points all around the eges. He looked very sad so that wasnt it. I said please let me try agen. Ill get it in a few minits becaus Im not so fast somtimes. Im a slow reeder too in Miss Kinnians class for slow adults but I'm trying very hard.

He gave me a chance with another card that had 2 kinds of ink spilled on it red and blue.

He was very nice and talked slow like Miss Kinnian does and he explaned it to me that it was a *raw shok.*[2] He said pepul see things in the ink. I said show me where. He said think. I told him I think a inkblot but that wasnt rite eather. He said what does it remind you—pretend something. I closd my eyes for a long time to pretend. I told him I pretned a fowntan pen with ink leeking all over a table cloth. Then he got up and went out.

I dont think I passd the *raw shok* test.

---

2. **raw shok:** Rorschach (rôr′shäk′) test, a psychological test in which people describe the images suggested to them by a series of inkblots.

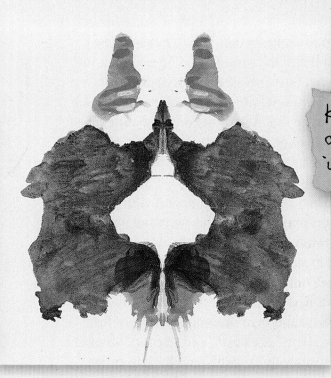

He gave me a chance with another card that had 2 kinds of ink spilled on it red and blue.

progris report 3—martch 7

Dr Strauss and Dr Nemur say it dont matter about the inkblots. I told them I dint spill the ink on the cards and I couldn't see anything in the ink. They said that maybe they will still use me. I said Miss Kinnian never gave me tests like that one only spelling and reading. They said Miss Kinnian told that I was her bestist pupil in the adult nite scool becaus I tryed the hardist and I reely wantid to lern. They said how come you went to the adult nite scool all by yourself Charlie. How did you find it. I said I askd pepul and sumbody told me where I shud go to lern to read and spell good. They said why did you want to. I told them becaus all my life I wantid to be smart and not dumb. But its very hard to be smart. They said you know it will probly be tempirery. I said yes. Miss Kinnian told me. I dont care if it herts.

Later I had more crazy tests today. The nice lady who gave it me told me the name and I asked her how do you spellit so I can rite it in my progris riport. THEMATIC APPERCEPTION TEST. I dont know the frist 2 words but I know what *test* means. You got to pass it or you get bad marks. This test lookd easy becaus I coud see the picturs. Only this time she dint want me to tell her the picturs. That mixd me up. I said the man yesterday said I shoud tell him what I saw in the ink she said that dont make no difrence. She said make up storys about the pepul in the picturs.

I told her how can you tell storys about pepul you never met. I said why shud I make up lies. I never tell lies any more becaus I always get caut.

She told me this test and the other one the raw-shok was for getting personalty. I laffed so hard. I said how can you get that thing from inkblots and fotos. She got sore and put her picturs away. I dont care. It was sily. I gess I faled that test too.

Later some men in white coats took me to a difernt part of the hospitil and gave me a game to play. It was like a race with a white mouse. They called the mouse Algernon. Algernon was in a box with a lot of twists and turns like all kinds of walls and they gave me a pencil and a paper with lines and lots of boxes. On one side it said START and on the other end it said FINISH. They said it was *amazed* and that Algernon and me had the same *amazed* to do. I dint see how we could have the same *amazed* if Algernon had a box and I had a paper but I dint say nothing. Anyway there wasnt time because the race started.

One of the men had a watch he was trying to hide so I wouldnt see it so I tryed not to look and that made me nervus.

Anyway that test made me feel worser than all the others because they did it over 10 times with difernt *amazeds* and Algernon won every time. I dint know that mice were so smart. Maybe thats because Algernon is a white mouse. Maybe white mice are smarter then other mice.

progis riport 4—Mar 8

Their going to use me! Im so exited I can hardly write. Dr Nemur and Dr Strauss had a argament about it first. Dr Nemur was in the office when Dr Strauss brot me in. Dr Nemur was worryed about using me but Dr Strauss told him Miss Kinnian rekemmended me the best from all the people who she was teaching. I like Miss Kinnian becaus shes a very smart teacher. And she said Charlie your going to have a second chance. If you volenteer for this experament you mite get smart. They dont know if it will be perminint but theirs a chance. Thats why I said ok even when I was scared because she said it was an operashun. She said dont be scared Charlie you done so much with so little I think you deserv it most of all.

So I got scaird when Dr Nemur and Dr Strauss argud about it. Dr Strauss said I had something that was very good. He said I had a good *motor-vation*.[3] I never even knew I had that. I felt proud when he said that not every body with an eye-q of 68 had that thing. I dont know what it is or where I got it but he said Algernon had it too. Algernons *motor-vation* is the cheese they put in his box. But it cant be that because I didnt eat any cheese this week.

Then he told Dr Nemur something I dint understand so while they were talking I wrote down some of the words.

He said Dr Nemur I know Charlie is not what you had in mind as the first of your new brede of intelek** (coudnt get the word) superman. But most people of his low ment** are host** and uncoop** they are usualy dull apath** and hard to reach. He has a good natcher hes intristed and eager to please.

Dr Nemur said remember he will be the first human beeng ever to have his intelijence trippled by surgicle meens.

Dr Strauss said exakly. Look at how well hes lerned to read and write for his low mentel age its as grate an acheve** as you and I lerning einstines therey of **vity[4] without help. That shows the intenss motor-vation. Its comparat** a tremen** achev** I say we use Charlie.

I dint get all the words and they were talking to fast but it sounded like Dr Strauss was on my side and like the other one wasnt.

Then Dr Nemur nodded he said all right maybe your right. We will use Charlie.

---

3. **motor-vation:** motivation, the force or inner drive that makes someone want to do or accomplish something; here, Charlie's desire to learn.
4. **einstines therey of **vity:** Einstein's theory of relativity, which was developed by the German-born American physicist Albert Einstein (1879–1955) and deals with matter, time, space, and energy.

When he said that I got so exited I jumped up and shook his hand for being so good to me. I told him thank you doc you wont be sorry for giving me a second chance. And I mean it like I told him. After the operashun Im gonna try to be smart. Im gonna try awful hard.

progris ript 5—Mar 10

Im skared. Lots of people who work here and the nurses and the people who gave me the tests came to bring me candy and wish me luck. I hope I have luck. I got my rabits foot and my lucky penny and my horse shoe. Only a black cat crossed me when I was comming to the hospitil. Dr Strauss says dont be supersitis Charlie this is sience. Anyway Im keeping my rabits foot with me.

I asked Dr Strauss if Ill beat Algernon in the race after the operashun and he said maybe. If the operashun works Ill show that mouse I can be as smart as he is. Maybe smarter. Then Ill be abel to read better and spell the words good and know lots of things and be like other people. I want to be smart like other people. If it works perminint they will make everybody smart all over the wurld.

They dint give me anything to eat this morning. I dont know what that eating has to do with getting smart. Im very hungry and Dr Nemur took away my box of candy. That Dr Nemur is a grouch. Dr Strauss says I can have it back after the operashun. You cant eat befor a operashun . . .

Progress Report 6—Mar 15

The operashun dint hurt. He did it while I was sleeping. They took off the bandijis from my eyes and my head today so I can make a PROGRESS REPORT. Dr Nemur who looked at some of my other ones says I spell PROGRESS wrong and he told me how to spell it and REPORT too. I got to try and remember that.

I have a very bad memary for spelling. Dr Strauss says its ok to tell about all the things that happin to me but he says I shoud tell more about what I feel and what I think. When I told him I dont know how to think he said try. All the time when the bandijis were on my eyes I tryed to think. Nothing happened. I dont know what to think about. Maybe if I ask him he will tell me how I can think now that Im suppose to get smart. What do smart people think about. Fancy things I suppose. I wish I knew some fancy things alredy.

Their really my friends
and they like me.

WEEKLY TIME CARD

DAY	IN	OUT	IN	OUT	IN	OUT	Total
M							
T							
W							
T							
F							
S							
S							

REG.   H O U R S

O.T.

Foreman Signature

Progress Report 7—mar 19

Nothing is happining. I had lots of tests and different kinds of races with Algernon. I hate that mouse. He always beats me. Dr Strauss said I got to play those games. And he said some time I got to take those tests over again. Thse inkblots are stupid. And those pictures are stupid too. I like to draw a picture of a man and a woman but I wont make up lies about people.

I got a headache from trying to think so much. I thot Dr Strauss was my frend but he dont help me. He dont tell me what to think or when Ill get smart. Miss Kinnian dint come to see me. I think writing these progress reports are stupid too.

Progress Report 8—Mar 23

Im going back to work at the factery. They said it was better I shud go back to work but I cant tell anyone what the operashun was for and I have to come to the hospitil for an hour evry night after work. They are gonna pay me mony every month for lerning to be smart.

Im glad Im going back to work because I miss my job and all my frends and all the fun we have there.

Dr Strauss says I shud keep writing things down but I dont have to do it every day just when I think of something or something speshul happins. He says dont get discoridged because it takes time and it happins slow. He says it took a long time with Algernon before he got 3 times smarter then he was before. Thats why Algernon beats me all the time because he had that operashun too. That makes me feel better. I coud probly do that *amazed* faster than a reglar mouse. Maybe some day Ill beat Algernon. Boy that would be something. So far Algernon looks like he mite be smart perminent.

Mar 25 (I dont have to write PROGRESS REPORT on top any more just when I hand it in once a week for Dr Nemur to read. I just have to put the date on. That saves time)

We had a lot of fun at the factery today. Joe Carp said hey look where Charlie had his operashun what did they do Charlie put some brains in. I was going to tell him but I remembered Dr Strauss said no. Then Frank Reilly said what did you do Charlie

forget your key and open your door the hard way. That made me laff. Their really my friends and they like me.

Sometimes somebody will say hey look at Joe or Frank or George he really pulled a Charlie Gordon. I don't know why they say that but they always laff. This morning Amos Borg who is the 4 man at Donnegans used my name when he shouted at Ernie the office boy. Ernie lost a packige. He said Ernie for godsake what are you trying to be a Charlie Gordon. I dont understand why he said that. I never lost any packiges.

Mar 28 Dr Strauss came to my room tonight to see why I dint come in like I was suppose to. I told him I dont like to race with Algernon any more. He said I dont have to for a while but I shud come in. He had a present for me only it wasnt a present but just for lend. I thot it was a little television but it wasnt. He said I got to turn it on when I go to sleep. I said your kidding why shud I turn it on when Im going to sleep. Who ever herd of a thing like that. But he said if I want to get smart I got to do what he says. I told him I dint think I was going to get smart and he put his hand on my sholder and said Charlie you dont know it yet but your getting smarter all the time. You wont notice for a while. I think he was just being nice to make me feel good because I dont look any smarter.

Oh yes I almost forgot. I asked him when I can go back to the class at Miss Kinnians school. He said I wont go their. He said that soon Miss Kinnian will come to the hospitil to start and teach me speshul. I was mad at her for not comming to see me when I got the operashun but I like her so maybe we will be frends again.

Mar 29 That crazy TV kept me up all night. How can I sleep with something yelling crazy things all night in my ears. And the nutty pictures. Wow. I dont know what it says when Im up so how am I going to know when Im sleeping.

Dr Strauss says its ok. He says my brains are lerning when I sleep and that will help me when Miss Kinnian starts my lessons in the hospitl (only I found out it isnt a hospitil its a labatory). I think its all crazy. If you can get smart when your sleeping why do people go to school. That thing I dont think will work. I use to watch the late show and the late late show on TV all the time and it never made me smart. Maybe you have to sleep while you watch it.

PROGRESS REPORT 9—April 3

Dr Strauss showed me how to keep the TV turned low so now I can sleep. I dont hear a thing. And I still dont understand what it says. A few times I play it over in the morning to find out what I lerned when I was sleeping and I dont think so. Miss Kinnian says Maybe its another langwidge or something. But most times it sounds american. It talks so fast faster then even Miss Gold who was my teacher in 6 grade and I remember she talked so fast I coudnt understand her.

I told Dr Strauss what good is it to get smart in my sleep. I want to be smart when Im awake. He says its the same thing and I have two minds. Theres the *subconscious* and the *conscious*[5] (thats how you spell it). And one dont tell the other one what its

doing. They don't even talk to each other. Thats why I dream. And boy have I been having crazy dreams. Wow. Ever since that night TV. The late late late late late show.

I forgot to ask him if it was only me or if everybody had those two minds.

(I just looked up the word in the dictionary Dr Strauss gave me. The word is *subconscious. adj. Of the nature of mental operations yet not present in consciousness; as, subconscious conflict of desires.*) Theres more but I still dont know what it means. This isnt a very good dictionary for dumb people like me.

Anyway the headache is from the party. My frends from the factery Joe Carp and Frank Reilly invited me to go with them to Muggsys Saloon for some drinks. I dont like to drink but they said we will have lots of fun. I had a good time.

Joe Carp said I shoud show the girls how I mop out the toilet in the factory and he got me a mop. I showed them and everyone laffed when I told that Mr Donnegan said I was the best janiter he ever had because I like my job and do it good and never come late or miss a day except for my operashun.

I said Miss Kinnian always said Charlie be proud of your job because you do it good.

Everybody laffed and we had a good time and they gave me lots of drinks and Joe said Charlie is a card when hes potted. I dont know what that means but everybody likes me and we have fun. I cant wait to be smart like my best frends Joe Carp and Frank Reilly.

I dont remember how the party was over but I think I went out to buy a newspaper and coffe for Joe and Frank and when I came back there was no one their. I looked for them all over till late. Then I dont remember so good but I think I got sleepy

---

5. **subconscious** (sub·kän**ʹ**shəs) *n.:* mental activity that takes place below the level of the **conscious** (kän**ʹ**shəs), or full awareness.

or sick. A nice cop brot me back home. Thats what my landlady Mrs Flynn says.

But I got a headache and a big lump on my head and black and blue all over. I think maybe I fell but Joe Carp says it was the cop they beat up drunks some times. I don't think so. Miss Kinnian says cops are to help people. Anyway I got a bad headache and Im sick and hurt all over. I dont think Ill drink anymore.

April 6 I beat Algernon! I dint even know I beat him until Burt the tester told me. Then the second time I lost because I got so exited I fell off the chair before I finished. But after that I beat him 8 more times. I must be getting smart to beat a smart mouse like Algernon. But I dont *feel* smarter.

I wanted to race Algernon some more but Burt said thats enough for one day. They let me hold him for a minit. Hes not so bad. Hes soft like a ball of cotton. He blinks and when he opens his eyes their black and pink on the eges.

I said can I feed him because I felt bad to beat him and I wanted to be nice and make frends. Burt said no Algernon is a very specshul mouse with an operashun like mine, and he was the first of all the animals to stay smart so long. He told me Algernon is so smart that every day he has to solve a test to get his food. Its a thing like a lock on a door that changes every time Algernon goes in to eat so he has to lern something new to get his food. That made me sad because if he couldnt lern he would be hungry.

I dont think its right to make you pass a test to eat. How woud Dr Nemur like it to have to pass a test every time he wants to eat. I think Ill be frends with Algernon.

April 9 Tonight after work Miss Kinnian was at the laboratory. She looked like she was glad to see me but scared. I told her dont worry Miss Kinnian Im not smart yet and she laffed. She said I have confidence in you Charlie the way you struggled so hard to read and right better than all the others. At werst you will have it for a littel wile and your doing somthing for sience.

We are reading a very hard book. I never read such a hard book before. Its called *Robinson Crusoe* about a man who gets merooned on a dessert Iland. Hes smart and figers out all kinds of things so he can have a house and food and hes a good swimmer. Only I feel sorry because hes all alone and has no frends. But I think their must be somebody else on the iland because theres a picture with his funny umbrella looking at footprints. I hope he gets a frend and not be lonely.

April 10 Miss Kinnian teaches me to spell better. She says look at a word and close your eyes and say it over and over until you remember. I have lots of truble with *through* that you say *threw* and *enough* and *tough* that you dont say *enew* and *tew*. You got to say *enuff* and *tuff*. Thats how I use to write it before I started to get smart. Im confused but Miss Kinnian says theres no reason in spelling.

Apr 14 Finished *Robinson Crusoe.* I want to find out more about what happens to him but Miss Kinnian says thats all there is. *Why*

Apr 15 Miss Kinnian says Im lerning fast. She read some of the Progress Reports and she looked at me kind of funny. She says Im a fine person and Ill show them all. I asked her why. She said never mind but I shoudnt feel bad if I find out that everybody isnt nice like I think. She said for a person who god gave so little to you done more then a lot of people with brains they never even used. I said all my frends are smart people but there good. They like me and they never did anything that wasnt nice. Then she got something in her eye and she had to run out to the ladys room.

Apr 16 Today, I lerned, the *comma*, this is a comma (,) a period, with a tail, Miss Kinnian, says its importent, because, it makes writing better, she said, sombeody, coud lose, a lot of money, if a comma, isnt, in the, right place, I dont have, any money, and I dont see, how a comma, keeps you from losing it,

But she says, everybody, uses commas, so Ill use, them too,

Apr 17 I used the comma wrong. Its punctuation. Miss Kinnian told me to look up long words in the dictionary to lern to spell them. I said whats the difference if you can read it anyway. She said its part of your education so now on Ill look up all the words Im not sure how to spell. It takes a long time to write that way but I think Im remembering. I only have to look up once and after that I get it right. Anyway thats how come I got the word *punctuation* right. (Its that way in the dictionary). Miss Kinnian says a period is punctuation too, and there are lots of other marks to lern. I told her I thot all the periods had to have tails but she said no.

You got to mix them up, she showed? me" how. to mix! them(up,. and now; I can! mix up all kinds" of punctuation, in! my writing? There, are lots! of rules? to lern; but Im gettin'g them in my head.

One thing I? like about, Dear Miss Kinnian: (thats the way it goes in a business letter if I ever go into business) is she, always gives me' a reason" when—I ask. She's a gen'ius! I wish! I cou'd be smart" like, her; (Punctuation, is; fun!)

April 18 What a dope I am! I didn't even understand what she was talking about. I read the grammar book last night and it explanes the whole thing. Then I saw it was the same way as Miss Kinnian was trying to tell me, but I didn't get it. I got up in the middle of the night, and the whole thing straightened out in my mind.

Miss Kinnian said that the TV working in my sleep helped out. She said I reached a plateau. Thats like the flat top of a hill.

After I figgered out how punctuation worked, I read over all my old Progress Reports from the beginning. Boy, did I have crazy spelling and punctuation! I told Miss Kinnian I ought to go over the pages and fix all the mistakes but she said, "No, Charlie, Dr. Nemur wants them just as they are. That's why he let you keep them after they were photostated, to see your own progress. You're coming along fast, Charlie."

That made me feel good. After the lesson I went down and played with Algernon. We don't race anymore.

April 20 I feel sick inside. Not sick like for a doctor, but inside my chest it feels empty like getting punched and a heartburn at the same time.

I wasn't going to write about it, but I guess I got to, because it's important. Today was the first time I ever stayed home from work.

Last night Joe Carp and Frank Reilly invited me to a party. There were lots of girls and some men from the factory. I remembered how sick I got last time I drank too much, so I told Joe I didn't want anything to drink. He gave me a plain Coke instead. It tasted funny, but I thought it was just a bad taste in my mouth.

We had a lot of fun for a while. Joe said I should dance with Ellen and she would teach me the steps. I fell a few times and I couldn't understand why because no one else was dancing besides Ellen and me. And all the time I was tripping because somebody's foot was always sticking out.

Then when I got up I saw the look on Joe's face and it gave me a funny feeling in my stomack. "He's a scream," one of the girls said. Everybody was laughing.

Frank said, "I ain't laughed so much since we sent him off for the newspaper that night at Muggsy's and ditched him."

"Look at him. His face is red."

"He's blushing. Charlie is blushing."

"Hey, Ellen, what'd you do to Charlie? I never saw him act like that before."

I didn't know what to do or where to turn. Everyone was looking at me and laughing and I felt naked. I wanted to hide myself. I ran out into the street and I threw up. Then I walked home. It's a funny thing I never knew that Joe and Frank and the

Last night Joe Carp and Frank Reilly invited me to a party.

others liked to have me around all the time to make fun of me.

Now I know what it means when they say "to pull a Charlie Gordon."

I'm ashamed.

PROGRESS REPORT 10

April 21 Still didn't go into the factory. I told Mrs. Flynn my landlady to call and tell Mr. Donnegan I was sick. Mrs. Flynn looks at me very funny lately like she's scared of me.

I think it's a good thing about finding out how everybody laughs at me. I thought about it a lot. It's because I'm so dumb and I don't even know when I'm doing something dumb. People think it's funny when a dumb person can't do things the same way they can.

Anyway, now I know I'm getting smarter every day. I know punctuation and I can spell good. I like to look up all the hard words in the dictionary and I remember them. I'm reading a lot now, and Miss Kinnian says I read very fast. Sometimes I even understand what I'm reading about, and it stays in my mind. There are times when I can close my eyes and think of a page and it all comes back like a picture.

Besides history, geography, and arithmetic, Miss Kinnian said I should start to learn a few foreign languages. Dr. Strauss gave me some more tapes to play while I sleep. I still don't understand how that conscious and unconscious mind works, but Dr. Strauss says not to worry yet. He asked me to promise that when I start learning college subjects next week I wouldn't read any books on psychology—that is, until he gives me permission.

I feel a lot better today, but I guess I'm still a little angry that all the time people

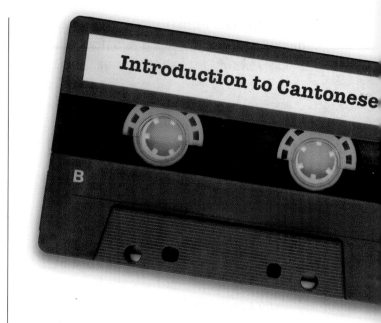

were laughing and making fun of me because I wasn't so smart. When I become intelligent like Dr. Strauss says, with three times my I.Q. of 68, then maybe I'll be like everyone else and people will like me and be friendly.

I'm not sure what an I.Q. is. Dr. Nemur said it was something that measured how intelligent you were—like a scale in the drugstore weighs pounds. But Dr. Strauss had a big argument with him and said an I.Q. didn't weigh intelligence at all. He said an I.Q. showed how much intelligence you could get, like the numbers on the outside of a measuring cup. You still had to fill the cup up with stuff.

Then when I asked Burt, who gives me my intelligence tests and works with Algernon, he said that both of them were wrong (only I had to promise not to tell them he said so). Burt says that the I.Q. measures a lot of different things including some of the things you learned already, and it really isn't any good at all.

So I still don't know what I.Q. is except that mine is going to be over 200 soon. I didn't want to say anything, but I don't see how if they don't know *what* it is, or *where* it is—I don't see how they know *how much* of it you've got.

Dr. Nemur says I have to take a *Rorschach Test* tomorrow. I wonder what *that* is.

April 22 I found out what a *Rorschach* is. It's the test I took before the operation—the one with the inkblots on the pieces of cardboard. The man who gave me the test was the same one.

I was scared to death of those inkblots. I knew he was going to ask me to find the pictures and I knew I wouldn't be able to. I was thinking to myself, if only there was some way of knowing what kind of pictures were hidden there. Maybe there weren't any pictures at all. Maybe it was just a trick to see if I was dumb enough to look for something that wasn't there. Just thinking about that made me sore at him.

"All right, Charlie," he said, "you've seen these cards before, remember?"

"Of course I remember."

The way I said it, he knew I was angry, and he looked surprised. "Yes, of course. Now I want you to look at this one. What might this be? What do you see on this card? People see all sorts of things in these inkblots. Tell me what it might be for you—what it makes you think of."

I was shocked. That wasn't what I had expected him to say at all. "You mean there are no pictures hidden in those inkblots?"

He frowned and took off his glasses. "What?"

"Pictures. Hidden in the inkblots. Last time you told me that everyone could see them and you wanted me to find them too."

He explained to me that the last time he had used almost the exact same words he was using now. I didn't believe it, and I still have the suspicion that he misled me at the time just for the fun of it. Unless—I don't know any more—could I have been *that* feebleminded?

· We went through the cards slowly. One of them looked like a pair of bats tugging at something. Another one looked like two men fencing with swords. I imagined all sorts of things. I guess I got carried away. But I didn't trust him any more, and I kept turning them around and even looking on the back to see if there was anything there I was supposed to catch. While he was making his notes, I peeked out of the corner of my eye to read it. But it was all in code that looked like this:

WF + A DdF-Ad orig. WF-A SF + obj

The test still doesn't make sense to me. It seems to me that anyone could make up lies about things that they didn't really see. How could he know I wasn't making a fool of him by mentioning things that I didn't really imagine? Maybe I'll understand it when Dr. Strauss lets me read up on psychology.

April 25 I figured out a new way to line up the machines in the factory, and Mr. Donnegan says it will save him ten thousand dollars a year in labor and increased production. He gave me a twenty-five-dollar bonus.

Vocabulary
misled (mis·led′) *v.:* fooled; led to believe something wrong.

I wanted to take Joe Carp and Frank Reilly out to lunch to celebrate, but Joe said he had to buy some things for his wife, and Frank said he was meeting his cousin for lunch. I guess it'll take a little time for them to get used to the changes in me. Everybody seems to be frightened of me. When I went over to Amos Borg and tapped him on the shoulder, he jumped up in the air.

People don't talk to me much anymore or kid around the way they used to. It makes the job kind of lonely.

April 27 I got up the nerve today to ask Miss Kinnian to have dinner with me tomorrow night to celebrate my bonus.

At first she wasn't sure it was right, but I asked Dr. Strauss and he said it was okay. Dr. Strauss and Dr. Nemur don't seem to be getting along so well. They're arguing all the time. This evening when I came in to ask Dr. Strauss about having dinner with Miss Kinnian, I heard them shouting. Dr. Nemur was saying that it was *his* experiment and *his* research, and Dr. Strauss was shouting back that he contributed just as much, because he found me through Miss Kinnian and he performed the operation. Dr. Strauss said that someday thousands of neurosurgeons might be using his technique all over the world.

Dr. Nemur wanted to publish the results of the experiment at the end of this month. Dr. Strauss wanted to wait a while longer to be sure. Dr. Strauss said that Dr. Nemur was more interested in the Chair of Psychology at Princeton than he was in the experiment. Dr. Nemur said that Dr. Strauss was nothing but an opportunist who was trying to ride to glory on *his* coattails.

When I left afterwards, I found myself trembling. I don't know why for sure, but it

was as if I'd seen both men clearly for the first time. I remember hearing Burt say that Dr. Nemur had a shrew of a wife who was pushing him all the time to get things published so that he could become famous. Burt said that the dream of her life was to have a big shot husband.

Was Dr. Strauss really trying to ride on his coattails?

April 28 I don't understand why I never noticed how beautiful Miss Kinnian really is. She has brown eyes and feathery brown hair

I don't understand why I never noticed how beautiful Miss Kinnian really is.

that comes to the top of her neck. She's only thirty-four! I think from the beginning I had the feeling that she was an unreachable genius—and very, very old. Now, every time I see her she grows younger and more lovely.

We had dinner and a long talk. When she said that I was coming along so fast that soon I'd be leaving her behind, I laughed.

"It's true, Charlie. You're already a better reader than I am. You can read a whole page at a glance while I can take in only a few lines at a time. And you remember every single thing you read. I'm lucky if I can recall the main thoughts and the general meaning."

"I don't feel intelligent. There are so many things I don't understand."

She took out a cigarette and I lit it for her. "You've got to be a *little* patient. You're accomplishing in days and weeks what it takes normal people to do in half a lifetime. That's what makes it so amazing. You're like a giant sponge now, soaking things in. Facts, figures, general knowledge. And soon you'll begin to connect them, too. You'll see how the different branches of learning are related. There are many levels, Charlie, like steps on a giant ladder that take you up higher and higher to see more and more of the world around you.

"I can see only a little bit of that, Charlie, and I won't go much higher than I am now, but you'll keep climbing up and up, and see more and more, and each step will open new worlds that you never even knew existed." She frowned. "I hope . . . I just hope to God—"

"What?"

"Never mind, Charles. I just hope I wasn't wrong to advise you to go into this in the first place."

I laughed. "How could that be? It worked, didn't it? Even Algernon is still smart."

We sat there silently for a while and I knew what she was thinking about as she watched me toying with the chain of my rabbit's foot and my keys. I didn't want to think of that possibility any more than elderly people want to think of death. I knew that this was only the beginning. I knew what she meant about levels because I'd seen some of them already. The thought of leaving her behind made me sad.

I'm in love with Miss Kinnian.

PROGRESS REPORT 11

April 30 I've quit my job with Donnegan's Plastic Box Company. Mr. Donnegan insisted that it would be better for all concerned if I left. What did I do to make them hate me so?

The first I knew of it was when Mr. Donnegan showed me the petition. Eight hundred and forty names, everyone connected with the factory, except Fanny Girden. Scanning the list quickly, I saw at

once that hers was the only missing name. All the rest demanded that I be fired.

Joe Carp and Frank Reilly wouldn't talk to me about it. No one else would either, except Fanny. She was one of the few people I'd known who set her mind to something and believed it no matter what the rest of the world proved, said, or did—and Fanny did not believe that I should have been fired. She had been against the petition on principle and despite the pressure and threats she'd held out.

"Which don't mean to say," she remarked, "that I don't think there's something mighty strange about you, Charlie. Them changes. I don't know. You used to be a good, dependable, ordinary man—not too bright maybe, but honest. Who knows what you done to yourself to get so smart all of a sudden. Like everybody around here's been saying, Charlie, it's not right."

"But how can you say that, Fanny? What's wrong with a man becoming intelligent and wanting to acquire knowledge and understanding of the world around him?"

She stared down at her work and I turned to leave. Without looking at me, she said: "It was evil when Eve listened to the snake and ate from the tree of knowledge. It was evil when she saw that she was naked. If not for that none of us would ever have to grow old and sick, and die."

Once again now I have the feeling of shame burning inside me. This intelligence has driven a wedge between me and all the people I once knew and loved. Before, they laughed at me and despised me for my ignorance and dullness; now, they hate me for my knowledge and understanding. What in God's name do they want of me?

They've driven me out of the factory. Now I'm more alone than ever before . . .

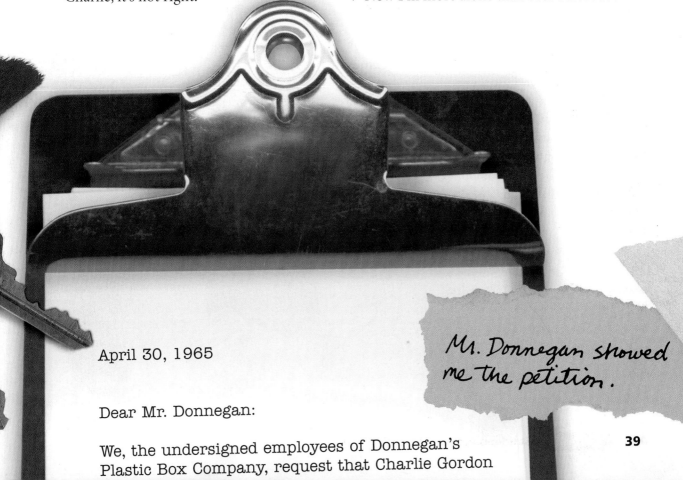

April 30, 1965

Mr. Donnegan showed me the petition.

Dear Mr. Donnegan:

We, the undersigned employees of Donnegan's Plastic Box Company, request that Charlie Gordon

Literary Response and Analysis
Part 1

Reading Check

1. What is the operation meant to do for Charlie?

2. Why does Dr. Strauss think Charlie would be a good subject for the experiment?

3. Who is Algernon? What happens when Charlie first races Algernon?

4. What are some signs that Charlie is changing now that he's had the operation?

Interpretations

5. Re-read your Quickwrite. Then, add two or three sentences connecting what you wrote earlier with your thoughts about what has happened in the story so far.

6. Go back to Charlie's March 7 entry (pages 25–26). What **context clues** did you use to figure out what "crazy tests" Charlie is taking (such as the "*amazed*" with Algernon)? Give some other examples of how you used context clues to figure out what Charlie is reporting.

7. Re-read Fanny's comments about the changes in Charlie (page 39). How are Charlie's experiences similar to those of Adam and Eve? (Look especially at Charlie's entry for April 20. You may want to compare his description with the biblical account, in Genesis 2:25–3:24.)

8. Early in the story, Dr. Strauss tells Dr. Nemur that Charlie's learning to read and write is as much of an achievement as their learning a difficult scientific theory without help (page 26). What does he mean? Challenge or defend his statement.

9. Think about the last few lines in Part 1. What do you think about people who dislike others who are different from them?

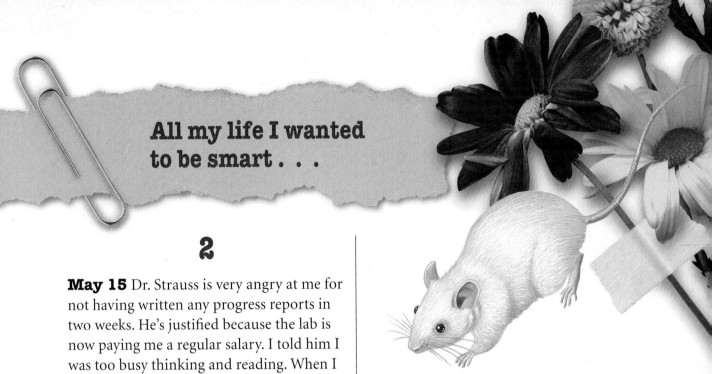

All my life I wanted to be smart . . .

2

May 15 Dr. Strauss is very angry at me for not having written any progress reports in two weeks. He's justified because the lab is now paying me a regular salary. I told him I was too busy thinking and reading. When I pointed out that writing was such a slow process that it made me impatient with my poor handwriting, he suggested that I learn to type. It's much easier to write now because I can type nearly seventy-five words a minute. Dr. Strauss continually reminds me of the need to speak and write simply so that people will be able to understand me.

I'll try to review all the things that happened to me during the last two weeks. Algernon and I were presented to the American Psychological Association sitting in convention with the World Psychological Association last Tuesday. We created quite a sensation. Dr. Nemur and Dr. Strauss were proud of us.

I suspect that Dr. Nemur, who is sixty—ten years older than Dr. Strauss—finds it necessary to see <u>tangible</u> results of his work. Undoubtedly the results of pressure by Mrs. Nemur.

Contrary to my earlier impressions of him, I realize that Dr. Nemur is not at all a genius. He has a very good mind, but it struggles under the specter of self-doubt. He wants people to take him for a genius. Therefore, it is important for him to feel that his work is accepted by the world. I believe that Dr. Nemur was afraid of further delay because he worried that someone else might make a discovery along these lines and take the credit from him.

Dr. Strauss on the other hand might be called a genius, although I feel that his areas of knowledge are too limited. He was educated in the tradition of narrow specialization; the broader aspects of background were neglected far more than necessary—even for a neurosurgeon.

I was shocked to learn that the only ancient languages he could read were Latin, Greek, and Hebrew, and that he knows almost nothing of mathematics beyond the elementary levels of the calculus

Vocabulary
tangible (tan′jə·bəl) *adj.*: capable of being seen or felt.

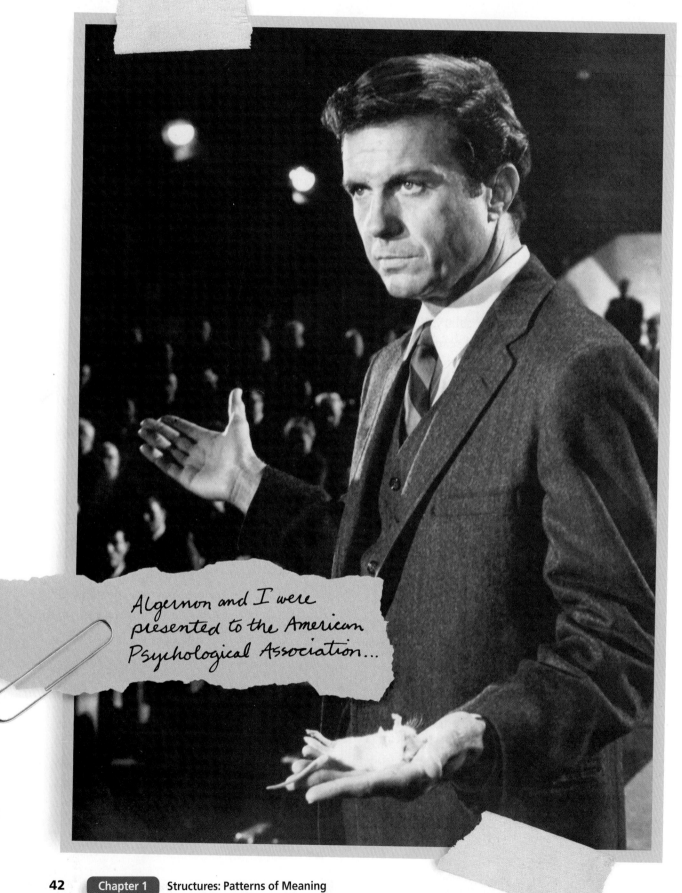

Algernon and I were presented to the American Psychological Association...

of variations. When he admitted this to me, I found myself almost annoyed. It was as if he'd hidden this part of himself in order to deceive me, pretending—as do many people, I've discovered—to be what he is not. No one I've ever known is what he appears to be on the surface.

Dr. Nemur appears to be uncomfortable around me. Sometimes when I try to talk to him, he just looks at me strangely and turns away. I was angry at first when Dr. Strauss told me I was giving Dr. Nemur an inferiority complex. I thought he was mocking me and I'm oversensitive at being made fun of.

How was I to know that a highly respected psychoexperimentalist like Nemur was unacquainted with Hindustani and Chinese? It's absurd when you consider the work that is being done in India and China today in the very field of his study.

I asked Dr. Strauss how Nemur could refute Rahajamati's attack on his method and results if Nemur couldn't even read them in the first place. That strange look on Dr. Strauss's face can mean only one of two things. Either he doesn't want to tell Nemur what they're saying in India, or else—and this worries me—Dr. Strauss doesn't know either. I must be careful to speak and write clearly and simply so that people won't laugh.

May 18 I am very disturbed. I saw Miss Kinnian last night for the first time in over a week. I tried to avoid all discussions of intellectual concepts and to keep the conversation on a simple, everyday level, but she just stared at me blankly and asked me what I meant about the mathematical variance equivalent in Dorbermann's Fifth Concerto.

When I tried to explain she stopped me and laughed. I guess I got angry, but I suspect I'm approaching her on the wrong level. No matter what I try to discuss with her, I am unable to communicate. I must review Vrostadt's equations on *Levels of Semantic Progression*. I find that I don't communicate with people much anymore. Thank God for books and music and things I can think about. I am alone in my apartment at Mrs. Flynn's boardinghouse most of the time and seldom speak to anyone.

May 20 I would not have noticed the new dishwasher, a boy of about sixteen, at the corner diner where I take my evening meals if not for the incident of the broken dishes.

They crashed to the floor, shattering and sending bits of white china under the tables. The boy stood there, dazed and frightened, holding the empty tray in his hand. The whistles and catcalls[1] from the customers (the cries of "Hey, there go the profits!" . . . "Mazel tov!"[2] . . . and "Well, *he* didn't work here very long . . ." which invariably seem to follow the breaking of glass or dishware in a public restaurant) all seemed to confuse him.

When the owner came to see what the excitement was about, the boy cowered as if he expected to be struck and threw up his arms as if to ward off the blow.

---

1. **catcalls** *n.:* shouts and whistles made to express disapproval or ridicule, so called because people used to make noises like a cat's cry to show disapproval.
2. **mazel tov** (mä′zəl tōv′): Yiddish expression meaning "congratulations."

Vocabulary
refute (ri·fyo͞ot′) *v.:* prove wrong using evidence.
invariably (in·ver′ē·ə·blē) *adv.:* always.

"All right! All right, you dope," shouted the owner, "don't just stand there! Get the broom and sweep that mess up. A broom . . . a broom, you idiot! It's in the kitchen. Sweep up all the pieces."

The boy saw that he was not going to be punished. His frightened expression disappeared and he smiled and hummed as he came back with the broom to sweep the floor. A few of the rowdier customers kept up the remarks, amusing themselves at his expense.

"Here, sonny, over here there's a nice piece behind you . . ."

"C'mon, do it again . . ."

"He's not so dumb. It's easier to break 'em than to wash 'em . . ."

As his vacant eyes moved across the crowd of amused onlookers, he slowly mirrored their smiles and finally broke into an uncertain grin at the joke which he obviously did not understand.

I felt sick inside as I looked at his dull, vacuous smile, the wide, bright eyes of a child, uncertain but eager to please. They were laughing at him because he was mentally retarded.

And I had been laughing at him too.

Suddenly, I was furious at myself and all those who were smirking at him. I jumped up and shouted, "Shut up! Leave him alone! It's not his fault he can't understand! He can't help what he is! But for God's sake . . . he's still a human being!"

The room grew silent. I cursed myself for losing control and creating a scene. I tried not to look at the boy as I paid my check and walked out without touching my food. I felt ashamed for both of us.

How strange it is that people of honest feelings and sensibility, who would not take advantage of a man born without arms or legs or eyes—how such people think nothing of abusing a man born with low intelligence. It infuriated me to think that not too long ago I, like this boy, had foolishly played the clown.

And I had almost forgotten.

I'd hidden the picture of the old Charlie Gordon from myself because now that I was intelligent it was something that had to be pushed out of my mind. But today in looking at that boy, for the first time I saw what I had been. *I was just like him!*

Only a short time ago, I learned that people laughed at me. Now I can see that unknowingly I joined with them in laughing at myself. That hurts most of all.

I have often re-read my progress reports and seen the illiteracy, the childish naiveté,[3] the mind of low intelligence peering from a dark room, through the keyhole, at the dazzling light outside. I see that even in my dullness I knew that I was inferior, and that other people had something I lacked—something denied me. In my mental blindness, I thought that it was somehow connected with the ability to read and write, and I was sure that if I could get those skills I would automatically have intelligence too.

Even a feeble-minded man wants to be like other men.

A child may not know how to feed itself, or what to eat, yet it knows of hunger.

This then is what I was like. I never knew. Even with my gift of intellectual awareness, I never really knew.

This day was good for me. Seeing the past more clearly, I have decided to use my knowledge and skills to work in the field of increasing human intelligence levels. Who is better equipped for this work? Who else has lived in both worlds? These are my people. Let me use my gift to do something for them.

Tomorrow, I will discuss with Dr. Strauss the manner in which I can work in this area. I may be able to help him work out the problems of widespread use of the technique which was used on me. I have several good ideas of my own.

There is so much that might be done with this technique. If I could be made into a genius, what about thousands of others like myself? What fantastic levels might be achieved by using this technique on normal people? On *geniuses*?

___
3. **naiveté** (nä·ēv·tā') *n.:* simplicity; foolish innocence.

There are so many doors to open. I am impatient to begin.

PROGRESS REPORT 12

May 23 It happened today. Algernon bit me. I visited the lab to see him as I do occasionally, and when I took him out of his cage, he snapped at my hand. I put him back and watched him for a while. He was unusually disturbed and vicious.

May 24 Burt, who is in charge of the experimental animals, tells me that Algernon is changing. He is less cooperative, he refuses to run the maze any more; general motivation has decreased. And he hasn't been eating. Everyone is upset about what this may mean.

May 25 They've been feeding Algernon, who now refuses to work the shifting-lock problem. Everyone identifies me with Algernon. In a way we're both the first of our kind. They're all pretending that Algernon's behavior is not necessarily significant for me. But it's hard to hide the fact that some of the other animals who were used in this experiment are showing strange behavior.

Dr. Strauss and Dr. Nemur have asked me not to come to the lab anymore. I know what they're thinking but I can't accept it. I am going ahead with my plans to carry their research forward. With all due respect to both of these fine scientists, I am well aware of their limitations. If there is an answer, I'll have to find it out for myself. Suddenly, time has become very important to me.

May 29 I have been given a lab of my own and permission to go ahead with the research. I'm on to something. Working day and night. I've had a cot moved into the lab. Most of my writing time is spent on the notes which I keep in a separate folder, but from time to time I feel it necessary to put down my moods and my thoughts out of sheer habit.

I find the *calculus of intelligence* to be a fascinating study. Here is the place for the application of all the knowledge I have acquired. In a sense it's the problem I've been concerned with all my life.

May 31 Dr. Strauss thinks I'm working too hard. Dr. Nemur says I'm trying to cram a lifetime of research and thought into a few weeks. I know I should rest, but I'm driven on by something inside that won't let me stop. I've got to find the reason for the sharp regression in Algernon. I've got to know *if* and *when* it will happen to me.

Vocabulary
regression (ri·gresh'ən) *n.*: return to an earlier or less advanced condition.

The Algernon-Gordon Effect:
A Study of Structure and Function

I have been given a lab of my own and permission to go ahead with the research.

June 4

LETTER TO DR. STRAUSS (*copy*)

Dear Dr. Strauss:

Under separate cover I am sending you a copy of my report entitled, "The Algernon-Gordon Effect: A Study of Structure and Function of Increased Intelligence," which I would like to have you read and have published.

As you see, my experiments are completed. I have included in my report all of my formulae, as well as mathematical analysis in the appendix. Of course, these should be verified.

Because of its importance to both you and Dr. Nemur (and need I say to myself, too?) I have checked and rechecked my results a dozen times in the hope of finding an error. I am sorry to say the results must stand. Yet for the sake of science, I am grateful for the little bit that I here add to the knowledge of the function of the human mind and of the laws governing the artificial increase of human intelligence.

I recall your once saying to me that an experimental *failure* or the *disproving* of a theory was as important to the advancement of learning as a success would be. I know now that this is true. I am sorry, however, that my own contribution to the field must rest upon the ashes of the work of two men I regard so highly.

Yours truly,
Charles Gordon
encl.: rept

June 5 I must not become emotional. The facts and the results of my experiments are clear, and the more sensational aspects of my own rapid climb cannot obscure the fact that the tripling of intelligence by the surgical technique developed by Drs. Strauss and Nemur must be viewed as having little or no practical applicability (at the present time) to the increase of human intelligence.

As I review the records and data on Algernon, I see that although he is still in his physical infancy, he has regressed mentally. Motor activity is impaired; there is a general reduction of glandular activity; there is an accelerated loss of coordination.

There are also strong indications of progressive amnesia.

As will be seen by my report, these and other physical and mental deterioration syndromes can be predicted with statistically significant results by the application of my formula.

The surgical stimulus to which we were both subjected has resulted in an intensification and acceleration of all mental processes. The unforeseen development, which I have taken the liberty of calling the *Algernon-Gordon Effect*, is the logical extension of the entire intelligence speed-up. The hypothesis here proven may be described simply in the following terms: Artificially increased intelligence deteriorates at a rate of time directly proportional to the quantity of the increase.

Vocabulary

verified (verʹə·fīdʹ) *v.*: confirmed; checked or tested for correctness.

obscure (əb·skyo͞orʹ) *v.*: hide.

deterioration (dē·tir'ē·ə·rāʹshən) *n.* used as *adj.*: worsening; decline.

hypothesis (hī·päthʹə·sis) *n.*: explanation or theory to be proved.

I feel that this, in itself, is an important discovery.

As long as I am able to write, I will continue to record my thoughts in these progress reports. It is one of my few pleasures. However, by all indications, my own mental deterioration will be very rapid.

I have already begun to notice signs of emotional instability and forgetfulness, the first symptoms of the burnout.

June 10 Deterioration progressing. I have become absent-minded. Algernon died two days ago. Dissection shows my predictions were right. His brain had decreased in weight and there was a general smoothing out of cerebral convolutions as well as a deepening and broadening of brain fissures.[4]

---

4. **brain fissures** (fish′ərz): grooves in the surface of the brain.

I guess the same thing is or will soon be happening to me. Now that it's definite, I don't want it to happen.

I put Algernon's body in a cheese box and buried him in the backyard. I cried.

June 15 Dr. Strauss came to see me again. I wouldn't open the door and I told him to go away. I want to be left to myself. I have become touchy and irritable. I feel the darkness closing in. It's hard to throw off thoughts of suicide. I keep telling myself how important this introspective journal will be.

It's a strange sensation to pick up a book that you've read and enjoyed just a few months ago and discover that you don't remember it. I remembered how great I thought John Milton was, but when I picked up *Paradise Lost* I couldn't understand it at all. I got so angry I threw the book across the room.

I've got to try to hold on to some of it. Some of the things I've learned. Oh, God, please don't take it all away.

June 19 Sometimes, at night, I go out for a walk. Last night I couldn't remember where I lived. A policeman took me home. I have the strange feeling that this has all happened to me before—a long time ago. I keep telling myself I'm the only person in the world who can describe what's happening to me.

June 21 Why can't I remember? I've got to fight. I lie in bed for days and I don't

Vocabulary

introspective (in′trə·spek′tiv) *adj.:* looking inward; observing one's own thoughts and feelings.

know who or where I am. Then it all comes back to me in a flash. Fugues of amnesia.[5] Symptoms of senility—second childhood. I can watch them coming on. It's so cruelly logical. I learned so much and so fast. Now my mind is deteriorating rapidly. I won't let it happen. I'll fight it. I can't help thinking of the boy in the restaurant, the blank expression, the silly smile, the people laughing at him. No—please—not that again . . .

June 22 I'm forgetting things that I learned recently. It seems to be following the classic pattern—the last things learned are the first things forgotten. Or is that the pattern? I'd better look it up again. . . .

I re-read my paper on the *Algernon-Gordon Effect* and I get the strange feeling that it was written by someone else. There are parts I don't even understand.

Motor activity impaired. I keep tripping over things, and it becomes increasingly difficult to type.

June 23 I've given up using the typewriter completely. My coordination is bad. I feel that I'm moving slower and slower. Had a terrible shock today. I picked up a copy of an article I used in my research, Krueger's *Uber psychische Ganzheit,* to see if it would help me understand what I had done. First I thought there was something wrong with my eyes. Then I realized I could no longer read German. I tested myself in other languages. All gone.

June 30 A week since I dared to write again. It's slipping away like sand through my fingers. Most of the books I have are too hard for me now. I get angry with them because I know that I read and understood them just a few weeks ago.

I keep telling myself I must keep writing these reports so that somebody will know what is happening to me. But it gets harder to form the words and remember spellings. I have to look up even simple words in the dictionary now and it makes me impatient with myself.

Dr. Strauss comes around almost every day, but I told him I wouldn't see or speak to anybody. He feels guilty. They all do. But I don't blame anyone. I knew what might happen. But how it hurts.

July 7 I don't know where the week went. Todays Sunday I know becuase I can see through my window people going to church. I think I stayed in bed all week but I remember Mrs. Flynn bringing food to me a few times. I keep saying over and over Ive got to do something but then I forget or maybe its just easier not to do what I say Im going to do.

I think of my mother and father a lot these days. I found a picture of them with me taken at a beach. My father has a big ball under his arm and my mother is holding me by the hand. I dont remember them the way they are in the picture. All I remember is my father drunk most of the time and arguing with mom about money.

He never shaved much and he used to scratch my face when he hugged me. My mother said he died but Cousin Miltie said he heard his mom and dad say that my father ran away with another woman. When I asked my mother she slapped my face and said my father was dead. I dont think I ever

---

5. **fugues** (fyo͞ogz) **of amnesia** (am·nē′zhə): temporary states of disturbed consciousness. A person who experiences fugues has no memory of them afterward.

found out which was true but I don't care much. (He said he was going to take me to see cows on a farm once but he never did. He never kept his promises . . .)

July 10 My landlady Mrs Flynn is very worried about me. She says the way I lay around all day and dont do anything I remind her of her son before she threw him out of the house. She said she doesn't like loafers. If Im sick its one thing, but if Im a loafer thats another thing and she wont have it. I told her I think Im sick.

I try to read a little bit every day, mostly stories, but sometimes I have to read the same thing over and over again because I dont know what it means. And its hard to write. I know I should look up all the words in the dictionary but its so hard and Im so tired all the time.

Then I got the idea that I would only use the easy words instead of the long hard ones. That saves time. I put flowers on Algernons grave about once a week. Mrs Flynn thinks Im crazy to put flowers on a mouses grave but I told her that Algernon was special.

July 14 Its sunday again. I dont have anything to do to keep me busy now because my television set is broke and I dont have any money to get it fixed. (I think I lost this months check from the lab. I dont remember)

I get awful headaches and asperin doesnt help me much. Mrs Flynn knows Im really sick and she feels very sorry for me. Shes a wonderful woman whenever someone is sick.

July 22 Mrs Flynn called a strange doctor to see me. She was afraid I was going to die.

I told the doctor I wasnt too sick and that I only forget sometimes. He asked me did I have any friends or relatives and I said no I dont have any. I told him I had a friend called Algernon once but he was a mouse and we used to run races together. He looked at me kind of funny like he thought I was crazy.

He smiled when I told him I used to be a genius. He talked to me like I was a baby and he winked at Mrs Flynn. I got mad and chased him out because he was making fun of me the way they all used to.

July 24 I have no more money and Mrs Flynn says I got to go to work somewhere and pay the rent because I havent paid for over two months. I dont know any work but the job I used to have at Donnegans Plastic Box Company. I dont want to go back there because they all knew me when I was smart and maybe theyll laugh at me. But I don't know what else to do to get money.

July 25 I was looking at some of my old progress reports and its very funny but I cant read what I wrote. I can make out some of the words but they dont make sense.

Miss Kinnian came to the door but I said go away I dont want to see you. She cried and I cried too but I wouldnt let her in because I didn't want her to laugh at me. I told her I didn't like her any more. I told her I didnt want to be smart any more. Thats not true. I still love her and I still want to be smart but I had to say that so shed go away. She gave Mrs Flynn money to pay the rent. I dont want that. I got to get a job.

Mr. Donnegan was very nice when I came back and asked him for my old job of janitor.

Please . . . please let me not forget how to read and write . . .

July 27 Mr Donnegan was very nice when I came back and asked him for my old job of janitor. First he was very suspicious but I told him what happened to me then he looked very sad and put his hand on my shoulder and said Charlie Gordon you got guts.

Everybody looked at me when I came downstairs and started working in the toilet sweeping it out like I used to. I told myself Charlie if they make fun of you dont get sore because you remember their not so smart as you once thot they were. And besides they were once your friends and if they laughed at you that doesnt mean anything because they liked you too.

One of the new men who came to work there after I went away made a nasty crack he said hey Charlie I hear your a very smart fella a real quiz kid. Say something intelligent. I felt bad but Joe Carp came over and grabbed him by the shirt and said leave him alone you lousy cracker or Ill break your neck. I didn't expect Joe to take my part so I guess hes really my friend.

Later Frank Reilly came over and said Charlie if anybody bothers you or trys to take advantage you call me or Joe and we will set em straight. I said thanks Frank and I got choked up so I had to turn around and go into the supply room so he wouldnt see me cry. Its good to have friends.

July 28 I did a dumb thing today I forgot I wasnt in Miss Kinnians class at the adult center any more like I use to be. I went in and sat down in my old seat in the back of the room and she looked at me funny and she said Charles. I dint remember she ever called me that before only Charlie so I said hello Miss Kinnian Im redy for my lesin today only I lost my reader that we was using. She startid to cry and run out of the room and everybody looked at me and I saw they wasnt the same pepul who used to be in my class.

Then all of a suddin I rememberd some things about the operashun and me getting smart and I said holy smoke I reely pulled a Charlie Gordon that time. I went away before she come back to the room.

Thats why Im going away from New York for good. I dont want to do nothing like that agen. I dont want Miss Kinnian to feel sorry for me. Evry body feels sorry at the factery and I dont want that eather so Im going someplace where nobody knows that Charlie Gordon was once a genus and now he cant even reed a book or rite good.

Im taking a cuple of books along and even if I cant reed them Ill practise hard and maybe I wont forget every thing I lerned. If I try reel hard maybe Ill be a littel bit smarter then I was before the operashun. I got my rabits foot and my luky penny and maybe they will help me.

If you ever reed this Miss Kinnian dont be sorry for me Im glad I got a second chanse to be smart becaus I lerned a lot of things that I never even new were in this world and Im grateful that I saw it all for a littel bit. I dont know why Im dumb agen or what I did wrong maybe its becaus I dint try hard enuff. But if I try and practis very hard maybe Ill get a littl smarter and know what all the words are. I remember a littel bit how nice I had a feeling with the blue book that has the torn cover when I red it. Thats why Im gonna keep trying to get smart so I can have that feeling agen. Its a good feeling to know things and be smart. I wish I had it rite now if I did I would sit down and reed all the time. Anyway I bet Im the first dumb person in the world who ever found out somthing importent for sience. I remember I did somthing but I dont remember what. So I gess its like I did it for all the dumb pepul like me.

Good-by Miss Kinnian and Dr Strauss and evreybody. And P.S. please tell Dr Nemur not to be such a grouch when pepul laff at him and he woud have more frends. Its easy to make frends if you let pepul laff at you. Im going to have lots of frends where I go.

P.P.S. Please if you get a chanse put some flowrs on Algernons grave in the bakyard . . .

Daniel Keyes

"Fascinated by the . . . Human Mind"

Daniel Keyes (1927–   ) says that he is "fascinated by the complexities of the human mind." Many people share his interest, as the enormous popularity of "Flowers for Algernon" shows. The story won the 1959 Hugo Award, given by the Science Fiction Writers of America, and it has been widely translated. Keyes expanded it into a novel, which won another science fiction prize, the Nebula Award, in 1966. The story was also made into a movie, *Charly*, a television play, *The Two Worlds of Charlie Gordon*, and even a Broadway musical, *Charlie and Algernon*.

Daniel Keyes was born in Brooklyn, New York. He has worked as an English teacher, a merchant seaman, an editor, and a fashion photographer.

For Independent Reading

Keyes has written a book about the process of writing his famous story. It is called *Algernon, Charlie and I*.

Literary Response and Analysis
Part 2

Reading Check

1. At the beginning of Part 2, what **conflicts** is Charlie having with the doctors? with himself?

2. How does Charlie react when the boy in the diner drops the dishes?

3. What does Charlie's research reveal about the results of the experiment?

4. What are some of the signals that tell you that Charlie's mental state is getting worse?

5. At the end of the story, why does Charlie decide to leave New York?

Interpretations

6. Why is Algernon important to Charlie?

7. Charlie takes a Rorschach test twice. These two incidents can be called **parallel episodes.** What other parallel episodes can you find in this story?

8. An important **subplot** in this story involves Charlie's relationship with Miss Kinnian. What is the **resolution** of that subplot?

9. Why would some people say that Charlie would be better off if he had not had the operation? What do you think?

10. At the end of the story, Charlie writes, "Its easy to make frends if you let pepul laff at you." Do you agree or disagree with Charlie's opinion? Explain.

11. What do you think becomes of Charlie after the story ends? Why?

12. Describe your feelings about "human engineering"—for example, using science to change a person's intelligence or personality.

Evaluation

13. Comment on whether you find the story believable. (Do you think the story shows how people really behave toward those who are mentally challenged? Do you think scientists will be able to increase intelligence someday?)

Writing

Dear Diary . . .

This story is made up of Charlie's progress reports, which are like a diary or journal. Pick another character from the story, and write a diary entry for him or her corresponding to one of Charlie's reports. For example, what might Miss Kinnian have written the night she and Charlie had dinner? What might Frank have written the day Charlie returned to work at the factory? Use the first-person pronoun *I* to write from your character's **point of view.**

BONUS QUESTION

What do *you* see in the inkblot on page 25?

Reading Standard 3.2
Evaluate the structural elements of the plot (for example, subplots, parallel episodes, climax), the plot's development, and the way in which conflicts are (or are not) addressed and resolved.

Vocabulary Development

History of the English Language

Digging into the Past. Where did English come from? England, of course! Not entirely. People didn't wake up one morning speaking the English of today. Today's English developed over a long period of time. The history of English can be divided into three periods: **Old English** (A.D. 450–1066), **Middle English** (1066–1485), and **Modern English** (1485 to the present).

Old English. In the fifth century, the Anglo-Saxons migrated from northern Europe to the island of Britain. There they found the Britons, a Celtic people who had earlier been conquered by the Romans. The Anglo-Saxons settled in and proceeded to develop a new language, combining bits from their old Germanic language and bits from the Celtic language of the natives. Soon Britain was invaded again, this time by the fierce Northmen, or Vikings, from Scandinavia. Their language, Norse, also was added to the language of Britain. We call this new language Old English. It was a spoken, or oral, language. Anyone who wanted to write something down wrote it in Latin. Here are three Old English words that survive today: *horse, night, wife.*

Middle English. In the year 1066, William the Conqueror, who was from Normandy, in France, conquered England. Soon French words were added to the mix. Because French developed from Latin, Latin also became an important influence on English. For several hundred years, England was a bilingual country. French was spoken by the upper classes and used in courts and government. English was spoken by the lower classes and used for the purposes of daily life. Latin was used by the Church. Most people spoke English, but they were borrowing words from French at a rapid rate. English continued to grow and change with all these borrowings—from Anglo-Saxon, Norse, Latin, French—resulting today in a language with a huge vocabulary that is both rich and international. Here are three words derived from French: *government, justice, literature.*

(*continued on next page*)

Reading Standard 1.2 Understand the most important points in the history of the English language, and use common word origins to determine the historical influences on English word meanings.

Modern English. In 1485, Henry VII, the first Tudor king, came to the throne of England. The House of Tudor helped to promote all things English—including the language. Printed books helped to make it possible for all English people to speak, read, and write the same language.

As you can see, there is more to an English word than its present-day definition. Our words have a past! You can dig into this past by looking up the **etymology** (et′ə·mäl′ə·jē), or origin and development of a word, in a dictionary. Consider this entry for the etymology of the word *obscure*. (The symbol < means "derived from" or "came from.")

> **obscure**   OFr *obscur* < L *obscurus*, "covered over"

Translated, this means "The word *obscure* evolved from the Old French word *obscur*, which in turn came from the Latin word *obscurus*, which means 'covered over.'"

PRACTICE

Dig into the past of three words from the Word Bank by using a good dictionary to look up their etymologies. You might have to go to more than one entry in the dictionary to get all your data for each word. Then, "translate" the story you discover behind each word. Make a word map, like the one below, based on the definitions and etymologies of the words. For each word, include a sentence that shows you understand the word's meaning.

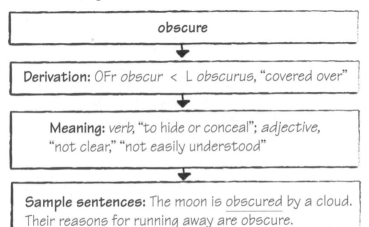

obscure

↓

Derivation: OFr *obscur* < L *obscurus*, "covered over"

↓

Meaning: *verb*, "to hide or conceal"; *adjective*, "not clear," "not easily understood"

↓

Sample sentences: The moon is obscured by a cloud. Their reasons for running away are obscure.

Word Bank

misled
tangible
refute
invariably
regression
verified
obscure
deterioration
hypothesis
introspective

Memory a Matter of Brains and Brawn

Analyzing Proposition and Support

Writers constantly try to persuade you to do things—to go somewhere, to buy something, to think a certain way. It's important to read persuasive arguments critically. You need to evaluate the writer's arguments to determine how credible—that is, how believable—they are.

The writer of a persuasive article usually begins with a **proposition,** which is an opinion. The proposition should be clearly stated. Then it's up to you to evaluate each reason that **supports** the proposition. A **reason** answers the question *why?* about the proposition statement.

Recognizing Support

A proposition can be supported with the following evidence:

- **facts,** including the results of scientific research and surveys

- **statistics**—facts in number form

- **examples**—specific instances that illustrate reasons or facts

- **anecdotes**—brief stories, such as personal experiences

- **definitions**

- **opinions from experts** on the subject, especially with direct quotations

Facts Versus Opinions

When you read persuasion, you must determine which statements are facts and which are opinions.

- A **fact** is something that can be proved true by direct observation or by checking a reliable reference source, such as an encyclopedia.

    The following statement is a **fact:** *I.Q. tests measure logical, verbal, and mathematical ability.*

    This statement is not a fact: *I.Q. tests are reliable measures of human ability.* It might sound like a fact, but it's the kind of statement that is impossible to prove.

- An **opinion** is a belief or an attitude. An opinion cannot be proved true or false, but it can be supported with facts.

    This statement is an **opinion:** *Albert Einstein is the greatest genius ever born.* It's a fact that Einstein was a genius, but no one can prove that he is the greatest genius ever born.

Vocabulary Development

The following words appear in the next article:

inevitable (in·ev′i·tə·bəl) *adj.:* unavoidable.

crucial (krōo′shəl) *adj.:* highly important.

provocative (prə·väk′ə·tiv) *adj.:* stirring up thoughts or feelings.

irrevocably (i·rev′ə·kə·blē) *adv.:* in a way that cannot be undone or changed.

cognitive (käg′nə·tiv) *adj.:* having to do with the process of knowing and being able to remember.

Reading Standard 2.2 Analyze text that uses proposition and support patterns.

Memory a Matter of Brains and Brawn

Mental, Physical Exertion Needed to Preserve the Mind

By Lauran Neergaard
ASSOCIATED PRESS

The brain is like a muscle: Use it or lose it.

That is the growing conclusion from research that shows fogged memory and slowed wit are not inevitable consequences of getting old, and there are steps people can take to protect their brains.

Mental exercise seems crucial. Benefits start when parents read to tots and depend heavily on education, but scientists say it is never too late to start jogging the gray matter.

People have to get physical, too. Bad memory is linked to heart disease, diabetes, and a high-fat diet—all risks that people can counter by living healthier lives.

In fact, provocative new research suggests these brain-protective steps, mental and physical, may be strong enough even to help influence who gets Alzheimer's disease.

"There are some things that,

if you know you have a family history (of Alzheimer's) and you're just 20 to 30 years old, you can start doing to increase your protective factors," said Dr. Amir Soas of Case Western Reserve University Medical School in Cleveland.

It is also good advice for the average baby boomer hoping to stay sharp, or the mom priming her child for a lifelong healthy brain.

Most important: "Read, read, read," Soas said. Do crossword puzzles. Pull out the chessboard or Scrabble. Learn a foreign language or a new hobby. "Anything that stimulates the brain to think," he said.

And cut back on television, Soas insists. "When you watch television, your brain goes into neutral," he said.

Just a few years ago, scientists believed the brain was wired forever before age 5 and that over the ensuing decades, a person irrevocably lost neurons and crucial brain circuitry

until mental decline became noticeable.

Scientists now know the brain continually rewires and adapts itself, even in old age; large brain-cell growth continues into the teen years; and even seniors can grow at least some new neurons.

What keeps brains healthy? Clues come from Alzheimer's research.

Numerous studies show people with less education have higher risks of Alzheimer's than the better-educated. Lead researcher Mary Haan of the University of Michigan found less than a ninth-grade education a key threshold; other studies suggest a difference even between holders of bachelor's and master's degrees.

It's not just formal education. Reading habits between ages 6 and 18 appear crucial predictors of cognitive function decades later, said Dr. David Bennett of Chicago's Rush University.

—from the *San Francisco Chronicle*

Reading Informational Materials

Reading Check

1. According to the article, how is the brain like a muscle?

2. At what point in life do the benefits of mental exercise begin?

3. What three factors are linked to bad memory?

4. According to one expert, what happens to people when they watch television?

5. What new brain-cell research makes scientists hopeful about preserving mental function?

6. Why is it important for people to get as much education as they can?

TestPractice

Memory a Matter of Brains and Brawn

1. Which of these statements is the **proposition** of this article?

   A "The brain is like a muscle: Use it or lose it."

   B Cut back on television.

   C Formal education is very important in keeping the brain healthy.

   D Alzheimer's disease can be prevented.

2. All of the following types of support are used in the article *except —*

   F facts

   G statistics

   H anecdotes

   J opinions

3. What is the writer's **attitude** about the possibility of increasing and preserving intelligence?

   A Hopeful

   B Neutral

   C Pessimistic

   D Angry

4. To keep the brain active, Dr. Amir Soas suggests all of the following *except —*

   F reading

   G playing chess

   H watching educational television

   J learning a foreign language

5. The experts quoted in this article agree on which one of the following statements?

   A People who read will not get Alzheimer's disease.

   B Reading and education can lower the risk of getting Alzheimer's disease.

   C Physical exercise can prevent Alzheimer's disease.

   D Memory is the most important function of the human mind.

Reading Standard 2.2
Analyze text that uses proposition and support patterns.

Vocabulary Development

Mapping Words

PRACTICE 1

Draw a word map like the one below for each word in the Word Bank. Here is a word map for *provocative:*

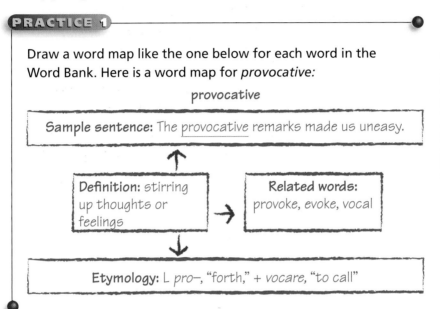

provocative

Sample sentence: The provocative remarks made us uneasy.

↑

Definition: stirring up thoughts or feelings → **Related words:** provoke, evoke, vocal

↓

Etymology: L *pro–,* "forth," + *vocare,* "to call"

Word Bank

inevitable
crucial
provocative
irrevocably
cognitive

Words and Tone

PRACTICE 2

This writer uses the informal language of popular culture. Informal language is often vivid because it uses unexpected connections. Think about the underlined word in each of these sentences, and answer the question that follows:

1. "Research . . . shows <u>fogged</u> memory and slowed wit are not inevitable consequences of getting old. . . ." What is a poor memory compared to?

2. "Scientists say it is never too late to start <u>jogging</u> the gray matter." In using the word *jogging,* what is the writer comparing mental exercise to?

3. "'When you watch television, your brain goes into <u>neutral</u>.' . . ." What is the writer comparing an idle brain to?

4. "Scientists now know the brain continually <u>rewires</u> and adapts itself. . . ." In using the word *rewires,* what is the writer comparing the brain to?

Reading Standard 1.1
Analyze metaphors to infer the literal and figurative meanings of phrases.

Reading Standard 1.2
Use common word origins to determine the historical influences on English word meanings.

The Landlady

Literary Focus
Foreshadowing

Writers make us feel suspense or anxiety by using **foreshadowing,** clues that hint at what will happen later. As you read "The Landlady," put yourself in the place of Billy, the main character. Pay close attention to what Billy sees and senses. Be on your toes—you may find yourself tripping over the many cleverly disguised clues.

Reading Skills
Predicting

As you read this story, you will probably find yourself **predicting,** or guessing, what will happen next. Your predictions might be based on what has already happened in the story and the clever clues the writer has left for you to figure out. They might also be based on similar events in other stories you know or in movies you have seen. As you read this story, look for the little open-book signs after some paragraphs. Stop at those points, and jot down what you think is going to happen to Billy.

Make the Connection
How Do You Picture It?

Picture this: You've just arrived in a new town by train, and you're looking for a place to stay. As you walk down the street, you see this sign in a boardinghouse window:

There are yellow flowers in a vase in the window and green curtains. You walk up to the window and look in. What do you see inside? What sort of a place is this boardinghouse?

Draw an outline of a house like the one below. Fill it with words and symbols showing what—and whom—you imagine you would find in the boardinghouse.

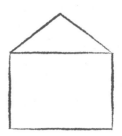

Grade 7 Review Reading Standard 3.2 Identify events that advance the plot, and determine how each event foreshadows future action(s).

The Landlady

Roald Dahl

Billy Weaver had traveled down from London on the slow afternoon train, with a change at Reading on the way, and by the time he got to Bath, it was about nine o'clock in the evening, and the moon was coming up out of a clear starry sky over the houses opposite the station entrance. But the air was deadly cold and the wind was like a flat blade of ice on his cheeks.

"Excuse me," he said, "but is there a fairly cheap hotel not too far away from here?"

"Try The Bell and Dragon," the porter[1] answered, pointing down the road. "They might take you in. It's about a quarter of a mile along on the other side."

Billy thanked him and picked up his suitcase and set out to walk the quarter-mile to The Bell and Dragon. He had never been to Bath before. He didn't know anyone who lived there. But Mr. Greenslade at the head office in London had told him it was a splendid town. "Find your own lodgings," he had said, "and then go along and report to the branch manager as soon as you've got yourself settled."

Billy was seventeen years old. He was wearing a new navy-blue overcoat, a new brown trilby hat,[2] and a new brown suit, and he was feeling fine. He walked briskly down the street. He was trying to do everything briskly these days. Briskness, he had decided, was the one common characteristic of all successful businessmen. The big shots up at the head office were absolutely fantastically brisk all the time. They were amazing.

There were no shops on this wide street that he was walking along, only a line of tall houses on each side, all of them identical. They had porches and pillars and four or five steps going up to their front doors, and it was obvious that once upon a time they had been very swanky residences. But now, even in the darkness, he could see that the paint was peeling from the woodwork on

---

1. **porter** *n.:* person hired to carry luggage.
2. **trilby hat:** soft hat with the top deeply indented.

their doors and windows and that the handsome white facades[3] were cracked and blotchy from neglect.

Suddenly, in a downstairs window that was brilliantly illuminated by a street lamp not six yards away, Billy caught sight of a printed notice propped up against the glass in one of the upper panes. It said "Bed and Breakfast." There was a vase of yellow chrysanthemums, tall and beautiful, standing just underneath the notice.

He stopped walking. He moved a bit closer. Green curtains (some sort of velvety material) were hanging down on either side of the window. The chrysanthemums looked wonderful beside them. He went right up and peered through the glass into the room, and the first thing he saw was a bright fire burning in the hearth. On the carpet in front of the fire, a pretty little dachshund was curled up asleep with its nose tucked into its belly. The room itself, so far as he could see in the half darkness, was filled with pleasant furniture. There was a baby grand piano and a big sofa and several plump armchairs, and in one corner he spotted a large parrot in a cage. Animals were usually a good sign in a place like this, Billy told himself; and all in all, it looked to him as though it would be a pretty decent house to stay in. Certainly it would be more comfortable than The Bell and Dragon.

On the other hand, a pub would be more congenial[4] than a boardinghouse. There would be beer and darts in the evenings, and lots of people to talk to, and it would probably be a good bit cheaper, too. He had stayed a couple of nights in a pub once before and he had liked it. He had never

stayed in any boardinghouses, and, to be perfectly honest, he was a tiny bit frightened of them. The name itself conjured up[5] images of watery cabbage, rapacious[6] landladies, and a powerful smell of kippers[7] in the living room.

After dithering about[8] like this in the cold for two or three minutes, Billy decided that he would walk on and take a look at The Bell and Dragon before making up his mind. He turned to go.

And now a queer thing happened to him. He was in the act of stepping back and turning away from the window when all at once his eye was caught and held in the most peculiar manner by the small notice that was there. BED AND BREAKFAST, it said. BED AND BREAKFAST, BED AND BREAKFAST, BED AND BREAKFAST. Each word was like a large black eye staring at him through the glass, holding him, compelling him, forcing him to stay where he was and not to walk away from that house, and the next thing he knew, he was actually moving across from the window to the front door of the house, climbing the steps that led up to it, and reaching for the bell.

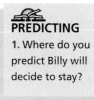

PREDICTING

1. Where do you predict Billy will decide to stay?

He pressed the bell. Far away in a back room he heard it ringing, and then *at once*—it must have been at once because he hadn't even had time to take his finger from the bell button—the door swung open and a woman was standing there.

---

3. **facades** (fə·sädz**ʹ**) *n.:* fronts of buildings.
4. **congenial** (kən·jēn**ʹ**yəl) *adj.:* agreeable; pleasant.
5. **conjured** (kun**ʹ**jərd) **up:** called to mind.
6. **rapacious** (rə·pā**ʹ**shəs) *adj.:* greedy.
7. **kippers** *n.:* fish that have been salted and smoked. Kippers are commonly eaten for breakfast in Great Britain.
8. **dithering about:** acting nervous and confused.

Normally you ring the bell and you have at least a half-minute's wait before the door opens. But this dame was like a jack-in-the-box. He pressed the bell—and out she popped! It made him jump.

She was about forty-five or fifty years old, and the moment she saw him, she gave him a warm, welcoming smile.

"*Please* come in," she said pleasantly. She stepped aside, holding the door wide open, and Billy found himself automatically starting forward. The compulsion or, more accurately, the desire to follow after her into that house was extraordinarily strong.

"I saw the notice in the window," he said, holding himself back.

"Yes, I know."

"I was wondering about a room."

"It's *all* ready for you, my dear," she said. She had a round pink face and very gentle blue eyes.

"I was on my way to The Bell and Dragon," Billy told her. "But the notice in your window just happened to catch my eye."

"My dear boy," she said, "why don't you come in out of the cold?"

"How much do you charge?"

"Five and sixpence a night, including breakfast."

It was fantastically cheap. It was less than half of what he had been willing to pay.

"If that is too much," she added, "then perhaps I can reduce it just a tiny bit. Do you desire an egg for breakfast? Eggs are expensive at the moment. It would be sixpence less without the egg."

"Five and sixpence is fine," he answered. "I should like very much to stay here."

"I knew you would. Do come in."

She seemed terribly nice. She looked exactly like the mother of one's best school friend welcoming one into the house to stay for the Christmas holidays. Billy took off his hat and stepped over the threshold.

"Just hang it there," she said, "and let me help you with your coat."

There were no other hats or coats in the hall. There were no umbrellas, no walking sticks—nothing.

"We have it *all* to ourselves," she said, smiling at him over her shoulder as she led the way upstairs. "You see, it isn't very often I have the pleasure of taking a visitor into my little nest."

The old girl is slightly dotty,[9] Billy told himself. But at five and sixpence a night, who cares about that? "I should've thought you'd be simply swamped with applicants," he said politely.

"Oh, I am, my dear, I am, of course I am. But the trouble is that I'm inclined to be just a teeny-weeny bit choosy and particular—if you see what I mean."

---

9. **dotty** *adj.:* crazy.

"Ah, yes."

"But I'm always ready. Everything is always ready day and night in this house just on the off chance that an acceptable young gentleman will come along. And it is such a pleasure, my dear, such a very great pleasure when now and again I open the door and I see someone standing there who is just *exactly* right." She was halfway up the stairs, and she paused with one hand on the stair rail, turning her head and smiling down at him with pale lips. "Like you," she added, and her blue eyes traveled slowly all the way down the length of Billy's body, to his feet, and then up again.

On the second-floor landing she said to him, "This floor is mine."

They climbed up another flight. "And this one is *all* yours," she said. "Here's your room. I do hope you'll like it." She took him into a small but charming front bedroom, switching on the light as she went in.

"The morning sun comes right in the window, Mr. Perkins. It *is* Mr. Perkins, isn't it?"

"No," he said. "It's Weaver."

"Mr. Weaver. How nice. I've put a water bottle between the sheets to air them out, Mr. Weaver. It's such a comfort to have a hot-water bottle in a strange bed with clean sheets, don't you agree? And you may light the gas fire at any time if you feel chilly."

"Thank you," Billy said. "Thank you ever so much." He noticed that the bedspread had been taken off the bed and that the bedclothes had been neatly turned back on one side, all ready for someone to get in.

"I'm so glad you appeared," she said, looking earnestly into his face. "I was beginning to get worried."

"That's all right," Billy answered brightly. "You mustn't worry about me."

He put his suitcase on the chair and started to open it.

"And what about supper, my dear? Did you manage to get anything to eat before you came here?"

"I'm not a bit hungry, thank you," he said. "I think I'll just go to bed as soon as possible because tomorrow I've got to get up rather early and report to the office."

"Very well, then. I'll leave you now so that you can unpack. But before you go to bed, would you be kind enough to pop into the sitting room on the ground floor and sign the book? Everyone has to do that because it's the law of the land, and we don't want to go breaking any laws at *this* stage in the proceedings, do we?" She gave him a little wave of the hand and went quickly out of the room and closed the door.

Now, the fact that his landlady appeared to be slightly off her rocker didn't worry Billy in the least. After all, she not only was harmless—there was no question about that—but she was also quite obviously a kind and generous soul. He guessed that she had probably lost a son in the war, or something like that, and had never gotten over it.

So a few minutes later, after unpacking his suitcase and washing his hands, he trotted downstairs to the ground floor and entered the living room. His landlady wasn't there, but the fire was glowing in the hearth, and the little dachshund was still sleeping soundly in front of it. The room was wonderfully warm and cozy. I'm a lucky fellow, he thought, rubbing his hands. This is a bit of all right.

PREDICTING

2. What prediction can you make about Billy's luck?

He found the guest book lying open on the piano, so he took

out his pen and wrote down his name and address. There were only two other entries above his on the page, and as one always does with guest books, he started to read them. One was a Christopher Mulholland from Cardiff. The other was Gregory W. Temple from Bristol.

That's funny, he thought suddenly. Christopher Mulholland. It rings a bell.

Now where on earth had he heard that rather unusual name before?

Was it a boy at school? No. Was it one of his sister's numerous young men, perhaps, or a friend of his father's? No, no, it wasn't any of those. He glanced down again at the book.

Christopher Mulholland
231 Cathedral Road, Cardiff

Gregory W. Temple
27 Sycamore Drive, Bristol

As a matter of fact, now he came to think of it, he wasn't at all sure that the second name didn't have almost as much of a familiar ring about it as the first.

"Gregory Temple?" he said aloud, searching his memory. "Christopher Mulholland? . . ."

"Such charming boys," a voice behind him answered, and he turned and saw his landlady sailing into the room with a large silver tea tray in her hands. She was holding it well out in front of her, and rather high up, as though the tray were a pair of reins on a frisky horse.

"They sound somehow familiar," he said.

"They do? How interesting."

"I'm almost positive I've heard those names before somewhere. Isn't that odd? Maybe it was in the newspapers. They weren't famous in any way, were they? I mean famous cricketers[10] or footballers or something like that?"

"Famous," she said, setting the tea tray down on the low table in front of the sofa. "Oh no, I don't think they were famous. But they were incredibly handsome, both of them, I can promise you that. They were tall and young and handsome, my dear, just exactly like you."

Once more, Billy glanced down at the book. "Look here," he said, noticing the dates. "This last entry is over two years old."

"It is?"

"Yes, indeed. And Christopher Mulholland's is nearly a year before that—more than *three years* ago."

"Dear me," she said, shaking her head and heaving a dainty little sigh. "I would never have thought it. How time does fly away from us all, doesn't it, Mr. Wilkins?"

"It's Weaver," Billy said. "W-e-a-v-e-r."

"Oh, of course it is!" she cried, sitting down on the sofa. "How silly of me. I do apologize. In one ear and out the other, that's me, Mr. Weaver."

"You know something?" Billy said. "Something that's really quite extraordinary about all this?"

"No, dear, I don't."

"Well, you see, both of these names—Mulholland and Temple—I not only seem to remember each one of them separately, so to speak, but somehow or other, in some peculiar way, they both appear to be sort of connected together as well. As though they were both famous for the same sort of thing, if you see what I mean—like . . . well . . . like Dempsey and Tunney, for example, or Churchill and Roosevelt."[11]

---

10. **cricketers** *n.:* people who play cricket, a game that is popular in Great Britain.

11. **Dempsey and Tunney . . . Churchill and Roosevelt:** Jack Dempsey and Gene Tunney were American boxers who competed for the world heavyweight championship in 1926. Winston Churchill was prime minister of Great Britain, and Franklin D. Roosevelt was president of the United States, during World War II.

There is nothing more tantalizing[13] than a thing like this that lingers just outside the borders of one's memory. He hated to give up.

"Now wait a minute," he said. "Wait just a minute. Mulholland . . . Christopher Mulholland . . . wasn't *that* the name of the Eton[14] schoolboy who was on a walking tour through the West Country, and then all of a sudden . . ."

"Milk?" she said. "And sugar?"

"Yes, please. And then all of a sudden . . ."

"Eton schoolboy?" she said. "Oh no, my dear, that can't possibly be right, because *my* Mr. Mulholland was certainly not an Eton schoolboy when he came to me. He was a Cambridge[15] undergraduate. Come over here now and sit next to me and warm yourself in front of this lovely fire. Come on. Your tea's all ready for you." She patted the empty place beside her on the sofa, and she sat there smiling at Billy and waiting for him to come over.

He crossed the room slowly and sat down on the edge of the sofa. She placed his teacup on the table in front of him.

"How amusing," she said. "But come over here now, dear, and sit down beside me on the sofa and I'll give you a nice cup of tea and a ginger biscuit[12] before you go to bed."

"You really shouldn't bother," Billy said. "I didn't mean you to do anything like that." He stood by the piano, watching her as she fussed about with the cups and saucers. He noticed that she had small, white, quickly moving hands and red fingernails.

"I'm almost positive it was in the newspapers I saw them," Billy said. "I'll think of it in a second. I'm sure I will."

---

12. **biscuit** (bis′kit) *n.:* British term meaning "cookie."

13. **tantalizing** (tan′tə·līz′iŋ) *adj.:* teasing by remaining unavailable or by withholding something desired by someone; tempting. (In Greek mythology, Tantalus was a king condemned after death to stand in water that moved away whenever he tried to drink it and to remain under branches of fruit that were just out of reach.)

14. **Eton:** boys' prep school near London.

15. **Cambridge:** famous university in England.

"*There* we are," she said. "How nice and cozy this is, isn't it?"

Billy started sipping his tea. She did the same. For half a minute or so, neither of them spoke. But Billy knew that she was looking at him. Her body was half turned toward him, and he could feel her eyes resting on his face, watching him over the rim of her teacup. Now and again, he caught a whiff of a peculiar smell that seemed to emanate[16] directly from her person. It was not in the least unpleasant, and it reminded him—well, he wasn't quite sure what it reminded him of. Pickled walnuts? New leather? Or was it the corridors of a hospital?

At length, she said, "Mr. Mulholland was a great one for his tea. Never in my life have I seen anyone drink as much tea as dear, sweet Mr. Mulholland."

"I suppose he left fairly recently," Billy said. He was still puzzling his head about the two names. He was positive now that he had seen them in the newspapers—in the headlines.

"Left?" she said, arching her brows. "But my dear boy, he never left. He's still here. Mr. Temple is also here. They're on the fourth floor, both of them together."

Billy set his cup down slowly on the table and stared at his landlady. She smiled back at him, and then she put out one of her white hands and patted him comfortingly on the knee. "How old are you, my dear?" she asked.

"Seventeen."

"Seventeen!" she cried. "Oh, it's the perfect age! Mr. Mulholland was also seventeen.

INFERRING

3. What do you think happened to Mr. Mulholland and Mr. Temple?

But I think he was a trifle shorter than you are; in fact I'm sure he was, and his teeth weren't *quite* so white. You have the most beautiful teeth, Mr. Weaver, did you know that?"

"They're not as good as they look," Billy said. "They've got simply masses of fillings in them at the back."

"Mr. Temple, of course, was a little older," she said, ignoring his remark. "He was actually twenty-eight. And yet I never would have guessed it if he hadn't told me, never in my whole life. There wasn't a *blemish* on his body."

"A what?" Billy said.

"His skin was *just* like a baby's."

There was a pause. Billy picked up his teacup and took another sip of his tea; then he set it down again gently in its saucer. He waited for her to say something else, but she seemed to have lapsed into another of her silences. He sat there staring straight ahead of him into the far corner of the room, biting his lower lip.

"That parrot," he said at last. "You know something? It had me completely fooled when I first saw it through the window. I could have sworn it was alive."

"Alas, no longer."

"It's most terribly clever the way it's been done," he said. "It doesn't look in the least bit dead. Who did it?"

"I did."

"*You* did?"

"Of course," she said. "And have you met my little Basil as well?" She nodded toward the dachshund curled up so comfortably in front of the fire. Billy looked at it. And suddenly, he realized that this animal had all the time been just as silent and motionless as the parrot. He put out a hand and

---

16. emanate (em′ə·nāt′) *v.*: come forth.

touched it gently on the top of its back. The back was hard and cold, and when he pushed the hair to one side with his fingers, he could see the skin underneath, grayish black and dry and perfectly preserved.

"Good gracious me," he said. "How absolutely fascinating." He turned away from the dog and stared with deep admiration at the little woman beside him on the sofa. "It must be most awfully difficult to do a thing like that."

"Not in the least," she said. "I stuff all my little pets myself when they pass away. Will you have another cup of tea?"

"No, thank you," Billy said. The tea tasted faintly of bitter almonds, and he didn't much care for it.

"You did sign the book, didn't you?"

"Oh, yes."

"That's good. Because later on, if I happen to forget what you were called, then I could always come down here and look it up. I still do that almost every day with Mr. Mulholland and Mr. . . . Mr. . . . "

"Temple," Billy said, "Gregory Temple. Excuse my asking, but haven't there been *any* other guests here except them in the last two or three years?"

Holding her teacup high in one hand, inclining her head slightly to the left, she looked up at him out of the corners of her eyes and gave him another gentle little smile.

"No, my dear," she said. "Only you."

PREDICTING

4. What happens now?

MEET THE WRITER

Roald Dahl

"A Persistent Muddler"

Roald (rōō′ôl) **Dahl** (1916–1990) was born in Wales, in Great Britain, to Norwegian parents. Many people believe that Dahl's dark humor had its source in his unpleasant experiences at boarding school. The brutal discipline at school apparently didn't help his writing at the time, however. One teacher said about young Roald, "A persistent muddler. Vocabulary negligible, sentences malconstructed. He reminds me of a camel."

For Independent Reading

Dahl wrote about boarding school and other childhood experiences in his autobiography *Boy*. Some of his most popular stories are in *The Wonderful Story of Henry Sugar and Six More*.

Literary Response and Analysis

Reading Check

1. What are Billy's first impressions when he peers through the window of the boardinghouse?

2. Why does Billy enter the boardinghouse even though he likes staying in pubs?

3. Describe the landlady's house. What in the house is not what it appears to be?

4. Billy keeps thinking he knows something about Mulholland and Temple. What is it that he knows but can't recall?

Interpretations

5. Through the window the boardinghouse looks cozy and comfortable. At what point in the story did you first become suspicious that things in the boardinghouse were not quite normal? When did you **predict** that something bad might happen?

6. What seems to be the landlady's idea of a perfect guest? What happens to her guests, and how do you know?

7. One important fact you may not know is that potassium cyanide, a favorite poison in mystery and suspense stories, has a faint bitter-almond taste. Go back to the text, and find where the writer plants this clue. What other clues in the story **foreshadow** Billy's fate? (Can you find a hint in the very first paragraph?)

8. The **climax** of a story is its most exciting point. It is also the moment at which the outcome of the conflict is decided. What do you think is the climax of this story? When does the reader know what will happen to Billy? (Different interpretations are possible.)

9. Skim through the story to find the points at which Billy makes fateful decisions. Choose one of these moments, and describe what Billy does and why he does it. How might a different decision have changed the **resolution,** or outcome, of the story?

Writing
Extend the End

What happens just after the story ends? Does Billy realize the danger he faces? If he does, is it too late, or does he escape? Write a paragraph or two that describes Billy's (and the landlady's) fate.

Reading Standard 3.2
Evaluate the structural elements of the plot (for example, subplots, parallel episodes, climax), the plot's development, and the way in which conflicts are (or are not) addressed and resolved.

Vocabulary Development

English from England

"The Landlady" is set in England, as you have already figured out. How did you know? Well, the geographic name *London* tips you off right in the first paragraph. The name *London* is followed by the names of two other famous English cities, *Reading* and *Bath*.

But there is another clue that this story was written by someone from England. The story uses many words that are part of British English but are not used in American English.

Is there more than one kind of English? Indeed, yes. Even though the English language originally came to North America from England, we have been busily making our own brand of English on our side of the Atlantic Ocean for hundreds of years. Differences are bound to occur when the same language is spoken in countries so far apart. Folks in America and in England understand one another just fine, but they often use different words to describe the same things. For example, a truck is called a lorry in England. A sweater is a jumper, and a cookie is a biscuit. Even though we have no trouble understanding the "British English" words in "The Landlady," they do tip us off that, well, we are definitely not in Kansas.

PRACTICE

Each sentence that follows uses words from "The Landlady" that are common in British English. What might an American say instead of the underlined word in each of the sentences below?

1. Billy had to find his own lodgings.
2. "The old girl is slightly dotty. . . ."
3. "'Pop into the sitting room. . . ."
4. "'Thank you ever so much.'"
5. "'This is a bit of all right.'"

Reading Standard 1.2
Understand the most important points in the history of the English language.

The Landlady   **71**

Grammar Link MINI-LESSON

Avoiding Double Comparisons

Billy thinks that the pub would be "cheaper" than a boardinghouse. He knows not to say "more cheaper." *More cheaper* is a double comparison, and it is wrong.

When you use an adjective to make a comparison, you should use only –er or *more,* and you should use only –est or *most.* You should never use both –er and *more* or –est and *most.* How do you know when to use one and when to use the other to form a comparison?

1. In general, add –er or –est to one-syllable modifiers, like *cheap.*
   cheap   cheaper   cheapest

2. Also add –er or –est to most two-syllable modifiers, like *pretty.*
   pretty   prettier   prettiest

3. Add *more* or *most* to adjectives of three or more syllables, like *beautiful.* (Think how hard it is to say "beautifuller" or "beautifullest.")
   beautiful   more beautiful   most beautiful

NONSTANDARD   The landlady gave Billy her most warmest smile.
STANDARD   The landlady gave Billy her warmest smile.

NONSTANDARD   The landlady was more choosier than she had to be.
STANDARD   The landlady was more choosy than she had to be.
STANDARD   The landlady was choosier than she had to be.

PRACTICE

Which comparisons need correction?

1. most smelliest
2. smallest
3. more shorter
4. most intelligent
5. more comfortable
6. more warmer
7. terriblest
8. most nastiest
9. most happiest
10. more sadder

For more help, see Use of Comparative and Superlative Forms in the *Holt Handbook,* pages 245–248.

Literary Response and Analysis

TestPractice DIRECTIONS: Read the story. Then, read each question, and write the letter of the best response.

Those Three Wishes

Judith Gorog

No one ever said that Melinda Alice was nice. That wasn't the word used. No, she was clever, even witty. She was called—never to her face, however—Melinda Malice. Melinda Alice was clever and cruel. Her mother, when she thought about it at all, hoped Melinda would grow out of it. To her father, Melinda's very good grades mattered.

It was Melinda Alice, back in the eighth grade, who had labeled the shy, myopic[1] new girl "Contamination" and was the first to pretend that anything or anyone touched by the new girl had to be cleaned, inoculated,[2] or avoided. High school had merely given Melinda Alice greater scope for her talents.

The surprising thing about Melinda Alice was her power; no one trusted her, but no one avoided her either. She was always included, always in the middle. If you had seen her, pretty and witty, in the center of a group of students walking past your house, you'd have thought, "There goes a natural leader."

Melinda Alice had left for school early. She wanted to study alone in a quiet spot she had because there was going to be a big math test, and Melinda Alice was not prepared. That A mattered; so Melinda Alice walked to school alone, planning her studies. She didn't usually notice nature much, so she nearly stepped on a beautiful snail that was making its way across the sidewalk.

"Ugh. Yucky thing," thought Melinda Alice, then stopped. Not wanting to step on the snail accidentally was one thing, but now she lifted her shoe to crush it.

"Please don't," said the snail.

"Why not?" retorted Melinda Alice.

"I'll give you three wishes," replied the snail evenly.

"Agreed," said Melinda Alice.

1. **myopic** (mī·äp′ik) *adj.*: nearsighted.
2. **inoculated** (i·näk′yə·lāt·id) *v.*: vaccinated.

(*continued on next page*)

Reading Standard 3.2
Evaluate the structural elements of the plot (for example, subplots, parallel episodes, climax), the plot's development, and the way in which conflicts are (or are not) addressed and resolved.

(*continued*)

"My first wish is that my next," she paused a split second, "my next thousand wishes come true." She smiled triumphantly and opened her bag to take out a small notebook and pencil to keep track.

Melinda Alice was sure she heard the snail say, "What a clever girl," as it made it to the safety of an ivy bed beside the sidewalk.

During the rest of the walk to school, Melinda was occupied with wonderful ideas. She would have beautiful clothes. "Wish number two, that I will always be perfectly dressed," and she was just that. True, her new outfit was not a lot different from the one she had worn leaving the house, but that only meant that Melinda Alice liked her own taste.

After thinking awhile, she wrote, "Wish number three. I wish for pierced ears and small gold earrings." Her father had not allowed Melinda to have pierced ears, but now she had them anyway. She felt her new earrings and shook her beautiful hair in delight. "I can have anything: stereo, tapes, TV videodisc, moped, car, anything! All my life!" She hugged her books to herself in delight.

By the time she reached school, Melinda was almost an altruist;[3] she could wish for peace. Then she wondered, "Is the snail that powerful?" She felt her ears, looked at her perfect blouse, skirt, jacket, shoes. "I could make ugly people beautiful, cure cripples . . ." She stopped. The wave of altruism had washed past. "I could pay people back who deserve it!" Melinda Alice looked at the school, at all the kids. She had an enormous sense of power. "They all have to do what I want now." She walked down the crowded halls to her locker. Melinda Alice could be sweet; she could be witty. She could—The bell rang for homeroom. Melinda Alice stashed her books, slammed the locker shut, and just made it to her seat.

"Hey, Melinda Alice," whispered Fred. "You know that big math test next period?"

"Oh, no," grimaced Melinda Alice. Her thoughts raced; "That stupid snail made me late, and I forgot to study."

"I'll blow it," she groaned aloud. "I wish I were dead."

---

3. **altruist** (al′tro͞o·ist) *n.:* person who helps others without expecting anything in return.

1. The writer leaves no doubt about what Melinda Alice is like. Which word does *not* describe her?
   A   clever
   B   pretty
   C   nice
   D   cruel

2. Which word best describes what Melinda Alice *wants*?
   F   love
   G   friends
   H   knowledge
   J   power

3. Why is Melinda Alice walking alone to school?
   A   No one likes her.
   B   She prefers to be alone.
   C   She wants to study.
   D   She is enjoying nature.

4. Melinda Alice does *not* step on the snail because —
   F   it is so beautiful
   G   it is too yucky
   H   it offers her three wishes
   J   she wants to be kind

5. Melinda Alice's wishes form **parallel episodes** in this short story. How many wishes does she make?
   A   A thousand
   B   Three
   C   Four
   D   Ten

6. Melinda Alice uses her wishes —
   F   for herself
   G   to benefit humanity
   H   to get even with enemies
   J   all of the above

7. Melinda Alice wishes for all of the following *except* —
   A   a thousand wishes
   B   to be perfectly dressed
   C   pierced ears and earrings
   D   a stereo, tapes, and a TV

8. The **climax** of a story is its most exciting point, the moment when the outcome of the plot is decided. In "Those Three Wishes" the climax occurs when —
   F   the snail gives Melinda Alice three wishes
   G   Melinda Alice wishes for a thousand more wishes
   H   Melinda Alice wishes she were dead
   J   Fred reminds Melinda Alice of the math test

9. The **resolution** of the story —
   A   is described by the writer in great detail
   B   is left undecided
   C   happens after the story ends
   D   never happens

10. Which of the following *best* sums up the **message** of this story?
    F   Be careful what you wish for. You may get it.
    G   Goodness wins in the end.
    H   You always get what you want.
    J   Mean people always triumph.

Reading Informational Materials

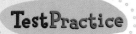 DIRECTIONS: Read the letter. Then, read each question, and write the letter of the best response.

Dear Councilman Duane:

More and more minors are smoking. When teens smoke, many problems arise. Something needs to be done to prove to minors that smoking is a bad thing. I am writing this letter to you in hopes that you will take steps to end this big problem.

Many problems develop when teenagers smoke. When teens smoke, laws are broken. Merchants break laws by intentionally selling cigarettes to minors. Teenage smokers damage their bodies permanently by smoking. Cigarettes cause addictions; even when teens want to quit, they often find they can't. Smoking can even affect a teenager's schooling. When a teenager needs a cigarette badly, he or she may ditch school to get one.

To help stop this problem, the city council could start a campaign against teenage smoking. You could make sure that schools with the sixth grade and older have a required class about the hazards of smoking, especially before the legal age. You could sponsor contests in each school for the best "Don't Smoke" posters, poems, essays, and stories. You could put the winners' posters and writing up around New York City. An educational campaign aimed at young teenagers would definitely help solve the problem of smoking by minors.

Some teenagers think, "It's my body, I can do what I want with it." Most smoking teenagers haven't fully matured emotionally. That means that what they believe now can change drastically in the following three to ten years of their lives. Therefore, as adults they may seriously regret decisions they made as teenagers.

Thank you for listening to my thoughts on this matter. I appreciate it and hope that you can do something to end the dilemma. Teenagers need to stop smoking, and you, as a person in power, can help them understand that it isn't all right to smoke.

—Hannah Fleury
St. Luke's School
New York, New York

Reading Standard 2.2
Analyze text that uses proposition and support patterns.

1. The writer's **purpose** in writing this letter is to —

   A describe

   B persuade

   C entertain

   D question

2. Which of the following sentences states the letter writer's **proposition**?

   F "More and more minors are smoking."

   G "When teens smoke, many problems arise."

   H "Something needs to be done to prove to minors that smoking is a bad thing."

   J "Cigarettes cause addictions."

3. Which of the following statements is an **opinion**?

   A "When teens smoke, laws are broken."

   B "More and more minors are smoking."

   C "Merchants break laws by intentionally selling cigarettes to minors."

   D "An educational campaign aimed at young teenagers would definitely help solve the problem of smoking by minors."

4. Which of the following sentences does *not* offer **support** for the letter writer's main idea?

   F "When teens smoke, laws are broken."

   G "Cigarettes cause addictions. . . . "

   H "Smoking can even affect a teenager's schooling."

   J "Teenagers need to stop smoking. . . . "

5. The **conclusion** of this letter —

   A restates the proposition

   B is a call to action

   C both of the above

   D none of the above

Vocabulary Development

TestPractice

Multiple-Meaning Words

DIRECTIONS: Choose the answer in which the underlined word is used in the same way it is used in the passage from "Flowers for Algernon."

1. "'You used to be a good, dependable, ordinary man—not too bright maybe, but honest. Who knows what you done to yourself to get so smart all of a sudden.'"

   A Your new outfit looks smart.

   B How smart do you think you are?

   C Don't be smart with me, young man!

   D Does the cut on your finger still smart?

2. "He hasn't been eating. Everyone is upset about what this may mean."

   F Charlie's friends were very mean to him.

   G The mean rainfall in that part of the world is one inch a year.

   H David Wells throws a mean fastball.

   J High intelligence doesn't necessarily mean high achievement.

3. "'I am grateful for the little bit that I here add to the knowledge of the function of the human mind.' . . ."

   A Did Charlie mind being teased?

   B Who will mind the lab tonight?

   C A mind is a terrible thing to waste.

   D That nasty dog should mind its owner.

4. "Then Frank Reilly said what did you do Charlie forget your key and open your door the hard way."

   F Play that song in the key of G major, please.

   G The homecoming game was a key event for everyone.

   H Ken locked the car door but left the key in the ignition.

   J Someone took the answer key to the test.

5. "I tried not to look at the boy as I paid my check and walked out without touching my food."

   A This test will check your word power.

   B Waiter, check, please.

   C The doctors tried to check Algernon's decline.

   D Have you cashed that check yet?

PERSONAL NARRATIVE

The Outsider

Many stories, as well as movies and TV shows, focus on the character of an outsider—a person excluded from the main group—such as Charlie Gordon in "Flowers for Algernon." Perhaps you know a person in actual life who was forced to be an outsider. You could write a **personal narrative** about your experience with that person. How did you treat him or her? Did you make fun of the person, or did you stand up for him or her? What happened to the person? Did you learn anything from the experience? Perhaps you have been the outsider on some occasion and wish to tell what happened to you. Before you write, gather your main details in a chart like this one:

Characters	Setting (if important)	Main Events	Focus (what I learned)

 Use "Writing a Personal Narrative," pages 588–603, for help with this assignment.

Other Choices

SHORT STORY

 ### 1 How It Feels

In "Broken Chain" you read about a boy named Alfonso who hates his crooked teeth and wants to make an impression on a girl. Write a **short story** of your own about a character who wants something very badly but is sure he or she will never get it. Remember that a short story is built on a **plot** that centers on a **conflict:** A character wants something so much that he or she takes certain steps to get it and then runs into complications.

PERSUASIVE ESSAY

2 Television Terror

You want to direct "The Landlady" for a TV movie. Write a letter to the producer, explaining why you think the story would make a successful movie. Be sure to address such issues as target audience, sponsors, and any changes needed to adapt the story for TV. State your position clearly in your first paragraph, and support it with convincing reasons and specific examples from the story and from current TV shows.

 Use "Writing a Persuasive Essay," pages 706–725, for help with this assignment.

Fiction

Can Heroes Rise?

Can you solve the mystery of *Jackaroo*? In this Cynthia Voigt novel, Gwen hears tales of Jackaroo, a swash-buckling hero who helps the hopeless and fights for justice, but she is too realistic to believe them to be true. Then a series of events changes her life, and she learns there may be more to Jackaroo than stories.

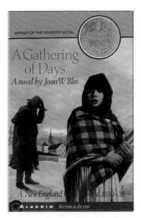

A Memorable Time

In Joan W. Blos's *A Gathering of Days*, teenaged Catherine Hall receives a journal and chronicles an eventful time of her life in it. Beginning in 1830, Catherine learns about racial prejudice from a man fleeing slavery, loses a close friend, and assumes greater responsibility on her family's New Hampshire farm as she journeys toward adulthood.

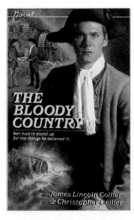

The Ties That Bind

In *The Bloody Country* by James Lincoln Collier and Christopher Collier, Ben Buck and his eighteenth-century Pennsylvania family may lose their home because of the threat of war. They also may lose Joe, a half-black, half-Indian boy whom they hold as a slave. Ben considers Joe his best friend.

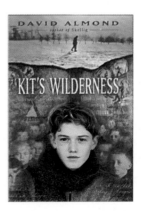

Searching for Sympathy

When a well-behaved thirteen-year-old named Kit Watson moves to Stoneygate, he encounters John Askew, a boy with a knack for getting into trouble. As they get to know each other, Kit finds they have something in common: Both can see ghosts of children who have died in Stoneygate's mines. In David Almond's *Kit's Wilderness*, Kit hopes this bond will help reveal John's goodness.

Nonfiction

Punishment Without Crime

In 1942, seven-year-old Jeanne Wakatsuki and her family were sent to the Manzanar internment camp. Jeanne Wakatsuki Houston and James D. Houston's *Farewell to Manzanar* is the true story of a native-born American who grew up behind barbed wire in her own country.

This title is available in the HRW Library.

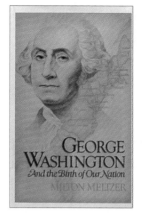

More Than a Dollar Bill

You know he was the first president, but have you ever wondered what George Washington was really like? Milton Meltzer answers that question in *George Washington and the Birth of Our Nation*. Meltzer looks at Washington's formative years as a surveyor and soldier in colonial Virginia, his role in the American Revolution, and his retirement in Mount Vernon.

Taking a Stand

In 1909, young women throughout the United States worked in factories under unhealthy conditions for low pay. In *We Shall Not Be Moved*, Joan Dash tells how a group of women in the shirtwaist industry in New York City battled for fair treatment by going on strike and struggling to form a union.

Days Gone By

In *Childtimes* by Eloise Greenfield and Lessie Jones Little, African American women from three generations look back on their childhoods. Some of their memories, such as the smell of home-baked rolls on a Sunday morning, are pleasant. But the writers also recall confrontations with racism at a very young age.

2 Characters
Doing the Right Thing

California Standards

Here are the Grade 8 standards you will study for mastery in Chapter 2. You will also review a standard from an earlier grade.

Word Analysis, Fluency, and Systematic Vocabulary Development

1.2 Understand the most important points in the history of the English language, and use common word origins to determine the historical influences on English word meanings.

Grade 6 Review

1.4 Use word, sentence, and paragraph clues to determine meaning of words.

Reading Comprehension (Focus on Informational Materials)

2.3 Find similarities and differences between texts in the treatment, scope, or organization of ideas.

Literary Response and Analysis

3.3 Compare and contrast motivations and reactions of literary characters from different historical eras confronting similar situations or conflicts.

KEYWORD:
HLLA 8-2

CALIFORNIA STANDARDS

Characters *by* John Leggett

THE HUMAN EXPERIENCE

Most of us are fascinated by other people. We like to know how other people deal with problems, disappointments, and temptations. A good story, whether it's true, made-up, or somewhere in between, reveals some truth about human experience. It does this through the people who live in its pages—its **characters.**

Characterization: The Breath of Life

The way a writer reveals character is called **characterization.** Poor characterization can make even a real person uninteresting. Good characterization can make readers feel that even fantasy characters—a bumbling teddy bear or a girl who is tossed by a tornado into an emerald city—live and breathe.

Creating Characters

A writer may simply *tell* us directly that a character is mean tempered or thrifty or brave or honest. This kind of characterization, called **direct characterization,** was often used by writers years ago. Present-day writers generally prefer to *show* their characters in action and let us decide for ourselves what kinds of people we are meeting. This method is called **indirect characterization.**

Direct Characterization

1 **Stating directly what the character is like.**

Sergeant Randolph was the cruelest drillmaster in the regiment.

Indirect Characterization

2 **Describing the appearance of the character.**

Wanda's hair was pink, and every pink hair stuck up from her head. Underneath all that pink hair, though, was a pair of innocent blue eyes.

3 **Showing the character in action.**

Toni glanced around, then tossed the empty soda can on the grass and kept walking.

4 **Allowing us to hear the character speak.**

"I don't have to do what you say," declared Darlene, pinching the new baby sitter.

5 **Revealing the character's thoughts and feelings.**

Ashley didn't like the looks of the squash pudding but decided to eat some to please the cook.

Reading Standard 3.3 Compare and contrast motivations and reactions of literary characters from different historical eras confronting similar situations or conflicts.

Peanuts reprinted by permission of United Feature Syndicate, Inc.

6 **Showing how others react to the character.**

"Go wake up my sister?" Lulu said. "Sure, Mom. Just give me armor and a twenty-foot pole, and I'll be all set to go."

How Could You Do That? Motivation

Why did your best friend suddenly get a crush on the biggest jerk in school? What could possibly have possessed your brother to think he could climb Mount McKinley?

We always wonder about people's **motivation**—that is, we wonder what makes people behave the way they do. In real life we may never learn the answer. Literature is different. In literature you'll find plenty of clues to characters' **motives**—why they do the things they do. One of the pleasures of literature is using these clues to figure out what makes people tick.

Practice

Choose a character from a story or novel you have read recently, and fill in a chart like the one below:

Method of Characterization	Details in Story
Appearance:	
Actions:	
Words spoken by character:	
Thoughts:	
Other characters' responses:	
Writer's direct comments:	

Character Profile of _____

from Harriet Tubman

Literary Focus
Characters in Biography

When we read a **biography**—the story of someone's life written by another person—we get to know the real people in the story. We get acquainted with the characters in a biography the same way we get to know people in our own lives. We observe their **actions**—what they say and do. We think about their **motivations,** the reasons for their actions. We learn something about their values. We watch the way they interact with other people. We compare these characters with the people we know (or with other people we have read about). Soon we feel we know them.

Reading Skills
Making Inferences

One of the pleasures of reading is making our own inferences about characters. **Inferences** are conclusions we come to based on information in the text and what we already know. An inference is an educated guess. As you read this biography, look for the little open-book signs. These signs indicate places where you must make inferences.

Make the Connection
Quickwrite ✏️

What have people over the centuries endured for the sake of freedom? What have people endured because their freedom was taken away? In your journal, jot down notes on these questions.

Reading Standard 3.3 Compare and contrast motivations and reactions of literary characters from different historical eras confronting similar situations or conflicts.

Background

In the biblical Book of Exodus, Moses is chosen by God to lead the people of Israel out of slavery in Egypt. Moses takes his people on a long, perilous desert journey and leads them to the Promised Land. As you read this biography, look for reasons why Harriet Tubman was called the Moses of her people.

Vocabulary Development

These are the words you'll need to know as you read the biography:

fugitives (fyoo′ji·tivz) *n.:* people fleeing from danger. *The fugitives escaped to the North, traveling by night.*

incomprehensible (in·käm′prē·hen′sə·bəl) *adj.:* impossible to understand. *The Fugitive Slave Law had once been an incomprehensible set of words.*

incentive (in·sent′iv) *n.:* reason to do something; motivation. *The incentive of a warm house and good food kept the fugitives going.*

dispel (di·spel′) *v.:* scatter; drive away. *Harriet tried to dispel the fugitives' fear of capture.*

eloquence (el′ə·kwəns) *n.:* ability to write or speak gracefully and convincingly. *Frederick Douglass was known for his eloquence in writing and speaking.*

Roots (1964) by Charles White. Chinese ink.

from Harriet Tubman
Conductor on the Underground Railroad
Ann Petry

If they were caught, she would probably be hanged.

The Railroad Runs to Canada

Along the Eastern Shore of Maryland, in Dorchester County, in Caroline County, the masters kept hearing whispers about the man named Moses, who was running off slaves. At first they did not believe in his existence. The stories about him were fantastic, unbelievable. Yet they watched for him. They offered rewards for his capture.

They never saw him. Now and then they heard whispered rumors to the effect that he was in the neighborhood. The woods were searched. The roads were watched. There was never anything to indicate his whereabouts. But a few days afterward, a goodly number of slaves would be gone from the plantation. Neither the master nor the overseer had heard or seen anything unusual in the quarter.[1] Sometimes one or the other would vaguely remember having heard a whippoorwill call somewhere in the woods, close by, late at night. Though it was the wrong season for whippoorwills.

Sometimes the masters thought they had heard the cry of a hoot owl, repeated, and would remember having thought that the intervals between the low moaning cry were wrong, that it had been repeated four times in succession instead of three. There was never anything more than that to suggest that all was not well in the quarter. Yet, when morning came, they invariably discovered that a group of the finest slaves had taken to their heels.

Unfortunately, the discovery was almost always made on a Sunday. Thus a whole day was lost before the machinery of pursuit could be set in motion. The posters offering rewards for the fugitives could not be printed until Monday. The men who made a living hunting for runaway slaves were out of reach, off in the woods with their dogs and their guns, in pursuit of four-footed game, or they were in camp meetings saying their prayers with their wives and families beside them.

Harriet Tubman could have told them that there was far more involved in this matter of running off slaves than signaling the would-be runaways by imitating the call of a whippoorwill, or a hoot owl, far more involved than a matter of waiting for a clear night when the North Star[2] was visible.

In December 1851, when she started out with the band of fugitives that she planned to take to Canada, she had been in the vicinity of the plantation for days, planning the trip, carefully selecting the slaves that she would take with her.

She had announced her arrival in the quarter by singing the forbidden spiritual[3]— "Go down, Moses, 'way down to Egypt Land"—singing it softly outside the door of a slave cabin, late at night. The husky voice was beautiful even when it was barely more than a murmur borne on the wind.

Once she had made her presence known,

---

1. **quarter** *n.:* area in a plantation where Africans lived. It consisted of windowless, one-room cabins made of logs and mud.

2. **North Star:** Runaways fleeing north used the North Star (Polaris) to help them stay on course.
3. **forbidden spiritual:** Spirituals are religious songs, some of which are based on the biblical story of the Israelites' escape from slavery in Egypt. Plantation owners feared that the singing of spirituals might lead to rebellion.

Vocabulary
fugitives (fyo͞o′ji·tivz) *n.:* people fleeing from danger.

word of her coming spread from cabin to cabin. The slaves whispered to each other, ear to mouth, mouth to ear, "Moses is here." "Moses has come." "Get ready. Moses is back again." The ones who had agreed to go North with her put ashcake[4] and salt herring in an old bandanna, hastily tied it into a bundle, and then waited patiently for the signal that meant it was time to start.

There were eleven in this party, including one of her brothers and his wife. It was the largest group that she had ever conducted, but she was determined that more and more slaves should know what freedom was like.

She had to take them all the way to Canada. The Fugitive Slave Law[5] was no longer a great many incomprehensible words written down on the country's lawbooks. The new law had become a reality. It was Thomas Sims, a boy, picked up on the streets of Boston at night and shipped back to Georgia. It was Jerry and Shadrach, arrested and jailed with no warning.

She had never been in Canada. The route beyond Philadelphia was strange to her. But she could not let the runaways who accompanied her know this. As they walked along, she told them stories of her own first flight; she kept painting vivid word pictures of what it would be like to be free.

> **MAKING INFERENCES**
>
> 1. What does it mean that the new law was Thomas Sims or Jerry and Shadrach?

But there were so many of them this time. She knew moments of doubt, when she was half afraid and kept looking back over her shoulder, imagining that she heard the sound of pursuit. They would certainly be pursued. Eleven of them. Eleven thousand dollars' worth of flesh and bone and muscle that belonged to Maryland planters. If they were caught, the eleven runaways would be whipped and sold South, but she—she would probably be hanged.

They tried to sleep during the day but they never could wholly relax into sleep. She could tell by the positions they assumed, by their restless movements. And they walked at night. Their progress was slow. It took them three nights of walking to reach the first stop. She had told them about the place where they would stay, promising warmth and good food, holding these things out to them as an incentive to keep going.

When she knocked on the door of a farmhouse, a place where she and her parties of runaways had always been welcome, always been given shelter and plenty to eat, there was no answer. She knocked again, softly. A voice from within said, "Who is it?" There was fear in the voice.

She knew instantly from the sound of the voice that there was something wrong. She said, "A friend with friends," the password on the Underground Railroad.

The door opened, slowly. The man who stood in the doorway looked at her coldly, looked with unconcealed astonishment and

---

4. **ashcake** *n.:* cornmeal bread baked in hot ashes.
5. **Fugitive Slave Law:** harsh federal law passed in 1850 stating that fugitives who escaped from slavery to free states could be forced to return to their owners. As a result, those who escaped were safe only in Canada. The law also made it a crime for a free person to help fugitives or to prevent their return.

Vocabulary

incomprehensible (in·kăm′prē·hen′sə·bəl) *adj.:* impossible to understand.

incentive (in·sent′iv) *n.:* reason to do something; motivation.

fear at the eleven disheveled[6] runaways who were standing near her. Then he shouted, "Too many, too many. It's not safe. My place was searched last week. It's not safe!" and slammed the door in her face.

She turned away from the house, frowning. She had promised her passengers food and rest and warmth, and instead of that, there would be hunger and cold and more walking over the frozen ground. Somehow she would have to instill courage into these eleven people, most of them strangers, would have to feed them on hope and bright dreams of freedom instead of the fried pork and corn bread and milk she had promised them.

They stumbled along behind her, half dead for sleep, and she urged them on, though she was as tired and as discouraged as they were. She had never been in Canada, but she kept painting wondrous word pictures of what it would be like. She managed to dispel their fear of pursuit so that they would not become hysterical, panic-stricken. Then she had to bring some of the fear back, so that they would stay awake and keep walking though they drooped with sleep.

Yet, during the day, when they lay down deep in a thicket, they never really slept, because if a twig snapped or the wind sighed in the branches of a pine tree, they jumped to their feet, afraid of their own shadows, shivering and shaking. It was very cold, but they dared not make fires because someone would see the smoke and wonder about it.

She kept thinking, eleven of them. Eleven thousand dollars' worth of slaves. And she had to take them all the way to Canada. Sometimes she told them about Thomas Garrett, in Wilmington.[7] She said he was their friend even though he did not know them. He was the friend of all fugitives. He called them God's poor. He was a Quaker[8] and his speech was a little different from that of other people. His clothing was different, too. He wore the wide-brimmed hat that the Quakers wear.

She said that he had thick white hair, soft, almost like a baby's, and the kindest eyes she had ever seen. He was a big man and strong, but he had never used his strength to harm anyone, always to help people. He would give all of them a new pair of shoes. Everybody. He always did. Once they reached his house in Wilmington, they would be safe. He would see to it that they were.

She described the house where he lived, told them about the store where he sold shoes. She said he kept a pail of milk and a loaf of bread in the drawer of his desk so that he would have food ready at hand for any of God's poor who should suddenly appear before him, fainting with hunger. There was a hidden room in the store. A whole wall swung open, and behind it was a room where he could hide fugitives. On the wall there were shelves filled with small boxes—boxes of shoes—so that you would never guess that the wall actually opened.

While she talked, she kept watching

MAKING INFERENCES
2. Why would shoes be so important to the fugitives?

---

7. **Wilmington:** city in Delaware.
8. **Quaker:** member of the Society of Friends, a religious group active in the movement to end slavery.

---

6. **disheveled** (di·shev'əld) *adj.:* untidy; rumpled.

Vocabulary
dispel (di·spel') *v.:* scatter; drive away.

them. They did not believe her. She could tell by their expressions. They were thinking. New shoes, Thomas Garrett, Quaker, Wilmington—what foolishness was this? Who knew if she told the truth? Where was she taking them anyway?

That night they reached the next stop—a farm that belonged to a German. She made the runaways take shelter behind trees at the edge of the fields before she knocked at the door. She hesitated before she approached the door, thinking, suppose that he too should refuse shelter, suppose— Then she thought, *Lord, I'm going to hold steady on to You and You've got to see me through*—and knocked softly.

MAKING INFERENCES

3. What inferences can you make about Tubman from this paragraph?

She heard the familiar guttural voice say, "Who's there?"

She answered quickly, "A friend with friends."

He opened the door and greeted her warmly. "How many this time?" he asked.

"Eleven," she said and waited, doubting, wondering.

He said, "Good. Bring them in."

He and his wife fed them in the lamp-lit kitchen, their faces glowing as they offered food and more food, urging them to eat, saying there was plenty for everybody, have more milk, have more bread, have more meat.

They spent the night in the warm kitchen. They really slept, all that night and until dusk the next day. When they left, it was with reluctance. They had all been warm and safe and well-fed. It was hard to exchange the security offered by that clean, warm kitchen for the darkness and the cold of a December night.

Go Down, Moses

traditional African American spiritual

When Israel was in Egypt land—
Let my people go.
Oppressed so hard they could not
   stand
Let my people go.
   CHORUS:
   Go down, Moses, way down in
      Egypt land;
   tell ole Pharaoh to let my people go.

Thus saith the Lord, bold Moses
   said—
Let my people go.
If not I'll smite your firstborn dead—
Let my people go.
   CHORUS

No more shall they in bondage toil—
Let my people go.
Let them come out with Egypt's
   spoil—
Let my people go.
   CHORUS

We need not always weep and
   mourn—
Let my people go.
And wear those slavery's chains
   forlorn—
Let my people go.
   CHORUS

"Go On or Die"

Harriet had found it hard to leave the warmth and friendliness, too. But she urged them on. For a while, as they walked, they seemed to carry in them a measure of contentment; some of the serenity and the cleanliness of that big, warm kitchen lingered on inside them. But as they walked farther and farther away from the warmth and the light, the cold and the darkness entered into them. They fell silent, sullen, suspicious. She waited for the moment when some one of them would turn mutinous.[9] It did not happen that night.

Two nights later, she was aware that the feet behind her were moving slower and slower. She heard the irritability in their voices, knew that soon someone would refuse to go on.

She started talking about William Still and the Philadelphia Vigilance Committee.[10] No one commented. No one asked any questions. She told them the story of William and Ellen Craft and how they escaped from Georgia. Ellen was so fair that she looked as though she were white, and so she dressed up in a man's clothing and she looked like a wealthy young planter. Her husband, William, who was dark, played the role of her slave. Thus they traveled from Macon, Georgia, to Philadelphia, riding on the trains, staying at the finest hotels. Ellen pretended to be very ill—her right arm was in a sling and her right hand was bandaged because she was supposed to have rheumatism.[11] Thus she avoided having to sign the register at the hotels, for she could not read or write. They finally arrived safely in Philadelphia and then went on to Boston.

No one said anything. Not one of them seemed to have heard her.

She told them about Frederick Douglass, the most famous of the escaped slaves, of his eloquence, of his magnificent appearance. Then she told them of her own first, vain effort at running away, evoking the memory of that miserable life she had led as a child, reliving it for a moment in the telling.

But they had been tired too long, hungry too long, afraid too long, footsore too long. One of them suddenly cried out in despair, "Let me go back. It is better to be a slave than to suffer like this in order to be free."

She carried a gun with her on these trips. She had never used it—except as a threat. Now, as she aimed it, she experienced a feeling of guilt, remembering that time, years ago, when she had prayed for the death of Edward Brodas, the Master, and then, not too long afterward, had heard that great wailing cry that came from the throats of the field hands, and knew from the sound that the Master was dead.

One of the runaways said again, "Let me go back. Let me go back," and stood still, and then turned around and said, over his shoulder, "I am going back."

She lifted the gun, aimed it at the

---

9. **mutinous** (myo͞ot′'n·əs) *adj.:* rebellious. *Mutiny* usually refers to a revolt of sailors against their officer.
10. **Philadelphia Vigilance Committee:** group that offered help to people escaping slavery. **William Still,** a free African American, was chairman of the committee.

---

11. **rheumatism** (ro͞o′mə·tiz′əm) *n.:* painful swelling and stiffness of the joints or muscles.

Vocabulary
eloquence (el′ə·kwəns) *n.:* ability to write or speak gracefully and convincingly.

Harriet (1972) by Charles White. Oil wash.
Courtesy Heritage Gallery, Los Angeles, California.

despairing slave. She said, "Go on with us or die." The husky, low-pitched voice was grim.

He hesitated for a moment and then he joined the others. They started walking again. She tried to explain to them why none of them could go back to the plantation. If a runaway returned, he would turn traitor; the master and the overseer would force him to turn traitor. The returned slave would disclose the stopping places, the hiding places, the corn stacks they had used with the full knowledge of the owner of the farm, the name of the German farmer who had fed them and sheltered them. These people who had risked their own security to help runaways would be ruined, fined, imprisoned.

She said, "We got to go free or die. And freedom's not bought with dust."

This time she told them about the long agony of the Middle Passage[12] on the old slave ships, about the black horror of the holds, about the chains and the whips. They too knew these stories. But she wanted to remind them of the long, hard way they had come, about the long, hard way they had yet to go. She told them about Thomas Sims, the boy picked up on the streets of Boston and sent back to Georgia. She said when they got him back to Savannah, got him in prison there, they whipped him until a doctor who was standing by watching said, "You will kill him if you strike him again!" His master said, "Let him die!"

MAKING INFERENCES
4. Why does Harriet Tubman make this threat?

Thus she forced them to go on. Sometimes she thought she had become nothing but a voice speaking in the darkness, cajoling,[13] urging, threatening. Sometimes she told them things to make them laugh; sometimes she sang to them and heard the eleven voices behind her blending softly with hers, and then she knew that for the moment all was well with them.

She gave the impression of being a short, muscular, indomitable woman who could never be defeated. Yet at any moment she was liable to be seized by one of those curious fits of sleep, which might last for a few minutes or for hours.[14]

Even on this trip, she suddenly fell asleep in the woods. The runaways, ragged, dirty, hungry, cold, did not steal the gun as they might have and set off by themselves or turn back. They sat on the ground near her and waited patiently until she awakened. They had come to trust her implicitly, totally. They, too, had come to believe her repeated statement, "We got to go free or die." She was leading them into freedom, and so they waited until she was ready to go on.

Finally, they reached Thomas Garrett's house in Wilmington, Delaware. Just as Harriet had promised, Garrett gave them all new shoes, and provided carriages to take them on to the next stop.

By slow stages they reached Philadelphia, where William Still hastily recorded their names, and the plantations whence they

---

12. **Middle Passage:** route traveled by ships carrying captured Africans across the Atlantic Ocean to the Americas. The captives endured the horrors of the Middle Passage crammed into **holds,** airless cargo areas below deck.

13. **cajoling** (kə·jōl′iŋ) v. used as adj.: coaxing.
14. Harriet's losses of consciousness were caused by a serious head injury that she had suffered as a teenager. Harriet had tried to protect someone else from punishment, and an enraged overseer threw a two-pound weight at her head.

The Underground Railroad runs to Canada.

had come, and something of the life they had led in slavery. Then he carefully hid what he had written, for fear it might be discovered. In 1872 he published this record in book form and called it *The Underground Railroad*. In the foreword to his book he said: "While I knew the danger of keeping strict records, and while I did not then dream that in my day slavery would be blotted out, or that the time would come when I could publish these records, it used to afford me great satisfaction to take them down, fresh from the lips of fugitives on the way to freedom, and to preserve them as they had given them."

William Still, who was familiar with all the station stops on the Underground Railroad, supplied Harriet with money and sent her and her eleven fugitives on to Burlington, New Jersey.

Harriet felt safer now, though there were danger spots ahead. But the biggest part of her job was over. As they went farther and farther north, it grew colder; she was aware of the wind on the Jersey ferry and aware of the cold damp in New York. From New York they went on to Syracuse,[15] where the temperature was even lower.

In Syracuse she met the Reverend J. W. Loguen, known as "Jarm" Loguen. This was the beginning of a lifelong friendship. Both Harriet and Jarm Loguen were to become friends and supporters of Old John Brown.[16]

From Syracuse they went north again, into a colder, snowier city—Rochester. Here they almost certainly stayed with Frederick Douglass, for he wrote in his autobiography:

"On one occasion I had eleven fugitives at the same time under my roof, and it was necessary for them to remain with me until I could collect sufficient money to get them to Canada. It was the largest number I ever had at any one time, and I had some difficulty in providing so many with food and shelter, but, as may well be imagined, they were not very fastidious[17] in either direction, and were well content with very plain food, and a strip of carpet on the floor for a bed, or a place on the straw in the barn loft."

Late in December 1851, Harriet arrived in St. Catharines, Canada West (now Ontario), with the eleven fugitives. It had taken almost a month to complete this journey.

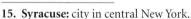

15. **Syracuse:** city in central New York.
16. **Old John Brown** (1800–1859): abolitionist (opponent of slavery) who was active in the Railroad. In 1859, Brown led a raid on the federal arsenal at Harpers Ferry, then in Virginia, in hopes of inspiring a slave uprising. Federal troops overpowered Brown and his followers, and Brown was convicted of treason and was hanged.
17. **fastidious** (fa·stid′ē·əs) *adj.*: fussy; hard to please.

Wanted Poster Series #17 (1971) by Charles White. Oil wash.

Flint Institute of Art/Courtesy Heritage Gallery, Los Angeles, California.

Ann Petry

"A Message in the Story"

A native of Old Saybrook, Connecticut, **Ann Petry** (1908–1997) was the granddaughter of a man who escaped from slavery on a Virginia plantation and came north by way of the Underground Railroad. As a young woman she worked as a pharmacist in her family's drugstores before moving to New York, where she became a writer of books for young people and adults. About her writing she said:

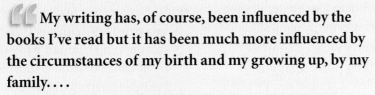

> My writing has, of course, been influenced by the books I've read but it has been much more influenced by the circumstances of my birth and my growing up, by my family. . . .
>
> We always had relatives visiting us. They added excitement to our lives. They brought with them the aura and the customs of a very different world. They were all storytellers, spinners of yarns. So were my mother and my father.
>
> Some of these stories had been handed down from one generation to the next, improved, embellished, embroidered. Usually there was a message in the story, a message for the young, a message that would help a young black child survive, help convince a young black child that black is truly beautiful.

For Independent Reading

Tituba of Salem Village is based on the true story of another heroic woman of African descent, who was accused of witchcraft in 1692.

Literary Response and Analysis

Reading Check

1. List at least five **facts** about the workings of the Underground Railroad that you learned from this biography.

2. List at least five **facts** you learned about Harriet Tubman.

3. List at least three **facts** you learned about slavery in the United States.

Interpretations

4. How was Tubman like Moses in the Bible? What was *her* Promised Land?

5. We sense **irony** when we notice that something is the opposite of what we think it should be. Why do we sense irony when we read that the men who hunted fugitives for money said prayers with their families on Sundays (page 88)?

6. What **inference** about Harriet Tubman's **character** can you draw from the incident with the gun? What other inferences can you make about the character of Harriet Tubman? Consider her words, her actions, and her effect on other people.

7. Think about another period in history when people were forced to leave behind everything they knew and loved. How would their experiences compare with the experiences of Harriet Tubman and her eleven fugitives? Think about your responses to the Quickwrite before you answer this question.

8. **Subjective writing** reveals the feelings of the writer; its aim is to present the writer's point of view. **Objective writing** is based completely on facts; the aim of objective writing is to inform, not to reveal the personal feelings of the writer. Is this biography of Tubman subjective, objective, or a combination of the two? Support your answer with details from the text.

9. Go back to the text, and find two **primary sources** (firsthand accounts) mentioned by Petry. What other firsthand sources might she have used to get all this factual information?

Writing

My Hero . . .

Most people would agree that Harriet Tubman is a hero. Heroism is also found in ordinary people, and it often goes unnoticed. Maybe there is someone in your family who has heroic qualities. Perhaps a teacher, a coach, a neighbor, or a friend is a real hero to you. Write a brief **biographical sketch** of someone you think is a hero. Your sketch should tell where and when the person was born, where the person lives now, and what he or she does. Be sure to explain why this person is a hero to you.

BONUS QUESTION

Tubman says, "Freedom's not bought with dust." What is it bought with?

Reading Standard 3.3
Compare and contrast motivations and reactions of literary characters from different historical eras confronting similar situations or conflicts.

Vocabulary Development

Influences on English: All in the Family

The histories of English words can give us a glimpse of the history of the English-speaking peoples themselves. Thousands of words that we use every day have come into English from other languages. Some countries, such as France and Germany, have tried to prevent their languages from borrowing foreign words. English, however, has always been like a giant sponge, absorbing words from every group it comes in contact with. The Vocabulary words in Petry's biography of Harriet Tubman all come from Latin. Latin is an ancient language that is no longer spoken. Because of its rich literature and its influence on English, however, it is still taught in some schools. The Word Bank, below, contains a list of the Vocabulary words and the Latin words they come from.

Word Bank

fugitives < L *fugere,* "to flee"

incomprehensible < L *prehendere,* "to seize, grasp, get hold of"

incentive < L *canere,* "to sing"

dispel < L *pellere,* "to drive, beat"

eloquence < L *loqui,* "to speak or talk"

Related Words

apprehend: capture; understand.

compel: force; overpower; control.

enchant: charm; bewitch.

expulsion: banishment.

impel: push; drive; urge; require.

loquacious: very talkative.

propel: send forcefully outward.

recant: take back one's words.

refuge: place safe from danger.

soliloquy: speech made by an actor alone onstage.

subterfuge: actions used to escape the consequences of one's misdeeds.

PRACTICE

Study the meaning of the words above, all of which come from Latin, and then look at the list called Related Words. The **related words** and some of the Vocabulary words have Latin roots in common. Make word trees grouping the words from each list that come from the same Latin word. One word tree has already been done for you. (Some trees will have just a few branches!)

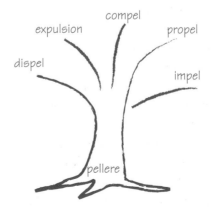

Reading Standard 1.2
Understand the most important points in the history of the English language, and use common word origins to determine the historical influences on English word meanings.

The Fugitive Slave Acts of 1793 and 1850

Using Text Structure to Organize Ideas

"Get organized!" Has anyone ever said that to you? What exactly does it mean? Let's look at the CDs floating around your room. If you have five CDs, you can probably stack them in one place. Then all the CDs are together—end of problem. If you have a lot of CDs, though, you may want to broaden the scope of your organization. You could alphabetize your CDs by artist or group, or you might put all the hip-hop together and all the classical together. As long as you are willing to live with it, almost anything you do will be fine.

Writers have a different problem. They have to organize ideas not just for themselves but also for their readers. So writers rely on certain **text structures** to help convey their ideas. Recognizing those structures can help you understand how the ideas are grouped and how they are connected.

Kinds of Text Structures

There are many kinds of text structures, but among the most commonly used are the following ones:

- **enumeration** (ē·nōō′mər·ā′shən)— explaining things first, second, third, and so on
- **chronology** (krə·näl′ə·jē)— describing events in the order in which they happen

- **comparison and contrast**—showing how one thing is similar to or different from another thing
- **cause and effect**—showing how one event causes another event, and so on

Background

The text that follows is a summary of two laws that were important in the lives of Harriet Tubman, Africans in America (whether held in slavery or free), slave owners, and ordinary citizens of the Northern states. The laws are called the Fugitive Slave Acts of 1793 and 1850.

The **Fugitive Slave Act of 1793** was a law with no provisions for enforcement. It did set a legal precedent, however. In the year 1850, the North and the South agreed to a compromise on the issue of slavery. The North got California admitted to the Union as a free state. The South got the **Fugitive Slave Act of 1850,** which required the federal government to capture fugitives from slavery in the North and return them to the South. The consequences of the 1850 act would soon echo in the gunfire of the Civil War.

Reading Standard 2.3
Find similarities and differences between texts in the treatment, scope, or organization of ideas.

The Fugitive Slave Acts of 1793 and 1850

The Fugitive Slave Act of 1793 stated that a person could not offer any form of protection to a fugitive from slavery; in fact, the law required that all runaways be captured and returned to the states they had fled from. The person protecting the fugitive was subject to a fine and was liable for any damages that the "owner" of the person might claim. This law was strongly opposed in the North, however, and was only loosely enforced. As a result, the South demanded that more severe legislation be passed—hence, the Fugitive Slave Act of 1850.

THE FUGITIVE SLAVE ACT OF 1850 HAD TEN SECTIONS, AS FOLLOWS:

SECTIONS 1, 2, AND 3 established the rules by which federal commissioners were appointed. These commissioners were then "authorized and required to exercise and discharge all the powers and duties conferred by this act."

SECTION 4 gave the appointed federal commissioners the authority to arrest and return alleged fugitives to the state or territory from which they had supposedly fled. This meant that the federal appointees who decided an alleged fugitive's fate did not belong to the community. Rather, they were strangers who came into the community to hold a hearing. Since the federal government was in charge, the local courts had no say in determining what would happen to the alleged fugitive.

SECTION 5 listed the penalties for failure to comply with warrants issued under the act: A federal marshal or deputy marshal who refused to serve a warrant was subject, on conviction, to a one-thousand-dollar fine. In 1850, one thousand dollars was enough to buy a good-sized house on a ten-acre plot of land.

This section also said that if an arrested person escaped a marshal's custody, the marshal was liable for "the full value of the service or labor of said fugitive in the State, Territory, or District whence he escaped."

In addition, this section empowered federal commissioners to deputize any bystander to serve on a posse or to do whatever was necessary to apprehend an alleged fugitive. The deputized person could not refuse to serve, although this would seem to have been a violation of the person's rights as a U.S. citizen.

SECTION 6 held that a fugitive from slavery was still a slave no matter where he or she was. This meant that fugitives crossing the Mason-Dixon line from the South into the North were no longer free. They now carried the legal status of slave. Free blacks in the North understood that this change in the law meant they were not safe in the "cradle of liberty," and thousands of them fled to Canada.

Section 6 also prohibited an alleged fugitive from testifying at his or her own trial. This meant that the defendant could not defend herself or himself. The only admissible evidence was testimony from the slave owner or his representative. The federal commissioners then judged whether that testimony was believable. In a speech on the Fugitive Slave Law of 1850, Frederick Douglass said that under this law the oaths of "any two villains" were sufficient to confine a free man to slavery for life.

SECTION 7 established penalties for interfering with the capture of an alleged fugitive: a fine "not exceeding one thousand dollars, and imprisonment not exceeding six months."

SECTION 8 dealt with fees paid to officials for their part in the arrest, custody, and delivery of a fugitive to his or her owner. It specified that these officials would not earn a salary. Instead, the more people they arrested, the more money they earned.

SECTION 9 stated that if the claimant suspected that an attempt would be made to rescue the fugitive by force, the arresting officer was required to keep the fugitive in custody, take him back to the state he fled, and deliver him to his "owner." This section more or less acknowledged that while many Northerners might not be particularly concerned about slavery as long as it was down South, they felt different when it affected their own communities. Seeing armed men on horses running down an unarmed person on foot forced them to make a choice between abiding by the law of the land and helping a fellow human being in trouble. Many ordinary Northerners, even those who did not consider themselves abolitionists,° chose to help.

SECTION 10 detailed the legal procedures to be followed when someone was claimed as a fugitive and handed over to his or her "owner."

—Flo Ota De Lange

° **abolitionists** *n.:* people dedicated to ending (abolishing) slavery.

The Harriet Tubman Series (1939–1940), No. 20, by Jacob Lawrence.

In 1850, the Fugitive Slave Law was passed, which bound the people north of the Mason and Dixon Line to return to bondage any fugitives found in their territories—forcing Harriet Tubman to lead her escaped slaves into Canada.

Hampton University Museum, Hampton, Virginia.

Reading Informational Materials

Reading Check

1. Under the Fugitive Slave Act of 1793, what would happen to someone who knowingly helped a person running away from slavery?

2. Under the Fugitive Slave Act of 1850, what would happen to a person who knowingly helped someone running away from slavery?

3. Under the Fugitive Slave Act of 1850, who was, and who was not, allowed to testify at the trial of an alleged runaway? (See Section 6.)

4. Under the Fugitive Slave Act of 1850, who was required to help catch a suspected runaway?

5. How did many Northerners react to the provisions of the Fugitive Slave Act of 1850?

Test Practice

The Fugitive Slave Acts of 1793 and 1850

1. How did the Fugitive Slave Act of 1850 differ from the Fugitive Slave Act of 1793?

   A It was broader in scope.

   B It gave fugitives more rights.

   C It had less severe penalties.

   D It opposed slavery.

2. Although Northerners could and did ignore the 1793 Fugitive Slave Act, the passage of the law was significant because —

   F it set a legal precedent

   G it caused the Civil War

   H it was a step toward abolishing slavery

   J blacks had voted for its passage

3. Section 6 of the Fugitive Slave Act of 1850 made it unsafe for black persons, whether free or fugitive, to be in any of the places below *except* —

   A the South

   B the North

   C the United States

   D Canada

4. The Fugitive Slave Acts were enacted to benefit —

   F the cause of justice

   G slave owners

   H all humanity

   J fugitives

5. To **organize** the ideas in this selection, the author used —

   A sequence

   B chronology

   C both of the above

   D none of the above

Reading Standard 2.3
Find similarities and differences between texts in the treatment, scope, or organization of ideas.

Vocabulary Development

Latin and the Law

The language of law and government uses many words derived from Latin. This reliance on Latin-based words sometimes makes reading legal materials a bit difficult, so let's take a closer look at some commonly used Latin words and their modern uses.

agere, "to act or do" *clamare,* "to call out; to shout" *dicere,* "to say; to tell"	*jurare,* "to swear" *legare,* "to send" *lex,* "law"

PRACTICE

Each passage below contains words formed from one of the Latin words listed above. First, identify the Latin root that is common to all the underlined words in each passage. Next, define each underlined word.

1. The enactment of the Fugitive Slave Act of 1850 pitted Northern and Southern activists against each other.
2. Abolitionists proclaimed the act unconstitutional and immoral. Slave owners wanted to reclaim their "property" in courts of law.
3. Abolitionists declared the Fugitive Slave Act of 1850 illegal because it threatened the safety of legitimately free persons.
4. Section 6 states that a black person would be arrested if someone alleged ownership. This allegation was legal and binding until a federal commissioner decided the case in court.
5. The law dictated that only the alleged "owner" could speak in court. The indicted person was thus left to the mercy of a prejudiced judicial proceeding.
6. Because a black person could not speak in his or her own defense, any "owner" could easily commit perjury by lying and obtaining an unjust verdict.

Reading Standard 1.2
Understand the most important points in the history of the English language, and use common word origins to determine the historical influences on English word meanings.

Grammar Link MINI-LESSON

Regular and Irregular Verbs

A **regular verb** forms its past tense and past participle by simply adding –d or –ed to its base form:

Base Form	Past Tense	Past Participle
escape	escaped	(have) escaped
disappear	disappeared	(have) disappeared

Irregular verbs are more complicated:

Base Form	Past Tense	Past Participle
leave	left	(have) left
eat	ate	(have) eaten
know	knew	(have) known

There are hundreds of irregular verbs, each with its own forms. Three of the most difficult irregular pairs follow.

Lie and *Lay*, *Sit* and *Set*, *Rise* and *Raise*

Lie and *lay*, *sit* and *set*, and *rise* and *raise* are pairs of irregular verbs that often cause confusion. Remember that the second verb in each pair expresses an action directed toward an object—a person or a thing named in the sentence; the first verb simply expresses an action. (For example, you *lie* down, but first you *lay* your schoolbag on the table.) Below are some of the forms of these six verbs. Notice that the past tense of *lie* is *lay*.

Base Form	Present Participle	Past Participle
lie	lying	(have) lain
lay	laying	(have) laid
sit	sitting	(have) sat
set	setting	(have) set
rise	rising	(have) risen
raise	raising	(have) raised

PRACTICE 1

Proofread the following paragraph, and correct all the incorrect verb forms.

The fugitives had leaved the plantation after they ate their evening meal. They knowed that the way would be hard but thinked that if they getted help along the way, they would be able to make it.

For more help, see Regular Verbs and Irregular Verbs in the *Holt Handbook*, pages 187–196.

PRACTICE 2

Copy the following paragraph, choosing the correct verb from each underlined pair.

The fugitives (1) sat/set on the ground and (2) lay/laid their bundles down for pillows. Soon they were (3) lying/laying fast asleep. They were sad when it was time to (4) rise/raise again; they wished they could have (5) lain/laid there longer.

For more help, see Irregular Verbs in the *Holt Handbook*, pages 188–196.

Barbara Frietchie

Literary Focus
A Character's Character

How a person reacts to a challenge can be considered a test of character. In that sentence the word *character* means "a person's essential quality or personality." A person's **character** can be described as kind, self-centered, outgoing, honest, brave, selfish, and so on. The word *character* can also mean "a person in a story, play, or poem." In the following poem, see what the *character* Barbara Frietchie reveals about her *character* when she decides to be different from the crowd.

Reading Skills
Paraphrasing: Saying It Your Way

Paraphrasing means restating a writer's text in your own words. A paraphrase differs from a **summary,** which retells only the most important points in a text. Here is a paraphrase of lines 1–4 of Whittier's poem: *The church spires of Frederick rise up from the cornfields, clear in the September morning. The spires are surrounded by the green hills of Maryland.*

Make the Connection
Quickwrite ✏️

Many of the people we most admire and think of as heroes have had to stand up for their beliefs. Use a chart like the one that follows to make a list of some of these individuals (contemporary, historical, fictional— maybe even yourself). You may want to brainstorm names with your classmates.

Name	Action	Belief

Background

"Barbara Frietchie" is set during the Civil War. In 1862, after defeating Union forces at the Second Battle of Bull Run, Confederate troops moved north into Maryland. Led by Generals Robert E. Lee and "Stonewall" Jackson, the troops marched into the town of Frederick. Lee and his men were expecting a warm welcome, but the people of Frederick were loyal to the Union. Whittier based "Barbara Frietchie" on these events.

Vocabulary Development

These words look familiar, but their use in the poem may surprise you:

staff (staf) *n.:* pole. *Frietchie hung the flag from a staff outside her window.*

tread (tred) *n.:* step. *The tread of the soldiers was echoed through the town.*

rent (rent) *v.:* tore. *The rifle blast rent a hole in the flag.*

stirred (sturd) *v.:* woke up. *The old woman stirred Jackson's feelings.*

host (hōst) *n.:* army. *The rebel host marched into Frederick, Maryland.*

Reading Standard 3.3
Compare and contrast motivations and reactions of literary characters from different historical eras confronting similar situations or conflicts.

Barbara Frietchie

John Greenleaf Whittier

Up from the meadows rich with corn,
Clear in the cool September morn,
The clustered spires of Frederick stand
Green-walled by the hills of Maryland.

5 Round about them orchards sweep,
Apple and peach tree fruited deep,
Fair as the garden of the Lord
To the eyes of the famished rebel horde,°
On that pleasant morn of the early fall

10 When Lee marched over the mountain wall;
Over the mountains winding down,
Horse and foot, into Frederick town.
Forty flags with their silver stars,
Forty flags with their crimson bars,

15 Flapped in the morning wind: the sun
Of noon looked down, and saw not one.
Up rose old Barbara Frietchie then,
Bowed with her fourscore years and ten;
Bravest of all in Frederick town,

20 She took up the flag the men hauled down
In her attic window the staff she set,
To show that one heart was loyal yet.
Up the street came the rebel tread,
Stonewall Jackson riding ahead.

25 Under his slouched hat left and right
He glanced; the old flag met his sight.
"Halt!"—the dust-brown ranks stood fast.
"Fire!"—out blazed the rifle blast.

8. horde (hôrd) *n.:* crowd.

Barbara Frietchie (1876) (detail) by Dennis Malone Carter (1827–1881). Oil on canvas (36¼″ × 46¼″).

Kirby Collection of Historical Paintings, Lafayette College, Easton, Pennsylvania. Photo by Thomas Kosa.

Vocabulary

staff (staf) *n.:* pole; stick. *Staff* also means "group of workers" and "lines on which musical notes are written."

tread (tred) *n.:* act of stepping or walking. *Tread* also means "the outer part of tires or of shoe soles."

It shivered the window, pane and sash;

30   It rent the banner with seam and gash.

Quick, as it fell, from the broken staff

Dame Barbara snatched the silken scarf.

She leaned far out on the windowsill,

And shook it forth with a royal will.

35   "Shoot, if you must, this old gray head,

But spare your country's flag," she said.

A shade of sadness, a blush of shame,

Over the face of the leader came;

The nobler nature within him stirred

40   To life at that woman's deed and word;

"Who touches a hair of yon gray head

Dies like a dog! March on!" he said.

All day long through Frederick street

Sounded the tread of marching feet:

45   All day long that free flag tossed

Over the heads of the rebel host.

Ever its torn folds rose and fell

On the loyal winds that loved it well;

And through the hill gaps sunset light

50   Shone over it with a warm good night.

Barbara Frietchie's work is o'er,

And the Rebel rides on his raids no more.

Honor to her! and let a tear

Fall, for her sake, on Stonewall's bier.°

55   Over Barbara Frietchie's grave,

Flag of Freedom and Union, wave!

Peace and order and beauty draw

Round thy symbol of light and law;

And ever the stars above look down

60   On thy stars below in Frederick town!

54. bier (bir) *n.*: coffin and the platform on which it rests. Stonewall Jackson died in 1863 after being wounded in battle.

Vocabulary

rent (rent) *v.* (past tense of *rend*, meaning "tear"): tore; ripped. *Rent* also means "pay money for use of a house or apartment or of things such as bowling shoes or ice skates."

stirred (sturd) *v.*: arose; woke up. *Stirred* also means "mixed a liquid or loose ingredients, as in a recipe."

host (hōst) *n.*: army; large number; crowd. *Host* also means "someone who entertains guests, at home or on TV."

John Greenleaf Whittier

John Greenleaf Whittier (1833) by Robert Peckham. Oil on canvas.

"Barbara Frietchie Was No Myth"

John Greenleaf Whittier (1807–1892) was born and raised on a farm in Haverhill, Massachusetts, where his Quaker family had lived since 1688. Whittier devoted most of his life to the antislavery movement. His poems reflect his dedication to freedom and justice and his deep religious faith. Whittier was born in the same year as Henry Wadsworth Longfellow (whose poem "Paul Revere's Ride" begins on page 410). Like Longfellow, Whittier was one of the hugely popular Fireside Poets, whose works sold the way bestselling novels do today. About "Barbara Frietchie," Whittier wrote:

> This poem was written in strict conformity to the account of the incident as I had it from respectable and trustworthy sources. It has since been the subject of a good deal of conflicting testimony, and the story was probably incorrect in some of its details. It is admitted by all that Barbara Frietchie was no myth, but a worthy and highly esteemed gentlewoman, intensely loyal and a hater of the slavery rebellion, holding her Union flag sacred and keeping it with her Bible; that when the Confederates halted before her house and entered her dooryard, she denounced them in vigorous language, shook her cane in their faces, and drove them out; and when General Burnside's [a Union general] troops followed close upon Jackson's, she waved her flag and cheered them. It is stated that May Quantrell, a brave and loyal lady in another part of the city, did wave her flag in sight of the Confederates. It is possible that there has been a blending of the two incidents.

Literary Response and Analysis

Reading Check

1. What is the **setting** of this poem—where and when does it take place?

2. **Paraphrase** lines 26–42, which describe the most important actions in the poem. In your own words, based on details in the poem, describe the picture Whittier creates.

3. In lines 53–54, what does the speaker say we should do?

4. In lines 55–60, the speaker addresses the flag. What does he ask the flag to do in lines 55–56? How would you **paraphrase** lines 57–60?

Interpretations

5. When writers use **allusions,** they refer to events, characters, or places in literature or history, or current events, and they expect us to understand what they are **alluding** to. What is the speaker alluding to in line 7, when he says the orchards of Maryland are as "fair as the garden of the Lord"?

6. In lines 15 and 16, something important happens, but we have to **infer** what it is. The speaker expects us to know, based on what he says next. What has happened by noontime in Frederick?

7. One definition of a hero is a person who does the right thing even though he or she might have to act alone. Could this definition apply to Barbara Frietchie and to Harriet Tubman (page 87)? How about

Reading Standard 3.3
Compare and contrast motivations and reactions of literary characters from different historical eras confronting similar situations or conflicts.

Stonewall Jackson? Could it apply to those heroes you cited in your Quickwrite notes? Consider the words and actions of these people in your responses.

Evaluation

8. Whittier's comment in Meet the Writer suggests that the incident described in this poem might not have occurred exactly the way he tells it. Does that comment affect your feelings about the poem? Why or why not?

Listening and Speaking
"Shoot, If You Must"

Alone or with a small group, prepare a **dramatic reading** of "Barbara Frietchie." You might want to have one person read Barbara Frietchie's lines, another person read Stonewall Jackson's, and a chorus read the rest. You could use pantomime, props, and sound effects. You might even set the poem to music. After your reading, ask your audience for feedback. Could your listeners understand everything that was said? How did hearing the poem read aloud compare with reading it silently?

BONUS QUESTION

Why was the general called "Stonewall" Jackson?

Vocabulary Development

History of the English Language: Finding Our Roots

The written record of English dates back about fourteen hundred years, but the ancestry of English goes back much further. Long ago, people living near the Caspian Sea (between what is now Asia and the Middle East) spoke a language we call Proto-Indo-European. (*Proto*– means "original or earliest." *Indo*– refers to India.) These people were fighters, farmers, and herders, and they had an urge to travel. Eventually they took to their great four-wheeled carts and spread east through modern-day Iran and India and west through Turkey and most of Europe. As groups settled in different areas, their language changed into the languages we now call Persian, Hindi, Armenian, Sanskrit, Greek, Russian, Polish, Irish, Italian, French, Spanish, German, Dutch, Swedish, Norwegian—and English. All these languages share ancient roots and are called Indo-European.

> **Word Bank**
>
> staff
> tread
> rent
> stirred
> host

PRACTICE 1

Look up *staff* and *tread* in a dictionary to discover their **Indo-European** (IE) **roots.** Then, with a small group of classmates, try to figure out how each word's different meanings might have derived from its one root.

Multiple-Meaning Words

PRACTICE 2

To practice using the **multiple meanings** of the Word Bank words, fill in the blanks in the paragraph below with the appropriate words. Then, write sentences of your own, using *another* meaning of each word. For extra credit, see if you can use all five words in one paragraph.

 At daybreak the enemy _____, which was camped on the plain, _____ into action. The _____ of their massive formations could be heard for miles around as they marched to battle. On the hilltop the lieutenant proudly planted the _____ holding the company flag, which was _____ and bloodied from the fighting.

Reading Standard 1.2
Understand the most important points in the history of the English language, and use common word origins to determine the historical influences on English word meanings.

Grammar Link MINI-LESSON

Keeping Tenses Consistent

Many writers tell their stories in the past tense, showing that the events have already happened.

> **The townspeople huddled indoors. Only Barbara Frietchie hung out the U.S. flag as the Confederate troops marched by.**

Writers sometimes tell their stories in the present tense instead, to give their readers the feeling that the events are happening right now.

> **The townspeople are huddling indoors. Only Barbara Frietchie hangs out the U.S. flag as the Confederate troops march by.**

Whichever tense you choose to write in, use it consistently. Either the events happened before, or they are happening now. You'll confuse your readers if you keep switching tenses.

Active and Passive Voice

When a verb is in the **active voice,** the subject of the verb does something. When a verb is in the **passive voice,** something is done to its subject.

ACTIVE **The father told a story to his sons.**
[The action is done *by* the subject, the father.]

PASSIVE **The sons were told a story by their father.**
[The action is done *to* the subject, the sons.]

Those two sentences convey the same information, but with different emphases. The first sentence stresses the doer of the action; the second sentence stresses the receiver of the action.

Try always to use the active voice, to give your writing a direct, lively tone.

PRACTICE 1

Select a story in this book, and rewrite its opening paragraph using a different tense. You might turn to "Raymond's Run" (page 367). How does the story sound when you rewrite the first paragraph in the past tense? How does "Broken Chain" (page 7) sound when you rewrite the first paragraph in the present tense?

For more help, see Verb Tense in the *Holt Handbook,* pages 196–199.

PRACTICE 2

Change the following sentences from the passive to the active voice. We think you'll like the difference.

(1) Her flag was waved by Barbara Frietchie. (2) Their rifles were fired by the troops. (3) Her now famous words were said by Barbara Frietchie. (4) Shame was felt by "Stonewall" Jackson.

For more help, see Active Voice and Passive Voice in the *Holt Handbook,* pages 200–201.

Too Soon a Woman

Literary Focus
Motivation

What makes people do the things they do? In literature as in life, a person's **motivation,** or reason for behavior, is not always clear. As you read this story, decide if the characters' actions make sense to you. Does each character's motivation become clearer as the story continues?

Reading Skills
Summarizing: Keep It Simple

A summary is a short restatement of the main events and essential ideas in a work. When you **summarize** a story, briefly identify the major characters. Then, in your own words, describe the characters' problems, state the main events, and explain how the problems are finally resolved. Remember to keep your summary simple and to leave out minor details. As you read "Too Soon a Woman," think about which events you would include if you had to summarize it for a friend.

Make the Connection
Quickwrite

Throughout history, people have risked everything—even life itself—in order to do the right thing. Harriet Tubman left all that she knew and everyone she loved to gain freedom from slavery. In this short story, set during pioneer days in North America, eighteen-year-old Mary risks her life to save three children in her care. Jot down some notes about other people who have chosen to do the right thing even when it was a hard choice.

Background

In 1803, with the Louisiana Purchase, the size of the United States doubled. By the 1880s, about one quarter of the nation's population lived in the West. In large part this mass resettlement was a result of the Homestead Act of 1862, which allowed a settler to earn up to 160 acres of land by living on it for five years and improving it. Homesteaders faced brutal hardships, though. Of the 400,000 families or more that homesteaded, nearly 60 percent failed.

Vocabulary Development

You'll find these words in the story:

skimpy (skim′pē) *adj.:* less than enough. *Their skimpy supplies wouldn't last long.*

grudging (gruj′iŋ) *v.* used as *adj.:* reluctant; unwilling. *Hungry travelers are glad for even a grudging bit of food.*

gaunt (gônt) *adj.:* very thin and bony. *The weary traveler had a gaunt face.*

rummaged (rum′ijd) *v.:* searched through the contents of a box, a drawer, and so on. *She rummaged around in the box for something to eat.*

savoring (sā′vər·iŋ) *v.* used as *adj.:* enjoying with great delight. *She sat up late at night, savoring life to the full.*

Reading Standard 3.3 Compare and contrast motivations and reactions of literary characters from different historical eras confronting similar situations or conflicts.

Too Soon a Woman

Dorothy M. Johnson

We left the home place behind, mile by slow mile, heading for the mountains, across the prairie where the wind blew forever.

At first there were four of us with the one-horse wagon and its skimpy load. Pa and I walked, because I was a big boy of eleven. My two little sisters romped and trotted until they got tired and had to be boosted up into the wagon bed.

That was no covered Conestoga,[1] like Pa's folks came West in, but just an old farm wagon, drawn by one weary horse, creaking and rumbling westward to the mountains, toward the little woods town where Pa thought he had an old uncle who owned a little two-bit sawmill.

Two weeks we had been moving when we picked up Mary, who had run away from somewhere that she wouldn't tell. Pa didn't want her along, but she stood up to him with no fear in her voice.

"I'd rather go with a family and look after kids," she said, "but I ain't going back. If you won't take me, I'll travel with any wagon that will."

Pa scowled at her, and her wide blue eyes stared back.

"How old are you?" he demanded.

"Eighteen," she said. "There's teamsters[2] come this way sometimes. I'd rather go with you folks. But I won't go back."

"We're prid' near out of grub," my father told her. "We're clean out of money. I got all I can handle without taking anybody else." He turned away as if he hated the sight of her. "You'll have to walk," he said.

So she went along with us and looked after the little girls, but Pa wouldn't talk to her.

On the prairie, the wind blew. But in the mountains, there was rain. When we stopped at little timber claims along the way, the homesteaders said it had rained all

---

2. **teamsters** *n.:* people who drive teams of horses.

---

1. **Conestoga** (kän′ə·stō′gə): covered wagon with wide wheels, used by American settlers to cross the prairies.

Vocabulary
skimpy (skim′pē) *adj.:* less than enough.

summer. Crops among the blackened stumps were rotted and spoiled. There was no cheer anywhere, and little hospitality. The people we talked to were past worrying. They were scared and desperate.

So was Pa. He traveled twice as far each day as the wagon, ranging through the woods with his rifle, but he never saw game. He had been depending on venison,[3] but we never got any except as a <u>grudging</u> gift from the homesteaders.

He brought in a porcupine once, and that was fat meat and good. Mary roasted it in chunks over the fire, half crying with the smoke. Pa and I rigged up the tarp[4] sheet for shelter to keep the rain from putting the fire clean out.

The porcupine was long gone, except for some of the tried-out fat[5] that Mary had saved, when we came to an old, empty cabin. Pa said we'd have to stop. The horse was wore out, couldn't pull anymore up those grades on the deep-rutted roads in the mountains.

At the cabin, at least there was shelter. We had a few potatoes left and some cornmeal. There was a creek that probably had fish in it, if a person could catch them. Pa tried it for half a day before he gave up. To this day I don't care for fishing. I remember my father's sunken eyes in his <u>gaunt</u>, grim face.

He took Mary and me outside the cabin to talk. Rain dripped on us from branches overhead.

"I think I know where we are," he said. "I calculate to get to old John's and back in about four days. There'll be grub in the town, and they'll let me have some whether old John's still there or not."

He looked at me. "You do like she tells you," he warned. It was the first time he had admitted Mary was on earth since we picked her up two weeks before.

"You're my pardner," he said to me, "but it might be she's got more brains. You mind what she says."

He burst out with bitterness, "There ain't anything good left in the world or people to care if you live or die. But I'll get grub in the town and come back with it."

He took a deep breath and added, "If you get too all-fired hungry, butcher the horse. It'll be better than starvin'."

He kissed the little girls good-bye and plodded off through the woods with one blanket and the rifle.

The cabin was moldy and had no floor. We kept a fire going under a hole in the roof, so it was full of blinding smoke, but we had to keep the fire so as to dry out the wood.

The third night we lost the horse. A bear scared him. We heard the racket, and Mary and I ran out, but we couldn't see anything in the pitch dark.

In gray daylight I went looking for him, and I must have walked fifteen miles. It seemed

---

3. **venison** (ven′i·sən) *n.:* deer meat.
4. **tarp** *n.:* short for *tarpaulin* (tär·pô′lin), or waterproof canvas.
5. **tried-out fat:** fat that has been melted down.

Vocabulary

grudging (gruj′iŋ) *v.* used as *adj.:* reluctant, unwilling.

gaunt (gônt) *adj.:* very thin and bony, as if from hunger or old age.

like I had to have that horse at the cabin when Pa came or he'd whip me. I got plumb lost two or three times and thought maybe I was going to die there alone and nobody would ever know it, but I found the way back to the clearing.

That was the fourth day, and Pa didn't come. That was the day we ate up the last of the grub.

The fifth day, Mary went looking for the horse. My sisters whimpered, huddled in a quilt by the fire, because they were scared and hungry.

I never did get dried out, always having to bring in more damp wood and going out to yell to see if Mary would hear me and not get lost. But I couldn't cry like the little girls did, because I was a big boy, eleven years old.

It was near dark when there was an answer to my yelling, and Mary came into the clearing.

Mary didn't have the horse—we never saw hide nor hair of that old horse again—

but she was carrying something big and white that looked like a pumpkin with no color to it.

She didn't say anything, just looked around and saw Pa wasn't there yet, at the end of the fifth day.

"What's that thing?" my sister Elizabeth demanded.

"Mushroom," Mary answered. "I bet it hefts[6] ten pounds."

"What are you going to do with it now?" I sneered. "Play football here?"

"Eat it—maybe," she said, putting it in a corner. Her wet hair hung over her shoulders. She huddled by the fire.

My sister Sarah began to whimper again. "I'm hungry!" she kept saying.

"Mushrooms ain't good eating," I said. "They can kill you."

"Maybe," Mary answered. "Maybe they can. I don't set up to know all about everything, like some people."

---

6. **hefts** *v.:* weighs.

"What's that mark on your shoulder?" I asked her. "You tore your dress on the brush."

"What do you think it is?" she said, her head bowed in the smoke.

"Looks like scars," I guessed.

"'Tis scars. They whipped me. Now mind your own business. I want to think."

Elizabeth whimpered, "Why don't Pa come back?"

"He's coming," Mary promised. "Can't come in the dark. Your pa'll take care of you soon's he can."

She got up and rummaged around in the grub box.

"Nothing there but empty dishes," I growled. "If there was anything, we'd know it."

Mary stood up. She was holding the can with the porcupine grease.

"I'm going to have something to eat," she said coolly. "You kids can't have any yet. And I don't want any squalling, mind."

It was a cruel thing, what she did then. She sliced that big, solid mushroom and heated grease in a pan.

The smell of it brought the little girls out of their quilt, but she told them to go back in so fierce a voice that they obeyed. They cried to break your heart.

I didn't cry. I watched, hating her.

I endured the smell of the mushroom frying as long as I could. Then I said, "Give me some."

"Tomorrow," Mary answered. "Tomorrow, maybe. But not tonight." She turned to me with a sharp command: "Don't bother me! Just leave me be."

She knelt there by the fire and finished frying the slice of mushroom.

If I'd had Pa's rifle, I'd have been willing to kill her right then and there.

She didn't eat right away. She looked at the brown, fried slice for a while and said, "By tomorrow morning, I guess you can tell whether you want any."

The little girls stared at her as she ate. Sarah was chewing an old leather glove.

When Mary crawled into the quilts with them, they moved away as far as they could get.

I was so scared that my stomach heaved, empty as it was.

Mary didn't stay in the quilts long. She took a drink out of the water bucket and sat down by the fire and looked through the smoke at me.

She said in a low voice, "I don't know how it will be if it's poison. Just do the best you can with the girls. Because your pa will come back, you know. . . . You better go to bed. I'm going to sit up."

And so would you sit up. If it might be your last night on earth and the pain of death might seize you at any moment, you would sit up by the smoky fire, wide awake, remembering whatever you had to remember, savoring life.

We sat in silence after the girls had gone to sleep. Once I asked, "How long does it take?"

Vocabulary

rummaged (rum′ijd) *v.:* searched through the contents of a box or another container.

savoring (sā′vər·iŋ) *v.* used as *adj.:* enjoying or appreciating with great delight.

"I never heard," she answered. "Don't think about it."

I slept after a while, with my chin on my chest. Maybe Peter dozed that way at Gethsemane as the Lord knelt praying.[7]

Mary's moving around brought me wide awake. The black of night was fading.

"I guess it's all right," Mary said. "I'd be able to tell by now, wouldn't I?"

I answered gruffly, "I don't know."

Mary stood in the doorway for a while, looking out at the dripping world as if she found it beautiful. Then she fried slices of the mushroom while the little girls danced with anxiety.

We feasted, we three, my sisters and I,

until Mary ruled, "That'll hold you," and would not cook any more. She didn't touch any of the mushroom herself.

That was a strange day in the moldy cabin. Mary laughed and was gay; she told stories, and we played "Who's Got the Thimble?" with a pine cone.

In the afternoon we heard a shout, and my sisters screamed and I ran ahead of them across the clearing.

The rain had stopped. My father came plunging out of the woods leading a pack horse—and well I remember the treasures of food in that pack.

He glanced at us anxiously as he tore at the ropes that bound the pack.

"Where's the other one?" he demanded.

Mary came out of the cabin then, walking sedately. As she came toward us, the sun began to shine.

My stepmother was a wonderful woman.

---

7. **Maybe Peter . . . knelt praying:** According to Matthew 26:36–46, Jesus spent an entire night praying in the Garden of Gethsemane, outside Jerusalem, knowing he would be arrested in the morning. He asked Peter and two other followers to stay awake with him, but they kept falling asleep.

MEET THE WRITER

Dorothy M. Johnson

"Kills-Both-Places"

Dorothy M. Johnson (1905–1984) was born in McGregor, Iowa, but made the West her home—in both a physical and a literary sense. After graduating from the University of Montana, she moved to New York City to work as a magazine editor but eventually returned to Montana to write the stories that would make her famous. Johnson is known for her sensitive, realistic portrayals of the American West. Three of her stories—"The Hanging Tree," "The Man Who Shot Liberty Valance," and "A Man Called Horse"—were made into movies.

The Blackfoot people of Montana made Johnson an honorary member and gave her the name Kills-Both-Places.

Literary Response and Analysis

Reading Check

1. **Summarize** the main events of the story, using the story map below to help you. Remember to include the main events only.

Characters:
Their problems:
Main events:
Resolution:

2. Who is telling this story?

3. What surprising fact do you learn at the story's end?

Interpretations

4. List three **conflicts** (internal or external) in this story. Which conflict seems to be the main one?

5. Think about the **title** of the story. In what way is Mary "too soon a woman"?

6. In your opinion, does the eleven-year-old narrator become "too soon a man" as well? Why or why not?

7. Explain the character's **motivation** for the actions involved in each of these questions:

   • At the beginning of the story, why does Pa refuse to talk to Mary?

   • Why does Mary refuse to give the children any of the mushroom at first?

   • Why does Mary laugh and tell stories and play games the day after she eats the mushroom?

   • Why does Pa ask about Mary when he returns?

8. Most people would consider Mary a hero because she risked her life for others. Do you think any teenagers today are heroes? What have they done to show their bravery? (You may want to consult your Quick-write notes.)

9. On page 115, Pa says, "There ain't anything good left in the world or people to care if you live or die." Do people feel that way today? How would you respond to a statement like Pa's?

Evaluation

10. "Too Soon a Woman" has also been published under the title "The Day the Sun Came Out." Which **title** do you like better? Why?

Writing
Analyzing Mary

What kind of a person is Mary? Write a paragraph in which you analyze Mary's character. In your character analysis, consider the following aspects:

• how Mary responds to the conflicts in her life

• why she makes the choices she does

• how people respond to her

• how she reacts to their responses

Use details from the text to support your analysis of Mary.

What *is* that giant mushroom?

Reading Standard 3.3
Compare and contrast motivations and reactions of literary characters from different historical eras confronting similar situations or conflicts.

Vocabulary Development

Ancient tribes.

History of the English Language: Review

Here is a time line to help you review some highlights in the development of the English language.

Historic Event	Time Frame	Effect on the English Language
Tribes living near the Caspian Sea migrate to Europe and Asia.	c. third millennium B.C.	Proto-Indo-European gradually changes into many languages.
The Romans conquer most of Europe, North Africa, and the Middle East.	27 B.C.–A.D. 476	Latin, the language of Roman soldiers, influences the language of the Britons.
Anglo-Saxons arrive in Britain, driving out the Britons.	fifth century A.D.	The Germanic language of the Anglo-Saxons replaces the Celtic spoken by the Britons.
Saint Augustine arrives in Britain to do missionary work on behalf of the Roman Catholic Church.	597	The Anglo-Saxons borrow many words from Latin, the language of the Roman Catholic Church.
Vikings from Scandinavia invade Britain.	end of the eighth century	Norse combines with the language of Britain to form what we now call **Old English.**
William the Conqueror, a Norman from France, conquers England.	1066	French and Latin influence the English language, and the period of **Middle English** begins.
William Caxton prints the first book in English.	1475	Written English reaches a large number of people.
Henry VII is crowned king of England.	1485	Henry VII promotes pride in all things English, including the language. The era of **Modern English** begins.
William Shakespeare is born.	1564	Shakespeare adds thousands of words and numerous phrases to the language.
Noah Webster publishes the *American Dictionary of the English Language*.	1828	Webster includes new American words and new meanings for older English words.
Americans move westward into territories originally settled by the Spanish.	middle of the nineteenth century	English-speaking Americans adopt many words of Spanish origin.
Science and technology advance at an unprecedented rate.	present	Use of English continues to spread around the world through the World Wide Web.

Reading Standard 1.2
Understand the most important points in the history of the English language, and use common word origins to determine the historical influences on English word meanings.

Romans.

Use the words from the Word Bank to solve the mystery-word questions below. You'll notice several of the historical influences listed in the time line on the previous page.

Word Bank

skimpy
grudging
gaunt
rummaged
savoring

1. This word is from Middle English, perhaps coming from the Icelandic word *gandur*, meaning "stick." Today it describes anyone who is overly thin and bony. *What word is it?*

2. This word is probably related to the Swedish word *skrympa*, meaning "to shrink." It describes quantities that are too small or that are less than what is needed. *What word is it?*

3. This word can be traced back to Middle English, from there to Old French, and finally to the Latin *sapor*, meaning "flavor." Today it has come to mean "enjoying and appreciating." *What word is it?*

4. This word is related to the Middle High German word *grogezen*, meaning "to howl or lament." It means "done or given unwillingly." *What word is it?*

5. This word comes from the Middle French verb *arrimer*, meaning "to pack or arrange cargo." Today's English word means "to search in or through something." *What word is it?*

Vikings.

Conestoga wagon.

William Shakespeare.

Union Pacific Railroad Poster *and* Home, Sweet Soddie

Comparing Texts: Treatment and Scope of Ideas

Home on the Range
Oh give me a home
Where the buffalo roam
Where the deer and the antelope play
Where seldom is heard
A discouraging word
And the skies are not cloudy all day

"Home on the Range" makes the prairie sound like a paradise, doesn't it? That must have been another prairie, not the one Mary encountered. Perhaps the ballad was written by a lonesome cowboy long after he'd left the prairie for the comforts of running tap water and home cooking.

But let's not be too hard on our singing cowboy, even though he has given us a **biased,** or one-sided, treatment of his subject. He has conveniently forgotten all unpleasant memories in order to paint a beautiful picture of the life he longs for.

An **objective,** or balanced, treatment presents all sides of a subject so that readers can draw their own conclusions. When the treatment covers many aspects of a topic, it is said to have a **broad scope,** unlike our ballad, which has a **limited scope.**

As you read the poster from the Union Pacific Railroad and the article "Home, Sweet Soddie," think about what they say and how they say it.

- Is there evidence of bias, or is the treatment balanced and objective?

- Is the focus on the big picture or on a small snapshot?

- How are the selections similar in their scope and treatment of ideas?

- How are they different?

Reading Standard 2.3
Find similarities and differences between texts in the treatment, scope, or organization of ideas.

RICH FARMING LANDS!

ON THE LINE OF THE
Union Pacific Railroad!

Located in the GREAT CENTRAL BELT of POPULA-
TION, COMMERCE and WEALTH, and adjoining the
WORLD'S HIGHWAY from OCEAN TO OCEAN.

12,000,000 ACRES!

*3,000,000 Acres in Central and Eastern Nebraska, in the
Platte Valley, now for sale!*

We invite the attention of all parties seeking a HOME,
to the LANDS offered for sale by this Company.

The Vast Quantity of Land from which to select enables everyone to secure such a location as he desires, suitable to any branch of farming or stock raising.

The Prices are Extremely Low. The amount of land owned by the Company is so large that they are determined to sell at the cheapest possible rates, ranging from $1.50 to $8.00 per acre.

The Terms of Payment are Easy. Ten years' credit at six percent interest. A deduction of ten percent for cash.

The Location is Central, along the 41st parallel, the favorite latitude of America. Equally well adapted to corn or wheat; free from the long, cold winters of the Northern, and the hot, unhealthy influences of the Southern States.

The Face of the Country is diversified with hill and dale, grain land and meadow, rich bottoms, low bluffs, and undulating tables, all covered with a thick growth of sweet nutritious grasses.

The Soil is a dark loam, slightly impregnated with lime, free from stone and gravel, and eminently adapted to grass, grain, and root crops; the subsoil is usually light and porous, retaining moisture with wonderful tenacity.

The Climate is mild and healthful; the atmosphere dry and pure. Epidemic diseases never prevail; Fever and Ague are unknown. The greatest amount of rain falls between March and October. The Winters are dry with but little snow.

Timber is found on the streams and grows rapidly.

The Title given the purchaser is absolute, in fee simple, and free from all encumbrances, derived directly from the United States.

Soldiers of the Late War are entitled to a Homestead of one hundred and sixty acres, within Railroad limits, which is equal to a bounty of $400.

Persons of Foreign Birth are also entitled to the benefits of the Free Homestead Law, on declaring their intentions of becoming citizens of the United States; this they may do immediately on their arrival in this country. . . .

Full information in regard to lands, prices, terms of sale, etc., together with pamphlets, circulars and maps, may be obtained from the Agents of the Department, also the
"PIONEER."
A handsome ILLUSTRATED PAPER, with maps, etc., and containing the HOMESTEAD LAW. Mailed free to all applicants. Address

O. F. DAVIS,
Land Commissioner, U. P. R. R.
OMAHA, NEB.

Home, Sweet Soddie

Here you are, a pioneer on the prairie, settled for your first night in your new Home Sweet Home. After you've traveled overland so many miles that it felt as though you'd gone halfway around the world, your straw mattress feels like heaven. But it sure is dark in here. Even though your fingers are right in front of your nose, you can't see them. The dark here is absolutely dark. There are no lights from other houses or from a town or city to reflect on the horizon. Outside there might be stars, but inside there is nothing but the velvety-black black.

Thousands of Worms

So when the first crack of dawn comes, you're anxious to check out your new world. But what's that? It looks like the ceiling above your head is moving. No, it couldn't be. Look again. Now it looks like the wall is moving too. Shut those eyes quick! While you're lying there trying to muster your forces to take another look, your parents wake up. Your mother exclaims, "This place is alive with worms!" You look again, and, sure enough, there are worms suspended from the ceiling, worms waving at you from the walls, and—what's that all over the floor? More worms! Hundreds—no, thousands of worms!

Houses Built of Soil

Where did all those worms

come from? Since there are hardly any trees out on the prairie, the pioneers built their first houses out of sod bricks cut from the surface layer of soil and including all the grasses and roots growing in it. It wasn't easy to build a house of sod. A twelve-by-fourteen-foot shelter required an acre of sod and a great deal of hard work. Because of the thick root system in the prairie grassland, walls built of sod were strong and long lasting. This was one of the advantages. Other advantages of sod houses included the fact that they were better insulated than wood houses, so they were cooler in summer and warmer in winter. They also offered more protection from tornadoes, wind, and fire.

No Sense Cleaning It!

What were the disadvantages? These: Sod blocks were essentially compacted soil, which tended to sift down from the ceiling and walls, making it hard, if not impossible, to keep the house clean. Sod also wasn't waterproof. In fact, it was quite the opposite. Whenever there was a heavy rain, water followed the root systems in the sod bricks right on down through the sod ceiling, soaking everything in the room and turning the sod floor to mud. All this dripping didn't stop when the rains stopped either. The roof could leak for days, and that meant people sometimes had to use boots and umbrellas indoors while the sun was shining brightly outside!

Bugs and Weather

The drawbacks of sod houses were not the only difficulties you would have faced as a pioneer on the prairie. Others included the unaccustomed vastness of the wide-open spaces, the endless blue sky, and the almost total lack of neighbors. There were also fleas, flies, mosquitoes, moths, bedbugs, field mice, rattlesnakes, grasshoppers, tornadoes, floods, hail, blizzards, prairie fires, dust storms, and drought. In summer the ground baked, and in winter it froze. The wind blew constantly, and water was as scarce as hens' teeth. One pioneer who couldn't take it anymore left this hard-earned lesson scrawled across the cabin door of his deserted homestead: "250 miles to the nearest post office, 100 miles to wood, 20 miles to water, 6 inches to hell. Gone to live with wife's folks."

No Warranties

Yes, sirree, homesteading on the prairie was hard work, and there were no warranties on claimed land. The buyers had to take all the risks upon themselves. The term for this arrangement is *caveat emptor*—"let the buyer beware." So what can you do but sweep all those worms out the front door and back onto the prairie? What else can happen, after all?

Well, newly cut sod is home to fleas, and bedbugs come crawling out of it at night. So every morning you have to take your bitten self and your infested bedding out-of-doors and pick off all those bugs. Then you head back inside armed with chicken

feathers dipped in kerosene to paint every crack and every crevice in every bit of that sod ceiling, wall, and floor.

Blizzards of Grasshoppers

One creature that doesn't come *out of* the sod, but instead comes *onto* the sod, is the grasshopper. You know, of course, about blizzards of snow. But what about a blizzard of grasshoppers? Enough grasshoppers to block out the sun? So many millions of grasshoppers that they can strip a farm bare in a matter of hours? Did you know that grasshoppers can chew their way through a plow handle? Did you know that grasshoppers are capable of eating almost everything in sight, including fences, bark, and that bedding that you just picked clean of fleas and bedbugs? If a pioneer family had dug 150 feet down for a well—the height of a thirteen-story building—grasshoppers falling into it could sour the water for weeks upon weeks. Grasshoppers could even stop a Union Pacific Railroad train from running. Piled some six inches deep on the tracks, their bodies so greased the rails that a train's wheels would spin but not move.

So, welcome to the good life out on the prairie, where "the skies are not cloudy all day." By the way, do you know what constantly blue skies mean for the average farmer?

—Flo Ota De Lange

PIONEER LIFE IN 1882

Reading Informational Materials

Reading Check

1. What is the **main point** of the Union Pacific Railroad poster?

2. What is the **main point** of "Home, Sweet Soddie"?

3. Find at least five details in the poster that would have motivated pioneers to buy land in Nebraska.

4. Find at least five details in "Home, Sweet Soddie" that might have discouraged pioneers from buying land in Nebraska.

5. **Exaggeration** is overstating something for an effect. What examples of exaggeration can you find in the poster and the article?

6. **Loaded words** are words that evoke a strong emotional reaction in the reader. What examples can you find in the poster?

TestPractice

Union Pacific Railroad Poster
Home, Sweet Soddie

1. The **purpose** of the Union Pacific Railroad poster was to —
   - **A** entertain railroad travelers passing through Nebraska
   - **B** persuade people to buy land in Nebraska
   - **C** provide information on Nebraska to scientists
   - **D** describe the good and bad qualities of Nebraska

2. The **purpose** of "Home, Sweet Soddie" is to —
   - **F** encourage people to move to the prairie
   - **G** praise the heroism of pioneers
   - **H** teach people how to build sod houses
   - **J** describe some of the difficulties of life on the prairie

3. The poster and the article are **similar** in that they both offer —
   - **A** an unbiased treatment
   - **B** a biased treatment
   - **C** an objective treatment
   - **D** a discouraging word

4. Which statement accurately describes the **tone** of these texts—that is, their attitudes toward their topics?
   - **F** "Home, Sweet Soddie" is humorous; the poster is enthusiastic.
   - **G** "Home, Sweet Soddie" is romantic; the poster is satiric.
   - **H** Both are romantic.
   - **J** Both are sarcastic.

5. The Union Pacific Railroad poster was intended as —
   - **A** a newspaper editorial
   - **B** an encyclopedia entry
   - **C** a travel magazine article
   - **D** an advertisement

Reading Standard 2.3 Find similarities and differences between texts in the treatment, scope, or organization of ideas.

Vocabulary Development

Who Am I? Diverse Derivations

No single person could travel the whole of the United States during the pioneer days, but the English language could and did. Some of the words commonly associated with the pioneers actually originated in far-off places. Play the word game below.

PRACTICE

Match the following words with the riddles that describe their origins:

beef jerky	muslin	siesta
calico	paddock	wilderness

1. I am a cotton fabric named for the place where I originated, Mosul, in what is now Iraq. My name came into English from Arabic, first through Italian (*mussolina*), then through French (*mousseline*).
2. If you take a nap in the afternoon, you know my name, but you might not know my origin. I came through Spanish from the Latin *sexta hora*, meaning "sixth hour," which refers to noon. Figure that one out.
3. I come from the American Spanish word *charqui,* which came from the Quechua *ch'arki*. I have nothing to do with tics or odd movements.
4. If you had a horse, you would keep it corralled in me. I came into use from the Old English *pearruc,* meaning "enclosure."
5. I am the cotton fabric used for most pioneer dresses. I come in many patterns, and I was named after the town in India where I originated, Calicut (now Kozhikode).
6. If you think I belong to America, think again. I existed in the English language long before anyone knew about the Wild West. I originally came from Old English and described the place where wild deer lived. (The word *deer* originally referred to any wild animals.)

Reading Standard 1.2
Understand the most important points in the history of the English language, and use common word origins to determine the historical influences on English word meanings.

Mrs. Flowers

Literary Focus
A Character's Influence

People often reveal their character—what they are made of—in hard times, when they face tough conflicts. People can also show their character in the way they live their everyday lives—especially in the way they treat other people. In this autobiographical story a woman named Mrs. Flowers has an important influence on a young girl named Marguerite.

Reading Skills
Determining the Main Idea: What's It All About?

The **main idea** is the message, opinion, or insight that is the focus of a piece of nonfiction writing. To find the main idea, look for key statements made by the writer. Look also at the details that the writer gives and think about what the details add up to. Then, try to put the main idea into your own words.

Make the Connection
Class Survey

Rate each of the statements that follow with a number from 0 to 4.

disagree 0 1 2 3 4 agree

1. Young people need older role models.
2. Friends should be the same age.
3. Adults can't understand how young people feel.
4. Everyone deserves to feel special.

Record your ratings on a sheet of paper. Then, with your class, tally the responses to each statement on the board.

Background

"Mrs. Flowers" is from a volume of Maya Angelou's autobiography. When Angelou (born Marguerite Johnson) was a little girl, her parents separated. She and her brother, Bailey, were sent to Stamps, Arkansas, to live with their grandmother (called Momma), who owned a general store. A year before meeting Mrs. Flowers, Marguerite had been violently assaulted by a friend of her mother's. In reaction she became depressed and withdrawn, and she stopped speaking.

Vocabulary Development

You'll learn these words as you read this autobiography:

taut (tôt) *adj.:* tightly stretched. *Though she was thin, Mrs. Flowers's skin was not taut.*

benign (bi·nīn′) *adj.:* kindly. *Marguerite loved Mrs. Flowers's benign smile.*

infuse (in·fyo͞oz′) *v.:* fill. *When Mrs. Flowers read aloud, she could infuse the words with great meaning.*

intolerant (in·täl′ər·ənt) *adj.:* unwilling to accept something. *Mrs. Flowers was intolerant of rudeness and ignorance.*

illiteracy (i·lit′ər·ə·sē) *n.:* inability to read or write. *Mrs. Flowers said we should be understanding of illiteracy.*

Reading Standard 3.3 Compare and contrast motivations and reactions of literary characters from different historical eras confronting similar situations or conflicts.

Mrs. Flowers

from I Know Why the Caged Bird Sings

Maya Angelou

For nearly a year, I sopped around the house, the Store, the school, and the church, like an old biscuit, dirty and inedible. Then I met, or rather got to know, the lady who threw me my first lifeline.

Mrs. Bertha Flowers was the aristocrat of Black Stamps. She had the grace of control to appear warm in the coldest weather, and on the Arkansas summer days it seemed she had a private breeze which swirled around, cooling her. She was thin without the taut look of wiry people, and her printed voile[1] dresses and flowered hats were as right for her as denim overalls for a farmer. She was our side's answer to the richest white woman in town.

Her skin was a rich black that would have peeled like a plum if snagged, but then no one would have thought of getting close enough to Mrs. Flowers to ruffle her dress, let alone snag her skin. She didn't encourage familiarity. She wore gloves too.

I don't think I ever saw Mrs. Flowers laugh, but she smiled often. A slow widening of her thin black lips to show even, small white teeth, then the slow effortless closing. When she chose to smile on me, I always wanted to thank her. The action was so graceful and inclusively benign.

She was one of the few gentlewomen I have ever known, and has remained throughout my life the measure of what a human being can be.

One summer afternoon, sweet-milk fresh in my memory, she stopped at the Store to buy provisions. Another Negro woman of her health and age would have been expected to carry the paper sacks home in one hand, but Momma said, "Sister Flowers, I'll send Bailey up to your house with these things."

She smiled that slow dragging smile, "Thank you, Mrs. Henderson. I'd prefer Marguerite, though." My name was beautiful when she said it. "I've been meaning to talk to her, anyway." They gave each other age-group looks.

There was a little path beside the rocky road, and Mrs. Flowers walked in front swinging her arms and picking her way over the stones.

She said, without turning her head, to me, "I hear you're doing very good schoolwork, Marguerite, but that it's all written. The teachers report that they have trouble getting you to talk in class." We passed the triangular farm on our left and the path widened to allow us to walk together. I hung back in the separate unasked and unanswerable questions.

"Come and walk along with me,

---

1. **voile** (voil) *n.* used as *adj.:* thin, sheer fabric.

Vocabulary

taut (tôt) *adj.:* tightly stretched.

benign (bi·nīn′) *adj.:* kindly. *Benign* can also mean "harmless."

Woman in Calico (1944) by William H. Johnson. Oil.

Marguerite." I couldn't have refused even if I wanted to. She pronounced my name so nicely. Or more correctly, she spoke each word with such clarity that I was certain a foreigner who didn't understand English could have understood her.

"Now no one is going to make you talk—possibly no one can. But bear in mind, language is man's way of communicating with his fellow man and it is language alone which separates him from the lower animals." That was a totally new idea to me, and I would need time to think about it.

"Your grandmother says you read a lot. Every chance you get. That's good, but not good enough. Words mean more than what is set down on paper. It takes the human voice to infuse them with the shades of deeper meaning."

I memorized the part about the human voice infusing words. It seemed so valid and poetic.

She said she was going to give me some books and that I not only must read them, I must read them aloud. She suggested that I try to make a sentence sound in as many different ways as possible.

"I'll accept no excuse if you return a book to me that has been badly handled." My imagination boggled at the punishment I would deserve if in fact I did abuse a book of Mrs. Flowers's. Death would be too kind and brief.

The odors in the house surprised me. Somehow I had never connected Mrs. Flowers with food or eating or any other common experience of common people. There must have been an outhouse, too, but my mind never recorded it.

The sweet scent of vanilla had met us as she opened the door.

"I made tea cookies this morning. You see, I had planned to invite you for cookies and lemonade so we could have this little chat. The lemonade is in the icebox."

It followed that Mrs. Flowers would have ice on an ordinary day, when most families in our town bought ice late on Saturdays only a few times during the summer to be used in the wooden ice cream freezers.

She took the bags from me and disappeared through the kitchen door. I looked around the room that I had never in my wildest fantasies imagined I would see. Browned photographs leered or threatened from the walls and the white, freshly done curtains pushed against themselves and against the wind. I wanted to gobble up the room entire and take it to Bailey, who would help me analyze and enjoy it.

"Have a seat, Marguerite. Over there by the table." She carried a platter covered with a tea towel. Although she warned that she hadn't tried her hand at baking sweets for some time, I was certain that like everything else about her the cookies would be perfect.

They were flat round wafers, slightly browned on the edges and butter-yellow in the center. With the cold lemonade they were sufficient for childhood's lifelong diet. Remembering my manners, I took nice little ladylike bites off the edges. She said she had made them expressly for me and that she had a few in the kitchen that I could take home to my brother. So I jammed one whole cake in my mouth and the rough crumbs scratched the insides of my jaws, and if I hadn't had to swallow, it would have been a dream come true.

Vocabulary
infuse (in·fyo͞oz′) v.: fill; inspire.

As I ate she began the first of what we later called "my lessons in living." She said that I must always be intolerant of ignorance but understanding of illiteracy. That some people, unable to go to school, were more educated and even more intelligent than college professors. She encouraged me to listen carefully to what country people called mother wit. That in those homely sayings was couched the collective wisdom of generations.

When I finished the cookies she brushed off the table and brought a thick, small book from the bookcase. I had read *A Tale of Two Cities* and found it up to my standards as a romantic novel. She opened the first page and I heard poetry for the first time in my life.

"It was the best of times, it was the worst of times. . . ." Her voice slid in and curved down through and over the words. She was nearly singing. I wanted to look at the pages. Were they the same that I had read? Or were there notes, music, lined on the pages, as in a hymn book? Her sounds began cascading gently. I knew from listening to a thousand preachers that she was nearing the end of her reading, and I hadn't really heard, heard to understand, a single word.

"How do you like that?"

It occurred to me that she expected a response. The sweet vanilla flavor was still on my tongue and her reading was a wonder in my ears. I had to speak.

I said, "Yes, ma'am." It was the least I could do, but it was the most also.

"There's one more thing. Take this book of poems and memorize one for me. Next time you pay me a visit, I want you to recite."

I have tried often to search behind the sophistication of years for the enchantment I so easily found in those gifts. The essence escapes but its aura[2] remains. To be allowed, no, invited, into the private lives of strangers, and to share their joys and fears, was a chance to exchange the Southern bitter wormwood[3] for a cup of mead with Beowulf[4] or a hot cup of tea and milk with Oliver Twist. When I said aloud, "It is a far, far better thing that I do, than I have ever done . . ."[5] tears of love filled my eyes at my selflessness.

On that first day, I ran down the hill and into the road (few cars ever came along it) and had the good sense to stop running before I reached the Store.

I was liked, and what a difference it made. I was respected not as Mrs. Henderson's grandchild or Bailey's sister but for just being Marguerite Johnson.

Childhood's logic never asks to be proved (all conclusions are absolute). I didn't question why Mrs. Flowers had singled me out for attention, nor did it occur to me that Momma might have asked her to give me a little talking-to. All I cared about was that she had made tea cookies for *me* and read to *me* from her favorite book. It was enough to prove that she liked me.

---

2. **aura** (ô′rə) *n.:* feeling or mood that seems to surround something like a glow.
3. **wormwood** *n.:* bitter-tasting plant. Angelou is referring to the harshness of life for African Americans in the South at that time.
4. **Beowulf** (bā′ə·woolf′): hero of an Old English epic. During the period portrayed in the epic, people drank **mead,** a drink made with honey.
5. **"It is . . . ever done":** another quotation from Charles Dickens's *A Tale of Two Cities.* One of the characters says these words as he goes voluntarily to die in place of another man.

Vocabulary

intolerant (in·tăl′ər·ənt) *adj.:* unwilling to accept something.
illiteracy (i·lit′ər·ə·sē) *n.:* inability to read or write.

Maya Angelou

"When You Get, Give"

On January 20, 1993, **Maya Angelou** (1928–   ) stood at a podium on Capitol Hill and recited her poem "On the Pulse of Morning" in honor of Bill Clinton's presidential inauguration. She may have thought at that moment that she had come a long way from her childhood in Stamps, Arkansas. Angelou has been an actor, a teacher, a speaker, a civil rights worker, and, above all, a writer—of poems, plays, songs, screenplays, and newspaper and magazine articles, as well as four autobiographies.

Angelou says that the two writers who have had the greatest influence on her work are William Shakespeare and the African American poet Paul Laurence Dunbar. (The title *I Know Why the Caged Bird Sings* is from Dunbar's poem "Sympathy.")

Angelou has in turn influenced the lives of many young people, both in person and through her writing. Six feet tall, gracious, and commanding, Angelou is as much a gentlewoman as her childhood friend Mrs. Flowers was. In an interview with *Essence* magazine, Angelou tells about a time when she was able to "throw a lifeline" to a young man she found cursing and fighting on a movie set in California:

> I went over and I said, 'Baby, may I speak to you for a minute?' He dropped his head, and I said, 'Come on, let's walk.'
>
> And I started talking to him and started crying. I said, 'Do you know how much at risk you are? Do you know how valuable you are to us? You're all we've got, baby.'
>
> He started crying and said to me, 'Don't cry.' I don't know who has cried for him. And let him see how much he means. . . .
>
> Black people say, when you get, give; when you learn, teach. As soon as that healing takes place, then we have to go out and heal somebody, and pass on the idea of a healing day—so that somebody else gets it and passes it on.

Literary Response and Analysis

Reading Check

1. This extract is from an **autobiography,** the story of the writer's own life. Angelou tells her story in **narrative form,** that is, as a series of related events. On your paper, draw a chart like the following one. Fill in the main events of the narrative, and sum up the resolution. You should be able to find five key events.

Problem:
Event 1:
Event 2:
Event 3:
Event 4:
Event 5:
Resolution:

Interpretations

2. At the beginning of "Mrs. Flowers," Maya Angelou says that she "sopped around" until Mrs. Flowers threw her a "lifeline." What **main idea** does Angelou suggest here? Find some quotations from the story that support the point Angelou makes about her experience.

3. Go back to the text, and find the only two words spoken by Marguerite. What do you think Angelou means when she writes, "It was the least I could do, but it was the most also" (page 133)? What does this tell you about Marguerite's **character?**

4. Throughout history, people have had to respond to difficult situations. Take three of the characters from this chapter, and compare their challenges and the ways they handled them.

Character	Historical Era	Conflict	Response to Problem

Evaluation

5. What do you think Mrs. Flowers meant when she told Marguerite that she "must always be intolerant of ignorance but understanding of illiteracy" (page 133)? Is that good advice for today? Draw on your own experience to support your answer.

Writing
Passing the Help On

Re-read Meet the Writer on page 134, and pay special attention to what Maya Angelou says about the young man in California. What words in this passage connect with the story of Mrs. Flowers? Write a paragraph in which you tell how Mrs. Flowers's talk with Marguerite is similar to what Angelou says here. Be sure to quote details from both the story and Angelou's comments.

Reading Standard 3.3
Compare and contrast motivations and reactions of literary characters from different historical eras confronting similar situations or conflicts.

Vocabulary Development

Context Clues: They Can Help

Sometimes (if you're lucky) the **context** of an unfamiliar word—the words, sentences, and paragraphs surrounding it—can help you figure out what the word means. The following terms are various kinds of **context clues.** (Which kind of context clue is used right here in the first sentence of this paragraph?)

- **Definitions and restatements.** Look for words that define the unfamiliar word or that restate it in other terms. *People should be intolerant of ignorance—they should not put up with it.*

- **Synonyms.** Look for words in the context that mean the same thing as the unfamiliar word. *Mrs. Flowers had a kindly, benign manner.*

- **Antonyms.** Look for words in the context that mean the opposite of the unfamiliar word. *Mrs. Flowers did not have the taut look thin people often have; she seemed relaxed and gracious.*

- **Cause and effect.** Look for words in the context that indicate that an unfamiliar word is the cause or the effect of some action. *Mrs. Flowers's benign smile caused Marguerite to glow with pleasure.*

- **Examples.** Look for examples that hint at the meaning of the unfamiliar word. *Mrs. Flowers's benign actions—giving Marguerite attention, baking cookies for her, lending her books—made the girl feel special.*

PRACTICE

Search for context clues that help you choose the correct meaning of the underlined words.

1. Mrs. Flowers was the aristocrat of black Stamps. Her noble behavior caused everyone to look up to her. *The word* aristocrat *means upper-class person / dictator / poor person.*

2. No one would have thought of getting close enough to touch Mrs. Flowers. She didn't encourage familiarity. *The word* familiarity *means family / closeness / distance.*

3. She stopped at the store to buy provisions, such as sugar, flour, and milk. *The word* provisions *means property / paper / food.*

4. Although they are not expressed in fancy language, the homely sayings of ordinary people often contain great wisdom. *The word* homely *means awful / simple / elegant.*

Grade 6 Review Reading Standard 1.4
Use word, sentence, and paragraph clues to determine meaning of words.

Mrs. Flowers's Recipes

Reading a Text Carefully

When you read most informational materials, you have to pay very close attention to every detail. This is especially true of recipes. If you don't read very carefully, you could easily confuse teaspoon (*tsp*) and tablespoon (*tbsp*). If you don't put the right amount of baking powder in Mrs. Flowers's cookies, they might come out like rocks.

There'll be no questions asked about these recipes, but we hope you'll try them out. You may want to get together with a few classmates and make enough for the class. Note that the cookies take two days to make. (Note also that they contain sugar.) Once you and your classmates have eaten cookies and drunk lemonade, you all can answer this:

BONUS QUESTION

How did they taste?

✳ Lemonade ✳

4–6 medium-sized lemons
1–2 cups sugar
2 quarts water
sprigs of mint (optional)

Squeeze lemons. Discard seeds. Add water. Add sugar to taste, stirring constantly until sugar is dissolved. (*Note:* Do not use chilled water, as sugar may clump instead of dissolving fully.) Chill and serve alone or over ice. (Optional: Garnish with sprigs of mint.)

✳ Crisp Sugar Cookies ✳

1/2 cup butter or margarine
1 cup sugar
1 egg

1 tbsp heavy cream
1 tsp vanilla
2 cups sifted all-purpose flour

1/2 tsp salt
1 tsp baking powder
extra sugar for topping (optional)

Cream butter or margarine with sugar in mixing bowl until light and fluffy. Add egg, heavy cream, and vanilla. Beat well. Sift flour with salt and baking powder. Add to creamed mixture, beating until well combined. Chill dough overnight. (*Note:* This step is essential. If not chilled, the dough will be too sticky to be rolled out smoothly.)

When ready to bake, preheat oven to 350° F (moderate).

Roll out the dough with a rolling pin until it is very thin, using only a small amount at a time, on a lightly floured board. Cut with a round cookie cutter or a glass. (Optional: Sprinkle cookies lightly with the extra sugar.) Place on ungreased cookie sheets.

Bake five minutes or until done. Makes 36–50 large cookies or about six dozen small cookies.

Literary Response and Analysis

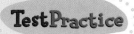 **TestPractice**   DIRECTIONS: Read this excerpt from an autobiography. Then, read each question, and write the letter of the best response.

This excerpt from an autobiography takes place in Sweden soon after World War II. The narrator, a Polish Jewish girl, and her younger brother had been in Nazi concentration camps. There they both contracted tuberculosis, a lung disease. The children were rescued from the camps and taken to a sanitarium in the Swedish countryside. The narrator has now recovered from her illness and is on her way to a shelter for Polish children in Stockholm, the capital of Sweden.

from No Pretty Pictures: A Child of War
Anita Lobel

It had been explained to me that I had recovered from my illness. I couldn't stay at a house for sick people anymore. When Herr[1] Nillson came to gather me up at the sanitarium, I had to accept that I was going with him alone. My brother was still sick. Lucky, I thought, to be allowed to stay for a little while longer at the sanitarium.

Herr Nillson was taking me to a shelter for Polish refugee kids. "You will like being with people from your own country again," he said. He must have sensed instantly that he had not reassured me. "It is a fine place," he said quietly. "You will see. And it is only temporary," he added. "Don't be frightened."

The trip to Stockholm had taken several hours. My recovery to good health was sending me into unwanted exile, but the journey did not feel like a deportation[2] or a flight. I loved sitting on a train with upholstered seats and watching the winter landscape rush by through the pristinely[3] polished window. In the January cold of Sweden there had been no possibility of sticking my head out an open window and letting the wind whip my face and hair. The hair that had grown to shoulder length and was at last braided into two thick, stubby braids. They were still too short. But there was no more concentration camp stubble to be ashamed of.

We came to a quiet street away from the tramways and neon lights. After a

---

1. **Herr:** Swedish for "Mr."

2. **deportation** (dē′pôr·tā′shən) *n.*: forcible removal; banishment.
3. **pristinely** (pris′tēn′lē) *adv.*: here, to the point of perfect cleanliness.

Reading Standard 3.3
Compare and contrast motivations and reactions of literary characters from different historical eras confronting similar situations or conflicts.

ride to the third floor in a small cage elevator, we stood in front of a door with a brass plaque with "A. Nillson" engraved on it. Herr Nillson rang the bell. The door was opened by a gaunt lady, in a prim white apron over a brown dress. Except that her gray hair was tightly wound into a bun and her head was not covered in a wimple, she made me think of a Benedictine nun. She curtsied to Herr Nillson. I curtsied to her. She took my little suitcase and my coat and scarf.

"If Miss Stina would be so kind," Herr Nillson said, "our young traveler will have some tea and sandwiches."

I was twelve years old that late January afternoon when I was ushered into A. Nillson's elegant apartment in Stockholm, Sweden. For seven years, in or out of danger, I had lived and slept in hovels[4] or public rooms with many other people. The convent. The concentration camp barracks. The sanitarium. Institutions. Since we had fled with Niania[5] away from Kraków,[6] I had not been in a private place where people had properly arranged tables and chairs and rugs and lamps. And servants.

---

4. **hovels** (huv′əlz) *n.:* small, miserable dwellings; huts.
5. **Niania:** the writer's nanny (a person who cares for young children).
6. **Kraków** (kra′kou′): city in Poland.

"You may sit down," Herr Nillson smiled. In the beautiful sitting room I eased myself cautiously onto the edge of a wooden chair that stood by the door. There were pots with plants by the windows. There were lace curtains. Several paintings on twisted silk cords hung from moldings. There was a rug on the floor that made me think of the old kilim in my parents' apartment in Kraków. One whole wall was covered with books. I heard the sounds of piano music from somewhere in the building.

"No, sit here," Herr Nillson said, pointing to an elegant chair covered in a silky blue striped fabric.

I wished I had been a doll or a puppet. I wished someone would come and bend my arms and legs into the right angles so that I knew how to fit myself properly into the seat of the beautiful chair I had been asked to occupy. I had seen a movie one afternoon in the big hall in the sanitarium. It took place in France. The people moved and posed gracefully in splendid rooms. Ladies in gowns of silk sat on silk sofas and took little sips of tea out of pretty porcelain cups and delicate bites of little cakes. Gentlemen bowed and kissed the hands of the ladies.

I knew my body was clean. There were no lice in my newly grown hair. Or in the seams of the skirt and blouse and sweater that had come out of a freshly donated bundle. When I carefully eased myself down onto the seat, I could feel my wool stockings pull around my thighs as the home-sewn garters with the buttons dug into my buttocks. I sat on Herr Nillson's silk chair, still fearing that shameful dirt would seep through. In my head there were echoes of the Nazis' shouts.

Herr Nillson sank easily into a large upholstered chair with curved arms.

Stina brought buttered bread and ham and tea on a tray. And cups and linen napkins. I took little bites of my sandwich and held my teacup as delicately as I could. I wanted to stay there with Herr Nillson forever.

Behind him I saw a half-opened door to a small room with a bed. Herr Nillson followed my gaze. "For tonight that is your room," he said. "Early tomorrow we will continue our journey." We both sipped from our teacups.

Herr Nillson told me about the work he did with refugees who had come to Sweden after the war. And about the interesting times I could expect at the Polish shelter and beyond. When it was time to go to bed, Herr Nillson took down a book from his crowded bookshelf. "This is for you," he said. "You may keep this."

Safely tucked in my suitcase were some catechism magazines that had been given out during Sunday school lessons at the sanitarium. And my miniature copy of the New Testament with pages thin and delicate and filled with beautiful pictures of the Holy Family, the gift from Sister Svea. Now I would add another book to my belongings. I thanked Herr Nillson for the volume of Selma Lagerlöf stories. I thanked the stern-looking Stina for the food. Everyone said, "*God natt.*"

I went into my private room and closed the door. Tomorrow I was going to a place that would have no barbed wire around it. There would be no Nazis with guns. There would be no shooting. But again I would be living in an institution. Under the large soft bolster with my head on a pillow edged with lace, I fell asleep reading a tale by Selma Lagerlöf.

1. In this selection from an **autobiography,** the narrator visits —
   A   a shelter for Polish refugees
   B   Herr Nillson's apartment
   C   a Nazi concentration camp
   D   a tuberculosis sanitarium

2. The narrator of this story is grateful for the special attention she receives. A character from another autobiography in this chapter is also appreciative of special attention. That **character** is —
   F   Harriet Tubman
   G   Barbara Frietchie
   H   Mrs. Flowers
   J   Marguerite

3. The narrator of this story fled with her brother and nanny to escape from the Nazis. Another character in this chapter also ran away from tyranny. That **character** is —
   A   Harriet Tubman
   B   Barbara Frietchie
   C   Mrs. Flowers
   D   Marguerite

4. The narrator of this story and Marguerite in "Mrs. Flowers" have similar reactions when they receive a book as a gift. Both girls —
   F   are pleased with the gift
   G   wish they were able to read
   H   refuse to accept the book
   J   spill their drinks on the book

5. Although they lived in different times, the narrator of this story and Barbara Frietchie have an experience in common. Both —
   A   told off a general
   B   protected their flag
   C   lived through a war
   D   recovered from tuberculosis

6. The writer doesn't tell you what a *sanitarium* is. The word is mentioned twice in the first paragraph. Re-read the surrounding sentences, and use **context clues** to determine which of the following definitions means *sanitarium.*
   F   Shelter for Polish children
   G   Place for sick people
   H   Train
   J   Concentration camp

7. Which of the following sentences *best* expresses the **main idea** of this extract from an autobiography?
   A   An act of kindness helps a child in many ways.
   B   The Swedes are very kind people.
   C   Children cannot accept change easily.
   D   Children need their parents.

8. Both "Mrs. Flowers" and this extract from a book called *No Pretty Pictures* feature all of the following characters *except* a —
   F   kind adult who helps a child
   G   child who cannot talk
   H   child who has suffered from violence
   J   child who loves books

Reading Informational Materials

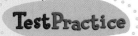

DIRECTIONS: Read the following two passages. Then, read each question, and write the letter of the best response.

Fragment on Slavery, 1854
Abraham Lincoln

If A can prove, however conclusively, that he may of right enslave B—why may not B snatch the same argument, and prove equally that he may enslave A?

You say A is white, and B is black. It is color, then, the lighter having the right to enslave the darker? Take care. By this rule you are to be slave to the first man you meet with a fairer skin than your own.

You do not mean color exactly? You mean the whites are intellectually the superior of the blacks and, therefore, have the right to enslave them? Take care again. By this rule, you are to be slave to the first man you meet with an intellect superior to your own.

But, say you, it is a question of interest; and, if you can make it your interest, you have the right to enslave another. Very well. And if he can make it his interest, he has the right to enslave you.

from What to the Slave Is the Fourth of July?
From an oration at Rochester, July 5, 1852
Frederick Douglass

Would you have me argue that man is entitled to liberty? that he is the rightful owner of his own body? . . . To do so, would be to make myself ridiculous, and to offer an insult to your understanding. There is not a man beneath the canopy of heaven that does not know that slavery is wrong for him.

What! am I to argue that it is wrong to make men brutes, to rob them of their liberty, to work them without wages, to keep them ignorant of their relations to their fellowmen, to beat them with sticks, to flay[1] their flesh with the lash, to load their limbs with irons, to hunt them with dogs, to sell them at auction, to sunder[2] their families, to knock out their teeth, to burn their flesh, to starve them into obedience and submission to their

---

1. **flay** *v.*: strip the skin off, as by whipping.
2. **sunder** *v.*: drive apart; separate.

Reading Standard 2.3
Find similarities and differences between texts in the treatment, scope, or organization of ideas.

masters? Must I argue that a system, thus marked with blood and stained with pollution, is wrong? No; I will not. . . .

At a time like this, scorching irony, not convincing argument, is needed. . . . We need the storm, the whirlwind, and the earthquake. The feeling of the nation must be quickened; the conscience of the nation must be roused; the propriety[3] of the nation must be startled; the hypocrisy[4] of the nation must be exposed; and its crimes against God and man must be proclaimed and denounced.

---

3. **propriety** (prə·prī**ʹ**ə·tē) *n.:* sense of correct behavior.
4. **hypocrisy** (hi·päk**ʹ**rə·sē) *n.:* pretense of virtue or goodness.

---

1. The passage by Abraham Lincoln presents an argument —
   A for light skin
   B against personal interest
   C for slavery
   D against slavery

2. Which of the following statements *best* expresses what Frederick Douglass is saying?
   F Arguments won't work against slavery; passions must be aroused.
   G We should sit down and talk calmly about the evils of slavery.
   H We don't need to do anything; everyone knows slavery is wrong.
   J The world needs more stormy weather and earthquakes.

3. The passage by Abraham Lincoln was intended as a —
   A personal narrative
   B persuasive argument
   C newspaper advertisement
   D poetic description

4. Douglass's passage was intended to do all of the following *except* to —
   F convince
   G rouse to action
   H work on listeners' feelings
   J amuse

5. The **treatment** of ideas in the passage by Douglass is —
   A detached
   B emotional
   C unfeeling
   D silly

6. The **treatment** of ideas in the passage by Abraham Lincoln is —
   F humorous
   G emotional
   H unfeeling
   J logical

7. The **subject** of both texts is —
   A the Union
   B the Civil War
   C slavery
   D the Fourth of July

Vocabulary Development

TestPractice

Synonyms

DIRECTIONS: Choose the word that is the best synonym of each underlined word from the literary selections in this chapter.

1. Something that is incomprehensible is —
   A not understandable
   B unconvincing
   C invented
   D misspelled

2. To have an incentive is to have —
   F incense
   G a motive
   H an interest
   J an invention

3. If you dispel a crowd, you _____ it.
   A join
   B challenge
   C scatter
   D control

4. A man who is gaunt is —
   F thin
   G heavy
   H disabled
   J muscular

5. If you go someplace with friends but you are grudging about it, you are —
   A unwilling
   B enthusiastic
   C annoyed
   D slow

6. If a rope is pulled taut, it is —
   F loose
   G tight
   H frayed
   J broken

7. If someone is benign, she is —
   A kindly
   B hostile
   C boring
   D sick

8. Lincoln could infuse speeches with feeling. *Infuse* means —
   F omit
   G lengthen
   H fill
   J ruin

9. If a student is intolerant of others, she is _____.
   A accepting
   B unaccepting
   C interested
   D uninterested

Mastering the Standards

RESPONSE TO A NOVEL

Character Matters

On page 146, you'll find descriptions of four novels that bring memorable characters to life. Choose one of these novels—or select another novel you have read recently—and evaluate it. In your evaluation, focus on the novel's main **character** or characters. To prepare, gather details about the novel in a chart like this one:

| Character's appearance: |
| Actions: |
| Key remarks: |
| How do others feel about him or her? |
| Does the writer characterize him or her directly? |
| Do we know the character's thoughts and feelings? |
| What is the character's **problem**? |
| How does he or she **resolve** it? |
| What **motivates** the actions of the character? |
| How does the character **change** during the story? |

▶ Use "Writing a Review of a Novel," pages 612–631, for help with this assignment.

Other Choices

RESPONDING TO A CHARACTER

 **She Made a Difference**

In Angelou's autobiography a woman named Mrs. Flowers has a strong effect on a young girl. Write an essay in which you analyze the character of Mrs. Flowers. Consider what the character looks like, how she acts, what she says, and how other characters respond to her. What direct comments does the writer make about Mrs. Flowers's character? Use details from the text to support your response to this unusual character.

HISTORICAL FICTION

 **Living History**

Writers often create fictional stories based on historical events. Go back to the Harriet Tubman story, and write a diary entry that might have been written by Harriet or one of the runaways. Try one of these characters. Write as "I."

- Harriet Tubman
- the man who wants to go back to the plantation
- the plantation owner
- the farmer who turns the group away

Fiction

Hard Travelin'

Bud—not Buddy—has had enough bad treatment in orphanages and foster homes, so he runs off in search of his father. Bud has never seen his dad, but he thinks he is a member of the famous jazz band the Dusky Devastators of the Depression!!!!!! Bud finds adventure and trouble in *Bud, Not Buddy.* This heartwarming and hilarious novel by Christopher Paul Curtis won a Newbery Medal.

This title is available in the HRW Library.

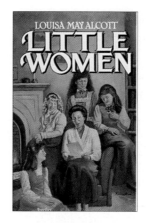

Civil War Sisters

In Louisa May Alcott's *Little Women,* Meg, Jo, Beth, and Amy March— four sisters—grow up in Massachusetts during the Civil War. This rich American classic of family love, a favorite of readers for more than a century, has been made into a movie four times (most recently in 1994).

A Helping Hand

Katherine Ayres's *North by Night: A Story of the Underground Railroad* is made up of fictional journal entries and letters written by sixteen-year-old Lucy Spenser. Lucy has been helping fugitives from slavery reach Canada for four years. When one of the fugitives dies while giving birth to a baby, Lucy is faced with a difficult decision.

History Lesson

Walter Dean Myers covers 250 years in the lives of an African American family in *The Glory Field.* From the family's early time in Africa until the end of segregation, the members of the Lewis family have supported one another despite persecution. Can they persuade one lost relative to return to their South Carolina home?

This title is available in the HRW Library.

Nonfiction

The Eyes of a Child

Grizzled men were not the only soldiers who fought in the Civil War. Many teenagers signed up to fight for both the Union and the Confederate causes. In *The Boys' War,* Jim Murphy tells of the excitement the young soldiers felt as they entered on this new experience and the horror they felt when they came face to face with the grim reality of war.

Master of Disguise

Determined to be a member of the Union army, Emma Edmonds presents herself as a man named Franklin Thompson and is made a private. Seymour Reit details her adventures in *Behind Rebel Lines.* When Edmonds is sent across Confederate lines to spy, she learns not just military secrets but the hardships of being a soldier on any side of a battle.

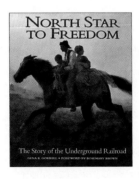

The Path to Freedom

Gena K. Gorrell offers a comprehensive history of the Underground Railroad in *North Star to Freedom: The Story of the Underground Railroad.* You will learn about the importance of figures such as William Lloyd Garrison and Frederick Douglass in the battle against slavery. Newspapers and photographs from the time depict acts of heroism during a tragic period in American history.

Problems in the Pacific

More than a hundred years ago Hawaii was an independent territory that the United States was anxious to acquire. However, Hawaii's seventeen-year-old Princess Ka'iulani cherished her country's independence. In *Princess Ka'iulani: Hope of a Nation, Heart of a People,* Sharon Linnéa describes the princess's struggle with the U.S. government and even with members of her own family.

3 Being There
Setting

California Standards

Here are the Grade 8 standards you will study for mastery in Chapter 3. You will also review standards from earlier grades.

Word Analysis, Fluency, and Systematic Vocabulary Development

1.3 Use word meanings within the appropriate context, and show ability to verify those meanings by definition, restatement, example, comparison, or contrast.

Grade 5 Review
1.3 Understand and explain frequently used synonyms, antonyms, and homographs.

Grade 6 Review
1.3 Recognize the origins and meanings of frequently used foreign words in English, and use these words accurately in speaking and writing.
1.4 Monitor expository text for unknown words or words with novel meanings by using word, sentence, and paragraph clues to determine meaning.

Reading Comprehension (Focus on Informational Materials)

Grade 5 Review
2.4 Draw inferences, conclusions, or generalizations about text, and support them with textual evidence and prior knowledge.

Grade 6 Review
2.1 Identify the structural features of popular media (for example, newspapers, magazines, online information), and use the features to obtain information.
2.2 Analyze text that uses the compare-and-contrast organizational pattern.

Grade 7 Review
2.3 Analyze text that uses the cause-and-effect organizational pattern.

Literary Response and Analysis

3.4 Analyze the relevance of the setting (for example, place, time, customs) to the mood, tone, and meaning of the text.

KEYWORD:
HLLA 8-3

CALIFORNIA STANDARDS

Setting *by* Mara Rockliff

YOU ARE THERE

Shipwrecked on a desert island in the novel *Robinson Crusoe*. Hiding from the Nazis in an Amsterdam attic during World War II in the play called *The Diary of Anne Frank*. Wandering through the crazy upside-down world of Lewis Carroll's *Alice's Adventures in Wonderland*. Where and when these famous works of literature take place— their **settings**—are at the heart of everything that happens. Without a setting, there simply would be no story.

Hey, Where Am I?

Opening a new book can be like dropping down the rabbit hole into Wonderland. One minute we're flopped in our favorite chair, feet up, one hand in a bowl of popcorn. The next minute we're in a spaceship on the cold, dark, silent surface of Pluto—or right in the middle of the Battle of Bull Run, bullets whistling past our ears.

Wherever we end up, we count on the writer to make it seem real. The writer can't tell us, "This story takes place in an eighteenth-century Mexican village," and then let the main character, Alfredo, order a large pepperoni pizza on his cell phone. The **customs** in the story have to fit the **time** and **place.**

Writers build believable settings by appealing to our senses. We *see*

Reading Standard 3.4 Analyze the relevance of the setting (for example, place, time, customs) to the mood, tone, and meaning of the text.

Alfredo's brightly dyed serape and *feel* the rough texture of the wool as he pulls it over his head. We *hear* his mother calling him down for breakfast and *smell* the sweet tamales in their corn husks before we *taste* them. These details make us feel that we are right there with Alfredo, ready to share whatever adventures come his way.

It Could Only Happen Here

Setting isn't just scenery, a colorful backdrop for the characters to stand in front of as they act out the plot. Setting, character, plot—they're all woven together as closely as the threads in Alfredo's serape. A teenage girl working in a mill factory in New England in the 1840s will not face the same challenges or make the same choices as a teenager trapped in a Chicago bank lobby during an armed robbery.

Sometimes the setting is responsible for the story's main **conflict.** A boy crash-lands alone in the Canadian wilderness, carrying nothing but a hatchet. A group of climbers is determined to reach the summit of Mount Everest, unaware of the deadly storm rolling in. In these situations, setting acts almost like another character, troubling and terrifying the main characters as no human villain ever could.

This Place Has Great Atmosphere

Even when the setting isn't the center of the action, it can still play a key role in creating **tone** and **mood,** or atmosphere. There will always be a murder in a murder mystery—but compare the coziness of a solution arrived at in an English drawing room with the gritty, edgy feel of clues dredged in the sewers. An August afternoon in a Mississippi swamp, a glamorous Hollywood premiere—setting can set a mood.

Language is what creates that setting. When you read a story with a vivid setting, look for words that help you use your senses. Find words that let you *see* the purple towers or the littered street, *smell* the arsenic poison or the musty closets, *hear* the sounds of creaky doors and droning bees, *taste* the hot chilies or the pancake syrup, *feel* the tropical breezes or the Arctic blasts.

Somewhere a Time and Place for Us . . .

When you're picking out something to read, the setting is often the first thing that helps you decide. Would you rather read a story set in a commune in rural America during the 1960s or one set in an Iroquois village in the 1690s? Would you rather immerse yourself in Renaissance Italy or in Tokyo in 2200? We all have special times and places that capture our imaginations. What are your favorites?

Practice

Choose a story you've read recently, perhaps one in this book or a novel you are reading independently. Describe its setting (both time and place) in a sentence or two. Now, choose a different setting for the story—your own neighborhood, for example, or another planet. List three important aspects of the story that would be affected by the switch in settings, and explain how they would change.

Title: _____

Setting: _____

Alternative setting: _____

Changes to the story:

1. _____
2. _____
3. _____

In Trouble

Literary Focus
Setting

Setting is often the first thing a writer tells you about. Here is the opening sentence of "The Landlady": "Billy Weaver had traveled down from London . . . and by the time he got to Bath, it was about nine o'clock in the evening. . . ." Setting can put you in a specific time and place or plunk you down in the middle of another culture. Setting can also affect the story's **mood,** or feeling. You may feel cheerful if you read that it's a sunny day, but you'll probably expect something bad to happen if you read that it's been raining for a week. Sometimes the setting goes even further and takes an active role in the **plot.** This happens when the character is in conflict with a force of nature—a mountain, a parched desert, bitterly cold weather. Setting is key in "In Trouble," as you'll learn in the very first sentence.

Reading Skills
Visualizing Setting

In a story in which setting is key, you have to use your imagination to try to *see* where you are and what is happening. In other words, you have to try to **visualize** what the writer is describing. As you read this story, try to picture where the man is and what his problem is. It may help if you draw a rough sketch of what you see.

Reading Standard 3.4
Analyze the relevance of the setting (for example, place, time, customs) to the mood, tone, and meaning of the text.

Make the Connection
Quickwrite 🖉

Think about settings that have had a strong effect on you. Where were you once very hot or very cold or very scared? What place made you feel especially safe and happy? Pick a setting you have strong feelings about, and jot down details that describe what you saw, heard, smelled, touched, and tasted.

Vocabulary Development

You'll meet up with these words as you read the story:

steeped (stēpt) *v.* used as *adj.:* filled with. *The sky was steeped in brilliant colors.*

alleviate (ə·lē′vē·āt′) *v.:* relieve. *Dogs need activities to alleviate boredom.*

contention (kən·ten′shən) *n.:* conflict. *There was contention among the dogs.*

exaltation (eg′zôl·tā′shən) *n.:* great joy. *Paulsen felt a sense of exaltation when he was with his dogs.*

chagrin (shə·grin′) *n.:* embarrassment. *Paulsen felt chagrin over his mistake.*

In Trouble

from *Woodsong*

Gary Paulsen

> I don't think
> I passed out so much
> as my brain simply
> exploded.

Background

This selection is taken from *Woodsong*, a book Gary Paulsen wrote about his adventures with dogs. Earlier in the book, Paulsen tells about how he had been trapping coyotes and beavers in Minnesota. He had been covering the sixty miles of his route on foot or on skis until a friend gave him a team of four sled dogs. Those dogs would change his life. "In Trouble" is about some of these changes.

Cold can be very strange. Not the cold felt running from the house to the bus or the car to the store, not the chill in the air on a fall morning, but deep cold.

Serious cold.

Forty, fifty, even sixty below zero—actual temperature, not windchill—seems to change everything. Steel becomes brittle and breaks, shatters; breath taken straight into the throat will freeze the lining and burst blood vessels; eyes exposed too long will freeze; fingers and toes freeze, turn black, and break off. These are all known, normal parts of intense cold.

But it changes beauty as well. Things are steeped in a new clarity, a clear focus. Sound seems to ring and the very air seems to be filled with diamonds when ice crystals form.

On a river in Alaska, while training, I once saw a place where a whirlpool had frozen into a cone, open at the bottom, like a beautiful trap waiting to suck the whole team down. When I stopped to look at it, with the water roaring through at the bottom, the dogs became nervous and stared down into the center as if mystified and were very glad when we moved on.

After a time I stopped trapping. That change—as with many changes—occurred because of the dogs. As mentioned, I had hunted when I was young, trapping and killing many animals. I never thought it wrong until the dogs came. And then it was a simple thing, almost a silly thing, that caused the change.

Columbia had a sense of humor and I saw it.

In the summer the dogs live in the kennel area, each dog with his own house, on a chain that allows him to move in a circle.

They can run only with the wheeled carts on cool nights, and sometimes they get bored being tied up. To alleviate the boredom, we give the dogs large beef bones to chew and play with. They get a new bone every other day or so. These bones are the center of much contention—we call them Bone Wars. Sometimes dogs clear across the kennel will hold their bones up in the air, look at each other, raise their hair, and start growling at each other, posturing and bragging about their bones.

But not Columbia.

Usually Columbia just chewed on his bone until the meat was gone. Then he buried it and waited for the next bone. I never saw him fight or get involved in Bone Wars and I always thought him a simple—perhaps a better word would be primitive—dog, basic and very wolflike, until one day when I was sitting in the kennel.

I had a notebook and I was sitting on the side of Cookie's roof, writing—the dogs are good company for working—when I happened to notice Columbia doing something strange.

He was sitting quietly on the outside edge of his circle, at the maximum length of his chain. With one paw he was pushing his bone—which still had a small bit of meat on it—out and away from him, toward the next circle.

Next to Columbia was a dog named Olaf.

Vocabulary

steeped (stēpt) v. used as adj.: filled with; saturated; soaked.

alleviate (ə·lē′vē·āt′) v.: relieve; reduce.

contention (kən·ten′shən) n.: conflict; struggle. Paulsen is playing on the phrase *bone of contention*, meaning "subject about which there is disagreement."

While Columbia was relatively passive, Olaf was very aggressive. Olaf always wanted to fight and he spent much time arguing over bones, females, the weather—anything and everything that caught his fancy. He was much scarred from fighting, with notched ears and lines on his muzzle, but he was a very good dog—strong and honest—and we liked him.

Being next to Columbia, Olaf had tried many times to get him to argue or bluster, but Columbia always ignored him.

Until this morning.

Carefully, slowly, Columbia pushed the bone toward Olaf's circle.

And of all the things that Olaf was—tough, strong, honest—he wasn't smart. As they say, some are smarter than others, and some are still not so smart, and then there was Olaf. It wouldn't be fair to call Olaf dumb—dogs don't measure those things like people—but even in the dog world he would not be known as a whip. Kind of a big bully who was also a bit of a doofus.

When he saw Columbia pushing the bone toward him, he began to reach for it. Straining against his chain, turning and trying to get farther and farther, he reached as far as he could with the middle toe on his right front foot, the claw going out as far as possible.

But not quite far enough. Columbia had measured it to the millimeter. He slowly pushed the bone until it was so close that Olaf's claw—with Olaf straining so hard his eyes bulged—just barely touched it.

Columbia sat back and watched Olaf straining and pushing and fighting, and when this had gone on for a long time—many minutes—and Olaf was still straining for all he was worth, Columbia leaned back and laughed.

"Heh, heh, heh . . ."

Then Columbia walked away.

And I could not kill or trap any longer.

It happened almost that fast. I had seen dogs with compassion for each other and their young and with anger and joy and hate and love, but this humor went into me more than the other things.

It was so complicated.

To make the joke up in his mind, the joke with the bone and the bully, and then set out to do it, carefully and quietly, to do it, then laugh and walk away—all of it was so complicated, so complex, that it triggered a chain reaction in my mind.

If Columbia could do that, I thought, if a dog could do that, then a wolf could do that. If a wolf could do that, then a deer could do that. If a deer could do that, then a beaver, and a squirrel, and a bird, and, and, and . . .

And I quit trapping then.

It was wrong for me to kill.

But I had this problem. I had gone over some kind of line with the dogs, gone back into some primitive state of exaltation that I wanted to study. I wanted to run them and learn from them. But it seemed to be wasteful (the word *immature* also comes to mind) to just run them. I thought I had to have a trap line to justify running the dogs, so I kept the line.

But I did not trap. I ran the country and camped and learned from the dogs and studied where I would have trapped if I were going to trap. I took many imaginary beaver and muskrat but I did no more sets and killed no more animals. I will not kill anymore.

Vocabulary
exaltation (eg′zôl·tā′shən) *n.:* great joy.

Yet the line existed. Somehow in my mind—and until writing this I have never told another person about this—the line still existed and when I had "trapped" in one area, I would extend the line to "trap" in another, as is proper when you actually trap. Somehow the phony trapping gave me a purpose for running the dogs and would until I began to train them for the Iditarod, a dog-sled race across Alaska, which I had read about in *Alaska* magazine.

But it was on one of these "trapping" runs that I got my third lesson,[1] or awakening.

There was a point where an old logging trail went through a small, sharp-sided gully—a tiny canyon. The trail came down one wall of the gully—a drop of fifty or so feet—then scooted across a frozen stream and up the other side. It might have been a game trail that was slightly widened or an old foot trail that had not caved in. Whatever it was, I came onto it in the middle of January. The dogs were very excited. New trails always get them tuned up and they were fairly smoking as we came to the edge of the gully.

I did not know it was there and had been letting them run, not riding the sled brake to slow them, and we virtually shot off the edge.

The dogs stayed on the trail, but I immediately lost all control and went flying out into space with the sled. As I did, I kicked sideways, caught my knee on a sharp snag, and felt the wood enter under the kneecap and tear it loose.

I may have screamed then.

The dogs ran out on the ice of the stream but I fell onto it. As these things often seem to happen, the disaster snowballed.

---

1. **my third lesson:** The first two lessons are described in the two previous chapters of *Woodsong.*

The trail crossed the stream directly at the top of a small frozen waterfall with about a twenty-foot drop. Later I saw the beauty of it, the falling lobes[2] of blue ice that had grown as the water froze and refroze, layering on itself. . . .

But at the time I saw nothing. I hit the ice of the streambed like dropped meat, bounced once, then slithered over the edge of the waterfall and dropped another twenty feet onto the frozen pond below, landing on the torn and separated kneecap.

I have been injured several times running dogs—cracked rib, a broken left leg, a broken left wrist, various parts frozen or cut or bitten while trying to stop fights—but nothing ever felt like landing on that knee.

I don't think I passed out so much as my brain simply exploded.

Again, I'm relatively certain I must have screamed or grunted, and then I wasn't aware of much for two, perhaps three minutes as I squirmed around trying to regain some part of my mind.

When things settled down to something I could control, I opened my eyes and saw that my snow pants and the jeans beneath were ripped in a jagged line for about a foot. Blood was welling out of the tear, soaking the cloth and the ice underneath the wound.

Shock and pain came in waves and I had to close my eyes several times. All of this was in minutes that seemed like hours, and I realized that I was in serious trouble. Contrary to popular belief, dog teams generally do not stop and wait for a musher[3] who falls off. They keep going, often for many miles.

Lying there on the ice, I knew I could not walk. I didn't think I could stand without some kind of crutch, but I knew I couldn't walk. I was a good twenty miles from home, at least eight or nine miles from any kind of farm or dwelling.

It may as well have been ten thousand miles.

There was some self-pity creeping in, and not a little chagrin at being stupid enough to just let them run when I didn't know the country. I was trying to skootch myself up to the bank of the gully to get into a more comfortable position when I heard a sound over my head.

I looked up, and there was Obeah looking over the top of the waterfall, down at me.

I couldn't at first believe it.

He whined a couple of times, moved back and forth as if he might be going to drag the team over the edge, then disappeared from view. I heard some more whining and growling, then a scrabbling sound, and was amazed to see that he had taken the team back up the side of the gully and dragged them past the waterfall to get on the gully wall just over me.

Vocabulary

chagrin (shə·grin′) *n.*: embarrassment and
   annoyance caused by disappointment or failure.

---

2. **lobes** *n.*: rounded pieces that jut out.
3. **musher** (mush′ər) *n.*: person who travels over snow
   by dog sled.

They were in a horrible tangle, but he dragged them along the top until he was well below the waterfall, where he scrambled down the bank with the team almost literally falling on him. They dragged the sled up the frozen streambed to where I was lying.

On the scramble down the bank Obeah had taken them through a thick stand of cockleburs. Great clumps of burs wadded between their ears and down their backs.

He pulled them up to me, concern in his eyes and making a soft whine, and I reached into his ruff and pulled his head down and hugged him and was never so happy to see anybody probably in my life. Then I felt something and looked down to see one of the other dogs—named Duberry— licking the wound in my leg.

She was licking not with the excitement that prey blood would cause but with the gentle licking that she would use when cleaning a pup, a wound lick.

I brushed her head away, fearing infection, but she persisted. After a moment I lay back and let her clean it, still holding on to Obeah's ruff, holding on to a friend.

And later I dragged myself around and untangled them and unloaded part of the sled and crawled in and tied my leg down. We made it home that way, with me sitting in the sled; and later, when my leg was sewed up and healing and I was sitting in my cabin with the leg propped up on pillows by the woodstove; later, when all the pain was gone and I had all the time I needed to think of it . . . later I thought of the dogs.

How they came back to help me, perhaps to save me. I knew that somewhere in the dogs, in their humor and the way they thought, they had great, old knowledge; they had something we had lost.

And the dogs could teach me.

Gary Paulsen

"I Had Been Dying of Thirst"

Gary Paulsen (1939–) lived all over the United States, as well as in the Philippines, when he was growing up. His father was an army officer who moved the family with each new assignment. Paulsen calls his boyhood a "rough run":

> The longest time I spent in one school was for about five months. I was an 'Army brat,' and it was a miserable life. School was a nightmare because I was unbelievably shy, and terrible at sports. I had no friends, and teachers ridiculed me. . . .
>
> One day, as I was walking past the public library in twenty-below temperatures, I could see the reading room bathed in a beautiful golden light. I went in to get warm, and to my absolute astonishment the librarian walked up to me and asked if I wanted a library card. She didn't care if I looked right, wore the right clothes, dated the right girls, was popular at sports—none of those prejudices existed in the public library. When she handed me the card, she handed me the world. I can't even describe how liberating it was. She recommended westerns and science fiction but every now and then would slip in a classic. I roared through everything she gave me and in the summer read a book a day. It was as though I had been dying of thirst and the librarian had handed me a five-gallon bucket of water. I drank and drank.

For Independent Reading

Woodsong is an autobiography, but Paulsen is best known for his young adult novels. These are two of the most popular:

- *Hatchet*, a thirteen-year-old boy survives alone in the Canadian wilderness.
- *Dogsong*, an Inuit youth treks across Alaska by dog sled.

Literary Response and Analysis

Reading Check

1. What did you learn about the **setting** in the first three paragraphs of this story?

2. Why did Paulsen stop trapping animals?

3. What mistake led to Paulsen's accident?

4. How did the dogs react to the accident?

5. Why was Paulsen surprised by the dogs' behavior?

Interpretations

6. Make a rough diagram illustrating the trick that Columbia played on Olaf. Explain Columbia's plan in terms of **causes** and **effects.**

7. How did the **setting** contribute to Paulsen's accident and make it worse?

8. Paulsen said of the frozen waterfall he fell over, "Later I saw the beauty of it. . . ." Why didn't he notice that beauty during the accident?

9. What do you think Paulsen learned from his accident and from the way his dogs responded?

Evaluation

10. As you read about Paulsen's terrible accident, were you able to **visualize** exactly where he was and why he was in such trouble? As you consider this question, discuss the story's illustrations: Did they help you visualize this setting? Did you try drawing this setting yourself? If so, compare your visual interpretation with the artist's.

11. Paulsen concludes by saying of the dogs that "they had great, old knowledge; they had something we had lost." What do you think he means by this?

12. In "Mrs. Flowers" (page 130), Mrs. Flowers says that it is language that sets humans apart from other animals. Other people believe that only humans have souls or laugh or behave unselfishly. What do *you* believe makes humans unique? Explain.

Writing

This Is How I See It

Write a brief descriptive essay about a place you know very well. Help your readers visualize the place by including details that help them *see* the setting, *smell* it, *hear* it, and perhaps *taste* it and *touch* it. Open your description with a topic statement that tells your readers what place you are going to describe and how you feel about it. Be sure to check your Quickwrite notes before you write.

▶ Use "Writing a Descriptive Essay," pages 768–770, for help with this assignment.

Reading Standard 3.4
Analyze the relevance of the setting (for example, place, time, customs) to the mood, tone, and meaning of the text.

Vocabulary Development

Verify Meanings

PRACTICE 1

Show that you understand the words in the Word Bank by answering the following questions.

1. What might cause <u>contention</u> between a person and a dog?
2. How would you <u>alleviate</u> someone's fear of dogs?
3. How would a dog show <u>chagrin</u>? How would you?
4. How would a dog show <u>exaltation</u>? How would you?
5. What is <u>steeped</u> every morning to drink for breakfast?

Word Bank

steeped
alleviate
contention
exaltation
chagrin

Sound-Alikes and Look-Alikes

Homophones (häm′ə·fōnz′) are words that sound the same but have different meanings and spellings. *Bear* and *bare* are homophones. **Homographs** (häm′ə·grafs′) are words that are spelled the same but have different meanings and origins and sometimes different pronunciations. *Wind* (rhymes with *pinned*) and *wind* (rhymes with *mind*) are homographs.

PRACTICE 2

For each sentence below, select the correct word from the two underlined **homophones.**

1. Paulsen felt the <u>would/wood</u> enter under his kneecap.
2. Paulsen hit the ice like a piece of dropped <u>meat/meet.</u>
3. The shock and <u>pain/pane</u> were hard to bear.
4. To steady himself, Paulsen held on to Obeah's <u>ruff/rough.</u>

Answer the question in parentheses about each **homograph.** Be sure to read each sentence <u>aloud</u> (or <u>allowed</u>?).

5. Paulsen felt the sharp snag <u>tear</u> his kneecap loose. (Does *tear* rhyme here with *pear* or *near*?)
6. One of the dogs was licking the <u>wound</u> in Paulsen's leg. (Does *wound* here rhyme with *sound* or *tuned*?)

Reading Standard 1.3
Show ability to verify word meanings by example.

Grade 5 Review Reading Standard 1.3
Understand and explain frequently used homographs.

Fast, Strong, and Friendly Too

Text Structure: Comparison and Contrast

Gary Paulsen describes his dogs as a team and also as individuals. Think for a moment about the dogs you have known. Do you agree that no two dogs are ever alike in personality, even those that have been raised together? Take a moment to complete a Venn diagram for two dogs—or cats or cows—you have known. In each circle, note the animals' differences. In the center, where the circles overlap, note the similarities.

When you note similarities, you are **comparing** features. When you note differences, you are **contrasting** features.

Differences   Similarities   Differences

As you read the next selection, watch for the ways in which the writer provides you with information about each breed. Where is comparison used? Where is contrast used?

In October 1999, a team of 230 huskies hauled a big-rig Kenworth flatbed truck with a huge load up Front Street in Whitehorse, Yukon Territory, Canada. The truck and load weighed 110,000 pounds.

Who were these dogs that performed this amazing feat? Huskies are thick-coated working dogs of the Arctic, often used as sled dogs. They can be of a number of breeds, including Siberian husky, Samoyed, and Alaskan malamute.

Siberian huskies are the typical sled dog. They were bred originally by the Chukchi people of Siberia, in northeastern Asia. The Chukchi trained them to run at a fast pace over great distances. That background probably accounts for the ability of the

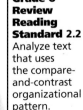

Grade 6 Review Reading Standard 2.2 Analyze text that uses the compare-and-contrast organizational pattern.

163

Siberian huskies to win races. For many years they won most of the dog-team-racing titles in Alaska. Their great endurance makes them ideally suited to take on the rugged terrain of the North.

The Chukchi upbringing may also account for the dogs' friendly nature. Siberian huskies are particularly good with children, and Chukchi tots were encouraged to play with the dogs.

Of all modern dog breeds the Samoyed is the one most closely related to the first ancestor dog. No wolf or fox bloodlines run in the Samoyed strain. For centuries the Samoyed has been bred true in its homeland—the vast stretches of tundra reaching from the White Sea to the Yenisei River in central Siberia. There they served as sled dogs, reindeer guards, and household companions.

Many dog lovers believe the Samoyed to be the ultimate canine companion. After centuries of living with humankind, this white-furred, smiling-faced dog has developed an almost uncanny understanding of people. Samoyeds are intelligent and good-natured; they always protect and never hurt their human families. Some people consider Samoyeds to be the most beautiful dogs in existence.

Alaskan malamutes are the largest of the sled dogs, standing some twenty-four inches high. These powerful-looking dogs have remarkable endurance and fortitude. They were bred in upper western Alaska by an Inuit people called Mahlemuts, or Malemutes. Like Siberian huskies and Samoyeds, Alaskan malamutes are known for their loyalty, understanding, and intelligence.

While Alaskan malamutes are the largest of the sled dogs, the smallest dog that *looks* like one is the American Eskimo dog. No one knows why the Eskie is called an Eskimo dog. This miniature animal probably couldn't find its way out of a tall northern snowbank. At nine inches short, the toy-sized Eskie looks like a full-sized sled dog in the same way that a toy version of a big-rig Kenworth flatbed truck looks like a full-sized one. Can't you just see it? Two hundred thirty less-than-one-foot-tall Eskies hauling a toy-sized big rig up Front Street in Whitehorse, Yukon Territory, Canada.

—Flo Ota De Lange

Reading Informational Materials

Reading Check

To **compare** and **contrast** the four breeds of dog you have just read about, complete a chart like the one opposite. It works on the same principle as the Venn diagram you filled in before reading the article, but it allows you to compare and contrast four things instead of just two.

Breed of Dog	Distinct Features	Similarities to Other Breeds
Siberian husky		
Samoyed		
Alaskan malamute		
American Eskimo dog		

TestPractice

Fast, Strong, and Friendly Too

1. The writer says that all the following breeds have been used as sled dogs *except* the —
   A   Alaskan malamute
   B   Siberian husky
   C   Samoyed
   D   American Eskimo dog

2. Samoyeds are different from Siberian huskies and Alaskan malamutes in that they —
   F   have no wolf bloodlines in their strain
   G   are intelligent and loyal
   H   are strong and hardworking
   J   like to play with children

3. The largest sled dog is the —
   A   Alaskan malamute
   B   Siberian husky
   C   Samoyed
   D   American Eskimo dog

4. The smallest dog that looks like a sled dog is the —
   F   Siberian husky
   G   Samoyed
   H   Alaskan malamute
   J   American Eskimo dog

Grade 6 Review Reading Standard 2.2 Analyze text that uses the compare-and-contrast organizational pattern.

Vocabulary Development

Context Clues: Reading Closely

Using a word's context—or surrounding words—to discover its meaning is especially useful when you're reading unfamiliar factual material.

PRACTICE

For each underlined word in the following passages from "Fast, Strong, and Friendly Too," fill in a chart like the one below. On a separate sheet of paper, write down your best guess at the word's meaning, and list the context clues in the passage that led you to that guess. Then, look up the dictionary definition. How close did you come? The first item has been completed for you.

1. "Of all modern dog breeds the Samoyed is the one most closely related to the first ancestor dog. No wolf or fox bloodlines run in the Samoyed strain. For centuries the Samoyed has been bred true in its homeland. . . ."

ancestor	My best guess: original (very first)
Context clues: first dog bred true no wolf or fox bloodlines	Dictionary definition: forefather; forebear further back in generations than a grandparent

2. "For many years [Siberian huskies] won most of the dog-team-racing titles in Alaska. Their great endurance makes them ideally suited to take on the rugged terrain of the north."

3. "For centuries the Samoyed has been bred true in its home-land—the vast stretches of tundra reaching from the White Sea to the Yenisei River in central Siberia."

4. "Many dog lovers believe the Samoyed to be the ultimate canine companion."

5. "After centuries of living with humankind, this white-furred, smiling-faced dog has developed an almost uncanny understanding of people."

6. "[Alaskan malamutes] were bred in upper western Alaska by an Inuit people called Mahlemuts, or Malemutes."

Grade 6 Review Reading Standard 1.4
Monitor expository text for unknown words or words with novel meanings by using word, sentence, and paragraph clues to determine meaning.

There Will Come Soft Rains

Literary Focus
Setting as Character

The setting of Gary Paulsen's "In Trouble" plays a major role in the story. An accident on a frozen riverbank miles from human habitation creates a life-threatening situation. In some stories the setting is even more important; it becomes a **character** in the story. If the dogs had not returned to rescue Paulsen, the setting might have become an opponent he had to battle to stay alive. As you read "There Will Come Soft Rains," you may be surprised at just how important a role the setting plays.

Reading Skills
Text Structures: Chronology

Have you ever asked a question like this after seeing a movie: "Did the holdup take place *before* or *after* the phone rang?" If you have, you were asking about chronology. **Chronology** is time order—what happens first, next, and last. A story written in **chronological order** presents events in the time sequence in which they occurred, one after the other.

As you read "There Will Come Soft Rains," use your reading notes to keep track of what's happening from hour to hour.

Make the Connection
Quickwrite 🖉

New technology changes the way people live. At the start of the twentieth century, most people had no cars, no electricity, no telephones. Most people didn't even have indoor toilets or running water. If someone had predicted an invention like the World Wide Web, people would have laughed. No one at that time could have imagined the way we live today. Jot down your ideas about what life might be like a hundred years from now. How do you think new technology will affect our lives?

Vocabulary Development

You'll learn these words as you read this story:

paranoia (par′ə·noi′ə) *n.:* mental disorder that causes people to feel unreasonable distrust and suspicion. *The house was so concerned with self-protection that it almost seemed to suffer from paranoia.*

cavorting (kə·vôrt′iŋ) *v.* used as *adj.:* leaping about. *Images of panthers could be seen cavorting on the walls of the nursery.*

tremulous (trem′yōō·ləs) *adj.:* trembling. *The tremulous branches swayed in the night breezes.*

oblivious (ə·bliv′ē·əs) *adj.:* unaware. *The mechanical house was oblivious of events in the world outside.*

sublime (sə·blīm′) *adj.:* majestic; grand. *The sublime poetry was recited until the very end.*

Reading Standard 3.4 Analyze the relevance of the setting (for example, place, time, customs) to the mood, tone, and meaning of the text.

The rain tapped on the empty house, echoing.

THERE WILL COME SOFT RAINS

Ray Bradbury

7:00 In the living room the voice-clock sang, *Ticktock, seven o'clock, time to get up, time to get up, seven o'clock!* as if it were afraid that nobody would. The morning house lay empty. The clock ticked on, repeating and repeating its sounds into the emptiness. *Seven-nine, breakfast time, seven-nine!*

In the kitchen the breakfast stove gave a hissing sigh and ejected from its warm interior eight pieces of perfectly browned toast, eight eggs sunny side up, sixteen slices of bacon, and two coffees.

"Today is August 4, 2026," said a second voice from the kitchen ceiling, "in the city of Allendale, California." It repeated the date three times for memory's sake. "Today is Mr. Featherstone's birthday. Today is the anniversary of Tilita's marriage. Insurance is payable, as are the water, gas, and light bills."

Somewhere in the walls, relays clicked, memory tapes glided under electric eyes.

8:01 *Eight-one, tick-tock, eight-one o'clock, off to school, off to work, run, run, eight-one!* But no doors slammed, no carpets took the soft tread of rubber heels. It was raining outside. The weather box on the front door sang quietly: "Rain, rain, go away; rubbers, raincoats for today . . ." And the rain tapped on the empty house, echoing.

Outside, the garage chimed and lifted its door to reveal the waiting car. After a long wait the door swung down again.

At eight-thirty the eggs were shriveled and the toast was like stone. An aluminum wedge scraped them into the sink, where hot water whirled them down a metal throat which digested and flushed them away to the distant sea. The dirty dishes were dropped into a hot washer and emerged twinkling dry.

Nine-fifteen, sang the clock, *time to clean.*

Out of warrens[1] in the wall, tiny robot mice darted. The rooms were acrawl with the small cleaning animals, all rubber and metal. They thudded against chairs, whirling their moustached runners, kneading the rug nap, sucking gently at hidden dust. Then, like mysterious invaders, they popped into their burrows. Their pink electric eyes faded. The house was clean.

10:00 *Ten o'clock.* The sun came out from behind the rain. The house stood alone in a city of rubble and ashes. This was the one house left standing. At night the ruined city gave off a radioactive glow which could be seen for miles.

Ten-fifteen. The garden sprinklers whirled up in golden founts, filling the soft morning air with scatterings of brightness. The water pelted windowpanes, running down the charred west side where the house had been burned evenly free of its white paint. The entire west face of the house was black, save for five places. Here the silhouette in paint of a man mowing a lawn. Here, as in a photograph, a woman bent to pick flowers. Still farther over, their images burned on wood in one titanic instant, a small boy, hands flung into the air; higher up, the image of a thrown ball, and opposite him a girl, hands raised to catch a ball which never came down.

The five spots of paint—the man, the woman, the children, the ball—remained. The rest was a thin charcoaled layer.

The gentle sprinkler rain filled the garden with falling light.

Until this day, how well the house had

---

1. **warrens** *n.*: small, crowded spaces. The little holes in the ground in which rabbits live are called warrens.

kept its peace. How carefully it had inquired, "Who goes there? What's the password?" and, getting no answer from lonely foxes and whining cats, it had shut up its windows and drawn shades in an old-maidenly preoccupation with self-protection which bordered on a mechanical paranoia.

It quivered at each sound, the house did. If a sparrow brushed a window, the shade snapped up. The bird, startled, flew off! No, not even a bird must touch the house!

The house was an altar with ten thousand attendants, big, small, servicing, attending, in choirs. But the gods had gone away, and the ritual of the religion continued senselessly, uselessly.

12:00 *Twelve noon.*

A dog whined, shivering, on the front porch.

The front door recognized the dog voice and opened. The dog, once huge and fleshy, but now gone to bone and covered with sores, moved in and through the house, tracking mud. Behind it whirred angry mice, angry at having to pick up mud, angry at inconvenience.

For not a leaf fragment blew under the door but what the wall panels flipped open and the copper scrap rats flashed swiftly out. The offending dust, hair, or paper, seized in miniature steel jaws, was raced back to the burrows. There, down tubes which fed into the cellar, it was dropped into the sighing vent of an incinerator which sat like evil Baal[2] in a dark corner.

The dog ran upstairs, hysterically yelping to each door, at last realizing, as the house realized, that only silence was here.

It sniffed the air and scratched the kitchen door. Behind the door, the stove was making pancakes which filled the house with a rich baked odor and the scent of maple syrup.

The dog frothed at the mouth, lying at the door, sniffing, its eyes turned to fire. It ran wildly in circles, biting at its tail, spun in a frenzy, and died. It lay in the parlor for an hour.

2:00 *Two o'clock,* sang a voice.

Delicately sensing decay at last, the regiments of mice hummed out as softly as blown gray leaves in an electrical wind.

Two-fifteen.

The dog was gone.

In the cellar, the incinerator glowed suddenly and a whirl of sparks leaped up the chimney.

Two thirty-five.

Bridge tables sprouted from patio walls. Playing cards fluttered onto pads in a shower of pips.[3] Martinis manifested on an oaken bench with egg-salad sandwiches. Music played.

But the tables were silent and the cards untouched.

At four o'clock the tables folded like great butterflies back through the paneled walls.

Four-thirty.

The nursery walls glowed. Animals took shape: yellow giraffes, blue lions, pink antelopes, lilac panthers cavorting in crystal

---

3. **pips** *n.:* figures on cards.

Vocabulary

paranoia (par′ə·noi′ə) *n.:* mental disorder that causes people to believe they are being persecuted; false suspicions.

cavorting (kə·vôrt′iŋ) *v.* used as *adj.:* leaping about; frolicking.

---

2. **Baal** (bā′əl): in the Bible, the god of Canaan, whom the Israelites came to regard as a false god.

substance. The walls were glass. They looked out upon color and fantasy. Hidden films clocked through well-oiled sprockets,[4] and the walls lived. The nursery floor was woven to resemble a crisp cereal[5] meadow. Over this ran aluminum roaches and iron crickets, and in the hot, still air butterflies of delicate red tissue wavered among the sharp aromas of animal spoors![6] There was the sound like a great matted yellow hive of bees within a dark bellows, the lazy bumble of a purring lion. And there was the patter of okapi[7] feet and the murmur of a fresh jungle rain, like other hoofs, falling upon the summer-starched grass. Now the walls dissolved into distances of parched weed, mile on mile, and warm endless sky. The animals drew away into thorn brakes[8] and water holes.

It was the children's hour.

 Five o'clock. The bath filled with clear hot water. *Six, seven, eight o'clock.* The dinner dishes manipulated like magic tricks, and in the study a *click.* In the metal stand opposite the hearth where a fire now blazed up warmly, a cigar popped out, half an inch of soft gray ash on it, smoking, waiting.

Nine o'clock. The beds warmed their hidden circuits, for nights were cool here.

Nine-five. A voice spoke from the study ceiling:

"Mrs. McClellan, which poem would you like this evening?"

The house was silent.

The voice said at last, "Since you express

no preference, I shall select a poem at random." Quiet music rose to back the voice. "Sara Teasdale. As I recall, your favorite. . . .

> *There will come soft rains and the smell of
>   the ground,*
> *And swallows circling with their shimmer-
>   ing sound;*
>
> *And frogs in the pools singing at night,*
> *And wild plum trees in tremulous white;*
>
> *Robins will wear their feathery fire,*
> *Whistling their whims on a low fence-wire;*
>
> *And not one will know of the war, not one*
> *Will care at last when it is done.*
>
> *Not one would mind, neither bird nor tree,*
> *If mankind perished utterly;*
>
> *And Spring herself, when she woke at dawn*
> *Would scarcely know that we were gone."*

The fire burned on the stone hearth, and the cigar fell away into a mound of quiet ash on its tray. The empty chairs faced each other between the silent walls, and the music played.

 At ten o'clock the house began to die.

The wind blew. A falling tree bough crashed through the kitchen window. Cleaning solvent,[9] bottled, shattered over the stove. The room was ablaze in an instant!

"Fire!" screamed a voice. The house lights flashed, water pumps shot water from the

---

4. **sprockets** *n.:* wheels with points designed to fit into the holes along the edges of a filmstrip.
5. **cereal** *n.:* grasses that produce grain.
6. **spoors** *n.:* animal tracks or droppings.
7. **okapi** (ō·kä′pē) *n.:* African animal related to the giraffe but with a much shorter neck.
8. **thorn brakes:** clumps of thorn bushes; thickets.

---

9. **solvent** *n.:* something that can dissolve something else (here, something that dissolves dirt). *Solvent, dissolve,* and *solution* have the same Latin root, *solvere,* which means "to loosen."

Vocabulary
tremulous (trem′yoo·ləs) *adj.:* trembling. *Tremulous* also means "fearful" or "timid."

ceilings. But the solvent spread on the linoleum, licking, eating, under the kitchen door, while the voices took it up in chorus: "Fire, fire, fire!"

The house tried to save itself. Doors sprang tightly shut, but the windows were broken by the heat and the wind blew and sucked upon the fire.

The house gave ground as the fire in ten billion angry sparks moved with flaming ease from room to room and then up the stairs. While scurrying water rats squeaked from the walls, pistoled their water, and ran for more. And the wall sprays let down showers of mechanical rain.

But too late. Somewhere, sighing, a pump shrugged to a stop. The quenching rain ceased. The reserve water supply which had filled baths and washed dishes for many quiet days was gone.

The fire crackled up the stairs. It fed upon Picassos and Matisses[10] in the upper halls, like delicacies, baking off the oily flesh, tenderly crisping the canvases into black shavings.

Now the fire lay in beds, stood in windows, changed the colors of drapes!

And then, reinforcements.

From attic trapdoors, blind robot faces peered down with faucet mouths gushing green chemical.

The fire backed off, as even an elephant must at the sight of a dead snake. Now there were twenty snakes whipping over the floor, killing the fire with a clear cold venom of green froth.

---

10. **Picassos and Matisses:** paintings by Pablo Picasso (1881–1973), a famous Spanish painter and sculptor who worked in France, and by Henri Matisse (än·rē′ mȧ·tēs′) (1869–1954), a famous French painter.

But the fire was clever. It had sent flame outside the house, up through the attic to the pumps there. An explosion! The attic brain which directed the pumps was shattered into bronze shrapnel on the beams.

The fire rushed back into every closet and felt of the clothes hung there.

The house shuddered, oak bone on bone, its bared skeleton cringing from the heat, its wire, its nerves revealed as if a surgeon had torn the skin off to let the red veins and capillaries quiver in the scalded air. Help, help! Fire! Run, run! Heat snapped mirrors like the first brittle winter ice. And the voices wailed, Fire, fire, run, run, like a tragic nursery rhyme, a dozen voices, high, low, like children dying in a forest, alone, alone. And the voices fading as the wires popped their sheathings[11] like hot chestnuts. One, two, three, four, five voices died.

In the nursery the jungle burned. Blue lions roared, purple giraffes bounded off. The panthers ran in circles, changing color, and ten million animals, running before the fire, vanished off toward a distant steaming river. . . .

Ten more voices died. In the last instant under the fire avalanche, other choruses, oblivious, could be heard announcing the time, playing music, cutting the lawn by remote-control mower, or setting an umbrella frantically out and in, the slamming and opening front door, a thousand things happening, like a clock shop when each clock strikes the hour insanely before or after the other, a scene of maniac confusion, yet unity; singing, screaming, a few last cleaning mice darting bravely out to carry the horrid ashes away! And one voice, with sublime disregard for the situation, read poetry aloud in the fiery study, until all the film spools burned, until all the wires withered and the circuits cracked.

The fire burst the house and let it slam flat down, puffing out skirts of spark and smoke.

In the kitchen, an instant before the rain of fire and timber, the stove could be seen making breakfasts at a psychopathic[12] rate, ten dozen eggs, six loaves of toast, twenty dozen bacon strips, which, eaten by fire, started the stove working again, hysterically hissing!

The crash. The attic smashing into kitchen and parlor. The parlor into cellar, cellar into subcellar. Deep freeze, armchair, film tapes, circuits, beds, and all like skeletons thrown in a cluttered mound deep under.

Smoke and silence. A great quantity of smoke.

Dawn showed faintly in the east. Among the ruins, one wall stood alone. Within the wall, a last voice said, over and over again and again, even as the sun rose to shine upon the heaped rubble and steam:

"Today is August 5, 2026, today is August 5, 2026, today is . . ."

---

11. **sheathings** *n.:* protective coverings.

12. **psychopathic** (sī′kō·path′ik) *adj.:* insane.

Vocabulary
oblivious (ə·bliv′ē·əs) *adj.:* unaware.
sublime (sə·blīm′) *adj.:* majestic; grand.

Ray Bradbury

"My Stories Have Led Me Through My Life"

At the age of twelve, **Ray Bradbury** (1920–   ) wrote his first short stories, in pencil on brown wrapping paper. He's been writing stories—and novels, poems, plays, and screenplays—ever since. Their settings range from Mars and Venus to Ireland and Green Town, a fictional town based on his birthplace, Waukegan, Illinois. Much of Bradbury's writing, like "There Will Come Soft Rains," expresses his belief that advances in science and technology should never come at the expense of human beings.

Bradbury advises young writers to keep writing:

> If you write a hundred short stories and they're all bad, that doesn't mean you've failed. You fail only if you stop writing. I've written about two thousand short stories; I've only published about three hundred, and I feel I'm still learning.

He follows his own advice and writes nearly every day. Although he has been writing for almost seventy years, he says he is still having fun.

> Writing is supposed to be difficult, agonizing, a dreadful exercise, a terrible occupation. But, you see, my stories have led me through my life. They shout, I follow. They run up and bite me on the leg—I respond by writing down everything that goes on during the bite. When I finish, the idea lets go and runs off.

For Independent Reading

Try *The Martian Chronicles,* the book that "There Will Come Soft Rains" appears in. Other popular books by Bradbury include the short story collection *The Illustrated Man* and the novel *Fahrenheit 451.*

Literary Response and Analysis

Reading Check

1. At the beginning of the story, what clues suggest that all is not well in the McClellan household?

2. Find details that tell you what has happened to the family.

3. Explain why there is still activity in the house. Who or what controls the house?

4. Describe how the house is finally destroyed.

Interpretations

5. Review the story by listing, in **chronological order,** the main events that take place in the house on August 4, 2026. Now, look at the little digital clocks that indicate the hours. How long does it take for the house to be destroyed?

6. In this story the house, the fire, and the appliances are **personified**— that is, they are described as if they were living, even human, beings. Find three examples of such personi- fication in the text.

7. A fully automated house is not only the **setting** of this story; it is also the main **character**—a role usually played by a person or an animal. What does the house do as its life is threatened and then destroyed?

8. Bradbury describes the house as "an altar with ten thousand attendants" (page 170). Who are the gods who are worshiped? What has happened to those gods?

9. On page 169, Bradbury writes, "At night the ruined city gave off a radioactive glow. . . ." What **inference,** or guess based on evidence, can you make to explain what caused this glow and destroyed the house?

10. Compare Bradbury's vision of the future with Sara Teasdale's, on page 171. Why might Bradbury have chosen to include Teasdale's poem in his story?

Evaluation

11. When Bradbury published this story back in 1950, the year 2026 seemed a lot further off than it does today. Describe what you think life in 2026 will be like. Go back to your Quick- write notes for ideas.

Writing
The Cutting Edge

Invent a new toy or labor-saving device for Bradbury's world of 2026 or for the world you imagined in your Quickwrite. Make a drawing of your invention, and attach a written explanation of what it does and how it works.

Dog-wash machine, designed by Kimberly Swift, Canyon Vista Middle School, Austin, Texas.

Reading Standard 3.4 Analyze the relevance of the setting (for example, place, time, customs) to the mood, tone, and meaning of the text.

Vocabulary Development

Word Analogies

A **word analogy** (ə·nal′ə·jē) is a word puzzle based on two pairs of words that have the same relationship. The words in each pair might have the same meaning or an opposite meaning, or they might share some other relationship, such as cause and effect or whole to part. For example, in the analogy "*Start* is to *stop* as *hate* is to _____," *start* and *stop* are opposites, so the word that would show the same relationship in the second pair is *love*, the opposite of *hate*.

> **Word Bank**
>
> paranoia
> cavorting
> tremulous
> oblivious
> sublime

PRACTICE 1

On a separate sheet of paper, complete each analogy by writing down the word from the Word Bank that best fits in the blank. These pairs are words with the same meanings or words with opposite meanings.

1. *Weary* is to *tired* as *shaky* is to _____.
2. *Depression* is to *sadness* as _____ is to *suspicion*.
3. *Afraid* is to *frightened* as *majestic* is to _____.
4. *Hit* is to *miss* as *aware* is to _____.
5. *Crying* is to *weeping* as _____ is to *frolicking*.

Words in Context

PRACTICE 2

On a separate sheet of paper, write down the words from the Word Bank that correctly fill the blanks.

    The old man watched the boys and girls _____ in the meadow. The setting was _____ , with mountains rising in all directions. However, instead of enjoying the happy scene, the old man was _____ to its charm. In his _____ , he imagined that the boys and girls were making fun of him. He shook his cane, _____ with rage, and yelled at them to leave him alone. So they did.

Reading Standard 1.3
Use word meanings within the appropriate context, and show ability to verify those meanings by comparison or contrast.

Destination: MARS

Text Structures: Magazines

Some magazines—like *Time* and *Newsweek*—cover a broad range of topics. Others deal specifically with a popular sport or hobby. No matter what you're interested in, you can probably find a magazine devoted to it.

All About Magazines

Magazines have structural features that tell you what's inside:

- **The cover.** A magazine's cover art and its main headline tell you what the lead article is. Often the cover will have one or two smaller headlines that announce other featured stories.

- **The contents page.** Usually found within the first few pages of a magazine, the contents page lists articles and regular features and tells you what page they are on. *National Geographic World*, the magazine that "Destination: Mars" comes from, calls its contents page "Inside this issue."

Before you read your next magazine article, take some time to look at the way it's structured. Along with the text, a magazine article may include the following features:

- **A title.** A magazine article usually has a title that is cleverly worded to get your attention.

- **A subtitle.** An article often has a subtitle—a secondary title that tells you more about the article.

- **Illustrations.** An article is usually illustrated with art or photographs that explain or enrich the text. **Captions** usually explain illustrations.

- **Sidebars.** Many articles feature a sidebar or two, short articles set off within the main article that focus on a topic related to the main story.

Grade 6 Review Reading Standard 2.1 Identify the structural features of popular media (for example, magazines), and use the features to obtain information.

Destination: MARS

Aline Alexander Newman

IN THE 21ST CENTURY THERE WILL BE LIFE ON MARS— HUMAN LIFE!

SO FAR only robots have visited Mars. Robots are safer and cheaper than manned missions. Scientists used to think sending humans would require hauling three years' worth of oxygen and water (for the round trip as well as the time spent on Mars) and enough rocket fuel to get them home. That's a bulky and expensive way to travel.

However, scientists are studying new ideas that would be less costly and also allow astronauts to "pack light." Using inflatable habitats, producing oxygen and rocket fuel on Mars instead of lugging it all from Earth, and recycling air and water would all lighten the load.

In 1997, engineer John Lewis took part in an experiment designed to see whether four people could survive in a closed-loop life-support system. That means nothing goes to waste—not even a drop of water—no matter where it comes from.

For about three months the crew was sealed inside a three-story chamber at Johnson Space Center in Houston, Texas. They washed their hands in recycled sweat, measured and weighed how much they went to the bathroom, and even drank each other's urine! Sounds disgusting, right? It wasn't. All the body wastes were collected and purified. "Our drinking water was cleaner than water out of a tap," says Lewis....

The Earthlings are coming! The Earthlings are coming!

Engineers at the National Aeronautics and Space Administration (NASA), in Houston, Texas, are preparing to send people to Mars. The mission is not official yet. "But it will happen," says John Connolly, NASA mission designer. "Probably before 2020."

Scientists give many reasons for going: to explore, to learn new things, to find important minerals, and maybe eventually to establish colonies so people can live there. But perhaps the most exciting reason to go is to search for evidence of past or present life, probably microscopic, on Mars.

"I want to believe it's there," says Connolly. "But the surface of Mars is a pretty nasty place. We may have to dig down to where we think it's wetter and warmer."

The mission will require an extended stay on a frozen planet that lacks breathable oxygen and has only trace amounts of water on its surface. Keep reading to learn how NASA is planning to get humans there and then keep them alive and safe.

"OUR EVENTUAL GOAL," explains aerospace engineer Scott Baird, "is to live off the land." In preparation for the astronauts' arrival, a cargo carrier will reach Mars first and drop off a large chemical maker° and inflatable habitat.

It will take six months for astronauts to travel to Mars. Once there, they will study and explore Mars for 500 days before returning to Earth. Their landing craft, expanded with the attached inflatable habitat, will serve as their home away from home.

"It'll be a blast," says Baird. "And by the time the kids of today grow up, they may be able to go."

° **chemical maker:** device that produces oxygen and fuel.

◀ Inside the "can," the nickname for the simulated capsule, the crew lived as they would during a long space voyage. Cut off from the world, they kept busy by exercising, maintaining the life-support systems, and keeping written logs.

COMPARING EARTH AND MARS

Earth	Mars
Nickname: the Blue Planet	Nickname: the Red Planet
Length of day: 23 hours, 56 minutes	Length of day: 24 hours, 37 minutes
Length of year: 365 days	Length of year: 687 Earth days
Moons: one	Moons: two
Planet surface: mostly wet and warm	Planet surface: cold and dry
Atmosphere: 98 percent oxygen and nitrogen mix	Atmosphere: 95 percent carbon dioxide
Weather highlights: temperatures range from below −100°F to above 120°F; most storms wet	Weather highlights: almost always below freezing; dry dust storms

Reading Informational Materials

Reading Check

1. What is the **subtitle** of the article?

2. According to information in the **sidebar,** when is it likely that people will land on Mars?

3. Give some reasons for scientists' wanting to travel to Mars. Where do you find this information?

4. What new ideas are scientists implementing to allow astronauts to "travel light"?

5. Name three differences between Earth and Mars. Where do you find this information?

Test Practice

Destination: MARS

1. In what part of "Destination: Mars" do you learn that the surface of Mars is "a pretty nasty place"?
   A The title
   B The subtitle
   C The caption
   D The sidebar

2. The explanation that accompanies the photo of the "can" is called —
   F a caption
   G a subtitle
   H an illustration
   J a sidebar

3. It is clear that the author of the article got some information from —
   A personal experience
   B interviews
   C photographs
   D travel magazines

4. All of the following statements about Mars are true *except* —
   F it lacks breathable oxygen
   G its surface is warm
   H it has more than one moon
   J it's nicknamed "the Red Planet"

5. According to the article, why have only robots traveled to Mars so far?
   A They are more efficient than humans.
   B They are safer and cheaper to send.
   C They produce their own oxygen and fuel.
   D They are not affected by dry dust storms.

Grade 6 Review Reading Standard 2.1 Identify the structural features of popular media (for example, magazines), and use the features to obtain information.

The Circuit

Literary Focus
Tone

Tone usually refers to the way a writer feels about a place or a character. Tone is revealed through word choice. In describing a setting, for example, a writer might use words that reveal his love for the twisty streets of his neighborhood. His tone will be upbeat, positive. Another writer might use words that suggest her hatred for the muddy fields and pig odor of the farm where she was born. Her tone will be negative. Notice how Francisco Jiménez describes the places where he and his family picked crops in California. How does he feel about these settings?

Reading Skills
Making Inferences

Part of the power of this story comes from the fact that the writer doesn't always tell you exactly what is happening. He depends on you to make **inferences,** or educated guesses based on clues in the story. As you read, look for the little open-book signs at the end of some paragraphs. Stop at those points to answer the questions that require you to make inferences.

Make the Connection
Quickwrite 🖉

The United States is often called a nation of immigrants, because almost every family has roots in other parts of the world. Draw a line down the middle of a page in your notebook. On the left, list the reasons families come to the United States today. On the right, list some of the difficulties you think they face.

Vocabulary Development

These words are used in Francisco Jiménez's story:

circuit (sʉr′kit) *n.:* regular route of a person doing a certain job. *Panchito and his family followed a crop-picking circuit.*

detect (dē·tekt′) *v.:* discover; notice. *His father did not detect any problems with the car.*

populated (päp′yə·lāt′id) *v.* used as *adj.:* lived in. *The dirt floor was populated by earthworms.*

drone (drōn) *n.:* continuous buzzing sound. *The drone of the insects made the hot day seem hotter.*

instinctively (in·stiŋk′tiv·lē) *adv.:* automatically. *Panchito instinctively hid when he saw the school bus.*

Reading Standard 3.4
Analyze the relevance of the setting (for example, place, time, customs) to the mood, tone, and meaning of the text.

THE CIRCUIT

Cajas de cartón

Francisco Jiménez

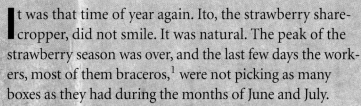

It was that time of year again. Ito, the strawberry share-cropper, did not smile. It was natural. The peak of the strawberry season was over, and the last few days the workers, most of them braceros,[1] were not picking as many boxes as they had during the months of June and July.

As the last days of August disappeared, so did the number of braceros. Sunday, only one—the best picker—came to work. I liked him. Sometimes we talked during our half-hour lunch break. That is how I found out he was from Jalisco,[2] the same state in Mexico my family was from. That Sunday was the last time I saw him.

When the sun had tired and sunk behind the mountains, Ito signaled us that it was time to go home. "Ya esora,"[3] he yelled in his broken Spanish. Those were the words I waited for twelve hours a day, every day, seven days a week, week after week. And the thought of not hearing them again saddened me.

As we drove home, Papá did not say a word. With both hands on the wheel, he stared at the dirt road. My older brother, Roberto, was also silent. He leaned his head back and closed his eyes. Once in a while he cleared from

---

1. **braceros** (brə·ser′ōz) *n.:* Mexican farm laborers brought into the United States for limited periods to harvest crops. *Bracero* comes from the Spanish word *brazo,* meaning "arm."
2. **Jalisco** (hä·lēs′kô).
3. **Ya esora** (yä es·ô′rä): *Ya es hora,* Spanish for "It's time."

Vocabulary

circuit (sʉr′kit) *n.:* route of a person doing a certain job.

his throat the dust that blew in from outside.

Yes, it was that time of year. When I opened the front door to the shack, I stopped. Everything we owned was neatly packed in cardboard boxes. Suddenly I felt even more the weight of hours, days, weeks, and months of work. I sat down on a box. The thought of having to move to Fresno and knowing what was in store for me there brought tears to my eyes.

That night I could not sleep. I lay in bed thinking about how much I hated this move.

A little before five o'clock in the morning, Papá woke everyone up. A few minutes later, the yelling and screaming of my little brothers and sisters, for whom the move was a great adventure, broke the silence of dawn. Shortly, the barking of the dogs accompanied them.

While we packed the breakfast dishes, Papá went outside to start the "Carcanchita." That was the name Papá gave his old '38 black Plymouth. He bought it in a used-car lot in Santa Rosa in the winter of 1949. Papá was very proud of his little jalopy. He had a right to be proud of it. He spent a lot of time looking at other cars before buying this one. When he finally chose the Carcanchita, he checked it thoroughly before driving it out of the car lot. He examined every inch of the car. He listened to the motor, tilting his head from side to side like a parrot, trying to detect any noises that spelled car trouble. After being satisfied with the looks and sounds of the car, Papá then insisted on knowing who the original owner was. He never did find out from the car salesman, but he bought the car anyway. Papá figured the original owner must have been an important man, because behind the rear seat of the car he found a blue necktie.

Papá parked the car out in front and left the motor running. "Listo,"[4] he yelled. Without saying a word, Roberto and I began to carry the boxes out to the car. Roberto carried the two big boxes and I carried the two smaller ones. Papá then threw the mattress on top of the car roof and tied it with ropes to the front and rear bumpers.

Everything was packed except Mamá's pot. It was an old, large galvanized pot[5] she had picked up at an army surplus store in Santa María the year I was born. The pot had many dents and nicks, and the more dents and nicks it acquired the more Mamá liked it. "Mi olla,"[6] she used to say proudly.

I held the front door open as Mamá carefully carried out her pot by both handles, making sure not to spill the cooked beans. When she got to the car, Papá reached out to help her with it. Roberto opened the rear car door and Papá gently placed it on the floor behind the front seat. All of us then climbed in. Papá sighed, wiped the sweat off his forehead with his sleeve, and said wearily: "Es todo."[7]

As we drove away, I felt a lump in my throat. I turned around and looked at our little shack for the last time.

At sunset we drove into a labor camp near Fresno. Since Papá did not speak English, Mamá asked the camp foreman if he needed any more workers. "We don't need no more," said the foreman, scratching his head. "Check with Sullivan down the road. Can't

MAKING INFERENCES

1. Why is the narrator so sad?

---

4. **listo** (lēsʹtô): Spanish for "ready."
5. **galvanized pot:** metal pot plated with zinc.
6. **mi olla** (mē ôʹyä): Spanish for "my pot."
7. **Es todo** (es tôʹdô): Spanish for "That's all."

Vocabulary
detect (dē·tektʹ) v.: discover; notice.

miss him. He lives in a big white house with a fence around it."

When we got there, Mamá walked up to the house. She went through a white gate, past a row of rosebushes, up the stairs to the front door. She rang the doorbell. The porch light went on and a tall, husky man came out. They exchanged a few words. After the man went in, Mamá clasped her hands and hurried back to the car. "We have work! Mr. Sullivan said we can stay there the whole season," she said, gasping and pointing to an old garage near the stables.

The garage was worn out by the years. It had no windows. The walls, eaten by termites, strained to support the roof, full of holes. The dirt floor, populated by earthworms, looked like a gray road map.

That night, by the light of a kerosene lamp, we unpacked and cleaned our new home. Roberto swept away the loose dirt, leaving the hard ground. Papá plugged the holes in the walls with old newspapers and tin can tops. Mamá fed my little brothers and sisters. Papá and Roberto then brought in the mattress and placed it on the far corner of the garage. "Mamá, you and the little ones sleep on the mattress. Roberto, Panchito, and I will sleep outside under the trees," Papá said.

Early next morning Mr. Sullivan showed us where his crop was, and after breakfast, Papá, Roberto, and I headed for the vineyard to pick.

Around nine o'clock the temperature had risen to almost one hundred degrees. I was completely soaked in sweat and my mouth felt as if I had been chewing on a handkerchief. I walked over to the end of the row, picked up the jug of water we had brought, and began drinking. "Don't drink too much; you'll get sick," Roberto shouted. No sooner had he said that than I felt sick to my stomach. I dropped to my knees and let the jug roll off my hands. I remained motionless with my eyes glued on the hot sandy ground. All I could hear was the drone of insects. Slowly I began to recover. I poured water over my face and neck and watched the dirty water run down my arms to the ground.

I still felt a little dizzy when we took a break to eat lunch. It was past two o'clock, and we sat underneath a large walnut tree that was on the side of the road. While we ate, Papá jotted down the number of boxes we had picked. Roberto drew designs on the ground with a stick. Suddenly I noticed Papá's face turn pale as he looked down the road. "Here comes the school bus," he whispered loudly in alarm. Instinctively, Roberto and I ran and hid in the vineyards. We did not want to get in trouble for not going to school. The neatly dressed boys about my age got off. They carried books under their arms. After they crossed the street, the bus drove away. Roberto and I came out from hiding and joined Papá. "Tienen que tener cuidado,"[8] he warned us.

8. **Tienen que tener cuidado** (tē·e'nen kā te·nār' kwē·dä'dô): Spanish for "You have to be careful."

Vocabulary

populated (päp'yə·lāt'id) v. used as adj.: inhabited; lived in or on.

drone (drōn) n.: continuous and monotonous buzzing or humming sound.

instinctively (in·stiŋk'tiv·lē) adv.: automatically; without thinking.

The next morning I could hardly move. My body ached all over. I felt little control over my arms and legs. This feeling went on every morning for days until my muscles finally got used to the work.

It was Monday, the first week of November. The grape season was over and I could now go to school. I woke up early that morning and lay in bed, looking at the stars and savoring[11] the thought of not going to work and of starting sixth grade for the first time that year. Since I could not sleep, I decided to get up and join Papá and Roberto at breakfast. I sat at the table across from Roberto, but I kept my head down. I did not want to look up and face him. I knew he was sad. He was not going to school today. He was not going tomorrow, or next week, or next month. He would not go until the cotton season was over, and that was sometime in February. I rubbed my hands together and watched the dry, acid-stained skin fall to the floor in little rolls.

When Papá and Roberto left for work, I felt relief. I walked to the top of a small grade[12] next to the shack and watched the Carcanchita disappear in the distance in a cloud of dust.

After lunch we went back to work. The sun kept beating down. The buzzing insects, the wet sweat, and the hot, dry dust made the afternoon seem to last forever. Finally the mountains around the valley reached out and swallowed the sun. Within an hour it was too dark to continue picking. The vines blanketed the grapes, making it difficult to see the bunches.

"Vámonos,"[9] said Papá, signaling to us that it was time to quit work. Papá then took out a pencil and began to figure out how much we had earned our first day. He wrote down numbers, crossed some out, wrote down some more. "Quince,"[10] he murmured.

When we arrived home, we took a cold shower underneath a water hose. We then sat down to eat dinner around some wooden crates that served as a table. Mamá had cooked a special meal for us. We had rice and tortillas with carne con chile, my favorite dish.

MAKING INFERENCES

4. What do you infer about the amount of time Roberto can spend in school? How does Roberto feel about it?

---

9. **Vámonos** (vä′mô·nôs): Spanish for "Let's go."
10. **quince** (kēn′sā): Spanish for "fifteen."

11. **savoring** (sā′vər·iŋ) *v.* used as *adj.*: enjoying, as if tasting something delicious.
12. **grade** *n.*: here, hill.

Two hours later, around eight o'clock, I stood by the side of the road waiting for school bus number twenty. When it arrived, I climbed in. Everyone was busy either talking or yelling. I sat in an empty seat in the back.

When the bus stopped in front of the school, I felt very nervous. I looked out the bus window and saw boys and girls carrying books under their arms. I put my hands in my pant pockets and walked to the principal's office. When I entered, I heard a woman's voice say: "May I help you?" I was startled. I had not heard English for months. For a few seconds I remained speechless. I looked at the lady, who waited for an answer. My first instinct was to answer her in Spanish, but I held back. Finally, after struggling for English words, I managed to tell her that I wanted to enroll in the sixth grade. After answering many questions, I was led to the classroom.

Mr. Lema, the sixth-grade teacher, greeted me and assigned me a desk. He then introduced me to the class. I was so nervous and scared at that moment when everyone's eyes were on me that I wished I were with Papá and Roberto picking cotton. After taking roll, Mr. Lema gave the class the assignment for the first hour. "The first thing we have to do this morning is finish reading the story we began yesterday," he said enthusiastically. He walked up to me, handed me an English book, and asked me to read. "We are on page 125," he said politely. When I heard this, I felt my blood rush to my head; I felt dizzy. "Would you like to read?" he asked hesitantly. I opened the book to page 125. My mouth was dry. My eyes began to water. I could not begin. "You can read later," Mr. Lema said understandingly.

For the rest of the reading period I kept getting angrier and angrier with myself. *I should have read,* I thought to myself.

During recess I went into the restroom and opened my English book to page 125. I began to read in a low voice, pretending I was in class. There were many words I did not know. I closed the book and headed back to the classroom.

Mr. Lema was sitting at his desk correcting papers. When I entered he looked up at me and smiled. I felt better. I walked up to him and asked if he could help me with the new words. "Gladly," he said.

The rest of the month I spent my lunch hours working on English with Mr. Lema, my best friend at school.

One Friday, during lunch hour, Mr. Lema asked me to take a walk with him to the music room. "Do you like music?" he asked me as we entered the building.

"Yes, I like corridos,"[13] I answered. He then picked up a trumpet, blew on it, and handed it to me. The sound gave me goose bumps. I knew that sound. I had heard it in many corridos. "How would you like to learn how to play it?" he asked. He must have read my face because before I could answer, he added: "I'll teach you how to play it during our lunch hours."

That day I could hardly wait to get home to tell Papá and Mamá the great news. As I got off the bus, my little brothers and sisters ran up to meet me. They were yelling and screaming. I thought they were happy to see me, but when I opened the door to our shack, I saw that everything we owned was neatly packed in cardboard boxes.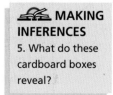

MAKING INFERENCES

5. What do these cardboard boxes reveal?

---

13. **corridos** (cō·rē′dôs) *n.:* Mexican folk ballads.

Francisco Jiménez

"The Events Were Not Experienced in the English Language"

Francisco Jiménez (1943–   ) was born in Mexico and came to the United States when he was four years old. At the age of six, he started working in the fields. The crop cycle took his family all over southern California. After many difficult years, Jiménez acquired U.S. citizenship and a doctoral degree in Latin American literature. Jiménez has won several awards for his short stories. He writes:

> 'The Circuit' is an autobiographical short story based on my experiences as a child growing up in a family of migrant farm workers. The setting is the San Joaquin Valley, a rich agricultural area in California, where my family made a living working in the fields. . . .
>
> I actually wrote the first version of the story in Spanish when I was a graduate student at Columbia University in 1972, and published it in a Spanish literary magazine in New York City. Later I expanded it and named it 'Cajas de cartón' ('Cardboard Boxes'), which I then translated into English under the title 'The Circuit.' I retitled 'Cajas de cartón' 'The Circuit' rather than 'Cardboard Boxes' because 'Cardboard Boxes' did not sound right to me.
>
> I wrote the original version of 'The Circuit' in Spanish because it was the language in which the events I describe occurred. In fact, I had difficulty finding the exact English words to translate the story because the events I describe in it were not experienced in the English language. This is why I kept some of the Spanish words in the translation. I write in both Spanish and English, but the language I write in is determined by what period in my life I write about. Since Spanish was the dominant language during my childhood, I generally write about those experiences in Spanish.

Literary Response and Analysis

Reading Check

1. Fill out this time line to show the main events in Panchito's story. At each point in the time line, sum up what happens to Panchito.

June–
July   Last days
        in August   November   December

Interpretations

2. Draw a large version of the thought bubble on the left. Fill it with words and symbols showing what Panchito might be thinking and feeling at one of the following points in the story:

- when he watches the neatly dressed boys getting off the school bus
- as he enters the school for the first time
- when he comes home and sees the cardboard boxes again

3. How do you think Papá feels about the fact that his children do not go to school regularly?

4. The narrator takes time to describe two **settings:** the old garage the family live in and Mr. Sullivan's vineyard, where the family pick grapes. Make a cluster diagram for each setting, and list the words that help you feel you are there in each setting. After you have completed each cluster, write at least one word describing the **tone** of the writer's description.

Mr. Sullivan's vineyard

Tone: _____

the garage

Tone: _____

5. **Setting** is not only a time and a place. What does the setting in this story tell you about the customs, foods, activities, clothing, and lifestyle of the migrant worker?

6. Go back to your Quickwrite chart. Circle any items in either column that you think apply to the family in the story. Then, in a different color, add any new information that you learned from the story.

Writing
"Dear Mr. Jiménez"

What does the **title** of the story mean to you? Do you agree with Jiménez's statement in Meet the Writer that "The Circuit" is a better title than "Cardboard Boxes"? Write a letter to the author giving your responses to these questions. For the "inside address" of your letter, write the name and address of your school.

Reading Standard 3.4
Analyze the relevance of the setting (for example, place, time, customs) to the mood, tone, and meaning of the text.

Vocabulary Development

Verify Meanings

PRACTICE

1. Which word is related to the word *circuit*?
   a. circumference   **b.** pursuit   **c.** citrus   **d.** electric

2. If Papá detects noises in the car's engine, has he discovered noises, or has he repaired them?

3. Which of these words is related to the word *detect*?
   a. defect   **b.** defeat   **c.** detective   **d.** defective

4. Is Mr. Sullivan's garage fit to be populated by a family? Why or why not?

5. What would the drone of insects sound like? What other sounds could be described as drones?

6. If people act instinctively, are they acting automatically or thoughtfully?

Word Bank

circuit
detect
populated
drone
instinctively

Grammar Link MINI-LESSON

Personal Pronouns

Here are some rules for choosing between the personal pronoun forms *I* and *me, she* and *her, he* and *him, we* and *us,* and *they* and *them:*

- When the pronoun is the **subject** of the verb, use *I, she, he, we,* or *they.*

  I worked with my family.

  We picked strawberries.

- When the pronoun is the **object** of the verb (the receiver of the action) or the **object** of a preposition, use *me, her, him, us,* or *them.*

  The long hours tired us.

  The hot sun beat down on me.

Reading Standard 1.3
Show ability to verify word meanings by example.

PRACTICE

For each of the following sentences, choose the correct pronoun from the underlined pair.

1. Papa was proud when he/him bought Carcanchita.
2. The garage served as a home for they/them all.
3. Roberto and I/me hid when the school bus came.
4. Panchito's teacher offered to teach he/him to play the trumpet.

For more help, see Using Pronouns Correctly in the *Holt Handbook,* pages 214–235.

Cesar Chavez: He Made a Difference

Text Structure: Cause and Effect

Think about a time when you or someone you know had a disagreement that turned into a fight or a shoving match. Jot down the details of that experience on a sheet of paper.

Finished? Whatever else you had to say about the incident, chances are you wrote down what started it (the **cause**) and what happened next (the **effect**). Human beings are naturally curious (OK, nosy). We like to know the reason (**cause**) for an action or reaction (**effect**). We want to know why (**cause**) something happened (**effect**). We make sense of events (**effects**) by looking carefully at what caused them. We sometimes even want to know what caused our mistakes.

Cause and Effect: It Happens in Real Life

Let's look back at "The Circuit" (page 183) and Panchito's life for a moment. The hardships he faces are familiar to thousands of migrant farmworkers in California: poor working and living conditions, low wages, lack of education. One of those thousands of workers, Cesar Chavez, set out to change things for the farmworkers by forming a union in order to fight for fair wages and

better working conditions. In 1962, he organized the National Farm Workers Association (later called the United Farm Workers of America). It took years of difficult and sometimes frightening struggle, but the farmworkers eventually prevailed.

Why did the farmworkers succeed despite all the odds against them? There was no single cause, but a major one was Chavez's belief in the power of nonviolence. Think back to the disagreement you wrote about at the start of this lesson. Did resorting to violence help things? Probably not. Chavez knew that resorting to violence would lead to defeat for the farmworkers. His decision to use nonviolent means was important to their success.

We might also wonder, "Why was Cesar Chavez so determined to change things, even to the point of risking his life? Why, out of the thousands of migrant workers in California, did this man make a difference? What goes into the making of such a person?" As you read the following biographical article, see if you can spot some causes of his actions.

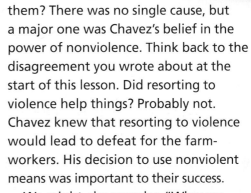

Mexican migratory workers in the fields of southern California, drinking soda pop. Photograph taken between 1945 and 1960.

Grade 7 Review Reading Standard 2.3 Analyze text that uses the cause-and-effect organizational pattern.

CESAR CHAVEZ: He Made a Difference

WHAT IS IT ABOUT THE PERSONAL experience of injustice that makes some people decide to help others while other people help only themselves?

One of the people who decided to help others was Cesar Chavez (1927–1993). When Chavez was growing up, his family members were migrant farmworkers. They traveled from region to region in California and worked long hours picking crops in the hot sun for very low wages. Since the whole family had to work to make enough money to survive, Chavez was able to go to school only when the harvests were in, and he had to quit school after eighth grade.

One year his father saw an opportunity to own his own land. He made an agreement with a landowner to clear eighty acres of the man's land and to take forty other acres of the man's land as payment for his work. Chavez's father cleared the eighty acres as promised, but when the time came for him to be paid, the landowner refused to give him the deed to the promised forty acres. Instead, he sold the land to another person.

When Cesar Chavez's father saw a lawyer about the matter, the lawyer advised him to borrow some money and buy the land from the other person. Chavez's father did just that. But cash was a difficult thing for his father to come by, and one day he didn't have the money to make an interest payment. The lawyer not only took the forty acres back but also sold it to the original owner—the man who had cheated Chavez's father in the first place.

Cesar Chavez says that he never forgot the injustice those men did to his father. For more than a hundred years, people like his father had been

allowed to toil in the fields but had not been allowed to enjoy the fruits of their toil. Chavez hoped to change this, a task many regarded as hopeless.

Chavez believed that migrant farmworkers needed a union to help them get fair wages and better working conditions. In 1962, he organized the National Farm Workers Association, later called the United Farm Workers of America. The union's five-year strike against California's grape growers drew support from around the country. Many people across the United States refused to buy or eat grapes until the strike was settled.

The union's actions were based on the non-violent principles of Mohandas K. Gandhi and Martin Luther King, Jr. However, many farm-workers were angry and believed that they could not win against the growers without violence. After all, the growers were using scare tactics and violence against them. Chavez met the threat of violence with a radical plan. He was willing to sacrifice his own life by going on a hunger strike to prevent violence and to ensure that the union would continue. His example won the angry workers over. By practicing nonviolence himself, Chavez inspired others in the farmworkers' movement to recommit themselves to the struggle for justice through nonviolence.

When Cesar Chavez died in 1993, more than fifty thousand mourners gathered to honor him at the United Farm Workers' field office in Delano, California. The field office is called Forty Acres.

—Flo Ota De Lange

Reading Informational Materials

Reading Check

This account of the life of Cesar Chavez is built on a series of **causes** and **effects**. Think about the succession of events, how one thing leads to another. Copy the chart on the right onto a separate sheet of paper, adding other examples from the article to complete the chart.

Cause	Effect
1. Family earns low wages.	1. All have to work.
2. Father sees chance to own land.	2.
3. [And so on]	3.

TestPractice

CESAR CHAVEZ: He Made a Difference

1. Which of the following situations was *not* a **cause** of Cesar Chavez's dedication to bettering the lives of migrant workers?

    A The way the landowner treated Chavez's father

    B The way the lawyer treated Chavez's father

    C The opportunity to purchase the Forty Acres field office

    D The possibility of achieving justice through nonviolent means

2. An **effect** of Cesar Chavez's dedication to bettering the lives of farmworkers was that the —

    F United Farm Workers was formed

    G farmworkers became angry

    H landowner cheated his father

    J lawyer gave his father advice

3. The **cause** of Cesar Chavez's hunger strike was —

    A imprisonment of strikers

    B possibility of violence from farmworkers

    C love of his father

    D deep religious beliefs

4. *Nonviolence* means —

    F "being too afraid to fight"

    G "being afraid of violence"

    H "refusing to use violence on principle"

    J "not wanting to be caught"

5. Cesar Chavez gave the name Forty Acres to the site of the United Farm Workers' field office at Delano. The name was —

    A symbolic

    B offensive

    C literal

    D humorous

Grade 7 Review Reading Standard 2.3
Analyze text that uses the cause-and-effect organizational pattern.

Vocabulary Development

Grade 6 Review Reading Standard 1.3 Recognize the origins and meanings of frequently used foreign words in English.

Spanish and English: All in the Family

Thousands of words from Spanish have become part of the English language, and more words from Spanish are entering English all the time. Many Spanish words were absorbed into the English language in the sixteenth and seventeenth centuries, when explorers from Spain gave Spanish names to mountains, rivers, lakes, and new settlements in North America.

PRACTICE

Copy the chart on the right, and fill in the meanings of the Spanish names. Use a dictionary if you need to.

Spanish Name	Meaning
Colorado	
Florida	
Los Angeles	
San Francisco	
Fresno	

Grammar Link MINI-LESSON

Pronoun Reference

When you use pronouns in your writing, make sure their **antecedents** (words they refer to) are clear.

UNCLEAR   **Chavez's father saw a lawyer, and he advised buying the land.** [Who advised buying the land, Chavez's father or the lawyer?]

CLEAR   **Chavez's father saw a lawyer, who advised buying the land.**

UNCLEAR   **The landowner made a promise to Chavez's father, but it didn't happen.** [What didn't happen?]

CLEAR   **The landowner made a promise to Chavez's father, but didn't keep the promise.**

PRACTICE

Find a piece of writing you've been working on, and exchange papers with a classmate. Circle every pronoun your partner used, and underline its antecedent. If you can't identify the antecedent, put a question mark in the margin. Exchange papers again, and revise any sentences with unclear pronoun references. **For more help, see Using Pronouns Correctly in the *Holt Handbook*, pages 214–235.**

Picking Strawberries: Could You Do It?

Take a Guess

Lance opened his eyes, glanced lazily at the clock, and was suddenly wide awake. Nine-thirty! Good grief, he must have overslept. . . . A slow smile spread across Lance's face and turned into a wide grin, which soon turned into a yawn. He stretched once, turned over, and thought, "Two weeks! No alarms, no bus, no homework." Ahhhhh . . . mmmmmmm . . . zzzzzzzzz.

Even though the writer of the passage above has left out quite a few details, it isn't difficult to figure out the situation. You don't need to have every fact spelled out to understand what is happening. That is because, like any good reader, you have made inferences and generalizations and drawn conclusions on your own.

Drawing Inferences

When you draw **inferences,** you make educated guesses based on the clues the writer gives and your own experience or knowledge. You can probably supply the following information about the passage above even though the writer has not given it to you directly:

- a possible time of year
- the situation
- why Lance doesn't have to worry
- Lance's feelings

Reaching Conclusions

A **conclusion** is your final thought or judgment about what you have read. It takes into account all the facts and all your inferences. A conclusion is **valid** (both true and logical) if it can be supported with information from the text and if no information in the text contradicts it. Let's return to Lance. You probably concluded that Lance is enjoying the first day of a two-week vacation. Absolutely.

Making Generalizations

A **generalization** is a broad statement that can apply to many situations. To be valid, generalizations, like conclusions, have to be supported by facts. For the "story" about Lance, one generalization might be "Waking up on the first morning of a two-week vacation is a pleasure." Generalizations unsupported by facts are untrue. "All vacations are relaxing" would be too general, since some vacations are hectic.

As you read the following article, think about the inferences you might draw from it. Also think about any conclusions or generalizations you might make based on facts in the article.

Grade 5 Review Reading Standard 2.4
Draw inferences, conclusions, or generalizations about text, and support them with textual evidence and prior knowledge.

PICKING STRAWBERRIES:
Could You Do It?

The following experiment will give you an idea of what it is like to pick strawberries for a living. One problem with picking a strawberry is that a ripe berry is easily bruised by handling, and if it is bruised, no one will buy it. So the strawberry picker must find a way to pluck the berry off the plant without hurting it. Sound easy? Well, maybe so—if you have all the time in the world and are picking only one berry. But what if, in order to earn enough money to provide your family with the basics, you have to pick about ten thousand strawberries in a twelve-hour workday? That increase in numbers turns strawberry picking into a very different situation, doesn't it?

To pick ten thousand strawberries in twelve hours, you have to pick about

- 1 strawberry every four seconds
- 14 strawberries every minute
- 840 strawberries every hour

So how can we get an idea of what the strawberry picker's hands are doing as she or he picks a berry? In the absence of a real strawberry plant, let's settle for a twelve-inch length of string. Anchor this piece of string around something stable, like a chair back or a door handle. Then, tie a granny knot. Have someone time you while you are doing it. How fast can you tie it? Practice doing it until you can tie a granny knot in four seconds or less. Then, try doing the same thing with fourteen separate lengths of twelve-inch string. The idea is to get fourteen separate knots tied in less than a minute. Now, imagine tying 840 knots in an hour and 10,080 knots in twelve hours. Are you getting an idea of what strawberry picking is like?

—Flo Ota De Lange

Reading Informational Materials

Reading Check

1. How many strawberries must a worker pick in an hour to support his or her family?

2. Why does the writer suggest that you try tying the knots?

TestPractice

PICKING STRAWBERRIES: Could You Do It?

1. "But what if, in order to earn enough money to provide your family with the basics, you have to pick about ten thousand straw-berries in a twelve-hour workday?" One **inference** that can be made from this sentence is that —

   A strawberry pickers and their families are wealthy

   B strawberry picking is slow and leisurely

   C strawberry pickers are paid by quantity

   D strawberry pickers are paid by the hour

2. All of the following **inferences** can be made from the knot-tying experiment *except* —

   F a strawberry picker needs to know many knot-tying styles

   G a strawberry picker must have good coordination

   H strawberry picking is repetitive work

   J a strawberry picker must be fast

3. Which of the following **conclusions** about strawberry picking could be drawn from this text?

   A It is easy money.

   B It is harder than you might think.

   C It requires maturity and strength.

   D It is impossible.

4. One **generalization** that could be made from this reading is that —

   F strawberries taste good

   G strawberry picking is hard

   H strawberries are hard to grow

   J strawberry pickers are nice

5. Based on this article, which **conclusion** could you make about the writer's beliefs?

   A Strawberry pickers work too hard.

   B Strawberry pickers could work harder.

   C Strawberry pickers should seek other work.

   D Management takes unfair advantage of strawberry pickers.

Grade 5 Review Reading Standard 2.4
Draw inferences, conclusions, or generalizations about text, and support them with textual evidence and prior knowledge.

Vocabulary Development

Context Clues: Multiple Meanings

The following exercise will give you practice in using context clues to figure out a word's meaning. In this exercise the words are simple. As you will see, however, they have multiple meanings.

PRACTICE

Each sentence below contains one underlined word followed by several definitions of that word. Choose the definition that best fits the sentence. Then, explain which words in the sentence led you to choose that definition. The first item has been done for you.

1. "The following experiment will give you an idea of what it is like to <u>pick</u> strawberries for a living."

    a. gather   **b.** choose   **c.** criticize

    Answer: The definition that works best is **a,** *gather*. The writer uses *pick* in the sense of gathering strawberries and carrying them away. This is not like choosing one special strawberry, and it certainly wouldn't make sense to criticize them!

2. "But what if, in order to earn enough money to provide your family with the basics, you <u>have</u> to pick about ten thousand strawberries in a twelve-hour workday?"

    a. own   **b.** get; acquire   **c.** are required

3. "That increase in numbers turns strawberry picking into a very different <u>situation</u>, doesn't it?"

    a. rank   **b.** location   **c.** circumstance

4. "In the absence of a real strawberry plant, let's settle for a twelve-inch <u>length</u> of string."

    a. distance   **b.** segment   **c.** duration

Grade 6 Review Reading Standard 1.4 Monitor expository text for unknown words or words with novel meanings by using word, sentence, and paragraph clues to determine meaning.

Literary Response and Analysis

 **TestPractice**

DIRECTIONS: Read the passage. Then, read each question, and write the letter of the best response.

from The Cay
Theodore Taylor

In the novel The Cay, *Phillip, an eleven-year-old boy who is blind, is shipwrecked on a very small island, or cay, with a West Indian seaman named Timothy and a cat. Timothy dies while protecting Phillip during a hurricane. In this part of the story, Phillip is trying to make it on his own.*

The sun came out strong in the morning. I could feel it on my face. It began to dry the island, and toward noon, I heard the first cry of a bird. They were returning.

By now, I had taught myself to tell time, very roughly, simply by turning my head toward the direct warmth of the sun. If the angle was almost overhead, I knew it was around noon. If it was low, then of course, it was early morning or late evening.

There was so much to do that I hardly knew where to start. Get a campfire going, pile new wood for a signal fire, make another rain catchment for the water keg, weave a mat of palm fibers to sleep on. Then make a shelter of some kind, fish the hole on the reef, inspect the palm trees to see if any coconuts

were left—I didn't think any could be up there—and search the whole island to discover what the storm had deposited. It was enough work for weeks, and I said to Stew Cat, "I don't know how we'll get it all done." But something told me I must stay very busy and not think about myself.

I accomplished a lot in three days, even putting a new edge on Timothy's knife by honing it on coral. I jabbed it into the palm nearest my new shelter, so that I would always know where it was if I needed it. Without Timothy's eyes, I was finding that in my world, everything had to be very precise; an exact place for everything.

On the fifth day after the storm, I began to scour the island to find out what had been cast up. It was exciting, and I knew it would take days or weeks to accomplish. I had made another cane and beginning with east beach, I felt my way back and forth, reaching down to touch everything that my cane struck; sometimes having to spend a long time trying to decide what it was that I held in my hands.

I found several large cans and used one of them to start the "time" can again, dropping five pebbles into it so that the reckoning would begin again from the night of the storm. I discovered

Reading Standard 3.4
Analyze the relevance of the setting (for example, place, time, customs) to the mood, tone, and meaning of the text.

200   Chapter 3   Being There: Setting

an old broom, and a small wooden crate that would make a nice stool. I found a piece of canvas, and tried to think of ways to make pants from it, but I had no needle or thread.

Other than that, I found many shells, some bodies of dead birds, pieces of cork, and chunks of sponge, but nothing I could really put to good use.

It was on the sixth day after the storm, when I was exploring on south beach, that I heard the birds. Stew Cat was with me, as usual, and he growled when they first screeched. Their cries were angry, and I guessed that seven or eight might be in the air.

I stood listening to them; wondering what they were. Then I felt a beat of wing past my face, and an angry cry as the bird dived at me. I lashed out at it with my cane, wondering why they were attacking me.

Another dived down, screaming at me, and his bill nipped the side of my head. For a moment, I was confused, not knowing whether to run for cover under sea grape, or what was left of it, or try to fight them off with my cane. There seemed to be a lot of birds.

Then one pecked my forehead sharply, near my eyes, and I felt blood run down my face. I started to walk back toward camp, but had taken no more than three or four steps when I tripped over a log. I fell into the sand, and at the same time, felt a sharp pain in the back of my head. I heard a raging screech as the bird soared up again. Then another bird dived at me.

I heard Stew Cat snarling and felt him leap up on my back, his claws digging into my flesh. There was another wild screech, and Stew Cat left my back, leaping into the air.

His snarls and the wounded screams of the bird filled the stillness over the cay. I could hear them battling in the sand. Then I heard the death caw of the bird.

I lay still a moment. Finally, I crawled to where Stew Cat had his victim. I touched him; his body was rigid and his hair was still on edge. He was growling, low and muted.

Then I touched the bird. It had sounded large, but it was actually rather small. I felt the beak; it was very sharp.

Slowly, Stew Cat began to relax.

Wondering what had caused the birds to attack me, I felt around in the sand. Soon, my hand touched a warm shell. I couldn't blame the birds very much. I'd accidentally walked into their new nesting ground.

They were fighting for survival, after the storm, just as I was. I left Stew Cat to his unexpected meal and made my way slowly back to camp.

1. What details tell you that the **setting** of this story is a tropical island?

   A   Palm trees and coconuts

   B   Warm sun

   C   A wooden crate

   D   Returning birds

2. Being blind and alone on a small island is scary enough for Phillip, but what detail of the setting adds horror to the **mood**?

   F   Timothy's knife

   G   Stew Cat

   H   A signal fire

   J   Attacking birds

3. Which sentence shows that Phillip is optimistic in spite of his troubles?

   A   "There was so much to do that I hardly knew where to start."

   B   "It was enough work for weeks, and I said to Stew Cat, 'I don't know how we'll get it all done.'"

   C   "I accomplished a lot in three days, even putting a new edge on Timothy's knife. . . ."

   D   "I found a piece of canvas, and tried to think of ways to make pants from it, but I had no needle or thread."

4. Which of the following **conclusions** can you reasonably make about Phillip's character?

   F   Phillip is self-pitying.

   G   Phillip is brave and intelligent.

   H   Phillip is fun-loving and lazy.

   J   Phillip lacks self-esteem.

5.

Phillip hears birds screeching.		Stew Cat kills a bird.

   If you were arranging the events of this passage in **chronological order,** which of the following events would you place in the empty box?

   A   Birds attack Phillip.

   B   Birds lay eggs in the sand.

   C   Stew Cat eats the bird.

   D   Phillip returns to camp.

6. Phillip says he accomplished a lot, "even putting a new edge on Timothy's knife by honing it on coral." *Honing* probably means —

   F   breaking

   G   sharpening

   H   coloring

   J   ruining

7. What does Phillip discover was the **cause** of the bird attack?

   A   The birds hate humans.

   B   The birds were hungry.

   C   The birds were protecting their eggs.

   D   The birds wanted to eat the cat.

8. What **inference** can you make at the end of the story?

   F   Stew Cat eats the eggs.

   G   The birds take the eggs to a safer place.

   H   Phillip packs the eggs in his sack.

   J   Stew Cat eats the bird.

Vocabulary Development

TestPractice

Context Clues

DIRECTIONS: Use context clues to guess the meaning of each underlined word or phrase in the following sentences.

1. "The peak of the strawberry season was over, and the last few days the workers, most of them braceros, were not picking as many boxes as they had during the months of June and July." In this sentence, *peak* means —

   A part of a baseball cap

   B crest of a hill

   C worst period

   D highest point

2. "The yelling and screaming of my little brothers and sisters . . . broke the silence of dawn. Shortly, the barking of the dogs accompanied them." In this sentence, *accompanied* means —

   F joined in with

   G fought against

   H quieted

   J awoke

3. "While we ate, Papá jotted down the number of boxes we had picked." In this sentence, *jotted down* means —

   A wrote a brief note about

   B analyzed completely

   C stacked up

   D summed up

4. "The vines blanketed the grapes, making it difficult to see the bunches." In this sentence, *blanketed* means —

   F revealed

   G destroyed

   H covered

   J exposed

5. "Papá sighed, wiped the sweat off his forehead with his sleeve, and said wearily: 'Es todo [That's all].'" In this sentence, *wearily* means —

   A weirdly

   B tiredly

   C meanly

   D angrily

Vocabulary Development

TestPractice

Synonyms

DIRECTIONS: Choose the word or group of words that has the same or about the same meaning as the underlined word. You studied some of these words in previous chapters.

1. Apparent means —
   A unknown
   B outrageous
   C visible
   D hidden

2. Someone who is sullen is —
   F grumpy
   G wealthy
   H jealous
   J funny

3. Someone who has been misled has been —
   A employed
   B fooled
   C deserted
   D ignored

4. A disheveled person is —
   F angry
   G prepared
   H easygoing
   J untidy

5. Sublime means —
   A grand
   B ancient
   C destructive
   D fortunate

6. To obscure something is to —
   F sell it
   G hide it
   H throw it
   J taste it

7. Intolerant means —
   A incurable
   B unaccepting
   C unbelievable
   D insincere

8. Someone who is gaunt is —
   F ill
   G quiet
   H thin
   J bright

Mastering the Standards

TECHNICAL DOCUMENT

Writers Wanted!

If you were on the Mars project described in the article on page 178, you would have to know how to operate many tools. Writing instructions on using tools—from simple household tools to the sophisticated tools used by NASA engineers—is an important skill. Practice your skill at writing instructions by describing in clear, easy-to-understand language how to use a tool you are familiar with. Assume your audience does not know anything about using this tool. Here are some tools you might write about: a bicycle, a lawn mower, a VCR, a can opener, a coffee maker. Before you start to write, list the tasks the tool can accomplish. Then, list in chronological order the steps that the user must follow in order to use the tool correctly. Also list some mistakes that the user might make. Your aim in writing a technical document is *clarity*—no figures of speech, no humor.

▷ **Use "Writing Instructions for Operating a Tool," pages 643–660, for help with this assignment.**

Other Choices

PERSUASION

1 Tomorrow Will Bring . . .

Ray Bradbury (page 174) tells stories about what life might be like in the future. What do you think the future will be like? Will genetic engineering of food make a difference? What about mapping the human genome sequence? Will space exploration (like that described in the article on Mars, page 178) affect human life on Earth? Think of a topic about the future, one that worries you or gives you hope. Then, write a report in which you state your opinion about possible developments in the future and provide facts to support it.
▷ **Use "Writing a Persuasive Essay," pages 706–725, for help with this assignment.**

TECHNICAL DOCUMENT

2 Bylaws and Aims

Cesar Chavez set up an organization representing the migrant farmworkers. Most organizations have bylaws, or sets of rules that govern an organization's meetings or affairs. Suppose you wish to organize a group of students who share your interest in something: band, a sport, a community project. Write a document that will serve as the bylaws of your group. Include (a) a statement of the group's aims, (b) a list of bylaws—that is, rules the group will observe during its activities and its meetings, and (c) a description of the group's organization. This is a project you might enjoy doing with a group of classmates.
▷ **Use "Writing Bylaws," pages 776–777, for help with this assignment.**

Fiction

Consequences of War

As World War II comes to a close, Yuki Sakane and her family are finally released from an internment camp and allowed to return home to Berkeley, California. However, the Sakanes quickly find that Berkeley has changed. Because of the war, former friends and other residents have become suspicious of returning Japanese Americans. Yuki and her family try to overcome this hostility in Yoshiko Uchida's novel *Journey Home.*

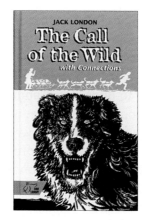

Change of Scenery

In Jack London's classic adventure story *The Call of the Wild,* Buck is stolen from his comfortable home and forced into service as a sled dog in the Alaskan wilderness. As he struggles to adapt to his new surroundings, Buck learns to draw on his instincts to survive among brutal owners and fierce competition.

This title is available in the HRW Library.

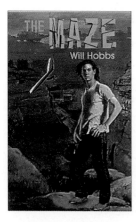

Lost and Found

Rick Walker doesn't know where to turn when he is lost and alone. Luckily, a biologist named Lon Peregrino befriends Rick. Lon is dedicated to preserving the nearly extinct California condors who reside by the Maze, a landscape of beautiful deep canyons. In Will Hobbs's novel *The Maze,* Rick helps Lon protect the condors from extinction while following his own dreams of flight.

Triumph and Tragedy

Patricia A. Cochrane's *Purely Rosie Pearl* tells the story of twelve-year-old Rosie Pearl Bush and her family, migrant workers in the Sacramento Valley. Rosie thinks her family's future looks bright after her father replaces the disagreeable Jake Porter as field boss. But her joy turns to sadness when a terrible event takes place.

Nonfiction

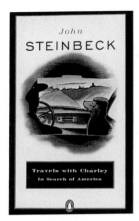

Across the Country

By the time John Steinbeck turned fifty-eight, he had written the classic American novels *Of Mice and Men* and *The Grapes of Wrath.* What remained was Steinbeck's desire to drive across the country that he had written about so eloquently. *Travels with Charley* is Steinbeck's chronicle of his journey. With his French poodle, Charley, by his side, Steinbeck encounters all the sides of America in the 1960s: beauty at Niagara Falls, racism in New Orleans, companionship in California.

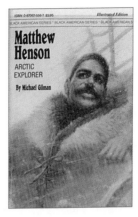

Overdue Recognition

When Robert Peary was searching for men to join him on the first expedition to the North Pole, he knew Matthew Henson would be a worthy partner. Peary recognized this African American's determination and resourcefulness, and their association led to a lifetime of exciting Arctic exploration for both men. Discover Henson's little-known contributions to a remarkable journey in Michael Gilman's *Matthew Henson: Arctic Explorer.*

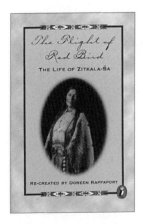

Cruel Decisions

When Gertrude Bonnin was eight years old, she was removed from her Sioux reservation in the Dakotas and placed in a boarding school in Indiana. Gertrude resisted when her instructors tried to make her renounce her Native American customs. Instead, she renamed herself Zitkala-Ša (Red Bird). As an adult, Zitkala-Ša made people aware of the harsh treatment of American Indians. Doreen Rappaport tells this brave woman's story in *The Flight of Red Bird: The Life of Zitkala-Ša.*

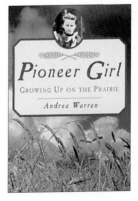

Nebraska Landscapes

Although living on the prairie could be physically and mentally grueling, Grace McCance loved it. Andrea Warren documents McCance's life on the Nebraska prairie in *Pioneer Girl: Growing Up on the Prairie.* Even when blizzards or thunderstorms damaged their land, Grace and her family found a way to survive, and even to triumph.

4 We Still Believe

California Standards

Here are the Grade 8 standards you will study for mastery in Chapter 4. You will also review standards from earlier grades.

Word Analysis, Fluency, and Systematic Vocabulary Development

1.3 Use word meanings within the appropriate context, and show ability to verify those meanings by definition, restatement, example, comparison, or contrast.

Grade 6 Review

1.4 Use word, sentence, and paragraph clues to determine meaning.

Reading Comprehension (Focus on Informational Materials)

Grade 5 Review

2.3 Discern main ideas and concepts presented in texts, identifying and assessing evidence that supports those ideas.

Grade 6 Review

2.2 Analyze text that uses the compare-and-contrast organizational pattern.

2.3 Connect and clarify main ideas by identifying their relationships to other sources and related topics.

2.4 Clarify an understanding of texts by creating outlines and logical notes.

Literary Response and Analysis

3.5 Identify and analyze recurring themes (for example, good versus evil) across traditional and contemporary works.

Grade 6 Review

3.6 Identify and analyze features of themes conveyed through characters, actions, and images.

3.7 Explain the effects of common literary devices (for example, symbolism, imagery, metaphor) in nonfictional texts.

Grade 7 Review

3.3 Analyze characterization as delineated through a character's thoughts, words, and actions.

KEYWORD:
HLLA 8-4

CALIFORNIA STANDARDS

Theme *by* Mara Rockliff
TRUTHS ABOUT OUR LIVES

Messages Are for E-mail

A lot of people call the theme the author's "message." If this were true, stories would be only the sugar coating that writers use to get us to swallow their messages. Stories are much more than this. We don't read stories for a moral lesson. We look to fiction for excitement, emotion, suspense, laughs, and the chance to meet interesting people doing interesting things. Yet when a story touches us, it usually *has* taught us something. The stories that have a meaning beyond the people and events on their pages—a meaning that *we* can use—are the ones that change our lives. This deeper meaning is called **theme.**

Most writers say they don't know their theme when they begin to write. They often start with just a character or a situation. "What would motivate someone to risk everything?" they wonder, or "How would a thirteen-year-old boy deal with his parents' divorce?" Then they start to write.

A theme will often emerge naturally from the story as it progresses and from what the writer believes about life. A writer who believes that a single mistake can haunt a person forever, for example, will write one kind of story. Someone who believes that what matters most is to learn from our mistakes and move on will write another kind. We, the readers, discover a truth about life as we share the characters' experiences. At the end of the story, what the characters have discovered we have discovered also.

Finding Meaning in It All

Like the truths we discover in real life, themes in stories can be complicated, open to interpretation, and sometimes difficult to put into words.

You might read about a family hiding from the Nazis and come away thinking the theme is: *Even in extraordinary circumstances, people still do ordinary things, like fight, make up, and fall in love.* One of your classmates might say the theme is: *The human spirit will always triumph over evil.* You both could be right.

Does that mean themes aren't really there in the story? It means that readers recognize themes when what the writer believes about life and wants to say coincides with what the reader believes about life and wants to hear. The meaning of a story comes from both the writer and the reader.

So how do you put your finger on what a story means to you? Try looking at these elements:

Reading Standard 3.5
Identify and analyze recurring themes (for example, good versus evil) across traditional and contemporary works.

The title. Often, but not always, writers use titles to hint at the story's theme. If the title is more than just the name of a character, consider what it suggests. Why do you think the writer chose this title?

The characters. How do the main characters change in the course of the story? What do they discover that could have meaning for other people's lives—including your own?

The big moments. Which scenes or passages in the story seem especially important? What revelations about life do they suggest to you?

The resolution. How are conflicts or problems in the story settled? How do you feel about the outcome? Does the resolution give you an idea of what the story means?

Recurring Themes the World Over

People all over the world share the same dreams and fears: They long for a vision of human life that gives meaning to their own existence. They long for heroes who will come to their rescue in times of danger. It is not surprising, then, that all over the world people tell the same stories—more or less. Characters change and settings change, but themes recur. The same themes can be found in ancient myths, in short stories published in today's magazines, in movies, and even on TV shows.

Practice

To begin your exploration of recurring themes, look again at the two themes mentioned on page 210: *Even in extraordinary circumstances, people still do ordinary things, like fight, make up, and fall in love* and *The human spirit will always triumph over evil*. Then, think of novels, stories, poems, and plays you have studied or read on your own. Think also of movies, plays, and TV shows you have seen. With a group of classmates, brainstorm titles of works that reflect those two themes.

The Diary of Anne Frank

Literary Focus
Theme

Plot answers the question "What happens?" **Theme** answers the question "What does this reveal?" Theme is the general idea or insight about human existence that is revealed in a story, poem, or play. Most works of literature do not have just one theme. A long work will often reveal many themes. Different readers may discover different themes, based on their own backgrounds and attitudes. See what themes you discover in this play as you experience with the characters the terror of hiding from enemies who want to destroy you.

Reading Skills
Using Resources

In this text are many **resources** that contain facts about the true story of Anne Frank and about the play. Those resources include **maps,** a **time line,** a drawing of the **stage set,** historical **photographs,** and entries from Anne Frank's diary. (The diary is an example of a **primary source,** that is, firsthand information.) As you read, use those background resources to deepen your understanding of what is happening in the play. The time line especially will help you trace what is going on in the war-torn world beyond Anne's attic. The stage design will help you visualize the action of the play.

Grade 6 Review Reading Standard 3.6 Identify and analyze features of themes conveyed through characters, actions, and images.

Vocabulary Development

These are some of the words you will learn as you read the play:

conspicuous (kən·spik′yo͞o·əs) *adj.:* noticeable. *The Nazis required all Jews to wear a conspicuous yellow Star of David on their clothing.*

unabashed (un′ə·basht′) *adj.:* unembarrassed. *Anne's unabashed comments sometimes embarrassed her mother.*

loathe (lōth) *v.:* hate. *Anne loathed having her mother treat her like a baby.*

indignantly (in·dig′nənt·lē) *adv.:* with anger caused by something felt to be unjust. *Anne indignantly claimed she had not been rude.*

fortify (fôrt′ə·fī′) *v.:* strengthen. *Dr. Dussel took pills to fortify himself.*

zeal (zēl) *n.:* great enthusiasm; devotion to a cause. *The Maccabees showed great zeal in their fight against tyranny.*

tyranny (tir′ə·nē) *n.:* cruel and unjust use of power. *The Maccabees' fight against tyranny and oppression two thousand years ago still inspires people today.*

gingerly (jin′jər·lē) *adv.:* cautiously. *Peter held Anne's gift gingerly, afraid it might jump out and hit him.*

ostentatiously (äs′tən·tā′shəs·lē) *adv.:* in a showy way. *Peter held his coat ostentatiously to pretend he was hiding his cat there.*

appalled (ə·pôld′) v. used as adj.: horrified. *Dussel's alarming news was met with a moment of appalled silence.*

disgruntled (dis·grunt′'ld) v. used as adj.: displeased; annoyed. *Dr. Dussel listened, disgruntled, to the conversation.*

inarticulate (in′är·tik′yoo·lit) adj.: unable to speak. *Peter was so furious at Dussel that he became inarticulate.*

forlorn (fôr·lôrn′) adj.: abandoned and lonely. *Dussel felt forlorn when Peter and Anne both closed their doors on him.*

animation (an′i·mā′shen) n.: liveliness. *Anne's animation could both delight and annoy her family.*

remorse (ri·môrs′) n.: deep feeling of guilt. *Mrs. Frank felt remorse for her angry outburst.*

Background
A True Story

❝ I hope I shall be able to confide in you completely, as I have never been able to do in anyone before, and I hope that you will be a great support and comfort to me. ❞

So begins the diary of a thirteen-year-old Jewish girl named Anne Frank. Anne's diary opens in 1942 with stories of boyfriends, parties, and school life. It closes two years later, just days before Anne is captured and imprisoned in a Nazi concentration camp.

Anne Frank was born in Frankfurt, Germany, in 1929. When she was four years old, her family immigrated to Amsterdam, the Netherlands, to escape the anti-Jewish measures being introduced in Germany. In Amsterdam, Otto Frank, Anne's father, managed a company that sold pectin, a substance used in making jams and jellies. Anne and her older sister, Margot, enjoyed a happy, carefree childhood until May 1940, when the Netherlands capitulated (surrendered) to the invading German army. Anne wrote in her diary about the Nazi occupation that followed:

❝ After May 1940, good times rapidly fled: first the war, then the capitulation, followed by the arrival of the Germans, which is when the sufferings of us Jews really began. Anti-Jewish decrees followed each other in quick succession. Jews must wear a yellow star, Jews must hand in their bicycles, Jews are banned from trains and are forbidden to drive. Jews are only allowed to do their shopping between three and five o'clock and then only in shops which bear the placard 'Jewish shop.' Jews must be indoors by eight o'clock and cannot even sit in their own gardens after that hour. Jews are forbidden to visit theaters, cinemas, and other places of entertainment. Jews may not take part in public sports. Swimming baths, tennis courts, hockey fields, and other sports grounds are all prohibited to them. Jews may not visit Christians. Jews must go to Jewish schools, and many more restrictions of a similar kind.

So we could not do this and were forbidden to do that. But life went on in spite of it all. ❞

Soon, however, the situation in the Netherlands grew much worse. As in other German-occupied countries, the Nazis began rounding up Jews and transporting them to concentration camps and death camps, where prisoners died from overwork, starvation, or disease or were murdered in gas chambers. Escaping Nazi-occupied territory became nearly impossible.

Europe Before World War II

See also the maps on page 293.

Like many other Jews trapped in Europe at the time, Anne and her family went into hiding to avoid capture. Others were not so lucky, as Anne knew:

❝ Countless friends and acquaintances have gone to a terrible fate. Evening after evening the green and gray army lorries [trucks] trundle past. The Germans ring at every front door to inquire if there are any Jews living in the house. If there are, then the whole family has to go at once. If they don't find any, they go on to the next house. No one has a chance of evading them unless one goes into hiding. Often they go around with lists and only ring when they know they can get a good haul. Sometimes they let them off for cash—so much per head. It seems like the slave hunts of olden times. . . . In the evenings when it's dark, I often see rows of good, innocent people accompanied by crying children, walking on and on, in the charge of a couple of these chaps,

bullied and knocked about until they almost drop. No one is spared—old people, babies, expectant mothers, the sick—each and all join in the march of death. ❞

The Frank family and four other Jews lived for more than two years hidden in a few cramped rooms (now known as the Secret Annex) behind Mr. Frank's office and warehouse. In August 1944, the Nazi police raided their hiding place and sent all eight of its occupants to concentration camps. Of the eight, only Otto Frank survived. Anne died of typhus in a camp in Germany called Bergen-Belsen. She was fifteen years old.

When she began her diary, Anne didn't intend to show it to anyone unless she found a "real friend." Through its dozens of translations and the stage adaptation you are about to read, Anne's diary has found her generations of friends all over the world.

ANNE FRANK'S LIFE		WORLD EVENTS
June 12: Anne Frank is born in Frankfurt, Germany.	**1929**	

Anne in 1933.

The Franks decide to leave Germany to escape Nazi persecution. While Mr. Frank looks for a new home in Amsterdam, the Netherlands, the rest of the family stays with relatives in Aachen, Germany.	**1930 to 1932**	The National Socialist German Workers' (Nazi) party begins its rise to power. The Nazis proclaim the superiority of the German "master race" and blame Jews for the German defeat in World War I and for the troubled economy.
	1933	**January 30:** The Nazi party leader, Adolf Hitler, becomes chancellor (head of the government) of Germany.

March 10: The first concentration camp is established by the Nazis, at Dachau, Germany.

April: The Nazis pass their first anti-Jewish law, banning the public employment of Jews.

Adolf Hitler.

1934	
1935	**September 15:** The Nuremberg Laws are passed, denying Jews German citizenship and forbidding marriage between Jews and non-Jews.

Anne with her father at Miep Santrouschitz and Jan Gies's wedding.

1936	**October 25:** Germany and Italy form an alliance (the Axis).

Summer: The Van Pels family (called the Van Daans in Anne's diary) flee Germany for the Netherlands.	**1937**	
December 8: Fritz Pfeffer (called Albert Dussel in Anne's diary) flees Germany for the Netherlands.	**1938**	**March 12–13:** The German army invades and annexes Austria.

September 29–30: The Munich Agreement, granting Germany the right to annex part of Czechoslovakia, is drafted and signed by representatives of France, Great Britain, Italy, and Germany.

November 9–10: Kristallnacht (Night of the Broken Glass). Led by the SS, the Nazi special police, Germans beat and kill Jews, loot Jewish stores, and burn synagogues.

Anne playing with her friend Sanne Ledermann in Amsterdam.

The Granger Collection, New York.

ANNE FRANK'S LIFE

Anne, second from left, with friends on her tenth birthday.

The Granger Collection, New York.

June 12: Anne receives a diary for her thirteenth birthday.

July 6: The Franks go into hiding after Margot receives an order to appear for deportation to a labor camp in Germany. The Van Pels family joins them one week later.

November 16: Fritz Pfeffer becomes the eighth occupant of the Secret Annex.

August 4: Nazi police raid the Secret Annex; the occupants are sent to concentration camps.

September: Mr. Van Pels dies in Auschwitz.

December 20: Fritz Pfeffer dies in Neuengamme.

Anne's mother, Edith Frank, dies in Auschwitz. Three weeks later Otto Frank is freed when Auschwitz is liberated by the Soviet army. Anne and Margot die in Bergen-Belsen a few weeks before British soldiers liberate the camp. Peter Van Pels dies in Mauthausen. Mrs. Van Pels dies in Theresienstadt.

WORLD EVENTS

1939

March: Germany invades and occupies most of Czechoslovakia.

September 1: Germany invades Poland. France and Great Britain declare war on Germany two days later.

1940

Spring: Germany invades Denmark, Norway, the Netherlands, Belgium, Luxembourg, and France.

September 27: Japan joins the Axis.

1941

June 22: Germany invades the Soviet Union.

December: The United States enters the war on the side of the Allied nations (including Great Britain, the Soviet Union, and other countries) after Japan attacks the U.S. naval base at Pearl Harbor.

1942

January: The "Final Solution" is secretly announced at a conference of Nazi officials: Europe's Jews are to be "exterminated," or murdered. Construction of death camps, equipped with gas chambers and huge incinerators for mass killing and cremation, begins in Poland. Millions of people (Jews and non-Jews) will die in those camps.

1943

1944

June 6: D-day. Allied forces land in Normandy, in northern France, and launch an invasion of western Europe.

Bombing of Hiroshima.

1945

May 8: The war in Europe ends with Germany's unconditional surrender to the Allies.

August 14: Japan surrenders after the United States drops atomic bombs on the Japanese cities of Hiroshima and Nagasaki.

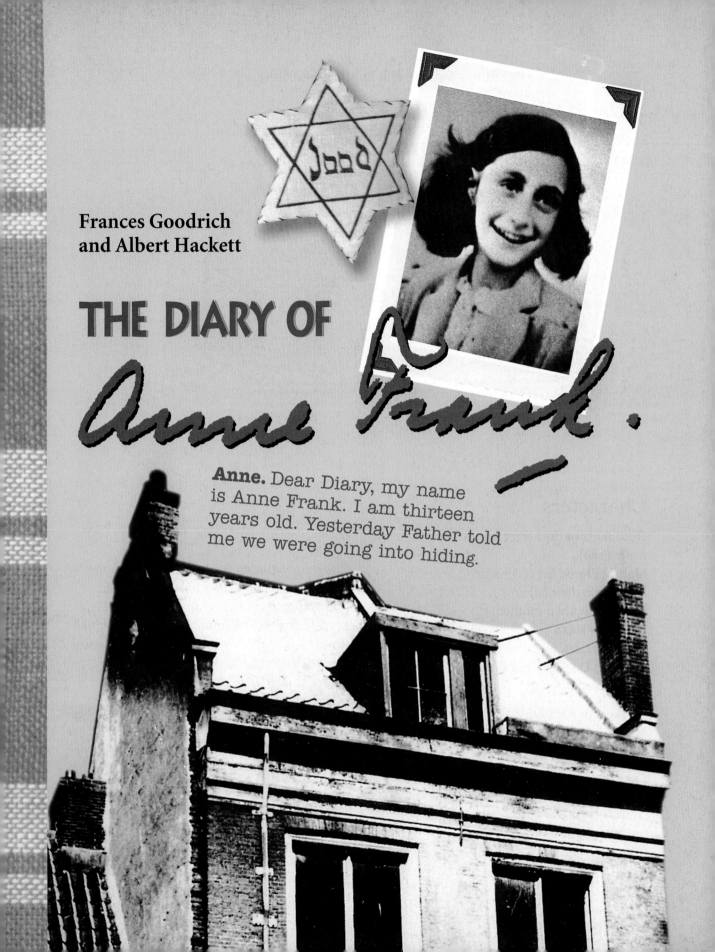

**Frances Goodrich
and Albert Hackett**

THE DIARY OF

Anne Frank.

Anne. Dear Diary, my name is Anne Frank. I am thirteen years old. Yesterday Father told me we were going into hiding.

Stage Set for *The Diary of Anne Frank*

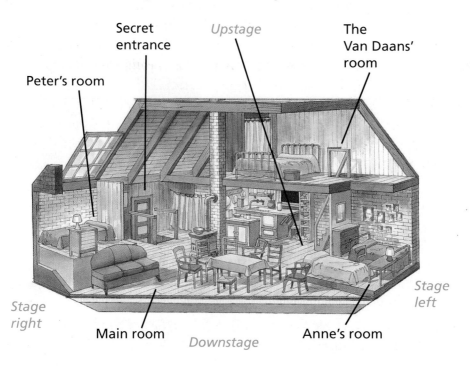

Secret entrance

Upstage

The Van Daans' room

Peter's room

Stage right

Stage left

Main room

Downstage

Anne's room

Characters

Occupants of the Secret Annex:
Anne Frank
Margot Frank, her older sister
Mr. Frank, their father
Mrs. Frank, their mother
Peter Van Daan
Mr. Van Daan, his father
Mrs. Van Daan, his mother
Mr. Dussel, a dentist

Workers in Mr. Frank's Business:
Miep Gies,[1] a young Dutchwoman
Mr. Kraler,[2] a Dutchman

Setting: Amsterdam, the Netherlands, July 1942 to August 1944; November 1945.

1. **Miep Gies** (mēp khēs).
2. **Kraler** (krä**'**lər).

Act One

■ SCENE 1

The scene remains the same throughout the play. It is the top floor of a warehouse and office building in Amsterdam, Holland. The sharply peaked roof of the building is outlined against a sea of other rooftops stretching away into the distance. Nearby is the belfry of a church tower, the Westertoren, whose carillon[3] rings out the hours. Occasionally faint sounds float up from below: the voices of children playing in the street, the tramp of marching feet, a boat whistle from the canal.[4]

3. **carillon** (kar**'**ə·län**'**) *n.:* set of bells, each of which produces a single tone.
4. **canal** *n.:* artificial waterway. Amsterdam, which was built on soggy ground, has more than one hundred canals, built to help drain the land. The canals are used like streets.

The three rooms of the top floor and a small attic space above are exposed to our view. The largest of the rooms is in the center, with two small rooms, slightly raised, on either side. On the right is a bathroom, out of sight. A narrow, steep flight of stairs at the back leads up to the attic. The rooms are sparsely furnished, with a few chairs, cots, a table or two. The windows are painted over or covered with makeshift blackout curtains. In the main room there is a sink, a gas ring for cooking, and a wood-burning stove for warmth.

The room on the left is hardly more than a closet. There is a skylight in the sloping ceiling. Directly under this room is a small, steep stairwell, with steps leading down to a door. This is the only entrance from the building below. When the door is opened, we see that it has been concealed on the outer side by a bookcase attached to it.

The curtain rises on an empty stage. It is late afternoon, November 1945.

The rooms are dusty, the curtains in rags. Chairs and tables are overturned.

The door at the foot of the small stairwell swings open. MR. FRANK *comes up the steps into view. He is a gentle, cultured European in his middle years. There is still a trace of a German accent in his speech.*

He stands looking slowly around, making a supreme effort at self-control. He is weak, ill. His clothes are threadbare.

After a second he drops his rucksack on the couch and moves slowly about. He opens the door to one of the smaller rooms and then abruptly closes it again, turning away. He goes to the window at the back, looking off at the Westertoren as its carillon strikes the hour of six; then he moves restlessly on.

From the street below we hear the sound of a barrel organ and children's voices at play.

There is a many-colored scarf hanging from a nail. MR. FRANK *takes it, putting it around his neck. As he starts back for his rucksack, his eye is caught by something lying on the floor. It is a woman's white glove. He holds it in his hand and suddenly all of his self-control is gone. He breaks down crying.*

We hear footsteps on the stairs. MIEP GIES *comes up, looking for* MR. FRANK. MIEP *is a Dutchwoman of about twenty-two. She wears a coat and hat, ready to go home. She is pregnant. Her attitude toward* MR. FRANK *is protective, compassionate.*

Miep. Are you all right, Mr. Frank?

Mr. Frank (*quickly controlling himself*). Yes, Miep, yes.

Miep. Everyone in the office has gone home . . . It's after six. (*Then, pleading*) Don't stay up here, Mr. Frank. What's the use of torturing yourself like this?

Mr. Frank. I've come to say goodbye . . . I'm leaving here, Miep.

Miep. What do you mean? Where are you going? Where?

Mr. Frank. I don't know yet. I haven't decided.

Miep. Mr. Frank, you can't leave here! This is your home! Amsterdam is your home. Your business is here, waiting for you. . . . You're needed here. . . . Now that the war is over, there are things that . . .

Mr. Frank. I can't stay in Amsterdam, Miep. It has too many memories for me. Everywhere, there's something . . . the house we lived in . . . the school . . . that street organ playing out there . . . I'm not the person you used to know, Miep. I'm a bitter old man. (*Breaking off*) Forgive me. I shouldn't speak to you like this . . . after all that you did for us . . . the suffering . . .

Miep. No. No. It wasn't suffering. You can't say we suffered. (*As she speaks, she straightens a chair which is overturned.*)

Mr. Frank. I know what you went through, you and Mr. Kraler. I'll remember it as long as I live. (*He gives one last look around.*) Come, Miep. (*He starts for the steps, then remembers his rucksack, going back to get it.*)

Miep (*hurrying up to a cupboard*). Mr. Frank, did you see? There are some of your papers here. (*She brings a bundle of papers to him.*) We found them in a heap of rubbish on the floor after . . . after you left.

Mr. Frank. Burn them. (*He opens his rucksack to put the glove in it.*)

Miep. But, Mr. Frank, there are letters, notes . . .

Mr. Frank. Burn them. All of them.

Miep. Burn *this*? (*She hands him a paperbound notebook.*)

Mr. Frank (*quietly*). Anne's diary. (*He opens the diary and begins to read.*) "Monday, the sixth of July, nineteen forty-two." (*To* MIEP) Nineteen forty-two. Is it possible, Miep? . . . Only three years ago. (*As he continues his reading, he sits down on the couch.*) "Dear Diary, since you and I are going to be great friends, I will start by telling you about myself. My name is Anne Frank. I am thirteen years old. I was born in Germany the twelfth of June, nineteen twenty-nine. As my family is Jewish, we emigrated to Holland when Hitler came to power."

[*As* MR. FRANK *reads on, another voice joins his, as if coming from the air. It is* ANNE'*s voice.*]

Mr. Frank and Anne's Voice. "My father

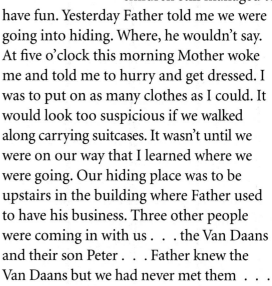
Miep Gies and Otto Frank.

started a business, importing spice and herbs. Things went well for us until nineteen forty. Then the war came, and the Dutch capitulation, followed by the arrival of the Germans. Then things got very bad for the Jews."

[MR. FRANK'*s voice dies out.* ANNE'*s voice continues alone. The lights dim slowly to darkness. The curtain falls on the scene.*]

Anne's Voice. You could not do this and you could not do that. They forced Father out of his business. We had to wear yellow stars.[5] I had to turn in my bike. I couldn't go to a Dutch school anymore. I couldn't go to the movies or ride in an automobile or even on a streetcar, and a million other things. But somehow we children still managed to have fun. Yesterday Father told me we were going into hiding. Where, he wouldn't say. At five o'clock this morning Mother woke me and told me to hurry and get dressed. I was to put on as many clothes as I could. It would look too suspicious if we walked along carrying suitcases. It wasn't until we were on our way that I learned where we were going. Our hiding place was to be upstairs in the building where Father used to have his business. Three other people were coming in with us . . . the Van Daans and their son Peter . . . Father knew the Van Daans but we had never met them . . .

---

5. yellow stars: The Nazis ordered all Jews to sew a large Star of David (a six-pointed star) on their outer clothing so that they could be easily recognized as Jews.

[*During the last lines the curtain rises on the scene. The lights dim on.* ANNE's *voice fades out.*]

■ SCENE 2

It is early morning, July 1942. The rooms are bare, as before, but they are now clean and orderly.

MR. VAN DAAN, *a tall, portly man in his late forties, is in the main room, pacing up and down, nervously smoking a cigarette. His clothes and overcoat are expensive and well cut.*

MRS. VAN DAAN *sits on the couch, clutching her possessions: a hatbox, bags, etc. She is a pretty woman in her early forties. She wears a fur coat over her other clothes.*

PETER VAN DAAN *is standing at the window of the room on the right, looking down at the street below. He is a shy, awkward boy of sixteen. He wears a cap, a raincoat, and long Dutch trousers, like plus fours.[6] At his feet is a black case, a carrier for his cat.*

The yellow Star of David is <u>conspicuous</u> on all of their clothes.

Mrs. Van Daan (*rising, nervous, excited*). Something's happened to them! I know it!

Mr. Van Daan. Now, Kerli!

Mrs. Van Daan. Mr. Frank said they'd be here at seven o'clock. He said . . .

Mr. Van Daan. They have two miles to walk. You can't expect . . .

Mrs. Van Daan. They've been picked up. That's what's happened. They've been taken . . .

[MR. VAN DAAN *indicates that he hears someone coming.*]

Mr. Van Daan. You see?

---

6. **plus fours** *n.:* baggy trousers that end in cuffs just below the knees.

[PETER *takes up his carrier and his school bag, etc., and goes into the main room as* MR. FRANK *comes up the stairwell from below.* MR. FRANK *looks much younger now. His movements are brisk, his manner confident. He wears an overcoat and carries his hat and a small cardboard box. He crosses to the* VAN DAANS, *shaking hands with each of them.*]

Mr. Frank. Mrs. Van Daan, Mr. Van Daan, Peter. (*Then, in explanation of their lateness*) There were too many of the Green Police[7] on the streets . . . we had to take the long way around.

[*Up the steps come* MARGOT FRANK, MRS. FRANK, MIEP (*not pregnant now*), *and* MR. KRALER. *All of them carry bags, packages, and so forth. The Star of David is conspicuous on all of the* FRANKS' *clothing.* MARGOT *is eighteen, beautiful, quiet, shy.* MRS. FRANK *is a young mother, gently bred, reserved. She, like* MR. FRANK, *has a slight German accent.* MR. KRALER *is a Dutchman, dependable, kindly.*

As MR. KRALER *and* MIEP *go upstage to put down their parcels,* MRS. FRANK *turns back to call* ANNE.]

Mrs. Frank. Anne?

[ANNE *comes running up the stairs. She is thirteen, quick in her movements, interested in everything, mercurial[8] in her emotions. She wears a cape and long wool socks and carries a school bag.*]

---

7. **Green Police:** Nazi police, who wore green uniforms.
8. **mercurial** (mər·kyoor′ē·əl) *adj.:* changeable.

Vocabulary
conspicuous (kən·spik′yoo·əs) *adj.:* obvious; noticeable.

Scene from the movie *The Diary of Anne Frank* (1959), starring Millie Perkins as Anne. Other scenes from the movie appear throughout the play.

Mr. Frank (*introducing them*). My wife, Edith. Mr. and Mrs. Van Daan (MRS. FRANK *hurries over, shaking hands with them.*) . . . their son, Peter . . . my daughters, Margot and Anne.

[ANNE *gives a polite little curtsy as she shakes* MR. VAN DAAN's *hand. Then she immediately starts off on a tour of investigation of her new home, going upstairs to the attic room.*

MIEP *and* MR. KRALER *are putting the various things they have brought on the shelves.*]

Mr. Kraler. I'm sorry there is still so much confusion.
Mr. Frank. Please. Don't think of it. After all, we'll have plenty of leisure to arrange everything ourselves.
Miep (*to* MRS. FRANK). We put the stores of food you sent in here. Your drugs are here . . . soap, linen here.

Mrs. Frank. Thank you, Miep.
Miep. I made up the beds . . . the way Mr. Frank and Mr. Kraler said. (*She starts out.*) Forgive me. I have to hurry. I've got to go to the other side of town to get some ration books[9] for you.
Mrs. Van Daan. Ration books? If they see our names on ration books, they'll know we're here.
Mr. Kraler. There isn't anything . . .
Miep. Don't worry. Your names won't be on them. (*As she hurries out*) I'll be up later. } *Together*
Mr. Frank. Thank you, Miep.
Mrs. Frank (*to* MR. KRALER). It's illegal, then, the ration books? We've never done anything illegal.

---

9. **ration books:** books of stamps or coupons issued by the government during wartime. People could purchase scarce items, such as food, clothing, and gasoline, only with these coupons.

Mr. Frank. We won't be living here exactly according to regulations.

[*As* MR. KRALER *reassures* MRS. FRANK, *he takes various small things, such as matches and soap, from his pockets, handing them to her.*]

Mr. Kraler. This isn't the black market,[10] Mrs. Frank. This is what we call the white market . . . helping all of the hundreds and hundreds who are hiding out in Amsterdam.

[*The carillon is heard playing the quarter-hour before eight.* MR. KRALER *looks at his watch.* ANNE *stops at the window as she comes down the stairs.*]

Anne. It's the Westertoren!

Mr. Kraler. I must go. I must be out of here and downstairs in the office before the workmen get here. (*He starts for the stairs leading out.*) Miep or I, or both of us, will be up each day to bring you food and news and find out what your needs are. Tomorrow I'll get you a better bolt for the door at the foot of the stairs. It needs a bolt that you can throw yourself and open only at our signal. (*To* MR. FRANK) Oh . . . You'll tell them about the noise?

Mr. Frank. I'll tell them.

Mr. Kraler. Goodbye, then, for the moment. I'll come up again, after the workmen leave.

Mr. Frank. Goodbye, Mr. Kraler.

Mrs. Frank (*shaking his hand*). How can we thank you?

[*The others murmur their goodbyes.*]

Mr. Kraler. I never thought I'd live to see the day when a man like Mr. Frank would

---

10. **black market** *n.:* place or system for buying and selling goods illegally, without ration stamps.

have to go into hiding. When you think—

[*He breaks off, going out.* MR. FRANK *follows him down the steps, bolting the door after him. In the interval before he returns,* PETER *goes over to* MARGOT, *shaking hands with her. As* MR. FRANK *comes back up the steps,* MRS. FRANK *questions him anxiously.*]

Mrs. Frank. What did he mean, about the noise?

Mr. Frank. First let us take off some of these clothes.

[*They all start to take off garment after garment. On each of their coats, sweaters, blouses, suits, dresses is another yellow Star of David.* MR. *and* MRS. FRANK *are under-dressed quite simply. The others wear several things: sweaters, extra dresses, bathrobes, aprons, nightgowns, etc.*]

Mr. Van Daan. It's a wonder we weren't arrested, walking along the streets . . . Petronella with a fur coat in July . . . and that cat of Peter's crying all the way.

Anne (*as she is removing a pair of panties*). A cat?

Mrs. Frank (*shocked*). Anne, please!

Anne. It's all right. I've got on three more.

[*She pulls off two more. Finally, as they have all removed their surplus clothes, they look to* MR. FRANK, *waiting for him to speak.*]

Mr. Frank. Now. About the noise. While the men are in the building below, we must have complete quiet. Every sound can be heard down there, not only in the work-rooms but in the offices too. The men come at about eight-thirty and leave at about five-thirty. So, to be perfectly safe, from eight in the morning until six in the evening we must move only when it is necessary, and then in stockinged feet. We must not speak above a whisper. We must not run any water. We cannot use the sink or even, forgive me, the w.c.[11] The pipes go down through the workrooms. It would be heard. No trash . . . (MR. FRANK *stops abruptly as he hears the sound of marching feet from the street below. Everyone is motionless, paralyzed with fear.* MR. FRANK *goes quietly into the room on the right to look down out of the window.* ANNE *runs after him, peering out with him. The tramping feet pass without stopping. The tension is relieved.* MR. FRANK, *followed by* ANNE, *returns to the main room and resumes his instructions to the group.*) . . . No trash must ever be thrown out which might reveal that someone is living up here . . . not even a potato paring. We must burn everything in the stove at night. This is the way we must live until it is over, if we are to survive.

[*There is silence for a second.*]

Mrs. Frank. Until it is over.

Mr. Frank (*reassuringly*). After six we can move about . . . we can talk and laugh and have our supper and read and play games . . . just as we would at home. (*He looks at his watch.*) And now I think it would be wise if we all went to our rooms, and we settled before eight o'clock. Mrs. Van Daan, you and your husband will be upstairs. I regret that there's no room for Peter. But he will be here, near us. This will be our common room, where we'll meet to talk and eat and read like one family.

Mr. Van Daan. And where do you and Mrs. Frank sleep?

Mr. Frank. This room is also our bedroom.

Mrs. Van Daan. That isn't right. We'll sleep here and you take the room upstairs. } *Together*

Mr. Van Daan. It's your place.

Mr. Frank. Please. I've thought this out for weeks. It's the best arrangement. The only arrangement.

Mrs. Van Daan (*to* MR. FRANK). Never, never can we thank you. (*Then, to* MRS. FRANK) I don't know what would have happened to us, if it hadn't been for Mr. Frank.

Mr. Frank. You don't know how your husband helped me when I came to this country . . . knowing no one . . . not able to speak the language. I can never repay him for that. (*Going to* MR. VAN DAAN) May I help you with your things?

Mr. Van Daan. No. No. (*To* MRS. VAN DAAN) Come along, liefje.[12]

Mrs. Van Daan. You'll be all right, Peter? You're not afraid?

Peter (*embarrassed*). Please, Mother.

[*They start up the stairs to the attic room above.* MR. FRANK *turns to* MRS. FRANK.]

Mr. Frank. You too must have some rest, Edith. You didn't close your eyes last night. Nor you, Margot.

Anne. I slept, Father. Wasn't that funny? I knew it was the last night in my own bed, and yet I slept soundly.

Mr. Frank. I'm glad, Anne. Now you'll be able to help me straighten things in here. (*To* MRS. FRANK *and* MARGOT) Come with me. . . . You and Margot rest in this room for the time being. (*He picks up their clothes, starting for the room on the right.*)

Mrs. Frank. You're sure . . . ? I could help

---

11. **w.c.:** short for "water closet," or toilet.

12. **liefje** (lēf'hyə): Dutch for "little dear one."

. . .And Anne hasn't had her milk . . .

Mr. Frank. I'll give it to her. (*To* ANNE *and* PETER) Anne, Peter . . .it's best that you take off your shoes now, before you forget. (*He leads the way to the room, followed by* MARGOT.)

Mrs. Frank. You're sure you're not tired, Anne?

Anne. I feel fine. I'm going to help Father.

Mrs. Frank. Peter, I'm glad you are to be with us.

Peter. Yes, Mrs. Frank.

[MRS. FRANK *goes to join* MR. FRANK *and* MARGOT.

During the following scene MR. FRANK *helps* MARGOT *and* MRS. FRANK *to hang up their clothes. Then he persuades them both to lie down and rest. The* VAN DAANS, *in their room above, settle themselves. In the main room* ANNE *and* PETER *remove their shoes.* PETER *takes his cat out of the carrier.*]

Anne. What's your cat's name?

Peter. Mouschi.[13]

Anne. Mouschi! Mouschi! Mouschi! (*She picks up the cat, walking away with it. To* PETER) I love cats. I have one . . .a darling little cat. But they made me leave her behind. I left some food and a note for the neighbors to take care of her . . . I'm going to miss her terribly. What is yours? A him or a her?

Peter. He's a tom. He doesn't like strangers. (*He takes the cat from her, putting it back in its carrier.*)

Anne (*unabashed*). Then I'll have to stop being a stranger, won't I? Is he fixed?

Peter (*startled*). Huh?

Anne. Did you have him fixed?

Peter. No.

Anne. I love cats. I have one . . .

Anne. Oh, you ought to have him fixed—to keep him from—you know, fighting. Where did you go to school?

Peter. Jewish Secondary.

Anne. But that's where Margot and I go! I never saw you around.

Peter. I used to see you . . . sometimes . . .

Anne. You did?

Peter. . . . in the schoolyard. You were always in the middle of a bunch of kids. (*He takes a penknife from his pocket.*)

Anne. Why didn't you ever come over?

Peter. I'm sort of a lone wolf. (*He starts to rip off his Star of David.*)

Vocabulary
unabashed (un′ə·basht′) *adj.:* unembarrassed; unashamed.

---

13. **Mouschi** (mōō′shē).

Anne. What are you doing?
Peter. Taking it off.
Anne. But you can't do that. They'll arrest you if you go out without your star.

[*He tosses his knife on the table.*]

Peter. Who's going out?
Anne. Why, of course! You're right! Of course we don't need them anymore. (*She picks up his knife and starts to take her star off.*) I wonder what our friends will think when we don't show up today?
Peter. I didn't have any dates with anyone.
Anne. Oh, I did. I had a date with Jopie to go and play ping-pong at her house. Do you know Jopie de Waal?[14]
Peter. No.
Anne. Jopie's my best friend. I wonder what she'll think when she telephones and there's no answer? . . . Probably she'll go over to the house. . . . I wonder what she'll think . . . we left everything as if we'd suddenly been called away . . . breakfast dishes in the sink . . . beds not made . . . (*As she pulls off her star, the cloth underneath shows clearly the color and form of the star.*) Look! It's still there! (PETER *goes over to the stove with his star.*) What're you going to do with yours?
Peter. Burn it.
Anne (*she starts to throw hers in, and cannot*). It's funny, I can't throw mine away. I don't know why.

Peter Van Pels
("Peter Van Daan").

Peter. You can't throw . . . ? Something they branded you with . . . ? That they made you wear so they could spit on you?

Anne. I know. I know. But after all, it *is* the Star of David, isn't it?

[*In the bedroom, right,* MARGOT *and* MRS. FRANK *are lying down.* MR. FRANK *starts quietly out.*]

Peter. Maybe it's different for a girl.

[MR. FRANK *comes into the main room.*]

Mr. Frank. Forgive me, Peter. Now let me see. We must find a bed for your cat. (*He goes to a cupboard.*) I'm glad you brought your cat. Anne was feeling so badly about hers. (*Getting a used small washtub*) Here we are. Will it be comfortable in that?
Peter (*gathering up his things*). Thanks.
Mr. Frank (*opening the door of the room on the left*). And here is your room. But I warn you, Peter, you can't grow anymore. Not an inch, or you'll have to sleep with your feet out of the skylight. Are you hungry?
Peter. No.
Mr. Frank. We have some bread and butter.
Peter. No, thank you.
Mr. Frank. You can have it for luncheon then. And tonight we will have a real supper . . . our first supper together.
Peter. Thanks. Thanks. (*He goes into his room. During the following scene he arranges his possessions in his new room.*)
Mr. Frank. That's a nice boy, Peter.
Anne. He's awfully shy, isn't he?

---

14. **Jopie de Waal** (yō′pē də väl′).

Mr. Frank. You'll like him, I know.

Anne. I certainly hope so, since he's the only boy I'm likely to see for months and months.

[MR. FRANK *sits down, taking off his shoes.*]

Mr. Frank. Annele,[15] there's a box there. Will you open it?

[*He indicates a carton on the couch.* ANNE *brings it to the center table. In the street below, there is the sound of children playing.*]

Anne (*as she opens the carton*). You know the way I'm going to think of it here? I'm going to think of it as a boardinghouse. A very peculiar summer boardinghouse, like the one that we—(*She breaks off as she pulls out some photographs.*) Father! My movie stars! I was wondering where they were! I was looking for them this morning . . . and Queen Wilhelmina![16] How wonderful!

Mr. Frank. There's something more. Go on. Look further. (*He goes over to the sink, pouring a glass of milk from a thermos bottle.*)

Anne (*pulling out a pasteboard-bound book*). A diary! (*She throws her arms around her father.*) I've never had a diary. And I've always longed for one. (*She looks around the room.*) Pencil, pencil, pencil, pencil. (*She starts down the stairs.*) I'm going down to the office to get a pencil.

Mr. Frank. Anne! No! (*He goes after her, catching her by the arm and pulling her back.*)

Anne (*startled*). But there's no one in the building now.

Mr. Frank. It doesn't matter. I don't want you ever to go beyond that door.

Anne (*sobered*). Never . . .? Not even at nighttime, when everyone is gone? Or on Sundays? Can't I go down to listen to the radio?

Mr. Frank. Never. I am sorry, Anneke.[17] It isn't safe. No, you must never go beyond that door.

[*For the first time* ANNE *realizes what "going into hiding" means.*]

Anne. I see.

Mr. Frank. It'll be hard, I know. But always remember this, Anneke. There are no walls, there are no bolts, no locks that anyone can put on your mind. Miep will bring us books. We will read history, poetry, mythology. (*He gives her the glass of milk.*) Here's your milk. (*With his arm about her, they go over to the couch, sitting down side by side.*) As a matter of fact, between us, Anne, being here has certain advantages for you. For instance, you remember the battle you had with your mother the other day on the subject of overshoes? You said you'd rather die than wear overshoes? But in the end you had to wear them? Well now, you see, for as long as we are here, you will never have to wear overshoes! Isn't that good? And the coat that you inherited from Margot, you won't have to wear that anymore. And the piano! You won't have to practice on the piano. I tell you, this is going to be a fine life for you!

[ANNE's *panic is gone.* PETER *appears in the doorway of his room, with a saucer in his hand. He is carrying his cat.*]

Peter. I . . . I . . . I thought I'd better get some water for Mouschi before . . .

---

15. **Annele** (än'ə·lə): Yiddish for "little Anne" (like "Annie").
16. **Queen Wilhelmina** (vil'hel·mē'nä) (1880–1962): queen of the Netherlands from 1890 to 1948.
17. **Anneke** (än'ə·kə): another affectionate nickname for Anne.

Anne. I've never had a diary. And I've always longed for one.

Mr. Frank. Of course.

[*As he starts toward the sink, the carillon begins to chime the hour of eight. He tiptoes to the window at the back and looks down at the street below. He turns to* PETER, *indicating in pantomime that it is too late.* PETER *starts back for his room. He steps on a creaking board. The three of them are frozen for a minute in fear. As* PETER *starts away again,* ANNE *tiptoes over to him and pours some of the milk from her glass into the saucer for the cat.* PETER *squats on the floor, putting the milk before the cat.* MR. FRANK *gives* ANNE *his fountain pen and then goes into the room at the right. For a second* ANNE *watches the cat; then she goes over to the center table and opens her diary.*

In the room at the right, MRS. FRANK *has sat up quickly at the sound of the carillon.* MR. FRANK *comes in and sits down beside her on the settee,[18] his arm comfortingly around her.*

---

18. **settee** (se·tē′) *n.:* small couch.

Upstairs, in the attic room, MR. *and* MRS. VAN DAAN *have hung their clothes in the closet and are now seated on the iron bed.* MRS. VAN DAAN *leans back, exhausted.* MR. VAN DAAN *fans her with a newspaper.*

ANNE starts to write in her diary. The lights dim out; the curtain falls.

In the darkness ANNE's *voice comes to us again, faintly at first and then with growing strength.]*

Anne's Voice. I expect I should be describing what it feels like to go into hiding. But I really don't know yet myself. I only know it's funny never to be able to go outdoors . . . never to breathe fresh air . . . never to run and shout and jump. It's the silence in the nights that frightens me most. Every time I hear a creak in the house or a step on the street outside, I'm sure they're coming for us. The days aren't so bad. At least we know that Miep and Mr. Kraler are down there below us in the office. Our protectors, we call them. I asked Father what would happen to them if the Nazis found out they were hiding us. Pim[19] said that they would suffer the same fate that we would. . . . Imagine! They know this, and yet when they come up here, they're always cheerful and gay, as if there were nothing in the world to bother them. . . . Friday, the twenty-first of August, nineteen forty-two. Today I'm going to tell you our general news. Mother is unbearable. She insists on treating me like a baby, which I loathe. Otherwise things are going better. The weather is . . .

[*As* ANNE's *voice is fading out, the curtain rises on the scene.*]

---

19. **Pim:** family nickname for Mr. Frank.

◼ SCENE 3

It is a little after six o'clock in the evening, two months later.

MARGOT *is in the bedroom at the right, studying.* MR. VAN DAAN *is lying down in the attic room above.*

The rest of the "family" is in the main room. ANNE *and* PETER *sit opposite each other at the center table, where they have been doing their lessons.* MRS. FRANK *is on the couch.* MRS. VAN DAAN *is seated with her fur coat, on which she has been sewing, in her lap. None of them are wearing their shoes.*

Their eyes are on MR. FRANK, *waiting for him to give them the signal which will release them from their day-long quiet.* MR. FRANK, *his shoes in his hand, stands looking down out of the window at the back, watching to be sure that all of the workmen have left the building below.*

After a few seconds of motionless silence, MR. FRANK *turns from the window.*

Mr. Frank (*quietly, to the group*). It's safe now. The last workman has left.

[*There is an immediate stir of relief.*]

Anne (*her pent-up energy explodes*). WHEE!
Mrs. Frank (*startled, amused*). Anne!
Mrs. Van Daan. I'm first for the w.c.

[*She hurries off to the bathroom.* MRS. FRANK *puts on her shoes and starts up to the sink to prepare supper.* ANNE *sneaks* PETER's *shoes from under the table and hides them behind her back.* MR. FRANK *goes into* MARGOT's *room.*]

Vocabulary
loathe (lōth) *v.*: hate.

Mr. Frank (*to* MARGOT). Six o'clock. School's over.

[MARGOT *gets up, stretching.* MR. FRANK *sits down to put on his shoes. In the main room* PETER *tries to find his.*]

Peter. (*to* ANNE). Have you seen my shoes?
Anne (*innocently*). Your shoes?
Peter. You've taken them, haven't you?
Anne. I don't know what you're talking about.
Peter. You're going to be sorry!
Anne. Am I?

[PETER *goes after her.* ANNE, *with his shoes in her hand, runs from him, dodging behind her mother.*]

Mrs. Frank (*protesting*). Anne, dear!
Peter. Wait till I get you!
Anne. I'm waiting! (PETER *makes a lunge for her. They both fall to the floor.* PETER *pins her down, wrestling with her to get the shoes.*) Don't! Don't! Peter, stop it. Ouch!
Mrs. Frank. Anne! . . . Peter!

[*Suddenly* PETER *becomes self-conscious. He grabs his shoes roughly and starts for his room.*]

Anne (*following him*). Peter, where are you going? Come dance with me.
Peter. I tell you I don't know how.
Anne. I'll teach you.
Peter. I'm going to give Mouschi his dinner.
Anne. Can I watch?
Peter. He doesn't like people around while he eats.
Anne. Peter, please.
Peter. No!

[*He goes into his room.* ANNE *slams his door after him.*]

Mrs. Frank. Anne, dear, I think you shouldn't play like that with Peter. It's not dignified.
Anne. Who cares if it's dignified? I don't want to be dignified.

[MR. FRANK *and* MARGOT *come from the room on the right.* MARGOT *goes to help her mother.* MR. FRANK *starts for the center table to correct* MARGOT'*s school papers.*]

Mrs. Frank (*to* ANNE). You complain that I don't treat you like a grown-up. But when I do, you resent it.
Anne. I only want some fun . . . someone to laugh and clown with . . . After you've sat still all day and hardly moved, you've got to have some fun. I don't know what's the matter with that boy.
Mr. Frank. He isn't used to girls. Give him a little time.
Anne. Time? Isn't two months time? I could cry. (*Catching hold of* MARGOT) Come on, Margot . . . dance with me. Come on, please.
Margot. I have to help with supper.
Anne. You know we're going to forget how to dance . . . When we get out, we won't remember a thing.

[*She starts to sing and dance by herself.* MR. FRANK *takes her in his arms, waltzing with her.* MRS. VAN DAAN *comes in from the bathroom.*]

Mrs. Van Daan. Next? (*She looks around as she starts putting on her shoes.*) Where's Peter?
Anne (*as they are dancing*). Where would he be!
Mrs. Van Daan. He hasn't finished his lessons, has he? His father'll kill him if he catches him in there with that cat and his work not done. (MR. FRANK *and* ANNE *finish their dance. They bow to each other with*

extravagant formality.) Anne, get him out of there, will you?

Anne (*at* PETER's *door*). Peter? Peter?

Peter (*opening the door a crack*). What is it?

Anne. Your mother says to come out.

Peter. I'm giving Mouschi his dinner.

Mrs. Van Daan. You know what your father says. (*She sits on the couch, sewing on the lining of her fur coat.*)

Peter. For heaven's sake, I haven't even looked at him since lunch.

Mrs. Van Daan. I'm just telling you, that's all.

Anne. I'll feed him.

Peter. I don't want you in there.

Mrs. Van Daan. Peter!

Peter (*to* ANNE). Then give him his dinner and come right out, you hear?

[*He comes back to the table.* ANNE *shuts the door of* PETER's *room after her and disappears behind the curtain covering his closet.*]

Mrs. Van Daan (*to* PETER). Now is that any way to talk to your little girlfriend?

Peter. Mother . . . for heaven's sake . . . will you please stop saying that?

Mrs. Van Daan. Look at him blush! Look at him!

Peter. Please! I'm not . . . anyway . . . let me alone, will you?

Mrs. Van Daan. He acts like it was something to be ashamed of. It's nothing to be ashamed of, to have a little girlfriend.

Peter. You're crazy. She's only thirteen.

Mrs. Van Daan. So what? And you're six-teen. Just perfect. Your father's ten years older than I am. (*To* MR. FRANK) I warn you, Mr. Frank, if this war lasts much longer, we're going to be related and then . . .

Mr. Frank. Mazel tov![20]

Mrs. Frank (*deliberately changing the conversation*). I wonder where Miep is. She's usually so prompt.

[*Suddenly everything else is forgotten as they hear the sound of an automobile coming to a screeching stop in the street below. They are tense, motionless in their terror. The car starts away. A wave of relief sweeps over them. They pick up their occupations again.* ANNE *flings open the door of* PETER's *room, making a dramatic entrance. She is dressed in* PETER's *clothes.* PETER *looks at her in fury. The others are amused.*]

Anne. Good evening, everyone. Forgive me if I don't stay. (*She jumps up on a chair.*) I have a friend waiting for me in there. My friend Tom. Tom Cat. Some people say that we look alike. But Tom has the most beautiful whiskers, and I have only a little fuzz. I am hoping . . . in time . . .

Peter. All right, Mrs. Quack Quack!

Anne (*outraged—jumping down*). Peter!

Peter. I heard about you . . . how you talked so much in class they called you Mrs. Quack Quack. How Mr. Smitter made you write a composition . . . "'Quack, quack,' said Mrs. Quack Quack."

Mrs. Van Pels ("Mrs. Van Daan").

---

20. **mazel tov** (mä′zəl tōv′): Yiddish expression meaning "congratulations."

Anne. Well, go on. Tell them the rest. How it was so good he read it out loud to the class and then read it to all his other classes!
Peter. Quack! Quack! Quack . . . Quack . . . Quack . . .

[ANNE *pulls off the coat and trousers.*]

Anne. You are the most intolerable, insufferable boy I've ever met!

[*She throws the clothes down the stairwell.* PETER *goes down after them.*]

Peter. Quack, quack, quack!
Mrs. Van Daan (*to* ANNE). That's right, Anneke! Give it to him!
Anne. With all the boys in the world . . . why I had to get locked up with one like you! . . .
Peter. Quack, quack, quack, and from now on stay out of my room!

[*As* PETER *passes her,* ANNE *puts out her foot, tripping him. He picks himself up and goes on into his room.*]

Mrs. Frank (*quietly*). Anne, dear . . . your hair. (*She feels* ANNE's *forehead.*) You're warm. Are you feeling all right?
Anne. Please, Mother. (*She goes over to the center table, slipping into her shoes.*)
Mrs. Frank (*following her*). You haven't a fever, have you?
Anne (*pulling away*). No. No.
Mrs. Frank. You know we can't call a doctor here, ever. There's only one thing to do . . . watch carefully. Prevent an illness before it comes. Let me see your tongue.
Anne. Mother, this is perfectly absurd.
Mrs. Frank. Anne, dear, don't be such a baby. Let me see your tongue. (*As* ANNE *refuses,* MRS. FRANK *appeals to* MR. FRANK.) Otto . . . ?

Mr. Frank. You hear your mother, Anne.

[ANNE *flicks out her tongue for a second, then turns away.*]

Mrs. Frank. Come on—open up! (*As* ANNE *opens her mouth very wide*) You seem all right . . . but perhaps an aspirin . . .
Mrs. Van Daan. For heaven's sake, don't give that child any pills. I waited for fifteen minutes this morning for her to come out of the w.c.
Anne. I was washing my hair!
Mr. Frank. I think there's nothing the matter with our Anne that a ride on her bike or a visit with her friend Jopie de Waal wouldn't cure. Isn't that so, Anne?

[MR. VAN DAAN *comes down into the room. From outside we hear faint sounds of bombers going over and a burst of ack-ack.*][21]

Mr. Van Daan. Miep not come yet?
Mrs. Van Daan. The workmen just left, a little while ago.
Mr. Van Daan. What's for dinner tonight?
Mrs. Van Daan. Beans.
Mr. Van Daan. Not again!
Mrs. Van Daan. Poor Putti! I know. But what can we do? That's all that Miep brought us.

[MR. VAN DAAN *starts to pace, his hands behind his back.* ANNE *follows behind him, imitating him.*]

Anne. We are now in what is known as the "bean cycle." Beans boiled, beans en casserole, beans with strings, beans without strings . . .

---

21. **ack-ack** *n.:* slang for "antiaircraft gunfire."

[PETER *has come out of his room. He slides into his place at the table, becoming immediately absorbed in his studies.*]

Mr. Van Daan (*to* PETER). I saw you . . . in there, playing with your cat.

Mrs. Van Daan. He just went in for a second, putting his coat away. He's been out here all the time, doing his lessons.

Mr. Frank (*looking up from the papers*). Anne, you got an "excellent" in your history paper today . . . and "very good" in Latin.

Anne (*sitting beside him*). How about algebra?

Mr. Frank. I'll have to make a confession. Up until now I've managed to stay ahead of you in algebra. Today you caught up with me. We'll leave it to Margot to correct.

Anne. Isn't algebra vile, Pim!

Mr. Frank. Vile!

Margot (*to* MR. FRANK). How did I do?

Anne (*getting up*). Excellent, excellent, excellent, excellent!

Mr. Frank (*to* MARGOT). You should have used the subjunctive here . . .

Margot. Should I? . . . I thought . . . look here . . . I didn't use it here . . .

[*The two become absorbed in the papers.*]

Anne. Mrs. Van Daan, may I try on your coat?

Mrs. Frank. No, Anne.

Mrs. Van Daan (*giving it to* ANNE). It's all right . . . but careful with it. (ANNE *puts it on and struts with it.*) My father gave me that the year before he died. He always bought the best that money could buy.

Anne. Mrs. Van Daan, did you have a lot of boyfriends before you were married?

Mrs. Frank. Anne, that's a personal question. It's not courteous to ask personal questions.

Mrs. Van Daan. Oh, I don't mind. (*To* ANNE) Our house was always swarming with boys. When I was a girl, we had . . .

Mr. Van Daan. Oh, God. Not again!

Mrs. Van Daan (*good-humored*). Shut up! (*Without a pause, to* ANNE. MR. VAN DAAN *mimics* MRS. VAN DAAN, *speaking the first few words in unison with her.*) One summer we had a big house in Hilversum. The boys came buzzing round like bees around a jam pot. And when I was sixteen! . . . We were wearing our skirts very short those days and I had good-looking legs. (*She pulls up her skirt, going to* MR. FRANK.) I still have 'em. I may not be as pretty as I used to be, but I still have my legs. How about it, Mr. Frank?

Mr. Van Daan. All right. All right. We see them.

Mrs. Van Daan. I'm not asking you. I'm asking Mr. Frank.

Peter. Mother, for heaven's sake.

Mrs. Van Daan. Oh, I embarrass you, do I? Well, I just hope the girl you marry has as good. (*Then, to* ANNE) My father used to worry about me, with so many boys hanging round. He told me, if any of them gets fresh, you say to him . . . "Remember, Mr. So-and-So, remember I'm a lady."

Anne. "Remember, Mr. So-and-So, remember I'm a lady." (*She gives* MRS. VAN DAAN *her coat.*)

Mr. Van Daan. Look at you, talking that way in front of her! Don't you know she puts it all down in that diary?

Mrs. Van Daan. So, if she does? I'm only telling the truth!

[ANNE *stretches out, putting her ear to the floor, listening to what is going on below. The sound of the bombers fades away.*]

Mrs. Frank (*setting the table*). Would you mind, Peter, if I moved you over to the couch?

Anne (*listening*). Miep must have the radio on.

[PETER *picks up his papers, going over to the couch beside* MRS. VAN DAAN.]

Mr. Van Daan (*accusingly, to* PETER). Haven't you finished yet?

Peter. No.

Mr. Van Daan. You ought to be ashamed of yourself.

Peter. All right. All right. I'm a dunce. I'm a hopeless case. Why do I go on?

Mrs. Van Daan. You're not hopeless. Don't talk that way. It's just that you haven't anyone to help you, like the girls have. (*To* MR. FRANK) Maybe you could help him, Mr. Frank?

Mr. Frank. I'm sure that his father . . .?

Mr. Van Daan. Not me. I can't do anything with him. He won't listen to me. You go ahead . . . if you want.

Mr. Frank (*going to* PETER). What about it, Peter? Shall we make our school co-educational?

Mrs. Van Daan (*kissing* MR. FRANK). You're an angel, Mr. Frank. An angel. I don't know why I didn't meet you before I met that one there. Here, sit down, Mr. Frank . . . (*She forces him down on the couch beside* PETER.) Now, Peter, you listen to Mr. Frank.

Mr. Frank. It might be better for us to go into Peter's room.

[PETER *jumps up eagerly, leading the way.*]

Mrs. Van Daan. That's right. You go in there, Peter. You listen to Mr. Frank. Mr. Frank is a highly educated man.

[*As* MR. FRANK *is about to follow* PETER *into*

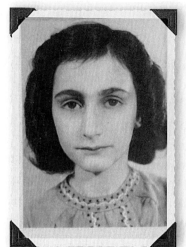

Anne Frank.

his room, MRS. FRANK *stops him and wipes the lipstick from his lips. Then she closes the door after them.*]

Anne (*on the floor, listening*). Shh! I can hear a man's voice talking.

Mr. Van Daan (*to* ANNE). Isn't it bad enough here without your sprawling all over the place?

[ANNE *sits up.*]

Mrs. Van Daan (*to* MR. VAN DAAN). If you didn't smoke so much, you wouldn't be so bad-tempered.

Mr. Van Daan. Am I smoking? Do you see me smoking?

Mrs. Van Daan. Don't tell me you've used up all those cigarettes.

Mr. Van Daan. One package. Miep only brought me one package.

Mrs. Van Daan. It's a filthy habit anyway. It's a good time to break yourself.

Mr. Van Daan. Oh, stop it, please.

Mrs. Van Daan. You're smoking up all our money. You know that, don't you?

Mr. Van Daan. Will you shut up? (*During this,* MRS. FRANK *and* MARGOT *have studiously kept their eyes down. But* ANNE, *seated on the floor, has been following the discussion interestedly.* MR. VAN DAAN *turns to see her staring up at him.*) And what are you staring at?

Anne. I never heard grown-ups quarrel before. I thought only children quarreled.

Mr. Van Daan. This isn't a quarrel! It's a discussion. And I never heard children so rude before.

Anne (*rising, indignantly*). I, rude!

Mr. Van Daan. Yes!

Mrs. Frank (*quickly*). Anne, will you get me my knitting? (ANNE *goes to get it.*) I must remember, when Miep comes, to ask her to bring me some more wool.

Margot (*going to her room*). I need some hairpins and some soap. I made a list. (*She goes into her bedroom to get the list.*)

Mrs. Frank (*to* ANNE). Have you some library books for Miep when she comes?

Anne. It's a wonder that Miep has a life of her own, the way we make her run errands for us. Please, Miep, get me some starch. Please take my hair out and have it cut. Tell me all the latest news, Miep. (*She goes over, kneeling on the couch beside* MRS. VAN DAAN.) Did you know she was engaged? His name is Dirk, and Miep's afraid the Nazis will ship him off to Germany to work in one of their war plants. That's what they're doing with some of the young Dutchmen . . . they pick them up off the streets—

Mr. Van Daan (*interrupting*). Don't you ever get tired of talking? Suppose you try keeping still for five minutes. Just five minutes.

[*He starts to pace again. Again* ANNE *follows him, mimicking him.* MRS. FRANK *jumps up and takes her by the arm up to the sink and gives her a glass of milk.*]

Mrs. Frank. Come here, Anne. It's time for your glass of milk.

Mr. Van Daan. Talk, talk, talk. I never heard such a child. Where is my . . . ? Every evening it's the same, talk, talk, talk. (*He looks around.*) Where is my . . . ?

Mrs. Van Daan. What're you looking for?

Mr. Van Daan. My pipe. Have you seen my pipe?

Mrs. Van Daan. What good's a pipe? You haven't got any tobacco.

Mr. Van Daan. At least I'll have something to hold in my mouth! (*Opening* MARGOT's *bedroom door*) Margot, have you seen my pipe?

Margot. It was on the table last night.

[ANNE *puts her glass of milk on the table and picks up his pipe, hiding it behind her back.*]

Mr. Van Daan. I know. I know. Anne, did you see my pipe? . . . Anne!

Mrs. Frank. Anne, Mr. Van Daan is speaking to you.

Anne. Am I allowed to talk now?

Mr. Van Daan. You're the most aggravating . . . The trouble with you is, you've been spoiled. What you need is a good old-fashioned spanking.

Anne (*mimicking* MRS. VAN DAAN). "Remember, Mr. So-and-So, remember I'm a lady." (*She thrusts the pipe into his mouth, then picks up her glass of milk.*)

Mr. Van Daan (*restraining himself with difficulty*). Why aren't you nice and quiet like your sister Margot? Why do you have to show off all the time? Let me give you a little advice, young lady. Men don't like that kind of thing in a girl. You know that? A man likes a girl who'll listen to him once in a while . . . a domestic girl, who'll keep her house shining for her husband . . . who loves to cook and sew and . . .

Anne. I'd cut my throat first! I'd open my veins! I'm going to be remarkable! I'm going to Paris . . .

Mr. Van Daan (*scoffingly*). Paris!

Anne. . . . . to study music and art.

Mr. Van Daan. Yeah! Yeah!

Vocabulary

indignantly (in·dig′nənt·lē) *adv.:* with anger caused by something felt to be unjust.

Anne. I'm going to be a famous dancer or singer . . . or something wonderful.

[*She makes a wide gesture, spilling the glass of milk on the fur coat in* MRS. VAN DAAN's *lap.* MARGOT *rushes quickly over with a towel.* ANNE *tries to brush the milk off with her skirt.*]

Mrs. Van Daan. Now look what you've done . . . you clumsy little fool! My beautiful fur coat my father gave me . . .
Anne. I'm so sorry.
Mrs. Van Daan. What do you care? It isn't yours. . . . So go on, ruin it! Do you know what that coat cost? Do you? And now look at it! Look at it!
Anne. I'm very, very sorry.
Mrs. Van Daan. I could kill you for this. I could just kill you!

[MRS. VAN DAAN goes *up the stairs, clutching the coat.* MR. VAN DAAN *starts after her.*]

Mr. Van Daan. Petronella . . . liefje! Liefje! . . . Come back . . . the supper . . . come back!
Mrs. Frank. Anne, you must not behave in that way.
Anne. It was an accident. Anyone can have an accident.
Mrs. Frank. I don't mean that. I mean the answering back. You must not answer back. They are our guests. We must always show the greatest courtesy to them. We're all living under terrible tension. (*She stops as* MARGOT *indicates that* MR. VAN DAAN *can hear. When he is gone, she continues.*) That's why we must control ourselves . . . You don't hear Margot getting into arguments with them, do you? Watch Margot. She's always courteous with them. Never familiar. She keeps her distance. And they respect her for it. Try to be like Margot.

Mrs. Van Daan. Now look what you've done!

Anne. And have them walk all over me, the way they do her? No, thanks!
Mrs. Frank. I'm not afraid that anyone is going to walk all over you, Anne. I'm afraid for other people, that you'll walk on them. I don't know what happens to you, Anne. You are wild, self-willed. If I had ever talked to my mother as you talk to me . . .
Anne. Things have changed. People aren't like that anymore. "Yes, Mother." "No, Mother." "Anything you say, Mother." I've got to fight things out for myself! Make something of myself!
Mrs. Frank. It isn't necessary to fight to do it. Margot doesn't fight, and isn't she . . . ?
Anne (*violently rebellious*). Margot! Margot! Margot! That's all I hear from everyone . . . how wonderful Margot is . . . "Why aren't you like Margot?"
Margot (*protesting*). Oh, come on, Anne, don't be so . . .

Anne (*paying no attention*). Everything she does is right, and everything I do is wrong! I'm the goat around here! . . . You're all against me! . . . And you worst of all!

[*She rushes off into her room and throws herself down on the settee, stifling her sobs.* MRS. FRANK *sighs and starts toward the stove.*]

Mrs. Frank (*to* MARGOT). Let's put the soup on the stove . . . if there's anyone who cares to eat. Margot, will you take the bread out? (MARGOT *gets the bread from the cupboard.*) I don't know how we can go on living this way . . . I can't say a word to Anne . . . she flies at me . . .

Margot. You know Anne. In half an hour she'll be out here, laughing and joking.

Mrs. Frank. And . . . (*She makes a motion upward, indicating the* VAN DAANS.) . . . I told your father it wouldn't work . . . but no . . . no . . . he had to ask them, he said . . . he owed it to him, he said. Well, he knows now that I was right! These quarrels! . . . This bickering!

Margot (*with a warning look*). Shush. Shush.

[*The buzzer for the door sounds.* MRS. FRANK *gasps, startled.*]

Mrs. Frank. Every time I hear that sound, my heart stops!

Margot (*starting for* PETER'*s door*). It's Miep. (*She knocks at the door.*) Father?

[MR. FRANK *comes quickly from* PETER'*s room.*]

Mr. Frank. Thank you, Margot. (*As he goes down the steps to open the outer door*) Has everyone his list?

Margot. I'll get my books. (*Giving her mother a list*) Here's your list. (MARGOT *goes into her and* ANNE'*s bedroom on the*

right. ANNE *sits up, hiding her tears, as* MARGOT *comes in.*) Miep's here.

[MARGOT *picks up her books and goes back.* ANNE *hurries over to the mirror, smoothing her hair.*]

Mr. Van Daan (*coming down the stairs*). Is it Miep?

Margot. Yes. Father's gone down to let her in.

Mr. Van Daan. At last I'll have some cigarettes!

Mrs. Frank (*to* MR. VAN DAAN). I can't tell you how unhappy I am about Mrs. Van Daan's coat. Anne should never have touched it.

Mr. Van Daan. She'll be all right.

Mrs. Frank. Is there anything I can do?

Mr. Van Daan. Don't worry.

[*He turns to meet* MIEP. *But it is not* MIEP *who comes up the steps. It is* MR. KRALER, *followed by* MR. FRANK. *Their faces are grave.* ANNE *comes from the bedroom.* PETER *comes from his room.*]

Mrs. Frank. Mr. Kraler!

Mr. Van Daan. How are you, Mr. Kraler?

Margot. This is a surprise.

Mrs. Frank. When Mr. Kraler comes, the sun begins to shine.

Mr. Van Daan. Miep is coming?

Mr. Kraler. Not tonight. (MR. KRALER *goes to* MARGOT *and* MRS. FRANK *and* ANNE, *shaking hands with them.*)

Mrs. Frank. Wouldn't you like a cup of coffee? . . . Or, better still, will you have supper with us?

Mr. Frank. Mr. Kraler has something to talk over with us. Something has happened, he says, which demands an immediate decision.

Mrs. Frank (*fearful*). What is it?

[MR. KRALER *sits down on the couch. As he*

talks he takes bread, cabbages, milk, etc., from his briefcase, giving them to MARGOT *and* ANNE *to put away.*]

Mr. Kraler. Usually, when I come up here, I try to bring you some bit of good news. What's the use of telling you the bad news when there's nothing that you can do about it? But today something has happened. . . . Dirk . . . Miep's Dirk, you know, came to me just now. He tells me that he has a Jewish friend living near him. A dentist. He says he's in trouble. He begged me, could I do anything for this man? Could I find him a hiding place? . . . So I've come to you . . . I know it's a terrible thing to ask of you, living as you are, but would you take him in with you?

Mr. Frank. Of course we will.

Mr. Kraler (*rising*). It'll be just for a night or two . . . until I find some other place. This happened so suddenly that I didn't know where to turn.

Mr. Frank. Where is he?

Mr. Kraler. Downstairs in the office.

Mr. Frank. Good. Bring him up.

Mr. Kraler. His name is Dussel[22] . . .

Mr. Frank. Dussel . . . I think I know him.

Mr. Kraler. I'll get him.

[*He goes quickly down the steps and out.* MR. FRANK *suddenly becomes conscious of the others.*]

Mr. Frank. Forgive me. I spoke without consulting you. But I knew you'd feel as I do.

Mr. Van Daan. There's no reason for you to consult anyone. This is your place. You have a right to do exactly as you please. The only thing I feel . . . there's so little food as it is . . . and to take in another person . . .

---

22. **Dussel** (dōos′əl).

[PETER *turns away, ashamed of his father.*]

Mr. Frank. We can stretch the food a little. It's only for a few days.

Mr. Van Daan. You want to make a bet?

Mrs. Frank. I think it's fine to have him. But, Otto, where are you going to put him? Where?

Peter. He can have my bed. I can sleep on the floor. I wouldn't mind.

Mr. Frank. That's good of you, Peter. But your room's too small . . . even for you.

Anne. I have a much better idea. I'll come in here with you and Mother, and Margot can take Peter's room and Peter can go in our room with Mr. Dussel.

Margot. That's right. We could do that.

Mr. Frank. No, Margot. You mustn't sleep in that room . . . neither you nor Anne. Mouschi has caught some rats in there. Peter's brave. He doesn't mind.

Anne. Then how about *this*? I'll come in here with you and Mother, and Mr. Dussel can have my bed.

Mrs. Frank. No. No. *No!* Margot will come in here with us and he can have her bed. It's the only way. Margot, bring your things in here. Help her, Anne.

[MARGOT *hurries into her room to get her things.*]

Anne (*to her mother*). Why Margot? Why can't I come in here?

Mrs. Frank. Because it wouldn't be proper for Margot to sleep with a . . . Please, Anne. Don't argue. Please.

[ANNE *starts slowly away.*]

Mr. Frank (*to* ANNE). You don't mind sharing your room with Mr. Dussel, do you, Anne?

Anne. No. No, of course not.

Mr. Frank. Good. (ANNE *goes off into her bedroom, helping* MARGOT. MR. FRANK *starts to search in the cupboards.*) Where's the cognac?[23]

Mrs. Frank. It's there. But, Otto, I was saving it in case of illness.

Mr. Frank. I think we couldn't find a better time to use it. Peter, will you get five glasses for me?

[PETER *goes for the glasses.* MARGOT *comes out of her bedroom, carrying her possessions, which she hangs behind a curtain in the main room.* MR. FRANK *finds the cognac and pours it into the five glasses that* PETER *brings him.* MR. VAN DAAN *stands looking on sourly.* MRS. VAN DAAN *comes downstairs and looks around at all the bustle.*]

Mrs. Van Daan. What's happening? What's going on?

Mr. Van Daan. Someone's moving in with us.

Mrs. Van Daan. In here? You're joking.

Margot. It's only for a night or two . . . until Mr. Kraler finds him another place.

Mr. Van Daan. Yeah! Yeah!

[MR. FRANK *hurries over as* MR. KRALER *and* DUSSEL *come up.* DUSSEL *is a man in his late fifties, meticulous, finicky . . . bewildered now. He wears a raincoat. He carries a briefcase, stuffed full, and a small medicine case.*]

Mr. Frank. Come in, Mr. Dussel.

Mr. Kraler. This is Mr. Frank.

Dussel. Mr. Otto Frank?

Mr. Frank. Yes. Let me take your things. (*He takes the hat and briefcase, but* DUSSEL *clings to his medicine case.*) This is my wife, Edith . . . Mr. and Mrs. Van Daan . . . their son, Peter . . . and my daughters, Margot and Anne.

[DUSSEL *shakes hands with everyone.*]

Mr. Kraler. Thank you, Mr. Frank. Thank you all. Mr. Dussel, I leave you in good hands. Oh . . . Dirk's coat.

[DUSSEL *hurriedly takes off the raincoat, giving it to* MR. KRALER. *Underneath is his white dentist's jacket, with a yellow Star of David on it.*]

Dussel (*to* MR. KRALER). What can I say to thank you . . . ?

Mrs. Frank (*to* DUSSEL). Mr. Kraler and Miep . . . They're our lifeline. Without them we couldn't live.

Mr. Kraler. Please. Please. You make us seem very heroic. It isn't that at all. We simply don't like the Nazis. (*To* MR. FRANK, *who offers him a drink*) No, thanks. (*Then, going on*) We don't like their methods. We don't like . . .

Mr. Frank (*smiling*). I know. I know. "No one's going to tell us Dutchmen what to do with our damn Jews!"

Mr. Kraler (*to* DUSSEL). Pay no attention to Mr. Frank. I'll be up tomorrow to see that they're treating you right. (*To* MR. FRANK) Don't trouble to come down again. Peter will bolt the door after me, won't you, Peter?

Peter. Yes, sir.

Mr. Frank. Thank you, Peter. I'll do it.

Mr. Kraler. Good night. Good night.

Fritz Pfeffer ("Dussel").

Group. Good night, Mr. Kraler. We'll see you tomorrow. (*Etc., etc.*)

[MR. KRALER *goes out with* MR. FRANK. MRS. FRANK *gives each one of the "grown-ups" a glass of cognac.*]

Mrs. Frank. Please, Mr. Dussel, sit down.

[DUSSEL *sinks into a chair.* MRS. FRANK *gives him a glass of cognac.*]

Dussel. I'm dreaming. I know it. I can't believe my eyes. Mr. Otto Frank here! (*To* MRS. FRANK) You're not in Switzerland, then? A woman told me . . . She said she'd gone to your house . . . the door was open, everything was in disorder, dishes in the sink. She said she found a piece of paper in the wastebasket with an address scribbled on it . . . an address in Zurich.[24] She said you must have escaped to Zurich.
Anne. Father put that there purposely . . . just so people would think that very thing!
Dussel. And you've been *here* all the time?
Mrs. Frank. All the time . . . ever since July.

[ANNE *speaks to her father as he comes back.*]

Anne. It worked, Pim . . . the address you left! Mr. Dussel says that people believe we escaped to Switzerland.
Mr. Frank. I'm glad. . . . And now let's have a little drink to welcome Mr. Dussel. (*Before they can drink,* DUSSEL *bolts his drink.* MR. FRANK *smiles and raises his glass.*) To Mr. Dussel. Welcome. We're very honored to have you with us.
Mrs. Frank. To Mr. Dussel, welcome.

[*The* VAN DAANS *murmur a welcome. The "grown-ups" drink.*]

Mrs. Van Daan. Um. That was good.
Mr. Van Daan. Did Mr. Kraler warn you that you won't get much to eat here? You can imagine . . . three ration books among the seven of us . . . and now you make eight.

[PETER *walks away, humiliated. Outside, a street organ is heard dimly.*]

Dussel (*rising*). Mr. Van Daan, you don't realize what is happening outside that you should warn me of a thing like that. You don't realize what's going on. . . . (*As* MR. VAN DAAN *starts his characteristic pacing,* DUSSEL *turns to speak to the others.*) Right here in Amsterdam every day hundreds of Jews disappear. . . . They surround a block and search house by house. Children come home from school to find their parents gone. Hundreds are being deported[25] . . . people that you and I know . . . the Hallensteins . . . the Wessels . . .
Mrs. Frank (*in tears*). Oh, no. No!
Dussel. They get their call-up notice . . . come to the Jewish theater on such and such a day and hour . . . bring only what you can carry in a rucksack. And if you refuse the call-up notice, then they come and drag you from your home and ship you off to Mauthausen. The death camp!
Mrs. Frank. We didn't know that things had got so much worse.
Dussel. Forgive me for speaking so.
Anne (*coming to* DUSSEL). Do you know the de Waals? . . . What's become of them? Their daughter Jopie and I are in the same class. Jopie's my best friend.

---

24. **Zurich** (zoor′ik): Switzerland's largest city. Because Switzerland remained neutral during World War II, many refugees sought safety there.

25. **deported** *v.*: forcibly sent away (to concentration camps and death camps).

Dussel. They are gone.

Anne. Gone?

Dussel. With all the others.

Anne. Oh, no. Not Jopie!

[*She turns away, in tears.* MRS. FRANK *motions to* MARGOT *to comfort her.* MARGOT *goes to* ANNE, *putting her arms comfortingly around her.*]

Mrs. Van Daan. There were some people called Wagner. They lived near us . . . ?

Mr. Frank (*interrupting, with a glance at* ANNE). I think we should put this off until later. We all have many questions we want to ask. . . . But I'm sure that Mr. Dussel would like to get settled before supper.

Dussel. Thank you. I would. I brought very little with me.

Mr. Frank (*giving him his hat and briefcase*). I'm sorry we can't give you a room alone. But I hope you won't be too uncomfortable. We've had to make strict rules here . . . a schedule of hours . . . We'll tell you after supper. Anne, would you like to take Mr. Dussel to his room?

Anne (*controlling her tears*). If you'll come with me, Mr. Dussel? (*She starts for her room.*)

Dussel (*shaking hands with each in turn*). Forgive me if I haven't really expressed my gratitude to all of you. This has been such a shock to me. I'd always thought of myself as Dutch. I was born in Holland. My father was born in Holland, and my grandfather. And now . . . after all these years . . . (*He breaks off.*) If you'll excuse me.

[DUSSEL *gives a little bow and hurries off after* ANNE. MR. FRANK *and the others are subdued.*]

Anne (*turning on the light*). Well, here we are.

[DUSSEL *looks around the room. In the main room* MARGOT *speaks to her mother.*]

Margot. The news sounds pretty bad, doesn't it? It's so different from what Mr. Kraler tells us. Mr. Kraler says things are improving.

Mr. Van Daan. I like it better the way Kraler tells it.

[*They resume their occupations, quietly.* PETER *goes off into his room. In* ANNE's *room,* ANNE *turns to* DUSSEL.]

Anne. You're going to share the room with me.

Dussel. I'm a man who's always lived alone. I haven't had to adjust myself to others. I hope you'll bear with me until I learn.

Anne. Let me help you. (*She takes his briefcase.*) Do you always live all alone? Have you no family at all?

Dussel. No one. (*He opens his medicine case and spreads his bottles on the dressing table.*)

Anne. How dreadful. You must be terribly lonely.

Dussel. I'm used to it.

Anne. I don't think I could ever get used to it. Didn't you even have a pet? A cat, or a dog?

Dussel. I have an allergy for fur-bearing animals. They give me asthma.

Anne. Oh, dear. Peter has a cat.

Dussel. Here? He has it here?

Anne. Yes. But we hardly ever see it. He keeps it in his room all the time. I'm sure it will be all right.

Dussel. Let us hope so. (*He takes some pills to fortify himself.*)

Anne. That's Margot's bed, where you're going to sleep. I sleep on the sofa there. (*Indicating the clothes hooks on the wall*) We cleared these off for your things. (*She goes over to the window.*) The best part about this

---

Vocabulary
fortify (fôrt′ə·fī′) *v.*: strengthen.

room . . . you can look down and see a bit of the street and the canal. There's a houseboat . . . you can see the end of it . . . a bargeman lives there with his family . . . They have a baby and he's just beginning to walk and I'm so afraid he's going to fall into the canal someday. I watch him . . .

Dussel (*interrupting*). Your father spoke of a schedule.

Anne (*coming away from the window*). Oh, yes. It's mostly about the times we have to be quiet. And times for the w.c. You can use it now if you like.

Dussel (*stiffly*). No, thank you.

Anne. I suppose you think it's awful, my talking about a thing like that. But you don't know how important it can get to be, especially when you're frightened. . . . About this room, the way Margot and I did . . . she had it to herself in the afternoons for studying, reading . . . lessons, you know . . . and I took the mornings. Would that be all right with you?

Dussel. I'm not at my best in the morning.

Anne. You stay here in the mornings, then. I'll take the room in the afternoons.

Dussel. Tell me, when you're in here, what happens to me? Where am I spending my time? In there, with all the people?

Anne. Yes.

Dussel. I see. I see.

Anne. We have supper at half past six.

Dussel (*going over to the sofa*). Then, if you don't mind . . . I like to lie down quietly for ten minutes before eating. I find it helps the digestion.

Anne. Of course. I hope I'm not going to be too much of a bother to you. I seem to be able to get everyone's back up.

[DUSSEL *lies down on the sofa, curled up, his back to her.*]

Dussel. I always get along very well with children. My patients all bring their children to me, because they know I get on well with them. So don't you worry about that.

[ANNE *leans over him, taking his hand and shaking it gratefully.*]

Anne. Thank you. Thank you, Mr. Dussel.

[*The lights dim to darkness. The curtain falls on the scene.* ANNE'*s voice comes to us, faintly at first and then with increasing power.*]

Anne's Voice. . . . And yesterday I finished Cissy Van Marxvelt's latest book. I think she is a first-class writer. I shall definitely let my children read her. Monday, the twenty-first of September, nineteen forty-two. Mr. Dussel and I had another battle yesterday. Yes, Mr. Dussel! According to him, nothing, I repeat . . . nothing is right about me . . . my appearance, my character, my manners. While he was going on at me, I thought . . . sometime I'll give you such a smack that you'll fly right up to the ceiling! Why is it that every grown-up thinks he knows the way to bring up children? Particularly the grown-ups that never had any. I keep wishing that Peter was a girl instead of a boy. Then I would have someone to talk to. Margot's a darling, but she takes everything too seriously. To pause for a moment on the subject of Mrs. Van Daan. I must tell you that her attempts to flirt with Father are getting her nowhere. Pim, thank goodness, won't play.

[*As she is saying the last lines, the curtain rises on the darkened scene.* ANNE'*s voice fades out.*]

Literary Response and Analysis
Act One, Scenes 1–3

Reading Check

1. A **flashback** is an interruption in the present action of a plot to show events that happened at an earlier time. Most of this play is told in the form of an extended flashback framed by the opening and closing scenes. Where in Scene 1 does the flashback begin? What do we learn about the characters and their basic situation before the flashback begins?

2. By the end of Scene 3, we have met all ten **characters** who appear in the play. List those characters, and choose two or three adjectives to describe each one.

3. When does Anne begin to understand what going into hiding will mean? Describe some of the ways life in the Secret Annex is different from life outside.

Interpretations

4. Sounds from outside the Secret Annex play an important part in the play. Some remind us of ordinary life going on in the city. Others punctuate the scene with reminders of the danger outside. List four of the sounds heard so far. Which sounds are pleasant? Which are threatening?

5. The story of a play usually follows the ups and downs of relationships. Describe how Anne and Peter hit it off in their first scene together.

6. What does Mrs. Frank mean by her comment to Anne that "you complain that I don't treat you like a grown-up. But when I do, you resent it"?

7. Do Anne and Peter seem to have typical teenage attitudes toward their families? Go back to the text for examples to support your response.

8. List the **conflicts** that have developed among the characters by the end of Scene 3. Why are these conflicts dangerous for the people in the Secret Annex? What other conflicts do you **predict** might arise?

9. **Compare** Mr. Frank's and Mr. Van Daan's reactions to the arrival of Albert Dussel. Which seems like the right way to respond? Why?

10. Mr. Frank tells Anne, "There are no walls, there are no bolts, no locks that anyone can put on your mind" (page 227). What does he mean?

Grade 6 Review Reading Standard 3.6 Identify and analyze features of themes conveyed through characters, actions, and images.

■ SCENE 4

It is the middle of the night, several months later. The stage is dark except for a little light which comes through the skylight in PETER'*s room.*

Everyone is in bed. MR. *and* MRS. FRANK *lie on the couch in the main room, which has been pulled out to serve as a makeshift double bed.*

MARGOT *is sleeping on a mattress on the floor in the main room, behind a curtain stretched across for privacy. The others are all in their accustomed rooms.*

From outside we hear two drunken soldiers singing "Lili Marlene." A girl's high giggle is heard. The sound of running feet is heard coming closer and then fading in the distance. Throughout the scene there is the distant sound of airplanes passing overhead.

A match suddenly flares up in the attic. We dimly see MR. VAN DAAN. *He is getting his bearings. He comes quickly down the stairs and goes to the cupboard where the food is stored. Again the match flares up, and is as quickly blown out. The dim figure is seen to steal back up the stairs.*

There is quiet for a second or two, broken only by the sound of airplanes and running feet on the street below. Suddenly, out of the silence and the dark, we hear ANNE *scream.*

Anne (*screaming*). No! No! Don't . . . don't take me!

[*She moans, tossing and crying in her sleep. The other people wake, terrified.* DUSSEL *sits up in bed, furious.*]

Dussel. Shush! Anne! Anne, for God's sake, shush!

Anne (*still in her nightmare*). Save me! Save me!

[*She screams and screams.* DUSSEL *gets out of bed, going over to her, trying to wake her.*]

Dussel. For God's sake! Quiet! Quiet! You want someone to hear?

[*In the main room* MRS. FRANK *grabs a shawl and pulls it around her. She rushes in to* ANNE, *taking her in her arms.* MR. FRANK *hurriedly gets up, putting on his overcoat.* MARGOT *sits up, terrified.* PETER'*s light goes on in his room.*]

Mrs. Frank (*to* ANNE, *in her room*). Hush, darling, hush. It's all right. It's all right. (*Over her shoulder, to* DUSSEL) Will you be kind enough to turn on the light, Mr. Dussel? (*Back to* ANNE) It's nothing, my darling. It was just a dream.

[DUSSEL *turns on the light in the bedroom.* MRS. FRANK *holds* ANNE *in her arms. Gradually* ANNE *comes out of her nightmare, still trembling with horror.* MR. FRANK *comes into the room, and goes quickly to the window, looking out to be sure that no one outside has heard* ANNE'*s screams.* MRS. FRANK *holds* ANNE, *talking softly to her. In the main room* MARGOT *stands on a chair, turning on the center hanging lamp. A light goes on in the* VAN DAANS' *room overhead.* PETER *puts his robe on, coming out of his room.*]

Mrs. Frank. Hush, darling, hush. It's all right.

Dussel (*to* MRS. FRANK, *blowing his nose*). Something must be done about that child, Mrs. Frank. Yelling like that! Who knows but there's somebody on the streets? She's endangering all our lives.

Mrs. Frank. Anne, darling.

Dussel. Every night she twists and turns. I don't sleep. I spend half my night shushing her. And now it's nightmares!

[MARGOT *comes to the door of* ANNE's *room, followed by* PETER. MR. FRANK *goes to them, indicating that everything is all right.* PETER *takes* MARGOT *back.*]

Mrs. Frank (*to* ANNE). You're here, safe, you see? Nothing has happened. (*To* DUSSEL) Please, Mr. Dussel, go back to bed. She'll be herself in a minute or two. Won't you, Anne?
Dussel (*picking up a book and a pillow*). Thank you, but I'm going to the w.c. The one place where there's peace!

[*He stalks out.* MR. VAN DAAN, *in underwear and trousers, comes down the stairs.*]

Mr. Van Daan (*to* DUSSEL). What is it? What happened?
Dussel. A nightmare. She was having a nightmare!
Mr. Van Daan. I thought someone was murdering her.
Dussel. Unfortunately, no.

[*He goes into the bathroom.* MR. VAN DAAN *goes back up the stairs.* MR. FRANK, *in the main room, sends* PETER *back to his own bedroom.*]

Mr. Frank. Thank you, Peter. Go back to bed.

[PETER *goes back to his room.* MR. FRANK *follows him, turning out the light and looking out the window. Then he goes back to the main room, and gets up on a chair, turning out the center hanging lamp.*]

Mrs. Frank (*to* ANNE). Would you like some water? (ANNE *shakes her head.*) Was it a very bad dream? Perhaps if you told me . . . ?
Anne. I'd rather not talk about it.
Mrs. Frank. Poor darling. Try to sleep, then. I'll sit right here beside you until you fall asleep. (*She brings a stool over, sitting there.*)
Anne. You don't have to.
Mrs. Frank. But I'd like to stay with you . . . very much. Really.
Anne. I'd rather you didn't.
Mrs. Frank. Good night, then. (*She leans down to kiss* ANNE. ANNE *throws her arm up over her face, turning away.* MRS. FRANK, *hiding her hurt, kisses* ANNE's *arm.*) You'll be all right? There's nothing that you want?
Anne. Will you please ask Father to come.
Mrs. Frank (*after a second*). Of course, Anne dear. (*She hurries out into the other room.* MR. FRANK *comes to her as she comes in.*) Sie verlangt nach Dir![1]
Mr. Frank (*sensing her hurt*). Edith, Liebe, schau . . .[2]
Mrs. Frank. Es macht nichts! Ich danke dem lieben Herrgott, dass sie sich wenigstens an Dich wendet, wenn sie Trost braucht! Geh hinein, Otto, sie ist ganz hysterisch vor Angst.[3] (*As* MR. FRANK *hesitates*) Geh zu ihr.[4] (*He looks at her for a second and then goes to get a cup of water for* ANNE. MRS. FRANK *sinks down on the bed, her face in her hands, trying to keep from sobbing aloud.* MARGOT *comes over to her, putting her arms around her.*) She wants nothing of me. She pulled away when I leaned down to kiss her.

---

1. **Sie . . . Dir:** German for "She's asking for you."
2. **Liebe, schau:** "Dear, look."
3. **Es . . . Angst:** "It doesn't matter! I thank the dear Lord that she turns at least to you when she needs comfort! Go to her, Otto, she's completely hysterical with fear."
4. **Geh zu ihr:** "Go to her."

Margot. It's a phase . . . You heard Father. . . Most girls go through it . . . they turn to their fathers at this age . . . they give all their love to their fathers.

Mrs. Frank. You weren't like this. You didn't shut me out.

Margot. She'll get over it. . . .

[*She smooths the bed for* MRS. FRANK *and sits beside her a moment as* MRS. FRANK *lies down. In* ANNE's *room* MR. FRANK *comes in, sitting down by* ANNE. ANNE *flings her arms around him, clinging to him. In the distance we hear the sound of ack-ack.*]

Anne. Oh, Pim. I dreamed that they came to get us! The Green Police! They broke down the door and grabbed me and started to drag me out the way they did Jopie.

Mr. Frank. I want you to take this pill.

Anne. What is it?

Mr. Frank. Something to quiet you.

[*She takes it and drinks the water. In the main room* MARGOT *turns out the light and goes back to her bed.*]

Mr. Frank (*to* ANNE). Do you want me to read to you for a while?

Anne. No. Just sit with me for a minute. Was I awful? Did I yell terribly loud? Do you think anyone outside could have heard?

Mr. Frank. No. No. Lie quietly now. Try to sleep.

Anne. I'm a terrible coward. I'm so disappointed in myself. I think I've conquered my fear . . . I think I'm really grown-up . . . and then something happens . . . and I run to you like a baby. . . . I love you, Father. I don't love anyone but you.

Mr. Frank (*reproachfully*). Annele!

Anne. It's true. I've been thinking about it for a long time. You're the only one I love.

Mr. Frank. It's fine to hear you tell me that you love me. But I'd be happier if you said you loved your mother as well. . . . She needs your help so much . . . your love . . .

Anne. We have nothing in common. She doesn't understand me. Whenever I try to explain my views on life to her, she asks me if I'm constipated.

Mr. Frank. You hurt her very much just now. She's crying. She's in there crying.

Anne. I can't help it. I only told the truth. I didn't want her here . . . (*Then, with sudden change*) Oh, Pim, I was horrible, wasn't I? And the worst of it is, I can stand off and look at myself doing it and know it's cruel and yet I can't stop doing it. What's the matter with me? Tell me. Don't say it's just a phase! Help me.

Mr. Frank. There is so little that we parents can do to help our children. We can only try to set a good example . . . point the way. The rest you must do yourself. You must build your own character.

Anne. I'm trying. Really I am. Every night I think back over all of the things I did that day that were wrong . . . like putting the wet mop in Mr. Dussel's bed . . . and this thing now with Mother. I say to myself, that was wrong. I make up my mind, I'm never going to do that again. Never! Of course, I may do something worse . . . but at least I'll never do *that* again! . . . I have a nicer side, Father . . . a sweeter, nicer side. But I'm scared to show it. I'm afraid that people are going to laugh at me if I'm serious. So the mean Anne comes to the outside and the good Anne stays on the inside, and I keep on trying to switch them around and have the good Anne outside and the bad Anne inside and be what I'd like to be . . . and might be . . . if only . . . only . . .

[*She is asleep.* MR. FRANK *watches her for a moment and then turns off the light, and starts out. The lights dim out. The curtain falls on the scene.* ANNE's *voice is heard, dimly at first and then with growing strength.*]

Anne's Voice. . . . The air raids[5] are getting worse. They come over day and night. The noise is terrifying. Pim says it should be music to our ears. The more planes, the sooner will come the end of the war. Mrs. Van Daan pretends to be a fatalist.[6] What will be, will be. But when the planes come over, who is the most frightened? No one else but Petronella! . . . Monday, the ninth of November, nineteen forty-two. Wonderful news! The Allies have landed in Africa. Pim says that we can look for an early finish to the war. Just for fun, he asked each of us what was the first thing we wanted to do when we got out of here. Mrs. Van Daan longs to be home with her own things, her needlepoint chairs, the Bechstein piano her father gave her . . . the best that money could buy. Peter would like to go to a movie. Mr. Dussel wants to get back to his dentist's drill. He's afraid he is losing his touch. For myself, there are so many things . . . to ride a bike again . . . to laugh till my belly aches . . . to have new clothes from the skin out . . . to have a hot tub filled to overflowing and wallow in it for hours . . . to be back in school with my friends . . .

---

5. **air raids** *n.:* Allied aircraft conducted air raids, or bombing attacks on ground targets, in the Netherlands because the country was occupied by the Germans.
6. **fatalist** (fāt′l·ist) *n.:* person who believes that all events are determined by fate and therefore cannot be prevented or affected by people's actions.

[*As the last lines are being said, the curtain rises on the scene. The lights dim on as* ANNE's *voice fades away.*]

■ SCENE 5

It is the first night of the Hanukkah[7] celebration. MR. FRANK *is standing at the head of the table on which is the menorah.[8] He lights the shamas, or servant candle, and holds it as he says the blessing. Seated, listening, are all of the "family," dressed in their best. The men wear hats;* PETER *wears his cap.*

Mr. Frank (*reading from a prayer book*). "Praised be Thou, oh Lord our God, Ruler of the universe, who has sanctified us with Thy commandments and bidden us kindle the Hanukkah lights. Praised be Thou, oh Lord our God, Ruler of the universe, who has wrought wondrous deliverances for our fathers in days of old. Praised be Thou, oh Lord our God, Ruler of the universe, that Thou has given us life and sustenance and brought us to this happy season." (MR. FRANK *lights the one candle of the menorah as he continues.*) "We kindle this Hanukkah light to celebrate the great and wonderful deeds wrought through the zeal with which God filled the

---

7. **Hanukkah** (khä′noo·kä′): joyous eight-day Jewish holiday, usually falling in December, celebrating the rededication of the holy Temple in Jerusalem in 164 B.C. The Temple had been taken over by the Syrians, who had conquered Jerusalem. The Maccabee family led the Jews in a successful rebellion against the Syrians and retook the Temple.
8. **menorah** (mə·nō′rə) *n.:* Hebrew for "lamp." Mr. Frank is lighting a menorah that holds nine candles: eight candles, one for each of the eight nights of Hanukkah, and the shamas, the candle used to light the others.

Vocabulary
zeal (zēl) *n.:* great enthusiasm; devotion to a cause.

Mr. Frank.
"They fought against indifference, against tyranny and oppression . . ."

hearts of the heroic Maccabees, two thousand years ago. They fought against indifference, against <u>tyranny</u> and oppression, and they restored our Temple to us. May these lights remind us that we should ever look to God, whence cometh our help." Amen. (*Pronounced "o-mayn"*)

All. Amen.

[MR. FRANK *hands* MRS. FRANK *the prayer book.*]

Mrs. Frank (*reading*). "I lift up mine eyes unto the mountains, from whence cometh my help. My help cometh from the Lord who made heaven and earth. He will not suffer thy foot to be moved. He that keepeth thee will not slumber. He that keepeth Israel doth neither slumber nor sleep. The Lord is thy keeper. The Lord is thy shade upon thy right hand. The sun shall not smite thee by

Vocabulary
tyranny (tĭr′ə·nē) *n.*: cruel and unjust rule or use of power.

day, nor the moon by night. The Lord shall keep thee from all evil. He shall keep thy soul. The Lord shall guard thy going out and thy coming in, from this time forth and forevermore."[9] Amen.

All. Amen.

[MRS. FRANK *puts down the prayer book and goes to get the food and wine.* MARGOT *helps her.* MR. FRANK *takes the men's hats and puts them aside.*]

Dussel (*rising*). That was very moving.

Anne (*pulling him back*). It isn't over yet!

Mrs. Van Daan. Sit down! Sit down!

Anne. There's a lot more, songs and presents.

Dussel. Presents?

Mrs. Frank. Not this year, unfortunately.

Mrs. Van Daan. But always on Hanukkah everyone gives presents . . . everyone!

Dussel. Like our St. Nicholas's Day.[10]

[*There is a chorus of no's from the group.*]

Mrs. Van Daan. No! Not like St. Nicholas! What kind of a Jew are you that you don't know Hanukkah?

Mrs. Frank (*as she brings the food*). I remember particularly the candles . . . First, one, as we have tonight. Then, the second night, you light two candles, the next night three . . . and so on until you have eight candles burning. When there are eight candles, it is truly beautiful.

Mrs. Van Daan. And the potato pancakes.

Mr. Van Daan. Don't talk about them!

---

9. Mrs. Frank is reading Psalm 121 from the Bible.

10. **St. Nicholas's Day:** Christian holiday celebrated in the Netherlands and other European countries on December 5, on which small gifts are given, especially to children.

Mrs. Van Daan. I make the best latkes[11] you ever tasted!

Mrs. Frank. Invite us all next year . . . in your own home.

Mr. Frank. God willing!

Mrs. Van Daan. God willing.

Margot. What I remember best is the presents we used to get when we were little . . . eight days of presents . . . and each day they got better and better.

Mrs. Frank (*sitting down*). We are all here, alive. That is present enough.

Anne. No, it isn't. I've got something. . . . (*She rushes into her room, hurriedly puts on a little hat improvised from the lampshade, grabs a satchel bulging with parcels, and comes running back.*)

Mrs. Frank. What is it?

Anne. Presents!

Mrs. Van Daan. Presents!

Dussel. Look!

Mr. Van Daan. What's she got on her head?

Peter. A lampshade!

Anne (*she picks out one at random*). This is for Margot. (*She hands it to* MARGOT, *pulling her to her feet.*) Read it out loud.

Margot (*reading*).

> You have never lost your temper.
> You never will, I fear,
> You are so good.
> But if you should,
> Put all your cross words here.

(*She tears open the package.*) A new crossword puzzle book! Where did you get it?

Anne. It isn't new. It's one that you've done. But I rubbed it all out, and if you wait a little and forget, you can do it all over again.

---

11. **latkes** (lät′kəz) *n.*: potato pancakes, a traditional Hanukkah food.

Margot (*sitting*). It's wonderful, Anne. Thank you. You'd never know it wasn't new.

[*From outside we hear the sound of a street-car passing.*]

Anne (*with another gift*). Mrs. Van Daan.
Mrs. Van Daan (*taking it*). This is awful . . . I haven't anything for anyone . . . I never thought . . .
Mr. Frank. This is all Anne's idea.
Mrs. Van Daan (*holding up a bottle*). What is it?
Anne. It's hair shampoo. I took all the odds and ends of soap and mixed them with the last of my toilet water.[12]
Mrs. Van Daan. Oh, Anneke!
Anne. I wanted to write a poem for all of them, but I didn't have time. (*Offering a large box to* MR. VAN DAAN) Yours, Mr. Van Daan, is *really* something . . . something you want more than anything. (*As she waits for him to open it*) Look! Cigarettes!
Mr. Van Daan. Cigarettes!
Anne. Two of them! Pim found some old pipe tobacco in the pocket lining of his coat . . . and we made them . . . or rather, Pim did.
Mrs. Van Daan. Let me see . . . Well, look at that! Light it, Putti! Light it.

[MR. VAN DAAN *hesitates.*]

Anne. It's tobacco, really it is! There's a little fluff in it, but not much.

[*Everyone watches intently as* MR. VAN DAAN *cautiously lights it. The cigarette flares up. Everyone laughs.*]

Peter. It works!
Mrs. Van Daan. Look at him.

----
12. **toilet water** *n.*: cologne.

Mr. Van Daan (*spluttering*). Thank you, Anne. Thank you.

[ANNE *rushes back to her satchel for another present.*]

Anne (*handing her mother a piece of paper*). For Mother, Hanukkah greeting. (*She pulls her mother to her feet.*)
Mrs. Frank (*she reads*).

> Here's an IOU that I promise to pay.
> Ten hours of doing whatever you say.
> Signed, Anne Frank.

(MRS. FRANK, *touched, takes* ANNE *in her arms, holding her close.*)
Dussel (*to* ANNE). Ten hours of doing what you're told? *Anything* you're told?
Anne. That's right.
Dussel. You wouldn't want to sell that, Mrs. Frank?
Mrs. Frank. Never! This is the most precious gift I've ever had!

[*She sits, showing her present to the others.* ANNE *hurries back to the satchel and pulls out a scarf, the scarf that* MR. FRANK *found in the first scene.*]

Anne (*offering it to her father*). For Pim.
Mr. Frank. Anneke . . . I wasn't supposed to have a present! (*He takes it, unfolding it and showing it to the others.*)
Anne. It's a muffler . . . to put round your neck . . . like an ascot, you know. I made it myself out of odds and ends. . . . I knitted it in the dark each night, after I'd gone to bed. I'm afraid it looks better in the dark!
Mr. Frank (*putting it on*). It's fine. It fits me perfectly. Thank you, Annele.

[ANNE *hands* PETER *a ball of paper with a string attached to it.*]

Anne. That's for Mouschi.

Peter (*rising to bow*). On behalf of Mouschi, I thank you.

Anne (*hesitant, handing him a gift*). And . . . this is yours . . . from Mrs. Quack Quack. (*As he holds it gingerly in his hands*) Well . . . open it . . . Aren't you going to open it?

Peter. I'm scared to. I know something's going to jump out and hit me.

Anne. No. It's nothing like that, really.

Mrs. Van Daan (*as he is opening it*). What is it, Peter? Go on. Show it.

Anne (*excitedly*). It's a safety razor!

Dussel. A what?

Anne. A razor!

Mrs. Van Daan (*looking at it*). You didn't make that out of odds and ends.

Anne (*to* PETER). Miep got it for me. It's not new. It's secondhand. But you really do need a razor now.

Dussel. For what?

Anne. Look on his upper lip . . . you can see the beginning of a moustache.

Dussel. He wants to get rid of that? Put a little milk on it and let the cat lick it off.

Peter (*starting for his room*). Think you're funny, don't you.

Dussel. Look! He can't wait! He's going in to try it!

Peter. I'm going to give Mouschi his present! (*He goes into his room, slamming the door behind him.*)

Mr. Van Daan (*disgustedly*). Mouschi, Mouschi, Mouschi.

[*In the distance we hear a dog persistently barking.* ANNE *brings a gift to* DUSSEL.]

Anne. And last but never least, my roommate, Mr. Dussel.

Dussel. For me? You have something for me? (*He opens the small box she gives him.*)

Anne. I made them myself.

Dussel (*puzzled*). Capsules! Two capsules!

Anne. They're earplugs!

Dussel. Earplugs?

Anne. To put in your ears so you won't hear me when I thrash around at night. I saw them advertised in a magazine. They're not real ones. . . . I made them out of cotton and candle wax. Try them . . . See if they don't work . . . See if you can hear me talk . . .

Dussel (*putting them in his ears*). Wait now until I get them in . . . so.

Anne. Are you ready?

Dussel. Huh?

Anne. Are you ready?

Dussel. Good God! They've gone inside! I can't get them out! (*They laugh as* DUSSEL *jumps about, trying to shake the plugs out of his ears. Finally he gets them out. Putting them away*) Thank you, Anne! Thank you!

Mr. Van Daan. A real Hanukkah!

Mrs. Van Daan. Wasn't it cute of her?

Mrs. Frank. I don't know when she did it.

Margot. I love my present.

⎫
⎬ *Together*
⎭

Anne (*sitting at the table*). And now let's have the song, Father . . . please . . . (*To* DUSSEL) Have you heard the Hanukkah song, Mr. Dussel? The song is the whole thing! (*She sings*) "Oh, Hanukkah! Oh, Hanukkah! The sweet celebration . . ."

Mr. Frank (*quieting her*). I'm afraid, Anne, we shouldn't sing that song tonight. (*To* DUSSEL) It's a song of jubilation, of rejoicing. One is apt to become too enthusiastic.

Vocabulary
gingerly (jin′jər′lē) *adv.:* carefully; cautiously.

Anne. Oh, please, please. Let's sing the song. I promise not to shout!

Mr. Frank. Very well. But quietly, now . . . I'll keep an eye on you and when . . .

[*As* ANNE *starts to sing, she is interrupted by* DUSSEL, *who is snorting and wheezing.*]

Dussel (*pointing to* PETER). You . . . You! (PETER *is coming from his bedroom, ostentatiously holding a bulge in his coat as if he were holding his cat, and dangling* ANNE'*s present before it.*) How many times . . . I told you . . . Out! Out!

Mr. Van Daan (*going to* PETER). What's the matter with you? Haven't you any sense? Get that cat out of here.

Peter (*innocently*). Cat?

Mr. Van Daan. You heard me. Get it out of here!

Peter. I have no cat.

[*Delighted with his joke, he opens his coat and pulls out a bath towel. The group at the table laugh, enjoying the joke.*]

Dussel (*still wheezing*). It doesn't need to be the cat . . . his clothes are enough . . . when he comes out of that room . . .

Mr. Van Daan. Don't worry. You won't be bothered anymore. We're getting rid of it.

Dussel. At last you listen to me. (*He goes off into his bedroom.*)

Mr. Van Daan (*calling after him*). I'm not doing it for you. That's all in your mind . . . all of it! (*He starts back to his place at the table.*) I'm doing it because I'm sick of seeing that cat eat all our food.

Peter. That's not true! I only give him bones . . . scraps . . .

Mr. Van Daan. Don't tell me! He gets fatter every day! Damn cat looks better than any of us. Out he goes tonight!

Peter. No! No!

Anne. Mr. Van Daan, you can't do that! That's Peter's cat. Peter loves that cat.

Mrs. Frank (*quietly*). Anne.

Peter (*to* MR. VAN DAAN). If he goes, I go.

Mr. Van Daan. Go! Go!

Mrs. Van Daan. You're not going and the cat's not going! Now please . . . this is Hanukkah . . . Hanukkah . . . this is the time to celebrate . . . What's the matter with all of you? Come on, Anne. Let's have the song.

Anne (*singing*).

Oh, Hanukkah!
Oh, Hanukkah!
The sweet celebration.

Mr. Frank (*rising*). I think we should first blow out the candle . . . then we'll have something for tomorrow night.

Margot. But, Father, you're supposed to let it burn itself out.

Mr. Frank. I'm sure that God understands shortages. (*Before blowing it out*) "Praised be Thou, oh Lord our God, who hast sustained us and permitted us to celebrate this joyous festival."

[*He is about to blow out the candle when*

Margot Frank.

Vocabulary

ostentatiously (ăs′tən·tā′shəs·lē) *adv.*: in a showy or exaggerated way.

suddenly there is a crash of something falling below. They all freeze in horror, motionless. For a few seconds there is complete silence. MR. FRANK *slips off his shoes. The others noiselessly follow his example.* MR. FRANK *turns out a light near him. He motions to* PETER *to turn off the center lamp.* PETER *tries to reach it, realizes he cannot, and gets up on a chair. Just as he is touching the lamp, he loses his balance. The chair goes out from under him. He falls. The iron lampshade crashes to the floor. There is a sound of feet below running down the stairs.*]

Mr. Van Daan (*under his breath*). God Almighty! (*The only light left comes from the Hanukkah candle.* DUSSEL *comes from his room.* MR. FRANK *creeps over to the stairwell and stands listening. The dog is heard barking excitedly.*) Do you hear anything?

Mr. Frank (*in a whisper*). No. I think they've gone.

Mrs. Van Daan. It's the Green Police. They've found us.

Mr. Frank. If they had, they wouldn't have left. They'd be up here by now.

Mrs. Van Daan. I know it's the Green Police. They've gone to get help. That's all. They'll be back!

Mr. Van Daan. Or it may have been the Gestapo,[13] looking for papers . . .

Mr. Frank (*interrupting*). Or a thief, looking for money.

Mrs. Van Daan. We've got to do something . . . Quick! Quick! Before they come back.

Mr. Van Daan. There isn't anything to do. Just wait.

[MR. FRANK *holds up his hand for them to be*

quiet. He is listening intently. There is complete silence as they all strain to hear any sound from below. Suddenly ANNE *begins to sway. With a low cry she falls to the floor in a faint.* MRS. FRANK *goes to her quickly, sitting beside her on the floor and taking her in her arms.*]

Mrs. Frank. Get some water, please! Get some water!

[MARGOT *starts for the sink.*]

Mr. Van Daan (*grabbing* MARGOT). No! No! No one's going to run water!

Mr. Frank. If they've found us, they've found us. Get the water. (MARGOT *starts again for the sink.* MR. FRANK, *getting a flashlight*) I'm going down.

[MARGOT *rushes to him, clinging to him.* ANNE *struggles to consciousness.*]

Margot. No, Father, no! There may be someone there, waiting. . . . It may be a trap!

Mr. Frank. This is Saturday. There is no way for us to know what has happened until Miep or Mr. Kraler comes on Monday morning. We cannot live with this uncertainty.

Margot. Don't go, Father!

Mrs. Frank. Hush, darling, hush. (MR. FRANK *slips quietly out, down the steps, and out through the door below.*) Margot! Stay close to me.

[MARGOT *goes to her mother.*]

Mr. Van Daan. Shush! Shush!

[MRS. FRANK *whispers to* MARGOT *to get the water.* MARGOT *goes for it.*]

Mrs. Van Daan. Putti, where's our money? Get our money. I hear you can buy the

---

13. Gestapo (gə·stä′pō): Nazi secret police.

Green Police off, so much a head. Go upstairs quick! Get the money!

Mr. Van Daan. Keep still!

Mrs. Van Daan (*kneeling before him, pleading*). Do you want to be dragged off to a concentration camp? Are you going to stand there and wait for them to come up and get you? Do something, I tell you!

Mr. Van Daan (*pushing her aside*). Will you keep still!

[*He goes over to the stairwell to listen.* PETER *goes to his mother, helping her up onto the sofa. There is a second of silence; then* ANNE *can stand it no longer.*]

Anne. Someone go after Father! Make Father come back!

Peter (*starting for the door*). I'll go.

Mr. Van Daan. Haven't you done enough?

[*He pushes* PETER *roughly away. In his anger against his father* PETER *grabs a chair as if to hit him with it, then puts it down, burying his face in his hands.* MRS. FRANK *begins to pray softly.*]

Anne. Please, please, Mr. Van Daan. Get Father.

Mr. Van Daan. Quiet! Quiet!

[ANNE *is shocked into silence.* MRS. FRANK *pulls her closer, holding her protectively in her arms.*]

Mrs. Frank (*softly, praying*). "I lift up mine eyes unto the mountains, from whence cometh my help. My help cometh from the Lord who made heaven and earth. He will not suffer thy foot to be moved . . . He that keepeth thee will not slumber . . ."

[*She stops as she hears someone coming. They all watch the door tensely.* MR. FRANK *comes quietly in.* ANNE *rushes to him, holding him tight.*]

Mr. Frank. It was a thief. That noise must have scared him away.

Mrs. Van Daan. Thank God.

Mr. Frank. He took the cash box. And the radio. He ran away in such a hurry that he didn't stop to shut the street door. It was swinging wide open. (*A breath of relief sweeps over them.*) I think it would be good to have some light.

Margot. Are you sure it's all right?

Mr. Frank. The danger has passed. (MARGOT *goes to light the small lamp.*) Don't be so terrified, Anne. We're safe.

Dussel. Who says the danger has passed? Don't you realize we are in greater danger than ever?

Mr. Frank. Mr. Dussel, will you be still! (MR. FRANK *takes* ANNE *back to the table, making her sit down with him, trying to calm her.*)

Dussel (*pointing to* PETER). Thanks to this clumsy fool, there's someone now who knows we're up here! Someone now knows we're up here, hiding!

Mrs. Van Daan (*going to* DUSSEL). Someone knows we're here, yes. But who is the someone? A thief! A thief! You think a thief is going to go to the Green Police and say . . . "I was robbing a place the other night and I heard a noise up over my head?" You think a thief is going to do that?

Dussel. Yes. I think he will.

Mrs. Van Daan (*hysterically*). You're crazy! (*She stumbles back to her seat at the table.* PETER *follows protectively, pushing* DUSSEL *aside.*)

Dussel. I think someday he'll be caught and then he'll make a bargain with the Green Police . . . if they'll let him off, he'll tell them where some Jews are hiding!

[*He goes off into the bedroom. There is a second of* appalled *silence.*]

Mr. Van Daan. He's right.

Anne. Father, let's get out of here! We can't stay here now . . . Let's go . . .

Mr. Van Daan. Go! Where?

Mrs. Frank (*sinking into her chair at the table*). Yes. Where?

Mr. Frank (*rising, to them all*). Have we lost all faith? All courage? A moment ago we thought that they'd come for us. We were sure it was the end. But it wasn't the end. We're alive, safe. (MR. VAN DAAN *goes to the table and sits.* MR. FRANK *prays*) "We thank Thee, oh Lord our God, that in Thy infinite mercy Thou hast again seen fit to spare us." (*He blows out the candle, then turns to* ANNE.) Come on, Anne. The song! Let's have the song! (*He starts to sing.* ANNE *finally starts falteringly to sing, as* MR. FRANK *urges her on. Her voice is hardly audible at first.*)

Anne (*singing*).

Oh, Hanukkah! Oh, Hanukkah!
The sweet . . . celebration . . .

[*As she goes on singing, the others gradually join in, their voices still shaking with fear.* MRS. VAN DAAN *sobs as she sings.*]

Group.

Around the feast . . . we . . . gather
In complete . . . jubilation . . .
Happiest of sea . . . sons
Now is here.
Many are the reasons for good cheer.

[DUSSEL *comes from the bedroom. He comes over to the table, standing beside* MARGOT, *listening to them as they sing.*]

Together
We'll weather
Whatever tomorrow may bring.

Anne. We can't stay here now . . .

[*As they sing on with growing courage, the lights start to dim.*]

So hear us rejoicing
And merrily voicing
The Hanukkah song that we sing.
Hoy!

[*The lights are out. The curtain starts slowly to fall.*]

Hear us rejoicing
And merrily voicing
The Hanukkah song that we sing.

[*They are still singing as the curtain falls.*]

Curtain

Vocabulary
appalled (ə·pôld′) *v.* used as *adj.:* horrified; shocked.

Literary Response and Analysis
Act One, Scenes 4–5

Reading Check

1. Anne's nightmare in Scene 4 reveals tensions between Anne and two other members of the household. What is the nightmare? What tensions does it reveal?

2. Describe how the Hanukkah celebration in Scene 5 is interrupted. What does Peter do that makes matters worse? According to Dussel, how will this incident lead to their discovery by the police?

Interpretations

3. Go back to the list of **characters** you made after you read Scenes 1–3. Which adjectives, if any, would you change now? Why?

4. Anne is a **dynamic character;** that is, she changes in the course of the play. How does she hurt her mother in Scene 4? How do her gifts to her mother and Peter show that she has changed?

5. Re-read Anne's conversation with her father on page 247. What does she say that reminds you the most— or the least—of yourself? Explain.

6. There are many events in our lives that involve rituals: birthdays, wedding anniversaries, Christmas, Hanukkah. When we take part in those rituals, we remember the past and look to the future. The theater often shows rituals being celebrated onstage. Discuss how the Hanukkah celebration contrasts with the harsh reality outside the hiding place. What is the **mood** of this Hanukkah scene?

7. During the dark days of World War II, when England stood alone against the Nazis, the English found courage in these words of their prime minister, Winston Churchill: "We shall fight on the beaches, we shall fight on the landing grounds, we shall fight in the fields and in the streets, we shall fight in the hills, we shall never surrender." In what moment of the play does a group of people find courage in the words of a song? Can you think of other episodes from plays or movies (or real life) in which people face danger and summon up courage from a speech or song?

8. Describe the **reversal**—the sudden change in the characters' fortunes— that occurs in Scene 5. How did it make you feel?

9. Imagine that you are watching this play in a theater. What questions do you have as the curtain comes down on Act One? What do you **predict** will happen in Act Two?

Grade 6 Review Reading Standard 3.6 Identify and analyze features of themes conveyed through characters, actions, and images.

Act Two

■ SCENE 1

In the darkness we hear ANNE*'s voice, again reading from the diary.*

Anne's Voice. Saturday, the first of January, nineteen forty-four. Another new year has begun and we find ourselves still in our hiding place. We have been here now for one year, five months, and twenty-five days. It seems that our life is at a standstill.

[*The curtain rises on the scene. It is late afternoon. Everyone is bundled up against the cold. In the main room* MRS. FRANK *is taking down the laundry, which is hung across the back.* MR. FRANK *sits in the chair down left, reading.* MARGOT *is lying on the couch with a blanket over her and the many-colored knitted scarf around her throat.* ANNE *is seated at the center table, writing in her diary.* PETER, MR. *and* MRS. VAN DAAN, *and* DUSSEL *are all in their own rooms, reading or lying down.*

As the lights dim on, ANNE*'s voice continues, without a break.*]

Anne's Voice. We are all a little thinner. The Van Daans' "discussions" are as violent as ever. Mother still does not understand me. But then I don't understand her either. There is one great change, however. A change in myself. I read somewhere that girls of my age don't feel quite certain of themselves. That they become quiet within and begin to think of the miracle that is taking place in their bodies. I think that what is happening to me is so wonderful . . . not only what can be seen, but what is taking place inside. Each time it has happened, I have a feeling that I have a sweet secret. (*We hear the chimes and then a hymn being played on the carillon outside.*) And in spite of any pain, I long for the time when I shall feel that secret within me again.

[*The buzzer of the door below suddenly sounds. Everyone is startled.* MR. FRANK *tiptoes cautiously to the top of the steps and listens. Again the buzzer sounds, in* MIEP's *V-for-victory signal.*][1]

Mr. Frank. It's Miep!

[*He goes quickly down the steps to unbolt the door.* MRS. FRANK *calls upstairs to the* VAN DAANS *and then to* PETER.]

Mrs. Frank. Wake up, everyone! Miep is here! (ANNE *quickly puts her diary away.* MARGOT *sits up, pulling the blanket around her shoulders.* DUSSEL *sits on the edge of his bed, listening, disgruntled.* MIEP *comes up the steps, followed by* MR. KRALER. *They bring flowers, books, newspapers, etc.* ANNE *rushes to* MIEP, *throwing her arms affectionately around her.*) Miep . . . and Mr. Kraler . . . What a delightful surprise!

Mr. Kraler. We came to bring you New Year's greetings.

Mrs. Frank. You shouldn't . . . you should have at least one day to yourselves. (*She goes quickly to the stove and brings down teacups and tea for all of them.*)

Anne. Don't say that, it's so wonderful to see them! (*Sniffing at* MIEP's *coat*) I can smell the wind and the cold on your clothes.

Miep (*giving her the flowers*). There you are. (*Then to* MARGOT, *feeling her forehead*) How are you, Margot? . . . Feeling any better?

Margot. I'm all right.

Anne. We filled her full of every kind of pill so she won't cough and make a noise.

[*She runs into her room to put the flowers in water.* MR. *and* MRS. VAN DAAN *come from upstairs. Outside there is the sound of a band playing.*]

Mrs. Van Daan. Well, hello, Miep. Mr. Kraler.

Mr. Kraler (*giving a bouquet of flowers to* MRS. VAN DAAN). With my hope for peace in the New Year.

Peter (*anxiously*). Miep, have you seen Mouschi? Have you seen him anywhere around?

Miep. I'm sorry, Peter. I asked everyone in the neighborhood had they seen a gray cat. But they said no.

[MRS. FRANK *gives* MIEP *a cup of tea.* MR. FRANK *comes up the steps, carrying a small cake on a plate.*]

Mr. Frank. Look what Miep's brought for us!

Mrs. Frank (*taking it*). A cake!

Mr. Van Daan. A cake! (*He pinches* MIEP's *cheeks gaily and hurries up to the cupboard.*) I'll get some plates.

[DUSSEL, *in his room, hastily puts a coat on and starts out to join the others.*]

Mrs. Frank. Thank you, Miepia. You shouldn't have done it. You must have used all of your sugar ration for weeks. (*Giving it to* MRS. VAN DAAN) It's beautiful, isn't it?

Mrs. Van Daan. It's been ages since I even saw a cake. Not since you brought us one last year. (*Without looking at the cake, to* MIEP) Remember? Don't you remember, you gave us one on New Year's Day? Just this time last year? I'll never forget it because you had "Peace in nineteen forty-three" on it.

---

1. **V-for-victory signal:** three short rings and one long ring, Morse code for the letter *V*, the Allied symbol for victory.

Vocabulary
disgruntled (dis·grunt′'ld) *v.* used as *adj.*: displeased; annoyed.

(*She looks at the cake and reads*) "Peace in nineteen forty-four!"

Miep. Well, it has to come sometime, you know. (*As* DUSSEL *comes from his room*) Hello, Mr. Dussel.

Mr. Kraler. How are you?

Mr. Van Daan (*bringing plates and a knife*). Here's the knife, liefje. Now, how many of us are there?

Miep. None for me, thank you.

Mr. Frank. Oh, please. You must.

Miep. I couldn't.

Mr. Van Daan. Good! That leaves one . . . two . . . three . . . seven of us.

Dussel. Eight! Eight! It's the same number as it always is!

Mr. Van Daan. I left Margot out. I take it for granted Margot won't eat any.

Anne. Why wouldn't she!

Mrs. Frank. I think it won't harm her.

Mr. Van Daan. All right! All right! I just didn't want her to start coughing again, that's all.

Dussel. And please, Mrs. Frank should cut the cake.

Mr. Van Daan. What's the difference?

Mrs. Van Daan. It's not Mrs. Frank's cake, is it, Miep? It's for all of us. } *Together*

Dussel. Mrs. Frank divides things better.

Mrs. Van Daan (*going to* DUSSEL). What are you trying to say?

Mr. Van Daan. Oh, come on! Stop wasting time! } *Together*

Mr. Kraler.

Mrs. Van Daan (*to* DUSSEL). Don't I always give everybody exactly the same? Don't I?

Mr. Van Daan. Forget it, Kerli.

Mrs. Van Daan. No. I want an answer! Don't I?

Dussel. Yes. Yes. Everybody gets exactly the same . . . except Mr. Van Daan always gets a little bit more.

[MR. VAN DAAN *advances on* DUSSEL, *the knife still in his hand.*]

Mr. Van Daan. That's a lie!

[DUSSEL *retreats before the onslaught of the* VAN DAANS.]

Mr. Frank. Please, please! (*Then, to* MIEP) You see what a little sugar cake does to us? It goes right to our heads!

Mr. Van Daan (*handing* MRS. FRANK *the knife*). Here you are, Mrs. Frank.

Mrs. Frank. Thank you. (*Then, to* MIEP, *as she goes to the table to cut the cake*) Are you sure you won't have some?

Miep (*drinking her tea*). No, really, I have to go in a minute.

[*The sound of the band fades out in the distance.*]

Peter (*to* MIEP). Maybe Mouschi went back to our house . . . they say that cats . . . Do you ever get over there . . . ? I mean . . . do you suppose you could . . . ?

Miep. I'll try, Peter. The first minute I get, I'll try. But I'm afraid, with him gone a week . . .

Dussel. Make up your mind, already some-one has had a nice big dinner from that cat!

[PETER *is furious, inarticulate. He starts toward* DUSSEL *as if to hit him.* MR. FRANK *stops him.* MRS. FRANK *speaks quickly to ease the situation.*]

Mrs. Frank (*to* MIEP). This is delicious, Miep!

Mrs. Van Daan (*eating hers*). Delicious!

Mr. Van Daan (*finishing it in one gulp*). Dirk's in luck to get a girl who can bake like this!

Miep (*putting down her empty teacup*). I have to run. Dirk's taking me to a party tonight.

Anne. How heavenly! Remember now what everyone is wearing and what you have to eat and everything, so you can tell us tomorrow.

Miep. I'll give you a full report! Goodbye, everyone!

Mr. Van Daan (*to* MIEP). Just a minute. There's something I'd like you to do for me. (*He hurries off up the stairs to his room.*)

Mrs. Van Daan (*sharply*). Putti, where are you going? (*She rushes up the stairs after him, calling hysterically.*) What do you want? Putti, what are you going to do?

Miep (*to* PETER). What's wrong?

Peter (*his sympathy is with his mother*). Father says he's going to sell her fur coat. She's crazy about that old fur coat.

Dussel. Is it possible? Is it possible that anyone is so silly as to worry about a fur coat in times like this?

Peter. It's none of your darn business . . . and if you say one more thing . . . I'll, I'll take you and I'll . . . I mean it . . . I'll . . .

[*There is a piercing scream from* MRS. VAN DAAN, *above. She grabs at the fur coat as* MR. VAN DAAN *is starting downstairs with it.*]

Mrs. Van Daan. No! No! No! Don't you dare take that! You hear? It's mine! (*Downstairs* PETER *turns away, embarrassed, miserable.*) My father gave me that! You didn't give it to me. You have no right. Let go of it . . . you hear?

[MR. VAN DAAN *pulls the coat from her hands and hurries downstairs.* MRS. VAN DAAN *sinks to the floor, sobbing. As* MR. VAN DAAN *comes into the main room, the others look away, embarrassed for him.*]

Mr. Van Daan (*to* MR. KRALER). Just a little—discussion over the advisability of selling this coat. As I have often reminded Mrs. Van Daan, it's very selfish of her to keep it when people outside are in such desperate need of clothing. . . . (*He gives the coat to* MIEP.) So if you will please to sell it for us? It should fetch a good price. And by the way, will you get me cigarettes. I don't care what kind they are . . . get all you can.

Miep. It's terribly difficult to get them, Mr. Van Daan. But I'll try. Goodbye.

[*She goes.* MR. FRANK *follows her down the steps to bolt the door after her.* MRS. FRANK *gives* MR. KRALER *a cup of tea.*]

Mrs. Frank. Are you sure you won't have some cake, Mr. Kraler?

Mr. Kraler. I'd better not.

Mr. Van Daan. You're still feeling badly? What does your doctor say?

Mr. Kraler. I haven't been to him.

Mrs. Frank. Now, Mr. Kraler! . . .

Mr. Kraler (*sitting at the table*). Oh, I tried. But you can't get near a doctor these days . . . they're so busy. After weeks I finally

---

Vocabulary

inarticulate (in′är·tik′yoō·lit) *adj.:* unable to speak. *Inarticulate* also means "unable to speak understandably or effectively."

managed to get one on the telephone. I told him I'd like an appointment . . . I wasn't feeling very well. You know what he answers . . . over the telephone . . . "Stick out your tongue!" (*They laugh. He turns to* MR. FRANK *as* MR. FRANK *comes back.*) I have some contracts here . . . I wonder if you'd look over them with me . . .

Mr. Frank (*putting out his hand*). Of course.

Mr. Kraler (*he rises*). If we could go downstairs . . . (MR. FRANK *starts ahead;* MR. KRALER *speaks to the others.*) Will you forgive us? I won't keep him but a minute. (*He starts to follow* MR. FRANK *down the steps.*)

Margot (*with sudden foreboding*). What's happened? Something's happened! Hasn't it, Mr. Kraler?

[MR. KRALER *stops and comes back, trying to reassure* MARGOT *with a pretense of casualness.*]

Mr. Kraler. No, really. I want your father's advice . . .

Margot. Something's gone wrong! I know it!

Mr. Frank (*coming back, to* MR. KRALER). If it's something that concerns us here, it's better that we all hear it.

Mr. Kraler (*turning to him, quietly*). But . . . the children . . . ?

Mr. Frank. What they'd imagine would be worse than any reality.

[*As* MR. KRALER *speaks, they all listen with intense apprehension.* MRS. VAN DAAN *comes down the stairs and sits on the bottom step.*]

Mr. Kraler. It's a man in the storeroom . . . I don't know whether or not you remember him . . . Carl, about fifty, heavyset, nearsighted . . . He came with us just before you left.

Mr. Frank. He was from Utrecht?

Mr. Kraler. That's the man. A couple of weeks ago, when I was in the storeroom, he closed the door and asked me . . . "How's Mr. Frank? What do you hear from Mr. Frank?" I told him I only knew there was a rumor that you were in Switzerland. He said he'd heard that rumor too, but he thought I might know something more. I didn't pay any attention to it . . . but then a thing happened yesterday . . . He'd brought some invoices to the office for me to sign. As I was going through them, I looked up. He was standing staring at the bookcase . . . your bookcase. He said he thought he remembered a door there . . . Wasn't there a door there that used to go up to the loft? Then he told me he wanted more money. Twenty guilders[2] more a week.

Mr. Van Daan. Blackmail!

Mr. Frank. Twenty guilders? Very modest blackmail.

Mr. Van Daan. That's just the beginning.

Dussel (*coming to* MR. FRANK). You know what I think? He was the thief who was down there that night. That's how he knows we're here.

Mr. Frank (*to* MR. KRALER). How was it left? What did you tell him?

Mr. Kraler. I said I had to think about it. What shall I do? Pay him the money? . . . Take a chance on firing him . . . or what? I don't know.

Dussel (*frantic*). For God's sake, don't fire him! Pay him what he asks . . . keep him here where you can have your eye on him.

Mr. Frank. Is it so much that he's asking? What are they paying nowadays?

Mr. Kraler. He could get it in a war plant. But

---

2. **guilders** (gil′dərz) *n.:* Dutch money.

this isn't a war plant. Mind you, I don't know if he really knows . . . or if he doesn't know.

Mr. Frank. Offer him half. Then we'll soon find out if it's blackmail or not.

Dussel. And if it is? We've got to pay it, haven't we? Anything he asks we've got to pay!

Mr. Frank. Let's decide that when the time comes.

Mr. Kraler. This may be all my imagination. You get to a point, these days, where you suspect everyone and everything. Again and again . . . on some simple look or word, I've found myself . . .

[*The telephone rings in the office below.*]

Mrs. Van Daan (*hurrying to* MR. KRALER). There's the telephone! What does that mean, the telephone ringing on a holiday?

Mr. Kraler. That's my wife. I told her I had to go over some papers in my office . . . to call me there when she got out of church. (*He starts out.*) I'll offer him half, then. Goodbye . . . we'll hope for the best!

[*The group call their goodbyes halfheartedly.* MR. FRANK *follows* MR. KRALER *to bolt the door below. During the following scene,* MR. FRANK *comes back up and stands listening, disturbed.*]

Dussel (*to* MR. VAN DAAN). You can thank your son for this . . . smashing the light! I tell you, it's just a question of time now. (*He goes to the window at the back and stands looking out.*)

Margot. Sometimes I wish the end would come . . . whatever it is.

Mrs. Frank (*shocked*). Margot!

[ANNE *goes to* MARGOT, *sitting beside her on the couch with her arms around her.*]

Margot. Then at least we'd know where we were.

Mrs. Frank. You should be ashamed of yourself! Talking that way! Think how lucky we are! Think of the thousands dying in the war, every day. Think of the people in concentration camps.

Anne (*interrupting*). What's the good of that? What's the good of thinking of misery when you're already miserable? That's stupid!

Mrs. Frank. Anne!

[*As* ANNE *goes on raging at her mother,* MRS. FRANK *tries to break in, in an effort to quiet her.*]

Anne. We're young, Margot and Peter and I! You grown-ups have had your chance! But look at us . . . If we begin thinking of all the horror in the world, we're lost! We're trying to hold on to some kind of ideals . . . when everything . . . ideals, hopes . . . everything is being destroyed! It isn't our fault that the world is in such a mess! We weren't around when all this started! So don't try to take it out on us! (*She rushes off to her room, slamming the door after her. She picks up a brush from the chest and hurls it to the floor. Then she sits on the settee, trying to control her anger.*)

Mr. Van Daan. She talks as if we started the war! Did we start the war? (*He spots* ANNE's *cake. As he starts to take it,* PETER *anticipates him.*)

Peter. She left her cake. (*He starts for* ANNE's *room with the cake. There is silence in the main room.* MRS. VAN DAAN *goes up to her room, followed by* MR. VAN DAAN. DUSSEL *stays looking out the window.* MR. FRANK *brings* MRS. FRANK *her cake. She eats it slowly, without relish.* MR. FRANK *takes his cake to* MARGOT *and sits quietly on the sofa*

Peter. You know just how to talk to them.

beside her. PETER *stands in the doorway of* ANNE'*s darkened room, looking at her, then makes a little movement to let her know he is there.* ANNE *sits up quickly, trying to hide the signs of her tears.* PETER *holds out the cake to her.*) You left this.

Anne (*dully*). Thanks.

[PETER *starts to go out, then comes back.*]

Peter. I thought you were fine just now. You know just how to talk to them. You know just how to say it. I'm no good . . . I never can think . . . especially when I'm mad . . .

That Dussel . . . when he said that about Mouschi . . . someone eating him . . . all I could think is . . . I wanted to hit him. I wanted to give him such a . . . a . . . that he'd . . . That's what I used to do when there was an argument at school. . . . That's the way I . . . but here . . . And an old man like that . . . it wouldn't be so good.

Anne. You're making a big mistake about me. I do it all wrong. I say too much. I go too far. I hurt people's feelings. . . .

[DUSSEL *leaves the window, going to his room.*]

Peter. I think you're just fine . . . What I want to say . . . if it wasn't for you around here, I don't know. What I mean . . .

[PETER *is interrupted by* DUSSEL'*s turning on the light.* DUSSEL *stands in the doorway, startled to see* PETER. PETER *advances toward him forbiddingly.* DUSSEL *backs out of the room.* PETER *closes the door on him.*]

Anne. Do you mean it, Peter? Do you really mean it?

Peter. I said it, didn't I?

Anne. Thank you, Peter!

[*In the main room* MR. *and* MRS. FRANK *collect the dishes and take them to the sink, washing them.* MARGOT *lies down again on the couch.* DUSSEL, *lost, wanders into* PETER'*s room and takes up a book, starting to read.*]

Peter (*looking at the photographs on the wall*). You've got quite a collection.

Anne. Wouldn't you like some in your room? I could give you some. Heaven knows you spend enough time in there . . . doing heaven knows what . . .

Peter. It's easier. A fight starts, or an argument . . . I duck in there.

Anne. You're lucky, having a room to go to.

His Lordship is always here . . . I hardly ever get a minute alone. When they start in on me, I can't duck away. I have to stand there and take it.

Peter. You gave some of it back just now.

Anne. I get so mad. They've formed their opinions . . . about everything . . . but we . . . we're still trying to find out . . . We have problems here that no other people our age have ever had. And just as you think you've solved them, something comes along and bang! You have to start all over again.

Peter. At least you've got someone you can talk to.

Anne. Not really. Mother . . . I never discuss anything serious with her. She doesn't understand. Father's all right. We can talk about everything . . . everything but one thing. Mother. He simply won't talk about her. I don't think you can be really intimate with anyone if he holds something back, do you?

Peter. I think your father's fine.

Anne. Oh, he is, Peter! He is! He's the only one who's ever given me the feeling that I have any sense. But anyway, nothing can take the place of school and play and friends of your own age . . . or near your age . . . can it?

Peter. I suppose you miss your friends and all.

Anne. It isn't just . . . (*She breaks off, staring up at him for a second.*) Isn't it funny, you and I? Here we've been seeing each other every minute for almost a year and a half, and this is the first time we've ever really talked. It helps a lot to have someone to talk to, don't you think? It helps you to let off steam.

Peter (*going to the door*). Well, any time you want to let off steam, you can come into my room.

Anne (*following him*). I can get up an awful lot of steam. You'll have to be careful how you say that.

Peter. It's all right with me.

Anne. Do you mean it?

Peter. I said it, didn't I?

[*He goes out.* ANNE *stands in her doorway looking after him. As* PETER *gets to his door, he stands for a minute looking back at her. Then he goes into his room.* DUSSEL *rises as he comes in, and quickly passes him, going out. He starts across for his room.* ANNE *sees him coming and pulls her door shut.* DUSSEL *turns back toward* PETER's *room.* PETER *pulls his door shut.* DUSSEL *stands there, bewildered,* forlorn.

The scene slowly dims out. The curtain falls on the scene. ANNE's *voice comes over in the darkness . . . faintly at first and then with growing strength.*]

Anne's Voice. We've had bad news. The people from whom Miep got our ration books have been arrested. So we have had to cut down on our food. Our stomachs are so empty that they rumble and make strange noises, all in different keys. Mr. Van Daan's is deep and low, like a bass fiddle. Mine is high, whistling like a flute. As we all sit around waiting for supper, it's like an orchestra tuning up. It only needs Toscanini[3] to raise his baton and we'd be off in the "Ride of the Valkyries."[4] Monday, the sixth

---

3. **Toscanini** (täs′kə·nē′nē): Arturo Toscanini (1867–1957), a famous orchestra conductor.
4. **"Ride of the Valkyries"** (val·kir′ēz): lively piece of music from an opera by the German composer Richard Wagner (1813–1883).

Vocabulary
forlorn (fôr·lôrn′) *adj.:* abandoned and lonely.

of March, nineteen forty-four. Mr. Kraler is in the hospital. It seems he has ulcers. Pim says we are his ulcers. Miep has to run the business and us too. The Americans have landed on the southern tip of Italy. Father looks for a quick finish to the war. Mr. Dussel is waiting every day for the warehouse man to demand more money. Have I been skipping too much from one subject to another? I can't help it. I feel that spring is coming. I feel it in my whole body and soul. I feel utterly confused. I am longing . . . so longing . . . for everything . . . for friends . . . for someone to talk to . . . someone who understands . . . someone young, who feels as I do . . .

[*As these last lines are being said, the curtain rises on the scene. The lights dim on.* ANNE*'s voice fades out.*]

■ SCENE 2

It is evening, after supper. From outside we hear the sound of children playing. The "grown-ups," with the exception of MR. VAN DAAN, *are all in the main room.* MRS. FRANK *is doing some mending.* MRS. VAN DAAN *is reading a fashion magazine.* MR. FRANK *is going over business accounts.* DUSSEL, *in his dentist's jacket, is pacing up and down, impatient to get into his bedroom.* MR. VAN DAAN *is upstairs working on a piece of embroidery in an embroidery frame.*

In his room PETER *is sitting before the mirror, smoothing his hair. As the scene goes on, he puts on his tie, brushes his coat and puts it on, preparing himself meticulously for a visit from* ANNE. *On his wall are now hung some of* ANNE*'s motion picture stars.*

In her room ANNE *too is getting dressed. She stands before the mirror in her slip, trying various ways of dressing her hair.* MARGOT *is seated on the sofa, hemming a skirt for* ANNE *to wear.*

In the main room DUSSEL *can stand it no longer. He comes over, rapping sharply on the door of his and* ANNE*'s bedroom.*

Anne (*calling to him*). No, no, Mr. Dussel! I am not dressed yet. (DUSSEL *walks away, furious, sitting down and burying his head in his hands.* ANNE *turns to* MARGOT.) How is that? How does that look?
Margot (*glancing at her briefly*). Fine.
Anne. You didn't even look.
Margot. Of course I did. It's fine.
Anne. Margot, tell me, am I terribly ugly?
Margot. Oh, stop fishing.
Anne. No. No. Tell me.
Margot. Of course you're not. You've got nice eyes . . . and a lot of <u>animation</u>, and . . .
Anne. A little vague, aren't you?

[*She reaches over and takes a brassiere out of* MARGOT*'s sewing basket. She holds it up to herself, studying the effect in the mirror. Outside,* MRS. FRANK, *feeling sorry for* DUSSEL, *comes over, knocking at the girls' door.*]

Mrs. Frank (*outside*). May I come in?
Margot. Come in, Mother.
Mrs. Frank (*shutting the door behind her*). Mr. Dussel's impatient to get in here.
Anne (*still with the brassiere*). Heavens, he takes the room for himself the entire day.
Mrs. Frank (*gently*). Anne, dear, you're not going in again tonight to see Peter?

Vocabulary
animation (an'i·mā'shen) *n.:* liveliness.

Anne (*dignified*). That is my intention.

Mrs. Frank. But you've already spent a great deal of time in there today.

Anne. I was in there exactly twice. Once to get the dictionary, and then three quarters of an hour before supper.

Mrs. Frank. Aren't you afraid you're disturbing him?

Anne. Mother, I have some intuition.

Mrs. Frank. Then may I ask you this much, Anne. Please don't shut the door when you go in.

Anne. You sound like Mrs. Van Daan! (*She throws the brassiere back in* MARGOT's *sewing basket and picks up her blouse, putting it on.*)

Mrs. Frank. No. No. I don't mean to suggest anything wrong. I only wish that you wouldn't expose yourself to criticism . . . that you wouldn't give Mrs. Van Daan the opportunity to be unpleasant.

Anne. Mrs. Van Daan doesn't need an opportunity to be unpleasant!

Mrs. Frank. Everyone's on edge, worried about Mr. Kraler. This is one more thing . . .

Anne. I'm sorry, Mother. I'm going to Peter's room. I'm not going to let Petronella Van Daan spoil our friendship.

[MRS. FRANK *hesitates for a second, then goes out, closing the door after her. She gets a pack of playing cards and sits at the center table, playing solitaire. In* ANNE's *room* MARGOT *hands the finished skirt to* ANNE. *As* ANNE *is putting it on,* MARGOT *takes off her high-heeled shoes and stuffs paper in the toes so that* ANNE *can wear them.*]

Margot (*to* ANNE). Why don't you two talk in the main room? It'd save a lot of trouble. It's hard on Mother, having to listen to those remarks from Mrs. Van Daan and not say a word.

Anne. Why doesn't she say a word? I think it's ridiculous to take it and take it.

Margot. You don't understand Mother at all, do you? She can't talk back. She's not like you. It's just not in her nature to fight back.

Anne. Anyway . . . the only one I worry about is you. I feel awfully guilty about you. (*She sits on the stool near* MARGOT, *putting on* MARGOT's *high-heeled shoes.*)

Margot. What about?

Anne. I mean, every time I go into Peter's room, I have a feeling I may be hurting you. (MARGOT *shakes her head.*) I know if it were me, I'd be wild. I'd be desperately jealous, if it were me.

Margot. Well, I'm not.

Anne. You don't feel badly? Really? Truly? You're not jealous?

Margot. Of course I'm jealous . . . jealous that you've got something to get up in the morning for . . . But jealous of you and Peter? No.

[ANNE *goes back to the mirror.*]

Anne. Maybe there's nothing to be jealous of. Maybe he doesn't really like me. Maybe I'm just taking the place of his cat . . . (*She picks up a pair of short white gloves, putting them on.*) Wouldn't you like to come in with us?

Margot. I have a book.

[*The sound of the children playing outside fades out. In the main room* DUSSEL *can stand it no longer. He jumps up, going to the bedroom door and knocking sharply.*]

Dussel. Will you please let me in my room!

Anne. Just a minute, dear, dear Mr. Dussel. (*She picks up her mother's pink stole and* *adjusts it elegantly over her shoulders, then gives a last look in the mirror.*) Well, here I go . . . to run the gantlet.[5] (*She starts out, followed by* MARGOT.)

Dussel (*as she appears—sarcastic*). Thank you so much.

[DUSSEL *goes into his room.* ANNE *goes toward* PETER'*s room, passing* MRS. VAN DAAN *and her parents at the center table.*]

Mrs. Van Daan. My God, look at her! (ANNE *pays no attention. She knocks at* PETER'*s door.*) I don't know what good it is to have a son. I never see him. He wouldn't care if I killed myself. (PETER *opens the door and stands aside for* ANNE *to come in.*) Just a minute, Anne. (*She goes to them at the door.*) I'd like to say a few words to my son. Do you mind? (PETER *and* ANNE *stand waiting.*) Peter, I don't want you staying up till all hours tonight. You've got to have your sleep. You're a growing boy. You hear?

Mrs. Frank. Anne won't stay late. She's going to bed promptly at nine. Aren't you, Anne?

Anne. Yes, Mother . . . (*To* MRS. VAN DAAN) May we go now?

Mrs. Van Daan. Are you asking me? I didn't know I had anything to say about it.

Mrs. Frank. Listen for the chimes, Anne dear.

[*The two young people go off into* PETER'*s room, shutting the door after them.*]

---

5. **run the gantlet** (gŏnt'lĭt): proceed while under attack from both sides.

Mrs. Van Daan (*to* MRS. FRANK). In my day it was the boys who called on the girls. Not the girls on the boys.

Mrs. Frank. You know how young people like to feel that they have secrets. Peter's room is the only place where they can talk.

Mrs. Van Daan. Talk! That's not what they called it when I was young.

[MRS. VAN DAAN *goes off to the bathroom.* MARGOT *settles down to read her book.* MR. FRANK *puts his papers away and brings a chess game to the center table. He and* MRS. FRANK *start to play. In* PETER'*s room,* ANNE *speaks to* PETER, *indignant, humiliated.*]

Anne. Aren't they awful? Aren't they impossible? Treating us as if we were still in the nursery.

[*She sits on the cot.* PETER *gets a bottle of pop and two glasses.*]

Peter. Don't let it bother you. It doesn't bother me.

Anne. I suppose you can't really blame them . . . they think back to what *they* were like at our age. They don't realize how much more advanced we are. . . . When you think what wonderful discussions we've had! . . . Oh, I forgot. I was going to bring you some more pictures.

Peter. Oh, these are fine, thanks.

Anne. Don't you want some more? Miep just brought me some new ones.

Peter. Maybe later. (*He gives her a glass of*

Mrs. Frank.

pop and, taking some for himself, sits down facing her.)

Anne (*looking up at one of the photographs*). I remember when I got that . . . I won it. I bet Jopie that I could eat five ice-cream cones. We'd all been playing ping-pong . . . We used to have heavenly times . . . we'd finish up with ice cream at the Delphi or the Oasis, where Jews were allowed . . . there'd always be a lot of boys . . . we'd laugh and joke . . . I'd like to go back to it for a few days or a week. But after that I know I'd be bored to death. I think more seriously about life now. I want to be a journalist . . . or something. I love to write. What do you want to do?

Peter. I thought I might go off some-place . . . work on a farm or something . . . some job that doesn't take much brains.

Anne. You shouldn't talk that way. You've got the most awful inferiority complex.

Peter. I know I'm not smart.

Anne. That isn't true. You're much better than I am in dozens of things . . . arithmetic and algebra and . . . well, you're a million times better than I am in algebra. (*With sudden directness*) You like Margot, don't you? Right from the start you liked her, liked her much better than me.

Peter (*uncomfortably*). Oh, I don't know.

[*In the main room* MRS. VAN DAAN *comes from the bathroom and goes over to the sink, polishing a coffeepot.*]

Anne. It's all right. Everyone feels that way. Margot's so good. She's sweet and bright and beautiful and I'm not.

Peter. I wouldn't say that.

Anne. Oh, no, I'm not. I know that. I know quite well that I'm not a beauty. I never have been and never shall be.

Peter. I don't agree at all. I think you're pretty.

Anne. That's not true!

Peter. And another thing. You've changed . . . from at first, I mean.

Anne. I have?

Peter. I used to think you were awful noisy.

Anne. And what do you think now, Peter? How have I changed?

Peter. Well . . . er . . . you're . . . quieter.

[*In his room* DUSSEL *takes his pajamas and toilet articles and goes into the bathroom to change.*]

Anne. I'm glad you don't just hate me.

Peter. I never said that.

Anne. I bet when you get out of here, you'll never think of me again.

Peter. That's crazy.

Anne. When you get back with all of your friends, you're going to say . . . now what did I ever see in that Mrs. Quack Quack.

Peter. I haven't got any friends.

Anne. Oh, Peter, of course you have. Everyone has friends.

Peter. Not me. I don't want any. I get along all right without them.

Anne. Does that mean you can get along without me? I think of myself as your friend.

Peter. No. If they were all like you, it'd be different.

[*He takes the glasses and the bottle and puts them away. There is a second's silence and then* ANNE *speaks, hesitantly, shyly.*]

Anne. Peter, did you ever kiss a girl?

Peter. Yes. Once.

Anne (*to cover her feelings*). That picture's crooked. (PETER *goes over, straightening the photograph.*) Was she pretty?

Peter. Huh?

Peter. I've always thought that when two people . . .

Peter. It didn't with me.

Anne. I've been kissed twice. Once a man I'd never seen before kissed me on the cheek when he picked me up off the ice and I was crying. And the other was Mr. Koophuis, a friend of Father's, who kissed my hand. You wouldn't say those counted, would you?

Peter. I wouldn't say so.

Anne. I know almost for certain that Margot would never kiss anyone unless she was engaged to them. And I'm sure too that Mother never touched a man before Pim. But I don't know . . . things are so different now . . . What do you think? Do you think a girl shouldn't kiss anyone except if she's engaged or something? It's so hard to try to think what to do, when here we are with the whole world falling around our ears and you think . . . well . . . you don't know what's going to happen tomorrow and . . . What do you think?

Peter. I suppose it'd depend on the girl. Some girls, anything they do's wrong. But others . . . well . . . it wouldn't necessarily be wrong with them. (*The carillon starts to strike nine o'clock.*) I've always thought that when two people . . .

Anne. Nine o'clock. I have to go.

Peter. That's right.

Anne (*without moving*). Good night.

[*There is a second's pause; then* PETER *gets up and moves toward the door.*]

Peter. You won't let them stop you coming?

Anne. No. (*She rises and starts for the door.*) Sometime I might bring my diary. There are so many things in it that I want to talk over with you. There's a lot about you.

Peter. What kind of thing?

Anne. I wouldn't want you to see some of it.

Anne. The girl that you kissed.

Peter. I don't know. I was blindfolded. (*He comes back and sits down again.*) It was at a party. One of those kissing games.

Anne (*relieved*). Oh. I don't suppose that really counts, does it?

I thought you were a nothing, just the way you thought about me.

Peter. Did you change your mind, the way I changed my mind about you?

Anne. Well . . . You'll see . . .

[*For a second* ANNE *stands looking up at* PETER, *longing for him to kiss her. As he makes no move, she turns away. Then suddenly* PETER *grabs her awkwardly in his arms, kissing her on the cheek.* ANNE *walks out dazed. She stands for a minute, her back to the people in the main room. As she regains her poise, she goes to her mother and father and* MARGOT, *silently kissing them. They murmur their good nights to her. As she is about to open her bedroom door, she catches sight of* MRS. VAN DAAN. *She goes quickly to her, taking her face in her hands and kissing her, first on one cheek and then on the other. Then she hurries off into her room.* MRS. VAN DAAN *looks after her and then looks over at* PETER'*s room. Her suspicions are confirmed.*]

Mrs. Van Daan (*she knows*). Ah hah!

[*The lights dim out. The curtain falls on the scene. In the darkness* ANNE'*s voice comes, faintly at first and then with growing strength.*]

Anne's Voice. By this time we all know each other so well that if anyone starts to tell a story, the rest can finish it for him. We're having to cut down still further on our meals. What makes it worse, the rats have been at work again. They've carried off some of our precious food. Even Mr. Dussel wishes now that Mouschi was here. Thursday, the twentieth of April, nineteen forty-four. Invasion fever is mounting every day. Miep tells us that people outside talk of nothing else. For myself, life has become much more pleasant. I often go to Peter's room after supper. Oh, don't think I'm in love, because I'm not. But it does make life more bearable to have someone with whom you can exchange views. No more tonight. P.S. . . . I must be honest. I must confess that I actually live for the next meeting. Is there anything lovelier than to sit under the skylight and feel the sun on your cheeks and have a darling boy in your arms? I admit now that I'm glad the Van Daans had a son and not a daughter. I've outgrown another dress. That's the third. I'm having to wear Margot's clothes after all. I'm working hard on my French and am now reading *La Belle Nivernaise*.[6]

[*As she is saying the last lines, the curtain rises on the scene. The lights dim on as* ANNE'*s voice fades out.*]

■ SCENE 3

It is night, a few weeks later. Everyone is in bed. There is complete quiet. In the VAN DAANS' *room a match flares up for a moment and then is quickly put out.* MR. VAN DAAN, *in bare feet, dressed in underwear and trousers, is dimly seen coming stealthily down the stairs and into the main room, where* MR. *and* MRS. FRANK *and* MARGOT *are sleeping. He goes to the food safe and again lights a match. Then he cautiously opens the safe, taking out a half loaf of bread. As he closes the safe, it creaks. He stands rigid.* MRS. FRANK *sits up in bed. She sees him.*

---

6. *La Belle Nivernaise* (nē·ver′nez′): children's story by the French writer Alphonse Daudet (1840–1897).

Mrs. Frank (*screaming*). Otto! Otto! Komme schnell![7]

[*The rest of the people wake, hurriedly getting up.*]

Mr. Frank. Was ist los? Was ist passiert?[8]

[DUSSEL, *followed by* ANNE, *comes from his room.*]

Mrs. Frank (*as she rushes over to* MR. VAN DAAN). Er stiehlt das Essen![9]

Dussel (*grabbing* MR. VAN DAAN). You! You! Give me that.

Mrs. Van Daan (*coming down the stairs*). Putti . . . Putti . . . what is it?

Dussel (*his hands on* MR. VAN DAAN's *neck*). You dirty thief . . . stealing food . . . you good-for-nothing . . .

Mr. Frank. Mr. Dussel! For God's sake! Help me, Peter!

[PETER *comes over, trying, with* MR. FRANK, *to separate the two struggling men.*]

Peter. Let him go! Let go!

[DUSSEL *drops* MR. VAN DAAN, *pushing him away. He shows them the end of a loaf of bread that he has taken from* MR. VAN DAAN.]

Dussel. You greedy, selfish . . . !

[MARGOT *turns on the lights.*]

Mrs. Van Daan. Putti . . . what is it?

[*All of* MRS. FRANK's *gentleness, her self-control, is gone. She is outraged, in a frenzy of indignation.*]

_____

7. **Komme schnell:** German for "Come quickly."
8. **Was . . . passiert:** "What's going on? What happened?"
9. **Er . . . Essen:** "He is stealing the food."

Mrs. Frank. The bread! He was stealing the bread!

Dussel. It was you, and all the time we thought it was the rats!

Mr. Frank. Mr. Van Daan, how could you!

Mr. Van Daan. I'm hungry.

Mrs. Frank. We're all of us hungry! I see the children getting thinner and thinner. Your own son Peter . . . I've heard him moan in his sleep, he's so hungry. And you come in the night and steal food that should go to them . . . to the children!

Mrs. Van Daan (*going to* MR. VAN DAAN *protectively*). He needs more food than the rest of us. He's used to more. He's a big man.

[MR. VAN DAAN *breaks away, going over and sitting on the couch.*]

Mrs. Frank (*turning on* MRS. VAN DAAN). And you . . . you're worse than he is! You're a mother, and yet you sacrifice your child to this man . . . this . . . this . . .

Mr. Frank. Edith! Edith!

[MARGOT *picks up the pink woolen stole, putting it over her mother's shoulders.*]

Mrs. Frank (*paying no attention, going on to* MRS. VAN DAAN). Don't think I haven't seen you! Always saving the choicest bits for him! I've watched you day after day and I've held my tongue. But not any longer! Not after this! Now I want him to go! I want him to get out of here!

Mr. Frank. Edith!

Mr. Van Daan. Get out of here?

Mrs. Van Daan. What do you mean?

} *Together*

Mrs. Frank. Just that! Take your things and get out!

Mr. Frank (*to* MRS. FRANK). You're speaking in anger. You cannot mean what you are saying.

Mrs. Frank. I mean exactly that!

[MRS. VAN DAAN *takes a cover from the* FRANKS' *bed, pulling it about her.*]

Mr. Frank. For two long years we have lived here, side by side. We have respected each other's rights . . . we have managed to live in peace. Are we now going to throw it all away? I know this will never happen again, will it, Mr. Van Daan?

Mr. Van Daan. No. No.

Mrs. Frank. He steals once! He'll steal again!

[MR. VAN DAAN, *holding his stomach, starts for the bathroom.* ANNE *puts her arms around him, helping him up the step.*]

Mr. Frank. Edith, please. Let us be calm. We'll all go to our rooms . . . and afterwards we'll sit down quietly and talk this out . . . we'll find some way . . .

Mrs. Frank. No! No! No more talk! I want them to leave!

Mrs. Van Daan. You'd put us out, on the streets?

Mrs. Frank. There are other hiding places.

Mrs. Van Daan. A cellar . . . a closet. I know. And we have no money left even to pay for that.

Mrs. Frank. I'll give you money. Out of my own pocket I'll give it gladly. (*She gets her purse from a shelf and comes back with it.*)

Mrs. Van Daan. Mr. Frank, you told Putti you'd never forget what he'd done for you when you came to Amsterdam. You said you could never repay him, that you . . .

Mrs. Frank (*counting out money*). If my husband had any obligation to you, he's paid it, over and over.

Mr. Frank. Edith, I've never seen you like this before. I don't know you.

Mrs. Frank. I should have spoken out long ago.

Dussel. You can't be nice to some people.

Mrs. Van Daan (*turning on* DUSSEL). There would have been plenty for all of us, if *you* hadn't come in here!

Mr. Frank. We don't need the Nazis to destroy us. We're destroying ourselves.

[*He sits down, with his head in his hands.* MRS. FRANK *goes to* MRS. VAN DAAN.]

Mrs. Frank (*giving* MRS. VAN DAAN *some money*). Give this to Miep. She'll find you a place.

Anne. Mother, you're not putting *Peter* out. Peter hasn't done anything.

Mrs. Frank. He'll stay, of course. When I say I must protect the children, I mean Peter too.

[PETER *rises from the steps where he has been sitting.*]

Peter. I'd have to go if Father goes.

[MR. VAN DAAN *comes from the bathroom.* MRS. VAN DAAN *hurries to him and takes him to the couch. Then she gets water from the sink to bathe his face.*]

Mrs. Frank (*while this is going on*). He's no father to you . . . that man! He doesn't know what it is to be a father!

Peter (*starting for his room*). I wouldn't feel right. I couldn't stay.

Mrs. Frank. Very well, then. I'm sorry.

Anne (*rushing over to* PETER). No, Peter! No! (PETER *goes into his room, closing the door after him.* ANNE *turns back to her mother, crying.*) I don't care about the food.

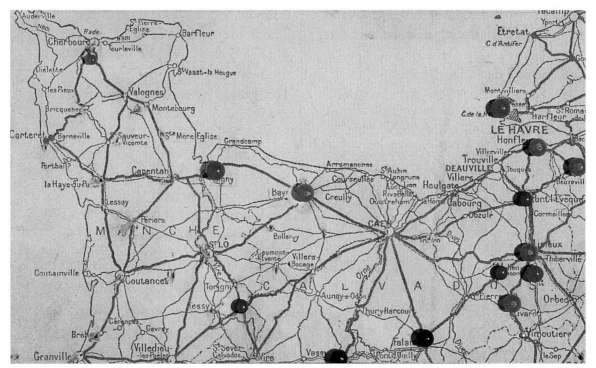

Map kept by Mr. Frank after the Allied invasion of Normandy. Colored pins show the progress of the Allied forces.

They can have mine! I don't want it! Only don't send them away. It'll be daylight soon. They'll be caught . . .

Margot (*putting her arms comfortingly around* ANNE). Please, Mother!

Mrs. Frank. They're not going now. They'll stay here until Miep finds them a place. (*To* MRS. VAN DAAN) But one thing I insist on! He must never come down here again! He must never come to this room where the food is stored! We'll divide what we have . . . an equal share for each! (DUSSEL *hurries over to get a sack of potatoes from the food safe.* MRS. FRANK *goes on, to* MRS. VAN DAAN) You can cook it here and take it up to him.

[DUSSEL *brings the sack of potatoes back to the center table.*]

Margot. Oh, no. No. We haven't sunk so far

that we're going to fight over a handful of rotten potatoes.

Dussel (*dividing the potatoes into piles*). Mrs. Frank, Mr. Frank, Margot, Anne, Peter, Mrs. Van Daan, Mr. Van Daan, myself . . . Mrs. Frank . . .

[*The buzzer sounds in* MIEP'*s signal.*]

Mr. Frank. It's Miep! (*He hurries over, getting his overcoat and putting it on.*)

Margot. At this hour?

Mrs. Frank. It is trouble.

Mr. Frank (*as he starts down to unbolt the door*). I beg you, don't let her see a thing like this!

Dussel (*counting without stopping*). . . . Anne, Peter, Mrs. Van Daan, Mr. Van Daan, myself . . .

Margot (*to* DUSSEL). Stop it! Stop it!

Dussel. . . . Mr. Frank, Margot, Anne,

Peter, Mrs. Van Daan, Mr. Van Daan, myself, Mrs. Frank . . .

Mrs. Van Daan. You're keeping the big ones for yourself! All the big ones . . . Look at the size of that! . . . And that! . . .

[DUSSEL *continues with his dividing.* PETER, *with his shirt and trousers on, comes from his room.*]

Margot. Stop it! Stop it!

[*We hear* MIEP's *excited voice speaking to* MR. FRANK *below.*]

Miep. Mr. Frank . . . the most wonderful news! . . . The invasion[10] has begun!

Mr. Frank. Go on, tell them! Tell them!

[MIEP *comes running up the steps, ahead of* MR. FRANK. *She has a man's raincoat on over her nightclothes and a bunch of orange-colored flowers in her hand.*]

Miep. Did you hear that, everybody? Did you hear what I said? The invasion has begun! The invasion!

[*They all stare at* MIEP, *unable to grasp what she is telling them.* PETER *is the first to recover his wits.*]

Peter. Where?

Mrs. Van Daan. When? When, Miep?

Miep. It began early this morning . . .

[*As she talks on, the realization of what she has said begins to dawn on them. Everyone goes crazy. A wild demonstration takes place.* MRS. FRANK *hugs* MR. VAN DAAN.]

Mrs. Frank. Oh, Mr. Van Daan, did you hear that?

[DUSSEL *embraces* MRS. VAN DAAN. PETER *grabs a frying pan and parades around the room, beating on it, singing the Dutch national anthem.* ANNE *and* MARGOT *follow him, singing, weaving in and out among the excited grown-ups.* MARGOT *breaks away to take the flowers from* MIEP *and distribute them to everyone. While this pandemonium is going on,* MRS. FRANK *tries to make herself heard above the excitement.*]

Mrs. Frank (*to* MIEP). How do you know?

Miep. The radio . . . The BBC![11] They said they landed on the coast of Normandy!

Peter. The British?

Miep. British, Americans, French, Dutch, Poles, Norwegians . . . all of them! More than four thousand ships! Churchill[12] spoke, and General Eisenhower![13] D-day, they call it!

Mr. Frank. Thank God, it's come!

Mrs. Van Daan. At last!

Miep (*starting out*). I'm going to tell Mr. Kraler. This'll be better than any blood transfusion.

Mr. Frank (*stopping her*). What part of Normandy did they land, did they say?

Miep. Normandy . . . that's all I know now . . . I'll be up the minute I hear some more! (*She goes hurriedly out.*)

Mr. Frank (*to* MRS. FRANK). What did I tell you? What did I tell you?

---

10. **the invasion:** On June 6, 1944, Allied forces landed in Normandy, a region of northern France, to launch a military campaign against the Germans.

11. **BBC:** British Broadcasting Corporation. People listened to the BBC, illegally, for news of the war that was more accurate than what German-controlled broadcasters offered.

12. **Churchill:** Sir Winston Churchill (1874–1965), British prime minister during World War II.

13. **General Eisenhower:** Dwight D. Eisenhower (1890–1969), commander of the Allied forces in western Europe. He later became president of the United States (1953–1961).

[MRS. FRANK *indicates that he has forgotten to bolt the door after* MIEP. *He hurries down the steps.* MR. VAN DAAN, *sitting on the couch, suddenly breaks into a convulsive sob. Everybody looks at him, bewildered.*]

Mrs. Van Daan (*hurrying to him*). Putti! Putti! What is it? What happened?
Mr. Van Daan. Please. I'm so ashamed.

[MR. FRANK *comes back up the steps.*]

Dussel. Oh, for God's sake!
Mrs. Van Daan. Don't, Putti.
Margot. It doesn't matter now!
Mr. Frank (*going to* MR. VAN DAAN). Didn't you hear what Miep said? The invasion has come! We're going to be liberated! This is a time to celebrate! (*He embraces* MRS. FRANK *and then hurries to the cupboard and gets the cognac and a glass.*)
Mr. Van Daan. To steal bread from children!
Mrs. Frank. We've all done things that we're ashamed of.
Anne. Look at me, the way I've treated Mother . . . so mean and horrid to her.
Mrs. Frank. No, Anneke, no.

[ANNE *runs to her mother, putting her arms around her.*]

Anne. Oh, Mother, I was. I was awful.
Mr. Van Daan. Not like me. No one is as bad as me!
Dussel (*to* MR. VAN DAAN). Stop it now! Let's be happy!
Mr. Frank (*giving* MR. VAN DAAN *a glass of cognac*). Here! Here! Schnapps![14] L'chaim![15]

[MR. VAN DAAN *takes the cognac. They all*

watch him. He gives them a feeble smile.
ANNE *puts up her fingers in a V-for-victory sign. As* MR. VAN DAAN *gives an answering V sign, they are startled to hear a loud sob from behind them. It is* MRS. FRANK, *stricken with remorse. She is sitting on the other side of the room.*]

Mrs. Frank (*through her sobs*). When I think of the terrible things I said . . .

[MR. FRANK, ANNE, *and* MARGOT *hurry to her, trying to comfort her.* MR. VAN DAAN *brings her his glass of cognac.*]

Mr. Van Daan. No! No! You were right!
Mrs. Frank. That I should speak that way to you! . . . Our friends! . . . Our guests! (*She starts to cry again.*)
Dussel. Stop it, you're spoiling the whole invasion!

[*As they are comforting her, the lights dim out. The curtain falls.*]

Anne's Voice (*faintly at first and then with growing strength*). We're all in much better spirits these days. There's still excellent news of the invasion. The best part about it is that I have a feeling that friends are coming. Who knows? Maybe I'll be back in school by fall. Ha, ha! The joke is on us! The warehouse man doesn't know a thing and we are paying him all that money! . . . Wednesday, the second of July, nineteen forty-four. The invasion seems temporarily to be bogged down. Mr. Kraler has to have an operation, which looks bad. The Gestapo have found the radio that was stolen. Mr. Dussel says

---

14. **schnapps** (shnäps) *n.*: strong liquor.
15. **l'chaim** (lə khä′yim) *interj.*: Hebrew toast meaning "to life."

Vocabulary
remorse (ri·môrs′) *n.*: deep feeling of guilt; self-reproach.

they'll trace it back and back to the thief, and then, it's just a matter of time till they get to us. Everyone is low. Even poor Pim can't raise their spirits. I have often been downcast myself . . . but never in despair. I can shake off everything if I write. But . . . and that is the great question . . . will I ever be able to write well? I want to so much. I want to go on living even after my death. Another birthday has gone by, so now I am fifteen. Already I know what I want. I have a goal, an opinion.

[*As this is being said, the curtain rises on the scene, the lights dim on, and* ANNE's *voice fades out.*]

▩ SCENE 4

It is an afternoon a few weeks later. . . . Everyone but MARGOT *is in the main room. There is a sense of great tension.*

Both MRS. FRANK *and* MR. VAN DAAN *are nervously pacing back and forth.* DUSSEL *is standing at the window, looking down fixedly at the street below.* PETER *is at the center table, trying to do his lessons.* ANNE *sits opposite him, writing in her diary.* MRS. VAN DAAN *is seated on the couch, her eyes on* MR. FRANK *as he sits reading.*

The sound of a telephone ringing comes from the office below. They all are rigid, listening tensely. DUSSEL *rushes down to* MR. FRANK.

Dussel. There it goes again, the telephone! Mr. Frank, do you hear?
Mr. Frank (*quietly*). Yes. I hear.
Dussel (*pleading, insistent*). But this is the third time, Mr. Frank! The third time in quick succession! It's a signal! I tell you it's

Miep, trying to get us! For some reason she can't come to us and she's trying to warn us of something!
Mr. Frank. Please. Please.
Mr. Van Daan (*to* DUSSEL). You're wasting your breath.
Dussel. Something has happened, Mr. Frank. For three days now Miep hasn't been to see us! And today not a man has come to work. There hasn't been a sound in the building!
Mrs. Frank. Perhaps it's Sunday. We may have lost track of the days.
Mr. Van Daan (*to* ANNE). You with the diary there. What day is it?
Dussel (*going to* MRS. FRANK). I don't lose track of the days! I know exactly what day it is! It's Friday, the fourth of August. Friday, and not a man at work. (*He rushes back to* MR. FRANK, *pleading with him, almost in tears.*) I tell you Mr. Kraler's dead. That's the only explanation. He's dead and they've closed down the building, and Miep's trying to tell us!
Mr. Frank. She'd never telephone us.
Dussel (*frantic*). Mr. Frank, answer that! I beg you, answer it!
Mr. Frank. No.
Mr. Van Daan. Just pick it up and listen. You don't have to speak. Just listen and see if it's Miep.
Dussel (*speaking at the same time*). For God's sake . . . I ask you.
Mr. Frank. No. I've told you, no. I'll do nothing that might let anyone know we're in the building.
Peter. Mr. Frank's right.
Mr. Van Daan. There's no need to tell us what side you're on.
Mr. Frank. If we wait patiently, quietly, I believe that help will come.

[*There is silence for a minute as they all listen to the telephone ringing.*]

Dussel. I'm going down. (*He rushes down the steps.* MR. FRANK *tries ineffectually to hold him.* DUSSEL *runs to the lower door, unbolting it. The telephone stops ringing.* DUSSEL *bolts the door and comes slowly back up the steps.*) Too late.

[MR. FRANK *goes to* MARGOT *in* ANNE'*s bedroom.*]

Mr. Van Daan. So we just wait here until we die.

Mrs. Van Daan (*hysterically*). I can't stand it! I'll kill myself! I'll kill myself!

Mr. Van Daan. For God's sake, stop it!

[*In the distance, a German military band is heard playing a Viennese waltz.*]

Mrs. Van Daan. I think you'd be glad if I did! I think you want me to die!

Mr. Van Daan. Whose fault is it we're here? (MRS. VAN DAAN *starts for her room. He follows, talking at her.*) We could've been safe somewhere . . . in America or Switzerland. But no! No! You wouldn't leave when I wanted to. You couldn't leave your things. You couldn't leave your precious furniture.

Mrs. Van Daan. Don't touch me!

[*She hurries up the stairs, followed by* MR. VAN DAAN. PETER, *unable to bear it, goes to his room.* ANNE *looks after him, deeply concerned.* DUSSEL *returns to his post at the window.* MR. FRANK *comes back into the main room and takes a book, trying to read.* MRS. FRANK *sits near the sink, starting to peel some potatoes.* ANNE *quietly goes to* PETER'*s room, closing the door after her.* PETER *is lying face down on the cot.* ANNE *leans over him, holding him in her arms, trying to bring him out of his despair.*]

Anne. Look, Peter, the sky. (*She looks up through the skylight.*) What a lovely, lovely day! Aren't the clouds beautiful? You know what I do when it seems as if I couldn't stand being cooped up for one more minute? I *think* myself out. I think myself on a walk in the park where I used to go with Pim. Where the jonquils and the crocuses and the violets grow down the slopes. You know the most wonderful part about *thinking* yourself out? You can have it any way you like. You can have roses and violets and chrysanthemums all blooming at the same time. . . . It's funny . . . I used to take it all for granted . . . and now I've gone crazy about everything to do with nature. Haven't you?

Peter. I've just gone crazy. I think if something doesn't happen soon . . . if we don't get out of here . . . I can't stand much more of it!

Anne (*softly*). I wish you had a religion, Peter.

Peter. No, thanks! Not me!

Anne. Oh, I don't mean you have to be Orthodox[16] . . . or believe in Heaven and Hell and Purgatory and things . . . I just mean some religion . . . it doesn't matter what. Just to believe in something! When I think of all that's out there . . . the trees . . . and flowers . . . and sea gulls . . . When I think of the dearness of you, Peter . . . and the goodness of the people we know . . . Mr. Kraler, Miep, Dirk, the vegetable man, all risking their lives for us every day . . . When I think of these good things, I'm not

---

16. **Orthodox:** Orthodox Jews strictly observe Jewish law.

afraid anymore . . . I find myself, and God, and I . . .

[PETER *interrupts, getting up and walking away.*]

Peter. That's fine! But when I begin to think, I get mad! Look at us, hiding out for two years. Not able to move! Caught here like . . . waiting for them to come and get us . . . and all for what?

Anne. We're not the only people that've had to suffer. There've always been people that've had to . . . sometimes one race . . . sometimes another . . . and yet . . .

Peter. That doesn't make me feel any better!

Anne (*going to him*). I know it's terrible, trying to have any faith . . . when people are doing such horrible . . . But you know what I sometimes think? I think the world may be going through a phase, the way I was with Mother. It'll pass, maybe not for hundreds of years, but someday . . . I still believe, in spite of everything, that people are really good at heart.

Peter. I want to see something now . . . not a thousand years from now! (*He goes over, sitting down again on the cot.*)

Anne. But, Peter, if you'd only look at it as part of a great pattern . . . that we're just a

Anne's Voice. And so it seems our stay here is over.

little minute in the life . . . (*She breaks off.*) Listen to us, going at each other like a couple of stupid grown-ups! Look at the sky now. Isn't it lovely? (*She holds out her hand to him.* PETER *takes it and rises, standing with her at the window looking out, his arms around her.*) Someday, when we're outside again, I'm going to . . .

[*She breaks off as she hears the sound of a car, its brakes squealing as it comes to a sudden stop. The people in the other rooms also become aware of the sound. They listen tensely. Another car roars up to a screeching stop.* ANNE *and* PETER *come from* PETER'*s room.* MR. *and* MRS. VAN DAAN *creep down the stairs.* DUSSEL *comes out from his room. Everyone is listening, hardly breathing. A doorbell clangs again and again in the building below.* MR. FRANK *starts quietly down the steps to the door.* DUSSEL *and* PETER *follow him. The others stand rigid, waiting, terrified.*

In a few seconds DUSSEL *comes stumbling back up the steps. He shakes off* PETER'*s help and goes to his room.* MR. FRANK *bolts the door below and comes slowly back up the steps. Their eyes are all on him as he stands there for a minute. They realize that what they feared has happened.* MRS. VAN DAAN *starts to whimper.* MR. VAN DAAN *puts her gently in a chair and then hurries off up the stairs to their room to collect their things.* PETER *goes to comfort his mother. There is a sound of violent pounding on a door below.*]

Mr. Frank (*quietly*). For the past two years we have lived in fear. Now we can live in hope.

[*The pounding below becomes more insistent. There are muffled sounds of voices, shouting commands.*]

Men's Voices. Aufmachen! Da drinnen!

Aufmachen! Schnell! Schnell! Schnell![17] (*Etc., etc.*)

[*The street door below is forced open. We hear the heavy tread of footsteps coming up.* MR. FRANK *gets two school bags from the shelves and gives one to* ANNE *and the other to* MARGOT. *He goes to get a bag for* MRS. FRANK. *The sound of feet coming up grows louder.* PETER *comes to* ANNE, *kissing her goodbye; then he goes to his room to collect his things. The buzzer of their door starts to ring.* MR. FRANK *brings* MRS. FRANK *a bag. They stand together, waiting. We hear the thud of gun butts on the door, trying to break it down.*

ANNE *stands, holding her school satchel, looking over at her father and mother with a soft, reassuring smile. She is no longer a child, but a woman with courage to meet whatever lies ahead.*

The lights dim out. The curtain falls on the scene. We hear a mighty crash as the door is shattered. After a second ANNE'*s voice is heard.*]

Anne's Voice. And so it seems our stay here is over. They are waiting for us now. They've allowed us five minutes to get our things. We can each take a bag and whatever it will hold of clothing. Nothing else. So, dear Diary, that means I must leave you behind. Goodbye for a while. P.S. Please, please, Miep, or Mr. Kraler, or anyone else. If you should find this diary, will you please keep it safe for me, because someday I hope . . .

[*Her voice stops abruptly. There is silence. After a second the curtain rises.*]

---

17. **Aufmachen . . . Schnell:** German for "Open up! You in there! Open up! Quickly! Quickly! Quickly!"

◼ SCENE 5

It is again the afternoon in November 1945. The rooms are as we saw them in the first scene. MR. KRALER *has joined* MIEP *and* MR. FRANK. *There are coffee cups on the table. We see a great change in* MR. FRANK. *He is calm now. His bitterness is gone. He slowly turns a few pages of the diary. They are blank.*

Mr. Frank. No more. (*He closes the diary and puts it down on the couch beside him.*)

Miep. I'd gone to the country to find food. When I got back, the block was surrounded by police . . .

Mr. Kraler. We made it our business to learn how they knew. It was the thief . . . the thief who told them.

[MIEP *goes up to the gas burner, bringing back a pot of coffee.*]

Mr. Frank (*after a pause*). It seems strange to say this, that anyone could be happy in a concentration camp. But Anne was happy in the camp in Holland where they first took us. After two years of being shut up in these rooms, she could be out . . . out in the sunshine and the fresh air that she loved.

Miep (*offering the coffee to* MR. FRANK). A little more?

Mr. Frank (*holding out his cup to her*). The news of the war was good. The British and Americans were sweeping through France. We felt sure that they would get to us in time. In September we were told that we were to be shipped to Poland. . . . The men to one camp. The women to another. I was sent to Auschwitz. They went to Belsen. In January we were freed, the few of us who were left. The war wasn't yet over, so it took us a long time to get home. We'd be sent here and there behind the lines where we'd be safe. Each time our train would stop . . . at a siding or a crossing . . . we'd all get out and go from group to group . . . Where were you? Were you at Belsen? At Buchenwald? At Mauthausen? Is it possible that you knew my wife? Did you ever see my husband? My son? My daughter? That's how I found out about my wife's death . . . of Margot, the Van Daans . . . Dussel. But Anne . . . I still hoped . . . Yesterday I went to Rotterdam. I'd heard of a woman there . . . She'd been in Belsen with Anne . . . I know now.

[*He picks up the diary again and turns the pages back to find a certain passage. As he finds it, we hear* ANNE's *voice.*]

Anne's Voice. In spite of everything, I still believe that people are really good at heart.

[MR. FRANK *slowly closes the diary.*]

Mr. Frank. She puts me to shame.

[*They are silent.*]

Curtain

Frances Goodrich and Albert Hackett

The cast of *The Diary of Anne Frank* on Broadway, in a 1997 adaptation by Wendy Kesselman. Anne is at the center, leaning on the table.

The Making of a Masterpiece

Frances Goodrich (1890–1984) and **Albert Hackett** (1900–1995) both started out as actors. They began writing plays and screenplays together and were married soon after. Working at desks facing in opposite directions in the same room, they would each write a version of a scene, then read and comment on the other's version before revising. In this way, Goodrich and Hackett created the scripts for many hit movies, including *Easter Parade, Father of the Bride*, and *It's a Wonderful Life*.

The Diary of Anne Frank, a work totally different from their other plays, is considered their masterpiece. Before they wrote the play, the playwrights spent ten days in Amsterdam visiting the Secret Annex, studying the neighborhood, and questioning Otto Frank (who came from Switzerland to help) on his memories and impressions. It took them two years and eight drafts to complete the play, which opened on Broadway in 1955 to great acclaim. The play won a Pulitzer Prize in 1956 and has since been performed countless times in countries around the world.

For Independent Reading

In addition to her diary, Anne wrote many short stories and autobiographical sketches during her time in hiding. You'll find a selection of these in *Anne Frank's Tales from the Secret Annex.*

Anne Frank Remembered is the story of Anne and the other occupants of the Secret Annex as told by their helper and protector, Miep Gies.

Literary Response and Analysis
Act Two and the Play as a Whole

Reading Check

1. How does Anne and Peter's relationship change in Act Two, Scene 1? In Scene 2, how do Mrs. Frank and Mrs. Van Daan respond to this change?

2. What news does Miep bring in Act Two, Scene 3?

3. At the beginning of Act Two, Scene 4, what is causing tension and fear in the household?

Interpretations

4. The **climax** of a play is its moment of greatest tension, when the main conflict is about to be resolved. What is this play's climax? How did you feel at this moment?

5. In Act One, Scene 4, Mr. Frank tells Anne, "You must build your own character." Has Anne done this by the end of the play? Explain.

6. What do you think is the main **conflict** in the play? Is it the conflict between the occupants of the Secret Annex and the Nazis, or is it something else?

7. Now that you have finished the play, which of the **resources** that accompany it—the maps, Anne's diary entries, the historical photographs, the time line—did you find most helpful? Are there other resources you wish had been included? Explain your answers.

8. Before *The Diary of Anne Frank* was first performed, Otto Frank wrote in a letter to the actor who would portray him, "Please don't play me as a 'hero.' . . . Nothing happened to me that did not happen to thousands upon thousands of other people." Do you see anyone in the play as a hero? In your answer, cite the qualities or actions that you think make someone a hero.

9. On page 277, Anne says, "I want to go on living even after my death." How has her wish come true?

Evaluation: The Play as a Whole

10. What do you think this play reveals about our need for freedom? about the power of love? about courage and hope? about good and evil? In your answers, consider how the play's **themes** relate to the themes in another work, such as Ann Petry's story of Harriet Tubman (page 87).

11. During the crisis in Act Two, Scene 3, Mr. Frank says, "We don't need the Nazis to destroy us. We're destroying ourselves." How would you describe the forces destroying the characters from inside? Do you think, given their desperate situation, that such behavior was inevitable?

12. The last thing Anne says in the play is "In spite of everything, I still believe that people are really good at heart." Given what actually happened to Anne Frank, some people have criticized the play for ending on a note of hope. When Anne

Grade 6 Review Reading Standard 3.6 Identify and analyze features of themes conveyed through characters, actions, and images.

wrote those words in her diary, she did not know what the Nazis would do to her and the other residents of the Secret Annex. Do you agree with the playwrights' choice of ending? Does the play support Anne's statement? Explain.

13. The play's version of events differs in many ways from what actually happened. For example:

- In real life, Anne was given the diary as a present for her thirteenth birthday, several weeks before her family went into hiding.
- The Frank family moved into the Secret Annex a week before the Van Pels family did. (Anne made up the names. She called the Van Pels family the Van Daans.)
- Margot was sixteen, not eighteen, when the Franks went into hiding.
- The occupants of the Secret Annex often went down to the lower floors of the office building after working hours.
- There is no evidence in Anne's diary that Mr. Van Daan stole food.

Why might the writers have chosen to change or invent these details? Do you think writers should change details in works based on real people and real events? Discuss your responses.

Writing
Compare and Contrast Characters

Whenever you **compare** two people or things, you tell how they're alike. When you **contrast** them, you point out their differences. Choose any two characters in this play who have at least one thing in common—young people (Anne, Margot, and Peter), for instance, or the two mothers or fathers. Think about how they're alike and how they're different, and jot down your ideas in a Venn diagram like the one begun below. Where the circles overlap, list the ways in which your characters are alike. Then, write a brief essay describing how your characters are alike and how they are different. A model of a student's essay comparing and contrasting Anne and Margot appears on page 291.

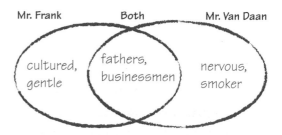

Report on Research

How does the Holocaust continue to affect the world today? Using the Internet and print sources in a library, research one of these topics: (1) the work of the Anne Frank Foundation or (2) the creation of the U.S. Holocaust Memorial Museum in Washington, D.C. Write a brief report on what you have learned.

Vocabulary Development

Verify Meanings

PRACTICE

With two classmates, divide up the list of words in the Word Bank. Write down your five words. Then, match each word with the name of a character or an event in the play. For example, you might make this match:

loathe—the way the residents of the Secret Annex feel toward the Nazis

Word Bank

conspicuous
unabashed
loathe
indignantly
fortify
zeal
tyranny
remorse
gingerly
ostentatiously
appalled
disgruntled
inarticulate
forlorn
animation

Reading Standard 1.3
Show ability to verify word meanings by definition, restatement, example, comparison, or contrast.

Grammar Link
MINI-LESSON

Dangling and Misplaced Modifiers

A modifying phrase or clause that doesn't clearly modify a word in a sentence is called a **dangling modifier.**

DANGLING   **Peeking out the window,** *the church tower* **could be seen.**

The church tower isn't peeking out the window. Rearranging and adding or changing words in the sentence can make the meaning clear.

CLEAR   **Peeking out the window,** *Anne* **could see the church tower.**

A **misplaced modifier** causes confusion because it seems to modify the wrong word in a sentence.

MISPLACED   **My grandmother** *told* **me about her experiences in Nazi-occupied Europe last week.**

CLEAR   **My grandmother** *told* **me last week about her experiences in Nazi-occupied Europe.**

The best way to catch dangling and misplaced modifiers, as with any error that causes confusion for readers, is to ask other people to read your drafts.

PRACTICE

Each of the following sentences contains a dangling or misplaced modifier. Rewrite each sentence so that it makes sense.

1. Anne watched the canal boats hiding in the Secret Annex.
2. Coughing and sneezing, Peter's cat was a problem for Dussel.
3. Hoping for a better future, the cake read, "Peace in 1944."
4. Miep discovered the diary in the Secret Annex, which had been thrown on the floor.

The Diary of Anne Frank   **285**

from The Diary of a Young Girl

Literary Focus
Comparing Characterization

The writers of *The Diary of Anne Frank* based their play on Anne's actual diary, which her father had published after the war, under the title *The Diary of a Young Girl*. The playwrights based the character of Anne on their own interpretation of the person revealed in the diary. They considered the opinions Anne expressed, the way she described herself, and the way she interacted with other people. They also talked with Anne's father, Otto Frank. Some critics have felt that the playwrights did not capture the real Anne. As you read the following excerpts from Anne's diary, try to decide what kind of person Anne might have been. How close do you think the playwrights came to portraying the real Anne?

Reading Skills
Comparing and Contrasting

When you **compare** people or things, you show their similarities—how they are alike. When you **contrast** people or things, you show how they are different. As you read the excerpts from Anne's diary, notice how this Anne is similar to or different from the Anne in the play.

Grade 7 Review Reading Standard 3.3
Analyze characterization as delineated through a character's thoughts, words, and actions.

from The Diary of a Young Girl

Anne Frank

Wednesday, 3 May, 1944

. . . Since Saturday we've changed over, and have lunch at half past eleven in the mornings, so we have to last out with one cupful of porridge; this saves us a meal. Vegetables are still very difficult to obtain; we had rotten boiled lettuce this afternoon. Ordinary lettuce, spinach, and boiled lettuce, there's nothing else. With these we eat rotten potatoes, so it's a delicious combination!

As you can easily imagine, we often ask ourselves here despairingly: "What, oh, what is the use of the war? Why can't people live peacefully together? Why all this destruction?"

The question is very understandable, but no one has found a satisfactory answer to it so far. Yes, why do they make still more gigantic planes, still heavier bombs, and, at the same time, prefabricated houses for reconstruction? Why should millions be spent daily on the war and yet there's not a penny available for medical services, artists, or poor people?

Why do some people have to starve while there are surpluses rotting in other parts of the world? Oh, why are people so crazy?

I don't believe that the big men, the politicians and the capitalists alone, are guilty of the war. Oh no, the little man is just as guilty; otherwise the peoples of the world would have risen in revolt long ago! There's in people simply an urge to destroy, an urge to kill, to murder and rage, and until all mankind, without exception, undergoes a great change, wars will be waged, everything that has been built up, cultivated, and grown will be destroyed and disfigured, after which mankind will have to begin all over again.

I have often been downcast, but never in despair; I regard our hiding as a dangerous adventure, romantic and interesting at the same time. In my diary I treat all the privations° as amusing. I have made up my mind now to lead a different life from other girls and, later on, different from ordinary housewives. My start has been so very full of interest, and that is the sole reason why I have to laugh at the humorous side of the most dangerous moments.

I am young and I possess many buried qualities; I am young and strong and am living a great adventure; I am still in the midst of it and can't grumble the whole day long. I have been given a lot: a happy nature, a great deal of cheerfulness and strength. Every day I feel that I am developing inwardly, that the liberation is drawing nearer, and how beautiful nature is, how good the

---

° **privations** (prī·vā′shənz) *n.:* lack of necessities.

people are about me, how interesting this adventure is! Why, then, should I be in despair?

Yours,

Anne

Saturday, 15 July, 1944

. . . "For in its innermost depths youth is lonelier than old age." I read this saying in some book and I've always remembered it, and found it to be true. Is it true, then, that grown-ups have a more difficult time here than we do? No. I know it isn't. Older people have formed their opinions about everything and don't waver before they act. It's twice as hard for us young ones to hold our ground and maintain our opinions in a time when all ideals are being shattered and destroyed, when people are showing their worst side and do not know whether to believe in truth and right and God.

Anyone who claims that the older ones have a more difficult time here certainly doesn't realize to what extent our problems weigh down on us, problems for which we are probably much too young but which thrust themselves upon us continually, until, after a long time, we think we've found a solution, but the solution doesn't seem able to resist the facts which reduce it to nothing again. That's the difficulty in these times: Ideals, dreams, and cherished hopes rise within us, only to meet the horrible truth and be shattered.

It's really a wonder that I haven't dropped

Anne in 1940.

all my ideals, because they seem so absurd and impossible to carry out. Yet I keep them, because in spite of everything I still believe that people are really good at heart. I simply can't build up my hopes on a foundation consisting of confusion, misery, and death. I see the world gradually being turned into a wilderness, I hear the ever approaching thunder, which will destroy us too, I can feel the sufferings of millions, and yet, if I look up into the heavens, I think that it will all come right, that this cruelty too will end, and that peace and tranquility will return again.

In the meantime, I must uphold my ideals, for perhaps the time will come when I shall be able to carry them out.

Yours,

Anne

Literary Response and Analysis

Reading Check

1. What does Anne complain about in the first entry?

2. How does Anne describe herself in the first entry?

3. In the second entry, what reasons does Anne give for thinking that young people have a harder time in the annex than older people?

4. In the second entry, what reasons does Anne give for keeping her ideals?

Interpretations

5. In **dramatic irony** the audience or reader knows something a character does not know. What do we know as we read Anne's diary that Anne does not know? How does the dramatic irony make you feel?

6. In her diary, Anne says that "the little man" is as guilty of the war as the politicians and the capitalists. What does she mean? What experiences did she have, according to the play, that might have led her to that conclusion?

7. After reading these excerpts, decide if you think the play captures the real Anne, or if you think important aspects of Anne's personality are missing from the character in the play. What can a play do that a diary cannot do? What can a diary tell us that a play cannot tell us?

8. What might Anne be thinking about when she says that someday she may be able to carry out her ideals? Base your response on details in the play or diary as well as on your own hopes for the future.

9. What questions does Anne ask in these diary entries that could still be asked today? What answers would you give to some of those questions?

Evaluation

10. In the first entry, Anne writes, "There's in people simply an urge to destroy, an urge to kill, to murder and rage. . . ." In the second entry she says that "in spite of everything I still believe that people are really good at heart." How do you think Anne could reconcile these seemingly contradictory opinions? (Cite evidence from the text in your response.) How do you feel about Anne's beliefs?

Writing

I Am Anne

Using details from the play and the diary, as well as your own ideas, write an "I am" poem for Anne Frank, using this framework:

I am . . .	I am . . .
I hear . . .	I feel . . .
I see . . .	I try . . .
I say . . .	I dream . . .
I cry . . .	I am . . .
I am . . .	

Grade 7 Review Reading Standard 3.3 Analyze characterization as delineated through a character's thoughts, words, and actions.

Anne and Margot Frank

Analyzing Compare-and-Contrast Text

You do it all the time. You meet someone who reminds you of someone else, or you don't like this week's episode of your favorite TV show as well as you liked last week's episode. You are **comparing** (seeing similarities) and **contrasting** (seeing differences). Writers do it too. You can see how a professional writer does it in the paragraph below from a review of *Parallel Journeys*, a book by Eleanor H. Ayer.

Compare-and-Contrast Organization

There are two basic ways in which writers can organize compare-and-contrast essays:

- **Block method.** Writers using the block method discuss all the features of the first subject, then discuss all the features of the second subject.

- **Point-by-point method.** Writers using the point-by-point method discuss one feature at a time, describing how it applies first to one subject and then to another.

The excerpt from the book review below uses the point-by-point method. First, the reviewer compares how Waterford and Heck grew up. Then, she compares what happened to each one in the war. Finally, she compares their postwar experiences. Watch to see which organizational method is used by the student who wrote the essay on the next page.

They grew up a few miles apart in Nazi Germany. Helen Waterford was Jewish; Alfons Heck was an ardent member of the Hitler Youth. . . . While she was crammed in a cattle car bound for Auschwitz, he was a teenage commander of frontline troops, ready to fight and die for the glory of Hitler and the Fatherland. Their postwar experiences in the U.S. are just as compelling: Helen trying to pick up the pieces of her shattered self; Alfons awakening to what he'd been part of, determined now to warn the world about it. . . . Both Germans speak quietly and honestly, without hand-wringing, coverup, or self-pity.

—Hazel Rochman, *Booklist*

Similarity 1.
Difference 1.
Difference 2.

Difference 3.

Similarity 2.

Grade 6 Review Reading Standard 2.2
Analyze text that uses the compare-and-contrast organizational pattern.

ANNE AND MARGOT FRANK

Thirteen-year-old Anne Frank and eighteen-year-old Margot Frank are sisters growing up in Amsterdam during World War II. Anne and Margot are alike and different in many ways, and in the play version of *The Diary of Anne Frank,* they are often compared to each other.

Margot is a mature, beautiful young lady. Even through the hardest times in the war, she would keep quiet. She was always obedient and polite; she did everything that she was told, like helping with supper and setting the table. Anne, on the other hand, had a mind of her own. She did not need people to tell her what to do. She was often active, loud, and curious. Anne was a daydreamer, and sometimes her dreams caused people to see her as a troublemaker. A perfect example is when Anne tried on Mrs. Van Daan's fur coat. While pretending she was a young Mrs. Van Daan, Anne spilled milk all over the coat.

Mrs. Frank would always compare Anne and Margot, which sometimes made Anne feel insecure. Margot was always known as the ladylike one, whereas Anne was known as the childish one. I do not think that Anne was treated like other girls her age because of Margot's maturity.

Anne was always outgoing. She had many school friends and grew to be Peter Van Daan's good friend. Margot was charming and polite, but very shy, so it was hard for her to be sociable. When Anne went to see Peter, Margot would always stay in her room and read a book.

Throughout the play Anne was usually cheerful and peppy. It might have been her way of making the war less painful. Though she would never say it, I think that Margot felt like she had been betrayed and had trouble trusting people. I also think that she felt that she should keep quiet and let others sort things out.

All in all, I believe that Anne and Margot are different, but they do share one thing: the strength to survive through the harsh times in the Secret Annex. I think they should have forgotten their petty differences and concentrated on what they believed in because they were all fighting for the same reasons.

—Hanna Jamal
United Nations International School
New York, New York

Reading Informational Materials

Reading Check

1. List five words the writer uses to describe Margot.

2. List five words the writer uses to describe Anne.

3. In what ways are Anne and Margot alike, according to the writer?

4. In what ways are they different, according to the writer?

TestPractice

ANNE AND MARGOT FRANK

1. Which of the following sentences *best* states the **main idea** of this essay?

   A "Mrs. Frank would always compare Anne and Margot. . . ."

   B "Margot is a mature, beautiful young lady."

   C "Anne was always outgoing."

   D "All in all, I believe that Anne and Margot are different. . . ."

2. Which of the following sentences uses a word or phrase that signals a difference in the sisters?

   F "Mrs. Frank would always compare Anne and Margot. . . ."

   G "Even through the hardest times in the war, [Margot] would keep quiet."

   H "Anne, on the other hand, had a mind of her own."

   J "When Anne went to see Peter, Margot would always stay in her room. . . ."

3. Which of the following sentences clearly expresses an **opinion**?

   A "[Margot] was always obedient and polite. . . ."

   B "[Anne] did not need people to tell her what to do."

   C "Margot was charming and polite, but very shy. . . ."

   D "I think they should have forgotten their petty differences. . . ."

4. Which of the following sentences shows a similarity between the sisters?

   F "They do share one thing: the strength to survive. . . ."

   G "Margot was always known as the ladylike one, whereas Anne was known as the childish one."

   H "[Margot] did everything that she was told, like helping with supper. . . ."

   J "[Anne's] dreams caused people to see her as a troublemaker."

Grade 6 Review Reading Standard 2.2
Analyze text that uses the compare-and-contrast organizational pattern.

A Tragedy Revealed: A Heroine's Last Days

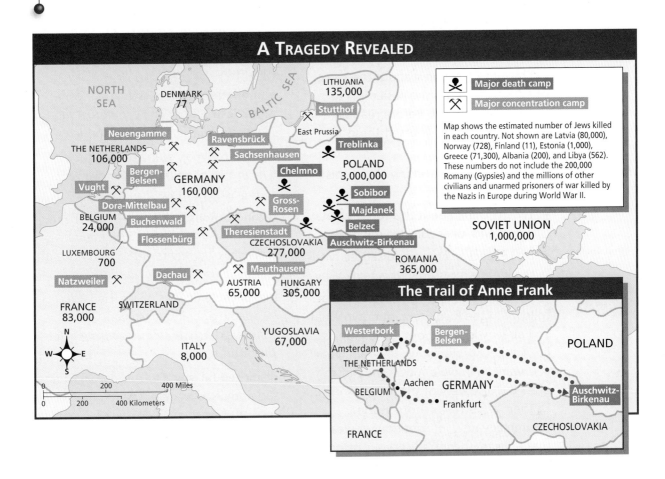

A TRAGEDY REVEALED

☠ Major death camp

✗ Major concentration camp

Map shows the estimated number of Jews killed in each country. Not shown are Latvia (80,000), Norway (728), Finland (11), Estonia (1,000), Greece (71,300), Albania (200), and Libya (562). These numbers do not include the 200,000 Romany (Gypsies) and the millions of other civilians and unarmed prisoners of war killed by the Nazis in Europe during World War II.

NORTH SEA

DENMARK 77

BALTIC SEA

LITHUANIA 135,000

Stutthof

East Prussia

Neuengamme

THE NETHERLANDS 106,000

Ravensbrück

Sachsenhausen

Treblinka

Bergen-Belsen

GERMANY 160,000

Chelmno

POLAND 3,000,000

Vught

Dora-Mittelbau

Gross-Rosen

Sobibor

BELGIUM 24,000

Buchenwald

Majdanek

Theresienstadt

Belzec

LUXEMBOURG 700

Flossenbürg

CZECHOSLOVAKIA 277,000

Auschwitz-Birkenau

SOVIET UNION 1,000,000

Natzweiler

Dachau

Mauthausen

AUSTRIA 65,000

HUNGARY 305,000

ROMANIA 365,000

FRANCE 83,000

SWITZERLAND

YUGOSLAVIA 67,000

ITALY 8,000

N W E S

0   200   400 Miles
0   200   400 Kilometers

The Trail of Anne Frank

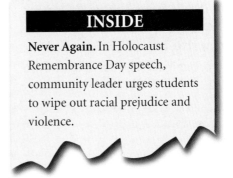

Westerbork

Amsterdam

THE NETHERLANDS

Bergen-Belsen

POLAND

Aachen

GERMANY

BELGIUM

Frankfurt

Auschwitz-Birkenau

FRANCE

CZECHOSLOVAKIA

Literary Focus
Factual Reporting: What's the Main Idea?

The factual article you're about to read, which was first published in 1958, starts where Anne Frank's diary and the play end—with the discovery of the Secret Annex and the arrest of its occupants. In articles like this one, writers often provide **key passages** or **key statements** that reveal their feelings about the topic. These key statements can clue you in to the writer's main idea.

Reading Skills
Using Prior Knowledge

Suppose you saw this item on the front page of a newspaper:

> ## INSIDE
>
> **Never Again.** In Holocaust Remembrance Day speech, community leader urges students to wipe out racial prejudice and violence.

Grade 5 Review Reading Standard 2.3 Discern main ideas and concepts presented in texts, identifying and assessing evidence that supports those ideas.

You probably wouldn't have any trouble understanding that information. In fact, from your knowledge of history and your understanding of current events, you'd probably have some idea of what to expect in the article.

The more you know about the topic of a text, of course, the easier it is to understand the text. Before reading a text, you might ask yourself these questions:

- What do I already know about this topic?
- When I think about this topic, what words and ideas come to mind?
- Do I expect to agree or disagree with the ideas expressed in this text? Why?

Make a **KWL chart** like the one that follows. In the K column, jot down what you already **k**now about Anne Frank's life. In the W column, write down what you **w**ant to know about Anne's fate after the discovery of the Secret Annex.

Then, as you read, note in the L column any new information you **l**earn that adds to or contradicts your **prior knowledge.** In the W column, check off any questions that are answered in the text.

K	W	L

Make the Connection
Quickwrite 🖊

If you could interview survivors of the Holocaust who knew Anne Frank, what would you ask them? Jot down some of your questions.

Vocabulary Development

These are the words you'll learn as you read the article:

indomitable (in·däm′i·tə·bəl) *adj.:* unconquerable. *Anne Frank's spirit was indomitable.*

annihilation (ə·nī′ə·lā′shən) *n.:* complete destruction. *We still mourn the Nazi annihilation of six million Jews.*

refuge (ref′yōōj) *n.:* place of safety. *The Franks found refuge for two years in the Secret Annex.*

reconciliations (rek′ən·sil′ē·ā′shənz) *n.:* acts of making up after arguments. *After the arguments in the Secret Annex came the tearful reconciliations.*

inexplicable (in·eks′pli·kə·bəl) *adj.:* incapable of being explained. *There were inexplicable sounds coming from the building.*

dispirited (di·spir′it·id) *v.* used as *adj.:* sad and discouraged. *The residents were often dispirited during their long confinement in the Secret Annex.*

premonition (prem′ə·nish′ən) *n.:* feeling that something bad will happen. *When the lamp crashed, the residents of the Secret Annex had a premonition that they would be discovered.*

emaciated (ē·mā′shē·āt′id) *v.* used as *adj.:* extremely thin, as from starvation or illness. *Anne's emaciated face showed suffering and hunger.*

raucous (rô′kəs) *adj.:* loud and rough. *They were frightened by the raucous shouting outside the window.*

clamorous (klam′ər·əs) *adj.:* loud and demanding. *They heard the clamorous voices of the Gestapo in the stairway.*

A Tragedy Revealed: A Heroine's Last Days

Ernst Schnabel

Statue of Anne Frank by Pieter L'Hont, Utrecht, the Netherlands.

Last year in Amsterdam I found an old reel of movie film on which Anne Frank appears. She is seen for only ten seconds and it is an accident that she is there at all.

The film was taken for a wedding in 1941, the year before Anne Frank and seven others went into hiding in their "Secret Annex." It has a flickering, Chaplinesque[1] quality, with people popping suddenly in and out of doorways, the nervous smiles and hurried waves of the departing bride and groom.

Then, for just a moment, the camera seems uncertain where to look. It darts to the right, then to the left, then whisks up a wall, and into view comes a window

---

1. **Chaplinesque** (chap'lin·esk'): like the old silent movies starring Charlie Chaplin (1889–1977).

Last year I set out to follow the fading trail of this girl who has become a legend.

crowded with people waving after the departing automobiles. The camera swings farther to the left, to another window. There a girl stands alone, looking out into space. It is Anne Frank.

Just as the camera is about to pass on, the child moves her head a trifle. Her face flits more into focus, her hair shimmers in the sun. At this moment she discovers the camera, discovers the photographer, discovers us watching seventeen years later, and laughs at all of us, laughs with sudden merriment and surprise and embarrassment all at the same time.

I asked the projectionist to stop the film for a moment so that we could stand up to examine her face more closely. The smile stood still, just above our heads. But when I walked forward close to the screen, the smile ceased to be a smile. The face ceased to be a face, for the canvas screen was granular and the beam of light split into a multitude of tiny shadows, as if it had been scattered on a sandy plain.

Anne Frank, of course, is gone too, but her spirit has remained to stir the conscience of the world. Her remarkable diary has been read in almost every language. I have seen a letter from a teenaged girl in Japan who says she thinks of Anne's Secret Annex as her second home. And the play based on the diary has been a great success wherever it is produced. German audiences, who invariably greet the final curtain of *The Diary of Anne Frank* in stricken silence, have jammed the theaters in what seems almost a national act of penance.

Last year I set out to follow the fading trail of this girl who has become a legend. The trail led from Holland to Poland and back to Germany, where I visited the moss-grown site of the old Bergen-Belsen concentration camp at the village of Belsen and saw the common graves shared by Anne Frank and thirty thousand others. I interviewed forty-two people who knew Anne or who survived the ordeal that killed her. Some had known her intimately in those last tragic months. In the recollections of others she appears only for a moment. But even these fragments fulfill a promise. They make explicit a truth implied in the diary. As we somehow knew she must be, Anne Frank, even in the most frightful extremity, was indomitable.

The known story contained in the diary is a simple one of human relationships, of the poignant maturing of a perceptive girl who is thirteen when her diary begins and only fifteen when it ends. It is a story without violence, though its background is the most dreadful act of violence in the history of man, Hitler's annihilation of six million European Jews.

In the summer of 1942, Anne Frank, her father, her mother, her older sister, Margot, and four others were forced into hiding during the Nazi occupation of Holland. Their refuge was a tiny apartment they called the Secret Annex, in the back of an Amsterdam office building. For twenty-five months the Franks, the Van Daan family, and later a dentist, Albert Dussel,[2] lived in

---

2. In her diary, Anne made up names. The Van Daans were really named Van Pels, and Albert Dussel was really Fritz Pfeffer.

Vocabulary
indomitable (in·däm′i·tə·bəl) *adj.:* unconquerable.
annihilation (ə·nī′ə·lā′shən) *n.:* complete destruction.
refuge (ref′yo͞oj) *n.:* place of safety.

the Secret Annex, protected from the Gestapo[3] only by a swinging bookcase which masked the entrance to their hiding place and by the heroism of a few Christians who knew they were there. Anne Frank's diary recounts the daily pressures of their cramped existence: the hushed silences when strangers were in the building, the diminishing food supply, the fear of fire from the incessant Allied air raids, the hopes for an early invasion, above all the dread of capture by the pitiless men who were hunting Jews from house to house and sending them to concentration camps. Anne's diary also describes with sharp insight and youthful humor the bickerings, the wounded pride, the tearful reconciliations of the eight human beings in the Secret Annex. It tells of Anne's wishes for the understanding of her adored father, of her despair at the gulf between her mother and herself, of her tremulous and growing love for young Peter Van Daan.

The actual diary ends with an entry for August 1, 1944, in which Anne Frank, addressing her imaginary friend Kitty, talks of her impatience with her own unpredictable personality. The stage version goes further: It attempts to reconstruct something of the events of August 4, 1944, the day the Secret Annex was violated and its occupants finally taken into a captivity from which only one returned.

What really happened on that August day fourteen years ago was far less dramatic than what is now depicted on the stage. The automobiles did not approach with howling sirens, did not stop with screaming brakes in front of the house on the Prinsengracht canal in Amsterdam. No rifle butt pounded against the door until it reverberated, as it now does in the theater every night somewhere in the world. The truth was, at first, that no one heard a sound.

It was midmorning on a bright summer day. In the hidden apartment behind the secret bookcase there was a scene of relaxed domesticity. The Franks, the Van Daans, and Mr. Dussel had finished a poor breakfast of ersatz[4] coffee and bread. Mrs. Frank and Mrs. Van Daan were about to clear the table. Mr. Van Daan, Margot Frank, and Mr. Dussel were resting or reading. Anne Frank was very likely at work on one of the short stories she often wrote when she was not busy with her diary or her novel. In Peter Van Daan's tiny attic room Otto Frank was chiding the eighteen-year-old boy for an error in his English lesson. "Why, Peter," Mr. Frank was saying, "you know that *double* is spelled with only one *b*."

In the main part of the building four other people, two men and two women, were working at their regular jobs. For more than two years these four had risked their lives to protect their friends in the hide-out, supplied them with food, and brought them news of a world from which they had disappeared. One of the women was Miep, who had just got married a few months earlier. The other was Elli, a pretty typist of twenty-three. The men were Kraler and Koophuis,

---

4. **ersatz** (er'zäts') *adj.*: artificial. Regular coffee beans were unavailable because of severe wartime shortages.

Vocabulary
reconciliations (rek'ən·sil'ē·ā'shənz) *n.*: acts of making up after arguments or disagreements.

---

3. **Gestapo** (gə·stä'pō): Nazi secret police force, known for its use of terror.

middle-aged spice merchants who had been business associates of Otto Frank's before the occupation. Mr. Kraler was working in one office by himself. Koophuis and the two women were in another.

I spoke to Miep, Elli, and Mr. Koophuis in Amsterdam. The two women had not been arrested after the raid on the Secret Annex. Koophuis had been released in poor health after a few weeks in prison, and Kraler, who now lives in Canada, had eventually escaped from a forced labor camp.

Elli, now a mother, whose coloring and plump good looks are startlingly like those of the young women painted by the Dutch masters,[5] recalled: "I was posting entries in the receipts book when a car drove up in front of the house. But cars often stopped, after all. Then the front door opened, and someone came up the stairs. I wondered who it could be. We often had callers. Only this time I could hear that there were several men. . . ."

Miep, a delicate, intelligent, still young-looking woman, said: "The footsteps moved along the corridor. Then a door creaked, and a moment later the connecting door to Mr. Kraler's office opened, and a fat man thrust his head in and said in Dutch: 'Quiet. Stay in your seats.' I started and at first did not know what was happening. But then, suddenly, I knew."

Mr. Koophuis is now in very poor health, a gaunt, white-haired man in his sixties. He added: "I suppose I did not hear them because of the rumbling of the spice mills in the warehouse. The fat man's head was the first thing I knew. He came in and planted himself in front of us. 'You three stay here, understand?' he barked. So we stayed in the office and listened as someone else went upstairs, and doors rattled, and then there were footsteps everywhere. They searched the whole building."

Mr. Kraler wrote me this account from Toronto: "A uniformed staff sergeant of the Occupation Police[6] and three men in civilian clothes entered my office. They wanted to see the storerooms in the front part of the building. All will be well, I thought, if they don't want to see anything else. But after the sergeant had looked at everything, he went out into the corridor, ordering me again to come along. At the end of the corridor they drew their revolvers all at once and the sergeant ordered me to push aside the bookcase and open the door behind it. I said: 'But there's only a bookcase there!' At that he turned nasty, for he knew everything. He took hold of the bookcase and pulled. It yielded and the secret door was exposed. Perhaps the hooks had not been properly fastened. They opened the door and I had to precede them up the steps. The policemen followed me. I could feel their pistols in my back. I was the first to enter the Franks' room. Mrs. Frank was standing at the table. I made a great effort and managed to say: 'The Gestapo is here.'"

Otto Frank, now sixty-eight, has remarried and lives in Switzerland. Of the eight who lived in the Secret Annex, he is the only survivor. A handsome, soft-spoken man of obviously great intelligence, he regularly answers correspondence that comes to him

---

5. **Dutch masters:** seventeenth-century painters including Rembrandt, Frans Hals (fräns häls), and Jan Vermeer (yän vər·mer′).

6. **Occupation Police:** police organized by the German forces while they occupied the Netherlands.

Bookcase hiding the entrance to the Secret Annex.

"It yielded and the secret door was exposed."

about his daughter from all over the world. He recently went to Hollywood for consultation on the movie version of *The Diary of Anne Frank.* About the events of that August morning in 1944 Mr. Frank told me: "I was showing Peter Van Daan his spelling mistakes when suddenly someone came running up the stairs. The steps creaked, and I started to my feet, for it was morning, when everyone was supposed to be quiet. But then the door flew open and a man stood before us holding his pistol aimed at my chest.

"In the main room the others were already assembled. My wife and the children and Van Daans were standing there with raised hands. Then Albert Dussel came in, followed by another stranger. In the middle of the room stood a uniformed policeman. He stared into our faces.

"'Where are your valuables?' he asked. I pointed to the cupboard where my cash box was kept. The policeman took it out. Then he looked around and his eye fell on the leather briefcase where Anne kept her diary and all her papers. He opened it and shook everything out, dumped the contents on the floor so that Anne's papers and notebooks and loose sheets lay scattered at our feet. No one spoke, and the policeman didn't even glance at the mess on the floor as he put our valuables into the briefcase and closed it. He asked us whether we had any weapons. But we had none, of course. Then he said, 'Get ready.'"

Who betrayed the occupants of the Secret Annex? No one is sure, but some suspicion centers on a man I can only call M., whom the living remember as a crafty and disagreeable sneak. He was a warehouse clerk hired after the Franks moved into the building, and he was never told of their presence. M. used to come to work early in the mornings, and he once found a locked briefcase which Mr. Van Daan had carelessly left in the office, where he sometimes worked in the dead of night. Though Kraler claimed it was his own briefcase, it is possible the clerk suspected. Little signs lead to bigger conclusions. In the course of the months he had worked in the building, M. might have gathered many such signs: the dial on the office radio left at BBC[7] by nocturnal listeners, slight rearrangements in the office furniture, and, of course, small inexplicable sounds from the back of the building.

M. was tried later by a war crimes court, denied everything, and was acquitted. No one knows where he is now. I made no effort to find him. Neither did I search out Silberthaler, the German police sergeant who made the arrest. The betrayers would have told me nothing.

Ironically enough, the occupants of the Secret Annex had grown optimistic in the last weeks of their self-imposed confinement. The terrors of those first nights had largely faded. Even the German army communiqués[8] made clear that the war was approaching an end. The Russians were well into Poland. On the Western front Americans had broken through at Avranches and were pouring into the heart of France. Holland must be liberated soon. In her diary Anne Frank wrote that she thought she might be back in school by fall.

Now they were all packing. Of the capture Otto Frank recalled: "No one wept. Anne was very quiet and composed, only just as dispirited as the rest of us. Perhaps that was why she did not think to take along her notebooks, which lay scattered about on the floor. But maybe she too had the premonition that all was lost now, everything, and so she walked back and forth and did not even glance at her diary."

As the captives filed out of the building, Miep sat listening. "I heard them going," she said, "first in the corridor and then down the stairs. I could hear the heavy boots and the footsteps, and then the very light footsteps of Anne. Through the years she had taught herself to walk so softly that you could hear her only if you knew what to listen for. I did not see her, for the office door was closed as they all passed by."

---

8. **communiqués** (kə·myoō′ni·kāz′) *n.:* official bulletins.

Vocabulary

inexplicable (in·eks′pli·kə·bəl) *adj.:* incapable of being explained.

dispirited (di·spir′it·id) *v.* used as *adj.:* sad and discouraged.

premonition (prem′ə·nish′ən) *n.:* feeling that something, especially something bad, will happen.

---

7. **BBC:** British Broadcasting Corporation.

At Gestapo headquarters the prisoners were interrogated only briefly. As Otto Frank pointed out to his questioners, it was unlikely, after twenty-five months in the Secret Annex, that he would know the whereabouts of any other Jews who were hiding in Amsterdam.

The Franks, the Van Daans, and Dussel were kept at police headquarters for several days, the men in one cell, the women in the other. They were relatively comfortable there. The food was better than the food they had had in the Secret Annex and the guards left them alone.

Suddenly, all eight were taken to the railroad station and put on a train. The guards named their destination: Westerbork, a concentration camp for Jews in Holland, about eighty miles from Amsterdam. Mr. Frank said: "We rode in a regular passenger train. The fact that the door was bolted did not matter very much. We were together and had been given a little food for the journey. We were actually cheerful. Cheerful, at least, when I compare that journey to our next. We had already anticipated the possibility that we might not remain in Westerbork to the end. We knew what was happening to Jews in Auschwitz. But weren't the Russians already deep into Poland? We hoped our luck would hold.

"As we rode, Anne would not move from the window. It was summer outside. Meadows, stubble fields, and villages flew by. The telephone wires along the right of way curved up and down along the windows. After two years it was like freedom for her. Can you understand that?"

Among the names given me of survivors who had known the Franks at Westerbork was that of a Mrs. de Wiek, who lives in Apeldoorn, Holland. I visited Mrs. de Wiek in her home. A lovely, gracious woman, she told me that her family, like the Franks, had been in hiding for months before their capture. She said: "We had been at Westerbork three or four weeks when the word went around that there were new arrivals. News of that kind ran like wildfire through the camp, and my daughter Judy came running to me, calling, 'New people are coming, Mama!'

"The newcomers were standing in a long row in the mustering square,[9] and one of the clerks was entering their names on a list. We looked at them, and Judy pressed close against me. Most of the people in the camp were adults, and I had often wished for a

---

9. **mustering square:** place of assembly for inspection and roll call.

> "As we rode, Anne would not move from the window. After two years it was like freedom for her."

young friend for Judy, who was only fifteen. As I looked along the line, fearing I might see someone I knew, I suddenly exclaimed, 'Judy, see!'

"In the long line stood eight people whose faces, white as paper, told you at once that they had been hiding and had not been in the open air for years. Among them was this girl. And I said to Judy, 'Look, there is a friend for you.'

"I saw Anne Frank and Peter Van Daan every day in Westerbork. They were always together, and I often said to my husband, 'Look at those two beautiful young people.'

"Anne was so radiant that her beauty flowed over into Peter. Her eyes glowed and her movements had a lilt to them. She was very pallid at first, but there was something so attractive about her frailty and her expressive face that at first Judy was too shy to make friends.

"Anne was happy there, incredible as it seems. Things were hard for us in the camp. We 'convict Jews' who had been arrested in hiding places had to wear blue overalls with a red bib and wooden shoes. Our men had their heads shaved. Three hundred people lived in each barracks. We were sent to work at five in the morning, the children to a cable workshop and the grown-ups to a shed where we had to break up old batteries and salvage the metal and the carbon rods. The food was bad, we were always kept on the run, and the guards all screamed 'Faster, faster!' But Anne was happy. It was as if she had been liberated. Now she could see new people and talk to them and could laugh. She could laugh while the rest of us thought nothing but: Will they send us to the camps in Poland? Will we live through it?

"Edith Frank, Anne's mother, seemed numbed by the experience. She could have been a mute. Anne's sister Margot spoke little and Otto Frank was quiet too, but his was a reassuring quietness that helped Anne and all of us. He lived in the men's barracks, but once when Anne was sick, he came over to visit her every evening and would stand beside her bed for hours, telling her stories. Anne was so like him. When another child, a twelve-year-old boy named David, fell ill, Anne stood by his bed and talked to him. David came from an Orthodox family, and he and Anne always talked about God."

Anne Frank stayed at Westerbork only three weeks. Early in September a thousand of the "convict Jews" were put on a freight train, seventy-five people to a car. Brussels fell to the Allies, then Antwerp, then the Americans reached Aachen. But the victories were coming too late. The Franks and their friends were already on the way to Auschwitz, the camp in Poland where four million Jews died.

Mrs. de Wiek was in the same freight car as the Franks on that journey from Westerbork to Auschwitz. "Now and then when the train stopped," she told me, "the SS guards[10] came to the door and held out their caps and we had to toss our money and valuables into the caps. Anne and Judy sometimes pulled themselves up to the small barred window of the car and described the villages we were passing through. We made the children repeat the addresses where we could meet after the war if we became separated in the camp. I remember that the Franks chose a meeting place in Switzerland.

"I sat beside my husband on a small box.

---

10. **SS guards:** Nazi special police, who ran the concentration camps.

On the third day in the train, my husband suddenly took my hand and said, 'I want to thank you for the wonderful life we have had together.'

"I snatched my hand away from his, crying, 'What are you thinking about? It's not over!'

"But he calmly reached for my hand again and took it and repeated several times, 'Thank you. Thank you for the life we have had together.' Then I left my hand in his and did not try to draw it away."

On the third night, the train stopped, the doors of the car slid violently open, and the first the exhausted passengers saw of Auschwitz was the glaring searchlights fixed on the train. On the platform, kapos (criminal convicts who were assigned to positions of authority over the other prisoners) were running back and forth shouting orders. Behind them, seen distinctly against the light, stood the SS officers, trimly built and smartly uniformed, many of them with huge dogs at their sides. As the people poured out of the train, a loudspeaker roared, "Women to the left! Men to the right!"

Mrs. de Wiek went on calmly: "I saw them all as they went away, Mr. Van Daan and Mr. Dussel and Peter and Mr. Frank. But I saw no sign of my husband. He had vanished. I never saw him again.

"'Listen!' the loudspeaker bawled again. 'It is an hour's march to the women's camp. For the children and the sick there are trucks waiting at the end of the platform.'

"We could see the trucks," Mrs. de Wiek said. "They were painted with big red crosses. We all made a rush for them. Who among us was not sick after those days on the train? But we did not reach them.

People were still hanging on to the backs of the trucks as they started off. Not one person who went along on that ride ever arrived at the women's camp, and no one has ever found any trace of them."

Mrs. de Wiek, her daughter, Mrs. Van Daan, Mrs. Frank, Margot, and Anne survived the brutal pace of the night march to the women's camp at Auschwitz. Next day their heads were shaved; they learned that the hair was useful as packing for pipe joints in U-boats.[11] Then the women were put to work digging sods of grass, which they placed in great piles. As they labored each day, thousands of others were dispatched with maniacal efficiency in the gas chambers, and smoke rising from the stacks of the huge crematoriums[12] blackened the sky.

Mrs. de Wiek saw Anne Frank every day at Auschwitz. "Anne seemed even more beautiful there," Mrs. de Wiek said, "than she had at Westerbork. Of course her long hair was gone, but now you could see that her beauty was in her eyes, which seemed to grow bigger as she grew thinner. Her gaiety had vanished, but she was still alert and sweet, and with her charm she sometimes secured things that the rest of us had long since given up hoping for.

"For example, we each had only a gray sack to wear. But when the weather turned cold, Anne came in one day wearing a suit of men's long underwear. She had begged it somewhere. She looked screamingly funny with those long white legs but somehow still delightful.

"Though she was the youngest, Anne was

---

11. **U-boats** *n.:* submarines.
12. **crematoriums** (krē′mə·tôr′ē·əmz) *n.:* furnaces in which prisoners' bodies were cremated (burned to ashes).

Prisoners arriving at Auschwitz.

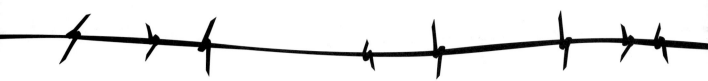

the leader in her group of five people. She also gave out the bread to everyone in the barracks and she did it so fairly there was none of the usual grumbling.

"We were always thirsty at Auschwitz, so thirsty that at roll call we would stick out our tongues if it happened to be raining or snowing, and many became sick from bad water. Once, when I was almost dead because there was nothing to drink, Anne suddenly came to me with a cup of coffee. To this day I don't know where she got it.

"In the barracks many people were dying, some of starvation, others of weakness and despair. It was almost impossible not to give up hope, and when a person gave up, his face became empty and dead. The Polish woman doctor who had been caring for the sick said to me, 'You will pull through. You still have your face.'

"Anne Frank, too, still had her face, up to the very last. To the last also she was moved by the dreadful things the rest of us had somehow become hardened to. Who bothered to look when the flames shot up into the sky at night from the crematoriums? Who was troubled that every day new people were being selected and gassed? Most of us were beyond feeling. But not Anne. I can still see her standing at the door and looking down the camp street as a group of naked Gypsy girls were driven by on their way to the crematorium. Anne watched them going and cried. And she also cried when we marched past the Hungarian children who had been waiting half a day in the rain in front of the gas chambers. And Anne nudged me and said, 'Look, look! Their eyes!' Anne cried. And you cannot imagine how soon most of us came to the end of our tears."

Late in October the SS selected the healthiest of the women prisoners for work in a munitions factory in Czechoslovakia. Judy de Wiek was taken from her mother, but Anne and her sister Margot were rejected because they had contracted scabies.[13] A few days later there was another selection for shipment from Auschwitz. Stripped, the women waited naked for hours on the mustering ground outside the barracks. Then, one by one, they filed into the barracks, where a battery of powerful lights had been set up and an SS doctor waited to check them over. Only those able to stand a trip and do hard work were being chosen for this new shipment, and many of the women lied about their age and condition in the hope that they would escape the almost certain death of Auschwitz. Mrs. de Wiek was rejected and so was Mrs. Frank. They waited, looking on.

"Next it was the turn of the two girls, Anne and Margot," Mrs. de Wiek recalled. "Even under the glare of that light Anne still had her face, and she encouraged Margot, and Margot walked erect into the light. There they stood for a moment, naked and shaven-headed, and Anne looked at us with her unclouded face, looked straight and stood straight, and then they were approved

---

13. **scabies** *n.:* skin disease that causes severe itching.

and passed along. We could not see what was on the other side of the light. Mrs. Frank screamed, 'The children! Oh, God!'"

The chronicle of most of the other occupants of the Secret Annex ends at Auschwitz. Mrs. Frank died there of malnutrition two months later. Mr. Frank saw Mr. Van Daan marched to the gas chambers. When the SS fled Auschwitz before the approaching Russians in January 1945, they took Peter Van Daan with them. It was bitter cold and the roads were covered with ice and Peter Van Daan, Anne Frank's shy beloved, was never heard of again.

From Auschwitz, Mr. Dussel, the dentist, was shipped to a camp in Germany, where he died. Only Otto Frank remained there alive until liberation. Anne Frank and Mrs. Van Daan and Margot had been selected for shipment to Bergen-Belsen.

Last year I drove the 225 miles from Amsterdam to Belsen and spent a day there walking over the heath.[14] The site of the old camp is near the city of Hannover, in the state of Lower Saxony. It was June when I arrived, and lupine was in flower in the scrubland.

My guide first showed me the cemetery where fifty thousand Russian prisoners of war, captured in one of Hitler's great early offensives, were buried in 1941. Next to them is a cemetery for Italians. No one knows exactly whether there are three hundred or three thousand in that mass grave.

About a mile farther we came to the main site of the Bergen-Belsen camp. Amid the low growth of pine and birches many large rectangular patches can be seen on the heath. The barracks stood on these, and between them the worn tracks of thousands of bare feet are still visible. There are more mass graves nearby, low mounds overgrown with heath grass or new-planted dwarf pines. Boards bearing the numbers of the dead stand beside some mounds, but others are unmarked and barely discernible. Anne Frank lies there.

The train that carried Anne from Auschwitz to Belsen stopped at every second station because of air raids. At Bergen-Belsen there were no roll calls, no organization, almost no sign of the SS. Prisoners lived on the heath without hope. The fact that the Allies had reached the Rhine encouraged no one. Prisoners died daily—of hunger, thirst, sickness.

The Auschwitz group had at first been assigned to tents on the Bergen-Belsen heath, tents which, one survivor recalls, gave an oddly gay, carnival aspect to the camp. One night that fall a great windstorm brought the tents crashing down, and their occupants were then put in wooden barracks. Mrs. B. of Amsterdam remembered about Anne: "We lived in the same block and saw each other often. In fact, we had a party together at Christmastime. We had saved up some stale bread, and we cut this up and put onions and boiled cabbage on the pieces. Over our feast we nearly forgot our misery for a few hours. We were almost happy. I know that it sounds ghastly now, but we really were a little happy in spite of everything."

One of Anne Frank's dearest childhood friends in Amsterdam was a girl named Lies Goosens.[15] Lies is repeatedly mentioned in

---

14. **heath** (hēth) *n.:* area of open wasteland covered with low-growing plants.

15. **Lies Goosens** (lēs khō′sins).

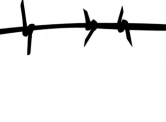

Anne in 1942. This may be the last photograph of her ever taken.

the diary. She was captured before the Franks were found in the Secret Annex, and Anne wrote of her great fears for the safety of her friend. Now the slim and attractive wife of an Israeli army officer, Lies lives in Jerusalem. But she was in Bergen-Belsen in February 1945, when she heard that a group of Dutch Jews had been moved into the next compound.

Lies said, "I waited until night. Then I stole out of the barracks and went over to the barbed wire which separated us from the newcomers. I called softly into the darkness, 'Is anyone there?'

"A voice answered, 'I am here. I am Mrs. Van Daan.'

"We had known the Van Daans in Amsterdam. I told her who I was and asked whether Margot or Anne could come to the fence. Mrs. Van Daan answered in a breathless voice that Margot was sick but that Anne could probably come and that she would go look for her.

"I waited, shivering in the darkness. It took a long time. But suddenly I heard a voice: 'Lies? Lies? Where are you?'

"I ran in the direction of the voice, and then I saw Anne beyond the barbed wire. She was in rags. I saw her emaciated, sunken

Vocabulary
emaciated (ē·mā′shē·āt′id) v. used as *adj.*:
extremely thin, as from starvation or illness.

face in the darkness. Her eyes were very large. We cried and cried as we told each other our sad news, for now there was only the barbed wire between us, nothing more, and no longer any difference in our fates.

"But there was a difference after all. My block still had food and clothing. Anne had nothing. She was freezing and starving. I called to her in a whisper, 'Come back tomorrow. I'll bring you something.'

"And Anne called across, 'Yes, tomorrow. I'll come.'

"I saw Anne again when she came to the fence on the following night," Lies continued. "I had packed up a woolen jacket and some zwieback[16] and sugar and a tin of sardines for her. I called out, 'Anne, watch now!' Then I threw the bundle across the barbed wire.

"But I heard only screams and Anne crying. I shouted, 'What's happened?' And she called back, weeping, 'A woman caught it and won't give it to me.' Then I heard rapid footsteps as the woman ran away. Next night I had only a pair of stockings and zwieback, but this time Anne caught it."

In the last weeks at Bergen-Belsen, as Germany was strangled between the Russians and the Western Allies, there was almost no food at all. The roads were blocked, the railroads had been bombed, and the SS commander of the camp drove around the district trying unsuccessfully to requisition supplies. Still, the crematoriums worked night and day. And in the midst of the starvation and the murder there was a great epidemic of typhus.

Both Anne and Margot Frank contracted the disease in late February or early March

of 1945. Margot lay in a coma for several days. Then, while unconscious, she somehow rolled from her bed and died. Mrs. Van Daan also died in the epidemic.

The death of Anne Frank passed almost without notice. For Anne, as for millions of others, it was only the final anonymity, and I met no one who remembers being with her in that moment. So many were dying. One woman said, "I feel certain she died because of her sister's death. Dying is easy for anyone left alone in a concentration camp." Mrs. B., who had shared the pitiful Christmastide feast with Anne, knows a little more: "Anne, who was very sick at the time, was not informed of her sister's death. But a few days later she sensed it and soon afterward she died, peacefully."

Three weeks later British troops liberated Bergen-Belsen.

Miep and Elli, the heroic young women who had shielded the Franks for two years, found Anne's papers during the week after the police raid on the Secret Annex. "It was terrible when I went up there," Miep recalled. "Everything had been turned upside down. On the floor lay clothes, papers, letters, and school notebooks. Anne's little wrapper hung from a hook on the wall. And among the clutter on the floor lay a notebook with a red-checked cover. I picked it up, looked at the pages, and recognized Anne's handwriting."

Elli wept as she spoke to me: "The table was still set. There were plates, cups, and spoons, but the plates were empty, and I was so frightened I scarcely dared take a step. We sat down on the floor and leafed through all the papers. They were all Anne's, the notebooks and the colored duplicate paper from the office too. We

---

16. zwieback (swē′bak′) *n.*: sweetened bread that is sliced and toasted after it is baked.

gathered all of them and locked them up in the main office.

"A few days later M. came into the office, M. who now had the keys to the building. He said to me, 'I found some more stuff upstairs,' and he handed me another sheaf of Anne's papers. How strange, I thought, that *he* should be the one to give these to me. But I took them and locked them up with the others."

Miep and Elli did not read the papers they had saved. The red-checked diary, the office account books into which it overflowed, the 312 tissue-thin sheets of colored paper filled with Anne's short stories and the beginnings of a novel about a young girl who was to live in freedom—all these were kept in the safe until Otto Frank finally returned to Amsterdam alone. Thus Anne Frank's voice was preserved out of the millions that were silenced. No louder than a child's whisper, it speaks for those millions and has outlasted the <u>raucous</u> shouts of the murderers, soaring above the <u>clamorous</u> voices of passing time.

Vocabulary
raucous (rô′kəs) *adj.:* loud and rowdy.
clamorous (klam′ər·əs) *adj.:* loud and demanding.

MEET THE WRITER

Ernst Schnabel

Following the Trail

As a young man, **Ernst Schnabel** (1913–1986) left his birthplace of Zittau, Germany, to become a sailor and travel the world. He served in the German marines during World War II, then gave up the seafaring life for a writing career. He was well-known in Germany for his radio plays, tales of his adventures at sea, and books linking classical mythology with modern-day situations. Schnabel's adventures didn't end when he began writing: In 1951, he flew around the world in nine days, then turned his experience into a novel.

For Independent Reading

"I have followed the trail of Anne Frank. It leads out of Germany and back into Germany, for there was no escape." So begins *Anne Frank: A Portrait in Courage* (1958). Based on interviews with forty-two people whose lives touched Anne's, this book enlarges on the story told in the article.

Literary Response and Analysis

Reading Check

1. This article contains a **chronological account** of what happened to Anne and the other residents of the Secret Annex after their arrest by the Gestapo. Draw a time line that shows what Ernst Schnabel discovered. Start with August 4, 1944. End with March 1945. For a model time line, see pages 215–216.

Interpretations

2. Fill in the L column of your **KWL chart.** Then, choose one or two interesting or surprising things that you learned, and discuss them with a partner.

3. Did reading this article by Ernst Schnabel change your feelings about Anne Frank's story or help you understand the events in the play? Explain.

4. How closely does the Anne that Mrs. de Wiek describes resemble the **character** Anne in the play? Explain.

5. Choose two quotations from the people Schnabel interviewed, and write the question you think he asked to get each response. Are any of these questions similar to ones you wrote in your Quickwrite notes?

6. This writer wanted to discover what happened to Anne Frank after her arrest. But he certainly had other **purposes** in writing this factual article. What do you think his purposes were? What would you say is the **main idea** of the article? Find

at least one passage in the article that supports the main idea.

7. Now that you've read Schnabel's article, how do you feel about Anne's statement that "people are really good at heart"? Explain whether your reading of the article tends to support or contradict Anne's belief.

8. Whom else do you know about whose "spirit has remained to stir the conscience of the world" (page 296)? Describe the lasting influence this person has had.

Evaluation

9. In his factual article, Schnabel uses the names that Anne made up for Mr. and Mrs. Van Pels (whom Anne calls Mr. and Mrs. Van Daan) and Fritz Pfeffer (whom Anne calls Albert Dussel). Why do you think he chose to do this? Do you think he should have used their real names? Why or why not?

Writing
Share Your Report

For further research into this period in history, read one of the books about the Holocaust or World War II recommended on pages 346–347. Write a brief report on that book, and present it to the class. Include a comparison of the new book with the other materials in this chapter. What new information did you find in the new book? Which work did you like best? Which one did you learn the most from?

**Grade 5
Review
Reading
Standard** 2.3
Discern main ideas and concepts presented in texts, identifying and assessing evidence that supports those ideas.

Vocabulary Development

Reading Standard 1.3
Show ability to verify meanings by comparison.

Word Ratings: Connotations

Connotations are the feelings associated with a word, feelings that go beyond its strict dictionary definition, or **denotation.** Often connotations show shades of meaning or intensity.

PRACTICE

Use the symbol "+" if the word on the right seems stronger than the numbered Word Bank word on the left. Use "−" if it seems weaker. Use a dictionary for help. (Try this exercise with a partner. You may not agree!)

1. indomitable ( ) strong
2. annihilation ( ) ruin
3. refuge ( ) shelter
4. reconciliations ( ) agreements
5. inexplicable ( ) mysterious
6. dispirited ( ) hopeless
7. premonition ( ) dread
8. emaciated ( ) skinny
9. raucous ( ) noisy
10. clamorous ( ) loud

Word Bank

indomitable
annihilation
refuge
reconciliations
inexplicable
dispirited
premonition
emaciated
raucous
clamorous

Grammar Link MINI-LESSON

Joining Independent Clauses

Use a semicolon between independent clauses joined by words and phrases such as these:

after all	in fact	otherwise
besides	instead	still
for example	meanwhile	therefore
however	on the other hand	unfortunately

The play tells the story of life in the Secret Annex; however, it does not always stick to what really happened.

The playwrights invented the howling siren and pounding rifle butt for the arrest scene; after all, it's more dramatic that way.

Note that a comma always follows a connecting word.

PRACTICE

Choose three of the words or phrases listed on the left. Use each one in a sentence of your own. Be sure your semicolons and commas are in the right places.
For more help, see Semicolons in the *Holt Handbook,* pages 331–334.

Walking with Living Feet

Connecting Main Ideas

Some people say that the best readers are able to find connections among all the different texts they read. As you read this personal essay, called "Walking with Living Feet," look for Dara Horn's **main idea**—the message, opinion, or insight that is central to a piece of nonfiction. Then, think about what you learned from "A Tragedy Revealed" by Ernst Schnabel (page 295). How does Schnabel's factual report deepen your understanding of Horn's personal essay?

Train destination sign.

Grade 6 Review Reading Standard 2.3 Connect and clarify main ideas by identifying their relationships to other sources and related topics.

WALKING WITH LIVING FEET

I had a very unusual fifteenth birthday. During my birthday week, at the end of April, I was traveling with five thousand high school students from around the world, visiting concentration camps in Poland. I learned more there than I learned during my entire life in school; once I stepped out of a gas chamber, I became a different person. When I turned fifteen, I discovered that no matter how much you read about the Holocaust, nothing can ever be like seeing it with your own eyes. The day after my fifteenth birthday was the turning point of my life. I was at Majdanek, one of the largest Nazi concentration camps. And I will never forget it.

Majdanek has been left exactly as it was when it was in use, so intact that if it were to be "plugged in," it could start gassing people tomorrow.

I stood in a gas chamber there, at Majdanek. I saw the blue stains of Zyklon B streaking the ceilings and walls, the poison used to kill the people who were crushed into this tiny, gray cement room. I could see how their fingers had scraped off the white paint, trying to escape. The cement floor that I sat on was cold and clammy; the air in the room seemed made of chills. When I first sat down, I did not notice, but soon those chilling waves were seeping into my skin, like so many tiny fingers trying to pull at my nerves and make my bones quiver. All around me, kids were crying hysterically, yet the chills that rankled the air around me hadn't reached my mind, and I could not feel. I hated myself for it. Anger, fear, pain, and shock—I could have felt all of those and more, but instead I felt nothing. That void was far worse: All the other emotions around me showed the presence of human hearts, but I was almost not there at all. I wanted to feel; I hated the guilt I had at my lack of reaction as much as I hated what happened there. Only my squirming skin could attest to my surroundings, and the crawling air made my lungs tighten. I wished I could cry, but I couldn't break down my mental blockade. Why?

The camp of Majdanek extends for miles, but one of the worst things about it is that it's right in a town, almost a city, called Lublin. There are actually houses right next to the barbed wire, the fence with its thorns that stabbed my frightened eyes, enough to separate a universe. The people of that city would have had to be dead not to notice the death which struck daily, right behind their backyards, where I saw children playing. People marched through Lublin from the train station, entered through the same barbed wire gate that I did, and left through the chimney. Nobody in Lublin noticed, because if they had, their fate would have been the same. And today the camp's long gray, barnlike barracks still extend forever, in endless rows, the sky a leaden weight blocking the colors that grace free life. Gray is the color of hell.

Inside each of the barracks is a new horror. Some are museum exhibits, with collections of people's toothbrushes (they were told that they were being "relocated" and to bring one suitcase, the contents of which were confiscated) and people's hair. All of the walls in one barracks are covered with people's hats, hanging in rows. But the worst were the shoes.

About five of the barracks are filled with nothing but the shoes of some of the people who were killed there—over 850,000 pairs. In one barracks, I sat on a platform about five feet off the ground, and surrounding it was an ocean of shoes, five feet deep. In the gas chamber I could not feel, but in that room filled with shoes, my mental blockade cracked. The photographs meant nothing to me, the history lessons and names and numbers were never strong enough. But here each shoe is different, a different size and shape: a high heel, a sandal, a baby's shoe so tiny that its owner couldn't have been old enough to walk, and shoes like mine. Each pair of those shoes walked a path all its own, guided its owner through his or her life and to all of their deaths. Thousands and thousands of shoes, each pair different, each pair silently screaming someone's murdered dreams. No book can teach me what I saw there with my own eyes!

I glanced at my own shoe, expecting it to be far different from those in that ocean of death, and my breath caught in my throat as I saw that my shoe seemed to be almost the same style as one, no, two, three, of the shoes I saw; it seemed as if every shoe there was my shoe. I touched the toe of one nearby and felt its dusty texture, certain that mine would be different. But as I touched my own toe, tears welled in my eyes as my fingers traced the edges of my dusty, living shoes. Eight hundred and fifty thousand pairs of shoes, but now I understood: They weren't numbers; they were people.

Soon I was crying, but for someone else: for the child whose mother's sandals rested on that pile, for the woman whose husband's shoes swam motionless in that sea, like the tears that streaked my face, for the girl whose best friend's slippers were buried in that ocean of grayness and silence. I was lost to the shoes there. I wished I could throw my shoes into that pile, to grasp and feel each shoe, to jump into the sea of shoes, to become a part of it, to take it with me. I wanted to add my own shoes to that ocean, but all I could leave there were my salty tears. My feet clumped on the wooden platform as I left, and I had never been more conscious of how my shoes fit my living feet.

At the very end of the camp was another gas chamber and the crematorium, its smokestack jutting through the leaden sky. This gas chamber did not have the blue poison stains that streaked the walls in the one I saw first, or maybe it did: The only light in that cement room was from dozens of memorial candles. It was too dark to see. The air inside was damp and suffocating, like a burial cave, and yet the air was savagely alive. It crawled down my neck and compressed me as the walls and ceiling seemed to move closer. No words can express how it felt to step out of that gas chamber alive, wearing my living shoes.

And I saw the crematorium where the corpses were burned, ovens shaped to fit a person. As I touched the brick furnaces with trembling fingers, my tears froze in my eyes and I could not cry. It was here that I felt my soul go up in flames, leaving me an empty shell.

Majdanek reeks of death everywhere. Even the reminders and signs of life that exist in a cemetery, like a footprint or rustling leaves, are absent here, every image of life erased. Even the wind does not ruffle the grass, which never used to grow here because the prisoners would eat it. But in the crematorium, I felt something I cannot express. No words exist to describe how I felt. It was someone else's nightmare, a nightmare that turned real before I even noticed it. It was a stark and chilling reality that struck me there, standing where people were slaughtered and burned, and my mind simply stopped. Have you ever been to Planet Hell? My people are numbers here, struck from a list and sent out the chimney, their children's bodies roasting. And I was there. You cannot visit this planet through any film or book; photographs cannot bring you here. Planet Hell is beyond the realm of tears. This is why I could not cry.

I left the camp. How many people, who had walked in those 850,000 pairs of shoes, once dreamed of doing what I had just done? And did they, too, forget how to cry?

In Israel I planted a tree with soil I had taken from concentration camps. In the soil were white specks, human bone ash. I am fifteen years old, and I know I can never forget.

—Dara Horn
Millburn High School
Millburn, New Jersey

First appeared in *Merlyn's Pen: The National Magazines of Student Writing.*

Reading Informational Materials

Reading Check

1. What does the writer do during her birthday week?

2. What does the writer see and experience in the first gas chamber at Majdanek?

3. Why does the writer finally cry when she sees the room full of shoes?

4. The writer calls the crematorium "Planet Hell." What evidence did she give to support this **analogy** comparing the crematorium to hell?

TestPractice

WALKING WITH LIVING FEET

1. The writer's **purpose** in writing about her visit to Majdanek was most likely to —
   A tell how it felt
   B entertain the reader
   C persuade the reader to take a stand
   D teach the history of the camp

2. Which of the following sentences do you think *best* states the writer's **main idea**?
   F "I had a very unusual fifteenth birthday."
   G "No matter how much you read about the Holocaust, nothing can ever be like seeing it with your own eyes."
   H "Nobody in Lublin noticed. . . ."
   J "No words exist to describe how I felt."

3. The writer says that no Lublin residents noticed anyone entering the camp through the barbed wire gate and leaving through the chimney because —
   A if they had, their fate would have been the same as the prisoners' fate
   B they could not see over the high walls around the camp
   C the camp was so far from town they could not see what went on inside
   D they did not want to know what was happening in the camp

4. Planting a tree in soil taken from a concentration camp is a **symbol** of —
   F good land management
   G good growing out of evil
   H a need for revenge
   J a misuse of resources

Grade 6 Review Reading Standard 2.3 Connect and clarify main ideas by identifying their relationships to other sources and related topics.

Vocabulary Development

Context Clues

PRACTICE 1

In the following passages from this essay, context clues for the underlined words are in italic type. Use the context clues to identify the meaning of each underlined word.

1. "The cement floor that I sat on was *cold* and clammy; *the air in the room seemed made of chills.*" *Clammy* means
   a. cold and damp
   b. warm and damp
   c. flooded
   d. rough

2. "Anger, fear, pain, and shock—I could have felt all of those and more, but instead *I felt nothing*. That void was far worse. . . ." *Void* means
   a. pit
   b. vista
   c. space
   d. emptiness

3. "I wished I could cry, but I couldn't *break down* my mental blockade." *Blockade* means
   a. barrier
   b. bombardment
   c. agony
   d. illness

4. "The air was savagely alive. It crawled down my neck and compressed me *as the walls and ceiling seemed to move closer.*" *Compressed* means
   a. squeezed together from pressure
   b. comforted by a parent
   c. released from prison
   d. relieved from anxiety

Words in Context

PRACTICE 2

The underlined words above can be used in other contexts. See if you can answer these questions:

1. How would a cave explorer use the word *clammy*?
2. How would a physicist use the word *void*?
3. How would a naval officer use the word *blockade*?
4. How would a pipe fitter use the word *compressed*?

Reading Standard 1.3
Use word meanings within the appropriate context.

Grade 6 Review Reading Standard 1.4
Use word, sentence, and paragraph clues to determine meaning.

Camp Harmony *and*
In Response to Executive Order 9066

Literary Focus
Recurring Themes

Because **themes** are general ideas about human experience, they have been repeated again and again in literature throughout the ages. For instance, a theme such as *Good can triumph over evil* can be found in ancient texts as well as in contemporary novels. As you read the following selections, look for themes you recognize from other works, including *The Diary of Anne Frank.*

Reading Skills
Making Generalizations: Putting It All Together

A **generalization** is a broad statement based on several particular situations. When you make a generalization, you combine new evidence in a text with what you already know. For example, after you have read about Monica Sone's experiences, you might make a generalization about the treatment of Japanese Americans during World War II.

Make the Connection
Quickwrite ✏️

Look at the paintings on pages 321 and 326. Freewrite in response to one of them. You might use this starter: "The first thing I noticed was . . ."

Background

In 1942, many thousands of Japanese Americans living on the West Coast were sent to internment camps. They had committed no crime, but the United States had gone to war with Japan. Executive Order 9066 made their confinement legal. Ironically, many of the evacuated families had sons or brothers serving with the U.S. Army in the war overseas. Most of the 120,000 Japanese Americans detained spent three years behind barbed wire. Released in 1945, at the end of World War II, they returned home to find their property stolen and their livelihoods gone. They had to wait more than forty years for an apology and compensation from the U.S. government.

Vocabulary Development

You will learn these words as you read "Camp Harmony":

tersely (tʉrs′lē) *adv.*: briefly and clearly. *The child tersely stated, "Pigs—dirty."*

laconically (lə·kän′ik·lē) *adv.*: with few words. *He answered laconically: "Soup."*

breach (brēch) *n.*: opening. *The narrator squeezed into a breach in the wall of people.*

riveted (riv′it·id) *v.*: fastened; held firmly. *The family watched, riveted with fear, as the stove turned red hot.*

vigil (vij′əl) *n.*: watch. *Armed guards kept an around-the-clock vigil in the camp.*

Reading Standard 3.5
Identify and analyze recurring themes (for example, good versus evil) across traditional and contemporary works.

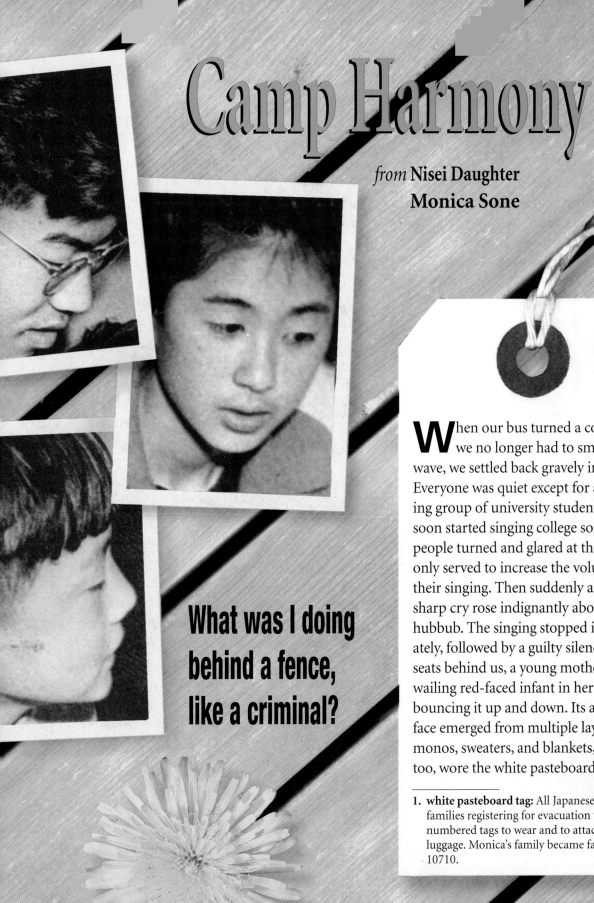

Camp Harmony

from **Nisei Daughter**
Monica Sone

What was I doing behind a fence, like a criminal?

When our bus turned a corner and we no longer had to smile and wave, we settled back gravely in our seats. Everyone was quiet except for a chattering group of university students, who soon started singing college songs. A few people turned and glared at them, which only served to increase the volume of their singing. Then suddenly a baby's sharp cry rose indignantly above the hubbub. The singing stopped immediately, followed by a guilty silence. Three seats behind us, a young mother held a wailing red-faced infant in her arms, bouncing it up and down. Its angry little face emerged from multiple layers of kimonos, sweaters, and blankets, and it, too, wore the white pasteboard tag[1]

---

1. **white pasteboard tag:** All Japanese American families registering for evacuation were given numbered tags to wear and to attach to their luggage. Monica's family became family number 10710.

pinned to its blanket. A young man stammered out an apology as the mother gave him a wrathful look. She hunted frantically for a bottle of milk in a shopping bag, and we all relaxed when she had found it.

We sped out of the city southward along beautiful stretches of farmland, with dark, newly turned soil. In the beginning we devoured every bit of scenery which flashed past our window and admired the massive-muscled workhorses plodding along the edge of the highway, the rich burnished copper color of a browsing herd of cattle, the vivid spring green of the pastures, but eventually the sameness of the country landscape palled[2] on us. We tried to sleep to escape from the restless anxiety which kept bobbing up to the surface of our minds. I awoke with a start when the bus filled with excited buzzing. A small group of straw-hatted Japanese farmers stood by the highway, waving at us. I felt a sudden warmth toward them, then a twinge of pity. They would be joining us soon.

About noon we crept into a small town. Someone said, "Looks like Puyallup, all right." Parents of small children babbled excitedly, "Stand up quickly and look over there. See all the chick-chicks and fat little piggies?" One little city boy stared hard at the hogs and said tersely, "They're bachi—dirty!"

Our bus idled a moment at the traffic signal, and we noticed at the left of us an entire block filled with neat rows of low shacks, resembling chicken houses. Someone commented on it with awe, "Just look at those chicken houses. They sure go in for poultry in a big way here." Slowly the bus made a left turn, drove through a wire-fence gate, and to our dismay, we were inside the oversized chicken farm. The bus driver opened the door, the guard stepped out and stationed himself at the door again. Jim, the young man who had shepherded us into the buses, popped his head inside and sang out, "OK, folks, all off at Yokohama, Puyallup."

We stumbled out, stunned, dragging our bundles after us. It must have rained hard the night before in Puyallup, for we sank ankle deep into gray, glutinous[3] mud. The receptionist, a white man, instructed us courteously, "Now, folks, please stay together as family units and line up. You'll be assigned your apartment."

We were standing in Area A, the mammoth parking lot of the state fairgrounds. There were three other separate areas, B, C, and D, all built on the fairgrounds proper, near the baseball field and the racetracks. This camp of army barracks was hopefully called Camp Harmony.

We were assigned to apartment 2–I–A, right across from the bachelor quarters. The apartments resembled elongated,[4] low stables about two blocks long. Our home was one room, about eighteen by twenty feet, the size of a living room. There was one small window in the wall opposite the one door. It was bare except for a small, tinny wood-burning stove crouching in the center. The flooring consisted of two-by-fours laid directly on the earth, and dandelions were already pushing their way up through the cracks. Mother was delighted when she saw their shaggy yellow heads. "Don't anyone pick them. I'm going to cultivate them."

---

3. **glutinous** (gl $\overline{oo}$ t″n·əs) *adj.*: sticky; gluey.
4. **elongated** (ē·lôŋ′gāt′id) *v.* used as *adj.*: lengthened.

Vocabulary
tersely (turs′lē) *adv.*: briefly and clearly; without unnecessary words.

---

2. **palled** (pôld) *v.*: became boring or tiresome.

Topaz, August 1943 (1943) by Suiko Mikami. Watercolor.

Father snorted, "Cultivate them! If we don't watch out, those things will be growing out of our hair."

Just then Henry stomped inside, bringing the rest of our baggage. "What's all the excitement about?"

Sumi replied laconically, "Dandelions."

Henry tore off a fistful. Mother scolded, "Arra! Arra! Stop that. They're the only beautiful things around here. We could have a garden right in here."

"Are you joking, Mama?"

I chided Henry, "Of course she's not. After all, she has to have some inspiration to write poems, you know, with all the 'nari keri's.'[5] I can think of a poem myself right now:

Oh, Dandelion, Dandelion,
Despised and uprooted by all,
Dance and bob your golden heads
For you've finally found your home
With your yellow fellows, nari keri, amen!"

Henry said, thrusting the dandelions in Mother's black hair, "I think you can do ten times better than that, Mama."

Sumi reclined on her sea bag[6] and fretted, "Where do we sleep? Not on the floor, I hope."

"Stop worrying," Henry replied disgustedly. Mother and Father wandered out to see

---

5. *Nari keri* (nä·*rē* ke·*rē*) is a phrase used to end many Japanese poems. It is meant to convey wonder and awe.

6. **sea bag** *n.:* large canvas bag like the ones sailors use to carry their personal belongings. Each person was allowed to bring only one sea bag of bedding and two suitcases of clothing to the internment camps.

Vocabulary

laconically (lə·kän′ik·lē) *adv.:* with few words. *Laconically* and *tersely* are synonyms.

Japanese-American History Archives.

what the other folks were doing and they found people wandering in the mud, wondering what other folks were doing. Mother returned shortly, her face lit up in an ecstatic smile, "We're in luck. The latrine is right nearby. We won't have to walk blocks."

We laughed, marveling at Mother who could be so poetic and yet so practical. Father came back, bent double like a woodcutter in a fairy tale, with stacks of scrap lumber over his shoulder. His coat and trouser pockets bulged with nails. Father dumped his loot in a corner and explained, "There was a pile of wood left by the carpenters and hundreds of nails scattered loose. Everybody was picking them up, and I hustled right in with them. Now maybe we can live in style, with tables and chairs."

The block leader knocked at our door and announced lunchtime. He instructed us to take our meal at the nearest mess hall. As I untied my sea bag to get out my pie plate, tin cup, spoon, and fork, I realized I was hungry. At the mess hall we found a long line of people. Children darted in and out of the line, skiing in the slithery mud. The young stood impatiently on one foot, then the other, and scowled, "The food had better be good after all this wait." But the issei[7] stood quietly, arms folded, saying very little. A light drizzle began to fall, coating bare black heads with tiny sparkling raindrops. The chow line inched forward.

Lunch consisted of two canned sausages, one lob of boiled potato, and a slab of bread. Our family had to split up, for the hall was too crowded for us to sit together. I wandered up and down the aisles, back and forth along the crowded tables and benches, looking for a few inches to squeeze into. A small issei woman finished her meal, stood up, and hoisted her legs modestly over the bench, leaving a space for one. Even as I thrust myself into the breach, the space had shrunk to two inches, but I worked myself into it. My dinner companion, hooked just inside my right elbow, was a baldheaded, gruff-looking issei man who seemed to resent nestling at mealtime. Under my left elbow was a tiny, mud-spattered girl. With busy, runny nose, she was belaboring her sausages, tearing them into shreds and mixing them into the potato gruel which she had made with water. I choked my food down.

We cheered loudly when trucks rolled by, distributing canvas army cots for the young and hardy, and steel cots for the older folks. Henry directed the arrangement of the cots. Father and Mother were to occupy the corner nearest the woodstove. In the other corner, Henry arranged two cots in an L shape and announced that this was the combination living room–bedroom area, to be occupied by Sumi and myself. He fixed a male den for himself in the corner nearest the door. If I had had my way, I would have arranged everyone's cots in one neat row, as in Father's hotel dormitory.

We felt fortunate to be assigned to a room at the end of the barracks, because we had just one neighbor to worry about. The partition wall separating the rooms was only seven feet high, with an opening of four feet at the top, so at night, Mrs. Funai next door could tell when Sumi was still sitting up in bed in the dark, putting her hair

---

7. **issei** (ē′sā′) *n.*: Japanese who immigrated to North America. Issei were forbidden by law to become U.S. citizens.

Vocabulary
breach (brēch) *n.*: opening. *Breach* usually refers to a breakthrough in a wall or in a line of defense.

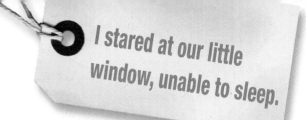

I stared at our little window, unable to sleep.

up. "Mah, Sumi-chan," Mrs. Funai would say through the plank wall, "are you curling your hair tonight, again? Do you put it up every night?" Sumi would put her hands on her hips and glare defiantly at the wall.

The block monitor, an impressive nisei[8] who looked like a star tackle, with his crouching walk, came around the first night to tell us that we must all be inside our room by nine o'clock every night. At ten o'clock, he rapped at the door again, yelling, "Lights out!" and Mother rushed to turn the light off not a second later.

Throughout the barracks, there was a medley[9] of creaking cots, whimpering infants, and explosive night coughs. Our attention was riveted on the intense little woodstove, which glowed so violently I feared it would melt right down to the floor. We soon learned that this condition lasted for only a short time, after which it suddenly turned into a deep freeze. Henry and Father took turns at the stove to produce the harrowing[10] blast which all but singed our army blankets but did not penetrate through them. As it grew quieter in the barracks, I could hear the light patter of rain. Soon I felt the *splat! splat!* of raindrops digging holes into my face. The dampness on my pillow spread like a mortal bleeding, and I finally had to get out and haul my cot toward the center of the room. In a short while, Henry was up. "I've got multiple leaks, too. Have to complain to the landlord first thing in the morning."

All through the night I heard people getting up, dragging cots around. I stared at our little window, unable to sleep. I was glad Mother had put up a makeshift curtain on the window, for I noticed a powerful beam of light sweeping across it every few seconds. The lights came from high towers placed around the camp, where guards with tommy guns kept a twenty-four-hour vigil. I remembered the wire fence encircling us, and a knot of anger tightened in my breast. What was I doing behind a fence, like a criminal? If there were accusations to be made, why hadn't I been given a fair trial? Maybe I wasn't considered an American anymore. My citizenship wasn't real, after all. Then what was I? I was certainly not a citizen of Japan, as my parents were. On second thought, even Father and Mother were more alien residents of the United States than Japanese nationals, for they had little tie with their mother country. In their twenty-five years in America, they had worked and paid their taxes to their adopted government as any other citizen.

Of one thing I was sure. The wire fence was real. I no longer had the right to walk out of it. It was because I had Japanese ancestors. It was also because some people had little faith in the ideas and ideals of democracy. They said that after all these were but words and could not possibly ensure loyalty. New laws and camps were surer devices. I finally buried my face in my pillow to wipe out burning thoughts and snatch what sleep I could.

---

8. nisei (nē′sā′) *n.*: native U.S. or Canadian citizen born of Japanese immigrant parents.
9. medley (med′lē) *n.*: jumble; mixture.
10. harrowing (har′ō·iŋ) *adj.*: extremely distressing.

Vocabulary

riveted (riv′it·id) *v.*: fastened or held firmly, as if by rivets (metal bolts or pins).
vigil (vij′əl) *n.*: watch; act of staying awake to keep watch.

Monica Sone

Monica Sone with her granddaughter.

"I Wanted to Tell Our Story"

Monica Sone (1919–   ) was born in Seattle, Washington. This is her explanation of how she came to write *Nisei Daughter:*

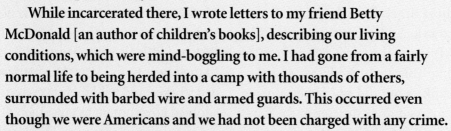 In the spring of 1942, shortly after Pearl Harbor [site of the U.S. naval base bombed by Japan], I was forced to leave my home in Seattle under U.S. Army orders. I was sent away to a prison camp built inside a state fairground in Puyallup, Washington. This camp, for some strange reason, was called Camp Harmony.

While incarcerated there, I wrote letters to my friend Betty McDonald [an author of children's books], describing our living conditions, which were mind-boggling to me. I had gone from a fairly normal life to being herded into a camp with thousands of others, surrounded with barbed wire and armed guards. This occurred even though we were Americans and we had not been charged with any crime.

Betty had apparently preserved all of my letters. One day she showed the packet of letters to an editor from Little, Brown and Co. He immediately became interested in my camp experiences, especially since at that time no details had come out of camp to be reported in the media. The editor reacted to my letters, sensing in them a human-interest story as well as a major historical event in our country.

The editor contacted me and inquired if I would be interested in expanding on my letters and writing a book. I was eager to do so. This was because after I eventually left camp and moved to the eastern part of the country, I discovered that the general public knew nothing about our evacuation and imprisonment of tens of thousands of Americans. I wanted to tell our story.

In Response to Executive Order 9066:

All Americans of Japanese Descent Must Report to Relocation Centers

Dwight Okita

Dear Sirs:
Of course I'll come. I've packed my galoshes
and three packets of tomato seeds. Denise calls them
"love apples." My father says where we're going
5   they won't grow.

I am a fourteen-year-old girl with bad spelling
and a messy room. If it helps any, I will tell you
I have always felt funny using chopsticks
and my favorite food is hot dogs.
10   My best friend is a white girl named Denise—
we look at boys together. She sat in front of me
all through grade school because of our names:
O'Connor, Ozawa. I know the back of Denise's head very well.
I tell her she's going bald. She tells me I copy on tests.
15   We're best friends.

I saw Denise today in Geography class.
She was sitting on the other side of the room.
"You're trying to start a war," she said, "giving secrets away
to the Enemy. Why can't you keep your big mouth shut?"
20   I didn't know what to say.
I gave her a packet of tomato seeds
and asked her to plant them for me, told her
when the first tomato ripened
she'd miss me.

Dwight Okita

Controversial Issues in a Charming Style

Dwight Okita (1958–   ) frequently looks to events from his own life as material for his poetry. His parents had to report to a Japanese American internment camp during World War II, a traumatic event that inspired "In Response to Executive Order 9066."

Okita does not shy away from controversial social and political issues, but he maintains a light, charming style that has made his writing popular with American readers. His poems also look at personal issues with a keen sense of humor. *Crossing with the Light*, the collection from which "In Response to Executive Order 9066" is taken, was published in 1992.

Department of Special Collections, Charles E. Yang Research Library, UCLA.

Progress After One Year, the Mess Hall Line (1943) by Kango Takamura. Watercolor.

Literary Response and Analysis

Reading Check

1. Write a one-paragraph **summary,** or short restatement, of the main events in "Camp Harmony."

2. Write a brief summary of the main events in "In Response to Executive Order 9066."

Interpretations

3. Sone says her camp "was hopefully called Camp Harmony" (see page 320). Do you think the name is appropriate? Support your opinion with evidence from the text.

4. Find several details that describe the conditions in Sone's camp. Using these details, make a **generalization** about the Japanese American internment camps.

5. What details in Okita's poem show that the narrator feels she is a real American? How is that girl betrayed by her friend?

6. The paintings on pages 321 and 326 were made by Japanese Americans living in internment camps during World War II. Choose one, and explain how it reminds you of, or seems different from, what you read in "Camp Harmony" or "In Response to Executive Order 9066." You may want to reread your Quickwrite before you respond.

7. Find two details in Sone's description of Camp Harmony that would be unlikely to appear in an encyclopedia entry about the internment camps. What information might the encyclopedia include that Sone's **autobiography** doesn't?

Evaluation

8. Sone says that she was imprisoned "because some people had little faith in the ideas and ideals of democracy" (page 323). What does she mean? Is she stating a **fact** or an **opinion**? Do you agree or disagree with her statement? Explain.

9. Here are two **themes:**

   • *Innocent people often bear the burden of blame for things they did not do.*

   • *In a struggle with the state, individuals are often helpless victims.*

   Choose one of those themes, and discuss how it is revealed in "Camp Harmony," in "In Response to Executive Order 9066," and in another story, movie, or TV show. How are the treatments of the theme similar, and how are they different?

Writing

Persuading FDR

Pretend you are Sone or the speaker of "In Response to Executive Order 9066." Write a letter to President Franklin D. Roosevelt to persuade him to cancel Executive Order 9066 and allow you and your family to go home. Use practical, moral, or legal arguments to make your case, supporting them with details from the text.

Reading Standard 3.5 Identify and analyze recurring themes (for example, good versus evil) across traditional and contemporary works.

Vocabulary Development

Verify Meanings: Restatement

PRACTICE

Change each of the following sentences so that you say the same thing using words that are different from the underlined words. You can restate just the underlined word or rewrite the whole sentence.

1. One little boy stared at the hogs and said <u>tersely</u>, "They're dirty."
2. Sumi answered <u>laconically</u>, "Dandelions."
3. Guards with tommy guns kept a twenty-four-hour <u>vigil</u> around the camp.
4. The narrator thrust herself into the tiny <u>breach</u> between two people sitting on the bench.
5. The family's attention was <u>riveted</u> on the stove.

Grammar Link
MINI-LESSON

Avoiding Double Negatives

A **double negative** occurs when two negative words express one negative idea. Avoid using double negatives in formal writing and speaking.

These are some commonly used negative words:

barely	never	none	nothing
hardly	no	no one	nowhere
neither	nobody	not *or* –n't	scarcely

NONSTANDARD	The room *did*n't *have* no furniture.
STANDARD	The room *had* no furniture. The room *did*n't *have* any furniture.
NONSTANDARD	It was so crowded they *could*n't hardly *sit* down.
STANDARD	It was so crowded they *could* hardly *sit* down.

PRACTICE

Proofread the following paragraph, correcting all double negatives.

   Monica and her family couldn't hardly believe dandelions were growing up through their floor. Nobody didn't like it when the rain came through the roof. Scarcely no one in the family slept the first night. They didn't have no privacy.
For more help, see The Double Negative in the *Holt Handbook*, page 249.

The Gettysburg Address

Literary Focus
Refrain

Like poets, good speakers appeal to our sense of hearing. One way they do this is by using refrains, which create echoes in listeners' ears. A **refrain** is a repeated sound, word, phrase, line, or group of lines. Refrains are used to build rhythm and emphasize important themes or messages. As you read the Gettysburg Address, look for the words and phrases that Lincoln chose to repeat.

Reading Skills
Dialogue with the Text: Slow Down to Understand

Read the Gettysburg Address at least twice. Read slowly and carefully, just as you'd read any difficult text. Record, in one column, any comments and questions suggested by your first reading. Then, in a second column, write down answers to your questions and additional thoughts as you read the speech a second time.

Make the Connection
A Class Quilt

Think about what America means to you. On an unlined sheet of paper, draw a symbol that represents your thoughts and feelings. Tape or staple your paper to your classmates' papers to create a class quilt, and explain the meaning of your symbol.

Background

The Battle of Gettysburg, which took place in Pennsylvania in 1863, was a turning point of the Civil War. In that bloody three-day battle, Union forces prevented Confederate forces from moving north, thus confining the war mainly to the South. The battle left at least 51,000 soldiers dead, wounded, or missing.

On November 19, 1863, part of the battlefield was dedicated as a military cemetery. President Abraham Lincoln was asked to make some remarks at the dedication. Although very brief, Lincoln's Gettysburg Address is considered one of the greatest speeches by a U.S. political leader. It is notable especially for its vision of American democracy.

First draft of the Gettysburg Address, in Lincoln's handwriting.
The Granger Collection, New York.

Executive Mansion,

Washington, _____, 186

Four score and seven years ago our fathers brought forth, upon this continent, a new nation, conceived in liberty, and dedicated to the proposition that "all men are created equal"

Now we are engaged in a great civil war, testing whether that nation, or any nation so conceived, I long endure, We are met

Grade 6 Review Reading Standard 3.7 Explain the effects of common literary devices in nonfictional texts.

The Gettysburg Address   329

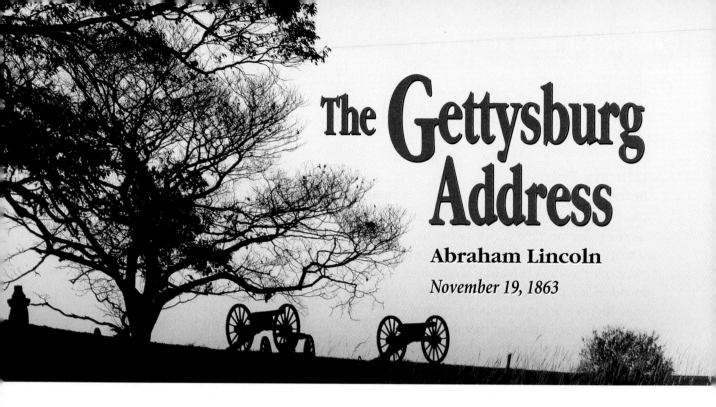

The Gettysburg Address

Abraham Lincoln
November 19, 1863

Four score and seven years ago our fathers brought forth on this continent a new nation, conceived in liberty, and dedicated to the proposition that all men are created equal.

Now we are engaged in a great civil war, testing whether that nation, or any nation so conceived and so dedicated, can long endure. We are met on a great battlefield of that war. We have come to dedicate a portion of that field, as a final resting place for those who here gave their lives that that nation might live. It is altogether fitting and proper that we should do this.

But, in a larger sense, we cannot dedicate—we cannot consecrate—we cannot hallow°—this ground. The brave men, living and dead, who struggled here, have consecrated it, far above our poor power to add or detract. The world will little note nor long remember what we say here, but it can never forget what they did here. It is for us the living, rather, to be dedicated here to the unfinished work which they who fought here have thus far so nobly advanced. It is rather for us to be here dedicated to the great task remaining before us—that from these honored dead we take increased devotion to that cause for which they gave the last full measure of devotion—that we here highly resolve that these dead shall not have died in vain—that this nation, under God, shall have a new birth of freedom—and that government of the people, by the people, for the people, shall not perish from the earth.

The Battle of Gettysburg (detail) (1870) by Peter Frederick Rothermel. Oil on canvas.

Pennsylvania Historical and Museum Commission, Harrisburg.

° *Consecrate* and *hallow* are synonyms meaning "make or declare holy." Lincoln is using repetition to create rhythm and emphasize his point.

Abraham Lincoln

Plain Speaking

Abraham Lincoln (1809–1865) was born in rural Kentucky. He spent his childhood there and in Indiana. At the age of twenty-one, he moved with his family to Illinois, where he taught himself law.

Lincoln soon became involved in politics, first at the state level and then at the national level. He was elected president in 1860, during a period of crisis that quickly erupted into war between the Northern and Southern states. In 1863, during the Civil War, he issued the Emancipation Proclamation. This proclamation led to the adoption of the Thirteenth Amendment to the Constitution, outlawing slavery.

Although Lincoln led the Union to victory, he did not live to see his country reunited. As he sat in a Washington theater, watching a play, Lincoln was shot by an assassin, John Wilkes Booth.

Lincoln believed in speaking and writing as clearly and simply as he could, so that people could understand exactly what he meant. He once explained:

> Among my earliest recollections I remember how, when a mere child, I used to get irritated when anybody talked to me in a way I could not understand. . . . I can remember going to my little bedroom, after hearing the neighbors talk of an evening with my father, and spending the night walking up and down and trying to make out what was the exact meaning of some of their, to me, dark sayings. I could not sleep when I got on such a hunt after an idea, until I had caught it; and when I thought I had got it, I was not satisfied until I had put it in language plain enough, as I thought, for any boy I knew to comprehend. This was a kind of passion with me, and it has stuck by me.

from I Have a Dream

Literary Focus
Allusion

An **allusion** is a reference to features of a culture that people share—literature, religion, history, mythology, sports. "I Have a Dream," a speech by Martin Luther King, Jr., draws much of its power from allusions to texts familiar to many Americans, such as this famous passage from the Bible, from Isaiah 40:4–5:

❝ Every valley shall be exalted, and every mountain and hill shall be made low: And the crooked shall be made straight, and the rough places plain. ❞

As you read "I Have a Dream," see what other allusions you recognize.

Make the Connection
Quickwrite ✏️

Pick one of the words from the list below, and create a **cluster map,** in which you write what you think of when you hear that word. Draw as many circles on your map as you like.

- freedom
- equality
- democracy
- liberty

Grade 6 Review Reading Standard 3.7 Explain the effects of common literary devices in nonfictional texts.

fair teachers

Supreme Court

justice

right to trial by jury

Background

On August 28, 1963, more than 200,000 Americans of all races and from almost every state in the Union took part in a march in Washington, D.C. The marchers called on Congress to pass a civil rights bill, and they demanded full equality for African Americans.

Late in the day, Martin Luther King, Jr., rose to speak. His words, which were heard by people across the country on TV and radio, deeply moved his listeners. King's concluding words are reprinted here as "I Have a Dream."

Vocabulary Development

Martin Luther King, Jr., uses these words in his "I Have a Dream" speech:

creed (krēd) *n.:* statement of belief or principles. *The Declaration of Independence is our nation's creed.*

oasis (ō·ā′sis) *n.:* place or thing offering relief. *King hopes to transform the United States into an oasis of freedom and justice.*

exalted (eg·zôlt′id) *v.:* lifted up. *King's stirring speech exalted his audience.*

discords (dis′kôrdz′) *n.:* conflicts. *King urges us to turn discords into harmony.*

prodigious (prō·dij′əs) *adj.:* huge; amazing. *King's dream involves a prodigious task: bringing justice to all people.*

from
I Have a Dream

Martin Luther King, Jr.
August 28, 1963

Marchers gather in front of the Lincoln Memorial in Washington, D.C., with the Washington Monument in the distance.

I say to you today, my friends, that in spite of the difficulties and frustrations of the moment I still have a dream. It is a dream deeply rooted in the American Dream.

I have a dream that one day this nation will rise up and live out the true meaning of its creed: "We hold these truths to be self-evident; that all men are created equal."

I have a dream that one day on the red hills of Georgia the sons of former slaves and the sons of former slave owners will be able to sit down together at the table of brotherhood.

I have a dream that one day even the state of Mississippi, a desert state sweltering with the heat of injustice and oppression, will be transformed into an oasis of freedom and justice.

I have a dream that my four little children will one day live in a nation where they will not be judged by the color of their skin but by the content of their character.

I have a dream today.

I have a dream that one day every valley shall be exalted, every hill and mountain shall be made low, the rough places will be made plain, and the crooked places will be made straight, and the glory of the Lord shall be revealed, and all flesh shall see it together.

This is our hope. This is the faith with which I return to the South. With this faith

Vocabulary

creed (krēd) *n.:* statement of belief or principles.
oasis (ō·ā'sis) *n.:* place in a desert with plants and a supply of water; place or thing offering relief.
exalted (eg·zôlt'id) *v.:* raised; lifted up.

Martin Luther King, Jr., delivers his "I Have a Dream" speech.

we will be able to hew out of the mountain of despair a stone of hope. With this faith we will be able to transform the jangling discords of our nation into a beautiful symphony of brotherhood. With this faith we will be able to work together, to pray together, to struggle together, to go to jail together, to stand up for freedom together, knowing that we will be free one day.

This will be the day when all of God's children will be able to sing with new meaning "My country 'tis of thee, sweet land of liberty, of thee I sing. Land where my fathers died, land of the pilgrim's pride, from every mountainside, let freedom ring."

And if America is to be a great nation, this must become true. So let freedom ring from the prodigious hilltops of New Hampshire. Let freedom ring from the mighty mountains of New York. Let freedom ring from the heightening Alleghenies of Pennsylvania!

Let freedom ring from the snowcapped Rockies of Colorado!

Let freedom ring from the curvaceous peaks of California!

But not only that; let freedom ring from Stone Mountain of Georgia!

Let freedom ring from Lookout Mountain of Tennessee!

Let freedom ring from every hill and molehill of Mississippi. From every mountainside, let freedom ring.

When we let freedom ring, when we let it ring from every village and every hamlet, from every state and every city, we will be able to speed up that day when all of God's children, black men and white men, Jews and Gentiles, Protestants and Catholics, will be able to join hands and sing in the words of the old Negro spiritual, "Free at last! Free at last! Thank God almighty, we are free at last!"

Vocabulary
discords (dis'kôrdz') *n.:* conflicts; disagreements.
prodigious (prō·dij'əs) *adj.:* huge; amazing.

Martin Luther King, Jr.

Martin Luther King, Jr., with picture of Gandhi.

"Nonviolence Is the Answer"

Martin Luther King, Jr. (1929–1968), grew up in Atlanta, Georgia. He started college at the age of fifteen. After he graduated, he went on to Crozer Theological Seminary in Pennsylvania to become a Baptist minister, like his father and grandfather. King continued his studies in Boston, where he received a doctorate degree. He then returned to the South to take a position as pastor of a church in Montgomery, Alabama. King was shocked by the intense racism and the strict segregation he saw in Montgomery. He helped organize the Montgomery bus boycott and went on to become a national leader in the civil rights movement, facing violence and risking arrest to spread his message of nonviolent resistance. In 1964, four years before he was assassinated, he accepted the Nobel Peace Prize with these words:

> Nonviolence is the answer to the crucial political and moral questions of our time; the need for man to overcome oppression and violence without resorting to oppression and violence.

King with Stokely Carmichael at a protest, 1966.

King with Ralph Abernathy, 1963.

Literary Response and Analysis

Reading Check

1. What happened in the past—eighty-seven years before Lincoln's speech?

2. What is happening in the present (in 1863)? How is that related to the past, according to Lincoln?

3. What hopes does Lincoln express for the future?

4. List three important things Martin Luther King, Jr., hopes to see come about in his dream.

Interpretations

5. What two American ideals seem most important to Abraham Lincoln? Do you agree with him?

6. What challenge does Lincoln propose for the future? Why is honoring the dead connected to that challenge?

7. Find two examples of **refrains** in Lincoln's speech. What idea is he trying to emphasize in each case?

8. In his speech, King makes **allusions,** or references, to the Declaration of Independence and to the patriotic hymn "My Country, 'Tis of Thee." Why would King want to remind his audience of those texts?

9. Find several examples of **refrain** (repeated words or sentences) in King's speech. What important ideas are being emphasized?

10. Describe in a sentence or two what you think the **theme,** or message, of the Gettysburg Address is. How is it similar to King's theme, or message? How is it different?

11. Choose either Lincoln's or King's speech, and describe how it makes you feel about being an American.

Evaluation

12. In Meet the Writer on page 331, Lincoln describes his efforts to express ideas in plain language. Do you think the Gettysburg Address is easy to understand? Support your opinion with examples from the text. Which passages, if any, gave you trouble? (Refer to the notes you made as you were reading.)

Writing

Fallen Heroes

Both Abraham Lincoln and Martin Luther King, Jr., were assassinated. Using the Internet or a library, research the life history of one of them or of another political leader who was assassinated, such as John F. Kennedy, Robert Kennedy, Malcolm X, or Mohandas Gandhi. Write a **poem,** a **letter,** or a **eulogy** (a speech praising a person who has died) from the point of view of one of that person's followers.

Speaking and Listening

Let It Ring!

Prepare and present a **dramatic reading** of either the Gettysburg Address or "I Have a Dream." Your delivery should be slow and clear. Pay special attention to **refrains.**

Vocabulary Development

Word Analogies

A **word analogy** is a puzzle that consists of two pairs of words that have the same relationship. (For a review of the types of analogies, see page 176.)

see page 176.

Word Bank

creed
oasis
exalted
discords
prodigious

PRACTICE 1

Complete each sentence below with the word from the Word Bank that fits best. Use each word only once.

1. *Suffering* is to *relief* as *desert* is to _____.
2. _____ is to *tiny* as *bright* is to *dim*.
3. *Arguments* is to _____ as *agreements* is to *harmonies*.
4. *Dream* is to *vision* as _____ is to *belief*.
5. *Raised* is to *sunken* as _____ is to *lowered*.

Words in Context

PRACTICE 2

Practice using word meanings within the appropriate context by filling in the blanks in the following paragraphs with the best word from the Word Bank. (Hint: You'll have to use each word twice.) You may recognize two characters from a famous novel, which has been made into many movies for screen and TV.

Ebenezer Scrooge took it as his _____ that money should be made and saved, not spent. For him the most _____ task of humankind was making money. His _____ talent for getting rich was legendary, as were his many _____ with anyone who tried to get money from him. He sought no _____ in which to rest from struggle and strife.

Bob Cratchit's _____ was to do the best he could in life, at work and at home. He put in a(n) _____ effort at his job, which was never appreciated by his stingy boss. He got through the trials and _____ of his workday by remembering his home, his _____. Cratchit's spirits were soothed and _____ each evening when he walked through his door and was greeted by his loving family.

What is the book (or movie)?

Reading Standard 1.3
Use word meanings within the appropriate context, and show ability to verify those meanings by comparison or contrast.

from The Power of Nonviolence

Taking Notes and Outlining

Good informational material is fascinating when you read it, but when you try to share your interest with a friend, you often cannot remember the details. You might even have forgotten the writer's main idea. Here are two good ways to keep track of important ideas and interesting details: (1) take notes, and (2) make an outline.

Notecards. Gather a stack of three-by-five-inch index cards. (You can substitute slips of paper of a similar size.)

Main ideas. As you read each paragraph, stop and ask yourself, "What is the main idea?" Some paragraphs may offer a new idea, while others will offer supporting evidence for an idea presented in a previous paragraph. Write each main idea at the top of a note card.

Details. On each card containing a main idea, write all the important supporting details. Try to use your own words. If you do use the writer's words, put quotation marks around them.

Outline. Once your cards are filled, you can organize your notes in an outline. Here is how an **informal outline** is set up:

Informal Outline
I. First main idea
    A. Supporting detail
    B. Supporting detail
    C. Supporting detail
II. Second main idea
[Etc.]

A formal outline is useful when you are preparing notes for a composition of your own, especially a research paper. Here is how a **formal outline** is set up:

Formal Outline
I. First main idea
    A. Supporting point
        1. Detail
        2. Detail
    B. Supporting point
II. Second main idea
    A. Supporting point
        1. Detail
        2. Detail
    B. Supporting point
[Etc.]

A formal outline must always have at least two items at each level. That is, if there is a I, there must be at least a II, if not a III; if there is an A, there must be at least a B, and so on.

Here's the start of an informal outline of the interview with the civil rights activist John Lewis that you are about to read. It's up to you to outline the rest.

I. Childhood experience of segregation
    A. Encountered separate water fountains
    B. Encountered separate seating in movie theaters
    C. Found experience differed from religious teaching

Grade 6 Review Reading Standard 2.4
Clarify an understanding of texts by creating outlines and logical notes.

from **The Power of Nonviolence**

John Lewis, *interviewed by Joan Morrison and Robert K. Morrison*

When I was a boy, I would go downtown to the little town of Troy, and I'd see the signs saying "White" and "Colored" on the water fountains. There'd be a beautiful, shining water fountain in one corner of the store marked "White," and in another corner was just a little spigot marked "Colored." I saw the signs saying "White Men," "Colored Men," and "White Women," "Colored Women." And at the theater we had to go upstairs to go to a movie. You bought your ticket at the same window that the white people did, but they could sit downstairs, and you had to go upstairs.

Lunch-counter segregation protest.

I wondered about that, because it was not in keeping with my religious faith, which taught me that we were all the same in the eyes of God. And I had been taught that all men are created equal.

It really hit me when I was fifteen years old, when I heard about Martin Luther King, Jr., and the Montgomery bus boycott. Black people were walking the streets for more than a year rather than riding segregated buses. To me it was like a great sense of hope, a light. Many of the teachers at the high school that I attended were from Montgomery, and they would tell us about what was happening there. That, more than any other event, was the turning point for me, I think. It gave me a way out. . . .

Lewis went on to college, where he attended workshops and studied the philosophy of non-violence.

In February 1960, we planned the first mass lunch-counter sit-in. About five hundred students, black and white, from various colleges showed up and participated in a nonviolent workshop the night before the sit-in. Some of them came from as far away as Pomona College in California and Beloit College in Wisconsin.

We made a list of what we called the "Rules of the Sit-in"—the do's and don'ts—and we mimeographed it on an old machine and passed it out to all the students. I wish I had a copy of this list today. I remember it said things like, "Sit up straight. Don't talk back. Don't laugh. Don't strike back." And at the end it said, "Remember the teachings of Jesus, Gandhi, Thoreau, and Martin Luther King, Jr."

Lunch-counter sit-in.

Then the next day it began. We wanted to make a good impression. The young men put on their coats and ties, and the young ladies their heels and stockings. We selected seven stores to go into, primarily the chain stores — Woolworth's, Kresge's, and the Walgreen drugstore—and

Empty bus during the Montgomery bus boycott.

we had these well-dressed young people with their books going to the lunch counters. They would sit down in a very orderly, peaceful, nonviolent fashion and wait to be served. They would be reading a book or doing their homework or whatever while they were waiting.

I was a spokesperson for one of these groups. I would ask to be served, and we would be told that we wouldn't be served. The lunch counter would be closed, and they would put up a sign saying "Closed—not serving." Sometimes they would lock the door, leave us in there, and turn out all the lights, and we would continue to sit.

After we had been doing this for a month, it was beginning to bother the business community and other people in Nashville. We heard that the city had decided to allow the police officials to stand by and allow the hoodlum element to come in and attack us—and that the police would arrest us—to try to stop the sit-ins. We had a meeting after we heard that, to decide did we still want to go down on this particular day. And we said yes.

I was with the group that went into the Woolworth's there. The lunch counter was upstairs—just a long row of stools in front of a counter. My group went up to sit there, and after we had been there for half an hour or so, a group of young white men came in and began pulling people off the lunch-counter stools, putting lighted cigarettes out in our hair or faces or down our backs, pouring ketchup and hot sauce all over us, pushing us down to the floor and beating us. Then the police came in and started arresting *us.* They didn't arrest a single person that beat us, but they arrested all of us and charged us with disorderly conduct.

That was the first mass arrest of students in the South for participating in a sit-in. Over one hundred of us were arrested that day. We were sentenced, all of us, to a fifty-dollar fine or thirty days in jail, and since we wouldn't pay the fine, we were put in jail. . . .

Lewis and his fellow students were jailed, but they continued their protests when they were released. In April 1960, the mayor of Nashville agreed that the lunch counters should be desegregated.

And so Nashville became the first major city in the South to desegregate its downtown lunch counters and restaurants. That was the power of nonviolence. . . .

I think one thing the movement did for all of us in the South, black and white alike, was to have a cleansing effect on our psyche. I think it brought up a great deal of the dirt and a great deal of the guilt from under the rug to the top, so that we could deal with it, so that we could see it in the light. And I think that in a real sense, we are a different people. We are better people. It freed even those of us who didn't participate—black people, white people alike—to be a little more human.

Civil rights activists march in Selma, Alabama.

Reading Informational Materials

Reading Check

1. What were the "Rules of the Sit-in"?

2. What did the students participating in the sit-ins do to make a good impression?

3. How did the lunch-counter workers respond to the sit-ins?

4. How did the city officials respond to the sit-ins?

5. What was the result of the sit-ins?

6. According to John Lewis, how did the nonviolent movement affect black people and white people?

TestPractice

from **The Power of Nonviolence**

1. Suppose an **outline** of this article listed these main ideas:

> **I.** Experiences of segregation
> **II.**
> **III.** Lunch-counter sit-ins
> **IV.** Effect of the movement

Which **main idea** should be II?
   A Segregated water fountains
   B Montgomery bus boycott
   C Rules of the sit-in
   D Woolworth's lunch counter

2. Suppose an **outline** of this article has a main heading that reads "Hoodlums Attack Demonstrators." Which of these details does *not* support that main idea?
   F Pulled demonstrators off stools
   G Poured hot sauce on demonstrators
   H Beat up demonstrators
   J Fined demonstrators fifty dollars

3. John Lewis said that the police "didn't arrest a single person that beat us, but they arrested all of us and charged us with disorderly conduct." This shows that the police were —
   A trying to keep law and order
   B prejudiced against the protesters
   C just doing their job
   D fair to everyone involved

4. Which of the following is the *best* statement of John Lewis's **main idea** in this article?
   F Nonviolence makes us all better people.
   G All men are created equal.
   H Police arrest protesters unfairly.
   J Injustice can be overcome with nonviolence.

Grade 6 Review Reading Standard 2.4 Clarify an understanding of texts by creating outlines and logical notes.

Literary Response and Analysis

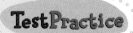
DIRECTIONS: Read the two stories. Then, read each question, and write the letter of the best response.

The Dog and the Wolf
Aesop (sixth century B.C.)

One cold and snowy winter the Wolf couldn't find enough to eat. She was almost dead with hunger when a House Dog happened by.

"Ah, Cousin," said the Dog, "you are skin and bones. Come, leave your life of roaming and starving in the forest. Come with me to my master and you'll never go hungry again."

"What will I have to do for my food?" said the Wolf.

"Not much," said the House Dog. "Guard the property, keep the Fox from the henhouse, protect the children. It's an easy life."

That sounded good to the Wolf, so the Dog and the Wolf headed to the village. On the way the Wolf noticed a ring around the Dog's neck where the hair had been rubbed off.

"What's that?" she asked.

"Oh, it's nothing," said the Dog. "It's just where the collar is put on at night to keep me chained up. I'm used to it."

"Chained up!" exclaimed the Wolf, as she ran quickly back to the forest.

Better to starve free than to be a well-fed slave.

The Puppy
Aleksandr Solzhenitsyn (twentieth century)

In our backyard a boy keeps his little dog Sharik chained up, a ball of fluff shackled since he was a puppy.

One day I took him some chicken bones that were still warm and smelled delicious. The boy had just let the poor dog off his lead to have a run round the yard. The snow there was deep and feathery; Sharik was bounding about like a hare, first on his hind legs, then on his front ones, from one corner of the yard to the other, back and forth, burying his muzzle in the snow.

He ran toward me, his coat all shaggy, jumped up at me, sniffed the bones—then off he went again, belly-deep in the snow.

I don't need your bones, he said. Just give me my freedom. . . .

—*translated by* Michael Glenny

Reading Standard 3.5 Identify and analyze recurring themes (for example, good versus evil) across traditional and contemporary works.

1. In the fable "The Dog and the Wolf," the Wolf decides to go to the village with the House Dog because she —

   A   is hungry

   B   wants an easier life

   C   wants to be chained up

   D   likes children

2. What does the Wolf notice on the way to the village?

   F   Children playing happily

   G   Well-fed people

   H   A ring on the Dog's neck

   J   The Dog limping

3. In "The Puppy," where is the little dog, Sharik, usually kept?

   A   Chained in the yard

   B   In a doghouse

   C   In the living room

   D   In the boy's bedroom

4. What do the House Dog and Sharik have in common?

   F   They both are chained at times.

   G   They both run away from home.

   H   They both are starving.

   J   They both hate their masters.

5. What do both the Wolf and Sharik want more than food?

   A   Love

   B   Freedom

   C   Security

   D   Fame

6. Which of the following sentences *best* expresses the **theme** that both the fable from ancient Greece and the story from modern-day Russia have in common?

   F   Nothing is worth more than freedom.

   G   Playing is more fun than eating.

   H   It is worth being chained up in order to be fed.

   J   One can never have both food and freedom.

7. In the first paragraph of "The Puppy," the writer uses the word shackled. Using context clues, you can guess that *shackled* means —

   A   punished

   B   chained up

   C   fed

   D   fenced in

Vocabulary Development

TestPractice

Multiple-Meaning Words

DIRECTIONS: Choose the answer in which the underlined word is used in the same way it is used in the quoted sentence. Items 1–3 are from *The Diary of Anne Frank*. Items 4–6 are from "Camp Harmony."

1. "The rooms are sparsely furnished, with a few chairs, cots, a <u>table</u> or two."
   - **A** The <u>table</u> of contents shows no listing for "Holocaust."
   - **B** The vote was to <u>table</u> the measure until the next meeting.
   - **C** The family gathered at the <u>table</u> as a platter of latkes was brought in.
   - **D** Because of the drought, the area's water <u>table</u> has dropped.

2. "Tomorrow I'll get you a better <u>bolt</u> for the door at the foot of the stairs."
   - **F** Please cut me three yards from this <u>bolt</u> of cloth.
   - **G** Hang on, or that horse will <u>bolt</u>.
   - **H** He installed a new double-<u>bolt</u> lock.
   - **J** That last lightning <u>bolt</u> struck the birdbath.

3. "I tell you, this is going to be a <u>fine</u> life for you!"
   - **A** What we need is a <u>fine</u> grade of sandpaper.
   - **B** The <u>fine</u> for littering has gone up.
   - **C** He's taking a course in <u>fine</u> wines.
   - **D** We all had a <u>fine</u> time.

4. "When our bus turned a corner and we no longer had to smile and <u>wave</u>, we settled back gravely in our seats."
   - **F** There was a <u>wave</u> of prejudice, and we could not escape it.
   - **G** Sometimes you just have to wait and see what comes in on the next <u>wave</u>.
   - **H** A <u>wave</u> of disapproval followed on our heels.
   - **J** <u>Wave</u> goodbye.

5. "Then suddenly a baby's <u>sharp</u> cry rose indignantly above the hubbub."
   - **A** Being deprived of one's rights is a very <u>sharp</u> blow.
   - **B** We tried to look <u>sharp</u> boarding the bus, but none of us felt that way.
   - **C** Barbed-wire fencing has <u>sharp</u> points.
   - **D** His voice gets <u>sharp</u> when he talks about those times.

6. "I awoke with a <u>start</u> when the bus filled with excited buzzing."
   - **F** The bombing of Pearl Harbor was more of an ending than a <u>start</u> for many of us.
   - **G** During the internment we had to <u>start</u> doing without many things.
   - **H** Sometimes I realized with a <u>start</u> that I was no longer free.
   - **J** When we came out of camp we literally had to <u>start</u> all over again.

RESEARCH REPORT

The Big Question

World War II got its name for a good reason: The war was fought all around the globe, and it affected almost everyone everywhere. Such an important event in world history offers endless possibilities for research. What questions would you like answered about this time period? Perhaps you want to know how the Nazis came to power, or why the Allied Forces were unable to reach Anne Frank in time to save her. You may wonder why the U.S. military didn't prevent the Japanese from bombing Pearl Harbor, or what has since happened to the inhabitants of the Pacific islands that the United States and Japan fought so hard to capture. Once you have decided on a question to research, look for sources of information in a library or on the Internet. Using at least three sources, write a research report on what you have learned.

 Use "Writing a Research Report," pages 668–695, for help with this assignment.

Other Choices

RESEARCH REPORT

1 **Protest Songs**

Songs often provide inspiration and support for protest movements. "We Shall Overcome" was the unofficial anthem of the civil rights movement. Buffy Sainte-Marie's "Now That the Buffalo's Gone" brought attention to Native American grievances. "Where Have All the Flowers Gone?" was sung at protests against the Vietnam War. The feminist movement of the 1970s had "Liberation, Now!" for a theme song. Pick one of those songs or another protest song of your choice. Research, and write a brief report on, the role of the song in the history of that protest movement.

 Use "Writing a Research Report," pages 668–695, for help with this assignment.

RESEARCH REPORT

2 **Getting Personal**

Monica Sone tells us in "Camp Harmony" what being sent to an internment camp was like for her and her family. Perhaps you would like to know what it was like for other people as well. Did other Japanese Americans have the same or different experiences? What were conditions like in their camps? How did they feel about their time imprisoned behind barbed-wire fencing? Look for other memoirs or reports about Japanese Americans' experiences during World War II. Write a report comparing three people's experiences. For one of your sources, you might want to read about what else happened to Monica Sone and her family. You can find the rest of her story in *Nisei Daughter*.

Use "Writing a Research Report," pages 668–695, for help with this assignment.

Fiction

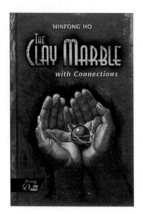

Never Tear Us Apart

Twelve-year-old Dara and her family flee war-torn Cambodia and find a haven at the refugee camp of Nong Chan. In *The Clay Marble* by Minfong Ho, Dara finds a new friend, Jantu, and for a short while their lives are peaceful. When the war brings chaos to the camp, however, Dara is separated from her family and Jantu. Now she must find the courage to reunite the people she loves.

This title is available in the HRW Library.

Another Dream

One of the messages in Martin Luther King's famous speech is that freedom does not come easily for everyone; some people must face injustice and treachery before they can be free. You'll find a character determined to find freedom no matter how dire the situation in Gloria Whalen's *Goodbye, Vietnam*. Thirteen-year-old Mai and her family are forced to leave Vietnam for Hong Kong. Although faced with unspeakable horrors on their voyage, they are determined to persevere so that they can reach their ultimate goal: a new life in America.

This title is available in the HRW Library.

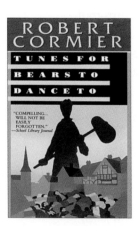

Aftermath

The Holocaust continues to affect people after all these years. In Robert Cormier's novel *Tunes for Bears to Dance To*, Henry is lonely until he meets Mr. Levine, a Holocaust survivor who continually works on a miniature re-creation of his old village. The two take comfort in one another. Then Mr. Hairston, Henry's racist employer, promises Henry a better life for his family if he ends the friendship.

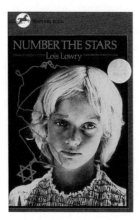

Perilous Mission

How far would you go to save a friend's life? In the 1990 Newbery Medal book by Lois Lowry, *Number the Stars*, Annemarie Johansen and Ellen Rosen, best friends living in peaceful Copenhagen, Denmark, don't concern themselves with questions like this—until the Nazis come for Ellen.

Nonfiction

Regrettable Action

After the bombing of Pearl Harbor, Japanese Americans were forced to abandon their homes and businesses and live in internment camps. Families were crowded into tiny, one-room apartments in long barracks behind fences guarded twenty-four hours a day by armed soldiers. Japanese Americans were essentially stripped of their human and civil rights. In *Behind Barbed Wire*, Daniel S. Davis describes the many difficulties they faced during World War II and the courage they showed in making a new start when they were finally released from the camps.

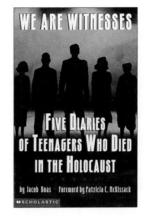

Persecuted

Jacob Boas looks at excerpts from the diaries of five teenagers who lived during World War II. Although they lived in different countries, each received a death sentence under Hitler's reign of terror. *We Are Witnesses: Five Diaries of Teenagers Who Died in the Holocaust* shows how the teenagers dealt with the worst kind of pain and oppression.

Real-Life Heroes

Under Nazi rule, even to be seen talking to a Jew was dangerous—yet all over Europe, non-Jews risked their lives to save neighbors and friends from the death camps. In *Rescue: The Story of How Gentiles Saved Jews in the Holocaust*, Milton Meltzer tells of their heroism.

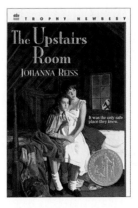

Undercover

In the Netherlands during World War II, Anne and Margot Frank went into hiding with their parents. At the same time, another pair of sisters escaped to the country to live through the war with a Dutch family in their farmhouse. *The Upstairs Room* and its sequel, *The Journey Back*, tell the true story of Johanna Reiss and her sister Sini.

5 | Imagine That!
Literary Devices

California Standards

Here are the Grade 8 standards you will study for mastery in Chapter 5. You will also review a standard from an earlier grade.

Reading

Word Analysis, Fluency, and Systematic Vocabulary Development

1.1 Analyze idioms, analogies, metaphors, and similes to infer the literal and figurative meanings of phrases.

Reading Comprehension (Focus on Informational Materials)

Grade 6 Review

2.8 Note instances of unsupported inferences and fallacious reasoning in text.

Literary Response and Analysis

3.6 Identify significant literary devices (for example, metaphor, symbolism, dialect, irony) that define a writer's style, and use those elements to interpret the work.

go.
hrw.
.com

KEYWORD:
HLLA 8-5

Elements of Style *by* Mara Rockliff

LITERARY DEVICES

Poem 1

from **Green Eggs and Ham**

I would not like them
here or there.
I would not like them
anywhere.
I do not like
green eggs and ham.
I do not like them,
Sam-I-am. . . .

Poem 2

who are you,little i

who are you,little i

(five or six years old)
peering from some high

window;at the gold

of november sunset

(and feeling:that if day
has to become night

this is a beautiful way)

If somebody gave you these two poems and told you one was written by E. E. Cummings and one by Dr. Seuss, would you be able to tell which was which? If you've ever read anything by either writer, you almost certainly would know the first is by Dr. Seuss and the second is by E. E. Cummings. But *how* would you know?

The answer is **style**—the way a writer uses language. The regular rhythm and the rhyme pattern we expect in a Dr. Seuss book, along with his silly-sounding invented words, make up his unique style. E. E. Cummings's use of lowercase letters, words that bump into each other, and unusual punctuation make up another style.

Every writer has a style, though some styles are more distinctive than others. Generations of beginning writers have tried to copy the unmistakable "plain style" of Ernest Hemingway. In fact, every year there's an Imitation Hemingway Contest, in which writers try to create the best "really good page of really bad Hemingway."

Unexpected Connections

Most writers don't self-consciously try to come up with a style. But style comes naturally from the choices writers make when they put words on a page. A long word or a short one? A simple sentence or one that's long and complex? A sarcastic and biting tone or one that is passionately sincere?

An important part of many writers' style is their use of **figures of speech,** expressions that are not literally true but that suggest similarities between usually unrelated things. Some figures of speech are so common that we use them without even noticing they're not literally true.

- He was tied up in traffic.
- That check you wrote bounced!
- I sat at the foot of the bed.

The bed doesn't actually have a foot; we're comparing it to a body, which has feet at the bottom. The check didn't really bounce like a rubber ball, and the man tied up in traffic wasn't tied with ropes—though he may have felt as if he were.

Here are some of the types of figurative language you're likely to come across:

Similes compare two unlike things using a word of comparison such as *like, than, as,* or *resembles.*

- Her hands were like ice.
- I feel lower than a snake in a ditch.

Metaphors compare two unlike things directly, without using a specific word of comparison.

- His heart is made of stone.
- Lewis is a rotten skunk!

In an **extended metaphor** the comparison is extended as far as the writer wants to take it.

> Fame is a bee.
> It has song—
> It has a sting—
> Ah, too, it has a wing.
> —Emily Dickinson

Personification speaks of a nonhuman or inanimate thing as if it had human or lifelike qualities.

- A falling leaf danced on the breeze.
- The train eats up the miles.
- The sun smiled on our cookout.

Symbols, in literature, are people, places, or events that have meaning in themselves but that also stand for something beyond themselves. Moby-Dick is a white whale hunted by Captain Ahab in the novel *Moby-Dick,* but he is also a symbol of evil. In everyday life we have many symbols. They are called public symbols because everyone knows what they mean: A dove with an olive branch symbolizes peace; a skull and crossbones symbolizes poison; a bearded man called Uncle Sam symbolizes the U.S. government.

(*continued on next page*)

Writers try to create fresh figures of speech to help us to see everyday things in a new way. "Her hands were as cold as ice" is a cliché—everyone's heard it before. But what about "Her handshake would make a snowman put on gloves"? or "Her hands were colder than a lizard in an ice chest"?

Unexpected Events

Another way writers create a fresh and exciting style is by playing with our expectations. When reality contradicts what we expect, it's called **irony.**

Verbal irony occurs when we say one thing and mean something else. "That's just great," your friend says in a disgusted tone, and you know she means it's *not* great at all.

Situational irony is a situation that turns out to be just the opposite of what we'd expect. The son of the police chief is arrested for burglary. The firehouse burns to the ground. The prize encyclopedia goes to the kid who never studied for the exam.

Dramatic irony occurs when we know something that a character in a book (or a movie or play) doesn't know. "Don't go down that dark hallway!" we want to scream, but the heroine goes anyway, and we know what she'll find there.

Putting Us There

Style also comes from the way a writer uses words so that they spring to life from the page. Vivid **imagery**—language that creates word pictures and appeals to the senses—makes us feel that we are seeing (or hearing, touching, tasting, or smelling) what the writer is describing. The poet John Greenleaf Whittier helps us experience the start of a New England blizzard with this image: "The sun that bleak December day / Rose cheerless over hills of gray."

Writers can also appeal to the ear with **dialect,** a way of speaking that's characteristic of a particular place or group of people. "Y'all come back now" tells us we're in the South. In older movies we'd hear a New York City cab-driver say: "Dat bum wanted me to take him and huh all da way to Noo Joisey."

Practice

Prepare a "literary devices" wall display for your classroom. You can keep adding to this display as your experience with literary devices grows. Here is how you do it:

Get seven poster boards, and give them the following labels:

- Symbols
- Images
- Irony
- Dialect
- Similes
- Metaphors
- Personification

Under each term, write its definition. Then, under each definition, write in examples that you think are interesting. You can find your examples in newspapers and magazines, as well as in the stories, poems, and novels you are reading in class and independently. Be sure to cite the author and title of the work you take each quotation from.

The Tell-Tale Heart

Literary Focus
Narrator: Who Says So?

When we read a story, we rely on the **narrator** (the person telling the story) to let us know what is going on. But what if the narrator can't be trusted? As you begin reading this story, decide if the narrator seems to be a reliable source of information.

Irony: The Unexpected!

Much of the horror in "The Tell-Tale Heart" comes from Poe's skillful use of **irony.** There are three kinds of irony:

- **Verbal irony**—we say just the opposite of what we mean.
- **Situational irony**—what happens is different from what we expect.
- **Dramatic irony**—we know something a character doesn't know.

Which types of irony work on your emotions in "The Tell-Tale Heart"? Pay particular attention to the narrator.

Reading Skills
Previewing: What's Ahead?

Preview this famous story by looking at the title and the illustrations. What do you think might happen in this story?

Make the Connection
Conduct a Survey: Top-Ten Terrors

Many people like a good scare now and then. Conduct a class poll to come up with a list of your top-ten terrors—choose details from scary TV shows, movies, books, and events.

Vocabulary Development

You'll learn these good, ordinary words as you read this strange story:

acute (ə·kyo͞ot′) *adj.:* sharp. *His nervousness increased his acute sense of hearing.*

vexed (vekst) *v.:* disturbed. *He was vexed by the old man's eye.*

sagacity (sə·gas′ə·tē) *n.:* intelligence and good judgment. *He was proud of his powers and of his sagacity.*

refrained (ri·frānd′) *v.:* held back. *Though furious, he refrained from action.*

wary (wer′ē) *adj.:* cautious. *He was too wary to make a careless mistake.*

suavity (swäv′ə·tē) *n.:* smooth manner. *The police showed perfect suavity.*

audacity (ô·das′ə·tē) *n.:* boldness. *He was impressed with his own audacity.*

vehemently (vē′ə·mənt·lē) *adv.:* forcefully. *He talked more vehemently, but he couldn't drown out the sound.*

gesticulations (jes·tik′yo͞o·lā′shənz) *n.:* energetic gestures. *His violent gesticulations did not disturb the policemen.*

derision (di·rizh′ən) *n.:* ridicule. *He hated the smiling derision of the police.*

Reading Standard 3.6 Identify significant literary devices (for example, irony) that define a writer's style, and use those elements to interpret the work.

Why will you say that I am mad?

The Tell-Tale Heart

Edgar Allan Poe

True!—nervous—very, very dreadfully nervous I had been and I am; but why *will* you say that I am mad? The disease had sharpened my senses—not destroyed—not dulled them. Above all was the sense of hearing acute. I heard all things in the heaven and in the earth. I heard many things in hell. How, then, am I mad? Hearken! and observe how healthily—how calmly I can tell you the whole story.

It is impossible to say how first the idea entered my brain; but once conceived, it haunted me day and night. Object[1] there was none. Passion there was none. I loved the old man. He had never wronged me. He had never given me insult. For his gold I had no desire. I think it was his eye! Yes, it was this! One of his eyes resem-

STYLE
1. Read this paragraph aloud. How does the style suggest the narrator's extreme nervousness?

---

1. object (äb′jikt) *n.:* purpose or goal.

Vocabulary
acute (ə·kyo͞ot′) *adj.:* sharp; sensitive; severe.

bled that of a vulture—a pale blue eye, with a film over it. Whenever it fell upon me, my blood ran cold; and so by degrees—very gradually—I made up my mind to take the life of the old man and thus rid myself of the eye forever.

Now this is the point. You fancy me mad. Madmen know nothing. But you should have seen *me*. You should have seen how wisely I proceeded—with what caution—with what foresight—with what dissimulation[2] I went to work! I was never kinder to the old man than during the whole week before I killed him. And every night, about midnight, I turned the latch of his door and opened it—oh, so gently! And then, when I had made an opening sufficient for my head, I put in a dark lantern, all closed, closed, so that no light shone out, and then I thrust in my head. Oh, you would have laughed to see how cunningly I thrust it in! I moved it slowly—very, very slowly, so that I might not disturb the old man's sleep. It took me an hour to place my whole head within the opening so far that I could see him as he lay upon his bed. Ha! Would a madman have been so wise as this? And then, when my head was well in the room, I undid the lantern cautiously—oh, so cautiously—cautiously (for the hinges creaked)—I undid it just so much that a single thin ray fell upon the vulture eye. And this I did for seven long nights—every night just at midnight—but I found the eye always closed; and so it was impossible to do the work; for it was not the old man who vexed me, but his Evil Eye. And

every morning, when the day broke, I went boldly into the chamber and spoke courageously to him, calling him by name in a hearty tone and inquiring how he had passed the night. So you see he would have been a very profound[3] old man, indeed, to suspect that every night, just at twelve, I looked in upon him while he slept.

MAKING INFERENCES
2. The narrator is talking to someone. Who might "you" be?

Upon the eighth night I was more than usually cautious in opening the door. A watch's minute hand moves more quickly than did mine. Never before that night had I *felt* the extent of my own powers—of my sagacity. I could scarcely contain my feelings of triumph. To think that there I was, opening the door, little by little, and he not even to dream of my secret deeds or thoughts. I fairly chuckled at the idea; and perhaps he heard me; for he moved on the bed suddenly, as if startled. Now you may think that I drew back—but no. His room was as black as pitch with the thick darkness (for the shutters were close fastened, through fear of robbers), and so I knew that he could not see the opening of the door, and I kept pushing it on steadily, steadily.

STYLE
3. Why is it ironic that the old man feared robbers? (What should he have feared?)

I had my head in, and was about to open the lantern, when my thumb slipped upon

---

2. **dissimulation** (di·sim′yo͞o·lā′shen) *n.:* disguising of intentions or feelings. (Look for a similar word at the end of the story.)

3. **profound** (prō·found′) *adj.:* deeply intellectual.

Vocabulary
vexed (vekst) *v.:* disturbed; annoyed.
sagacity (sə·gas′ə·tē) *n.:* intelligence and good judgment.

The illustrations on pages 356 and 359 are from a short movie based on "The Tell-Tale Heart."

the tin fastening, and the old man sprang up in the bed, crying out—"Who's there?"

I kept quite still and said nothing. For a whole hour I did not move a muscle, and in the meantime I did not hear him lie down. He was still sitting up in the bed listening—just as I have done, night after night, hearkening to the deathwatches[4] in the wall.

Presently I heard a slight groan, and I knew it was the groan of mortal terror. It was not a groan of pain or of grief—oh, no!—it was the low, stifled sound that arises from the bottom of the soul when overcharged with awe. I knew the sound well. Many a night, just at midnight, when all the world slept, it has welled up from my own bosom, deepening, with its dreadful echo, the terrors that distracted me. I say I knew it well. I knew what the old man felt, and pitied him, although I chuckled at heart. I knew that he had been lying awake ever since the first slight noise, when he had turned in the bed. His fears had been ever since growing upon him. He had been trying to fancy them causeless but could not. He had been saying to himself—"It is nothing but the wind in the chimney—it is only

---

4. deathwatches *n.:* beetles that burrow into wood and make tapping sounds, which some people believe are a sign of approaching death.

a mouse crossing the floor," or "It is merely a cricket which has made a single chirp." Yes, he had been trying to comfort himself with these suppositions; but he had found all in vain. *All in vain;* because Death, in approaching him, had stalked with his black shadow before him and enveloped the victim. And it was the mournful influence of the unperceived shadow that caused him to feel—although he neither saw nor heard— to *feel* the presence of my head within the room.

When I had waited a long time, very patiently, without hearing him lie down, I resolved to open a little—a very, very little crevice in the lantern. So I opened it—you cannot imagine how stealthily, stealthily— until, at length, a single dim ray, like the thread of the spider, shot from out the crevice and full upon the vulture eye.

STYLE
4. What simile does Poe use to help us see the ray of light from the lantern?

It was open—wide, wide open—and I grew furious as I gazed upon it. I saw it with perfect distinctness—all a dull blue, with a hideous veil over it that chilled the very marrow in my bones; but I could see nothing else of the old man's face or person, for I had directed the ray, as if by instinct, precisely upon the damned spot.

And now have I not told you that what you mistake for madness is but overacuteness of the senses?—now, I say, there came to my ears a low, dull, quick sound, such as a watch makes when enveloped in cotton. I knew *that* sound well too. It was the beating of the old man's heart. It increased my fury, as the beating of a drum stimulates the soldier into courage.

But even yet I refrained and kept still. I scarcely breathed. I held the lantern motionless. I tried how steadily I could maintain the ray upon the eye. Meantime the hellish tattoo[5] of the heart increased. It grew quicker and quicker and louder and louder every instant. The old man's terror *must* have been extreme! It grew louder, I say, louder every moment!—do you mark me well? I have told you that I am nervous: So I am. And now at the dead hour of the night, amid the dreadful silence of that old house, so strange a noise as this excited me to uncontrollable terror. Yet for some minutes longer I refrained and stood still. But the beating grew louder, louder! I thought the heart must burst. And now a new anxiety seized me—the sound would be heard by a neighbor! The old man's hour had come! With a loud yell, I threw open the lantern and leaped into the room. He shrieked once—once only. In an instant I dragged him to the floor and pulled the heavy bed over him. I then smiled gaily to find the deed so far done. But, for many minutes, the heart beat on with a muffled sound. This, however, did not vex me; it would not be heard through the wall. At length it ceased. The old man was dead. I removed the bed and examined the corpse. Yes, he was stone, stone dead. I placed my hand upon the heart and held it there many minutes. There was no pulsation. He was stone dead. His eye would trouble me no more.

STYLE
5. Where does Poe use repetition in this paragraph? Read the paragraph aloud to emphasize the repeated words.

---

5. **tattoo** *n.:* steady beat.

Vocabulary
refrained (ri·frānd′) *v.:* held back.

If still you think me mad, you will think so no longer when I describe the wise precautions I took for the concealment of the body. The night waned,[6] and I worked hastily but in silence. First of all I dismembered the corpse. I cut off the head and the arms and the legs.

I then took up three planks from the flooring of the chamber and deposited all between the scantlings.[7] I then replaced the boards so cleverly, so cunningly, that no human eye—not even *his*—could have detected anything wrong. There was nothing to wash out—no stain of any kind—no blood spot whatever. I had been too wary for that. A tub had caught all—ha! ha!

When I had made an end of these labors, it was four o'clock—still dark as midnight. As the bell sounded the hour, there came a knocking at the street door. I went down to open it with a light heart—for what had I *now* to fear? There entered three men, who introduced themselves, with perfect suavity, as officers of the police. A shriek had been heard by a neighbor during the night; suspicion of foul play had been aroused; information had been lodged at the police office, and they (the officers) had been deputed[8] to search the premises.

I smiled—for *what* had I to fear? I bade the gentlemen welcome. The shriek, I said, was my own in a dream. The old man, I mentioned, was absent in the country. I took my visitors all over the house. I bade them search—search *well*. I led them, at length, to *his* chamber. I showed them his treasures, secure, undisturbed. In the enthusiasm of my confidence, I brought chairs into the room and desired them *here* to rest from their fatigues, while I myself, in the wild audacity of my perfect triumph, placed my own seat upon the very spot beneath which reposed the corpse of the victim.

The officers were satisfied. My *manner* had convinced them. I was singularly at ease. They sat, and while I answered cheerily, they chatted familiar things. But, ere long, I felt myself getting pale and wished them gone. My head ached, and I fancied a ringing in my ears; but still they sat and still chatted. The ringing became more distinct—it continued and became more distinct: I talked more freely to get rid of the feeling: but it continued and gained definitiveness—until, at length, I found that the noise was *not* within my ears.

No doubt I now grew *very* pale—but I talked more fluently and with a heightened voice. Yet the sound increased—and what could I do? It was *a low, dull, quick sound— much such a sound as a watch makes when enveloped in cotton*. I gasped for breath— and yet the officers heard it not. I talked more quickly—more vehemently; but the noise steadily increased. I arose and argued about trifles, in a high key and with violent gesticulations, but the noise steadily increased. Why *would* they not be gone? I paced the floor to and fro with heavy strides, as if excited to fury by the observation of the men—but the noise steadily increased. Oh

---

6. **waned** (wānd) *v.:* gradually drew to a close.
7. **scantlings** *n.:* small beams of wood.
8. **deputed** (dē·pyo͞ot′id) *v.:* appointed.

Vocabulary

wary (wer′ē) *adj.:* cautious.
suavity (swäv′ə·tē) *n.:* smoothness; politeness.
audacity (ô·das′ə·tē) *n.:* boldness.
vehemently (vē′ə·mənt·lē) *adv.:* forcefully; passionately.
gesticulations (jes·tik′yo͞o·lā′shənz) *n.:* energetic gestures.

God! what *could* I do? I foamed—I raved—I swore! I swung the chair upon which I had been sitting and grated it upon the boards, but the noise arose over all and continually increased. It grew louder—louder—*louder!* And still the men chatted pleasantly, and smiled. Was it possible they heard not? Almighty God!—no, no! They heard!—they suspected!—they *knew!*—they were making a mockery of my horror!—this I thought, and this I think. But anything was better than this agony! Anything was more tolerable than this derision! I could bear those hypocritical smiles no longer! I felt that I must scream or die!—and now—again!—hark! louder! *louder!* louder! louder!—

"Villains!" I shrieked, "dissemble no more! I admit the deed!—tear up the planks!—here, here!—it is the beating of his hideous heart!"

STYLE
6. How do punctuation and repetition build a sense of horror in this paragraph? What do you imagine the police are really thinking by now?

Vocabulary
derision (di·riᴢh′ən) *n.:* contempt; ridicule.

Edgar Allan Poe

The Dark Side

Born in Boston, **Edgar Allan Poe** (1809–1849) was the son of traveling actors. When Poe was a baby, his father deserted the family; his mother died before his third birthday. Poe was taken in by the wealthy Allan family of Richmond, Virginia, and given a first-class education. At the age of twelve, he had already written enough poems (mainly love poems to girls he knew) to fill a book. By the time he was twenty, he had published two volumes of poetry.

Poe constantly argued with his foster father, John Allan, about money. Allan eventually broke all ties with Poe, leaving him penniless. In 1831, Poe moved in with his aunt, Maria Clemm, and her children in Baltimore, probably in an attempt to find a new family. He married his young cousin Virginia Clemm five years later.

Poe became as celebrated for his tales of horror and mystery as for his poetry. He made very little money from his writing, though—one of his most famous poems, "The Raven," earned him only about fifteen dollars. He seemed to live on the brink of disaster. His wife's death from tuberculosis in 1847 brought on a general decline in his physical and emotional health. He was found very ill and probably flooded with drink in a Baltimore tavern on a rainy day in 1849; he died four days later of unknown causes.

For Independent Reading

Poe was one of the first American writers to explore the dark side of the imagination. His horror tales include "The Masque of the Red Death," "The Pit and the Pendulum," and "The Fall of the House of Usher."

Literary Response and Analysis

Reading Check

1. For seven nights at midnight, the narrator watches the old man sleep. What happens on the eighth night? Fill in a chart like the one below to trace the events of the eighth night. Add as many boxes as you need.

> Event 1.

Then

> Event 2.

Then

> Event 3.

Then

Interpretations

2. We feel a strong sense of **dramatic irony** in this story: The narrator keeps claiming to be sane, but we become more and more certain that he is insane. What details in the story indicate that the narrator is insane?

3. Go back to your reading notes. Did **previewing** the story help you make accurate predictions? Why or why not?

4. How does the opening paragraph **foreshadow,** or hint at, the events of the story?

5. What is your explanation for the "heartbeat" noise that drives the narrator to confess?

6. Mood, or atmosphere, is the overall feeling in a story. How would you describe the mood of this story? What details does Poe use to create that mood?

7. The final paragraph of the story builds to a kind of mad **climax.** How does the writer use words and punctuation to create tension—and even the rhythm of a heartbeat?

8. To whom could the narrator be telling this horrible story?

9. Why is the story called "The Tell-Tale Heart"? (Could the title have more than one meaning?)

Evaluation

10. How is this story like other stories that scare people? Refer to your class survey of Top-Ten Terrors for examples.

Writing
Evaluating Style

Edgar Allan Poe once wrote that every word in a story should help create a "single overwhelming impression." How well has he done that in "The Tell-Tale Heart"? In a paragraph or two, describe the story's overall impact on you. Mention at least three details from the story that help create this impression.

Reading Standard 3.6 Identify significant literary devices (for example, irony) that define a writer's style, and use those elements to interpret the work.

Vocabulary Development

Searching for Synonyms

PRACTICE 1

Imagine that you are the editor of a magazine for teenagers. You want to include "The Tell-Tale Heart" in your Spooky Stories issue, but you think Poe's vocabulary is too hard and old-fashioned. Divide the words in the Word Bank with a partner (five apiece). Find the sentences in the story in which your words appear, and copy the sentences onto a blank sheet of paper. Rewrite each sentence to make it easier for today's teens to understand. Substitute more familiar words or phrases for the Word Bank words as well as for any other difficult words in the sentence. To locate **synonyms**— words with similar meanings—use a **thesaurus** (a dictionary of synonyms), a **synonym finder,** or a thesaurus that is part of your computer's **software.**

Word Bank

acute
vexed
sagacity
refrained
wary
suavity
audacity
vehemently
gesticulations
derision

Explaining Figures of Speech

PRACTICE 2

Each underlined phrase below contains a figure of speech from the story. Tell what two things are being compared in each sentence. Then, explain what each figure of speech means.

1. The narrator says the old man's eye resembled that of a vulture.
2. He said the eye makes his blood run cold.
3. He is moving in a room as black as pitch.
4. He sees the single ray of light from his lantern shoot out like the thread of the spider.
5. The heartbeat caused fury in the narrator the way the beating of a drum stimulates the soldier into courage.

Reading Standard 1.1
Analyze metaphors and similes to infer the literal and figurative meanings of phrases.

Reading Standard 1.3
Show ability to verify meanings by restatement.

Choose one of the phrases above, and make a drawing to illustrate its literal meaning. For example, if you were going to illustrate the figure of speech *I feel like a million bucks,* you might draw a person with money sprouting from her head, hands, and feet. Got the idea? Give it a try.

AN EXAMPLE OF FALLACIOUS REASONING

Edgar Allan Poe: His Life Revealed in His Work

Fallacious Reasoning

Fallacious (fə·lā′shəs) **reasoning** means simply "false thinking." People reason fallaciously when they draw incorrect or false conclusions. Such conclusions may be illogical, or they may be based on incomplete information.

"Because the world is flat, you'll fall off if you sail to the end of it" sounds funny today, but centuries ago uneducated people in Europe believed this fallacy. It was considered fact because, after all, when you looked at the world, it was flat for as far as you could see. This is the problem with fallacious reasoning: People believe it because they do not realize that it is based on incomplete or incorrect information.

For an argument to be convincing, it must be based on **logic,** or correct reasoning. Opinions should be supported by reasons and evidence, such as **facts, statistics, examples,** or **expert testimony.** When you decide whether or not you agree with an argument, you probably look automatically for reasons that you can agree or disagree with.

New clothes will make me more popular.

Are you also on the lookout for **fallacious reasoning**? Fallacious, or faulty, reasoning can be hard to spot, so it's important to watch for it whenever you evaluate an argument. Here are some common kinds of logical fallacies. Which ones do you recognize?

- **Hasty generalization**—a conclusion drawn from weak or insufficient evidence: *Harry and Joe didn't help when I dropped my books: Everyone in my school is so rude and uncaring.*

- **False cause and effect**—assuming that event A caused event B simply because A came first: *After I wore my new shirt to school, Mary invited me to her party. New clothes will make me more popular.*

- **Either/or fallacy**—the assumption that a problem or situation has only one possible cause or resolution when there may be several: *If we don't elect Jane class president, girls will have no say in running the school.*

- **Stereotyping**—believing that all members of a group share a certain characteristic: *All teenagers are angry and rebellious, and they all sleep late too.*

- **Name-calling** or **attacking the person**—attacking the person who's making the argument rather than the argument itself: *Ray's in favor of school uniforms. Big surprise—we all know how badly he dresses.*

- **Begging the question**—assuming that everyone agrees that something is true: *We all know that Samantha is the nicest girl in school.*

Grade 6 Review Reading Standard 2.8 Note instances of fallacious reasoning in text.

Edgar Allan Poe: His Life Revealed in His Work

Edgar Allan Poe was a very, very disturbed man. Every single story and poem he ever wrote is about disturbed, usually insane people. He writes about murderers, people buried alive, people being tortured, people killed by the Black Death. His characters imagine weird things, like a raven that croaks in English and plunges his beak into someone's heart.

No one could write stories like this without being crazy. How else could Poe have known what it is like to be insane? The only way he could have known is by being insane himself.

Poe's stories also show that he was a drug addict or an alcoholic. We know that he was always drunk. That probably accounts for the strange style of his writing. His stories are often very choppy. They use a lot of dashes and exclamation points, which suggests that a very nervous person wrote them, or someone on drugs.

We know that all writers are strange anyway, especially writers who specialize in horror.

I hope I have convinced you that Poe's writing reflects his sick mind.

(Despite all this, I love Poe's stories!)

—F. Reasoner

Reading Informational Materials

TestPractice

An Example of Fallacious Reasoning
Edgar Allan Poe: His Life Revealed in His Work

1. "Every single story and poem he ever wrote is about disturbed, usually insane people" is a **hasty generalization** because the writer —
   A probably hasn't read everything Poe wrote
   B was in a hurry when he or she wrote it
   C is not of Poe's generation
   D carefully considered the evidence

2. "The only way he could have known is by being insane himself" is another **hasty generalization** because —
   F the statement shows how insane the writer is
   G there is insufficient evidence support the statement
   H the statement assumes we all agree on something
   J the statement is an unfair attack on Poe

3. By saying that Poe's use of dashes and exclamation points suggests that a very nervous person or someone on drugs wrote the text, the writer is —
   A using the either/or fallacy
   B using false cause and effect
   C stereotyping
   D begging the question

4. By implying that we shouldn't take Poe's stories seriously because he was always drunk, the writer is —
   F using false cause and effect
   G begging the question
   H name-calling
   J using the either/or fallacy

5. Which two **fallacies** does the writer use in the statement "We know that all writers are strange anyway"?
   A False cause and effect and name-calling
   B Hasty generalization and stereotyping
   C Stereotyping and name-calling
   D Begging the question and stereotyping

Grade 6 Review Reading Standard 2.8 Note instances of fallacious reasoning in text.

Raymond's Run

Literary Focus
Style: Allusions

Squeaky, the girl who tells this story, likes allusions, especially to mythology and to an old TV show called *Gunsmoke*. An **allusion** is a reference to something in current events, on TV, in history, in literature, and so on. When writers use allusions, they expect readers to understand what they are referring to. Usually allusions refer to an aspect of culture that people share—literature, history, religion, mythology, politics, sports. The risk in using allusions is that some people may not make the connection. Sometimes allusions become dated. Footnotes in "Raymond's Run" explain a few allusions that may not make sense to you.

Style: Dialect

When you read this story, you hear Squeaky's own true voice—her dialect. A **dialect** is a way of speaking that is characteristic of a certain geographical area or a certain group of people. Dialect can involve special pronunciation, vocabulary, and grammar. Everyone speaks a dialect of some kind. No matter how close your dialect is to standard English, it will still show regional or group differences. Dialect is used by writers to capture the voice of a particular person. Squeaky and most of the other characters in "Raymond's Run" speak in a dialect used in Harlem, a neighborhood in New York City.

Reading Skills
Making Judgments

As you read, you continually make **judgments** about what you are reading. You form opinions about the story's characters, plot, and style. You decide if the plot or characters are believable. You find that you like or dislike individual characters or the way the story is told. As the story goes on, you might revise your judgments. As you read "Raymond's Run," make notes on your judgments about the story's characters, events, and style. See if your feelings change as the story progresses.

Make the Connection
Quickwrite

Squeaky, the narrator of the story you are about to read, is a tough, smart, funny, streetwise girl with strong opinions. She thinks she can tell what other people are like just from the way they look and talk. Like many of us, she sometimes forgets that there's much more to people than what appears on the surface. Have you ever been surprised to discover something new about someone? Take a few minutes to jot down what you've discovered.

Reading Standard 3.6 Identify significant literary devices (for example, dialect) that define a writer's style, and use those elements to interpret the work.

RAYMOND'S RUN

Toni Cade Bambara

I don't have much work to do around the house like some girls. My mother does that. And I don't have to earn my pocket money by hustling; George runs errands for the big boys and sells Christmas cards. And anything else that's got to get done, my father does. All I have to do in life is mind my brother Raymond, which is enough.

Sometimes I slip and say my little brother Raymond. But as any fool can see he's much bigger and he's older too. But a lot of people call him my little brother cause he needs looking after cause he's not quite right. And a lot of smart mouths got lots to say about that too, especially when George was minding him. But now, if anybody has anything to say to Raymond, anything to say about his big head, they have to come by me. And I don't play the dozens[1] or believe in standing around with somebody in my face doing a lot of talking. I much rather just knock you down and take my chances even if I am a little girl with skinny arms and a squeaky voice, which is how I got the name Squeaky. And if things get too rough, I run. And as anybody can tell you, I'm the fastest thing on two feet.

STYLE

1. What details in Squeaky's comments here reveal her special personality? What kind of person is Squeaky?

There is no track meet that I don't win the first-place medal. I used to win the twenty-yard dash when I was a little kid in kindergarten. Nowadays, it's the fifty-yard dash. And tomorrow I'm subject to run the quarter-meter relay all by myself and come in first, second, and third. The big kids call me

---

1. **play the dozens:** slang for "trade insults."

I'm the fastest and that goes for Gretchen, too, who says she's going to win this year. Ridiculous.

Mercury[2] cause I'm the swiftest thing in the neighborhood. Everybody knows that— except two people who know better, my father and me. He can beat me to Amsterdam Avenue with me having a two-fire-hydrant head start and him running with his hands in his pockets and whistling. But that's private information. Cause can you imagine some thirty-five-year-old man stuffing himself into PAL[3] shorts to race little kids? So as far as everyone's concerned, I'm the fastest and that goes for Gretchen, too, who has put out the tale that she is going to win the first-place medal this year. Ridiculous. In the second place, she's got short legs. In the third place, she's got freckles. In the first place, no one can beat me and that's all there is to it.

I'm standing on the corner admiring the weather and about to take a stroll down Broadway so I can practice my breathing exercises, and I've got Raymond walking on the inside close to the buildings, cause he's subject to fits of fantasy and starts thinking he's a circus performer and that the curb is a tightrope strung high in the air. And sometimes after a rain he likes to step down off his tightrope right into the gutter and slosh around getting his shoes and cuffs wet. Then I get hit when I get home. Or sometimes if you don't watch him he'll dash across traffic to the island[4] in the middle of Broadway and give the pigeons a fit. Then I have to go behind him apologizing to all the old people sitting around trying to get some sun and getting all upset with the pigeons fluttering

around them, scattering their newspapers and upsetting the waxpaper lunches in their laps. So I keep Raymond on the inside of me, and he plays like he's driving a stage-coach which is OK by me so long as he doesn't run me over or interrupt my breathing exercises, which I have to do on account of I'm serious about my running, and I don't care who knows it.

Now some people like to act like things come easy to them, won't let on that they practice. Not me. I'll high-prance down 34th Street like a rodeo pony

---

2. **Mercury:** in Roman mythology, messenger of the gods, known for his speediness.
3. **PAL:** Police Athletic League.
4. **island** *n.:* traffic island, a car-free area in the middle of the street.

to keep my knees strong even if it does get my mother uptight so that she walks ahead like she's not with me, don't know me, is all by herself on a shopping trip, and I am somebody else's crazy child. Now you take Cynthia Procter for instance. She's just the opposite. If there's a test tomorrow, she'll say something like, "Oh, I guess I'll play handball this afternoon and watch television tonight," just to let you know she ain't thinking about the test. Or like last week when she won the spelling bee for the millionth time, "A good thing you got 'receive,' Squeaky, cause I would have got it wrong. I completely forgot about the spelling bee." And she'll clutch the lace on her blouse like it was a narrow escape. Oh, brother. But of course when I pass her house on my early morning trots around the block, she is practicing the scales on the piano over and over and over and over. Then in music class she always lets herself get bumped around so she falls accidentally on purpose onto the piano stool and is so surprised to find herself sitting there that she decides just for fun to try out the ole keys. And what do you

know—Chopin's[5] waltzes just spring out of her fingertips and she's the most surprised thing in the world. A regular prodigy. I could kill people like that. I stay up all night studying the words for the spelling bee. And you can see me any time of day practicing running. I never walk if I can trot, and shame on Raymond if he can't keep up. But of course he does, cause if he hangs back someone's liable to walk up to him and get smart, or take his allowance from him, or ask him where he got that great big pumpkin head. People are so stupid sometimes.

So I'm strolling down Broadway breathing out and breathing in on counts of seven, which is my lucky number, and here comes Gretchen and her sidekicks: Mary Louise, who used to be a friend of mine when she

5. **Chopin's:** Frédéric François Chopin (shō′pan) (1810–1849), Polish composer and pianist.

first moved to Harlem from Baltimore and got beat up by everybody till I took up for her on account of her mother and my mother used to sing in the same choir when they were young girls, but people ain't grateful, so now she hangs out with the new girl Gretchen and talks about me like a dog; and Rosie, who is as fat as I am skinny and has a big mouth where Raymond is concerned and is too stupid to know that there is not a big deal of difference between herself and Raymond and that she can't afford to throw stones. So they are steady coming up Broadway and I see right away that it's going to be one of those Dodge City scenes[6] cause the street ain't that big and they're close to the buildings just as we are. First I think I'll step into the candy store and look over the new comics and let them pass. But that's chicken and I've got a reputation to consider. So then I think I'll just walk straight on through them or even over them if necessary. But as they get to me, they slow down. I'm ready to fight, cause like I said I don't feature a whole lot of chit-chat, I much prefer to just knock you down right from the jump and save everybody a lotta precious time.

"You signing up for the May Day races?" smiles Mary Louise, only it's not a smile at all. A dumb question like that doesn't deserve an answer. Besides, there's just me and Gretchen standing there really, so no use wasting my breath talking to shadows.

"I don't think you're going to win this time," says Rosie, trying to signify[7] with her hands on her hips all salty, completely forgetting that I have whupped her behind many times for less salt than that.

"I always win cause I'm the best," I say straight at Gretchen who is, as far as I'm concerned, the only one talking in this ventriloquist-dummy routine. Gretchen smiles, but it's not a smile, and I'm thinking that girls never really smile at each other because they don't know how and don't want to know how and there's probably no one to teach us how, cause grown-up girls don't know either. Then they all look at Raymond who has just brought his mule team to a standstill. And they're about to see what trouble they can get into through him. 📖

📚 **STYLE**

3. Explain the comparison Squeaky makes between Rosie and Gretchen and the "ventriloquist-dummy routine."

"What grade you in now, Raymond?"

"You got anything to say to my brother,

---

6. **Dodge City scenes:** showdowns like those in the television western *Gunsmoke*, which was set in Dodge City, Kansas. In a typical scene a marshal and an outlaw face off with pistols on an empty street.

7. **signify** *v.*: slang for "act boastful or insult someone."

you say it to me, Mary Louise Williams of Raggedy Town, Baltimore."

"What are you, his mother?" sasses Rosie.

"That's right, Fatso. And the next word out of anybody and I'll be their mother too." So they just stand there and Gretchen shifts from one leg to the other and so do they. Then Gretchen puts her hands on her hips and is about to say something with her freckle-face self but doesn't. Then she walks around me looking me up and down but keeps walking up Broadway, and her sidekicks follow her. So me and Raymond smile at each other and he says, "Gidyap" to his team and I continue with my breathing exercises, strolling down Broadway toward the iceman on 145th with not a care in the world cause I am Miss Quicksilver[8] herself.

I take my time getting to the park on May Day because the track meet is the last thing on the program. The biggest thing on the program is the May Pole dancing, which I can do without, thank you, even if my mother thinks it's a shame I don't take part and act like a girl for a change. You'd think my mother'd be grateful not to have to make me a white organdy dress with a big satin sash and buy me new white baby-doll shoes that can't be taken out of the box till the big day. You'd think she'd be glad her daughter ain't out there prancing around a May Pole getting the new clothes all dirty and sweaty and trying to act like a fairy or a flower or whatever you're supposed to be when you should be trying to be yourself, whatever that is, which is, as far as I am concerned, a poor black girl who really can't afford to buy shoes and a new dress you only wear once a lifetime cause it won't fit next year.

I was once a strawberry in a Hansel and Gretel pageant when I was in nursery school and didn't have no better sense than to dance on tiptoe with my arms in a circle over my head doing umbrella steps and being a perfect fool just so my mother and father could come dressed up and clap. You'd think they'd know better than to encourage that kind of nonsense. I am not a strawberry. I do not dance on my toes. I run. That is what I am all about. So I always come late to the May Day program, just in time to get my number pinned on and lay in the grass till they announce the fifty-yard dash.

I put Raymond in the little swings, which is a tight squeeze this year and will be impossible next year. Then I look around for Mr. Pearson, who pins the numbers on. I'm really looking for Gretchen if you want to know the truth, but she's not around. The park is jam-packed. Parents in hats and corsages and breast-pocket handkerchiefs peeking up. Kids in white dresses and light-blue suits. The parkees unfolding chairs and chasing the rowdy kids from Lenox[9] as if they had no right to be there. The big guys with their caps on backwards, leaning against the fence swirling the basketballs on the tips of their fingers, waiting for all these crazy people to clear out the park so they can play. Most of the kids in my class are carrying bass drums and glockenspiels[10] and flutes. You'd think they'd put in a few bongos or something for real like that.

Then here comes Mr. Pearson with his

---

8. **Quicksilver:** another name for mercury, a silver-colored liquid metal that flows rapidly.

9. **Lenox:** Lenox Avenue, a major street in Harlem.
10. **glockenspiels** (gläk′ən·spēlz′) *n.*: musical instruments with flat metal bars that are struck with small hammers and produce bell-like sounds. Glockenspiels are often used in marching bands.

clipboard and his cards and pencils and whistles and safety pins and fifty million other things he's always dropping all over the place with his clumsy self. He sticks out in a crowd because he's on stilts. We used to call him Jack and the Beanstalk to get him mad. But I'm the only one that can outrun him and get away, and I'm too grown for that silliness now.

"Well, Squeaky," he says, checking my name off the list and handing me number seven and two pins. And I'm thinking he's got no right to call me Squeaky, if I can't call him Beanstalk.

"Hazel Elizabeth Deborah Parker," I correct him and tell him to write it down on his board.

"Well, Hazel Elizabeth Deborah Parker, going to give someone else a break this year?" I squint at him real hard to see if he is seriously thinking I should lose the race on purpose just to give someone else a break. "Only six girls running this time," he continues, shaking his head sadly like it's my fault all of New York didn't turn out in sneakers. "That new girl should give you a run for your money." He looks around the park for Gretchen like a periscope in a submarine movie. "Wouldn't it be a nice gesture if you were . . . to ahhh . . ."

I give him such a look he couldn't finish putting that idea into words. Grown-ups got a lot of nerve sometimes. I pin number seven to myself and stomp away, I'm so burnt. And I go straight for the track and stretch out on the grass while the band winds up with "Oh, the Monkey Wrapped His Tail Around the Flag Pole," which my teacher calls by some other name. The man on the loudspeaker is calling everyone over

to the track and I'm on my back looking at the sky, trying to pretend I'm in the country, but I can't, because even grass in the city feels hard as sidewalk, and there's just no pretending you are anywhere but in a "concrete jungle" as my grandfather says.

The twenty-yard dash takes all of two minutes cause most of the little kids don't know no better than to run off the track or run the wrong way or run smack into the fence and fall down and cry. One little kid, though, has got the good sense to run straight for the white ribbon up ahead so he wins. Then the second-graders line up for the thirty-yard dash and I don't even bother to turn my head to watch cause Raphael Perez always wins. He wins before he even begins by psyching the runners, telling them they're going to trip on their shoelaces and fall on their faces or lose their shorts or something, which he doesn't really have to do since he is very fast, almost as fast as I am. After that is the forty-yard dash which I used to run when I was in first grade. Raymond is hollering from the swings cause he knows I'm about

STYLE

4. What values does Squeaky reveal in her remarks about Mr. Pearson and other grown-ups? How do you think she feels when she makes her last remark?

to do my thing cause the man on the loud-speaker has just announced the fifty-yard dash, although he might just as well be giving a recipe for angel food cake cause you can hardly make out what he's sayin for the static. I get up and slip off my sweat pants and then I see Gretchen standing at the starting line, kicking her legs out like a pro. Then as I get into place I see that ole Raymond is on line on the other side of the fence, bending down with his fingers on the ground just like he knew what he was doing. I was going to yell at him but then I didn't. It burns up your energy to holler.

Every time, just before I take off in a race, I always feel like I'm in a dream, the kind of dream you have when you're sick with fever and feel all hot and weightless. I dream I'm flying over a sandy beach in the early morning sun, kissing the leaves of the trees as I fly by. And there's always the smell of apples, just like in the country when I was little and used to think I was a choo-choo train, running through the fields of corn and chugging up the hill to the orchard. And all the time I'm dreaming this, I get lighter and lighter until I'm flying over the beach again, getting blown through the sky like a feather that weighs nothing at all. But once I spread my fingers in the dirt and crouch over the Get on Your Mark, the dream goes and I am solid again and am telling myself, Squeaky you must win, you must win, you are the fastest thing in the world, you can even beat your father up Amsterdam if you really try. And then I feel my weight coming back just behind my knees then down to my feet then into the earth and the pistol shot explodes in my blood and I am off and weightless again, flying past the other runners, my arms pumping up and down and the whole world is quiet except for the crunch as I zoom over the gravel in the track. I glance to my left and there is no one. To the right, a blurred Gretchen, who's got her chin jutting out as if it would win the race all by itself. And on the other side of the fence is Raymond with his arms down to his side and the palms tucked up behind him, running in his very own style, and it's the first time I ever saw that and I almost stop to watch my brother Raymond on his first run. But the white ribbon is bouncing toward me and I tear past it, racing into the distance till my feet with a mind of their own start digging up footfuls of dirt and brake me short. Then all the kids standing on the side pile on me, banging me on the back and slapping my head with their May Day programs, for I have won again and everybody on 151st Street can walk tall for another year.

STYLE

5. Read parts of this paragraph aloud to hear how the sentences imitate the rhythm of Squeaky's run.

"In first place . . ." the man on the loudspeaker is clear as a bell now. But then he pauses and the loudspeaker starts to whine. Then static. And I lean down to catch my breath and here comes Gretchen walking back, for she's overshot the finish line too, huffing and puffing with her hands on her hips taking it slow, breathing in steady time like a real pro and I sort of like her a little for the first time. "In first place . . ." and then three or four voices get all mixed up on the loudspeaker and I dig my sneaker into the grass and stare at Gretchen who's staring back, we both wondering just who did win. I can hear old Beanstalk arguing with the man on the loudspeaker and then a few others running their mouths about what the stopwatches say. Then I hear Raymond yanking at the fence to call me and I wave to shush him, but he keeps rattling the fence like a gorilla in a cage like in them gorilla movies, but then like a dancer or something he starts climbing up nice and easy but very fast. And it occurs to me, watching how smoothly he climbs hand over hand and remembering how he looked running with his arms down to his side and with the wind pulling his mouth back and his teeth showing and all, it occurred to me that Raymond would make a very fine runner. Doesn't he always keep up with me on my trots? And he surely knows how to breathe in counts of seven cause he's always doing it at the dinner table, which drives my brother George up the wall. And I'm smiling to beat the band cause if I've lost this race, or if me and Gretchen tied, or even if I've won, I can always retire as a runner and begin a whole new career as a coach with Raymond as my champion. After all, with a little more study I can beat Cynthia and her phony self at the spelling bee. And if I bugged my mother, I could get piano lessons and become a star. And I have a big rep[11] as the baddest thing around. And I've got a roomful of ribbons and medals and awards. But what has Raymond got to call his own?

So I stand there with my new plans, laughing out loud by this time as Raymond jumps down from the fence and runs over with his teeth showing and his arms down to the side, which no one before him has quite mastered as a running style. And by the time he comes over I'm jumping up

and down so glad to see him—my brother Raymond, a great runner in the family tradition. But of course everyone thinks I'm jumping up and down because the men on the loudspeaker have finally gotten themselves together and compared notes and are announcing "In first place—Miss Hazel Elizabeth Deborah Parker." (Dig that.) "In second place—Miss Gretchen P. Lewis." And I look over at Gretchen wondering what the "P" stands for. And I smile. Cause she's good, no doubt about it. Maybe she'd like to help me coach Raymond; she obviously is serious about running, as any fool can see. And she nods to congratulate me and then she smiles. And I smile. We stand there with this big smile of respect between us. It's about as real a smile as girls can do for each other, considering we don't practice real smiling every day, you know, cause maybe we too busy being flowers or fairies or strawberries instead of something honest and worthy of respect . . . you know . . . like being people.

---

11. **rep** *n.*: slang for "reputation." People often create slang by clipping off parts of words.

MEET THE WRITER

Toni Cade Bambara

"I Deal in Straight-Up Fiction Myself"

Toni Cade Bambara (1939–1995) grew up in New York City, where "Raymond's Run" takes place. Bambara's writing drew on the voices of her childhood: street-corner speechmakers, barbershop storytellers, performers at Harlem's legendary Apollo Theater. She said her stories came from her imagination, though:

> It does no good to write autobiographical fiction, cause the minute the book hits the stand here comes your mama screamin how could you. . . . And it's no use using bits and snatches even of real events and real people, even if you do cover, guise, switch-around, and change-up, cause next thing you know your best friend's laundry cart is squeaking past but your bell ain't ringing so you trot down the block after her and there's this drafty cold pressure front the weatherman surely did not predict and your friend says in this chilly way that it's really something when your own friend stabs you in the back with a pen. . . . So I deal in straight-up fiction myself, cause I value my family and friends, and mostly cause I lie a lot anyway.

Toni Cade adopted the name Bambara from a signature on a sketchbook she found in her great-grandmother's trunk. The Bambara are a people of northwestern Africa known for their skill in woodcarving.

For Independent Reading

"Raymond's Run" comes from a collection of short stories called *Gorilla, My Love*. Other stories in the collection with characters like Squeaky are "Blues Ain't No Mockin Bird" and the title story, "Gorilla, My Love."

Literary Response and Analysis

Reading Check

1. Explain why taking care of Raymond is not an easy job. How does Squeaky protect Raymond?

2. What does Mr. Pearson want Squeaky to do in the race? How does she react to his suggestion?

3. What does Squeaky decide to do for Raymond?

Interpretations

4. What do you think is the most important **conflict** in this story? Why?

5. Squeaky and Gretchen almost get into a fight before the race. Why, then, do they smile at each other after the race?

6. Go back to the notes you made while reading the story. What **judgments** did you make that you changed over the course of the story? Explain why you first made them and why you changed your mind. If you never changed your mind, describe one of your judgments, and explain why it did not change.

7. Find Squeaky's **allusions** (references to literature, history, sports, and so on), and explain what they reveal about Squeaky's interests and education.

8. In a **dialect,** words can have special meaning, pronunciation, or spelling. What do you think the italicized words in the following sentence from "Raymond's Run" mean?

"'I don't think you're going to win this time,' says Rosie, trying to *signify* with her hands on her hips *all salty*, completely forgetting that I have *whupped* her behind many times for less *salt* than that" (page 370). Rewrite the sentence as someone in your neighborhood might say it.

Evaluation

9. Would you have called this story "Raymond's Run"? Defend Bambara's choice, or invent a new title and explain why you think it's better.

Writing

False Impressions

Write a brief narrative about an incident (something that happened) in your life in which a first impression turned out to be wrong or someone you thought you knew well did something that surprised you. Answer these questions:

• What happened during this incident?

• Why was this incident important to you? What did you learn from it?

• What details (sights, feelings, things people said) do you remember?

Reading Standard 3.6
Identify significant literary devices (for example, dialect) that define a writer's style, and use those elements to interpret the work.

Vocabulary Development

Explaining Figures of Speech

Squeaky speaks in a colorful way and uses a lot of slang. The slang terms are usually based on **metaphors,** in which one thing is compared to something quite different. Squeaky also sprinkles her talk with **similes,** in which she compares one thing to another using *like, as, than*, or *resembles*. She also uses an **analogy,** a comparison of two things to show how they are alike. Analogies are often used to explain one concept by showing how it is similar to another concept, perhaps one that is more easily understood. Squeaky uses an analogy when she helps us understand her state of mind before the race by comparing it to a dream of flying.

PRACTICE 1

Identify each figure of speech that follows as a metaphor or as a simile. (Hint: Two are similes; two are metaphors.) Then, explain the comparison each figure of speech is based on.

1. Squeaky prances down the street like a rodeo pony to keep her knees strong.
2. Squeaky gets angry when people ask Raymond where he got that great big pumpkin head.
3. She thinks it is chicken to hide from the girls in the candy store.
4. She says that Mr. Pearson looks around the park like a periscope in a submarine movie.

PRACTICE 2

In a long paragraph on page 373, Squeaky uses an **analogy** to compare her state of mind before the race to a dream of flying. Re-read this analogy. Then, write an analogy of your own. You might compare playing football to playing a game of chess, or you might compare being sent to your room to being sent to jail. Open your analogy with words like these: "Playing football is like . . ." or "Being sent to my room is like . . ." Try to describe at least two ways in which your analogy works.

Reading Standard 1.1 Analyze analogies, metaphors, and similes to infer the literal and figurative meanings of phrases.

Olympic Games *and*

AN EXAMPLE OF UNSUPPORTED INFERENCES

The Old Olympic Games: A Report

Supported and Unsupported Inferences

"Hi, Mrs. Johnson. Got a minute?"

"Sure, Ted. What's up?"

"I was just wondering about this grade on my essay. I thought I did better than that."

"Well, Ted, you really went out on a limb with unsupported inferences."

"Unsupported what?"

"Inferences. You know, when you take the writer's clues and put two and two together."

"I did it wrong?"

"Well, in this essay you sometimes took two and two and came up with twenty-two. At other times you took two and two into orbit."

An **inference** is an educated guess. When you read, you make inferences by combining information in the text with what you already know. When you're evaluating a text or presenting an argument, make sure your inferences are supported—make sure you base them on information in the text and on reasonable prior knowledge. Ted's problem was that he made unsupported inferences. Instead of basing his inferences on the text, he went "into orbit."

Supported inferences are based on details in a writer's text. You can pose any number of possibilities as long as you can find evidence in the text to sup-

Ruins at Olympia in Greece, the site of the ancient Olympic Games.

port your ideas. In "Raymond's Run" you could support an inference that Squeaky and Gretchen will become friends because of the new respect they feel for each other at the end of the race. You could not find evidence to support an inference that Raymond will suddenly behave more like other people because he'll take up running. Nothing in the story supports that inference. When making inferences about a character in a story, you cannot ignore facts in the text.

Unsupported inferences are not based on details in the text. They might ignore facts or misinterpret details. They might draw conclusions that are not logical. Unsupported inferences can also go too far. Carrying inferences too far from the text is what Mrs. Johnson, in the dialogue above, means by going into orbit.

You'll find two readings in the pages that follow. One is an encyclopedia article about the Olympic Games. The second, a report based on the first article, is full of **unsupported inferences.**

Grade 6 Review Reading Standard 2.8
Note instances of unsupported inferences in text.

Olympic Games

THE ANCIENT GAMES. Athletics played an important role in the religious festivals of ancient Greece. Historians believe the ancient Greeks first organized athletic games as part of funeral ceremonies for important people. This practice probably existed by the 1200s B.C. Later, games became part of religious festivals honoring the gods. Many Greek cities held festivals every two or four years.

Over time, four great religious festivals developed that brought together people from throughout the Greek world. These festivals were the Isthmian, Nemean, Pythian, and Olympic games. The Olympic Games, which ranked as the most important, honored Zeus, the king of the gods.

The first recorded Olympic contest took place in 776 B.C. at Olympia in western Greece. The first winner was Koroibos (later spelled Coroebus), a cook from Elis. The Olympic Games were held every four years. They were so important to the ancient Greeks that time was measured in *Olympiads,* the four-year intervals between games. The only event in the first thirteen games was the *stadion,* a running race of 192 meters (210 yards). Through the years, longer running races were added.

Other types of competition became part of the ancient Olympics. In 708 B.C., wrestling and the pentathlon were added. The pentathlon was a combination of jumping, running, the discus throw, the javelin throw, and wrestling. Boxing joined the program in 688 B.C., and the four-horse chariot race was added in 680 B.C. Horse racing was included in 648 B.C., as was the *pancratium* (also spelled *pankration*), a combination of boxing, wrestling, and kicking. Some unusual events were included in the Olympics, such as a race in armor, a chariot race called the *apene,* in which two mules pulled the chariot, and a competition for trumpeters. . . .

Javelin thrower.

The Romans conquered Greece during the 140s B.C., and the games soon lost their religious meaning. In A.D. 393, Emperor Theodosius I banned the games.

THE MODERN GAMES. In 1857, a group of German archaeologists began to excavate the ruins of the stadium and temples of Olympia, which had been destroyed by an earthquake and buried by a landslide and floods. Their discoveries inspired Baron Pierre de Coubertin, a French educator, to organize a modern international Olympics. He first proposed the idea publicly in 1892. In 1894, the first IOC was formed.

The first modern Olympic Games were held in Athens, Greece, in 1896. The athletes competed in nine sports: (1) cycling, (2) fencing, (3) gymnastics, (4) lawn tennis, (5) shooting, (6) swimming, (7) track and field, (8) weight lifting, and (9) wrestling. James B. Connolly of the United States became the first modern Olympic champion, winning the triple jump (then known as the hop, step, and jump).

—from *The World Book Encyclopedia*

The Old Olympic Games:
A Report

The Olympic Games began in Greece a long time ago, before anyone knew how to write or play basketball. People weren't as smart back then as we are today. They played games for dead people, and they believed in lots of gods. They even thought the gods had a king, named Zeus. They didn't have clocks or watches, either, so they told time by counting games.

At first the only thing the old Greeks could do was race. They weren't very strong, so they could run only 210 yards. Later they got stronger and ran farther. Then they learned how to wrestle, jump, and throw things. They didn't play fair, though, and kicked each other when they were boxing and wrestling. They also raced chariots using four horses, which seems like three too many to me. Some of them raced chariots using mules! If they were that silly, it's no wonder the Romans conquered them and banned the games.

An earthquake and a landslide buried the old stadium. After a German dug it up, for some reason—I don't know what—a Frenchman decided to hold games again. The modern games began in 1896. They had nine cool events but no winter sports because it is too hot in Greece. An American won the hop, step, and jump. It's nice that an American won, but I don't get why winning a dance contest made him a champion.

—Anonymous

The Discus Thrower. An ancient Roman copy of a 2nd-century B.C. sculpture by Myron.

Reading Informational Materials

Reading Check

Base your answers to the following questions on "Olympic Games," the article from *The World Book Encyclopedia.*

1. When was the first recorded Olympic contest held?

2. Why were the ancient Olympic Games held?

3. List four events in the ancient Olympic Games.

4. Why did the ancient Olympic Games end?

5. When did the modern Olympic Games begin?

Test Practice

An Example of Unsupported Inferences
The Old Olympic Games: A Report

1. Which of the following statements from the report can be **supported** by details in the encyclopedia article?

   A "The Olympic Games began in Greece. . . ."

   B "People weren't as smart back then. . . ."

   C "They played games for dead people. . . ."

   D "They didn't have clocks or watches. . . ."

2. Which of the following statements from the report is an **unsupported inference**?

   F "The only thing the old Greeks could do was race."

   G "They also raced chariots using four horses. . . ."

   H "The Romans conquered them. . . ."

   J "The modern games began in 1896."

3. The following statements from the report are all **unsupported inferences** *except* —

   A "They even thought the gods had a king, named Zeus."

   B "They told time by counting games."

   C "They weren't very strong. . . ."

   D "They didn't play fair, though. . . ."

4. The report ends with the **unsupported inference** that the hop, step, and jump was —

   F a triple jump

   G a track-and-field event

   H a dance contest

   J won by an American

Grade 6 Review Reading Standard 2.8 Note instances of unsupported inferences in text.

My Mother Pieced Quilts *and* Suéter / Sweater

Literary Focus
Symbolism

People are symbol makers. A **symbol** is a person, a place, a thing, or an event that stands for something beyond itself. Some of our symbols are traditional. We easily understand them because people have agreed on their meaning. For example, a blindfolded woman holding scales symbolizes justice. In cartoons a lightbulb over someone's head symbolizes a bright idea.

Literary symbols are created by individual writers. Literary symbols stand for themselves in a story or a poem, but they stand for something else as well. Here is what writer Gary Soto (see "Broken Chain," page 7) says about symbols in poetry:

❝ Poetry is a concentrated form of writing; so much meaning is packed into such a little space. Therefore, each word in a poem is very important and is chosen very carefully to convey just the right meaning. For example, the word *tree* might stand for more than a tree in an orchard. It might symbolize life itself, or it might symbolize the strength of your grandfather or your father. *Rain* may symbolize tears; *dusk* may symbolize approaching death. ❞

Reading Skills
Reading Poetry: Watch the Sense of the Lines

Poetry is written in lines—some long and some very short. Some poets use punctuation in their lines; some poets do not. When you read a poem that does not use punctuation, you have to read the lines as thought units. That means you do not come to a dead stop at the end of every line. You have to see if the sense of the line carries over to the next line. In the first two lines of "My Mother Pieced Quilts," for example, you should not stop at the end of line 1. Instead, you should read on to line 2, which completes the meaning.

Read the poem three times. The second time, note where you should not pause and where you should make brief or full pauses. The third time, read the poem aloud.

Make the Connection
Quickwrite ✏

Teresa Palomo Acosta has her mother's quilt, and Alberto Forcada has his grandmother's sweater. Is there an object in your life that symbolizes something important to you? It could be an old toy or a favorite book or maybe a food that brings back memories. Your object may represent happy times or sad times. Jot down some notes about this important object. How does it make you feel?

Reading Standard 3.6 Identify significant literary devices (for example, symbolism) that define a writer's style, and use those elements to interpret the work.

Woman Sewing (1948) by Jacob Lawrence.

My Mother Pieced Quilts

TERESA PALOMO ACOSTA

they were just meant as covers
in winters
as weapons
against pounding january winds

5 but it was just that every morning I awoke to these
october ripened canvases
passed my hand across their cloth faces
and began to wonder how you pieced
all these together
these strips of gentle communion cotton and flannel
10 nightgowns
wedding organdies
dime store velvets

how you shaped patterns square and oblong and round
positioned
15 balanced
then cemented them
with your thread
a steel needle
a thimble

20   how the thread darted in and out
      galloping along the frayed edges, tucking them in
      as you did us at night
      oh how you stretched and turned and rearranged
      your michigan spring faded curtain pieces
25   my father's santa fe work shirt
      the summer denims, the tweeds of fall

      in the evening you sat at your canvas
      —our cracked linoleum floor the drawing board
      me lounging on your arm
30   and you staking out the plan:
      whether to put the lilac purple of easter against the red plaid of
        winter-going-
      into-spring
      whether to mix a yellow with blue and white and paint the
      corpus christi noon when my father held your hand
35   whether to shape a five-point star from the
      somber black silk you wore to grandmother's funeral

      you were the river current
      carrying the roaring notes . . .
      forming them into pictures of a little boy reclining
40   a swallow flying
      you were the caravan master at the reins
      driving your threaded needle artillery across the mosaic cloth bridges
      delivering yourself in separate testimonies°

      oh mother you plunged me sobbing and laughing
45   into our past
      into the river crossing at five
      into the spinach fields
      into the plainview cotton rows
      into tuberculosis wards
50   into braids and muslin dresses
      sewn hard and taut to withstand the thrashing of twenty-five years

      stretched out they lay
      armed/ready/shouting/celebrating

      knotted with love
55   the quilts sing on

---

43. testimonies *n.:* declarations. For example, people make testimonies of faith or of love.

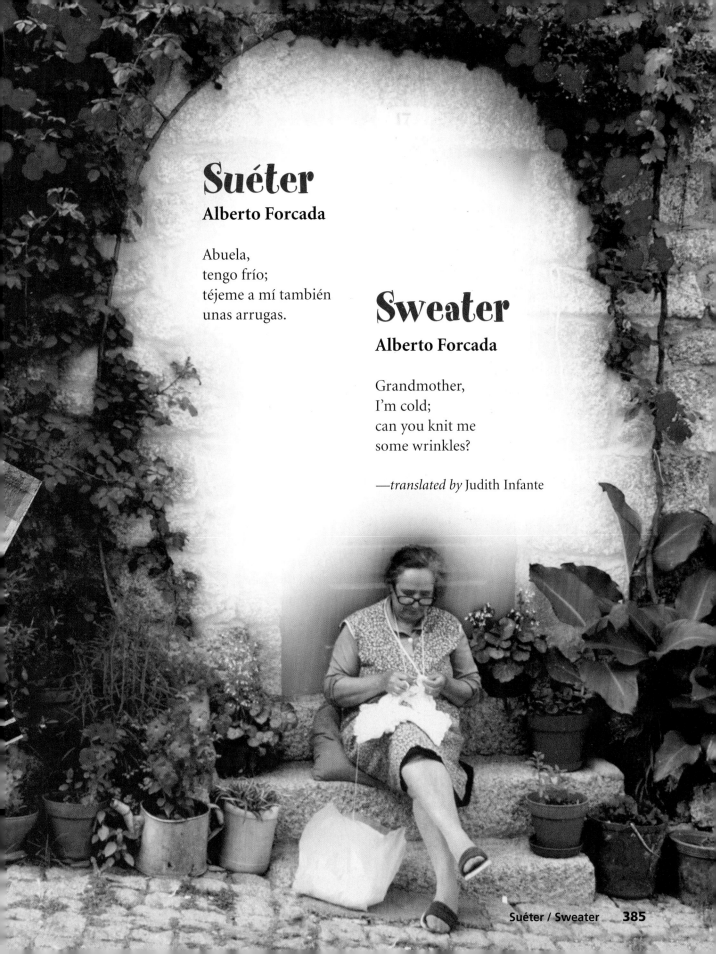

Suéter

Alberto Forcada

Abuela,
tengo frío;
téjeme a mí también
unas arrugas.

Sweater

Alberto Forcada

Grandmother,
I'm cold;
can you knit me
some wrinkles?

—*translated by* Judith Infante

Teresa Palomo Acosta

A Love of Poetry

Teresa Acosta (1949–   ) began writing poetry when she was sixteen and published her first poem in 1976. As a teenager she enjoyed European and early American poetry. Later she was inspired by African American and Mexican American poetry, when it became available to her. Acosta grew up in McGregor, Texas, and now teaches at the University of Texas at Austin.

Alberto Forcada

Despertar

The poems of **Alberto Forcada** (1969–   ) that appear in *Despertar (Awaking)*—"Suéter" is one of them—describe the dreams and fantasies of children. Forcada has a degree in philosophy from the National University of Mexico. His poems have been collected in three books and have been published in such magazines as *De Polanco para Polanco*, which serves a neighborhood in Mexico City.

Literary Response and Analysis

Reading Check

1. "My Mother Pieced Quilts" opens with the pronoun *they*. To whom or what does the pronoun refer?

2. When the speaker of "My Mother Pieced Quilts" wakes up in the morning, what does she wonder about her mother's quilts? See the second and third stanzas.

3. Quilts are made from scraps of many different kinds of material. What materials in her mother's quilts does the speaker remember? Make a list of them.

4. What decisions does her mother have to make as she plans her quilts? See lines 30–36.

5. Beginning in line 37 of "My Mother Pieced Quilts," the speaker identifies her mother with two things. What are they?

6. In lines 44–51, the speaker says that the quilts make her remember her family history. What can you **infer,** or guess, about that history, based on the details in these lines?

7. Who is speaking in "Sweater"?

8. What does the speaker of "Sweater" ask the grandmother to do?

Interpretations

9. **Personification** is a figure of speech in which an inanimate object is given human or lifelike qualities. List three or more examples of personification in Acosta's description of the quilts.

10. What would you say the quilts **symbolize** for the speaker of "My Mother Pieced Quilts"?

11. What does the speaker of "Sweater" compare the sweater to? Do you think he would have used this comparison if the poem had been addressed to his sister?

12. Would you have known what "Sweater" was about without having read the title? Explain why or why not.

Evaluation

13. If you know Spanish, check the translation of "Suéter." What word has the translator omitted from the English translation? What do you think of this omission?

Writing
My Symbol

In your Quickwrite you took notes on an object that symbolizes something important to you. In a paragraph or a poem, describe the object, and tell what you remember when you see it, taste it, smell it, or feel it. If you write a poem, you could imitate the style used by Acosta. Try to use figures of speech in your poem or paragraph.

Reading Standard 3.6 Identify significant literary devices (for example, symbolism) that define a writer's style, and use those elements to interpret the work.

Vocabulary Development

More on Metaphors

Metaphors are an important part of everyday speech. They make our language colorful and fun. They are even more essential to poetry. It would be unusual to find a poem without at least one metaphor in it.

PRACTICE 1

The following statements refer to metaphors in "My Mother Pieced Quilts." For each statement, tell what is being compared to what. Then, explain how the metaphor works—what is the poet *saying* about the quilts and the quilter in each metaphor? In some cases you will have to use your imagination. The first one has been completed for you.

1. Quilts were meant as <u>weapons against pounding january winds</u>.
   Answer: Quilts are compared to weapons. The metaphor means that the quilts protect the sleeper against the cold winds of January, just as weapons may protect someone from harm.
2. Quilts are <u>october ripened canvases</u>.
3. The quilter is said to have <u>cemented</u> the quilt pieces with her thread.
4. The thread is described as <u>galloping along the frayed edges</u>.
5. The speaker says the quilt maker was <u>the river current / carrying the roaring notes</u>.
6. The speaker says the quilt maker was <u>the caravan master at the reins / driving your threaded needle artillery across the mosaic cloth bridges</u>.
7. The quilts are said to be <u>armed/ready/shouting/celebrating</u>.
8. In the last line, the quilts <u>sing</u> on.

PRACTICE 2

For fun, make a drawing of the literal meanings of one or more of the images above. For example, for item 8, you could draw several quilts with faces, singing into microphones.

A word is dead *and* The Word / La palabra

Literary Focus
Figures of Speech

Figures of speech are important tools of poetry—and all imaginative writing. Figures of speech are built on comparisons and are not literally true. The two most common figures of speech are the metaphor and the simile.

- The **metaphor** directly compares two very different things: *The moon was a golden grapefruit high up in the sky.*

- The **simile** also compares two distinct things, but it does so using a word or phrase of comparison—such as *like, such as, as, than,* or *resembles: The moon looked like a gleaming new penny.*

A third common figure of speech is **personification,** in which a nonhuman or inanimate (not living) thing is described as if it were human or alive and did something that only living things do: *The moon smiled down on all the creatures of the forest. The wind tapped at my window.*

Make the Connection
Quickwrite

We all use words every day to communicate our needs, our thoughts, our feelings. But what do words themselves mean to you? Are they tools you use without thinking about them? Do you hate them for their hidden meanings or because you forget their definitions when you have to take a test? Do you delight in their possibilities and their variety? Jot down whatever comes into your mind when you think about words.

Reading Standard 3.6 Identify significant literary devices that define a writer's style, and use those elements to interpret the work.

A word is dead

Emily Dickinson

A word is dead
When it is said,
Some say.

I say it just
Begins to live
That day.

Sketch of a rabbit by
Seiho Takeuchi.

The Word

Manuel Ulacia

comes out from the pen
like a rabbit from a magician's hat
astronaut who knows itself alone
and weightless suspended on a line
in space

—*translated by* Jennifer Clement

La palabra

Manuel Ulacia

sale de la pluma
como el conejo del sombrero de un mago
astronauta que se sabe sola y sin peso
suspendida en una línea
en el espacio

Emily Dickinson

"Letter to the World"

Although today **Emily Dickinson** (1830–1886) is one of the most respected poets in the world, her work was almost completely unknown during her lifetime. Dickinson led an extremely private life in her family home in Amherst, Massachusetts. After she died, her sister Lavinia discovered the poems— almost eighteen hundred—that Dickinson had gathered into handmade booklets. Dickinson said that her poems were her "letter to the world" that never wrote to her.

Manuel Ulacia

Professor and Poet

When **Manuel Ulacia** (1954–   ) was a student, he studied architecture as well as literature. He went on to become a professor at Yale University and has also taught at Mexico City's Universidad Autónoma. In addition to his own poetry, Ulacia has studied and written about the work of his mentor, Octavio Paz, a Latin American poet and essayist who won the Nobel Prize in 1990.

Literary Response and Analysis

Reading Check

1. What is the subject of each poem?
2. In Emily Dickinson's poem, what do some people say happens to a word when it is spoken? What does the speaker say happens?

Interpretations

3. Dickinson uses **personification** when she says that a word begins to "live." How do you think a word can begin to live after it has been spoken?
4. What do the **similes** in lines 2–4 of Ulacia's poem make you see?
5. A children's rhyme goes, "Sticks and stones / Can break my bones / But names can never hurt me." How would Dickinson feel about that saying? How do you feel about it?

Evaluation

6. If you know Spanish, read the original text of Ulacia's poem aloud. Does it use rhyme? What is your evaluation of the translation into English?

Writing

A Word Is . . .

Before you read these poems, you took notes on your own feelings about words. Refer to your notes now, and write a paragraph—or a poem—expressing your personal feelings about words. Try to use some comparisons in your work: What do words remind *you* of? You could start off with Dickinson's beginning: "A word is . . ."

Words, Words, Words

Write a brief story for children, using a word as a character. It could be a particular word—*blue*, for example. Think of your word as a person; let your word tell how he or she is used and how he or she feels about other people and the way they use language. You can tell your story in the form of a poem or as a brief narrative. Illustrations would be more than acceptable.

Reading Standard 3.6
Identify significant literary devices that define a writer's style, and use those elements to interpret the work.

Vocabulary Development

Metaphors, Similes, and Personification

The most common figures of speech are metaphors, similes, and personification. **Metaphors** directly compare two unlike things. **Similes** also compare two unlike things but use *like*, *than*, *as*, or *resembles* to introduce the comparison. **Personification** gives human or lifelike qualities or behavior to nonhuman things.

PRACTICE

The following lines from famous poems include figures of speech. Decide if each quotation uses a metaphor, a simile, or personification. (Watch out: Personification is a type of metaphor.) Then, tell what two things are being compared.

1. "'Hope' is the thing with feathers" —Emily Dickinson
2. "I wandered lonely as a cloud" —William Wordsworth
3. "The road was a ribbon of moonlight" —Alfred Noyes
4. "O my Luve is like a red, red rose" —Robert Burns
5. "I hear America singing . . ." —Walt Whitman
6. "The sea is a hungry dog, / Giant and gray. / He rolls on the beach all day." —James Reeves
7. "The fog comes / on little cat feet" —Carl Sandburg
8. "I stepped on the toe / Of an unemployed hoe. It rose in offense / And struck me a blow. . . ." —Robert Frost

Reading Standard 1.1 Analyze metaphors and similes to infer the literal and figurative meanings of phrases.

Literary Response and Analysis

DIRECTIONS: Read the following little story. Then, read each multiple-choice question, and on a separate sheet of paper, write the letter of the best response.

Gil's Furniture Bought & Sold

Sandra Cisneros

There is a junk store. An old man owns it. We bought a used refrigerator from him once, and Carlos sold a box of magazines for a dollar. The store is small with just a dirty window for light. He doesn't turn the lights on unless you got money to buy things with, so in the dark we look and see all kinds of things, me and Nenny. Tables with their feet upside-down and rows and rows of refrigerators with round corners and couches that spin dust in the air when you punch them and a hundred T.V.'s that don't work probably. Everything is on top of everything so the whole store has skinny aisles to walk through. You can get lost easy.

The owner, he is a black man who doesn't talk much and sometimes if you didn't know better you could be in there a long time before your eyes notice a pair of gold glasses floating in the dark. Nenny who thinks she is smart and talks to any old man, asks lots of questions. Me, I never said nothing to him except once when I bought the Statue of Liberty for a dime.

But Nenny, I hear her asking one time how's this here and the man says, This, this is a music box, and I turn around quick thinking he means a *pretty* box with flowers painted on it, with a ballerina inside. Only there's nothing like that where this old man is pointing, just a wood box that's old and got a big brass record in it with holes. Then he starts it up and all sorts of things start happening. It's like all of a sudden he let go a million moths all over the dusty furniture and swan-neck shadows and in our bones. It's like drops of water. Or like marimbas only with a funny little plucked sound to it like if you were running your fingers across the teeth of a metal comb.

And then I don't know why, but I have to turn around and pretend I don't care about the box so Nenny won't see how stupid I am. But Nenny, who is stupider, already is asking how much and I can see her fingers going for the quarters in her pants pocket.

This, the old man says shutting the lid, this ain't for sale.

Reading Standard 3.6 Identify significant literary devices (for example, metaphor, symbolism, dialect, irony) that define a writer's style, and use those elements to interpret the work.

1. Cisneros writes: "Me, I never said nothing to him" and "I hear her asking one time how's this here." She uses **dialect** to do all of the following *except* —

   A give her characters a voice

   B make her characters come alive

   C make fun of her characters

   D show how her characters really speak

2. The narrator of this story says, "It's like all of a sudden he let go a million moths all over the dusty furniture and swan-neck shadows and in our bones." She uses these **figures of speech** to describe —

   F the magical power of music

   G how dirty the owner keeps his store

   H how creepy she thinks insects are

   J the animal shadows on the walls of the store

3. When the narrator says that the music is "like drops of water," she is using —

   A a simile

   B a metaphor

   C personification

   D irony

4. This little story is told by —

   F Nenny

   G Gil, the store owner

   H a young narrator who speaks as "I"

   J Carlos

5. The narrator turns around "so Nenny won't see how stupid I am." She is embarrassed —

   A because she has no money for the music box

   B by how much she likes the music

   C to be in such a dusty junk shop

   D to be seen with Nenny

6. When the narrator says that Nenny is "stupider" than she is, she is using **verbal irony.** What she really means is that —

   F Nenny is as moved by the music as she is

   G she's mad because Nenny has enough money to buy the box

   H she doesn't think Nenny is smart

   J she is embarrassed to be seen with Nenny

7. The **situational irony** in this story involves the fact that —

   A the girls are in an uncomfortable situation

   B the girls find beauty in a dirty, messy junk store

   C the junk store is dirty and crowded

   D the junk store is full of moths

8. For the narrator, the store owner, and Nenny, the music box is a **symbol** of —

   F joy that can come from surprising places

   G the store owner's inability to sell anything

   H how old things are just junk

   J the girls' love of shopping

Vocabulary Development

TestPractice

Synonyms

DIRECTIONS: Choose the word or words that mean the same, or about the same, as the underlined word. These are the words you learned while reading "The Tell-Tale Heart."

1. Acute means —
   A heavy
   B sharp
   C full
   D attractive

2. Sagacity means —
   F intelligence
   G sneakiness
   H safety
   J innocence

3. Refrained means —
   A redid
   B directed
   C held back
   D trained

4. Vexed means —
   F cursed
   G voted
   H annoyed
   J announced

5. Derision means —
   A decision
   B ridicule
   C division
   D pleasure

6. Audacity means —
   F boldness
   G bitterness
   H speediness
   J niceness

7. Wary means —
   A nice
   B very
   C annoyed
   D cautious

8. Vehemently means —
   F forcefully
   G verbally
   H viciously
   J gently

9. Suavity means —
   A smoothness
   B safety
   C seriousness
   D carelessness

10. Gesticulations are —
    F funny jokes
    G energetic gestures
    H angry words
    J math problems

Mastering the Standards

DESCRIPTION

Make It Real

In "Raymond's Run," Squeaky describes scenes in her neighborhood, such as the old people sitting in the sun on Broadway. Write a description of a place you know well. You might focus on your house or apartment building, your school bus or classroom, a mall or movie complex, your backyard or kitchen. In your description, include **factual details** (*My building has six floors with four apartments on each floor*) and **sensory details** that will help your readers see, hear, touch, smell, even taste your place (*As I climb the stairs, I smell fried dumplings from 1A, spaghetti sauce from 2B, pot roast from 3D, and chili from 4C*). You might even include **figures of speech** that will tell your reader what this place reminds you of (*In the morning the building sounds like a drum band, with dogs barking, doors slamming, and footsteps clumping down the stairs*). To collect details for your description, fill in a chart like this one:

 Use **"Writing a Descriptive Essay," pages 768–770, for help with this assignment.**

Place: _____
What I observe (see):
What I hear, smell, taste, touch:
What I am reminded of:

Other Choices

DESCRIPTION

1 Sell Your Product

For an electronic bulletin board posting, write a description of something you want to sell or give away, such as the bike or dollhouse you have outgrown or the kittens that are ready to leave their mama. Use specific details that are both **factual** (*seven weeks old*) and **appealing** (*soft, friendly, housebroken*).

▶ Use **"Writing a Descriptive Essay," pages 768–770, for help with this assignment.**

DESCRIPTION

2 To the Touch

Write a poem describing how things in your neighborhood feel. Start by listing images describing textures and temperatures (*soft grass, rough bricks, cold railings*). Then, think of **figures of speech**—metaphors, similes, personification—that will help your reader feel the details too (*fuzzy dandelions tickle like my kitten's whiskers*). You may want to write each image and figure of speech on a small slip of paper and then tape or paste the slips onto a large sheet of paper. Put your details in the order you like best. There! You have "found" a poem.

Fiction *and* Poetry

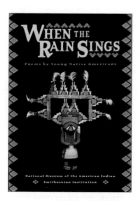

Making Their Voices Heard

When the Rain Sings is a collection of poetry written by Native Americans ages seven through seventeen. These young writers look back on their own lives and the history of their people in their lively, moving poems. Accompanying the poems are photographs of Native American ancestors and artifacts, along with historical overviews of each of the eight peoples represented in the book.

The Loner

You know her: the new kid in class no one wants for a friend. In *The Friends* by Rosa Guy, the new girl is Phyllisia Cathy, and she is from the West Indies. The only person who will befriend her is Edith, a Harlem-born girl trying to keep her family together despite the hardships of poverty.

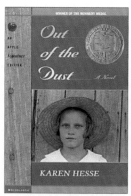

Picking Up the Pieces

While dust storms are devastating her family's Oklahoma farm in 1934, Billie Jo finds joy only in playing the piano. Then a terrible accident takes that joy away and changes her life forever. *Out of the Dust*, Karen Hesse's Newbery Medal–winning novel, tells the story of Billie Jo's coming to terms with her struggles and misfortunes. The story is told through a series of free-verse poems written in everyday language.

Survival of the Fittest

Young Brian finds himself stranded alone in the Canadian wilderness after a plane crash. With only his wits and a hatchet to rely on for survival, Brian learns some memorable lessons about nature, growing up, and himself in Gary Paulsen's Newbery Honor book *Hatchet*.

This title is available in the HRW Library.

Nonfiction

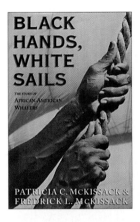

Finally Recognized

In *Black Hands, White Sails,* Patricia C. and Fredrick L. McKissack bring attention to African Americans who worked in the whaling industry from Colonial times until the nineteenth century. Some were to become captains and shipowners, and others played key roles in the Civil War and the Underground Railroad.

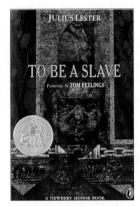

From Slavery to Freedom

In *To Be a Slave,* a Newbery Honor book by Julius Lester, men and women who lived through slavery tell their stories in their own words. Lester's *Long Journey Home,* six true stories of freedom, is an uplifting sequel.

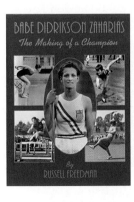

Battling the Odds

The athletic achievements of Babe Didrikson Zaharias could probably fill a book as large as this one! For starters, she was a championship golfer, a gold medalist in track and field, and an outstanding basketball player. More impressive, her accomplishments took place at a time when women had few opportunities for competition. Russell Freedman tells her story in *Babe Didrikson Zaharias: The Making of a Champion.*

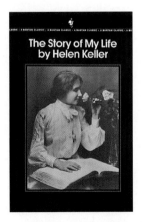

A Portrait of Bravery

Even though Helen Keller was left blind and deaf by an illness when she was nineteen months old, she was determined to read and write. In *The Story of My Life,* Keller writes about her refusal to give up in the face of unthinkable adversity. The book includes letters she wrote to friends and personal records that will lead readers to a greater understanding of her life.

6

Sound and Sense
Forms of Poetry

California Standards

Here are the Grade 8 standards you will study for mastery in Chapter 6:

Reading

Reading Comprehension (Focus on Informational Materials)

2.4 Compare the original text to a summary to determine whether the summary accurately captures the main ideas, includes critical details, and conveys the underlying meaning.

Literary Response and Analysis

3.1 Determine and articulate the relationship between the purposes and characteristics of different forms of poetry (for example, ballad, lyric, couplet, epic, elegy, ode, sonnet).

KEYWORD:
HLLA 8-6

Poetry *by* Mara Rockliff
SOUND AND SENSE

Words with Their Own Music

Did you ever unwrap a new CD and read the song lyrics before playing the disc? Often the words by themselves don't seem all that special. It takes music to bring them to life.

Poetry is different. The words in a good poem create their own music. The English poet Samuel Taylor Coleridge once defined poetry as "the best words in their best order." Listen to how one of his own poems begins:

> In Xanadu did Kubla Khan
> A stately pleasure-dome decree:
> Where Alph, the sacred river, ran
> Through caverns measureless to man
> Down to a sunless sea.
> —from "Kubla Khan"

All Coleridge gave us were words on a page, and yet more than two centuries after he wrote them down, the music still comes through. How did he do it?

Moving to the Beat

If words can create the haunting music of a poem, **rhythm**—the repetition of stressed and unstressed syllables—provides the poem's beat. Like many other languages, English is accented: Certain syllables get a stronger beat than other syllables. The beat of a poem comes from the patterns made by the stressed and unstressed syllables. If you say a few English words aloud, you'll hear the beat built into them: MOUN-tain, be-CAUSE, Cin-cin-NAT-i. Say your name aloud, and notice its beat.

Read aloud this little elegy (an **elegy** is a poem for someone who has died). Listen to the way your voice rises and falls as you pronounce the stressed and unstressed syllables.

For My Grandmother
This lovely flower fell to seed;
  Work gently, sun and rain;
She held it as her dying creed
  That she would grow again.
—Countee Cullen

You probably stressed the words this way (**'** indicates a stressed syllable; ˘ indicates an unstressed syllable):

˘ ' ˘ ' ˘ ' ˘ '
This lovely flower fell to seed.

A regular pattern of stressed and unstressed syllables is called **meter.** Cullen's simple meter, along with the short, plain words and few, short lines, helps us share the simple loveliness and faith Cullen saw in his grandmother.

Chiming Sounds

The chiming effect of **rhyme** adds to the music of a poem, like the tinkling of a bell or the clash of cymbals. Most rhymes

Reading Standard 3.1
Determine and articulate the relationship between the purposes and characteristics of different forms of poetry (for example, ballad, lyric, couplet, epic, elegy, ode, sonnet).

in poetry are **end rhymes.** In "For My Grandmother" the end rhymes are *seed* and *creed*, *rain* and *again* (pronounced the old-fashioned way, ə·gān′). When the two rhyming lines are consecutive, they're called a **couplet.** Here is a couplet with end rhymes that are spelled differently—but they rhyme:

The panther is like a leopard,
Except it hasn't been peppered.
　　　　　—Ogden Nash,
　　　　　　from "The Panther"

Rhymes can also occur within lines; these are called **internal rhymes.**

While I nodded, nearly napping,
　　suddenly there came a tapping,
As of someone gently rapping, rapping
　　at my chamber door—

　　　　　　—Edgar Allan Poe,
　　　　　　from "The Raven"

Napping, *tapping*, and *rapping* are **exact rhymes,** as are *leopard* and *peppered*. Many modern poets prefer **approximate rhymes** (also called near rhymes, off rhymes, imperfect rhymes, or slant rhymes). Approximate rhymes use sounds that are similar but not exactly the same, like *fellow* and *hollow* or *cat* and *catch* or *bat* and *bit*.

Some people think approximate rhymes sound less artificial than exact rhymes, more like real speech. Some poets use approximate rhymes because they feel that all the good exact rhymes have already been used too many times.

The Beat Goes On

Many poets today prefer to work in **free verse.** With free verse they do not have to write in meter or use a regular rhyme scheme, but that doesn't mean that "anything goes." Even when they write free verse, poets work to make their lines rhythmic. One way they do this is by repeating sentence patterns. You can't miss the rhythm in these lines by Walt Whitman, one of the first American poets to use free verse:

Give me the splendid silent sun with
　　all his beams full-dazzling,
Give me juicy autumnal fruit ripe and
　　red from the orchard,
Give me a field where the unmowed
　　grass grows,
Give me an arbor, give me the trellised
　　grape . . .
　　　　　　—from "Give Me the
　　　　　　Splendid Silent Sun"

Meter and rhyme aren't the only ways in which a poet can create music with words. Note all the *s* sounds as you read aloud this line from "The Raven":

And the silken, sad, uncertain rustling
　　of each purple curtain

Do you hear the rustling of that curtain in all those *s* sounds? This is **alliteration** (ə·lit′ər·ā′shən), the repetition of consonant sounds in several words that are close together. When vowel sounds are repeated, it's called **assonance** (as′ə·nəns).

(continued)

Poe's line also provides an example of **onomatopoeia** (än'ō·mat'ō·pē'ə), a long word that refers to the use of words with sounds that imitate or suggest their meaning—such as *rustle*. Doesn't *sizzle* sound like bacon frying on the grill? How about *snap*, *crackle*, *pop*? Words like these help poets bring sound and sense together.

Some Types of Poems

ballad: songlike poem that tells a story, often a sad story of betrayal, death, or loss. Ballads usually have a regular, steady rhythm, a simple rhyme pattern, and a refrain, all of which make them easy to memorize.

epic: long narrative poem about the many deeds of a great hero. Epics are closely connected to a particular culture. The hero of an epic embodies the important values of the society he comes from. (Heroes of epics have—so far—been male.)

narrative poem: poem that tells a story—a series of related events.

lyric poem: poem that does not tell a story but expresses the personal feelings of a speaker.

ode: long lyric poem, usually praising some subject, and written in dignified language.

sonnet: fourteen-line lyric poem that follows strict rules of structure, meter, and rhyme.

Practice

Find a poem you like, and prepare it for reading aloud. Here are some tips:

- Be aware of punctuation, especially periods and commas. A period signals the end of a sentence—which is not always at the end of a line. You should make a full stop when you come to a period.
- If a line of poetry doesn't end with punctuation, don't stop. Continue reading until you reach a punctuation mark.
- If the poem is written in meter, don't read it in a singsong way. Read the poem for its meaning, using a natural voice. Let the music come through on its own.

"I think that I shall never see, a poem as lovely as a bee, flea, sea, ski, plea, key . . ."

Valentine for Ernest Mann

Literary Focus
Lyric Poetry

Poems can tell stories, or they can just express the personal feelings or thoughts of the speaker. Poems that express feelings and do not tell stories are called **lyrics.** Lyric poems are usually short, and they imply—rather than state directly—a single, strong emotion. The word *lyric* comes from the word *lyre* (līr), which refers to a stringed instrument something like a small harp. In ancient Greece, people used to recite poems to the strumming of a lyre. (At poetry readings today music is still sometimes used to set the beat or create atmosphere.)

Reading Skills
Reading a Poem

All reading requires skill, but you may have to work a little harder to read a poem well. You'll find it easier if you use these strategies:

1. **Pay attention to punctuation.** Most poetry is written in sentences, but the sentences don't necessarily end at the ends of lines. Don't stop reading at the end of a line unless you see punctuation there. Pause briefly for a comma, colon, semicolon, or dash, but don't make a full stop till you come to a period. If a poet doesn't use any punctuation (some poets don't), it's up to you to figure out where a sentence—or a thought—begins and ends.

2. **Find the subject and verb.** When you are confused by a passage, look for the subject and verb. Then, decide how the other words in the sentence are used. Usually you'll find that they are modifiers.

3. **Look for figures of speech.** Figurative language is at the heart of most poems. Look for **metaphors** and **similes.** What comparisons are they revealing to you?

4. **Listen to the poem.** Read a poem aloud. You may find that the sounds add meaning to the poem.

5. **Read it again.** Read a poem over till you feel it's "yours."

6. **Have fun.** Poems are not written to torment you. Even the most serious poem, written to express the deepest emotion, involves a kind of play. Poets play with words, sounds, rhythms, rhymes. As you work at interpreting a poem, you are playing a game with the poet.

Make the Connection
Quickwrite ✏️

Think about the poems you have read or heard. Do you have any favorites? What do you think most poems are about? Jot down some of your feelings about poetry. Then, see if the poem that follows surprises you.

Reading Standard 3.1 Determine and articulate the relationship between the purposes and characteristics of different forms of poetry (for example, lyric).

Valentine for Ernest Mann

Naomi Shihab Nye

You can't order a poem like you order a taco.
Walk up to the counter, say, "I'll take two"
and expect it to be handed back to you
on a shiny plate.

5   Still, I like your spirit.
Anyone who says, "Here's my address,
write me a poem," deserves something in reply.
So I'll tell a secret instead:
poems hide. In the bottoms of our shoes,
10   they are sleeping. They are the shadows
drifting across our ceilings the moment
before we wake up. What we have to do
is live in a way that lets us find them.

Once I knew a man who gave his wife
15   two skunks for a valentine.
He couldn't understand why she was crying.
"I thought they had such beautiful eyes."
And he was serious. He was a serious man
who lived in a serious way. Nothing was ugly
20   just because the world said so. He really
liked those skunks. So, he re-invented them
as valentines and they became beautiful.
At least, to him. And the poems that had been hiding
in the eyes of skunks for centuries
25   crawled out and curled up at his feet.

Maybe if we re-invent whatever our lives give us
we find poems. Check your garage, the odd sock
in your drawer, the person you almost like, but not quite.
And let me know.

Naomi Shihab Nye

A Poet of the Familiar

Naomi Shihab Nye (1952–   ) often runs workshops in schools to help students find the poetry hidden in their imaginations. Nye grew up in St. Louis, lived in Jerusalem with her father's family for a year, and settled in San Antonio, Texas. Since Nye was born to an American mother and a Palestinian father, it's not surprising that she often celebrates in her writing the diversity of American culture. Wherever she lived, Nye carefully observed the activities of her friends and neighbors:

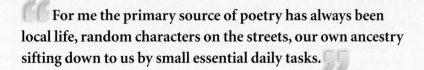

> For me the primary source of poetry has always been local life, random characters on the streets, our own ancestry sifting down to us by small essential daily tasks.

These "daily tasks" have continually inspired some of Nye's most powerful work. She can make the tiniest details seem exceptional. She once said:

> Familiar sights, sounds, smells have always been my necessities. Let someone else think about future goals and professional lives! I will keep track of the bucket and the hoe, billowing leaves, and clouds drifting in from the horizon.

For Independent Reading

Nye's first young-adult novel, *Habibi*, is autobiographical, about an American teenager who, on moving to Jerusalem, finds that suddenly *she* is the immigrant.

Literary Response and Analysis

Reading Check

1. What do you know about Ernest Mann, the person this poem is addressed to?

2. What reason does the speaker give for writing this poem?

3. What secret about poetry does the speaker share with Ernest Mann?

4. What reason did the man in the poem give for choosing two skunks for a valentine?

5. Where does the speaker say we might find poems?

Interpretations

6. In the first stanza the poet uses a **simile.** What two very different things is she comparing? What is she saying about poems by using this simile?

7. In the second stanza the poet **personifies** poems. What human things does she say poems can do? What is she telling us about poems by using this figure of speech?

8. The second stanza also includes a **metaphor.** What are poems compared to? What does this metaphor tell us about poems?

9. Why does the speaker tell us about the man and the skunks in the third stanza? (What do skunks have to do with poetry?)

10. What final advice does the speaker give Ernest Mann?

Writing

Finding a Poem

Follow Naomi Shihab Nye's advice, and try to find a lyric poem in your life. Use words that will help your reader see or touch or smell an object or person the way you do. Help your reader feel the way you feel about the object or person. For a structure you might spell out the name of your subject and start each line with a letter of the word, as in this example:

Soggy socks hang on the line,
Or rest in my drawer rolled up and dry.
Crew socks once smelly,
Kneesocks once fuzzy,
Soon will look like new!

Paul Revere's Ride

Literary Focus
Narrative Poem

A **narrative poem** is a poem that tells a story. The poem you are about to read tells an exciting story about a historical event.

Galloping Rhythm

People love rhythm. We love the rhythm of music, the rhythm of dance, the rhythm of our language. Rhythm is not only pleasing to the ear (and eye); it also affects our moods. A slow rhythm can make us feel sad or dreamy. A fast rhythm can make us feel like dancing. Rhythm is as essential to language as it is to music. In language, **rhythm** is the rise and fall of the voice, produced by sounds. When the sounds occur in a particular pattern, we call it **meter.**

"Paul Revere's Ride" is written with a strong meter. Notice, when you read it aloud, how the meter sounds like a galloping horse: da da DUM da da DUM da da DUM da da DUM. The story of Paul Revere has been told many times and in many different ways, but this poem is the most famous version of what happened on that fateful night. What makes everyone remember this poem is its rhythm.

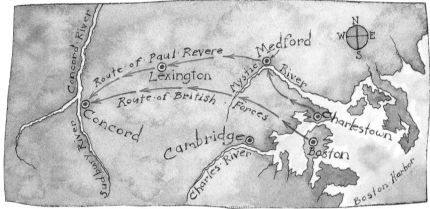

Make the Connection
Quickwrite ✏️

Many countries have heroes whom they honor for their courage in standing up for justice and freedom. Work with a partner to make a list of some of these heroes. Tell who they are, what country honors them, and what they did to help their people.

Background

This poem is based loosely on historical events. On the night of April 18, 1775, Paul Revere, William Dawes, and Dr. Samuel Prescott set out from Boston to warn American colonists of a planned British raid on Concord, Massachusetts. The British wanted to arrest two Americans who were calling for armed resistance to England. The British also wanted to destroy a supply of arms in Concord. The next day armed volunteers known as minutemen confronted the British at Lexington and Concord. These were the first battles of the American Revolution.

Reading Standard 3.1 Determine and articulate the relationship between the purposes and characteristics of different forms of poetry.

Paul Revere's Ride

Henry Wadsworth Longfellow

Listen, my children, and you shall hear
Of the midnight ride of Paul Revere,
On the eighteenth of April, in Seventy-five;
Hardly a man is now alive
5   Who remembers that famous day and year.

He said to his friend, "If the British march
By land or sea from the town tonight,
Hang a lantern aloft in the belfry° arch
Of the North Church tower as a signal light—
10   One, if by land, and two, if by sea;
And I on the opposite shore will be,
Ready to ride and spread the alarm
Through every Middlesex village and farm,
For the country folk to be up and to arm."

15   Then he said, "Good night!" and with muffled oar
Silently rowed to the Charlestown shore,
Just as the moon rose over the bay,
Where swinging wide at her moorings° lay
The Somerset, British man-of-war;
20   A phantom ship, with each mast and spar°
Across the moon like a prison bar,
And a huge black hulk, that was magnified
By its own reflection in the tide.

Meanwhile, his friend, through alley and street,
25   Wanders and watches with eager ears,
Till in the silence around him he hears
The muster° of men at the barrack door,
The sound of arms, and the tramp of feet,

---

8. **belfry** (bel′frē) *n.* used as *adj.*: steeple of a church where bells are hung.
18. **moorings** *n.*: cables holding a ship in place so that it doesn't float away.
20. **mast and spar**: poles supporting a ship's sails.
27. **muster** *n.*: assembly; gathering.

And the measured tread of the grenadiers,°
30 Marching down to their boats on the shore.

Then he climbed the tower of the Old North Church,
By the wooden stairs, with stealthy tread,
To the belfry chamber overhead,
And startled the pigeons from their perch
35 On the somber rafters, that round him made
Masses and moving shapes of shade—
By the trembling ladder, steep and tall,
To the highest window in the wall,
Where he paused to listen and look down
40 A moment on the roofs of the town,
And the moonlight flowing over all.

Beneath, in the churchyard, lay the dead,
In their night encampment on the hill,
Wrapped in silence so deep and still
45 That he could hear, like a sentinel's° tread,
The watchful night wind, as it went
Creeping along from tent to tent,
And seeming to whisper, "All is well!"
A moment only he feels the spell
50 Of the place and the hour, and the secret dread
Of the lonely belfry and the dead;
For suddenly all his thoughts are bent
On a shadowy something far away,
Where the river widens to meet the bay—
55 A line of black that bends and floats
On the rising tide, like a bridge of boats.

Meanwhile, impatient to mount and ride,
Booted and spurred, with a heavy stride
On the opposite shore walked Paul Revere.
60 Now he patted his horse's side,
Now gazed at the landscape far and near,
Then, impetuous,° stamped the earth,
And turned and tightened his saddle girth;

---

29. grenadiers (gren′ə·dirz′) *n.:* foot soldiers who carry and throw grenades.
45. sentinel's: guard's.
62. impetuous (im·pech′o͞o·əs) *adj.:* impulsive; eager.

The Midnight Ride of Paul Revere (detail) (1985) by Barbara Olsen.
Oil on canvas.

But mostly he watched with eager search
65 The belfry tower of the Old North Church,
As it rose above the graves on the hill,
Lonely and spectral° and somber and still.
And lo! as he looks, on the belfry's height
A glimmer, and then a gleam of light!
70 He springs to the saddle, the bridle he turns,
But lingers and gazes, till full on his sight
A second lamp in the belfry burns!

A hurry of hoofs in a village street,
A shape in the moonlight, a bulk in the dark,
75 And beneath, from the pebbles, in passing, a spark
Struck out by a steed flying fearless and fleet:
That was all! And yet, through the gloom and the light,
The fate of a nation was riding that night;
And the spark struck out by that steed, in his flight,
80 Kindled the land into flame with its heat.

---

67. spectral *adj.*: ghostly.

He has left the village and mounted the steep,
And beneath him, tranquil and broad and deep,
Is the Mystic, meeting the ocean tides;
And under the alders° that skirt its edge,
85 Now soft on the sand, now loud on the ledge,
Is heard the tramp of his steed as he rides.

It was twelve by the village clock,
When he crossed the bridge into Medford town.
He heard the crowing of the cock,
90 And the barking of the farmer's dog,
And felt the damp of the river fog,
That rises after the sun goes down.

It was one by the village clock,
When he galloped into Lexington.
95 He saw the gilded weathercock°
Swim in the moonlight as he passed,
And the meetinghouse windows, blank and bare,
Gaze at him with a spectral glare,
As if they already stood aghast°
100 At the bloody work they would look upon.

It was two by the village clock,
When he came to the bridge in Concord town.
He heard the bleating of the flock,
And the twitter of birds among the trees,
105 And felt the breath of the morning breeze
Blowing over the meadows brown.
And one was safe and asleep in his bed
Who at the bridge would be first to fall,
Who that day would be lying dead,
110 Pierced by a British musket ball.

You know the rest. In the books you have read,
How the British Regulars fired and fled—
How the farmers gave them ball for ball,

---

84. **alders** (ôl′dərz) *n.*: shrubs and trees of the birch family.
95. **weathercock** *n.*: weathervane made to look like a rooster (cock).
   Weathervanes indicate the direction in which the wind is blowing.
99. **aghast** (ə·gast′) *adj.*: shocked; horrified.

From behind each fence and farmyard wall,
115 Chasing the redcoats down the lane,
Then crossing the fields to emerge again
Under the trees at the turn of the road,
And only pausing to fire and load.

So through the night rode Paul Revere;
120 And so through the night went his cry of alarm
To every Middlesex village and farm—
A cry of defiance and not of fear,
A voice in the darkness, a knock at the door,
And a word that shall echo forevermore!
125 For, borne on the night wind of the Past,
Through all our history, to the last,
In the hour of darkness and peril and need,
The people will waken and listen to hear
The hurrying hoofbeats of that steed,
130 And the midnight message of Paul Revere.

MEET THE WRITER

Henry Wadsworth Longfellow

"Footprints on the Sands of Time"

If you went to school a hundred years ago, you and all your friends would probably be able to recite by heart several of the poems of **Henry Wadsworth Longfellow** (1807–1882). Born in Portland, Maine, Longfellow became the most popular poet of his day. Many of Longfellow's poems, such as *Evangeline* (1847), *The Song of Hiawatha* (1855), and *The Courtship of Miles Standish* (1858), were inspired by people and events in American history. As "Paul Revere's Ride" shows,

Henry Wadsworth Longfellow (1871) by Theodore Wust. Watercolor on ivory.
National Portrait Gallery, Smithsonian Institution, Washington, D.C./Art Resource, N.Y.

Longfellow believed that one person's actions could make a difference. In an early piece of verse, he wrote:

> Lives of great men all remind us
> We can make our lives sublime.
> And, departing, leave behind us
> Footprints on the sands of time.

Literary Response and Analysis

Reading Check

1. What is the purpose of Paul Revere's ride?

2. Describe the system of signals Revere arranges with his friend. What signal does he finally see?

3. A **narrative poem** relates a series of events, just as a short story does. Trace the main events of Revere's ride, as it is described in lines 81–106.

4. According to Longfellow, what were the results of Revere's midnight ride?

Interpretations

5. Read aloud the first stanza. Then, mark its stressed and unstressed syllables to indicate its **meter.** You will notice that the poet varies the pattern to avoid monotony. One thing that never varies is the stress on the last syllable of each line. (For help in marking the syllables, see page 402.)

6. What does the poet mean when he says, "The fate of a nation was riding that night" (line 78)? What does he mean by saying that the spark struck by the horse's hoof "kindled the land into flame" (line 80)?

7. What do you think the word or words are "that shall echo forever-more" (line 124)? Write what Revere might have said as he knocked on each door.

8. Re-read the last six lines of the poem. Why does the poet believe that "in the hour of darkness and peril and need," Americans will remember Paul Revere's message? What significance do you think this story has today?

9. What other Paul Reveres, from history or living today, have rallied their people with cries "of defiance and not of fear" (line 122)?

Writing

A New Narrative

"Paul Revere's Ride" is a **narrative poem,** that is, a poem that tells a story. Think of an exciting story you could tell using a strong **rhythm** just like the meter in this poem. Open your poem with Longfellow's first line. Your story could be based on a real or an imaginary person. For example, you might begin:

Listen, my children, and you shall hear
Of the scooter ride of Lily de Vere.

Reading Standard 3.1 Determine and articulate the relationship between the purposes and characteristics of different forms of poetry.

The Cremation of Sam McGee *and* The Dying Cowboy *and* Maiden-Savin' Sam

Literary Focus
Ballad

A **ballad** is a song or a songlike poem that tells a story, usually about lost love or betrayal or death. Ballads can be sad or humorous. They usually use simple language and a great deal of repetition, including a refrain. Their simple, regular meters and their rhyme patterns make them easy to memorize. All those sound patterns also make ballads fun to sing or read aloud.

The most famous ballads are old songs that were passed on orally for many years before they were written down. The authors of these old ballads are unknown, and the songs were often changed as they were handed down. That's why the most popular ballads come in many versions.

The strange story of Sam McGee is not a ballad in this traditional sense. After all, we know who wrote the poem. However, its writer calls it a ballad, and as you will see, he has told his story in a form that imitates the old ballads. Two other ballads follow: a traditional ballad by our old friend Anonymous and a student's ballad that includes a lot of exaggeration and a refrain.

Make the Connection
Quickwrite ✏️

Two of the ballads you are about to read are tall tales. A **tall tale** is an exaggerated, farfetched story that is obviously untrue but is told as though it were absolutely factual.

Exaggerations, which stretch the truth about as high and wide as it will go, are generally used for humor. Can you top this old standard: It was so hot, you could fry an egg on the sidewalk? Choose two of the starters below, and make up your own humorous exaggerations.

- It was so cold . . .
- It rained so hard . . .
- The snow was so deep . . .

Reading Standard 3.1 Determine and articulate the relationship between the purposes and characteristics of different forms of poetry (for example, ballad).

In the 1890s, thousands of fortune hunters rushed north, braving bitter cold and deep snow. Gold had been found in northwestern Canada, in the Klondike region of the Yukon Territory. The town of Dawson, at the center of the region, became the Yukon's capital.

Like many other gold seekers, Sam McGee is unprepared for the Klondike's seven-month winter, when the temperature sometimes falls as low as minus sixty-eight degrees Fahrenheit. This poem tells his story. (Cremation is the burning of a body to ashes.)

The Cremation of Sam McGee

Robert W. Service

There are strange things done in the midnight sun
*   By the men who moil° for gold;*
The Arctic trails have their secret tales
*   That would make your blood run cold;*
5 *The Northern Lights have seen queer sights,*
*   But the queerest they ever did see*
Was that night on the marge° of Lake Lebarge
*   I cremated Sam McGee.*

2. **moil** *v.:* labor.

7. **marge** *n.:* edge.

Now Sam McGee was from Tennessee, where the
    cotton blooms and blows.
Why he left his home in the South to roam 'round the
10   Pole, God only knows.
He was always cold, but the land of gold seemed to
    hold him like a spell;
Though he'd often say in his homely way that he'd
    "sooner live in hell."

On a Christmas Day we were mushing our way over the
    Dawson trail.
Talk of your cold! through the parka's fold it stabbed
    like a driven nail.
If our eyes we'd close, then the lashes froze till some-
15   times we couldn't see;
It wasn't much fun, but the only one to whimper was
    Sam McGee.

And that very night, as we lay packed tight in our robes
    beneath the snow,
And the dogs were fed, and the stars o'erhead were
    dancing heel and toe,
He turned to me, and "Cap," says he, "I'll cash in this
    trip, I guess;
And if I do, I'm asking that you won't refuse my last
20   request."

Well, he seemed so low that I couldn't say no; then he
    says with a sort of moan:
"It's the cursèd cold, and it's got right hold till I'm
    chilled clean through to the bone.
Yet 'tain't being dead—it's my awful dread of the icy
    grave that pains;
So I want you to swear that, foul or fair, you'll cremate
    my last remains."

A pal's last need is a thing to heed, so I swore I would
25   not fail;
And we started on at the streak of dawn; but God! he
    looked ghastly pale.

He crouched on the sleigh, and he raved all day of his
      home in Tennessee;
And before nightfall a corpse was all that was left of
      Sam McGee.

There wasn't a breath in that land of death, and I
      hurried, horror-driven,
With a corpse half hid that I couldn't get rid, because
30   of a promise given;
It was lashed to the sleigh, and it seemed to say: "You
      may tax your brawn and brains,
But you promised true, and it's up to you to cremate
      those last remains."

Now a promise made is a debt unpaid, and the trail has
      its own stern code.
In the days to come, though my lips were dumb, in my
      heart how I cursed that load.
In the long, long night, by the lone firelight, while the
35   huskies, round in a ring,
Howled out their woes to the homeless snows—
      O God! how I loathed° the thing.

37. loathed (lō*th*d) *v.:*
hated.

And every day that quiet clay seemed to heavy and
      heavier grow;
And on I went, though the dogs were spent° and the
      grub was getting low;

38. spent *adj.:* worn-out.

The trail was bad, and I felt half mad, but I swore I
      would not give in;
And I'd often sing to the hateful thing, and it
40   hearkened° with a grin.

40. hearkened
(här′kənd) *v.:*
listened carefully.

Till I came to the marge of Lake Lebarge, and a
      derelict° there lay;

41. derelict (der′ə·likt′)
n.: abandoned ship.

It was jammed in the ice, but I saw in a trice it was
      called the "Alice May."
And I looked at it, and I thought a bit, and I looked at
      my frozen chum;
Then "Here," said I, with a sudden cry, "is my cre-ma-
      tor-ium."

Some planks I tore from the cabin floor, and I lit the
boiler fire;
Some coal I found that was lying around, and I heaped
the fuel higher;
The flames just soared, and the furnace roared—such a
blaze you seldom see;
And I burrowed a hole in the glowing coal, and I
stuffed in Sam McGee.

Then I made a hike, for I didn't like to hear him sizzle
    so;
And the heavens scowled, and the huskies howled, and
50   the wind began to blow.
It was icy cold, but the hot sweat rolled down my
    cheeks, and I don't know why;
And the greasy smoke in an inky cloak went streaking
    down the sky.

I do not know how long in the snow I wrestled with
    grisly° fear;
But the stars came out and they danced about ere again
    I ventured near;
I was sick with dread, but I bravely said: "I'll just take a
55   peep inside.
I guess he's cooked, and it's time I looked"; . . . then
    the door I opened wide.

53. grisly *adj.:* here, caused by something horrible.

And there sat Sam, looking cool and calm, in the heart
    of the furnace roar;
And he wore a smile you could see a mile, and he said:
    "Please close that door.
It's fine in here, but I greatly fear you'll let in the cold
    and storm—
Since I left Plumtree, down in Tennessee, it's the first
60   time I've been warm."

There are strange things done in the midnight sun
    By the men who moil for gold;
The Arctic trails have their secret tales
    That would make your blood run cold;
65   *The Northern Lights have seen queer sights,*
    But the queerest they ever did see
Was that night on the marge of Lake Lebarge
    I cremated Sam McGee.

Robert W. Service

"A Story Jack London Never Got"

Born in Lancashire, England, **Robert W. Service** (1874–1958) immigrated to Canada in his early twenties. After traveling along the Canadian Pacific coast, he took a job with a bank and was transferred to the Yukon Territory. He wrote his most popular poems there, including "The Cremation of Sam McGee." The poem was inspired by a story Service heard at a party where he was feeling awkward and out of place:

> I was staring gloomily at a fat fellow across the table. He was a big mining man from Dawson, and he scarcely acknowledged his introduction to a little bank clerk. Portly and important, he was smoking a big cigar with a gilt band. Suddenly he said: 'I'll tell you a story Jack London never got.' Then he spun a yarn of a man who cremated his pal. It had a surprise climax which occasioned much laughter. I did not join, for I had a feeling that here was a decisive moment of destiny. I still remember how a great excitement usurped me. Here was a perfect ballad subject. The fat man who ignored me went his way to bankruptcy, but he had pointed me the road to fortune.

Service left the party and spent the next six hours wandering through the frozen woods in the bright moonlight, writing verse after verse in his head. When he finally went to bed, the poem was complete and Service was satisfied; he didn't even put it on paper until the next day.

For Independent Reading

You'll find "The Cremation of Sam McGee," along with "The Shooting of Dan McGrew" and other poems, in *The Best of Robert Service*.

Ballads like this one were sung by cowboys in the American West. They helped make the long, lonely nights on the prairie pass more quickly. This ballad is based on an eighteenth-century Irish tune, and it gave rise to the famous blues song "St. James Infirmary." The ballad also provided the title and the haunting theme music for Bang the Drum Slowly, *a movie about the death of a young baseball player.*

The Dying Cowboy
traditional American ballad

As I rode out by Tom Sherman's barroom,
As I rode out so early one day,
'Twas there I espied a handsome young cowboy,
All dressed in white linen, all clothed for the grave.

5 "I see by your outfit that you are a cowboy,"
These words he did say as I boldly stepped by.
"Come sit down beside me and hear my sad story,
For I'm shot in the breast and I know I must die.

"Then beat your drum slowly and play your fife lowly,
10 And play the dead march as you carry me along,
And take me to the graveyard and throw the sod o'er me,
For I'm a young cowboy and I know I've done wrong.

"'Twas once in the saddle I used to go dashing,
'Twas once in the saddle I used to go gay,
15 But I first took to drinking and then to card playing,
Got shot in the body and I'm dying today.

"Let sixteen gamblers come handle my coffin,
Let sixteen young cowboys come sing me a song,
Take me to the green valley and lay the sod o'er me,
20 For I'm a poor cowboy and I know I've done wrong.

"Go bring me back a cup of cool water
To cool my parched lips," this cowboy then said.
Before I returned, his soul had departed
And gone to his Maker—the cowboy lay dead.

25 We swung our ropes slowly and rattled our spurs lowly,
And gave a wild whoop as we carried him on,
For we all loved our comrade, so brave, young and handsome,
We all loved our comrade, although he'd done wrong.

The Cowboy (c. 1897) by Frederic Remington. Watercolor on paper.

Maiden-Savin' Sam

In the wild ol' West there lived a man,
A man by the title of Maiden-Savin' Sam.
Saving maidens was his hobby and he did it
    very well,
Bragged about his victories—great stories
    did he tell.

> *Sam, Sam, Maiden-Savin' Sam,*
> *Greatest maiden saver in all of the land.*
> *Saved all the short ones, all the tall ones,*
>   *too,*
> *With his hat on his head and spurs on*
>   *his shoes.*

"One day a herd of buffalo crossed the land,
Biggest gaw-darned herd in all the land!
I was a-watchin' them, watchin' was I,"
Sam began the story, with a twinkle in his
    eye.

> *Sam, Sam, Maiden-Savin' Sam . . .*

"Now as I was watchin'—'Uh-oh,' says I,
'In the herd's way a pretty maiden does lie.
She's gonna get trampled,' I thought to
    myself.
'No longer will she be in such radiatin'
    health.'"

> *Sam, Sam, Maiden-Savin' Sam . . .*

"I looked all around, and what did I see?
A big, shiny pitchfork just a-waitin' for me.
I picked it up, threw it far and wide,
And now them buffalo are buffalo hide."

> *Sam, Sam, Maiden-Savin' Sam . . .*

Sam now lies deep in his grave,
Chased one too many bears into a cave.
But never we'll forget him—he was the very
    best
Of all the maiden savers in all of the West!

—Jenny Ellison
    Webb School of Knoxville
    Knoxville, Tennessee

Literary Response and Analysis

Reading Check

1. Why is Sam McGee in the Klondike?

2. What does Sam ask the speaker to do? Why?

3. What surprise does the speaker meet with when he carries out Sam's request?

Interpretations

4. Pick two or three details from "The Cremation of Sam McGee" that help you picture the frozen landscape or feel the cold.

5. The poem about Sam McGee uses both end rhymes and **internal rhymes**—rhymes contained within lines, such as *done* and *sun* in line 1. List three more pairs of internal rhymes in the poem.

6. Sam McGee's story is fun to read aloud for many reasons, most of them having to do with its sound effects. Look now at the use of **alliteration** in the poem. Alliteration is the repetition of consonant sounds in words close together in a text. The repeated sounds can be in the beginning or middle of the word: "In the *l*ong, *l*ong night, by the *l*one fire*l*ight . . ." See how many uses of alliteration you can find in this poem. Be sure to read the lines aloud to *hear* the sound effects.

7. Traditional **ballads** usually have these features:

- They tell a story.
- They use simple language.
- They have a refrain, usually at the end of each stanza.
- They have simple rhymes.
- They have regular meters.
- They often describe supernatural events.

Use these ballad characteristics to compare, point by point, Sam McGee's story with "The Dying Cowboy" and with "Maiden-Savin' Sam." Which poem is closer to the old ballad form?

Writing

Anything You Can Do, I Can Do Better

Refer to the examples of **exaggeration** you made up for the Quickwrite. Can you top yourself? Write some more exaggerations based on those statements about the weather, adding at least three more to your list. Then, exchange your exaggerations in class. Which exaggeration is—well—the most exaggerated?

(continued)

Reading Standard 3.1 Determine and articulate the relationship between the purposes and characteristics of different forms of poetry (for example, ballad).

Listening and Speaking
Sam McGee Live

The story of Sam McGee's fantastic rebirth has been recited around many campfires over the years. Now it's your chance to prepare the poem for a **choral reading.** First, form a group, and assign different stanzas or lines to different voices. (You might want to use a chorus for the refrain.) Then, prepare the script, marking carefully on each person's copy where he or she is to start and stop reading. As you rehearse, work on your presentation until you are satisfied that you have it right. It will help to assign a group of students to act as critics. After each rehearsal, ask for feedback from your listeners. Listeners, meanwhile, should prepare a list of standards they would look for in a good oral presentation. For the performance you might want to wear costumes or use some props.

from Beowulf *and* Casey at the Bat

Literary Focus
Epic

An **epic** is a long narrative poem written in formal, elegant language that tells about a series of quests undertaken by a great hero. In the ancient epics this hero is a warrior who embodies the values cherished by the culture that recites the epic.

The oldest stories in the world are epics. In ancient Mesopotamia around 2000 B.C., people told the epic of the hero Gilgamesh, who was searching for the secret of immortal life. In ancient Greece around 500 B.C., children learned values by studying the *Iliad* and the *Odyssey*, Homer's great epics about the Trojan War heroes. In India, children know the adventures of the heroes in the *Mahabharata* and *Ramayana*. In Anglo-Saxon England around A.D. 700, people passed the long, dark nights listening to bards tell the story of the hero Beowulf, who saved a kingdom from two swamp monsters.

A mock-heroic story. "Casey at the Bat" is a short narrative poem that imitates the old epic tales, but in a comical way. Instead of a warrior we have a small-town baseball player. Instead of a quest focused on saving a great kingdom, we have a quest for a home run to save Mudville's home team. Instead of the epic poet's elegant similes, metaphors, and alliteration, we have sports slang.

Sutton Hoo helmet (7th century) from the Sutton Hoo ship treasure, Suffolk, England.
British Museum, London.

Make the Connection
Quickwrite ✏️

The old epic heroes were larger-than-life warriors. They were usually the saviors of their people. What do our sports heroes today have in common with those epic heroes? How are they different? Jot down your ideas.

Reading Standard 3.1 Determine and articulate the relationship between the purposes and characteristics of different forms of poetry (for example, epic).

Beowulf *is the first great work of English literature. Since it was written in Old English, which is very different from the English used today, the epic has been translated into Modern English many times. In the excerpt that follows, Beowulf, a warrior from the land of the Geats (in Scandinavia), has arrived at the court of Hrothgar, a Danish king. Beowulf gives his credentials; that is, he tells the king why he should be chosen to face Grendel, a huge monster who has been devouring Hrothgar's followers. Beowulf is speaking to the king in the section that follows.*

Beowulf and the Dragon (1932)
by Rockwell Kent. Lithograph.
The Granger Collection, New York.

from BEOWULF

"Hail, Hrothgar!
Higlac is my cousin° and my king; the days
Of my youth have been filled with glory. Now Grendel's
Name has echoed in our land: Sailors
5   Have brought us stories of Herot, the best
Of all mead-halls,° deserted and useless when the moon
Hangs in skies the sun had lit,
Light and life fleeing together.
My people have said, the wisest, most knowing
10   And best of them, that my duty was to go to the Danes'
Great King. They have seen my strength for themselves,
Have watched me rise from the darkness of war,
Dripping with my enemies' blood. I drove

2. **cousin** *n.:* any relative. Higlac is Beowulf's uncle and his king.

6. **mead-halls:** Mead is a drink made from honey, water, yeast, and malt. The hall was a central gathering place where warriors could feast, listen to a bard's stories, and sleep in safety.

Five great giants into chains, chased
15   All of that race from the earth. I swam
In the blackness of night, hunting monsters
Out of the ocean, and killing them one
By one; death was my errand and the fate
They had earned. Now Grendel and I are called
20   Together, and I've come. Grant me, then,
Lord and protector of this noble place,
A single request! I have come so far,
Oh shelterer of warriors and your people's loved friend,
That this one favor you should not refuse me—
25   That I, alone and with the help of my men,
May purge all evil from this hall. I have heard,
Too, that the monster's scorn of men
Is so great that he needs no weapons and fears none.
Nor will I. My lord Higlac
30   Might think less of me if I let my sword
Go where my feet were afraid to, if I hid
Behind some broad linden shield:° My hands
Alone shall fight for me, struggle for life
Against the monster. God must decide
Who will be given to death's cold grip.

—*translated by* Burton Raffel

A knight, from a chess set carved from walrus ivory (12th century).
British Museum, London.

32. linden shield: shield made from wood of the linden tree.

Gundestrup caldron.
National Museum, Copenhagen.

CASEY AT THE BAT

Ernest Lawrence Thayer

The outlook wasn't brilliant for the Mudville nine that day;
The score stood four to two, with but one inning more to play;
And so, when Cooney died at first, and Burrows did the same,
A sickly silence fell upon the patrons of the game.

5   A straggling few got up to go in deep despair. The rest
Clung to the hope which springs eternal in the human breast;
They thought, if only Casey could but get a whack, at that,
They'd put up even money now, with Casey at the bat.

But Flynn preceded Casey, as did also Jimmy Blake,
10   And the former was a pudding, and the latter was a fake;

So upon that stricken multitude grim melancholy sat,
For there seemed but little chance of Casey's getting to the bat.

But Flynn let drive a single, to the wonderment of all,
And Blake, the much-despised, tore the cover off the ball;
15 And when the dust had lifted, and they saw what had occurred,
There was Jimmy safe on second, and Flynn a-hugging third.

Then from the gladdened multitude went up a joyous yell;
It bounded from the mountaintop, and rattled in the dell;
It struck upon the hillside, and recoiled upon the flat;
20 For Casey, mighty Casey, was advancing to the bat.

There was ease in Casey's manner as he stepped into his place;
There was pride in Casey's bearing, and a smile on Casey's face;
And when, responding to the cheers, he lightly doffed his hat,
No stranger in the crowd could doubt 'twas Casey at the bat.

25 Ten thousand eyes were on him as he rubbed his hands with dirt;
Five thousand tongues applauded when he wiped them on his shirt;
Then while the writhing pitcher ground the ball into his hip,
Defiance gleamed in Casey's eye, a sneer curled Casey's lip.

And now the leather-covered sphere came hurtling through the air,
30 And Casey stood a-watching it in haughty grandeur there;
Close by the sturdy batsman the ball unheeded sped.
"That ain't my style," said Casey. "Strike one," the umpire said.

From the benches, black with people, there went up a muffled roar,
Like the beating of the storm waves on a stern and distant shore;
35 "Kill him! Kill the umpire!" shouted someone on the stand;
And it's likely they'd have killed him had not Casey raised his hand.

With a smile of Christian charity great Casey's visage shone;
He stilled the rising tumult; he bade the game go on;
He signaled to the pitcher, and once more the spheroid flew;
40 But Casey still ignored it, and the umpire said, "Strike two."

"Fraud!" cried the maddened thousands, and the echo answered, "Fraud!"
But a scornful look from Casey, and the audience was awed;
They saw his face grow stern and cold, they saw his muscles strain,

And they knew that Casey wouldn't let that ball go by again.

45 The sneer is gone from Casey's lips, his teeth are clenched in hate,
  He pounds with cruel violence his bat upon the plate;
  And now the pitcher holds the ball, and now he lets it go,
  And now the air is shattered by the force of Casey's blow.

  Oh! somewhere in this favored land the sun is shining bright;
50 The band is playing somewhere, and somewhere hearts are light;
  And somewhere men are laughing, and somewhere children shout,
  But there is no joy in Mudville—mighty Casey has struck out!

MEET THE WRITER

Ernest Lawrence Thayer

Shunning the Limelight

When the journalist **Ernest Lawrence Thayer** (1863–1940) submitted "Casey at the Bat" to the San Francisco *Examiner* in 1888, he had no idea it would become the most famous baseball poem ever written. In fact, he didn't even sign his own name to his work, choosing instead to use a nickname from his Harvard college days, Phin.

Shortly after the poem appeared in the California newspaper, a copy was given to a vaudeville entertainer named William De Wolf Hopper, who was about to appear in a Baseball Night performance in New York. Hopper must have recognized a winner. After quickly memorizing the poem, he went onstage and recited it; the audience went wild. Hopper went on to make a successful career of touring the country reciting "Casey at the Bat."

Despite the poem's popularity, Thayer considered it badly written and for years would not admit authorship. Many people tried to take credit for writing the poem, and a number of baseball players claimed the dubious distinction of having been the model for Casey. When the author was finally identified, he refused to take money for the poem's many reprintings. "All I ask," he said, "is never to be reminded of it again."

Literary Response and Analysis

FOCUS ON

Reading Check

1. What credentials does Beowulf give King Hrothgar to prove he is worthy of fighting the monster Grendel?

2. What request does Beowulf make of King Hrothgar?

3. At the beginning of "Casey at the Bat," why are the Mudville fans in despair?

4. What happens in "Casey at the Bat" when Flynn and Blake come to bat?

5. What happens when the mighty Casey comes to bat?

Interpretations

6. Beowulf is a typical **epic hero** in that he is enormously strong and has come to save a kingdom. Find places where the poet makes Casey seem like a great epic hero.

7. Epic heroes embody the values that their society holds dear—traits like courage, humility, strength, generosity, selflessness. What values do you think Casey embodies? Do you think these values are especially American? ✏️

8. Beowulf has come to Herot, the great hall of King Hrothgar, where he expects to perform mighty deeds. Casey is expected to perform his mighty deeds in a baseball stadium. How is this **setting** like Herot? How is it different?

9. The epics of ancient Greece and Rome are marked by long, beautiful similes and metaphors. Ernest

Lawrence Thayer also uses figures of speech to describe Casey and the ballgame in heroic language. The poem includes **similes** (comparisons of different things, using *like* or *as*), **metaphors** (direct comparisons of different things, without using *like* or *as*), and **personification** (speaking of something that is not human as if it had human qualities). Find figures of speech in lines 3, 6, 10, and 33–34. In each instance, tell what is being compared to what.

10. To elevate his language, Thayer often uses fancy words. Find examples of fancy words in lines 29, 37, and 39. What simpler words could he have used that mean the same thing?

Animal head from Viking ship (c. 800).

University Museum of National Antiquities, Oslo, Norway. Photo by Eirik Irgens Johnsen.

Writing

It's Off to School I Go . . .

Try your hand at writing a mock epic. Pick an everyday event in your life— such as getting ready for school or walking the dog or playing soccer—and describe it in the heightened language of an epic. A regular meter and rhymes would make it more fun, but if those are too hard to come up with, write your mock epic in free verse. That means that you don't have to use rhymes, but you do have to pay attention to the sound and rhythm of your poem. Make it sound grand!

Reading Standard 3.1 Determine and articulate the relationship between the purposes and characteristics of different forms of poetry (for example, epic).

Summaries of "Casey at the Bat"

What Goes into a Summary

"Hey, did you read that story? It's due tomorrow."

"I read it. But it had so many details! What's the point of it, anyway?"

Details. Which are critical? Which are not so critical? How do you tell the difference? A **critical detail** is one that must be included for the summary of a text to make sense. If the detail is not included, the summary falls apart, has a big gap, or is illogical. On the other hand, if you can do without it, the detail probably isn't critical.

A good summary of a story can help you understand important elements like **main events, cause and effect,** and **theme.** Here is a checklist of what you should look for in a good summary of a story, including the story in a narrative poem.

Reading Standard 2.4
Compare the original text to a summary to determine whether the summary accurately captures the main ideas, includes critical details, and conveys the underlying meaning.

Summary of a Story: A Checklist

1. The summary of a story should cite the story's **author** and **title.**
2. The summary should identify the **main characters,** the **problem** or **conflict** in the story, the **main events,** and the **resolution** of the problem.
3. The summary should list the main events of the plot, in the **order** in which they occur and in a way that shows the relationship of one event to another. (In other words, the summary should show **cause-and-effect** relationships. This means it should use words and phrases like *because, as a result of, since, therefore, so.*)
4. The summary should state the story's **theme.**
5. If the writer's words are quoted exactly in the summary, quotation marks should be used.

"Casey at the Bat"

SUMMARY 1

In the bottom of the ninth, Mudville trails. The last outs go to Cooney, Burrows, and Casey. Mudville loses 4–2.

"Casey at the Bat"

SUMMARY 2

The poem "Casey at the Bat" by Ernest Lawrence Thayer is about a baseball hero named Casey who plays for the Mudville nine. At the opening the game looks bad for Mudville. They are losing 4–2 in the bottom of the ninth. Then Cooney and Burrows are both out at first. If Casey gets to bat, he'll surely save the day; but Flynn and Blake go to bat first, and neither is likely to score. But, look! Each player bags a hit, and the crowd goes wild with joy. With two men on, up steps the mighty Casey. Strike one! Then strike two! The crowd screams. Casey signals for silence. His smile turns to a frown; his anger signals his resolve. He'll slam the next ball out of the park. But the air is shattered by his swing. Somewhere men are laughing, the poet says. But there is no joy in Mudville—mighty Casey has struck out! "Casey at the Bat" in its comic way reminds us that even the mighty can fall.

Reading Informational Materials

Reading Check

1. Which summary contains all or most of the poem's **critical details**? List three of these details.

2. Which summary states a **theme,** or **underlying meaning,** of the poem? What is that theme?

TestPractice

"Casey at the Bat"
SUMMARIES 1 AND 2

1. Summary 1 should be made stronger by doing all of the following *except* —

   A conveying the main ideas more clearly

   B adding more critical details

   C conveying the author's underlying meaning

   D using fewer details and sticking to the details in the poem

2. Which of the following **critical details** from the poem is included in both summaries?

   F Mudville is losing in the bottom of the ninth.

   G Cooney and Burrows are out at first.

   H Casey strikes out.

   J Even the mighty can fall.

3. Which of the following sentences from Summary 2 is not an important detail?

   A "They are losing 4–2 in the bottom of the ninth."

   B "Then Cooney and Burrows are both out at first."

   C "The crowd goes wild with joy."

   D "Mighty Casey has struck out!"

4. Which passage in Summary 2 should be put in quotation marks because it is a direct quote from the poem?

   F "The game looks bad for Mudville."

   G "He'll surely save the day."

   H "The crowd screams."

   J "Somewhere men are laughing."

Reading Standard 2.4
Compare the original text to a summary to determine whether the summary accurately captures the main ideas, includes critical details, and conveys the underlying meaning.

Oda a las gracias / Ode to Thanks *and*
Birdfoot's Grampa *and*
Ode to a Toad

Literary Focus
Ode

The **ode** originated in ancient Greece. For centuries, poets imitated these long, complex poems, which celebrated, in elegant language, one person or thing. Over the centuries famous odes have been written to nightingales, Greek vases, autumn, melancholy, joy, Britain, solitude, and winners in the Olympic Games.

Today odes are looser in form and subject matter, but they still celebrate a particular person or thing. The great Chilean poet Pablo Neruda has written several books of odes, most of which celebrate ordinary objects and everyday experiences.

Neruda dedicates "Ode to Thanks" to a word that most of us use every day. (The first twenty-two lines of the Spanish original are at the right.) The two other poems in this grouping are about toads. Only one of them is an ode; the other is a lyric (the titles will tell you which).

Make the Connection
Quickwrite ✏

What would you like to celebrate in your life? It could be a person, place, or thing. *Thing* may include many things— animals, food, flowers, machines, laughter, justice. Make a list of five subjects worthy of celebration.

from Oda a las gracias
Pablo Neruda

Gracias a la palabra
que agradece.
Gracias a *gracias*
por
5   cuanto esta palabra
derrite nieve o hierro.

El mundo parecía amenazante
hasta que suave
como pluma
10 clara,
o dulce como pétalo de azúcar,
de labio en labio
pasa,
gracias,
15 grandes a plena boca
o susurrantes,
apenas murmulladas,
y el ser volvió a ser hombre
y no ventana,
20 alguna claridad
entró en el bosque:
fue posible cantar bajo las
    hojas. . . .

Reading Standard 3.1 Determine and articulate the relationship between the purposes and characteristics of different forms of poetry (for example, ode).

Ode to Thanks

Pablo Neruda

Thanks to the word
that says *thanks!*
Thanks to *thanks,*
word
5   that melts
iron and snow!

The world is a threatening place
until
thanks
10   makes the rounds
from one pair of lips to another,
soft as a bright
feather
and sweet as a petal of sugar,
15   filling the mouth with its sound
or else a mumbled
whisper.
Life becomes human again:
it's no longer an open window.
20   A bit of brightness
strikes into the forest,
and we can sing again beneath the leaves.
Thanks, you're the medicine we take
to save us from
25   the bite of scorn.
Your light brightens the altar of harshness.
Or maybe
a tapestry
known
30   to far distant peoples.
Travelers
fan out
into the wilds,
and in that jungle
35   of strangers,

merci°
rings out
while the hustling train
changes countries,
40   sweeping away borders,
then *spasibo*°
clinging to pointy
volcanoes, to fire and freezing cold,
or *danke,*° yes! and *gracias,*° and
45   the world turns into a table:
a single word has wiped it clean,
plates and glasses gleam,
silverware tinkles,
and the tablecloth is as broad as a
     plain.

50   Thank you, *thanks,*
for going out and returning,
for rising up
and settling down.
We know, *thanks,*
55   that you don't fill every space—
you're only a word—
but
where your little petal
appears
60   the daggers of pride take cover,
and there's a penny's worth of
     smiles.

—*translated by* Ken Krabbenhoft

---

36. *merci* (mer·sē′): French for "thanks."
41. *spasibo* (spa·sē′bə): Russian for "thanks."
44. *danke* (dän′kə): German for "thanks."
    gracias (grä′sē·äs′): Spanish for "thanks."

Birdfoot's Grampa

Joseph Bruchac

The old man
must have stopped our car
two dozen times to climb out
and gather into his hands
5   the small toads blinded
by our lights and leaping,
live drops of rain.

The rain was falling,
a mist about his white hair
10   and I kept saying
you can't save them all
accept it, get back in
we've got places to go.

But, leathery hands full
15   of wet brown life,
knee deep in the summer
roadside grass,
he just smiled and said
they have places to go to
20   *too.*

Ode to a Toad

I was out one day for my usual jog
(I go kinda easy, rarely full-hog)
When I happened to see right there on the road
The squishy remains of a little green toad.

5   I thought to myself, where is his home?
Down yonder green valley, how far did he
     roam?
From out on the pond I heard sorrowful croaks,
Could that be the wailing of some of his folks?

I felt for the toad and his pitiful state,
But the day was now fading, and such was his
10   fate.
In the grand scheme of things, now I confess,
What's one little froggie more or less?

—Anne-Marie Wulfsberg
    Concord-Carlisle High School
    Concord, Massachusetts

Pablo Neruda

A Poet for All People

Pablo Neruda (1904–1973) was born and died in his beloved Chile, but he lived many years abroad, sometimes as a diplomat for his country and sometimes in political exile. Neruda won the Nobel Prize in literature in 1971, but he was only in his twenties when he first became famous—for his love poems. Those poems are recited often throughout the Spanish-speaking world. In his odes, Neruda gave up a complex, formal style and adopted a plainer one, using simple words and short lines so that his poems could be enjoyed by all people. He said of his new style:

> My poetry became clear and happy when it branched off toward humbler subjects and things.

Joseph Bruchac

"One Lesson I Was Taught"

Joseph Bruchac (1942–   ) was born in Saratoga Springs, New York, and was raised there by his grandmother and his grandfather, who was a member of the Abenaki people. Bruchac studied wildlife conservation in college. Today he is a well-known editor, publisher, poet, and collector of folk tales. Bruchac says that this poem describes one lesson he was taught "in the way most good lessons come to you—when you least expect them."

Literary Response and Analysis

Reading Check

1. In the first stanza of "Ode to Thanks," what does the speaker say the word *thanks* can do?

2. In lines 7–17, how does the speaker say the word *thanks* travels?

3. According to lines 23–25, what can the word *thanks* save us from?

4. In lines 50–61 of "Ode to Thanks," what does the speaker thank *thanks* for?

5. What does Birdfoot's grandfather say when he's told that he can't save all the toads?

6. What does the speaker in "Ode to a Toad" decide at the end of her ode?

Interpretations

7. What do you think the speaker of "Ode to Thanks" means when he says in lines 3–6 that *thanks* "melts iron and snow"?

8. What does the speaker compare *thanks* to in lines 12–15? How is a thank-you like these things?

9. In lines 31–44 of "Ode to Thanks," what effect does the poem say the word *thanks* has all over the world?

10. According to lines 45–49 of "Ode to Thanks," the word *thanks* turns the world into a table. How is thanking someone like setting a beautiful table for dinner?

11. In lines 58–61, what does the speaker say the word *thanks* does to pride?

12. The last line of "Ode to Thanks" is "and there's a penny's worth of smiles." What do you think this line means?

Evaluation

13. If you know Spanish, compare this translation with the original Spanish of lines 1–22 on page 437. Would you make any changes in word choice?

14. Review the definition of **ode** on page 437. How is "Ode to Thanks" like classical odes? How is it different? Cite details from the poem to support your answer.

15. Many people, like Birdfoot's Grampa, believe that their actions can make a difference even if they can't save everyone. Think of someone you know (or someone you know of) who has acted on that belief. What actions has this person taken? Do you believe the action was worth doing?

Writing

Ode to a . . .

Pick a person, place, or thing you would like to celebrate, and write an **ode.** Your purpose is to express your strong, positive feelings about all aspects of your subject. Try to talk directly to your subject, as Neruda does.

Reading Standard 3.1 Determine and articulate the relationship between the purposes and characteristics of different forms of poetry (for example, ode).

On the Grasshopper and the Cricket

Literary Focus
Sonnet

Imagine that you live in nineteenth-century England. You're a well-educated young person, and you want to impress a friend. Forget gifts of flowers. You would write your friend a poem. You'd most likely write a sonnet.

Every sonnet has fourteen lines, usually in iambic pentameter. **Iambic** refers to verse in which the beat or stress is on every other syllable, starting with the unstressed beat, like this:

From hedge to hedge.

Pentameter is verse in which there are five stressed beats in every line (*pente* is Greek for "five"). Occasional variations are OK. On top of that, if you were writing an **Italian sonnet** (also called **Petrarchan,** for the fourteenth-century Italian poet Petrarch, who mastered the form), you'd pose a question or make a point in the first eight lines. Then, in the last six lines, you'd respond to your own question or point.

Another sonnet form, called the **English,** or **Shakespearean, sonnet,** is made up of three units with four lines in each one. Each unit expresses related ideas. Two rhymed lines (called a **couplet**) sum up the poem.

John Keats, a great English poet, wrote many sonnets and sent them to friends. "On the Grasshopper and the Cricket" is one of his early sonnets. He wrote it in the Italian form.

Reading Standard 3.1 Determine and articulate the relationship between the purposes and characteristics of different forms of poetry (for example, sonnet).

Reading Skills
Using Form to Find Meaning

Knowing the form of a poem helps you figure out its meaning. You know that "On the Grasshopper and the Cricket" is a sonnet written in the Italian form. That means you can divide it into two chunks of meaning. First you look for a problem, a question, or an idea in the first eight lines. Then you see how the final six lines resolve the problem, answer the question, or comment on the idea.

Make the Connection
Quickwrite ✏

Nineteenth-century writers, like many others through the ages, shared their ideas and feelings about nature. How do you feel about nature? What do you see in nature that scares or disgusts you? What scenes, creatures, and patterns in nature fill you with wonder and awe? Think about the natural world for a minute or two, and jot down some of your thoughts.

(Opposite)
Landscape (detail) (19th century) by Patrick Nasmyth.
Ray Miles Gallery, London.

On the Grasshopper and the Cricket

John Keats

The poetry of earth is never dead:
    When all the birds are faint with the hot sun,
    And hide in cooling trees, a voice will run
From hedge to hedge about the new-mown mead;°
5   That is the Grasshopper's—he takes the lead
In summer luxury—he has never done
With his delights; for when tired out with fun
He rests at ease beneath some pleasant weed.
The poetry of earth is ceasing never:
10   On a lone winter evening, when the frost
       Has wrought a silence, from the stove there shrills
The Cricket's song, in warmth increasing ever,
    And seems to one in drowsiness half lost,
       The Grasshopper's among some grassy hills.

---

4. mead (mēd) *n.:* meadow.

John Keats

John Keats
by Charles Armitage Brown.
By courtesy of the National Portrait Gallery, London.

He Won the Contest

"On the Grasshopper and the Cricket" was the result of a sonnet-writing contest that **John Keats** (1795–1821) had with another poet, his friend Leigh Hunt. Snug indoors on a winter's night in 1816, the two poets heard the chirping of a cricket. Hunt challenged Keats to see which of them could write the best sonnet on the subject of the grasshopper and the cricket—within fifteen minutes.

At that time, Keats had only begun to write sonnets. He had trained to be a doctor for six years and had passed his examinations for a license to practice medicine, but he disliked surgery. What he really wanted was to become a poet.

Keats did become a poet, one of the greatest in the English language, although he lived for only twenty-five years. In physical size, Keats was a small man. When fully grown, he was barely five feet tall, and he was always slender. At school he was strong and athletic, however, admired by his many friends for having the courage and fighting spirit of a terrier.

The oldest of four children, John Keats was born into a middle-class family. Shortly after he was sent away to boarding school, at the age of eight, his father was killed in an accident. His mother died of tuberculosis when Keats was only fourteen. That event ended his formal education. Keats was apprenticed to a surgeon shortly afterward.

Keats's first book of poetry (1817) was not received well by critics, but despite many personal difficulties he continued to write. His beloved brother Tom died of tuberculosis in 1818, and then Keats himself began to show early signs of the disease. Meanwhile, he had fallen deeply in love with a young woman named Fanny Brawne. He knew, however, that his sickness would keep them from marrying. Even though he was dying, Keats continued to write poems of such beauty and depth of meaning that they are still read and admired today.

Literary Response and Analysis

Reading Check

1. In the first eight lines of the poem, what season is described?

2. Why aren't the birds singing? What are they doing instead?

3. Whose voice can be heard?

4. What kind of life does the grasshopper have?

5. In the last six lines of the poem, what season is described?

6. Where is the cricket singing? Whose song does the cricket's song sound like?

Interpretations

7. In this Italian **sonnet,** Keats describes two poets of the natural world. Who is the poet of summer in the first eight lines? Who is the poet of winter in the last six lines?

8. What simple words does Keats use to describe the hot, sleepy feeling of a summer day? What words does he use to describe his winter evening?

9. Which line of the poem echoes the first line? How do the changed words affect the meaning?

10. In this brief sonnet, Keats makes points about several things: nature, sound and silence, the heat of summer (and life), the cold of winter (and death). Sum up in your own words *one* point that the poet makes in the first eight lines of the sonnet. What point, related to the first one you mentioned, does he make in the last six lines?

Writing

Inspired by Nature

Look back at your Quickwrite notes to find something in nature that has special meaning for you. Write a poem in which you help your reader *picture* something in the world of nature and understand how you feel about it. You may choose to rhyme your poem and follow a regular meter, or you may choose to write in free verse, without regular rhymes or a pattern of rhythm. Perhaps you'll try to follow the strict form of an Italian sonnet—and challenge a friend to a sonnet-writing contest!

BONUS QUESTION

What gift from someone your own age is likely to impress you?

Reading Standard 3.1 Determine and articulate the relationship between the purposes and characteristics of different forms of poetry (for example, sonnet).

O Captain! My Captain!

Abraham Lincoln.

Literary Focus
Elegy

An **elegy** (el′ə·jē) is a poem of mourning. Most elegies are about someone who has died. Some elegies mourn a way of life that is gone forever. "O Captain! My Captain!" mourns the tragic death of President Abraham Lincoln. This elegy uses an **extended metaphor.** That means that a metaphor is stated, and the comparison is extended as far as the poet can take it—in this case, through the entire poem! As you read, decide who the captain really is and what the ship represents.

Make the Connection
Quickwrite

Although you are still young, you have probably lost someone or something you cared about. A person you were close to may have died. Perhaps you have lost a beloved pet. Maybe you had to move away from a place you loved. Perhaps a favorite hill or stream has been lost to a housing development. Think about someone or something that meant a lot to you and is now gone. Jot down some quick notes about how that loss affected you.

Background

Walt Whitman lived in Washington, D.C., during the Civil War. He worked as a government clerk and a war correspondent. He also served as a volunteer nurse, caring for the thousands of wounded soldiers who filled the nearby military hospitals. The Saturday before Lincoln's second inauguration, Whitman attended a reception at the White House. On inauguration day, March 4, 1865, Whitman twice saw Lincoln pass by in his carriage. He commented that the president "looked very much worn and tired; the lines, indeed, of vast responsibilities, intricate questions, and demands of life and death, cut deeper than ever upon his dark brown face; yet all the old goodness, tenderness, sadness, and canny shrewdness, underneath the furrows." The president was assassinated just a month later, on April 14, 1865. The country had just concluded a terrible civil war. The difficult job of healing had just begun.

Reading Standard 3.1 Determine and articulate the relationship between the purposes and characteristics of different forms of poetry (for example, elegy).

O Captain! My Captain!

Walt Whitman

O Captain! my Captain! our fearful trip is done,
The ship has weathered every rack,° the prize we sought is won,
The port is near, the bells I hear, the people all exulting,°
While follow eyes the steady keel, the vessel grim and daring;
       But O heart! heart! heart!
         O the bleeding drops of red,
           Where on the deck my Captain lies,
             Fallen cold and dead.

O Captain! my Captain! rise up and hear the bells;
Rise up—for you the flag is flung—for you the bugle trills,
For you bouquets and ribboned wreaths—for you the shores a-crowding,
For you they call, the swaying mass, their eager faces turning;
       Here Captain! dear father!
         The arm beneath your head!
           It is some dream that on the deck,
             You've fallen cold and dead.

My Captain does not answer, his lips are pale and still,
My father does not feel my arm, he has no pulse nor will,
The ship is anchored safe and sound, its voyage closed and done,
From fearful trip the victor° ship comes in with object won:
       Exult O shores, and ring O bells!
        But I with mournful tread,
          Walk the deck my Captain lies,
            Fallen cold and dead.

---

2. **rack** *n.:* here, violent change or disorder, like that caused by a storm.
3. **exulting** (eg·zult′iŋ) *v.* used as *adj.:* rejoicing.
20. **victor** *n.* used as *adj.:* winner.

Walt Whitman

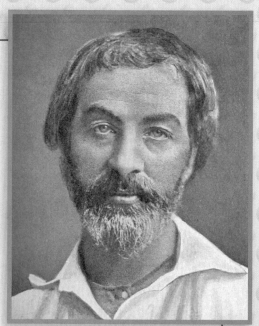

An American Original

Walt Whitman (1819–1892) is one of the finest and most original American poets. Born on Long Island, New York, Whitman had to leave school at age eleven to go to work. On weekends he continued his education by reading widely. He would sit on the beach and read Sir Walter Scott, the Bible, and Shakespeare. Whitman dressed and behaved in a manner all his own.

According to one story, Whitman once drove a horse-drawn carriage along Broadway, reciting Shakespeare at the top of his lungs. Whitman was also very talented and very persistent. When he couldn't find a publisher for *Leaves of Grass*, he published it himself, in 1855. He even wrote his own reviews. Whitman never stopped working on his "leaves." He revised his book and added poems to it until his death.

With *Leaves of Grass*, Whitman became an original voice of the still-new United States. Whitman embraced and celebrated all aspects of his country and its people—especially its workers. In "I Hear America Singing" (see page 451), he celebrates mechanics, carpenters, masons, woodcutters, shoemakers, girls sewing or washing. In "Song of Myself," he sings of boatmen, clam diggers, trappers, and men fleeing slavery.

Leaves of Grass is now recognized as a masterpiece, but that wasn't always so. At first many readers criticized Whitman's poems because they were about common people and common experiences. Readers also hated the poems because they were written in free verse instead of strictly rhymed and metered lines. For more than a century now, however, Americans and people all over the world have been strengthened and inspired by the poetry of Walt Whitman. We take great joy in it.

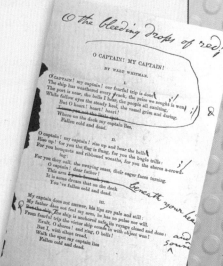

Literary Response and Analysis

Reading Check

1. In the first stanza of this poem, where is the ship?

2. What has happened to the captain of the ship?

3. In the second stanza, what does the speaker ask the captain to do?

4. In the third stanza, where is the ship?

5. At the end of the poem, what is the speaker doing?

Interpretations

6. "O Captain! My Captain!" is built on an **extended metaphor.** The poet speaks of a captain and a ship all the way through the poem, but we sense that he is not talking about an actual captain and an actual ship. What clues tell you that the captain is Lincoln, the assassinated president, and the ship is the country?

7. The poet uses a second **metaphor** for the president in lines 13 and 18. What is it, and how does this metaphor make the poem even sadder?

8. In line 20, the poet says, "From fearful trip the victor ship comes in with object won." If the ship is a metaphor for the country, what "trip" has the country made? What "object" has it won?

A sketch of Lincoln dying, by Hermann Faber.

9. What **refrain,** or repeated line, is used in the poem? Why is this situation **ironic,** or not what we would expect when a captain has brought his ship home victorious?

Writing

I Miss You

Write a little **elegy** about someone or something you cared deeply about but lost. You may want to use your notes from your Quickwrite, or you may prefer to choose another topic. Let the reader understand why the subject is important to you. You do not have to use rhyme and a strict meter. Try writing your elegy in free verse.

Reading Standard 3.1 Determine and articulate the relationship between the purposes and characteristics of different forms of poetry (for example, elegy).

I Hear America Singing
and I, Too

Literary Focus
Free Verse

Free verse does not follow a regular rhyme scheme or meter, but that doesn't mean that anything goes. Without a strict pattern to follow, poets writing free verse have to rely on their own sense of balance and measure. Poets writing free verse also use the following devices (for more information on these devices, turn to the definitions in the Handbook of Literary Terms in the back of this book):

- **alliteration** (ə·lit′ər·ā′shən)—repetition of consonant sounds (snow *falling fast*)

- **onomatopoeia** (än′ō·mat′ō·pē′ə)—the use of words whose sounds echo their meaning (the chain saw's *buzz*)

- **imagery**—language that evokes sensations of sight, sound, smell, taste, and touch

- **figures of speech**—language that is based on comparisons and is not literally true (metaphors, similes, personification)

- **rhythm**—a musical quality produced by repetition

Walt Whitman was the first American poet to use free verse. Today many poets write in free verse, so we take it for granted. In Whitman's day, however, people were used to poems written in "poetic" language, which used strict rhyme schemes and meters. These people were shocked by Whitman's sprawling lines and use of slang. In time many critics came to feel that Walt Whitman was the first and greatest poet to "give voice" to America. "I Hear America Singing" offers a good example of why they came to think so.

Make the Connection
Quickwrite 🖉

Think about the sounds you hear around you. If you live in a city, you may hear the rumble of a subway, the roar of traffic, people arguing, pigeons cooing. In the suburbs you might hear a gentler whoosh of traffic, kids shouting, birds singing, the drone of a lawn mower. In the country you might hear the wind blowing, a meadowlark singing, cicadas humming. Wherever you are, sit quietly and listen. Then, jot down all the sounds you hear.

Reading Standard 3.1 Determine and articulate the relationship between the purposes and characteristics of different forms of poetry.

I Hear America Singing

Walt Whitman

I hear America singing, the varied carols I hear,
Those of mechanics, each one singing his as it should
    be blithe° and strong,
The carpenter singing his as he measures his plank or
    beam,
The mason singing his as he makes ready for work, or
    leaves off work,
The boatman singing what belongs to him in his boat,
5   the deckhand singing on the steamboat deck,
The shoemaker singing as he sits on his bench, the
    hatter singing as he stands,
The woodcutter's song, the plowboy's on his way in
    the morning, or at noon intermission or at sundown,
The delicious singing of the mother, or of the young
    wife at work, or of the girl sewing or washing,
Each singing what belongs to him or her and to none
    else,
The day what belongs to the day—at night the party of
10   young fellows, robust, friendly,
Singing with open mouths their strong melodious
    songs.

----

2. **blithe** (blīth) *adj.:* lighthearted.

*For biographical information on
Walt Whitman, see page 448.*

Walt Whitman.
Courtesy of Ohio Wesleyan University,
Bayley-Whitman Collection, Delaware, Ohio.

I, Too

Langston Hughes

I, too, sing America.

I am the darker brother.
They send me to eat in the kitchen
When company comes,
5 But I laugh,
And eat well,
And grow strong.

Tomorrow,
I'll sit at the table
10 When company comes.
Nobody'll dare
Say to me,
"Eat in the kitchen,"
Then.

15 Besides,
They'll see how beautiful I am
And be ashamed—

I, too, am America.

Langston Hughes

"Poems Are Like Rainbows"

Born in Joplin, Missouri, **Langston Hughes** (1902–1967) began writing poetry in his early teens. As a young man he traveled around the world and held many jobs.

In his autobiography *The Big Sea* (1940), Hughes describes his writing process:

> There are seldom many changes in my poems, once they're down. Generally, the first two or three lines come to me from something I'm thinking about, or looking at, or doing, and the rest of the poem (if there is to be a poem) flows from those first few lines, usually right away. If there is a chance to put the poem down then, I write it down. If not, I try to remember it until I get to a pencil and paper; for poems are like rainbows: They escape you quickly.

For more biographical information on Langston Hughes, see page 455.

Literary Response and Analysis

Reading Check

1. List five working people Walt Whitman says he hears singing.

2. Who does Langston Hughes say is also singing?

Interpretations

3. "I, Too" was written in response to "I Hear America Singing." Whitman's poem is about inclusion. What is Hughes's poem about?

4. Do any of the singers in Whitman's poem sing about sad things or about poor working conditions? Do you think Whitman is making working life in the nineteenth century too pretty? Explain your answers.

5. "I Hear America Singing" and "I, Too" are both **free-verse** poems—they do not have a regular rhyme scheme or meter. They do, however, use repetition to create **rhythm.** In each poem, find examples of repeated words, lines, and sentence patterns.

Writing

I Hear . . .

Write a free-verse poem about the sounds you hear around you. Go back to your Quickwrite for ideas. Structure your poem the way Whitman structured his—as a list of sounds you hear. Try to build your sentences so that most of them have the same structure—just as Whitman does. (This repetition of sentence patterns will give your poem rhythm.) In your poem, simply describe the sounds you hear, or include your feelings about the "songs." Whatever your plan, be sure to use words and images that will help your reader hear the sounds.

Shipyards by Thomas Hart Benton (1889–1975). Mural, Equitable Life Insurance Company, New York.

Langston Hughes: A Biography *and* "Langston Hughes": A Summary

What Goes into a Summary?

Writing a good **summary** of an informational text is not easy. You have to restate the main ideas, include critical details, and sum up the underlying meaning of the text. Here is what to look for in a good summary of informational nonfiction:

Summary of an Informational Text: A Checklist

1. The summary should open with the **title** and **author** of the text.
2. The summary should state the **topic** of the text.
3. The summary should state the **main ideas,** in the **order** in which they occur in the text.
4. The summary should include important **supporting details.**
5. Quotation marks should be put around any words from the text that are quoted exactly.

Read the biography of Langston Hughes and the summary that follows. What makes the summary a good—or bad—summary?

Langston Hughes: A Biography

Langston Hughes was born in 1902 in Joplin, Missouri, but he spent most of his childhood in Lawrence, Kansas, with his grandmother. When he was twelve, he moved to Lincoln, Illinois, and then to Cleveland, Ohio, to live with his mother and stepfather. Hughes died in 1967 in his home in his beloved Harlem, in New York City.

According to a popular story, Langston Hughes first tasted fame when he was twenty-three years old. When the poet Vachel Lindsay came to dine at the Wardman Park Hotel in Washington, D.C., where Hughes was working as a busboy, Hughes left three poems by Lindsay's plate. Lindsay was so impressed by the poems that he presented them that night at a reading, saying he had discovered a true poet, a young black man who was working as a busboy in a nearby restaurant. For the next few days, newspapers up and down the East Coast ran articles acclaiming the "busboy poet."

That story is a good one, but it's a little misleading. Hughes was not really an overnight success. He had already put in a long apprenticeship as a writer. He had written his first poem when he was in eighth grade and was first published in his high school literary magazine. Hughes had also read a great deal of poetry, especially the works of Edgar Lee Masters, Vachel Lindsay, Amy Lowell, Carl Sandburg, and Walt Whitman. Whitman and Sandburg had a strong

Langston Hughes outside his house in Harlem.

Reading Standard 2.4 Compare the original text to a summary to determine whether the summary accurately captures the main ideas, includes critical details, and conveys the underlying meaning.

influence on Hughes because they celebrated the humanity of all people regardless of age, gender, race, or class. Hughes had already seen many of his own poems published in journals and magazines. What's more, a book of his poetry, *The Weary Blues,* was soon to be published by a famous New York publisher.

As the anecdote about Vachel Lindsay shows, Hughes was energetic and ambitious. Before he met Lindsay, he had attended Columbia University and had worked as a crew member on a freighter crossing the Atlantic to Africa and back. He spoke German and Spanish and had lived in Mexico (where his father also lived), France, and Italy. After meeting Lindsay, Hughes went on to earn a college degree at Lincoln University and to write fifteen volumes of poetry, six novels, three books of short stories, eleven plays, and a variety of nonfiction works. Hughes worked in Harlem during the heady days of the Harlem Renaissance, when that New York City neighborhood was teeming with talent—poets, musicians, artists.

About his poetry, Hughes said, "Perhaps the mission of an artist is to interpret beauty to the people—the beauty within themselves." Hughes also interpreted—and celebrated— the experiences of African Americans. Some of his most famous poems imitated jazz rhythms and the repetitive structure of the blues. Later in life he wrote poems specifically designed for jazz accompaniment. He also helped found several black theater companies and wrote and translated plays for them to perform. Langston Hughes is perhaps the most famous and original of all African American poets. He said his work was an attempt to "explain and illuminate the Negro condition in America." Hughes succeeded in that and more: His work illuminates the condition of all people everywhere.

"Langston Hughes": A Summary

"Langston Hughes: A Biography" focuses on the life and works of the poet Langston Hughes. The main point made in this biographical sketch is that Langston Hughes wrote about the experiences of African Americans but his work "illuminates the condition of all people everywhere." Hughes became famous when he was twenty-three, when the poet Vachel Lindsay read his poems at a poetry reading. Hughes had been writing since eighth grade, however, and had published a poem in a high school literary magazine. He was especially influenced by Whitman and Sandburg because they celebrated all humanity. Hughes accomplished a lot both before and after meeting Lindsay. He attended Columbia and graduated from Lincoln University. He traveled widely and spoke three languages. He was part of the Harlem Renaissance and published many books of poetry, plays, fiction, and nonfiction. Langston Hughes is probably the most famous and original of all African American poets.

Reading Informational Materials

Reading Check
Langston Hughes: A Biography

1. According to the biography, how did Vachel Lindsay help Langston Hughes?

2. According to the biography, which poets most influenced Hughes?

3. How did Hughes use the experiences of African Americans in his poetry?

4. What did Hughes say was the mission of an artist?

5. What did Hughes say he attempted to do in his work?

TestPractice

"Langston Hughes": A Summary

1. Which of the following **details** is included in *both* the summary and the biography?

   A Hughes was influenced by Whitman and Sandburg.

   B Hughes read Masters, Lindsay, Lowell, Sandburg, and Whitman.

   C Hughes spoke German and Spanish.

   D Hughes traveled to Africa, Mexico, France, and Italy.

2. Which detail in the summary is probably *not* important and could have been omitted?

   F Hughes became famous at age twenty-three.

   G Hughes was part of the Harlem Renaissance.

   H Hughes wrote about African Americans.

   J Hughes was published in a high school literary magazine.

3. Which **critical details** from the biography does the summary omit?

   A Hughes's birth and death dates

   B Influences on Hughes

   C Colleges Hughes attended

   D Hughes's subject matter

4. Which passage in the summary should be placed in **quotation marks** because it uses the exact words of the writer of the biography?

   F attended Columbia and graduated from Lincoln University

   G accomplished a lot both before and after meeting Lindsay

   H traveled widely and spoke three languages

   J the most famous and original of all African American poets

Reading Standard 2.4 Compare the original text to a summary to determine whether the summary accurately captures the main ideas, includes critical details, and conveys the underlying meaning.

Literary Response and Analysis

TestPractice

POETRY

DIRECTIONS: Read each question, and write the letter of the best response.

1. Many old songs survive from the Middle Ages in England. These old songs often tell stories of betrayal, murder, and love. They have simple meters, use simple rhymes, and include a refrain. These old songs are called —

   A ballads

   B sonnets

   C epics

   D couplets

2. Read this short poem by Langston Hughes, and answer the question that follows.

   > O God of dust and rainbows help us see
   >
   > That without dust the rainbow would not be.

   This poem could *best* be described as —

   F a ballad

   G a sonnet

   H an epic

   J a lyric

3. In the poem above, the rhyme could *best* be described as —

   A free verse

   B a couplet

   C meter

   D approximate rhyme

4. Homer's great stories of the heroes of the Trojan War, the *Iliad* and the *Odyssey;* the ancient Mesopotamian story of the hero-king Gilgamesh; the story of the warrior Beowulf, who saves a people from monsters—all of these are called —

   F ballads

   G epics

   H lyrics

   J elegies

5. Read these famous lines from the Bible, and answer the question that follows.

   > To every thing there is a season,
   > And a time to every purpose under the heaven:
   > A time to be born, and a time to die;
   > A time to plant, and a time to pluck up that which is planted. . . .
   > —Ecclesiastes 3:1–2

   Which of the following comments about these lines is correct?

   A The lines are in free verse.

   B The lines are in couplets.

   C The lines are a ballad.

   D The lines are written in strict meter.

Reading Standard 3.1
Determine and articulate the relationship between the purposes and characteristics of different forms of poetry (for example, ballad, lyric, couplet, epic, elegy, ode, sonnet).

6. Read the following poem, and answer the question that follows. (Be sure to note the number of lines in the poem. Also note that *D.R.* in line 6 means "Dominican Republic.")

> I've heard said that among the
>   eskimos
> there are over a hundred words
>   for snow:
> the soft kind, the hard-driving
>   kind, the roll
> a snowball kind: snow being such
>   a force   ✓
> in their lives, it needs a blizzard
> 5   of words.
> In my own D.R. we have many rains:
> the sprinkle, the shower, the
>   hurricane,
> the tears, the many tears for our
>   many dead.
> I've asked around and find that in
>   all tongues
> there are at least a dozen words
> 10   for talk:
> the heart-to-heart, the chat, the
>   confession,
> the juicy gossip, the quip, the
>   harangue—
> no matter where we're from we
>   need to talk
> about snow, rain, about being human.
>   —Julia Alvarez

This poem is an example of —

F an elegy
G an ode
H a ballad
J a sonnet

7. Which of the following statements *best* expresses the **main idea** of Julia Alvarez's poem? (See item 6.)

A Eskimos have many words for snow.
B People in the Dominican Republic have many words for rain.
C All languages have many words for talk.
D Communication is important for all people.

8. If you were reading a serious poem written to mourn someone who has died, you would probably be reading—

F an ode
G a ballad
H an epic
J an elegy

9. If you read a poem called "Ode to the West Wind," you could expect —

A a poem that was light and humorous
B a song with a refrain
C a mournful poem about someone who has died
D a serious poem written in formal language

Reading Informational Materials

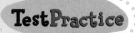 **DIRECTIONS:** Read the poem and the summary that follows. Then, read each question, and write the letter of the best response.

Oranges

Gary Soto

The first time I walked
With a girl, I was twelve,
Cold, and weighted down
With two oranges in my jacket.
5 December. Frost cracking
Beneath my steps, my breath
Before me, then gone,
As I walked toward
Her house, the one whose
10 Porch light burned yellow
Night and day, in any weather.
A dog barked at me, until
She came out pulling
At her gloves, face bright
15 With rouge. I smiled,
Touched her shoulder, and led
Her down the street, across
A used car lot and a line
Of newly planted trees,
20 Until we were breathing
Before a drugstore. We
Entered, the tiny bell
Bringing a saleslady
Down a narrow aisle of goods.
25 I turned to the candies
Tiered like bleachers,
And asked what she wanted—
Light in her eyes, a smile
Starting at the corners

30 Of her mouth. I fingered
A nickel in my pocket,
And when she lifted a chocolate
That cost a dime,
I didn't say anything.
35 I took the nickel from
My pocket, then an orange,
And set them quietly on
The counter. When I looked up,
The lady's eyes met mine,
40 And held them, knowing
Very well what it was all
About.

    Outside,
A few cars hissing past,
Fog hanging like old
45 Coats between the trees.
I took my girl's hand
In mine for two blocks,
Then released it to let
Her unwrap the chocolate.
50 I peeled my orange
That was so bright against
The gray of December
That, from some distance,
Someone might have thought
55 I was making a fire in my hands.

Reading Standard 2.4
Compare the original text to a summary to determine whether the summary accurately captures the main ideas, includes critical details, and conveys the underlying meaning.

"Oranges": A Summary

The poem "Oranges" by Gary Soto is about the bittersweet experience of a first date. As the boy walks to the girl's house, with a nickel and two oranges in his pocket, his breath is visible in the December chill. A dog barks at him till the girl appears; then all is well. They walk together to the drugstore. Offered her choice, the girl picks a chocolate that costs a dime. The boy pays for the candy with his nickel, which is all the money he has, and offers an orange as well. The saleslady understands, her eyes holding his for a moment. Back on the street again, the boy takes his girl's hand for two blocks and then releases it so she can unwrap her chocolate. He peels his orange, which is so bright in the darkness he says someone might have thought I was making a fire in my hands. The brightness of that moment will live in his memory like a flame.

1. Which phrase from the summary contains a **critical detail**?
   A "As the boy walks"
   B "with a nickel and two oranges in his pocket"
   C "his breath is visible"
   D "Back on the street again"

2. Which item below contains a less important detail, one that could have been omitted from the summary?
   F "A dog barks at him. . . ."
   G "They walk together to the drugstore."
   H "The saleslady understands. . . ."
   J "The boy takes his girl's hand. . . ."

3. Which of the following passages from the summary suggests the poem's **underlying meaning,** or **main idea**?
   A "The poem . . . is about the bittersweet experience of a first date."
   B "The saleslady understands, her eyes holding his for a moment."
   C "As the boy walks to the girl's house, with a nickel and two oranges . . ."
   D "The brightness of that moment will live in his memory like a flame."

4. Which passage from the summary is a **direct quote** and should be in quotation marks?
   F the bittersweet experience of a first date
   G all is well
   H The saleslady understands
   J someone might have thought I was making a fire in my hands

Vocabulary Development

TestPractice

Multiple-Meaning Words

DIRECTIONS: Choose the answer in which the underlined word is used the same way it is used in the quotation from "The Cremation of Sam McGee."

1. "Now Sam McGee was from Tennessee, where the cotton blooms and blows."
   A   The boxer's blows were swift and deadly.
   B   The milkweed seed blows over the fields.
   C   Joshua blows his trumpet, and the walls come tumbling down.
   D   The boy blows his nose in his hand-kerchief.

2. "Talk of your cold! through the parka's fold it stabbed like a driven nail."
   F   Jake had no friends because of his cold personality.
   G   The ponies shivered all night in the cold.
   H   When Angela got a cold, she couldn't stop sneezing.
   J   Mara prefers cold colors, like blue, to warm ones, like red.

3. "And that very night, as we lay packed tight in our robes beneath the snow . . ."
   A   No one knew who would win the tight race for class president.
   B   Scrooge was so tight he wouldn't pay fair wages.
   C   The puppies snuggled tight against their mother.
   D   The salesclerk said, "Sit tight. I'll be right with you."

4. "And the dogs were fed, and the stars o'erhead were dancing heel and toe . . ."
   F   Maria got a blister on her heel while hiking in the woods.
   G   Jim felt like a heel when he was mean to his brother.
   H   The well-behaved dog would heel behind his trainer.
   J   Paulie threw the heel of bread to the hungry ducks.

5. "Some planks I tore from the cabin floor, and I lit the boiler fire. . . ."
   A   The candidate had twelve planks in her platform.
   B   Ivan built his cabin out of oak planks.
   C   The pirates made their prisoners walk the plank.
   D   Mary served the fish on a wooden plank.

Mastering the Standards

RESPONSE TO LITERATURE

Sound and Sense

When you respond to a poem, you do two things. First, you analyze the poem—you take the poem apart to see how it works. Second, you explain how the poem's message and language affect you.

- Your first task is to select a poem. This chapter contains many poems. (Don't overlook the poem by Julia Alvarez on page 459.)
- Once you have your poem, take notes, using a chart like the one below:

Who is the **speaker** of the poem? What is the poem about?
Does the poem tell a **story**? If so, tell who the main characters are, and summarize the main events.
Is the poem a lyric poem? What feeling does it express?
Is the poem written with **rhyme** and **meter**, or is it in **free verse**? Does it use **alliteration** or **onomatopoeia**? Does it use **metaphors**, **similes**, or **personification**?
Explain how the poem affects you, using specific details from the poem.

 Use "Writing a Response to a Poem," pages 773–775, for help with this assignment.

Other Choices

PERFORMANCE

1 Reader's Theater

Select a group of poems from this chapter for performance in a reader's theater. You can prepare the poems for delivery by a single reader, by two or three readers, or by a chorus. You can also have two or three actors dramatize your poem. You can wear costumes and use props, lighting, and sound effects to make your reader's theater come alive.

 Use "Reciting and Listening to a Literary Work," pages 637–640, for help with this assignment.

POEM

2 Answering a Poem

Write a poem that responds to another poem. For example, you might want to answer the poem by Julia Alvarez on page 459, about our need for communication. You might want to write a response to "Paul Revere's Ride," dedicated to the other rider, William Dawes. You might want to write a poem like Langston Hughes's "I, Too," in which you tell about a particular American voice. Choose your own form; the voice in the poem must be your own.

Fiction *and* Poetry

Full Speed Ahead!

Robert Lawson presents a different perspective on Paul Revere's ride in his novel *Mr. Revere and I.* Lawson writes about Revere's famous ride from the point of view of the horse! The book contains humor as well as useful historical information about the beginning of the American Revolution.

Wonders of Nature

You will gain an appreciation of Japanese poetry in *In the Eyes of the Cat.* The editor and illustrator Demi has selected short poems about animals, from the gnat to the monkey, and arranged them according to the seasons. The illustrations help make this a thoroughly enjoyable book for all readers.

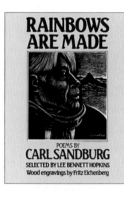

An American Icon

Carl Sandburg's interest in America was boundless. He composed poems about American workers and cities, played folk songs, and wrote a six-volume biography of Abraham Lincoln. *Rainbows Are Made* is a collection of Sandburg's poems. They are sometimes funny, occasionally grim, and always enlightening.

The Power of Imagination

The popular poet Naomi Shihab Nye chose the poems that make up the bilingual collection called *The Tree Is Older Than You Are.* Famous poets such as Octavio Paz and Alberto Blanco take scenes from everyday life and make them extraordinary. Illustrations by Mexican painters complement the poems.

Nonfiction

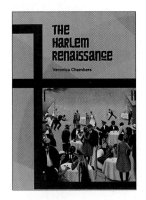

Cultural Revolution

In *The Harlem Renaissance,* Veronica Chambers looks back at a special time in American history. During the 1920s, African American musicians such as Duke Ellington, writers such as Zora Neale Hurston, and painters such as William H. Johnson produced visionary art. Their work continues to influence American society to this day.

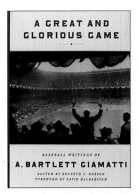

The National Pastime

Baseball was more than a game to A. Bartlett Giamatti; each game was a drama that gave insight into the American character. *A Great and Glorious Game* collects some of Giamatti's writings about the game he loved, from the time he was a literature professor at Yale University through the period when he served as commissioner of baseball.

Honest Abe

Russell Freedman's *Lincoln: A Photo-biography* takes an intimate look at the man who has been called our greatest president. Freedman writes about Abraham Lincoln's childhood, his legendary debates with Stephen Douglas, and his struggles as president during the years of civil war. The photographs and text of this Newbery Medal winner are complemented by illustrations and historical documents.

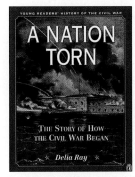

A Nation Divided

Delia Ray looks at the forces that created the Civil War in *A Nation Torn: The Story of How the Civil War Began.* In the years leading up to the war, the North and the South were growing increasingly passionate about their opposing views of slavery, which finally made war inevitable. Ray also highlights the major political figures involved in the war.

7 Literary Criticism

The Person Behind the Text

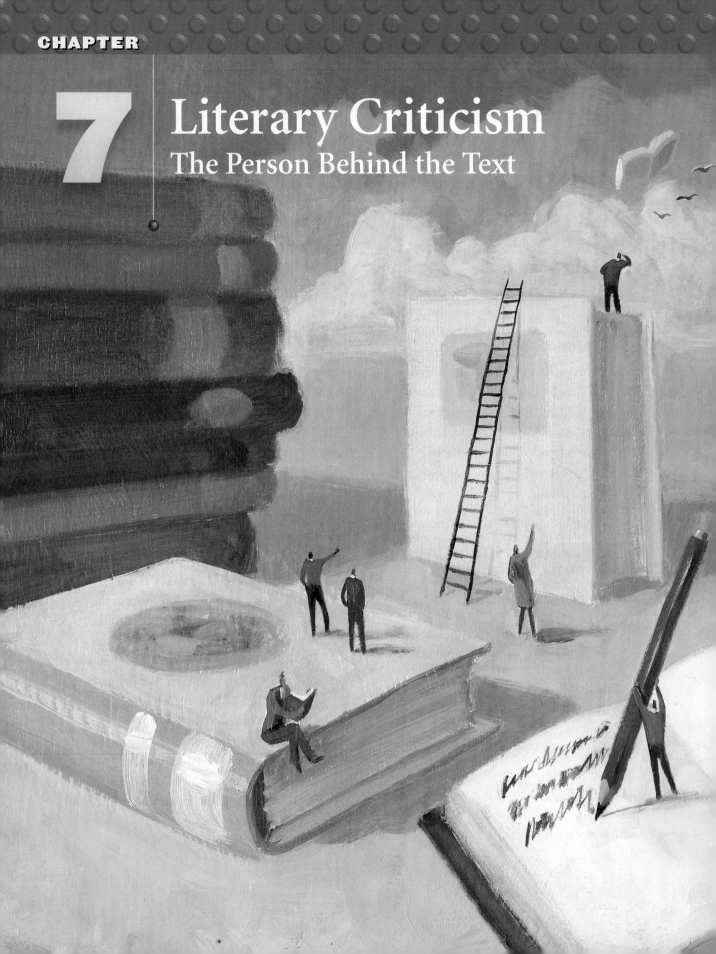

California Standards

Here are the Grade 8 standards you will study for mastery in Chapter 7. You will also review standards from an earlier grade.

Word Analysis, Fluency, and Systematic Vocabulary Development

1.1 Analyze idioms to infer the literal and figurative meanings of phrases.

1.3 Use word meanings within the appropriate context, and show ability to verify those meanings by definition, restatement, example, comparison, or contrast.

Grade 6 Review
1.4 Use word, sentence, and paragraph clues to determine meaning.

Reading Comprehension (Focus on Informational Materials)

2.7 Evaluate the unity, coherence, logic, internal consistency, and structural patterns of text.

Literary Response and Analysis

3.7 Analyze a work of literature, showing how it reflects the heritage, traditions, attitudes, and beliefs of its author (biographical approach).

KEYWORD:
HLLA 8-7

Literary Criticism *by* Mara Rockliff

DOES FICTION REFLECT THE WRITER'S LIFE?

The Person on the Page

The great French essayist Michel de Montaigne once wrote, "Everyone recognizes me in my book, and my book in me." Other writers, however, have complained that readers are mistaken when they believe that a fictional character is actually the writer.

Using Their Lives

There is no question that writers' lives often influence their subject matter. Gary Paulsen wasn't stranded alone in the Canadian wilderness at the age of thirteen, as was his hero in *Hatchet*. However, his adult adventures training sled dogs in Alaska surely made their way into his novel *Dogsong,* about a boy's trek across Alaska by dog sled.

Writers' lives can play into their writing in a multitude of ways. A British writer might set a story in a location he knows well—perhaps an English country home or a boarding school—and then fill his plot with bizarre, completely imaginary events. A fantasy writer might set her story in a place and time that never existed, but her hero's mother might behave very much like someone she once knew—her great-aunt, for example.

However, it's important not to mistake fiction for autobiography. Many of Gary Soto's stories and poems take place in the Mexican American neighborhood where he grew up, but not everything he writes about really happened to him. For example, he says he would have loved to have a girlfriend riding on the handlebars of his bicycle, as Alfonso does in Soto's story "Broken Chain." Instead, he had only his little brother, Jimmy, to share his bike.

Still, it can be intriguing to connect what we know about a writer's life with his or her work. Why does one writer make all of her teenage characters outsiders and rebels? Why does another seem especially interested in divorce? Only the writer can answer these questions for sure.

Writing from Experience

At one time almost all the books published in America were written by people of European descent. These writers wrote not just about their own lives and traditions but about everyone else's too.

Today if you want to read about Native American experiences, you might choose a book by Virginia Driving Hawk Sneve or Joseph Bruchac. A hundred years ago it would have been James Fenimore Cooper's *The Last of the Mohicans.* Today if you want to read about African American experiences,

Reading Standard 3.7 Analyze a work of literature, showing how it reflects the heritage, traditions, attitudes, and beliefs of its author (biographical approach).

you might pick up a book by Virginia Hamilton or Christopher Paul Curtis. A hundred years ago it might have been Harriet Beecher Stowe's wildly popular *Uncle Tom's Cabin.* Today if you want to read about Asian experiences, you might pick up a book by Amy Tan or Laurence Yep. Years ago it would have been *The Good Earth* by Pearl Buck.

Writing from Imagination

There are limits to the idea that writers should write about only what they know. In Laurence Yep's science fiction novel *Sweetwater,* for example, none of the main characters are Asian, like the writer. Some aren't even human! But Yep *is* writing about what he knows— the fear we all may feel in the face of the unknown.

Over a hundred years ago, sitting in her room in Amherst, Massachusetts, the poet Emily Dickinson wrote:

I never saw a moor,
I never saw the sea;
Yet know I how the heather looks.
And what a wave must be.

Can a person who has spent her whole life far from the sea write about the ocean? Can a grown woman write from the point of view of a little boy? Can a writer who's never solved a crime write convincingly, book after book, about all kinds of mysteries?

In fact, good writers deal successfully with challenges like these all the time. Research helps. So does the ability to take what they *know* about life—how people think, act, feel—and apply it to an imagined situation. Today, as they have for thousands of years, writers start with some basic truths, and their imaginations fill in the rest.

Practice

Each school year you are expected to read a variety of books. In your reading you have almost certainly found a special writer whose stories you love. As the school year goes on, keep records of your favorite reading experiences on note cards like the one below. You can find answers to the last three items below by reading about the writer's life.

Author:

Favorite titles:

What he/she writes about:

How stories show author's
  heritage:
  beliefs:
  experiences:

Ribbons

Literary Focus
The Speaker

The **speaker** in a story or poem is the person who tells you the story or talks to you in the poem. It is important to remember, though, that the speaker is not always the writer. In "Ribbons," the speaker is a young girl named Stacy. A man named Laurence Yep wrote the story, so obviously the speaker is not the writer.

No matter how a writer tells a story, it usually reveals something about the writer's background or experiences. As you read this story, look for details that reflect Laurence Yep's heritage. Why do you think he chose a girl to tell you about an ancient Chinese custom that left millions of women with horribly deformed feet that made walking painful?

Reading Skills
Asking Questions

As a reader you do not have to know anything about the writer to appreciate or understand a story. Sometimes, though, you may want to be sure that a writer really knows the subject he or she is writing about. As you read "Ribbons," note any questions you have about the historical or factual details in the story.

Reading Standard 3.7
Analyze a work of literature, showing how it reflects the heritage, traditions, attitudes, and beliefs of its author (biographical approach).

Make the Connection
Quickwrite ✏️

The grandmother and granddaughter in this story grew up in very different cultures. How is your childhood different from the childhoods of your parents, grandparents, or any other adults you know well?

Vocabulary Development

You'll come across these words as you read this short story:

harassed (har′əst, hə·rast′) *v.* used as *adj.*: troubled; bothered. *Father looked harassed by all the work he had to do.*

laborious (lə·bôr′ē·əs) *adj.*: hard; difficult. *With difficulty, Grandma made the laborious climb up the stairs.*

exotic (eg·zät′ik) *adj.*: foreign; strange in a fascinating way. *Stacy noticed the exotic scent of her grandmother's belongings.*

exertion (eg·zur′shən) *n.*: hard work or effort. *Stacy's father was tired from the exertion of carrying many boxes.*

exile (ek′sīl′) *n.*: living away from one's country or community. Exile is usually forced. *Stacy felt she was in exile from ballet classes. Her grandma lived in exile from her home.*

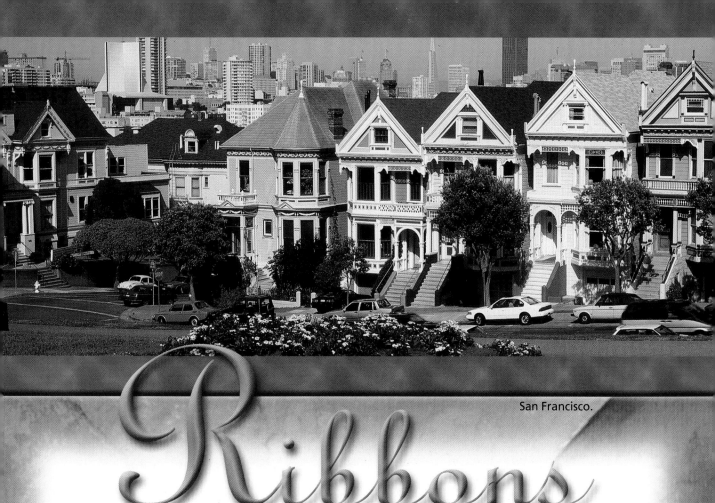

San Francisco.

Ribbons

Laurence Yep

The sunlight swept over the broad grassy square, across the street, and onto our living room rug. In that bright, warm rectangle of light, I practiced my ballet. Ian, my little brother, giggled and dodged around me while I did my exercises.

A car stopped outside, and Ian rushed to the window. "She's here! She's here!" he shouted excitedly. "Paw-paw's here!" *Paw-paw* is Chinese for grandmother—for "mother's mother."

I squeezed in beside Ian so I could look out the window, too. Dad's head was just disappearing as he leaned into the trunk of the car. A pile of luggage and cardboard boxes wrapped in rope sat by the curb. "Is that all Grandmother's?" I said. I didn't see how it would fit into my old bedroom.

Mom laughed behind me. "We're lucky she had to leave her furniture behind in Hong Kong." Mom had been trying to get her mother to come to San Francisco for years. Grandmother had finally agreed, but only because the British were going to return the city to the Chinese Communists in 1997. Because Grandmother's airfare and legal expenses had been so high, there wasn't room in the family budget for Madame

Oblomov's ballet school. I'd had to stop my daily lessons.

The rear car door opened, and a pair of carved black canes poked out like six-shooters. "Wait, Paw-paw," Dad said, and slammed the trunk shut. He looked sweaty and <u>harassed</u>.

Grandmother, however, was already using her canes to get to her feet. "I'm not helpless," she insisted to Dad.

Ian was relieved. "She speaks English," he said.

"She worked for a British family for years," Mom explained.

Turning, Ian ran toward the stairs. "I've got the door," he cried. Mom and I caught up with him at the front door and made him wait on the porch. "You don't want to knock her over," I said. For weeks, Mom had been rehearsing us for just this moment. Ian was supposed to wait, but in his excitement he began bowing to Grandmother as she struggled up the outside staircase.

Grandmother was a small woman in a padded silk jacket and black slacks. Her hair was pulled back into a bun behind her head. On her small feet she wore a pair of quilted cotton slippers shaped like boots, with furred tops that hid her ankles.

"What's wrong with her feet?" I whispered to Mom.

"They've always been that way. And don't mention it," she said. "She's sensitive about them."

I was instantly curious. "But what happened to them?"

"Wise grandchildren wouldn't ask," Mom warned.

Vocabulary
harassed (har′əst, hə·rast′) v. used as *adj.*: troubled; bothered.

Mom bowed formally as Grandmother reached the porch. "I'm so glad you're here," she said.

Grandmother gazed past us to the stairway leading up to our second-floor apartment. "Why do you have to have so many steps?" she said.

Mom sounded as meek as a child. "I'm sorry, Mother," she said.

Dad tried to change the subject. "That's Stacy, and this little monster is Ian."

"*Joe sun, Paw-paw,*" I said. "Good morning, Grand-mother." It was afternoon, but that was the only Chinese I knew, and I had been practicing it.

Mother had coached us on a proper Chinese greeting for the last two months, but I thought Grandmother also deserved an American-style bear hug. However, when I tried to put my arms around her and kiss her, she stiffened in surprise. "Nice children don't drool on people," she snapped at me.

To Ian, anything worth doing was worth repeating, so he bowed again. "*Joe sun, Paw-paw.*"

Grandmother brightened in an instant. "He has your eyes," she said to Mom.

Mom bent and hefted Ian into her arms. "Let me show you our apartment. You'll be in Stacy's room."

Grandmother didn't even thank me. Instead, she stumped up the stairs after Mom, trying to coax a smile from Ian, who was staring at her over Mom's shoulder.

Grandmother's climb was long, slow, laborious. *Thump, thump, thump.* Her

---

Vocabulary
laborious (lə·bôr′ē·əs) *adj.:* hard; difficult.

canes struck the boards as she slowly mounted the steps. It sounded like the slow, steady beat of a mechanical heart.

Mom had told us her mother's story often enough. When Mom's father died, Grandmother had strapped my mother to her back and walked across China to Hong Kong to escape the Communists who had taken over her country. I had always thought her trek was heroic, but it seemed even braver when I realized how wobbly she was on her feet.

I was going to follow Grandmother, but Dad waved me down to the sidewalk. "I need you to watch your grandmother's things until I finish bringing them up," he said. He took a suitcase in either hand and set off, catching up with Grandmother at the foot of the first staircase.

While I waited for him to come back, I inspected Grandmother's pile of belongings. The boxes, webbed with tight cords, were covered with words in Chinese and English. I could almost smell their exotic scent, and in my imagination I pictured sunlit waters lapping at picturesque docks. Hong Kong was probably as exotic to me as America was to Grandmother. Almost without thinking, I began to dance.

Dad came back out, his face red from exertion. "I wish I had half your energy," he said. Crouching, he used the cords to lift a box in each hand.

I pirouetted,[1] and the world spun round and round. "Madame Oblomov said I should still practice every day." I had waited for this day not only for Grandmother's sake but for my own. "Now that Grandmother's here, can I begin my ballet lessons again?" I asked.

Dad turned toward the house. "We'll see, hon."

Disappointment made me protest. "But you said I had to give up the lessons so we could bring her from Hong Kong," I said. "Well, she's here."

Dad hesitated and then set the boxes down. "Try to understand, hon. We've got to set your grandmother up in her own apartment. That's going to take even more money. Don't you want your room back?"

Poor Dad. He looked tired and worried. I should have shut up, but I loved ballet almost as much as I loved him. "Madame put me in the fifth division even though I'm only eleven. If I'm absent much longer, she might make me start over again with the beginners."

"It'll be soon. I promise." He looked guilty as he picked up the boxes and struggled toward the stairs.

Dad had taken away the one hope that had kept me going during my exile from Madame. Suddenly I felt lost, and the following weeks only made me more

---

1. **pirouetted** (pir′o͞o·et′id) *v.:* whirled around on one foot or on the point of the toe.

Vocabulary

exotic (eg·zät′ik) *adj.:* foreign; strange in a fascinating way.

exertion (eg·zur′shən) *n.:* hard work or effort.

exile (ek′sīl′) *n.:* living away from one's country, usually not by choice.

Street in Hong Kong.

confused. Mom started laying down all sorts of new rules. First, we couldn't run around or make noise because Grandmother had to rest. Then, we couldn't watch our favorite TV shows because Grandmother couldn't understand them. Instead, we had to watch westerns on one of the cable stations because it was easier for her to figure out who was the good guy and who was the bad one.

Worst of all, Ian got all of her attention—and her candy and anything else she could bribe him with. It finally got to me on a warm Sunday afternoon a month after she had arrived. I'd just returned home from a long walk in the park with some friends. I was looking forward to something cool and sweet when I found her giving Ian an ice-cream bar I'd bought for myself. "But that was *my* ice-cream bar," I complained as he gulped it down.

"Big sisters need to share with little brothers," Grandmother said, and she patted him on the head to encourage him to go on eating.

When I complained to Mom about how Grandmother was spoiling Ian, she only sighed. "He's a boy, Stacy. Back in China, boys are everything."

It wasn't until I saw Grandmother and Ian together the next day that I thought I really understood why she treated him so much better. She was sitting on a kitchen chair with her head bent over next to his. She had taught Ian enough Chinese so that they could hold short, simple conversations. With their faces so close, I could see how much alike they were.

Ian and I both have the same brown eyes, but his hair is black, while mine is brown, like Dad's. In fact, everything about Ian looks more Chinese. Except for the shape of my eyes, I look as Caucasian as Dad.

And yet people sometimes stare at me as if I were a freak. I've always told myself that it's because they're ignorant and never learned manners, but it was really hard to have my own grandmother make me feel that way.

Even so, I kept telling myself: Grandmother is a hero. She saved my mother. She'll like me just as much as she likes Ian once she gets to know me. And, I thought in a flash, the best way to know a person is to know what she loves. For me, that was the ballet.

Ever since Grandmother had arrived, I'd been practicing my ballet privately in the room I now shared with Ian. Now I got out the special box that held my satin toeshoes. I had been so proud when Madame said I was ready to use them. I was the youngest girl on *pointe*[2] at Madame's school. As I lifted them out, the satin ribbons fluttered down around my wrists as if in a welcoming caress. I slipped one of the shoes onto my foot, but when I tried to tie the ribbons around my ankles, the ribbons came off in my hands.

I could have asked Mom to help me re-attach them, but then I remembered that at one time Grandmother had supported her family by being a seamstress.

Grandmother was sitting in the big recliner in the living room. She stared uneasily out the window as if she were gazing not upon the broad, green lawn of the square but upon a Martian desert.

"Paw-paw," I said, "can you help me?"

Grandmother gave a start when she turned around and saw the ribbons dangling from my hand. Then she looked down at my

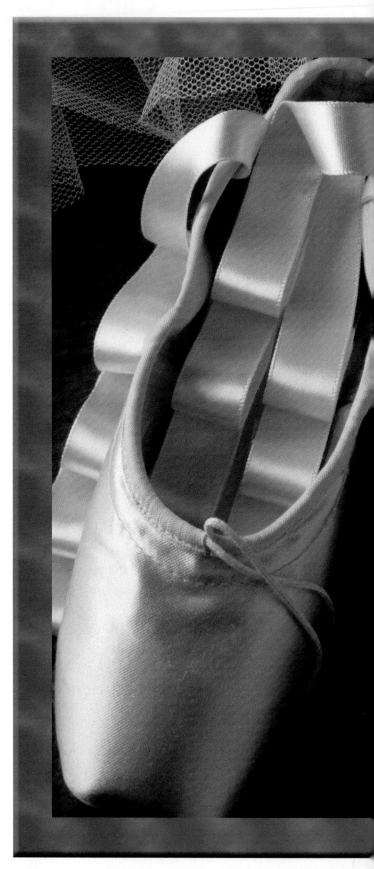

---

2. ***pointe*** (point) *n.:* ballet position on the tip of the toe. In French the pronunciation is pwa*n*t.

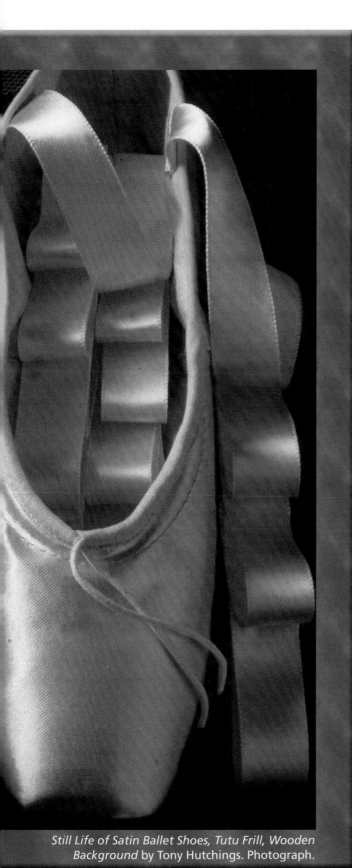

Still Life of Satin Ballet Shoes, Tutu Frill, Wooden Background by Tony Hutchings. Photograph.

bare feet, which were calloused from three years of daily lessons. When she looked back at the satin ribbons, it was with a hate and disgust that I had never seen before. "Give those to me." She held out her hand.

I clutched the ribbons tightly against my stomach. "Why?"

"They'll ruin your feet." She lunged toward me and tried to snatch them away.

Angry and bewildered, I retreated a few steps and showed her the shoe. "No, they're for dancing!"

All Grandmother could see, though, was the ribbons. She managed to totter to her feet without the canes and almost fell forward on her face. Somehow, she regained her balance. Arms reaching out, she stumbled clumsily after me. "Lies!" she said.

"It's the truth!" I backed up so fast that I bumped into Mom as she came running from the kitchen.

Mom immediately assumed it was my fault. "Stop yelling at your grandmother!" she said.

By this point, I was in tears. "She's taken everything else. Now she wants my toeshoe ribbons."

Grandmother panted as she leaned on Mom. "How could you do that to your own daughter?"

"It's not like you think," Mom tried to explain.

However, Grandmother was too upset to listen. "Take them away!"

Mom helped Grandmother back to her easy chair. "You don't understand," Mom said.

All Grandmother did was stare at the ribbons as she sat back down in the chair. "Take them away. Burn them. Bury them."

Mom sighed. "Yes, Mother."

As Mom came over to me, I stared at her in amazement. "Aren't you going to stand up for me?"

But she acted as if she wanted to break any ties between us. "Can't you see how worked up Paw-paw is?" she whispered. "She won't listen to reason. Give her some time. Let her cool off." She worked the ribbons away from my stunned fingers. Then she also took the shoe.

For the rest of the day, Grandmother just turned away every time Mom and I tried to raise the subject. It was as if she didn't want to even think about satin ribbons.

That evening, after the dozenth attempt, I finally said to Mom, "She's so weird. What's so bad about satin ribbons?"

"She associates them with something awful that happened to her," Mom said.

That puzzled me even more. "What was that?"

She shook her head. "I'm sorry. She made me promise never to talk about it to anyone."

The next morning, I decided that if Grandmother was going to be mean to me, then I would be mean to her. I began to ignore her. When she entered a room I was in, I would deliberately turn around and leave.

For the rest of the day, things got more and more tense. Then I happened to go into the bathroom early that evening. The door wasn't locked, so I thought it was unoccupied, but Grandmother was sitting fully clothed on the edge of the bathtub. Her slacks were rolled up to her knees, and she had her feet soaking in a pan of water.

"Don't you know how to knock?" she snapped, and dropped a towel over her feet.

However, she wasn't quick enough, because I saw her bare feet for the first time. Her feet were like taffy that someone had stretched out and twisted. Each foot bent downward in a way that feet were not meant to, and her toes stuck out at odd angles, more like lumps than toes. I didn't think she had all ten of them, either.

"What happened to your feet?" I whispered in shock.

Looking ashamed, Grandmother flapped a hand in the air for me to go. "None of your business. Now get out."

She must have said something to Mom, though, because that night Mom came in and sat on my bed. Ian was outside playing with Grandmother. "Your grandmother's very upset, Stacy," Mom said.

"I didn't mean to look," I said. "It was horrible." Even when I closed my eyes, I could see her mangled feet.

I opened my eyes when I felt Mom's hand on my shoulder. "She was so ashamed of them that she didn't like even me to see them," she said.

"What happened to them?" I wondered.

Mom's forehead furrowed as if she wasn't sure how to explain things. "There was a time back in China when people thought women's feet had to be shaped a certain way to look beautiful. When a girl was about five, her mother would gradually bend her toes under the sole of her foot."

"Ugh." Just thinking about it made my own feet ache. "Her own mother did that to her?"

Mom smiled apologetically. "Her mother and father thought it would make their little girl attractive so she could marry a rich man. They were still doing it in some of the back areas of China long after it was outlawed in the rest of the country."

I shook my head. "There's nothing lovely about those feet."

"I know. But they were usually bound up in silk ribbons." Mom brushed some of the hair from my eyes. "Because they were a symbol of the old days, Paw-paw undid the ribbons as soon as we were free in Hong Kong—even though they kept back the pain."

I was even more puzzled now. "How did the ribbons do that?"

Mom began to brush my hair with quick, light strokes. "The ribbons kept the blood from circulating freely and bringing more feeling to her feet. Once the ribbons were gone, her feet ached. They probably still do."

I rubbed my own foot in sympathy. "But she doesn't complain."

"That's how tough she is," Mom said.

Finally the truth dawned on me. "And she mistook my toeshoe ribbons for her old ones."

Mom lowered the brush and nodded solemnly. "And she didn't want you to go through the same pain she had."

I guess Grandmother loved me in her own way. When she came into the bedroom with Ian later that evening, I didn't leave. However, she tried to ignore me—as if I had become tainted by her secret.

When Ian demanded a story, I sighed. "All right. But only one."

Naturally, Ian chose the fattest story he could, which was my old collection of fairy tales by Hans Christian Andersen. Years of

Illustration by E. S. Hardy (late 19th century), from "The Little Mermaid" by Hans Christian Andersen.

reading had cracked the spine so that the book fell open automatically in his hands to the story that had been my favorite when I was small. It was the original story of "The Little Mermaid"—not the cartoon. The picture illustrating the tale showed the mermaid posed like a ballerina in the middle of the throne room.

"This one," Ian said, and pointed to the picture of the Little Mermaid.

When Grandmother and Ian sat down on my bed, I began to read. However, when I got to the part where the Little Mermaid could walk on land, I stopped.

Ian was impatient. "Come on, read," he ordered, patting the page.

"After that," I went on, "each step hurt her as if she were walking on a knife." I couldn't help looking up at Grandmother.

This time she was the one to pat the page. "Go on. Tell me more about the mermaid."

So I went on reading to the very end, where the Little Mermaid changes into sea foam. "That's a dumb ending," Ian said. "Who wants to be pollution?"

"Sea foam isn't pollution. It's just bubbles," I explained. "The important thing was that she wanted to walk even though it hurt."

"I would rather have gone on swimming," Ian insisted.

"But maybe she wanted to see new places and people by going on the land," Grandmother said softly. "If she had kept her tail, the land people would have thought she was odd. They might even have made fun of her."

When she glanced at her own feet, I thought she might be talking about herself— so I seized my chance. "My satin ribbons aren't like your old silk ones. I use them to tie my toeshoes on when I dance." Setting the book down, I got out my other shoe. "Look."

Grandmother fingered the dangling ribbons and then pointed at my bare feet. "But you already have calluses there."

I began to dance before Grandmother could stop me. After a minute, I struck a pose on half-toe. "See? I can move fine."

She took my hand and patted it clumsily. I think it was the first time she had showed me any sign of affection. "When I saw those ribbons, I didn't want you feeling pain like I do."

I covered her hands with mine. "I just wanted to show you what I love best— dancing."

"And I love my children," she said. I could hear the ache in her voice. "And my grandchildren. I don't want anything bad to happen to you."

Suddenly I felt as if there were an invisible ribbon binding us, tougher than silk and satin, stronger even than steel; and it joined her to Mom and Mom to me.

I wanted to hug her so badly that I just did. Though she was stiff at first, she gradually softened in my arms.

"Let me have my ribbons and my shoes," I said in a low voice. "Let me dance."

"Yes, yes," she whispered fiercely.

I felt something on my cheek and realized she was crying, and then I began crying, too.

"So much to learn," she said, and began hugging me back. "So much to learn."

Laurence Yep

"Being an Outsider"

Laurence Yep (1948–   ) believes his sympathy for the outcast is the main reason for his success, particularly with younger readers. He says:

> *I'm always pursuing the theme of being an outsider—an alien—and many teenagers feel they're aliens.*

Indeed, Yep's ability to relate to these feelings has made him popular with readers from all backgrounds for nearly thirty years.

Laurence Yep was born in San Francisco and grew up in an African American neighborhood while commuting to an elementary school in Chinatown. He then went to a predominantly white high school. Although Yep was exposed to many cultures, he felt he had no culture to call his own. His family had lost touch with the traditions of China, their homeland. Perhaps this is why much of Yep's fiction deals with the quest for identity. In *Child of the Owl* the heroine is an American girl named Casey who yearns to connect with her Chinese background. In *Sea Glass* a boy named Craig feels excluded from both white and Chinese American cultures before he finds his own identity.

Maxine Hong Kingston once wrote that Laurence Yep makes readers "gasp with recognition. 'Hey! that happened to me! I did that. I saw that,' the young reader will say, and be glad that a writer set it down, and feel comforted, less eccentric, less alone."

For Independent Reading

Dragonwings is one of Yep's most beloved novels. Set in San Francisco in the early twentieth century, it features a boy who dreams of building the ideal flying machine with his father. *Dragon's Gate* is a more challenging book. It tells the story of fourteen-year-old Otter, a Chinese immigrant who works on the transcontinental railroad under brutal conditions.

Literary Response and Analysis

Reading Check

1. Map out the structure of this story, using a graphic like the one that follows:

Main characters:
Their problem or conflict:
Main events (list as many as you need):
Climax:
Resolution:

Interpretations

2. Stacy and her grandmother come from very different cultures. Fill in a Venn diagram like the one below to show what the story reveals about the two cultures: the grandmother's Chinese culture and Stacy's American culture. In the shaded part, tell what the two cultures share.

Reading Standard 3.7
Analyze a work of literature, showing how it reflects the heritage, traditions, attitudes, and beliefs of its author (biographical approach).

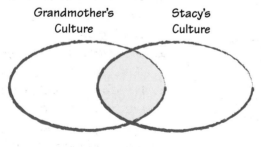

Grandmother's Culture   Stacy's Culture

3. Why does Stacy's grandmother favor Stacy's brother, Ian?

4. What misunderstanding about the ribbons causes the **conflict** between Stacy and her grandmother? How is this conflict between Stacy and her grandmother finally resolved?

5. Think about questions you have after reading this story. Consider the following details, which are presented as facts. Where could you go to check them out—to find out if they are accurate?

- Foot binding was once practiced in China.
- "In China, boys are everything."
- The Communists took over China.
- Many Chinese fled to Hong Kong.
- In 1997, Hong Kong was returned to Chinese control.

Evaluation

6. Why, in your opinion, did Yep choose a girl to be the **speaker**? Do you think Stacy is a believable character— that is, does she speak and behave the way girls her age actually speak and behave? Support your evaluation with specific details from the story.

Writing
Two Childhoods

Write an essay comparing two childhoods: your own childhood and the childhood of an adult you know. Try to show how they are different and how they are similar. You could compare things such as homes, games, chores, schools, clothes, music, and fads.

Vocabulary Development

Reading Standard 1.3
Show ability to verify meanings by definition, example, or contrast.

Verify Meanings: Examples

PRACTICE

1. Describe three situations in which someone would feel harassed. Describe three situations in which someone would *not* feel harassed.
2. How would someone feel after a laborious day? What is the opposite of a laborious day?
3. Name an animal, a plant, and a food that you see as exotic. Name an animal, a plant, and a food that do *not* seem exotic to you.
4. Name three tasks that require exertion. Name three that do *not* require any exertion at all.
5. The term *political exile* is often used today. What does it mean? Give an example of a famous person who was in political exile.

Word Bank

harassed
laborious
exotic
exertion
exile

Grammar Link MINI-LESSON

Its or *It's*?

Confusing *its* and *it's* is one of the most common errors writers make.

- *Its* is the **possessive** form of *it*. A possessive form shows ownership or belonging.

  Stacy held her toeshoe, with its [the shoe's] **satin ribbons, in her hand.**

The possessive form of a noun—such as *shoe's*—has an apostrophe. The possessive form of a personal pronoun—such as *its*—does not.

- *It's* is a **contraction** of *it is* or *it has*. A contraction shortens words by replacing one letter or more with an apostrophe.

  Stacy loves dancing on *pointe* even though it's hard work.

If you're not sure which form is correct, try using *it is* in the sentence. You'll see right away that *Stacy held her toeshoe, with it is satin ribbons, in her hand* doesn't make sense.

PRACTICE

Copy the following sentences, filling in the correct word: *its* or *it's*.

1. When her grandmother comes to live with them, _____ hard for Stacy to adjust.
2. She gives Ian the ice-cream bar even though _____ Stacy's.
3. Ian loves the book, with _____ pretty illustrations.
4. The fairy tale and _____ message help Stacy and her grandmother to understand each other.

For more help, see A Glossary of Usage in the *Holt Handbook*, pages 262–282.

Getting to the *Pointe*

Unity and Text Structure

A friend calls to tell you about something, but his story is so confusing that you ask him to start over again. You can't follow what your friend is saying because he's having trouble with the unity and structure of his story. Here's what to look for in a text when you're evaluating its unity and structure:

A Text Should Have Unity

When a text has **unity,** all its details support the main idea or topic. If your friend's story is about his sister, all the details should involve the sister. He shouldn't add details about his math test. If he sticks to his topic, his story will be unified.

A Text Should Have Structure

A text should have a clear structure. Most texts are organized according to one of the following **structural patterns:**

- **Chronological order.** In chronological order, events are described in the order in which they happen. This pattern is often used in narrative writing. Chronological order is also often used in historical writing and in compositions that explain a process. "Mrs. Flowers's Recipes," on page 137, uses chronological order to explain how to bake sugar cookies. When a text uses chronological order, it usually makes **cause-and-effect** relationships clear. If you are writing about the Civil War, for example, you might want to make clear what **caused** the war and what **effect** the war had on the country.

- **Order of importance.** When you use the order of importance to express your opinion, you give your strongest reason first and then move through less important reasons. For example, you might say, "Getting an education is important because you learn things that will help you all through life. You also need education to get a good job and to earn people's respect." You could also reverse the order, giving the weakest reason first, followed by the stronger ones, saving your strongest point for last.

- **Logical order.** You use logical order when you arrange your supporting details in related groups so that their connections are clear. For example, an article about a dog show might describe first how the dogs are groomed and then how they are paraded before the judges. Next it might list the standards for judging different breeds. When it talks about breed standards, similar breeds might be grouped together and compared. This would be a logical order.

You can use printed texts as models for writing well-organized texts of your own. Start by evaluating the unity and structure of the following article.

Reading Standard 2.7
Evaluate the unity and structural patterns of text.

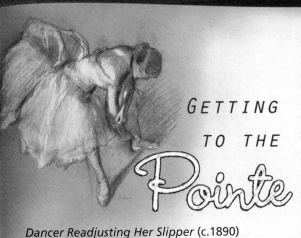

GETTING

TO THE

Pointe

Dancer Readjusting Her Slipper (c.1890)
by Edgar Degas. Pastel and charcoal.

❶ When you think of extreme sports, what's on your list? Snowboarding? Rock climbing? Ballet? . . . What? Not ballet? Think again. Although we think of dancers primarily as artists, they also need the skills of an extreme athlete. A ballet dancer must have the strength of a rock climber, the balance of a snowboarder, and the flexibility of a gymnast. As artists, ballet dancers are capable of casting a spell on an audience; but to cast that spell, they need to be first-rate athletes.

The *Pointe*—A Platform the Size of a Silver Dollar

❷ Gymnasts perform tremendous feats of balance. Ballet dancers, however, perform on the *pointe* of their toeshoes—a platform about the size of a silver dollar. During a performance the force on the *pointe* of their shoes can equal ten times their body's weight. And what about those shoes? If someone hit you on the head with a brand-new ballet shoe, you might think it had

a block of wood in its toe. What's really in it? Most *pointe* shoes are made from paper or burlap that has been soaked in glue, shaped, and covered in satin. Although the shoes are stiff at first, they break down quickly when used. Makers of *pointe* shoes are testing materials that are now used in athletic shoes, but most dancers still prefer the old-fashioned paper-and-glue version. These shoes don't give the foot much padding or protection, but they allow the dancer to "feel" the floor in much the same way that rock climbers must feel the surfaces of the rocks they are climbing. Footing is particularly important to ballet dancers because of the surfaces they perform on.

The *Floor*—It Should Protect the Dancer

❸ Most of the stages that dancers perform on were designed for opera, not dance. Their wood floors are often laid directly on concrete or steel beams. Thus, they lack the spring, or resilience, that could protect a dancer's legs and feet. To see for yourself, try doing jumping jacks on a concrete driveway and then on dirt or a lawn. (You can also try the basketball floor at your school, since most basketball floors are designed to "float" over concrete foundations.) It won't be difficult for your legs, ankles, and feet to feel the differences in these surfaces. Good ballet studios have sprung-wood floors with an inch or two of space between the floor and its concrete foundation. However, since most stages do not offer such a specialized floor, the quality of a ballet studio's flooring is less important than the excellence of the studio's training.

Ballet—A Risky Art

④ Ballet dancers must follow a long, demanding training program because tremendous risks are built into this extreme art form. Ballet training does more than just build strength; it changes the shape of the body. You may have observed that dancers walk, move, and carry their weight differently. This difference reflects the way they must move to stay strong and healthy as they dance. The importance of correct form and technique cannot be overstated. If a dancer shifts balance even slightly to one side rather than directly over the ankle, an additional forty pounds of pressure may be transferred to the delicate foot and ankle. Over time that can lead to stress fractures, tendonitis, and ankle strains or sprains—and a great deal of pain. A good ballet teacher corrects the tiniest errors in foot placement, and ballet students come to welcome such corrections as a means to avoid injury. As much as young dancers long for toeshoes, good ballet teachers know that this step should not be rushed. Experts suggest that *pointe* work should not begin before ages ten to twelve, while a dancer's feet are still growing, and once begun, it should proceed very slowly.

Dance—A Conversation Between Dancer and Audience

⑤ Though their movements are carefully controlled, ballet dancers must learn to make it all look effortless. Dance is an art form, so it is not judged by the same standards that athletic contests are. The longest leap doesn't win a medal. The best dancers may not have the longest leaps, but they have something else: They are able to enchant an audience with the power, grace, and courage of their movement. The length of a leap is less important than the story the dancer tells in leaping. Thus, a leap becomes a sentence in a conversation between the dancer and the audience. When audience members are so involved in the conversation that they forget to notice that the leap itself is spectacular, the dancer has been successful.

Why Do It?

⑥ If you were to ask any extreme athletes why they do what they do, despite the risks of pain and injury, they would probably tell you about the freedom and joy that come with defying gravity, with challenging one's limits, with beating the odds. There is a thrill that comes with holding an audience spellbound. For ballet dancers the joy of performing their art well is as necessary as breathing.

—Sheri Henderson

Reading Informational Materials

Reading Check

To review the structure of this article, make an **outline** that shows the main topic of each paragraph and its supporting details. The outline is begun for you here:

I. Ballet is an extreme sport
   A. It requires strength
   B. It requires balance
   C. It requires flexibility
II. [And so on]

For help in making an outline, see page 338.

Test Practice

GETTING TO THE *Pointe*

1. Which sentence *best* expresses the **main idea** of the entire article?
   A Ballet dancers are better athletes than gymnasts are.
   B A ballet dancer is both an extreme athlete and an artist.
   C It is really hard to be a ballet dancer.
   D Ballet dancing is a dangerous profession.

2. Which of the following sentences could be added to paragraph 2 without destroying its **unity**?
   F Dancers wear many types of warm-up gear.
   G A sprung-wood floor is the best kind for ballet.
   H Dancers soften brand-new *pointe* shoes by hitting them with hammers or slamming them into doors.
   J Tap shoes can badly damage a wood floor.

3. Which of the following sentences could be added to paragraph 4 without destroying its **unity**?
   A Exercises on *pointe* should be increased gradually.
   B Dance costumes should not get in the dancer's way.
   C Try to do fifty jumping jacks every day.
   D Basketball is also a good sport to learn.

4. You can tell that the details in this article are organized in a **logical order** because —
   F the details are organized into related groups
   G the text uses cause-and-effect arguments
   H the text relates events in the order in which they happen
   J the text starts with the most important point and ends with the least important point

Reading Standard 2.7
Evaluate the unity and coherence of text.

Vocabulary Development

Context Clues

PRACTICE

Use **context** clues to guess at the meaning of each underlined word in the following sentences from "Getting to the *Pointe*."

1. "Gymnasts perform tremendous <u>feats</u> of balance."
   Feats are —
   - **a.** sly tricks
   - **b.** remarkable acts
   - **c.** tasty meals
   - **d.** toeholds

2. "Their wood floors are often laid directly on concrete or steel beams. Thus, they lack the spring, or <u>resilience</u>. . . ." *Resilience* means —
   - **a.** ability to bounce back into position
   - **b.** ability to change shape
   - **c.** warmth when touched
   - **d.** hardness and firmness

3. "If a dancer shifts balance even slightly to one side rather than directly over the ankle, an additional forty pounds of pressure may be <u>transferred</u> to the delicate foot and ankle." *Transferred* means —
   - **a.** moved from one place to another
   - **b.** changed completely
   - **c.** sent to a new job
   - **d.** lost on the way

4. "They would probably tell you about the freedom and joy that come with <u>defying</u> gravity. . . ." *Defying* means —
   - **a.** obeying fearfully
   - **b.** defining carefully
   - **c.** defending strongly
   - **d.** resisting boldly

Dancers (detail) by Edgar Degas (1834–1917).

Grade 6 Review Reading Standard 1.4
Use word, sentence, and paragraph clues to determine meaning.

The Treasure of Lemon Brown

Literary Focus
Writer's Background

Writers often draw on their own backgrounds to create a story. The setting may be a place they once lived. The characters may be based on people they knew. The theme may involve issues that especially concern them. The plot might even include events from their own lives. The setting of "The Treasure of Lemon Brown" is Harlem, the neighborhood in New York City where Walter Dean Myers grew up in the 1940s. Myers describes Harlem this way:

66 Thinking back to my boyhood days, I remember the bright sun on Harlem streets, the easy rhythms of black and brown bodies moving along the tar-and-asphalt pavement, the sounds of hundreds of children streaming in and out of red-brick tenements. . . . I remember playing basketball in Morningside Park until it was too dark to see the basket and then climbing over the fence to go home.

Harlem was a place of affirmation. The excitement of city living exploded in the teeming streets. 99

After you have finished the story and read Myers's biography, think about how the writer has used aspects of his life experiences to write this fictional story.

Reading Skills
Retelling

To be certain you understand what you are reading, stop from time to time and retell what has happened so far. As you read this story, stop at the little open-book signs alongside the text. Tell a partner what has happened.

Make the Connection
Quickwrite ✏️

Everyone's background is unique. Jot down some notes about your own background: where you live, the customs of your family, the beliefs you live by. What do you treasure most about your background?

Vocabulary Development

Review these words before you read "The Treasure of Lemon Brown":

impromptu (im·prämp′tōō′) *adj.:* unplanned. *Greg's friends had an impromptu checkers tournament.*

tentatively (ten′tə·tiv·lē) *adv.:* in an uncertain or hesitant way. *Greg pushed tentatively on the tenement door.*

intently (in·tent′lē) *adv.:* with close attention. *Greg listened intently to the sounds in the room.*

brittle (brit′l) *adj.:* having a sharp, hard quality; ready to break. *The man's voice sounded high and brittle.*

ominous (äm′ə·nəs) *adj.:* threatening. *After the crash, Greg heard only an ominous silence.*

Reading Standard 3.7
Analyze a work of literature, showing how it reflects the heritage, traditions, attitudes, and beliefs of its author (biographical approach).

The Treasure of Lemon Brown **489**

Studio View (1977) by Gilbert Fletcher (24" × 20").

The Treasure of Lemon Brown

Walter Dean Myers

The dark sky, filled with angry, swirling clouds, reflected Greg Ridley's mood as he sat on the stoop of his building. His father's voice came to him again, first reading the letter the principal had sent to the house, then lecturing endlessly about his poor efforts in math.

"I had to leave school when I was thirteen," his father had said; "that's a year younger than you are now. If I'd had half the chances that you have, I'd . . ."

Greg had sat in the small, pale-green kitchen listening, knowing the lecture would end with his father saying he couldn't play ball with the Scorpions. He had asked his father the week before, and his father had said it depended on his next report card. It wasn't often the Scorpions took on new players, especially fourteen-year-olds, and this was a chance of a lifetime for Greg. He hadn't been allowed to play high school ball, which he had really wanted to do, but playing for the Community Center team was the next best thing. Report cards were due in a week, and Greg had been hoping for the best. But the principal had ended the suspense early when she sent that letter saying Greg would probably fail math if he didn't spend more time studying.

"And you want to play *basketball*?" His father's brows knitted over deep-brown eyes. "That must be some kind of a joke. Now you just get into your room and hit those books."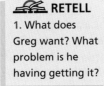

"And you want to play basketball?"

That had been two nights before. His father's words, like the distant thunder that now echoed through the streets of Harlem, still rumbled softly in his ears.

It was beginning to cool. Gusts of wind made bits of paper dance between the parked cars. There was a flash of nearby lightning, and soon large drops of rain splashed onto his jeans. He stood to go upstairs, thought of the lecture that probably awaited him if he did anything except shut himself in his room with his math book, and started walking down the street instead. Down the block there was an old tenement that had been abandoned for some months. Some of the guys had held an impromptu checkers tournament there the week before, and Greg had noticed that the door, once boarded over, had been slightly ajar.

Pulling his collar up as high as he could, he checked for traffic and made a dash across the street. He reached the house just as another flash of lightning changed the night to day for an instant, then returned the graffiti-scarred building to the grim shadows. He vaulted over the outer stairs and pushed tentatively on the door. It was open, and he let himself in.

The inside of the building was dark except for the dim light that filtered through the dirty windows from the street lamps. There

RETELL

1. What does Greg want? What problem is he having getting it?

Vocabulary

impromptu (im·prämp′to͞o′) *adj.:* unplanned; made or done without preparation.

tentatively (ten′tə·tiv·lē) *adv.:* in an uncertain or hesitant way.

was a room a few feet from the door, and from where he stood at the entrance, Greg could see a squarish patch of light on the floor. He entered the room, frowning at the musty smell. It was a large room that might have been someone's parlor at one time. Squinting, Greg could see an old table on its side against one wall, what looked like a pile of rags or a torn mattress in the corner, and a couch, with one side broken, in front of the window.

> **RETELL**
> 2. How does Greg end up in this old tenement?

He went to the couch. The side that wasn't broken was comfortable enough, though a little creaky. From this spot he could see the blinking neon sign over the bodega[1] on the corner. He sat awhile, watching the sign blink first green, then red, allowing his mind to drift to the Scorpions, then to his father. His father had been a postal worker for all Greg's life and was proud of it, often telling Greg how hard he had worked to pass the test. Greg had heard the story too many times to be interested now.

For a moment Greg thought he heard something that sounded like a scraping against the wall. He listened carefully, but it was gone.

Outside, the wind had picked up, sending the rain against the window with a force that shook the glass in its frame. A car passed, its tires hissing over the wet street and its red taillights glowing in the darkness.

Greg thought he heard the noise again. His stomach tightened as he held himself still and listened intently. There weren't any more scraping noises, but he was sure he had heard something in the darkness—something breathing!

He tried to figure out just where the breathing was coming from; he knew it was in the room with him. Slowly he stood, tensing. As he turned, a flash of lightning lit up the room, frightening him with its sudden brilliance. He saw nothing, just the overturned table, the pile of rags, and an old newspaper on the floor. Could he have been imagining the sounds? He continued listening, but heard nothing and thought that it might have just been rats. Still, he thought, as soon as the rain let up he would leave. He went to the window and was about to look out when he heard a voice behind him.

"Don't try nothin', 'cause I got a razor here sharp enough to cut a week into nine days!"

Greg, except for an involuntary tremor in his knees, stood stock-still. The voice was high and brittle, like dry twigs being broken, surely not one he had ever heard before. There was a shuffling sound as the person who had been speaking moved a step closer. Greg turned, holding his breath, his eyes straining to see in the dark room.

The upper part of the figure before him was still in darkness. The lower half was in the dim rectangle of light that fell unevenly from the window. There were two feet, in cracked, dirty shoes from which rose legs that were wrapped in rags.

"Who are you?" Greg hardly recognized his own voice.

"I'm Lemon Brown," came the answer. "Who're you?"

"Greg Ridley."

Vocabulary

intently (in·tent′lē) *adv.:* with close attention.
brittle (brit′′l) *adj.:* having a sharp, hard quality. *Brittle* also means "touchy or unbending."

---

1. **bodega** (bō·dā′gə) *n.:* small grocery store.

Children in Their Moments Alone Dare (1978) by Gilbert Fletcher.

"What you doing here?" The figure shuffled forward again, and Greg took a small step backward.

"It's raining," Greg said.

"I can see that," the figure said.

The person who called himself Lemon Brown peered forward, and Greg could see him clearly. He was an old man. His black, heavily wrinkled face was surrounded by a halo of crinkly white hair and whiskers that seemed to separate his head from the layers of dirty coats piled on his smallish frame.

His pants were bagged to the knee, where they were met with rags that went down to the old shoes. The rags were held on with strings, and there was a rope around his middle. Greg relaxed. He had seen the man before, picking through the trash on the corner and pulling clothes out of a Salvation Army box. There was no sign of the razor that could "cut a week into nine days."

"What are you doing here?" Greg asked.

"This is where I'm staying," Lemon Brown said. "What you here for?"

"Told you it was raining out," Greg said, leaning against the back of the couch until he felt it give slightly.

"Ain't you got no home?"

"I got a home," Greg answered.

"You ain't one of them bad boys looking for my treasure, is you?" Lemon Brown cocked his head to one side and squinted one eye. "Because I told you I got me a razor."

"I'm not looking for your treasure," Greg answered, smiling. "*If* you have one."

"What you mean, *if* I have one," Lemon Brown said. "Every man got a treasure. You don't know that, you must be a fool!"

"Sure," Greg said as he sat on the sofa and put one leg over the back. "What do you have, gold coins?"

"Don't worry none about what I got," Lemon Brown said. "You know who I am?"

"You told me your name was orange or lemon or something like that."

"Lemon Brown," the old man said, pulling back his shoulders as he did so, "they used to call me Sweet Lemon Brown."

"Sweet Lemon?" Greg asked.

"Yessir. Sweet Lemon Brown. They used to say I sung the blues so sweet that if I sang at a funeral, the dead would commence to rocking with the beat. Used to travel all over Mississippi and as far as Monroe, Louisiana, and east on over to Macon, Georgia. You mean you ain't never heard of Sweet Lemon Brown?"

"Afraid not," Greg said. "What . . . what happened to you?"

"Hard times, boy. Hard times always after a poor man. One day I got tired, sat down to rest a spell and felt a tap on my shoulder. Hard times caught up with me."

"Sorry about that."

"What you doing here? How come you didn't go on home when the rain come? Rain don't bother you young folks none."

"Just didn't." Greg looked away.

"I used to have a knotty-headed boy just like you." Lemon Brown had half walked, half shuffled back to the corner and sat down against the wall. "Had them big eyes like you got. I used to call them moon eyes. Look into them moon eyes and see anything you want."

"How come you gave up singing the blues?" Greg asked.

"Didn't give it up," Lemon Brown said. "You don't give up the blues; they give you up. After a while you do good for yourself, and it ain't nothing but foolishness singing about how hard you got it. Ain't that right?"

"I guess so." ✎

📖 RETELL
3. Who is Lemon Brown? What is *his* problem?

"What's that noise?" Lemon Brown asked, suddenly sitting upright.

Greg listened, and he heard a noise outside. He looked at Lemon Brown and saw the old man was pointing toward the window.

Greg went to the window and saw three men, neighborhood thugs, on the stoop. One was carrying a length of pipe. Greg looked back toward Lemon Brown, who moved quietly across the room to the window. The old man looked out, then beckoned frantically for Greg to follow him. For a moment Greg couldn't move. Then he found himself following Lemon Brown into the hallway and up darkened stairs. Greg followed as closely as he could. They reached the top of the stairs, and Greg felt Lemon Brown's hand first lying on his

Street Person (1982)
by Tom McKinney.
Watercolor
(16″ × 20″).

shoulder, then probing down his arm until he finally took Greg's hand into his own as they crouched in the darkness.

"They's bad men," Lemon Brown whispered. His breath was warm against Greg's skin.

"Hey! Ragman!" a voice called. "We know you in here. What you got up under them rags? You got any money?"

Silence.

"We don't want to have to come in and hurt you, old man, but we don't mind if we have to."

Lemon Brown squeezed Greg's hand in his own hard, gnarled fist.

There was a banging downstairs and a light as the men entered. They banged around noisily, calling for the ragman.

"We heard you talking about your treasure." The voice was slurred. "We just want to see it, that's all."

"You sure he's here?" One voice seemed to come from the room with the sofa.

"Yeah, he stays here every night."

"There's another room over there; I'm going to take a look. You got that flashlight?"

"Yeah, here, take the pipe too."

Greg opened his mouth to quiet the sound of his breath as he sucked it in uneasily. A beam of light hit the wall a few feet opposite him, then went out.

"Ain't nobody in that room," a voice said. "You think he gone or something?"

"I don't know," came the answer. "All I know is that I heard him talking about some kind of treasure. You know they found that shopping-bag lady with that money in her bags."

"Yeah. You think he's upstairs?"

"HEY, OLD MAN, ARE YOU UP THERE?"

Silence.

"Watch my back, I'm going up."

There was a footstep on the stairs, and the beam from the flashlight danced crazily along the peeling wallpaper. Greg held his breath. There was another step and a loud crashing noise as the man banged the pipe against the wooden banister. Greg could feel his temples throb as the man slowly neared them. Greg thought about the pipe, wondering what he would do when the man reached them—what he *could* do.

Then Lemon Brown released his hand and moved toward the top of the stairs. Greg looked around and saw stairs going up to the next floor. He tried waving to Lemon Brown, hoping the old man would see him in the dim light and follow him to the next floor. Maybe, Greg thought, the man wouldn't follow them up there. Suddenly, though, Lemon Brown stood at the top of the stairs, both arms raised high above his head.

"There he is!" a voice cried from below.

RETELL

4. What has happened to put Greg and Lemon Brown in danger?

"Throw down your money, old man, so I won't have to bash your head in!"

Lemon Brown didn't move. Greg felt himself near panic. The steps came closer, and still Lemon Brown didn't move. He was an eerie sight, a bundle of rags standing at the top of the stairs, his shadow on the wall looming over him. Maybe, the thought came to Greg, the scene could be even eerier.

Greg wet his lips, put his hands to his mouth, and tried to make a sound. Nothing came out. He swallowed hard, wet his lips once more, and howled as evenly as he could.

"*What's that?*"

As Greg howled, the light moved away from Lemon Brown, but not before Greg saw him hurl his body down the stairs at the men who had come to take his treasure. There was a crashing noise, and then footsteps. A rush of warm air came in as the downstairs door opened; then there was only an <u>ominous</u> silence.

Greg stood on the landing. He listened, and after a while there was another sound on the staircase.

"Mr. Brown?" he called.

"Yeah, it's me," came the answer. "I got their flashlight."

RETELL

5. How do Lemon Brown and Greg scare off the men?

Greg exhaled in relief as Lemon Brown made his way slowly back up the stairs.

"You OK?"

"Few bumps and bruises," Lemon Brown said.

"I think I'd better be going," Greg said, his breath returning to normal. "You'd

Vocabulary

ominous (äm′ə·nəs) *adj.:* threatening; seeming to indicate that something bad will happen.

better leave, too, before they come back."

"They may hang around outside for a while," Lemon Brown said, "but they ain't getting their nerve up to come in here again. Not with crazy old ragmen and howling spooks. Best you stay awhile till the coast is clear. I'm heading out west tomorrow, out to East St. Louis."

"They were talking about treasures," Greg said. "You *really* have a treasure?"

"What I tell you? Didn't I tell you every man got a treasure?" Lemon Brown said. "You want to see mine?"

"If you want to show it to me," Greg shrugged.

"Let's look out the window first, see what them scoundrels be doing," Lemon Brown said.

They followed the oval beam of the flashlight into one of the rooms and looked out the window. They saw the men who had tried to take the treasure sitting on the curb near the corner. One of them had his pants leg up, looking at his knee.

"You sure you're not hurt?" Greg asked Lemon Brown.

"Nothing that ain't been hurt before," Lemon Brown said. "When you get as old as me, all you say when something hurts is, 'Howdy, Mr. Pain, sees you back again.' Then when Mr. Pain see he can't worry you none, he go on mess with somebody else."

Greg smiled.

"Here, you hold this." Lemon Brown gave Greg the flashlight.

He sat on the floor near Greg and carefully untied the strings that held the rags on his

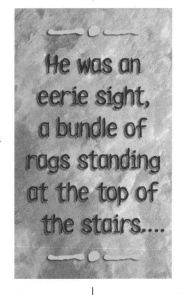

He was an eerie sight, a bundle of rags standing at the top of the stairs....

right leg. When he took the rags away, Greg saw a piece of plastic. The old man carefully took off the plastic and unfolded it. He revealed some yellowed newspaper clippings and a battered harmonica.

"There it be," he said, nodding his head. "There it be."

Greg looked at the old man, saw the distant look in his eye, then turned to the clippings. They told of Sweet Lemon Brown, a blues singer and harmonica player who was appearing at different theaters in the South. One of the clippings said he had been the hit of the show, although not the headliner. All of the clippings were reviews of shows Lemon Brown had been in more than fifty years ago. Greg looked at the harmonica. It was dented badly on one side, with the reed holes on one end nearly closed.

"I used to travel around and make money for to feed my wife and Jesse—that's my boy's name. Used to feed them good, too. Then his mama died, and he stayed with his mama's sister. He growed up to be a man, and when the war come, he saw fit to go off and fight in it. I didn't have nothing to give him except these things that told him who I was, and what he come from. If you know your pappy did something, you know you can do something too.

"Anyway, he went off to war, and I went off still playing and singing. 'Course by then I wasn't as much as I used to be, not without somebody to make it worth the while. You know what I mean?"

"Yeah," Greg nodded, not quite really knowing.

"I traveled around, and one time I come home, and there was this letter saying Jesse got killed in the war. Broke my heart, it truly did.

"They sent back what he had with him over there, and what it is is this old mouth fiddle and these clippings. Him carrying it around with him like that told me it meant something to him. That was my treasure, and when I give it to him, he treated it just like that, a treasure. Ain't that something?"

"Yeah, I guess so," Greg said.

"You *guess* so?" Lemon Brown's voice rose an octave[2] as he started to put his treasure back into the plastic. "Well, you got to guess, 'cause you sure don't know nothing. Don't know enough to get home when it's raining."

"I guess . . . I mean, you're right."

"You OK for a youngster," the old man said as he tied the strings around his leg, "better than those scalawags what come here looking for my treasure. That's for sure."

"You really think that treasure of yours was worth fighting for?" Greg asked. "Against a pipe?"

"What else a man got 'cepting what he can pass on to his son, or his daughter, if she be his oldest?" Lemon Brown said. "For a big-headed boy, you sure do ask the foolishest questions."

> **RETELL**
> 6. What do you learn about the treasure?

---

2. **octave** (äk′tiv) *n.*: eight whole notes.

"If you know your pappy did something, you know you can do something too."

Lemon Brown got up after patting his rags in place and looked out the window again.

"Looks like they're gone. You get on out of here and get yourself home. I'll be watching from the window, so you'll be all right."

Lemon Brown went down the stairs behind Greg. When they reached the front door, the old man looked out first, saw the street was clear, and told Greg to scoot on home.

"You sure you'll be OK?" Greg asked.

"Now, didn't I tell you I was going to East St. Louis in the morning?" Lemon Brown asked. "Don't that sound OK to you?"

"Sure it does," Greg said.

"Sure it does. And you take care of that treasure of yours."

"That I'll do," Lemon said, the wrinkles about his eyes suggesting a smile. "That I'll do."

The night had warmed and the rain had stopped, leaving puddles at the curbs. Greg didn't even want to think how late it was. He thought ahead of what his father would say and wondered if he should tell him about Lemon Brown. He thought about it until he reached his stoop, and decided against it. Lemon Brown would be OK, Greg thought, with his memories and his treasure.

Greg pushed the button over the bell marked "Ridley," thought of the lecture he knew his father would give him, and smiled.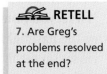

> **RETELL**
> 7. Are Greg's problems resolved at the end?

Walter Dean Myers

Photograph © 1994
by Jill Krementz.

"He Gave Me the Most Precious Gift"

Walter Dean Myers (1937–   ) was born in Martinsburg, West Virginia; he was one of eight children. Myers's mother died when he was two, and when he was three, his father sent him and two of his sisters to New York City to be raised by foster parents, the Deans. When he became a published writer, Myers added their name to his to show how important they were to him.

> My foster father was a wonderful man. He gave me the most precious gift any father could give to a son: He loved me. . . . My foster mother understood the value of education, even though neither she nor my father had more than a rudimentary education. She also understood the value of story, how it could serve as a refuge for people, like us, who couldn't afford the finer things in life or even all of what came to be the everyday things.

Myers has been an editor and a teacher as well as a writer of books for children and young adults. He says:

> Every time I sit down to write, I think of television as a value setter. I may write about a moral kid. Good. But TV says being tough is better. The TV people know that a certain kind of value system—'cool' masculine—is what sells beer and blue jeans. I have to counter that.

For Independent Reading

Hoops is a novel about a Harlem teenager contending for a citywide basketball title against powerful opposition—both on and off the court.

Literary Response and Analysis

Reading Check

1. Work out the main events that advance the **plot** of the story by filling in a diagram like this one. You should find at least three key events that lead to the **climax** and one key event before the **resolution**.

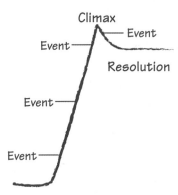

Climax

Event

Event

Resolution

Event

Event

Basic situation
(characters and their problems)

Interpretations

2. Why does Greg smile at the thought of the lecture he will get from his father?

3. In your opinion, why does Greg decide not to tell his father about Lemon Brown?

4. What do you think Greg has learned from Lemon Brown?

5. What does Lemon Brown mean when he says that everyone's got a treasure (page 494)?

6. Lemon Brown says, "If you know your pappy did something, you know you can do something too" (page 497). What does he mean? Do you agree? Explain.

7. Now that you've read the story, as well as Walter Dean Myers's own words about his life, how would you explain the way this **writer's background** is reflected in his story? Include details from the story and from Myers's personal background in your response.

Evaluation

8. Myers says that in his writing he has to "counter" values conveyed by TV (page 499). Is that a worthwhile goal? If Myers asked you whether his story challenges the values communicated by TV, what would you say?

Writing

Everybody's Got a Treasure

Write a children's story that includes parts of your own background. Set your story in a location you know well. Base your characters on people you know, even if you turn them into elves or dragons or puppy dogs. Focus your plot on something that you treasure—a photograph, an old toy, a person, a place. Make your children's story sad or silly or sweet, but make it *yours*.

Reading Standard 3.7
Analyze a work of literature, showing how it reflects the heritage, traditions, attitudes, and beliefs of its author (biographical approach).

Vocabulary Development

Reading Standard 1.3
Use word meanings within the appropriate context.

Vocabulary in Context

In "The Treasure of Lemon Brown," the words in the Word Bank are used in the context of an adventure in a Harlem tenement. The following questions ask you to think of other contexts for these words.

PRACTICE

1. How would an actor use the word *impromptu*?
2. How would the director of a play use the word *tentatively* in telling you that you might have won a part?
3. How would you use the word *intently* in talking about a book you can't put down?
4. How would a doctor use the word *brittle* in talking about an elderly person's bones?
5. How would a weather forecaster use the word *ominous*?

Word Bank

impromptu
tentatively
intently
brittle
ominous

Grammar Link MINI-LESSON

Don't or *Doesn't*?

When you use the contractions *don't* and *doesn't,* be sure they agree with their subjects.

- *Don't* is a contraction of *do not.* Use *don't* with plural subjects and with the pronouns *I* and *you.*

  Greg's dad said, "Get good grades or <u>you</u> <u>don't</u> play basketball."

  The <u>thugs</u> <u>don't</u> know where Greg and Lemon Brown are hiding.

- *Doesn't* is a contraction of *does not.* Use *doesn't* with singular subjects (except *I* and *you*).

  <u>Lemon Brown</u> <u>doesn't</u> want to lose his treasure.

  <u>Something</u> <u>doesn't</u> have to be worth a lot of money to be a treasure.

If you're unsure whether to use *don't* or *doesn't* in a sentence, try substituting *do not* and *does not* for the contractions. You can tell that *she does not* is correct and that *she do not* is incorrect.

PRACTICE

Copy the following sentences, and fill in each blank with the correct contraction: *don't* or *doesn't*.

1. Even though it's raining, Greg _____ want to go home.
2. At first, Greg and Lemon Brown _____ trust each other.
3. Their distrust _____ stop them from hiding together when the thugs enter.
4. The thugs _____ know what kind of treasure Lemon Brown has.
5. "I _____ want to hurt you, old man. Just give me your money."

For more help, see Other Problems in Agreement in the *Holt Handbook,* pages 166–173.

Little Walter

Logic, Coherence, and Consistency

What do you think of this brief response to "The Treasure of Lemon Brown"?

Text 1: An *Illogical* Response

Lemon Brown is a homeless person; therefore, he could not have been a good blues player. I once knew someone who played the harmonica really well. He had red hair and was on my baseball team. I think homeless people should all be given a place to stay so they don't have to sleep on the sidewalk. Lemon Brown should get a job so he could get an apartment.

A Text Should Be Logical

It's pretty obvious that Text 1 is not logical, but why is that? **Logic** means correct reasoning. To be logical, statements should be supported by reasons, evidence, and examples. Statements are *illogical* if the evidence does *not* support what is being said. The statement that Lemon Brown could not have been a good blues singer because he is now homeless is illogical. It is illogical because Lemon Brown's current living situation tells us nothing about his past achievements.

A Text Should Be Coherent

For a text to be logical, it also needs **coherence** (kō·hir′əns). That means that all of its parts must stick together and be clearly understood. Text 1 is not coherent because the writer jumps from one idea to another without making a connection between them.

Transitional words can help the reader follow the coherence of a text. Transitional words connect sentences and ideas. If you pay attention to transitional words when you read, you may find your text easier to understand. The following list shows some situations in which transitional words are used, as well as some transitional words used in these situations:

- connecting ideas **chronologically,** or in time sequence—*first, next, before, then, when, while, meanwhile, at last*
- connecting things in **space**—*above, across, among, before, below, here, in, near, there, under, next to*
- connecting ideas in **order of importance**—*first, mainly, more important, to begin with, then, last*
- **comparing** ideas—*also, and, another, just as, like, similarly*
- **contrasting** ideas—*although, but, however, still, yet, on the other hand*

A Text Should Be Consistent

If a text is logical and coherent, it also has **internal consistency,** which means that all of its parts are connected and agree with what came before. Because Text 1 has no internal consistency, we cannot tell what topic or main idea is intended.

Here is another brief response to "The Treasure of Lemon Brown":

Reading Standard 2.7
Evaluate the coherence, logic, and internal consistency of text.

Text 2: A *Logical* Response

The character of Lemon Brown reminds us of the humanity of homeless people. They are not just misfits who embarrass us by sleeping on our sidewalks and begging for change. Before their problems left them with no place to live, they too had jobs and families. We should always remember that they are human beings with ideas, opinions, and a life history. We should treat them with concern and respect.

This second response *is* logical, because it is based on evidence in the text that shows us Lemon Brown's humanity. It is coherent, because the ideas follow logically from one to the other. It has internal consistency, because all of it is about why homeless people are worthy of our concern and respect.

Background

"The Treasure of Lemon Brown" is a fictional story about a man who once played the harmonica and sang the blues. The article that follows is about Little Walter, a famous real-life blues singer and harmonica player. It's by the Pulitzer Prize–winning writer Studs Terkel, who often writes about life in Chicago. Terkel's text is taken from the jacket copy of a recording of Little Walter's music.

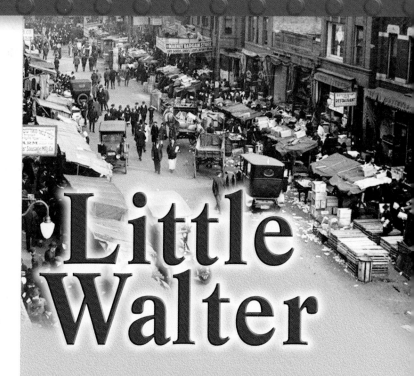

Little Walter

1 Marion Walter Jacobs, age fourteen, stood on the corner blowing wildly into his harmonica.

2 It was the colorful Chicago neighborhood known as the Maxwell Street Market. Here, wares, second- and thirdhand, were displayed out along the sidewalks or high on the open pushcarts. You could buy anything from used coffee grinders to slightly rusty fenders off a 1928 Cadillac to scratchy Victoria Spivey records. Here, too, wandering street musicians, blind and sighted, offered their wares: spirituals, blues, stomps, and pop tunes.

3 Sunday mornings were the choice sessions. It was then the crowds were largest. From all over the city and its environs they came: to gawk,[1] to bargain, perchance to buy. They remained to listen.

4 Young Jacobs ran his mouth and fingers across the harmonica like a magician performing sleight of hand. Passersby were . . . impressed. "Ooowee! Listen to Little

---

1. **gawk** (gôk) *v.:* stare.

Little Walter.

Walter!" It was this moniker[2] that stuck. Certainly, Marion was no name for a wild mouth harpist.

⑤ Little Walter had been playing the harmonica ever since he was six. Why did he take to this humble instrument? His reply is that of the bold spirit to whom all of life is a challenge: "If a guy could pick up a peanut and make something out of it (note: a reference to the deeds of George Washington Carver),[3] I figure I could take the harp an' make something out of it." (Artists of the harmonica seldom refer to it in this four-syllable manner. Always it's the "harp.")

⑥ He was born in Alexandria, Louisiana. . . . As a grocer's delivery boy, he offered the customers waltzes as well as vegetables—the harp was always in his back pocket. "Me an' my harp" were a love affair from way back.

⑦ In 1938, his family was part of the Deep South migration to Chicago. Our man was eight at the time. In this big, sprawling, booming city he heard new sounds. Here it was the great blues artists congregated: the legendary Big Bill, whose life and art were a saga in themselves; Big Maceo Merriwether, Tampa Red, Memphis Minnie. At first, the boy was not attuned to the blues; thus, his playing of polkas and waltzes and pop hits. Bit by bit, by a process of osmosis,[4] the richness of the blues found its way into his harp.

⑧ The young teenager tried to crash various clubs on Chicago's South and West Sides. Invariably he was booted out: "too young." But he was not to be denied, not for long. The veteran bluesmen took to the moans and cries that shouted their way out of his instrument. He was their man. During many of the personal appearances, his harmonica was heard italicizing the vocals of Big Bill, Muddy Waters, and many of their blues brethren. (Muddy insists that Little Walter accompany him on his recordings.)

⑨ His singing came out of Mother Necessity. He had no alternative. "I needed breathing time. If I blowed that harp without any rest, I'd never make it. Not the way *I* blow. So I began to sing in between my blowing, just to rest my lips an' my harp."

⑩ As much as any one man in recent years, . . . he's responsible for the resurgence[5] in the popularity of the blues harmonica. Says he wistfully: "Not so long ago, harp sold for a quarter. Now it cost two dollars. It'd be nice if that company'd remember who helped raise that price."

—Studs Terkel

---

2. **moniker** (män'i·kər) *n.*: slang for "nickname."
3. **George Washington Carver** (1864–1943): African American botanist famous for developing more than three hundred products from peanuts.

4. **osmosis** (äs·mō'sis) *n.*: in science, the passage of liquid through a membrane; here, absorption of ideas, feelings, and so on.
5. **resurgence** (ri·sur'jənts) *n.*: rising up again; re-emergence.

Reading Informational Materials

Reading Check

1. When did Little Walter start playing the harmonica?

2. What do harmonica players call their instrument?

3. What happened when Little Walter and his family moved from Louisiana to Chicago?

4. Why did Little Walter start singing as well as playing his harmonica?

TestPractice

Little Walter

1. We can tell that this article has **internal consistency** because all of it is about —

   A life on the streets of Chicago in 1938

   B the different blues players in Chicago

   C the development of Little Walter as a blues player

   D the family history of Marion Walter Jacobs

2. Which of the following transitional expressions could make a **coherent** connection between these two sentences from paragraph 3?

   "Sunday mornings were the choice sessions. It was then the crowds were largest."

   F in spite of

   G although

   H because

   J eventually

3. Which of the following sentences would make a **logical** addition to the conclusion of paragraph 4?

   A From then on he was Little Walter.

   B Passersby ignored the street musicians.

   C People could get great bargains on Maxwell Street.

   D Harmonicas cost more now than when he began.

4. In paragraph 8, the writer says, "The veteran bluesmen took to the moans and cries that shouted their way out of his instrument." This means that —

   F veteran bluesmen liked Little Walter's harmonica playing

   G veteran bluesmen stole Little Walter's songs

   H Little Walter was too much competition for the veteran bluesmen

   J Little Walter became very sad

Reading Standard 2.7 Evaluate the coherence, logic, and internal consistency of text.

Vocabulary Development

Idioms

In our ordinary, everyday conversation we use idioms without even noticing them. **Idioms** (id′ē·əmz) are expressions particular to a language or group. Idioms mean something other than the literal meanings of their words. *My heart is broken* is an idiom. So are these common expressions:

- It's raining cats and dogs.
- That book blew me away.
- The senator will twist some arms to pass the bill.
- I knocked myself out to finish on time.

PRACTICE 1

Take each idiom listed above, and tell what it means literally. Then, tell what it means figuratively. *My heart is broken,* for example, means literally "my heart is in at least two pieces" or "my heart can no longer pump blood." Figuratively it means "I am very sad and hurt."

Little Walter.

PRACTICE 2

Many of the titles and lyrics of blues songs are based on idioms. Below you will find three blues titles based on idioms, followed by an idiom used by Studs Terkel in the jacket notes for Little Walter's recording. What does each idiom mean literally? What does each one mean figuratively? (Notice how silly the literal meanings of the idioms are.)

1. A well-known blues song goes by the title "Nobody Knows You When You're Down and Out."
2. Little Walter uses some idioms as titles. "You Better Watch Yourself" is one.
3. "Off the Wall" is another of Little Walter's titles.
4. Terkel tells us that as a teenager, Little Walter tried to crash Chicago's blues clubs. (You might find this idiom more familiar in this form: *They weren't invited, so they tried to crash the party.*)

Chicago, 1924.

Reading Standard 1.1
Analyze idioms to infer the literal and figurative meanings of phrases.

A Smart Cookie / Bien águila

Literary Focus

Themes Cross Cultures

Whatever their heritage or traditions, people share certain dreams and fears. For example, people all over the world are likely to say, "I want my children to have everything I missed." In "A Smart Cookie" a mother talks about her missed opportunities and hopes that her daughter, Esperanza, will have a better future. (*Esperanza* means "hope" in Spanish.) As you read this story, look for a line spoken by the mother that expresses its **theme.** Remember that a theme reveals a truth about all our lives—often something that springs from our dreams or fears.

Reading Skills

Understanding Idioms

"A Smart Cookie" appears here in both English, the language in which Sandra Cisneros writes, and Spanish, her parents' language. When Elena Poniatowska translated the story into Spanish, the title posed a special problem because it is an **idiom,** an expression peculiar to a particular language. An idiom means something different from the literal meaning of each word. Do you know what the expression *smart cookie* means?

The translator could have simply used the Spanish words for *smart* and *cookie,* but in Spanish the phrase would just mean "intelligent pastry." To a Spanish speaker it would make no sense. She chose instead to change the title to

"Bien águila" ("A Real Eagle"), a Spanish idiom that means something close to "smart cookie" in English.

Make the Connection

Quickwrite ✏️

Esperanza's mother has hopes for her daughter. Write briefly about someone's hopes for you or about your own hopes for your future.

Background

In this character sketch, the speaker is Esperanza, the young girl who narrates all the stories in Sandra Cisneros's book *The House on Mango Street.* In this sketch, Esperanza lets her mother do a lot of the talking.

Esperanza's mother refers to the tragic opera *Madama Butterfly* by Giacomo Puccini. Butterfly, the heroine of that opera, is a young Japanese woman who falls deeply in love with a U.S. naval officer and marries him. Shortly after their marriage her husband returns to America. Butterfly waits for years and years for him to come back to her and their child. When he does finally return, he has an American wife with him. Butterfly, in despair, gives them her beloved child and then takes her own life.

Reading Standard 3.7 Analyze a work of literature, showing how it reflects the heritage, traditions, attitudes, and beliefs of its author (biographical approach).

A Smart Cookie

Sandra Cisneros

I could've been somebody, you know? my mother says and sighs. She has lived in this city her whole life. She can speak two languages. She can sing an opera. She knows how to fix a TV. But she doesn't know which subway train to take to get downtown. I hold her hand very tight while we wait for the right train to arrive.

She used to draw when she had time. Now she draws with a needle and thread, little knotted rosebuds, tulips made of silk thread. Someday she would like to go to the ballet. Someday she would like to see a play. She borrows opera records from the public library and sings with velvety lungs powerful as morning glories.

Today while cooking oatmeal she is Madame Butterfly until she sighs and points the wooden spoon at me. I could've been somebody, you know? Esperanza, you go to school. Study hard. That Madame Butterfly was a fool. She stirs the oatmeal. Look at my comadres.° She means Izaura whose husband left and Yolanda whose husband is dead. Got to take care all your own, she says shaking her head.

Then out of nowhere:

Shame is a bad thing, you know. It keeps you down. You want to know why I quit school? Because I didn't have nice clothes. No clothes, but I had brains.

Yup, she says disgusted, stirring again. I was a smart cookie then.

° **comadres** (kô·mä′drās) *n.:* Spanish for "close female friends" (literally, a child's mother and godmother).

Bien águila

Sandra Cisneros *translated by Elena Poniatowska*

Yo pude haber sido alguien, ¿sabes? dice mi madre y suspira. Toda su vida ha vivido en esta ciudad. Sabe dos idiomas. Puede cantar una ópera. Sabe reparar la tele. Pero no sabe qué metro tomar para ir al centro. La tomo muy fuerte de la mano mientras esperamos a que llegue el tren.

Cuando tenía tiempo dibujaba. Ahora dibuja con hilo y aguja, pequeños botones de rosa, tulipanes de hilo de seda. Algún día le gustaría ir al ballet. Algún día también, a ver una obra de teatro. Pide discos de ópera en la biblioteca pública y canta con pulmones aterciopelados y poderosos como glorias azules.

Hoy, mientras cuece la avena, es Madame Butterfly hasta que suspira y me señala con la cuchara de palo. Yo pude haber sido alguien, ¿sabes? Ve a la escuela, Esperanza. Estudia macizo. Esa Madame Butterfly era una tonta. Menea la avena. Fíjate en mis comadres. Se refiere a Izaura, cuyo marido se largó, y a Yolanda, cuyo marido está muerto. Tienes que cuidarte solita, dice moviendo la cabeza.

Y luego, nada más porque sí:

La vergüenza es mala cosa, ¿sabes? No te deja levantarte. ¿Sabes por qué dejé la escuela? Porque no tenía ropa bonita. Ropa no, pero cerebro sí.

¡Ufa! dice disgustada, meneando de nuevo. Yo entonces era bien águila.

Mercy (detail) (1992)
by Nick Quijano.

Sandra Cisneros

Crossing the Threshold

Like Esperanza, **Sandra Cisneros** (1954–   ) grew up in a Mexican American family in Chicago. She writes:

> I've managed to do a lot of things in my life I didn't think I was capable of and which many others didn't think me capable of either. Especially because I am a woman, a Latina, an only daughter in a family of six men. My father would've liked to have seen me married long ago. In our culture, men and women don't leave their father's house except by way of marriage. I crossed my father's threshold with nothing carrying me but my own two feet.

For Independent Reading

"A Smart Cookie" comes from *The House on Mango Street,* a collection of short sketches narrated by Esperanza. It was published in Spanish as *La Casa en Mango Street.*

Literary Response and Analysis

Reading Check

1. What is Esperanza's mother good at?

2. What has she never done?

3. What does she want Esperanza to do?

4. Why did Esperanza's mother quit school?

Interpretations

5. When people use **verbal irony,** they mean just the opposite of what they say. When Esperanza's mother uses the **idiom** *smart cookie* to describe herself, what does she really mean?

6. What does Esperanza's mother mean when she says to her daughter, "Got to take care all your own"?

7. What lines in this sketch do you think express most strongly the **theme** of the mother's story? Be sure to compare your choices in class.

8. Read the biography of Sandra Cisneros carefully (see page 510). Can you find any links between the sketch of Esperanza's mother and Cisneros's life story? (Be sure to read Cisneros's own words, within the big quotation marks.) Refer to details from each text in your answer.

9. Look back at your Quickwrite. What connections, if any, do you see between what you wrote there and "A Smart Cookie"?

10. Describe Esperanza's mother's attitude toward education. Do you think it is an attitude people share across cultures? Do you agree with the mother about the effects of shame? Explain.

Writing
What I Think

Write two or three paragraphs responding to one of these opinions:

- Parents put too much pressure on children by wanting their children to have better lives than they had.

- Children need to know the mistakes their parents made so that they can avoid making the same mistakes.

- Education is the key to independence.

- Shame is a bad thing. It keeps you down.

Use examples from real life (from your own life or from the lives of people you know), from literature, or from newspapers or magazines to support your response.

Picnic en el Coche by Theresa Rosado. Acrylic on wood.

Collection of Don Spyke.

Reading Standard 3.7 Analyze a work of literature, showing how it reflects the heritage, traditions, attitudes, and beliefs of its author (biographical approach).

Vocabulary Development

Idioms

An **idiom** is an expression that is peculiar to one language and means something different from the literal meaning of its words. *Hold your tongue* ("Don't speak") is an idiom of American English. If you didn't know this idiom, you might wonder why someone would want to hold on to a tongue! *Hold your horses* ("Be patient") is another idiom. If you didn't know this one, you might wonder, "What horses?"

PRACTICE

Each of the following statements contains an idiom, which is underlined. First, tell what the idiom means literally. Next, tell what the idiom means figuratively. The first item has been completed for you.

1. Joe has to stop beating around the bush and answer the question.

   Literal meaning: Joe is beating on some bushes with a stick.
   Figurative meaning: Joe is trying to avoid answering the question.

2. The rowdy class clammed up when the principal came in.

3. When I met you, I started dancing on air.

4. Shaquille lost his head when he decided to try out for varsity.

5. Liu couldn't get a handle on his math assignment.

6. Sharon went overboard decorating for her party.

7. The candidate hit the nail on the head when she said taxes are too high.

8. The surprise quiz was a piece of cake.

9. Luz fell for José the first time she saw him.

10. Our plans for vacation went down the tube.

Reading Standard 1.1
Analyze idioms to infer the literal and figurative meanings of phrases.

Saying Yes

Literary Focus
Epilogue

An **epilogue** (ep′ə·lôg′), or afterword, is a brief closing section to a piece of literature. In a play the epilogue is often spoken directly to the audience by an actor. In a novel an epilogue might supply information about what happens to the characters after the novel ends. In nonfiction an epilogue might be a critical commentary. In this chapter, selections have been chosen that reflect the heritage, traditions, attitudes, and beliefs of their authors. As you read "Saying Yes," see if you think it is an appropriate epilogue for this chapter.

Reading Skills
Reading a Dialogue

The first part of "Saying Yes" is set up as a dialogue. A person asks questions, and a speaker answers—or tries to answer. The second part of the poem is a commentary on the questions. In lines 9–18, you will have to decide when to pause at the ends of lines and when to read on without pausing—in order to get the sense of the lines. Try reading this poem aloud with a partner.

Make the Connection
Conduct a Survey

Most people living in the United States come from someplace else. You might have come to these shores as an immigrant yourself. Perhaps your parents or grandparents or great-grandparents came here from another place in the world. Even if your family has been here for many generations, chances are that they have moved around, from East to West, or from North to South, or from city to suburbs. Take a class poll to find out all the places your classmates and their families have come from. Think of a good way to display your findings graphically.

Reading Standard 3.7 Analyze a work of literature, showing how it reflects the heritage, traditions, attitudes, and beliefs of its author (biographical approach).

Saying Yes

Diana Chang

"Are you Chinese?"
"Yes."

"American?"
"Yes."

5   "*Really* Chinese?"
"No . . . not quite."

"*Really* American?"
"Well, actually, you see . . ."

But I would rather say
10   yes

Not neither-nor,
not maybe,
but both, and not only

The homes I've had,
15   the ways I am

I'd rather say it
twice,
yes

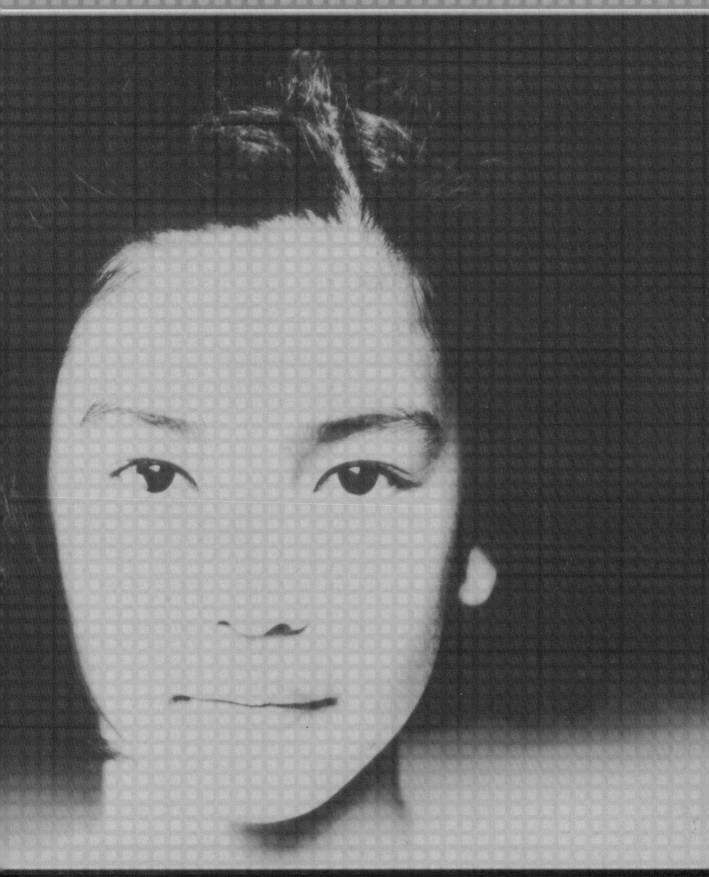

Diana Chang

"Jot It Down on Anything!"

Born in the United States to a Eurasian mother and a Chinese father, **Diana Chang** (1934–   ) currently lives on Long Island, New York. She is an adjunct associate professor at Barnard College in New York City, where she teaches creative writing. Chang warns her students to be prepared to write down their ideas for poems at any time:

> As it comes, wherever it waylays you, jot it down. You may be writing when you are not writing—on the bus or while lugging groceries or avoiding cigarette smoke in an elevator. Jot it down on anything—the hem of a dress if necessary—or it'll leave with no trace, a snowflake on a warm skillet.

Chang's poems have appeared in many magazines. About "Saying Yes," Chang has written:

> To my surprise, 'Saying Yes' has been reprinted very often. I can only suppose it's because it is sincere and simple.

In addition to her poems, Chang has published novels, including *The Frontiers of Love.* That novel takes place in the Chinese city of Shanghai in 1945, a time when it was losing its distinctive cultural identity as its residents began to embrace Western values. Chang is also an accomplished painter and has exhibited her work in one-woman shows.

Literary Response and Analysis

Interpretations

1. How does the speaker answer when people ask if she is *really* Chinese and American?

2. In the second part of the poem, she reflects on her answers. What would she *like* to say?

Evaluation

3. Do you think a person can identify equally with two different backgrounds? Or do you think a person has one primary identity? Explain your response.

4. What do you think of Chang's comment about this poem in her biography?

5. Do you think this poem makes a fitting **epilogue** to this chapter? Why or why not?

Writing

I Am . . .

Write a poem explaining how you feel about your own heritage or heritages. You could structure your poem, as Chang does, as a series of questions and answers. Display your poem, along with those of your classmates, as a a mosaic representing your class. You could call your poetry display "Saying Yes." You might want to add photographs to the mosaic.

October Light by Diana Chang. Acrylic.
Photographer: Joan G. Anderson.

Reading Standard 3.7
Analyze a work of literature, showing how it reflects the heritage, traditions, attitudes, and beliefs of its author (biographical approach).

Vermont Verge by Diana Chang. Acrylic.
Photographer: Joan G. Anderson.

Literary Response and Analysis

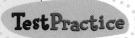 DIRECTIONS: Read the story. Then, read each question, and write the letter of the best response.

This excerpt is from a story that takes place during Hanukkah, the Jewish Festival of Lights, which usually begins in December. Hanukkah celebrates the rededication of the Temple in Jerusalem in 165 B.C. Another Jewish holiday, Purim, mentioned in the first paragraph, is a spring festival that honors Queen Esther.

from Just Enough Is Plenty: A Hanukkah Tale
Barbara Diamond Goldin

Malka's family lived in a village in Poland. They were poor, but not so poor. They had candles for the Sabbath, noisemakers for Purim, and spinning tops for Hanukkah.

Mama was busy preparing for tonight, the first of the eight nights of Hanukkah. She peeled onions and grated potatoes for the latkes, the potato pancakes.

Malka's younger brother Zalman carved a dreidel, a spinning top.

"This dreidel will spin the fastest of all," he boasted.

Papa was working long hours in his tailor shop so they could buy more food for the holiday. More potatoes, more onions, more flour, more oil.

For on the first night of Hanukkah, Malka's family always invited many guests. But this year only Aunt Hindy and Uncle Shmuel were coming to visit.

"Only two guests?" Malka asked. "Last year, we had so many guests that Papa had to put boards over the pickle barrels to make the table big enough."

"That was last year," Mama said gently. "This year has not been a good one for Papa in the shop. People bring him just a little mending here, a little mending there. He cannot afford to buy new material to sew fancy holiday dresses and fine suits."

"But it's Hanukkah," Malka reminded Mama.

Mama patted Malka's shoulder. "Don't worry, Malkaleh. We know how to stretch. We're poor, but not so poor. Now go. Ask Papa if he has a few more coins. I need more eggs for the latkes."

Reading Standard 3.7 Analyze a work of literature, showing how it reflects the heritage, traditions, attitudes, and beliefs of its author (biographical approach).

Meet the Writer

When she wrote this story, **Barbara Diamond Goldin** was a preschool teacher and storyteller who lived with her husband and two children in Northampton, Massachusetts. Three of her grandparents came from Poland. It was only in doing research for this book that she learned how they probably lived before coming to America. Perhaps this fictional story could be *their* true story!

1. The setting, a village in Poland, reflects the writer's **heritage** because —
   A   Poland is where she was born
   B   some of her grandparents came from Poland
   C   many Americans came from Poland
   D   Poland is a good place for a story

2. "She peeled onions and grated potatoes for the latkes, the potato pancakes." **Context clues** in this sentence tell you that *latkes* are —
   F   peeled onions
   G   grated potatoes
   H   potato pancakes
   J   Polish lakes

3. Hanukkah **traditions** mentioned in this excerpt include —
   A   eating potato pancakes
   B   working long hours
   C   blowing loud noisemakers
   D   living in Poland

4. This story excerpt mentions all of the following Hanukkah **traditions** *except* —
   F   latkes
   G   dreidels
   H   eight nights
   J   menorahs

5. When Mama says, "We're poor, but not so poor," she is expressing the **belief** that —
   A   they have enough
   B   they are really rich
   C   poverty doesn't matter
   D   it's better to be poor

6. In doing research for this book, the writer learned more about —
   F   teaching preschool
   G   life in Massachusetts
   H   Polish immigration
   J   her Polish heritage

Reading Informational Materials

 DIRECTIONS: Read the article. Then, read each question, and write the letter of the best response.

Blasting Through Bedrock: The Central Pacific Railroad Workers

Flo Ota De Lange

1 In the winter of 1866–1867, blizzards gripped the Sierra Nevada. Dwellings were buried in blowing, shifting, drifting, driving snow. Men who were building the western portion of the country's first transcontinental railroad had to tunnel from their camp to the mountainside, where they spent long, cold days digging out rock so tracks could be laid. The Central Pacific Railroad was building east from California to meet the Union Pacific Railroad, which was working west from Omaha, Nebraska.

2 Who were these hardy workers who survived the blizzards and helped build the nation's first transcontinental railroad? Most of them were immigrants from China. When other railroad hands saw the newly hired Chinese workers, they were scornful. How could these young men, averaging about four feet ten inches in height, heave a large shovelful of rock? The other workers either didn't know or had forgotten that the ancestors of

these men had built one of the Seven Wonders of the World—the Great Wall of China—which was begun in 221 B.C. The wall extends more than four thousand miles and averages about twenty-six feet high and twenty feet wide!

3 At the start the Central Pacific Railroad hired fifty Chinese laborers. These men knew little about railroad grading, but they learned quickly. Eventually the Chinese labor force grew to between ten thousand and twelve thousand workers. These men dug, blasted tunnels, and laid track up the Sierra Nevada, over the Donner Pass, and down through the deserts of Nevada.

4 People often credit the transcontinental railroad to men of vision—engineers, financiers, and politicians—without acknowledging the way their vision became a reality. As the president of the Central Pacific Railroad and former governor of California, Leland Stanford, wrote to

Reading Standard 2.7
Evaluate the unity, coherence, logic, internal consistency, and structural patterns of text.

President Andrew Johnson on October 19, 1865, "The greater portion of the laborers employed by us are Chinese. . . . Without them it would be impossible to complete the western portion of this great national enterprise within the time required by the Acts of Congress."

5 Complete it these workers did! Cannons roared in New York City and San Francisco when the telegraph lines carried the news: The Union Pacific and the Central Pacific Railroad lines had met at Promontory, Utah, on May 10, 1869.

---

1. Which statement *best* expresses the **main idea** of this article?

   A The winter of 1866 is famous for its terrible snowstorms and blizzards.

   B Chinese workers were important in building the transcontinental railroad.

   C The Great Wall of China is one of the Seven Wonders of the World.

   D Cannons were set off to celebrate the completion of the transcontinental railroad.

2. Which of the following details would be consistent with the **unity** of paragraph 1?

   F The Great Pyramids are also among the Seven Wonders of the World.

   G The Great Wall of China ascends steep ridges angled at seventy degrees.

   H Many people died from cave-ins and avalanches during the blizzards.

   J Building model trains is a rewarding and enjoyable hobby.

3. Read these sentences from paragraph 1. Which of the transition words that follow could be used to connect the two sentences **coherently**?

   "Dwellings were buried in blowing, shifting, drifting, driving snow. Men . . . had to tunnel from their camp to the mountainside. . . ."

   A before

   B however

   C although

   D therefore

4. Which of the following sentences could be added to this article without destroying its **internal consistency**?

   F During blizzards, people cannot see in front of them, and so they bump into things.

   G Chinese workers did backbreaking work from sunup to sundown six days a week.

   H Asa Whitney was the first to see the importance of a transcontinental railroad.

   J It took fourteen train lines to get Lincoln's body from Washington, D.C., to Illinois.

Vocabulary Development

Multiple-Meaning Words

DIRECTIONS: Use context clues to identify the meaning of each underlined word as it is used in the sentence. (Sentences are taken from "Ribbons.")

1. "Dad's head was just disappearing as he leaned into the trunk of the car." In this sentence, *trunk* means —
   - **A** large stem of a tree
   - **B** long snout
   - **C** large suitcase
   - **D** luggage compartment

2. "Because Grandmother's airfare and legal expenses had been so high, there wasn't room in the family budget for Madame Oblomov's ballet school." In this sentence, *high* means —
   - **F** tall
   - **G** lofty
   - **H** costly
   - **J** excited

3. "'Nice children don't drool on people,' she snapped at me." In this sentence, *snapped* means —
   - **A** bit suddenly
   - **B** snatched quickly
   - **C** spoke sharply
   - **D** broke apart

4. "Crouching, he used the cords to lift a box in each hand." In this sentence, *lift* means —
   - **F** raise
   - **G** ride
   - **H** steal
   - **J** elevator

5. "Suddenly I felt lost, and the following weeks only made me more confused." In this sentence, *lost* means —
   - **A** mislaid
   - **B** unseen
   - **C** bewildered
   - **D** wasted

6. "When I complained to Mom about how Grandmother was spoiling Ian, she only sighed." In this sentence, *spoiling* means —
   - **F** destroying
   - **G** decaying
   - **H** marring
   - **J** overindulging

Mastering the Standards

PERSUASIVE ESSAY

Grades or Sports?

In "The Treasure of Lemon Brown," Greg's father will not let Greg play basketball unless he gets good grades. Do you agree with Greg's father that getting good grades is more important than playing sports? Do you think that playing sports is just as important for a student's development? Do you think taking sports away is suitable punishment for poor grades? Write a **persuasive essay** explaining your opinion on this issue of sports and grades. First, write down your opinion. Next, choose your audience: Whom do you want to convince? Then, brainstorm or research a list of reasons to support your opinion. Your essay could be structured in the way shown at the right.

> **Introduction**
> Attention-grabbing beginning
> Statement of opinion

> **Body**
> Reason 1
> Evidence
> Reason 2
> Evidence
> [Etc. *Give at least three reasons.*]

> **Conclusion**
> Brief restatement of opinion
> Summary of reasons
> Strong closing statement

▶ **Use "Writing a Persuasive Essay," pages 706–725, for help with this assignment.**

Other Choices

RESEARCH / MUSIC / ORAL PRESENTATION

1 Those Sweet Sounds

Lemon Brown played some sweet blues sounds in his day. Esperanza's mother sings along to recordings of operas. Research some aspect of one of these very different types of music. You will first have to limit your subject. You might research the life of a blues musician like Little Walter (see page 503), or you might research the story of an opera like *Madama Butterfly.* Present your findings to the class in an **oral report.** Try to get recordings to share with the class.

DESCRIPTION

2 Family Keepsakes

A keepsake is an item that is valued as a reminder of something. Lemon Brown has his harmonica and newspaper clippings. In "Ribbons," Stacy's grandmother probably has important keepsakes in the boxes she brought from China. Do you or your family have any keepsakes? Choose an item that means a lot to you, and write a **description** of it. Tell what it looks like, even what it feels and smells like. Then, tell why it is important to you.

▶ **Use "Writing a Descriptive Essay," pages 768–770, for help with this assignment.**

Fiction

Serious Consequences

Ailin's family resists breaking with ancient Chinese traditions in a time of social change. On the other hand, Ailin does not wish to have her feet bound and does not wish to be married to someone who has been selected for her. In Lensey Namioka's *Ties That Bind, Ties That Break,* Ailin must choose between pleasing her family and pleasing herself.

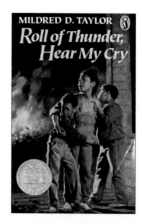

I'll Stand My Ground

Eight-year-old Cassie Logan does not understand the startling actions of white landowners in Depression-era Mississippi. Over the course of a year, she learns another lesson—why her family is desperately fighting to hold on to the land they call home. In *Roll of Thunder, Hear My Cry,* Mildred Taylor tells a story of pride and courage that all families can learn from.

A Blessing or a Curse?

Ella received a gift from a fairy on the day she was born. While this may sound exciting, Ella has never appreciated the gift because it is the gift of obedience. She has to do whatever anyone tells her to do. In Gail Carson Levine's Newbery Medal winner *Ella Enchanted,* Ella goes on a mission to change the way things are. She won't allow ogres, elves, or fairy godmothers to get in her way in this retelling of the Cinderella story.

The Meaning of Christmas

During his lifetime, Charles Dickens was known for his acts of charity. Perhaps that aspect of Dickens's character inspired his holiday classic, *A Christmas Carol.* Ebenezer Scrooge, a bitter, selfish old man, is unmoved by the holiday season. With the help of three Christmas spirits, he is able to change the course of his life and discover the joys of giving and of love.

This title is available in the HRW Library.

Nonfiction

Oh, Freedom

What was it like to walk through angry, violent mobs to integrate an all-white school? to be arrested for refusing to give up a seat at the front of a bus? to fight for freedom when other people your age were going to sports practice or attending their first dance? In *Freedom's Children,* Ellen Levine presents oral histories by African Americans who were involved as children or teenagers in the civil rights movement of the 1950s and 1960s.

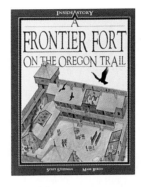

Settling Down

In *A Frontier Fort on the Oregon Trail,* Scott Steedman and Mark Bergin look at the way people lived in the Old West. Bergin's detailed illustrations present a typical day in the life of a soldier, a homemaker, and a trapper. Steedman fleshes out the illustrations with helpful text, including an explanation of how a cabin and a fort were built in the "New World."

Starting Out

Today, the only work most children in the United States have to worry about is schoolwork. Sadly, this was not always the case. In *Immigrant Kids,* Russell Freedman looks at how young people lived in the late nineteenth and early twentieth centuries, when children often had to take jobs and work under unsafe and exhausting conditions. Photographs from the period help us empathize with the sufferings of these children.

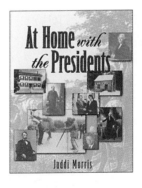

Not in the Newspapers

Do you ever wonder how social functions are conducted at the White House? Are you ever curious about where America's leaders grew up? Do you want to know how they lived after they left office? You can find out in *At Home with the Presidents* by Juddi Morris. The book also contains a wealth of information about First Ladies and describes a variety of historic sites you can visit.

8 Reading for Life

by Flo Ota De Lange and Sheri Henderson

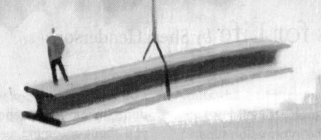

 # California Standards

Here are the Grade 8 standards you will study for mastery in Chapter 8:

Reading

Reading Comprehension (Focus on Informational Materials)

2.1 Compare and contrast the features and elements of consumer materials to gain meaning from documents (for example, warranties, contracts, product information, instruction manuals).

2.5 Understand and explain the use of a complex mechanical device by following technical directions.

2.6 Use information from a variety of consumer, workplace, and public documents to explain a situation or decision and to solve a problem.

KEYWORD:
HLLA 8-8

Skateboard Park Documents

M E M O R A N D U M

From: A. Longboard, Assistant Director of Parks and Recreation
To: J. Cool, Director of Parks and Recreation
Re: Establishment of a Permanent Skateboard Park

Critical Issues

A. Need. Ten percent of the families in this city, about seven thousand households, include at least one skateboarder. The city provides no designated space for skateboarding. Police reports show that citations for illegal skating are rising every month. This problem is particularly acute in downtown areas, leading to complaints from businesses. The nearest public skateboard park is twenty miles to the east in Mogul, where illegal skating dropped sharply when its park opened last year.

B. Liability. California AB 1296 states that persons who skateboard on public property are expected to know that it is a potentially dangerous sport. They cannot sue the city, county, or state for their injuries as long as the city has passed an ordinance requiring

- helmet, kneepads, and elbow pads for all skaters in the park
- clear and visible signs warning citizens of this requirement
- citations for skaters who violate the ordinance

Such an ordinance was enacted by our city council on July 15, 2000. Therefore, building a skateboard park would not pose a liability risk to the city as long as the above requirements are met.

C. Cost. Local groups have raised half the necessary $140,000. The Parks and Recreation Department's budget can fund the other half. Costs will be minimal—only inspection for damage and yearly maintenance.

D. Location. The city already owns two sites:

- 1.3 acres of the park area between 180th Avenue and 360th Drive, bordered by Drab Street and Grinding Drive, two heavily used thoroughfares. On two sides of the park are neighborhood houses.

- 2.1 acres in the 15-acre sports park at Ramp and Spin avenues. This site is set back from heavily traveled roads but still offers excellent access and visibility from service roads within the park. It is also three tenths of a mile from the fire station and paramedic aid. There are no residential neighborhoods bordering the complex.

The City Beat

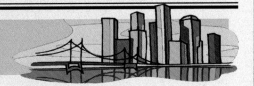

by N. Parker

A lively debate occurred at last Tuesday's packed city council meeting on the subject of whether to establish a skateboard park. Mayor Gridlock made a few opening remarks and then turned the microphone over to J. Cool, Director of Parks and Recreation. Mr. Cool read from portions of a report prepared by his staff, who had investigated the need for and the liability, risks, cost, and possible location of a park. Several members of the community spoke.

> *A packed meeting? Looks as if there's a lot of interest.*

K. Skater said, "Skateboarding is a challenging sport. It's good for us. But right now we have no place to skate, and so kids are getting tickets for illegal skating. Lots of people say it's too dangerous, but that's not true. Kids get hurt in every sport, but you can make it a lot less dangerous for us if you give us a smooth place to practice. Still, we skaters have to be responsible and only take risks we can handle. That teaches us a lot."

> *The right space would cut risks. Sports help kids learn to judge their strengths and limitations.*

D. T. Merchant remarked, "I am a store owner downtown. These skaters use our curbs and handrails as their personal skating ramps. They threaten pedestrians and scare people. If we build them an alternative, I believe most will use it. Then the police can concentrate on the few who break the rules."

> *Merchants need relief. Illegal skating is unsafe for everyone. Park may reduce police time spent citing skaters.*

G. Homeowner had this to say: "Skaters are illiterate bums. They think safety gear means thick hair gel. They have no respect. They will disturb my neighborhood all night long with their subhuman noise. I would like to remind the city council—I pay taxes and I

> *This guy really hates site 1.*

vote. A skateboard park? Not in my backyard!"

F. Parent: "My son is an outstanding citizen. He is respectful and well behaved. He also lives to skateboard. This city has placed my son at risk by failing to give him a safe place to skate. If we were talking about building a basketball court, nobody would think twice before agreeing. I'm a voter too, and I expect the city council to be responsive to the needs of *all* citizens."

> *Safety again. Good point.*

Finally, S. B. Owner said, "I am the owner of the Skate Bowl. Skateboarding is not a fad. It is here to stay. You may not like the way some skaters act or look, but I know them all. They're great kids. Seems like most of the good folks here tonight are worried about safety. So here's what I propose: I will sell all safety gear in my store at 50 percent off. That's less than it costs me, folks. All that you parents have to do is fill out an emergency-information card for your skater and return it to me. I'll see that the information is entered in a database that paramedics, hospital workers, and police officers can access. I'll also make sure that everyone who comes to my store knows what the Consumer Product Safety Commission says: 'Kids who want to skate are going to skate. Let's help them skate safely.'"

> *Affordable safety gear, emergency contacts, consumer education— I think I'll write a letter in support of this.*

Mr. Owner's proposal was met with a standing ovation. Plans to move ahead with the skateboard-park project will be formally put to a vote at next month's regular session.

> *It looks as if this could pass. Now they will have to decide where to put the park.*

DISCOUNT COUPON FOR

50% OFF   **50% OFF**   **50% OFF**

S. B. Owner's

SKATE BOWL

This coupon entitles bearer,

_____,

to **50 PERCENT OFF**

the regular list price on all helmets, kneepads, and elbow pads.

Discount does not extend to shoes, padded clothing, boards, trucks, stickers, or any other equipment. Discount does not include state or local sales tax. Discount is not good in combination with any other discount or coupon. Bearer must show photo identification, such as a school ID or a yearbook photograph.

> Read the fine print. Not all protective items are reduced in price. Kids will need a photo ID too.

excerpts from

Consumer Product Safety Commission
Document 93

Approximately 26,000 persons go to hospital emergency rooms each year for skateboard-related injuries. Several factors—lack of protective equipment, poor board maintenance, and irregular riding surfaces—are involved in these accidents.

> Board maintenance? Nobody ever thinks about that.

Who gets injured. Six of every ten skateboard injuries happen to children under fifteen years of age. Skateboarders who have been skating for less than a week suffer one third of the injuries; riders with a year or

> Let's hold beginner safety classes.

more of experience have the next highest number of injuries.

Injuries to first-time skateboarders are, for the most part, caused by falls. Experienced riders suffer injuries mainly when they fall after their skateboards strike rocks and other irregularities in the riding surface, or when they attempt difficult stunts.

Environmental hazards. Irregular surfaces account for more than half the skateboarding injuries caused by falls. Before riding, skateboarders should check the surface for holes, bumps, rocks, and debris. Areas set aside for skateboarding generally have smoother riding surfaces. Skateboarding in the street can result in collisions with cars, causing serious injury or even death.

> This section certainly supports the need to build a park and then inspect it regularly. It also supports arguments for site 2.

The skateboard. Before using their boards, riders should check them for hazards, such as loose, broken, or cracked parts; sharp edges; slippery top surfaces; and wheels with nicks and cracks. Serious defects should be corrected by a qualified repair person.

> Let's hold yearly skateboard checkup clinics.

Protective gear. Protective gear—such as slip-resistant, closed shoes, helmets, and specially designed padding—may not fully protect skateboarders from fractures, but its use is recommended because such gear can reduce the number and severity of injuries.

The protective gear currently on the market is not subject to federal performance standards, and so careful selection by consumers is necessary. In a helmet, look for proper fit and a chin strap; make sure the helmet does not block the rider's vision and hearing. Body padding should fit comfortably. If it is tight, it can restrict circulation and reduce the skater's ability to move freely. Loose-fitting padding, on the other hand, can slip off or slide out of position.

> Kids grow quickly. Parents need to be alert to changes in fit.

Source: U.S. Consumer Product Safety Commission, Washington, D.C. 20207.

PRACTICE

Writing a Letter

Have you reached a decision? We're betting you have. Now all you have to do is write to your city council in support of the plan. Cite information from the Skateboard Park documents to support your position. Don't forget to include suggestions for yearly inspection clinics and beginner safety classes. By the way, which do you think is the better site (see page 532)? Can you explain why?

Reading Standard 2.6
Use information from a variety of consumer, workplace, and public documents to explain a situation or decision and to solve a problem.

Leash-Free Dog Run Documents

You Decide

Here's another citywide problem to solve: Read the following **public, workplace,** and **consumer documents.** What's the situation? What decision must be made? What's the best solution? This time, make your own notes as you read.

Back   Forward   Reload   Home   Search

Location: http://www.southpaws.com/home

SouthPaws

Welcome to the SouthPaws Web site. SouthPaws is a not-for-profit group dedicated to creating and maintaining a leash-free space on the south side of our city for its 165,000 canine (that's dog) citizens. Please consider joining our 3,300+ members. Your membership fees are tax-deductible and will help give our dogs their own space! If you are interested in volunteering, please check out <u>Volunteer Want Ads.</u> Finally, you might want to consider SouthPaws T-shirts, sweats, caps, or leashes as a gift or for yourself. All proceeds support SouthPaws.

What's New?

Congratulations to the hundreds of volunteers who gathered signatures on the SouthPaws petition. All that hard work last spring paid off! The residents of our city have voted to establish a park or a beach where our dogs can run unleashed. This space will be jointly funded by the city and SouthPaws donations. SouthPaws volunteers will supervise the space during daylight hours and will be empowered to ticket dog owners who do not observe cleanup and safety rules. We will have one trial year after the space officially opens to prove that the idea works. Now we need your help more than ever.

We are working with the city Parks and Recreation Department to choose a location. These are the most likely locations:

Cameo Park

Pro
- is centrally located
- has convenient access roads
- has street parking

Con
- will incur high maintenance costs
- is smallest, at 1.2 residential acres
- is now a popular family park
- may lead nearby residents to object to noise, nuisances

Rocky Point Beach

Pro
- is little used
- consists of 5 nonresidential acres
- has ample parking
- will incur low start-up and maintenance costs

Con
- is inconveniently located
- has nonsand beach; smooth but potentially slippery rocks

Main Beach

Pro
- is centrally located
- consists of 7.3 nonresidential acres
- has sand beach

Con
- is heavily used all year
- may cause conflicts with businesses
- has limited, costly parking
- will require 24-hour security and maintenance staffing
- will incur high maintenance costs

<u>Pick a Site</u>

Click here to cast your vote in our survey.

SouthPaws

SouthPaws · 1111 South P Street · South City, CA · 90123

December 12, 2002

Ms. T. Wagger
Director of Parks and Recreation
2222 Central Avenue
South City, CA 90123

Dear Ms. Wagger,

SouthPaws members would like you to take their concerns into account when choosing the site of the proposed dog run. Here they are, in order of importance:

1. Space. Healthy dogs need ample space in which to run. The park needs to be large enough for a fair number of dogs to run around in it without colliding with one another. Ample size will minimize the possibility of dogfights.

2. Conflicts. A site that is already popular for sports, family activities, or tourism will likely be a problem.

3. Site. Our research shows that dog beaches are preferable to dog parks. Dogs are hard on park grass, which quickly turns to mud in rainy weather. Sand or shells can be brushed off a dog, but mud requires a bath. Dog beaches are also easier to supervise and clean.

Thank you for working with us to find a solution that is in the best interests of the most people. We are looking forward to meeting with you next week.

Sincerely,

A. K. Nine

A. K. Nine
Chairperson
SouthPaws Site Committee

Back   Forward   Reload   Home   Search

Location: http://www.southpaws.com/home

SouthPaws

Did You Know?

- In our city there are 165,000 licensed dogs.
- The city devotes a total of 10 acres to leash-free dog areas.
- The city devotes 1,050 acres to softball, 1,040 acres to golf, 287 acres to tennis.
- Eastside Leash-Free Dog Park accommodates 2,000 dogs per week on its 1-acre site.

SouthPaws Membership Information

Annual Tax-Deductible Membership Fees

Basic: $15 per year; entitles you to newsletter and voting rights

Deluxe: $25 per year; entitles you to the above plus one T-shirt or cap

Sponsor: $100 per year; entitles you to all of the above plus discounted dog-obedience classes and merchandise from local merchants

Angel: $250 per year; entitles you to all of the above plus your name on our Wall of Fame

New!

Help SouthPaws while you tell the world about your best friend. Buy a brick in the new Dog Walk of Fame. Your pet's name and a short message will be inscribed. Be sure to provide your pet's name, your name, and your message (up to 45 letter spaces). (Available to SouthPaws members only; $50 per pet's name.)

Membership in SouthPaws makes a great gift. Print out a membership application, complete it, and mail it with your donation.

Don't want to join? Then how about making a donation? We appreciate contributions in any amount.

Reading Informational Materials

Reading Check

1. What problem is the SouthPaws Web site concerned with?

2. What three concerns do SouthPaws members have?

3. Which proposed site addresses *most* of SouthPaws' concerns? Why?

TestPractice

Leash-Free Dog Run Documents

1. The decision to build the dog run was made by —

   A the city council

   B Parks and Recreation

   C SouthPaws

   D voters

2. If you were not a SouthPaws member but wanted to buy a brick in the new Dog Walk of Fame, it would cost you a minimum of —

   F $15

   G $25

   H $50

   J $65

3. How many acres are already devoted to leash-free zones?

   A 1

   B 10

   C 287

   D 1,050

4. SouthPaws members are *most* concerned about —

   F access

   G conflicts

   H space

   J type of area

5. The site that *best* meets the needs and concerns of SouthPaws members is —

   A Cameo Park

   B Rocky Point Beach

   C Main Beach

   D either Rocky Point or Main Beach

Reading Standard 2.6 Use information from a variety of consumer, workplace, and public documents to explain a situation or decision and to solve a problem.

WarpSpeedNet Documents *and* SweetPlayer Documents

Elements and Features of Consumer Materials

What has two wheels, pedals to make it go, and handles for steering the front wheel? A _____. That was easy to figure out, because the question names a bicycle's most basic elements. Still, is that all there is to a bicycle? Is that how you'd describe a bicycle you want? No way. You want stuff on your bike— maybe for mountain biking, maybe for racing, maybe for just looking cool. You want a bicycle that stands out in your crowd. You want features that make it unique.

Bicycles have common elements as well as special features. So do consumer documents. The **elements** that make up consumer materials define what the document is— warranty, contract, product

information, or instruction manual. The **features** are what make consumer documents unique. For example, all contracts spell out what you get and what you give. Without those two elements a contract isn't really a contract. Features are described in the details. Some features may be to your advantage; others may not. Understanding the details of a contract before you sign it will help you avoid problems later.

Let's look at some **consumer materials.** The notes in the margin will help you identify the elements and features of each type of document.

Reading Standard 2.1
Compare and contrast the features and elements of consumer materials to gain meaning from documents (for example, warranties, contracts, product information, instruction manuals).

WarpSpeedNet Documents

Choosing a High-Speed Internet Service Provider

Juan's family phone line is always busy, because everyone uses the Internet. They have decided that the family's big yearly purchase will be high-speed Internet access. The best price was offered by a cable company, and they decided to try it. The first **product information** they got was contained in the **advertisement** below:

Recognizing the Elements and Features of an Advertisement

With **WARPSPEEDNET**

You Get What You Want—*Now.*

Only WarpSpeedNet provides all the cable equipment and services you need for a lightning-fast Internet connection through your home computer. *Never wait again* to dial in, log on, or connect. WarpSpeedNet is always on, always ready to go. You'll never be disconnected in the middle of a download again!

WarpSpeedNet is point-and-click easy to use. Get weather reports *now*, news *now*, Web shopping *now*, music *now*, games *now*. Anything the World Wide Web offers, WarpSpeedNet brings to you—*Now!*

CALL DURING THE NEXT TWO WEEKS TO RECEIVE **FREE** INSTALLATION AND A RISK-FREE 30-DAY MONEY-BACK GUARANTEE

Call now and mention priority code RIW.
1-555-WarpNet

Service subject to availability in your area. Offer good in South and North County areas only. Minimum computer-system requirements apply. Offer expires 12/31/03.

Element—description of selling points.
Features—no equipment to buy; speedy, convenient, easy.

Element—enticements to buy.
Features—free installation, money-back guarantee, short-term offer.

Element—contact information.

Element—limitations.
Features—is not available everywhere, does not work with all computers, has expiration date.

PRACTICE

Analyzing an Advertisement

The purpose of an advertisement is, of course, to make you want a product. One of the ways it does this is to emphasize the good points and de-emphasize the limitations. Jot down on your own paper a few notes about how the emphasis and lack of emphasis were achieved in the advertisement above.

Reading Standard 2.1
Compare and contrast the features and elements of consumer materials to gain meaning from documents.

Reading a Service Agreement

Let's say that Juan's family decides to give WarpSpeedNet a try. We'll assume that they live in South County, meet the minimum computer-system requirements, and call within the two-week deadline. Juan's family is now entitled to everything the company promised: free installation, thirty-day money-back trial, and all the necessary cable equipment. This is what they receive when they sign up, along with a few more consumer documents. Let's take a closer look at those documents.

Don't let the word *agreement* in the following example fool you. This is a **contract,** and like most contracts, it is long and complicated to read. We won't print the whole thing, but here are two important sections:

SERVICE AGREEMENT

1. Equipment

A. Equipment includes rental of cable modem and necessary connections to permit use of one (1) computer to WarpSpeedNet service.

B. WarpSpeedNet will install equipment. Subscriber will grant company reasonable access to install, inspect, repair, maintain, or disconnect the equipment. Refusal to do so may result in discontinued service.

C. Cable equipment remains the property of WarpSpeedNet. Upon termination of service, equipment shall be returned in original condition, ordinary wear and tear excepted.

2. Charges

A. Subscriber agrees to pay for the monthly service subscribed to, including charges for installation, in advance. Monthly charges are set forth on a separate price list and are subject to change.

B. Subscribers who discontinue service will be required to pay all due and past-due charges. If the subscriber reconnects service, a charge will apply.

C. If cable equipment is lost, damaged, or stolen, subscriber must pay $300 to WarpSpeedNet for replacement.

_____
Company representative signature and date

_____
Subscriber signature and date

Element— services (what Juan's family gets). **Features—** cable service and equipment for one computer, installation, and setup.

Element— costs (what Juan's family pays). **Features—** payments per agreement, including all fees, charges, and replacement costs.

Element— signatures (no contract is valid without them).

Reading Standard 2.1
Compare and contrast the features and elements of consumer materials to gain meaning from documents.

BONUS QUESTION

Did you notice a mismatch between the advertisement and item 2.A under "Charges" in the contract? What is it? Which do you think will apply to Juan's family?

PRACTICE

Comparing and Contrasting
Take a few minutes to jot down the ways in which the advertisement and the contract are similar and the ways in which they are different.

Reading an Instruction Manual

Juan's family also received an instruction manual. Let's take a closer look.

WELCOME TO

WARPSPEEDNET

Element—table of contents.

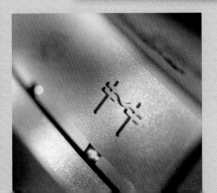

PRACTICE

Finding Information in an Instruction Manual
Some of the lights on the cable modem flash on and off, and Juan wonders if something is wrong. According to the table of contents, what page would tell him what he wants to know?

Cable Modem Lights

There are four lights on the front of your cable modem.

1. Power	**Steady green:** Power is on.
2. Cable	**Steady green:** Cable is ready to use. **Flashing red-green:** Cable is setting up connection. Wait. **Flashing red:** Connection has a problem. See Troubleshooting, page 33. **No light:** There is no cable connection. Call for service.
3. Computer link	**Steady green:** Connection is working. **Flashing red:** There is a connection problem. See Troubleshooting, page 33. **No light:** Computer has been turned off or disconnected.
4. Data	**Flashing light:** Modem is sending or receiving data.

15

Element—
explanation
of product.
Features—
specific meaning
of each light.

PRACTICE

Following Directions

1. Juan notices that lights 1 and 2 are always green. What does that mean?
2. Light 3 is on only sometimes. When should it be on?
3. Light 4 flashes on and off a great deal. Why is it flashing?
4. Is the cable modem working properly, or is there a problem? What do you think?
5. What is the **purpose** of the instruction manual? How is this purpose different from that of the contract and the advertisement? How is it the same?

Reading a Warranty

If the cable modem isn't working as promised, what can Juan's family do? Let's check the warranty.

The purpose of a warranty is _____. Yes! It tells when, how, and for how long you can get your money back. Take another look at WarpSpeedNet's warranty. What does it really offer? If the equipment fails during the first year, Juan's family can get a refund for the amount they paid. But hold on a minute! That doesn't really apply to Juan's family. Can you figure out why? (Hint: Go back and read the contract.)

This is all there is to it: product information, contract, instruction manual, warranty.

LIMITED WARRANTY

The WarpSpeedNet modem is guaranteed to be free of defects in material or workmanship under normal use for a period of one (1) year from the date of purchase. If the product malfunctions during this period, call WarpSpeedNet Customer Service to obtain a return authorization.

YOU MUST OBTAIN THIS AUTHORIZATION BEFORE RETURNING THE PRODUCT. PRODUCTS RECEIVED WITHOUT AUTHORIZATION WILL BE RETURNED TO SENDER. WHEN YOU CALL, BE PREPARED TO PROVIDE YOUR PROOF OF PURCHASE (RECEIPT NUMBER AND PRODUCT SERIAL NUMBER).

Clearly mark your return-authorization number on the box, and include sales receipt inside the box. In no event will WarpSpeedNet provide a refund in excess of the amount paid for the product.

Element—information on what is and is not guaranteed.
Features—specific information on when and how a refund may be obtained.

SweetPlayer Documents

Now Juan is ready to use that high-speed modem. His first stop? MP3 and *fast* downloads!

MP3? What is that? MP3 is an audio format, a software code that turns sounds into information a computer can understand. MP3 is nonproprietary. That means no one can claim ownership— anyone who wants to write a software program using it can legally do so. MP3 squeezes good sound quality into a small package. The sound-size combination makes MP3 the most popular audio format used today.

Juan can't wait to start listening to music on the family's computer. He has a collection of CDs from which he wants to rip (copy) his favorite tracks. He wants to explore Web radio and find new artists with cool tunes on sites where music is posted for free downloading. He needs the right software and has narrowed his search to a product called SweetPlayer, but which version should he get? Let's look at the Internet **advertisement.**

Reading Standard 2.1
Compare and contrast the features and elements of consumer materials to gain meaning from documents (for example, warranties, contracts, product information, instruction manuals).

Is it legal? The Internet is full of music. You can get your favorite hit in MP3 with a single click. It's easy, it's free—and it could be illegal. Many music sites contain music that someone has copied from a CD by digitizing it for use on computers and then placing it where other people can download it. It's a convenient and popular practice, but it is *not* legal. So what *is* legal?

1. You may rip tracks from a CD you own to a computer or to the Internet as long as they are for your own use and not for the use of other people.
2. You may download free promotional tracks. This is an increasingly popular way for artists to introduce their work to you. All music is legal on sites where the works are posted by the artists and record companies that created them. Free and promotional tracks are clearly marked, usually under the heading "Free Music." There are often CDs for sale by the artist too. Watch out, though. If a friend wants the same track, he or she will have to download it. It is not legal for you to copy a CD you downloaded from the Net.
3. You may buy the track for your own use. Many sites, including those of more and more record companies, are now offering tracks for sale in this manner.

Rule of thumb: If the way in which music is to be downloaded doesn't fit any of the three situations described above, the process probably isn't legal. When in doubt, check the copyright notice on the site.

Reading an Internet Advertisement and Instructions

 Back **Forward** **Reload** **Home** **Search**

Location: http://www.sweetplayer.com

SWEETPLAYER
The Best Free MP3 Player in Town!

SWEETPLAYER GIVES YOU

- fast and easy one-click downloading of MP3 files
- access to any of 2,500+ Web radio stations
- close to CD-quality sound with 128 Kbps sampling

And for a limited time you get

- SweetPlayer Deluxe for the introductory price of $19.95 (suggested retail price $29.95)*

Try it for 30 days, risk free.**

SweetPlayer Deluxe offers all the features of SweetPlayer *plus* it

- creates, edits, and organizes play lists
- rips CDs to MP3 files quickly and easily
- provides 256 Kbps, which means CD-quality sound
- personalizes your look with a choice of 100+ skins

*Special offer ends 6/15/02.
**After 30 days, software will require an activation code. Upon receipt of payment, purchaser will be sent the activation code by e-mail, fax, or U.S. mail.

Juan clicks on "SweetPlayer Deluxe." The following downloading directions appear on the screen:

DOWNLOAD DIRECTIONS

1. Shut down all open applications except your Internet browser.
2. Click on "Download Now."
3. Note where you are saving the download.
4. When download is complete, double-click on the saved file.
5. Fill in the requested registration information, and follow the instructions on your screen.
6. You must click "Accept" in the software-user's-agreement box to continue.
7. Click on "Yes" to reboot your computer once installation is complete. The computer will reboot automatically, and the program icon will appear on your desktop or on your "Start" menu.

Reading a Software User's Agreement and Warranty

Even though he plans to click on "Accept," Juan reads the software user's agreement carefully. (Remember that a user agreement is a form of **contract.**) It is long and complicated. Here are the parts that grab Juan's attention:

SOFTWARE USER'S AGREEMENT

IMPORTANT—READ CAREFULLY: This license agreement for SweetPlayer Deluxe is a legal agreement. By clicking on "Accept" or installing, copying, or using the software, you agree to abide by the terms and conditions of this license agreement. If you do not agree, click on "I Do Not Accept," and do not install the software.

1. License. The purchaser is granted a license to use this software on any single computer or on any two computers as long as the computers are not in use at the same time.

2. Use. In using this software, the purchaser agrees to comply with all laws, including applicable restrictions concerning copyright and other intellectual property rights.

3. This software is for *individual use only.* Files that are downloaded with this software, and are subject to copyright restrictions, may not be distributed to third parties or shared outside your normal circle of family and friends.

4. Title. The software is protected by copyright laws of the United States. This agreement relates to software use. Title and ownership rights and intellectual property rights remain with SweetPlayer, Inc.

Before clicking on "Accept," Juan also reads the **warranty.**

LIMITED WARRANTY

SweetPlayer, Inc., warrants that for a period of sixty (60) days from the date of purchase, the software will perform as described if operated as directed. SweetPlayer, Inc., makes no other warranties. This warranty will immediately terminate upon improper use or violations of the software user's agreement.

SweetPlayer, Inc., may, at its choice (1) replace defective media, (2) advise you how to achieve described performance, (3) refund the license-agreement fee. SweetPlayer, Inc., will be obligated to honor this warranty only if you inform SweetPlayer, Inc., of the problem during the warranty period and provide evidence of the date you acquired the software.

Under no circumstances will SweetPlayer, Inc., be held liable for more than the licensing cost of the product.

Now Juan is ready to go! He knows what he can legally do and what the company must legally provide. He clicks on "Accept." It is time to turn up the sound and— ba-boom, ba-boom, ba-dub-ba-duh-ba-BOOM.

Reading Informational Materials

Reading Check

1. Describe the basic **elements** of the SweetPlayer **advertisement.**

2. What special **features** does the ad offer? When will Juan be required to pay for his software? What will happen if he fails to make a payment?

3. Describe the basic **elements** of the **software user's agreement.**

4. What special **features** does the agreement detail?

5. In a few sentences, explain the difference between the advertisement and the agreement. What happens if Juan does not agree to the terms of the software user's agreement?

TestPractice

SWEETPLAYER Documents

1. Which of the following documents are the **download directions** *most* like?
   A   A warranty
   B   A contract
   C   Product information
   D   An instruction manual

2. The "Accept" button on the software user's agreement takes the place of a —
   F   description of services
   G   catalog of equipment
   H   signature on a contract
   J   feature of a warranty

3. By buying this product, Juan has purchased —
   A   the copyright and ownership title to the software
   B   shares of stock in the company
   C   the right to use the software
   D   the right to share the software with others

4. The **advertisement** and the **software user's agreement** are *alike* in that they both —
   F   offer important information about the product and its use
   G   entice the reader to buy the product
   H   discuss the legal terms and conditions of use
   J   tell the buyer how to get a refund

5. The **software user's agreement** and the **warranty** are *different* in that the first —
   A   describes the product, and the second describes the company
   B   is a legal document, but the second is not a legal document
   C   mainly outlines what the seller must do, and the second mainly outlines what the buyer must do
   D   mainly outlines what the buyer must do, and the second mainly outlines what the seller must do

Reading Standard 2.1 Compare and contrast the features and elements of consumer materials to gain meaning from documents (for example, warranties, contracts, product information, instruction manuals).

Computers *from* Holt Science and Technology

Following Technical Directions

When you want to make or do something new, you usually consult directions. To find out how long to boil spaghetti, you read the directions on the box. To do yoga exercises, you might follow the directions on a videotape. The directions for operating scientific and mechanical devices are called **technical directions.**

**Reading
Standard 2.5**
Understand and explain the use of a complex mechanical device by following technical directions.

Computers

Did you use a computer to wake up this morning? You might think of a computer as something you use to send e-mail or surf the Net, but computers are around you all the time. Computers are in automobiles, VCRs, and telephones. Even an alarm clock is a computer! An alarm clock, like the one in **Figure 1,** lets you program the time you want to wake up, and it will wake you up at that time.

Figure 1 *Believe it or not, this alarm clock is a computer!*

What Is a Computer?

A **computer** is an electronic device that performs tasks by processing and storing information. A computer performs a task when it is given a command and has the instructions necessary to carry out that command. Computers do not operate by themselves, or "think."

Basic Functions The basic functions a computer performs are shown in **Figure 2.** The information you give to a computer is called *input.* Setting your alarm clock is a type of input. To perform a task, a computer *processes* the input, changing it to a desirable form. Processing could mean adding a list of numbers, executing a drawing, or even moving a piece of equipment. Input doesn't have to be processed immediately; it can be stored until it is needed. Computers store information in their *memory.* For example, your alarm clock stores the time you want to wake up. It can then process this stored information by going off at the programmed time. *Output* is the final result of the task performed by the computer. What's the output of an alarm clock? The sound that wakes you up!

**Figure 2
The Functions of a Computer**

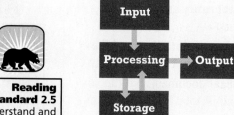

Computer Hardware

For each function of a computer, there is a corresponding part of the computer where each function occurs. **Hardware** refers to the parts, or equipment, that make up a computer. As you read about each piece of hardware, refer to **Figure 3.**

Input Devices Instructions given to a computer are called input. An *input device* is the piece of hardware that feeds information to the computer. You can enter information into a computer using a keyboard, a mouse, a scanner, a digitizing pad and pen—even your own voice!

Central Processing Unit A computer performs tasks within an area called the *central processing unit,* or CPU. In a personal computer, the CPU is a microprocessor. Input goes through the CPU for immediate processing or for storage in memory. The CPU is where the computer does calculations, solves problems, and executes the instructions given to it.

Figure 3 Computer Hardware

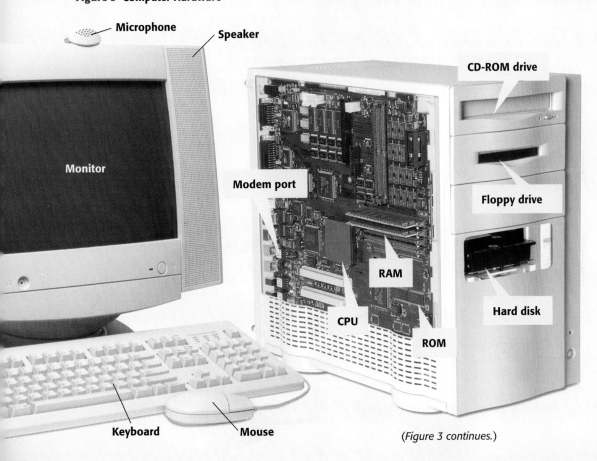

Microphone
Speaker
Monitor
Modem port
RAM
CPU
ROM
CD-ROM drive
Floppy drive
Hard disk
Keyboard
Mouse

(*Figure 3 continues.*)

Memory Information can be stored in the computer's memory until it is needed. Hard disks inside a computer and floppy disks or CD-ROMs inserted into a computer have memory to store information. Two other types of memory are *ROM* (read-only memory) and *RAM* (random-access memory).

ROM is permanent. It handles functions such as computer start-up, maintenance, and hardware management. ROM normally cannot be added to or changed, and it cannot be lost when the computer is turned off. On the other hand, RAM is temporary. It stores information only while that information is being used. RAM is sometimes called working memory. Large amounts of RAM allow more information to be input, which makes for a more powerful computer.

Output Devices Once a computer performs a task, it shows the results on an *output device*. Monitors, printers, and speaker systems are all examples of output devices.

Modems One piece of computer hardware that serves as an input device as well as an output device is a *modem*. Modems allow computers to communicate. One computer can input information into another computer over a telephone line, as long as each computer has its own modem. As a result, modems permit computers to "talk" with other computers.

Figure 3 Computer Hardware (*continued*)

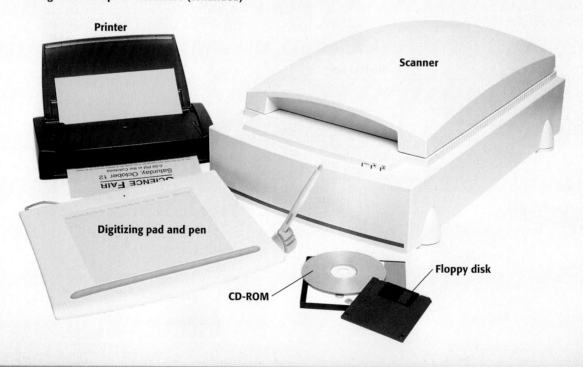

Printer

Scanner

Digitizing pad and pen

CD-ROM

Floppy disk

The Internet—A Global Network

Thanks to modems and computer software, it is possible to connect many computers and allow them to communicate with one another. That's what the **Internet** is—a huge computer network consisting of millions of computers that can all share information with one another.

How the Internet Works Computers can connect to one another on the Internet by using modems to dial into an Internet service provider, or ISP. A home computer connects to an ISP over a normal phone line. A school, business, or other group can have a local area network (LAN) that connects to an ISP using one phone line. As depicted in **Figure 4,** ISPs are connected globally by satellite. And that's how computers go global!

Figure 4 *Through a series of connections like this, every computer on the Internet can share information.*

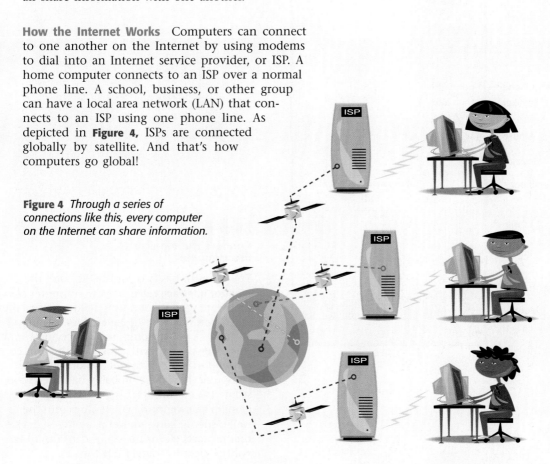

How to Set Up a Computer

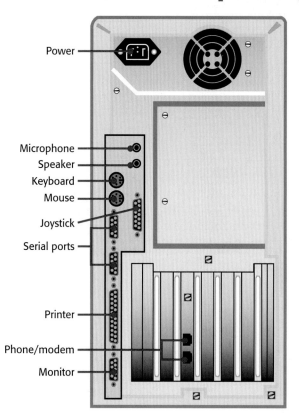

Power

Microphone
Speaker
Keyboard
Mouse
Joystick
Serial ports

Printer

Phone/modem
Monitor

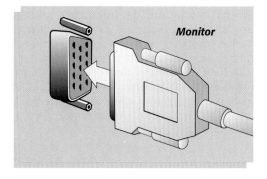

Monitor

Step 1
Connect the monitor to the computer.

The monitor has two cords: One cord, the **monitor interface cable,** lets the computer communicate with the monitor. It connects to the video port (the port designated for monitors) at the back of the computer. The connector on this cord is a plug with pins in it; the pins correspond to holes in the video port on the computer. This cable probably has screws to secure the connection. The other cord is the **monitor's power cord,** which plugs into the wall outlet or **surge protector,** a plug-in device that protects electronic equipment from high-voltage electrical surges (see Step 5).

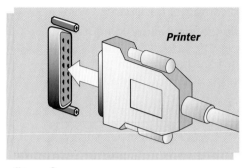

Printer

Step 2
Connect the printer to the computer.

The cable connectors that fit parallel ports, which your printer uses, have pins like those on the monitor cable and are usually secured with screws. Connect one end to the back of your printer and then connect the other end to the back of your computer where you see a **printer icon.**

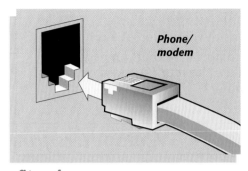

Phone/ modem

Step 4
Connect the phone line and phone to the modem.

Most computers come with **internal modems.** All you need to do is bring a line from the wall phone jack to the phone jack on the modem, which is visible on the back of your computer, and plug your telephone into the other jack on the modem.

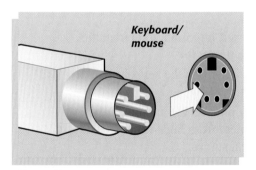

Keyboard/ mouse

Step 3
Connect the keyboard and mouse.

The connectors at the ends of the cords for the mouse and keyboard are round, and if you look inside them, you'll see small metal pins. These must be lined up correctly with the holes in the ports for the parts to fit together. Do not force the connectors together if they are not fitting properly; take another look to see whether you have them lined up correctly. Plug each connector into its labeled port on the back of your computer.

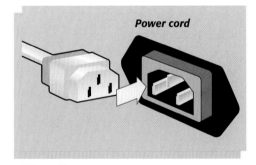

Power cord

Step 5
Connect the power cords.

The **power cord** is a three-prong, grounded cord you attach to your computer. Attach the power cord to the computer first; then, plug it into a surge protector. Do the same with the monitor's power cord. The surge protector then plugs into a grounded wall outlet. Turn on the monitor first, then the computer, and you're ready to go!

Reading Informational Materials

Reading Check

1. What is the definition of a computer?
2. According to the chart on page 550, what are the four functions of a computer?
3. What is computer hardware?
4. What do modems allow computers to do?
5. What is the Internet?

TestPractice Computers *from* Holt Science and Technology

1. What is the *best* answer to this question: Can computers operate by themselves?

   A No, because they need a command and instructions in order to operate

   B Yes, because they can operate without a command

   C No, because they can't get information stored in their memory

   D Yes, because they can check spelling and count words

2. Which of the following parts is *not* an example of an **output device**?

   F Monitor

   G Printer

   H Speaker system

   J Mouse

3. According to the illustration on page 551, which of the following is *not* housed with the central processing unit?

   A Modem port

   B Monitor

   C RAM

   D CD-ROM drive

4. What is the first thing you should do when you set up a computer?

   F Connect the keyboard and mouse

   G Connect the phone line to the modem

   H Connect the monitor to the computer

   J Connect the power cords

5. Why is it important to plug in the **surge protector**?

   A It connects the keyboard to the mouse.

   B It protects electronic equipment from high-voltage electrical surges.

   C It hooks up the phone line to the modem.

   D It turns the power off.

6. Which components of your computer do you *not* have to connect before you can use the Internet?

   F Monitor to computer

   G Printer to computer

   H Keyboard and mouse

   J Telephone line to modem

Reading Standard 2.5
Understand and explain the use of a complex mechanical device by following technical directions.

Mastering the Standards

BUSINESS LETTER

This Is What I Think

This chapter presents two town problems. Think about problems in your town that interest you. With a group of classmates, make a list of problems, and brainstorm possible solutions. Then, choose one problem, and write a formal business letter to the appropriate government official, proposing the solution you think is best. In your argument, try to answer any objections your reader might have. Be sure to include all these **parts of a business letter:**

- Heading—your address and the date
- Inside address—the name and address of the person you are writing to
- Salutation—your greeting
- Body—your message
- Closing—a respectful conclusion
- Signature—your signature and your name printed or typed

▶ Use "Writing for Life: Business Letters," pages 741–748, for help with this assignment.

Other Choices

RÉSUMÉ

 This Is Who I Am

To get a job baby-sitting or cutting lawns, you usually need only a friendly conversation. To work where no one knows you, however, you'll need a résumé, a summary of information about yourself. Your résumé should include your name, address, and phone number; the schools you've attended; any job experience you've had; your extracurricular activities; and references to people who will recommend you for a job.

▶ Use "Writing for Life: Job Applications," pages 751–752, for help with this assignment.

BUSINESS LETTER

 The Best Person for the Job

When you apply for a job by mail, send both your résumé and a cover letter. In the letter, state the job you are applying for, the reasons you are interested in the job, and your qualifications. Find a job that interests you in the classified ads of your local newspaper, or dream up your ideal job. Write a formal business letter applying for that job. (If you have made up the job, also make up the name and address of the person you are writing to.)

▶ Use "Writing for Life: Business Letters," pages 741–748, for help with this assignment.

Reading for Life: Magazines *and* Web Sites

So Many Roads

Each issue of *Cobblestone* focuses on an important aspect of the history of the United States. You might read about a historic figure like Robert E. Lee, a famous event like the California gold rush, or a document like the Bill of Rights. There's even been an issue dedicated to American cartoons! *Cobblestone* brings history to life with informative feature stories, engaging activities, and riveting photographs.

Whatever You Want

Cricket magazine has been capturing the imagination of kids for more than twenty-five years. In a typical issue you'll find folk tales, poetry, biographies, and just about any other style of writing you can think of. *Cricket* also features word games, story contests, and plenty of illustrations.

All Over the Map

In *National Geographic World* magazine you will read reports of developments in technology and features on exotic animals. You'll find *Kids Did It!,* profiles of young people who are making great achievements in science, sports, and music. Check out the Web site at www.nationalgeographic.com/kids.

How Things Work

Explore! is dedicated to explaining how the world works. Learn about everything from submarines to pipe organs to spelunking (exploring caves). Featured in every issue of this magazine are—among other columns—*Imagine That!,* which showcases science oddities, and *Then and Now,* which traces the effects of technological progress on a scientific invention throughout the years.

The Truth Is in Here

Have you ever wanted the inside scoop on outer space? Now you can find it on the Web at www.kids.msfc.nasa.gov/. You'll discover a three-dimensional map of the solar system, biographical pieces about astronauts, and information on how NASA keeps track of all those spaceships. The site is also loaded with games and even features an art gallery.

By Students, for Students

MidLink, an online magazine, fosters creativity in students around the globe through international poetry exchanges. Kids also build Web sites on topics such as favorite authors, historic landmarks, and camping experiences. With its links to sites on social studies, science, and more, *MidLink* can also serve as a research tool. You'll find *MidLink* at longwood.cs.ucf.edu/~MidLink/.

The Door's Wide Open

Kids' Castle is an online magazine developed by *Smithsonian* magazine. You will discover a variety of worlds inside: air and space, history, the arts, animals, science, and personalities. Click on the history link, and you might learn the story behind postage stamps. Follow the sports links, and you could discover vintage baseball leagues, where the rules of the game were different from today's. That's just the beginning: For more, log on at www.kidscastle.si.edu.

Where Have We Been?

The Library of Congress has a Web site that offers an overview of America's past: *America's Story from America's Library,* at www.americaslibrary.gov, introduces you to famous Americans as diverse as Harry Houdini and Langston Hughes. It also invites you to jump back in time to join America at play. Check out "See, Hear, and Sing" if you want to watch a movie, hear a song, or play a tune from America's past at this lively, interactive site.

Reading Matters

by Kylene Beers

Jenny made this list of things she was reading as an eighth-grader:

- library books
- schoolbooks
- school assignments
- letters from grandparents
- e-mail
- Internet sites
- magazines—lots
- newspaper—sports and movies mostly
- volleyball handbook
- job applications
- directions from parents for kids I baby-sit for

That's a long list, especially when you know that *Jenny doesn't like to read!* As Jenny explains, "You can't get away with not reading. Words are everywhere."

In this section of the book, you'll find strategies that will help you become a better reader—no matter how good a reader you already are. You're going to discover just how much reading matters!

Lesson

1. **Finding a Plot's Structure**
2. **Comparing and Contrasting Characters**
3. **The Power of Place**
4. **Analyzing Recurring Themes**
5. **Interpreting a Literary Work**
6. **Analyzing Forms of Poetry**
7. **Ask Questions About the Writer**
8. **Reading for Information**

Finding a Plot's Structure

Somebody Wanted But So

The Downfall of an Egg

First character is introduced.

Second character is introduced.

Humpty Dumpty sat on a wall. Humpty, who was afraid of heights to begin with, had never wanted to sit on that wall. As a result of losing his bet to Jack—his bet about jumping over the candlestick (Jack cleared the candle, but Humpty didn't)—he had to sit there for an hour. That wouldn't have been hard to do if Humpty weren't an egg and therefore oval shaped.

A third character is introduced. A problem is also introduced: Wolf wants an egg.

While Humpty was trying to stay balanced on the wall, Mr. B. B. Wolf, at the other end of the village, had just finished a tasty snack of pork chops. "Ah," thought Wolf, "if only I had some eggs. Nothing beats pork chops and eggs." He liked his idea so much that he let out a tremendous howl. Back at the wall, Humpty heard the howl. It startled him so much that he began wobbling. He teetered off the edge of the wall and landed—*splat*—on the ground.

Two major events.

The climax of the story.

The resolution of the story starts here.

The king's men were out patrolling that morning, looking for some sheep. The sheep, it was rumored, had been lost because the Little Blue Boy had fallen asleep while tending them. When the king's men came across the broken Humpty, they tried to put him back together but had no luck. Then they saw Jack lurking nearby. When they asked him why a good egg like Humpty had been up on a wall, Jack told them about the bet. He was arrested for reckless endangerment of an egg. The king's men completely forgot about the sheep, so the Little Blue Boy slept on. Wolf decided to skip the eggs and go for some cookies that a little girl was carrying in her basket. ■

Reading Standard 3.2
Evaluate the structural elements of the plot (for example, subplots, parallel episodes, climax), the plot's development, and the way in which conflicts are (or are not) addressed and resolved.

Find the Allusions

An **allusion** is a reference to someone or something in history, literature, sports, politics—something the writer figures the reader will recognize. In addition to the big allusion to "Humpty Dumpty," this story alludes to four other children's stories. Can you name them?

Allusions are to "Jack Be Nimble," "The Three Little Pigs," "Little Boy Blue," and "Little Red Riding Hood."

Understanding Plot Structure

"The Downfall of an Egg" is a simple story, but when you have a story with subplots, keeping track of the main plot structure can be difficult.

For help identifying the basic structural elements of a plot, use a strategy called **Somebody Wanted But So**. First, jot down those four words on a piece of paper (see below). Next, write the main character's name under the heading "Somebody." Then, under the heading "Wanted," write down what the character wants. In the "But" column, write down what prevents the character from getting what he or she wants. In the "So" column, write the story's resolution. When you're finished, you'll have one sentence. It might take more Somebody Wanted But So statements to cover the entire plot. If so, just use a word like *then* or *later* or *but* or *therefore*—whichever one makes sense—to connect the statements.

Somebody	Wanted	But	So
Humpty	wanted to win the bet with Jack,	but he lost,	so he had to sit on the wall for an hour.

Then,

Somebody	Wanted	But	So
Humpty	wanted to stay balanced on the wall though that was hard for an ovoid,	but a loud howl startled him,	so he fell and splattered.

Now, ask yourself if there's information about the plot that didn't show up in those two sentences. If you answer yes, write another SWBS statement.

PRACTICE

1. Review the stories in Chapter 1. Reduce one of them to the Somebody Wanted But So framework. You might try "Flowers for Algernon" (page 23) or "The Landlady" (page 62). You might also try one of the **subplots** in "Flowers for Algernon."

2. The **climax** of a story is its most exciting moment—the moment when the outcome of the conflict is determined. On your SWBS chart, circle the climax. Then, compare your charts in class. Readers won't always agree.

2 Comparing and Contrasting Characters

Semantic Differential Scales

Scales. There are fish scales, piano scales, and the scales of justice. Your skin can be dry and scaly, you can scale a fence, and you can weigh fruit on the scales in the grocery store. You can also use scales—not the ones in the bathroom—to compare characters. This special character-comparing scale is called a **semantic differential scale.**

A **semantic differential scale** can help you when you are comparing the traits of two or more characters or people.

Semantic Differential Scales

Semantic differential scales sound complex, but they are not. The word *semantic* refers to meanings of words. The word *differential* has to do with differences. To make a scale, simply place words that are opposite in meaning at opposite ends of a scale, like this:

kind_____ mean

Then, think of a person (say, your brother or sister), and decide where you'd place that person on this scale. If the person is kind, put a mark above the word *kind.* If the person is pretty mean, put your mark on the other end of the scale, as close to the word *mean* as you want it to be. Next, think of a second person (maybe your best friend), and rate that person on the same scale—using a different color ink. Notice how the scale helps you see at a glance how those two people are alike or different.

When You Read

When you are reading, you can easily make semantic differential scales in your notebook. As you think about the characters, make marks on the scales to remind you of the qualities they reveal. You'll probably notice that characters change. A character who is timid at the beginning of a story might be bold at the end. You can compare two or more characters on the same scale by using a different color ink for each character.

The key to a good scale is the words you choose for your comparisons. Brainstorming a list of qualities with a partner or group will help you find your words.

Here's a list of words you might use to create your scales:

A Box of Traits

brave/fearful	generous/stingy	optimistic/pessimistic
compassionate/cruel	happy/unhappy	powerful/weak
curious/indifferent	joyful/sad	selfless/selfish
dependable/undependable	kind/mean	sincere/insincere
fair/unfair	loyal/disloyal	truthful/untruthful
forgiving/unforgiving	obedient/disobedient	wise/foolish

PRACTICE

Think about Abraham Lincoln and Martin Luther King, Jr., well-known leaders who lived at different times in history, each associated with human rights. Now, decide where you'd place each of them on the following semantic differential scales. (If you prefer, select two contemporary leaders you know something about, and put them on the scales.)

powerful _____ weak
brave _____ fearful
compassionate _____ cruel

The Power of Place

If...Then...

Reading Standard 3.4
Analyze the relevance of the setting (for example, place, time, customs) to the mood, tone, and meaning of the text.

Where Am I?

Suppose you are the director of a movie, but you have only three lines of the script. Here are the three lines:

Actor One. You're late.

Actor Two. I'm sorry.

Actor One. It doesn't matter.

At this point you can't give the actors much direction on how to say the lines. You don't know if Actor One is angry or not or if Actor Two is really sorry or not. There's a lot you don't know because you don't even know where this conversation takes place. So, let's add some settings:

1. an empty church decorated for a wedding

2. a football field during a neighborhood afternoon pickup game

3. a football field during the Super Bowl

4. a busy airport

Now you've got some help in deciding what the problem might be. What does each setting suggest the play might be about? What problem could be connected to one of these settings? Is there a setting in which it really doesn't matter that Actor Two is late? Is there a setting in which Actor One actually does think it matters that Actor Two is late? As the director, show your actors how you want the lines said in each setting. How does their tone change as their setting changes?

What you can quickly see in this short exercise is that *place* makes a difference. As writers change their settings, plots or problems may also change.

Changing Places

To understand the power of a setting, think about what would happen if you changed it. Think in terms of **If . . . Then . . .**
For example, *if* the setting is the early 1900s in Pittsburgh, *then* what happens if I change the setting to the early 3000s? *If* the setting is downtown Los Angeles, *then* what happens if I change it to a beach in Maine? *If* the setting is an ocean liner, *then* what happens if I change it to a rocketship?

Setting and Mood

The setting of a story strongly affects its mood. A story set in a dark cave or in a place where the sun shines only a few months a year would probably not make you feel very cheerful. A sunny garden creates feelings of pleasure and freedom. A dungeon creates feelings of doom and entrapment.

PRACTICE

Below are two conversations. Read both conversations, and choose the one you like better. Then, describe three different settings, and place the characters and their dialogue in each setting. How does a change in setting change the scene?

Choice 1
Character One: You stole it.
Character Two: Was that a good idea?
Character One: Who said you could do that?

Choice 2
Character One: I'll go last.
Character Two: No, I'll go last.
Character One: No, I insist. I'll go last.

Before you describe your setting, gather your details in a diagram like the one below:

special features ← setting → weather

customs ← setting → threats

"Is this the right setting?"

Analyzing Recurring Themes

Most Important Word

Recurring Themes

The more you read, the more you'll discover that certain themes show up repeatedly in literary works. These are called **recurring themes.** *Recurring* simply means "happening over and over again." Here's a list of some themes that have been expressed in literature for thousands of years:

- Innocence has the power to conquer evil.
- Nature renews itself, just as people can renew themselves.
- Love endures.
- People will forever search for freedom.
- The power of imagination can transform the world.
- Heroism can come from unexpected sources.
- Our dreams of a perfect world often end in disappointment.

To see how themes can recur over time, think about Daniel Defoe's *Robinson Crusoe* (published in 1719) and Gary Paulsen's *Hatchet* (published in 1987). In both stories a castaway must survive in a wilderness. Each castaway survives his quest. Each one creates in the wilder-ness a kind of human home. Each emerges from the wilder-ness a wiser person. The theme of both stories has to do with what we learn about ourselves when all the trappings of civi-lization are taken from us. From this quest to survive, we learn truths about ourselves.

Most Important Word

To identify themes, you can use a strategy called **Most Important Word.** With this strategy you decide which word from the text you think is the most important word (or words—there can be more than one). Here are some of the rules:

- Don't use a character's name.
- Look for a word that is often used; that is used at a key point in the story, as in the climax; or that is used at the beginning and then again at the end.
- Think about how the word relates to the characters, set-ting, conflict, and resolution of the story.

Reading Standard 3.5
Identify and analyze recurring themes (for example, good versus evil) across traditional and contemporary works.

Here's an example of how the most important word helped a reader identify theme:

Character
The Rough-Faced Girl is always kind to others.

Plot
Many girls want to be chosen as the chief's bride. They are unkind girls.

Conflict
The Rough-Faced Girl suffers cruel taunts because of her looks.

Kindness
Most important word for the Rough-Faced Girl (a Native American Cinderella story)

Resolution
Because of her kindness, she is chosen to be the chief's bride.

Theme
Kindness toward others will be rewarded.

PRACTICE

Fill out a chart like the one that follows. Write down the titles of two books you have read that show similar themes. Then, briefly state the way the theme is handled in each book.

Display your charts in class.

Theme: _____

Story 1: _____

Story 2: _____

Interpreting a Literary Work

Logographic Clues

Writers use devices that help you interpret their works. For instance, a writer might have a character speak in a **dialect** to tell something about that character's education or background. A writer might use **symbolism** to deepen your understanding of a text. Imagine, for example, a scene in which a character sees a rainbow in the sky—that rainbow could symbolize hope. A writer might also use **metaphors** to provide clues to the text's deeper meaning. A character who is described as "prickly as a cactus" is a character who causes trouble. A writer might even make a point by using **irony**—a contrast between what you expect to happen and what really happens. You'd probably feel a sense of irony if you read a story about a Great Dane who runs away from a mouse.

Spotting Literary Devices

All those literary devices can help you interpret the text only if you can (1) identify them and (2) keep up with them! Lots of activities in this book help you identify literary devices. On the side of this page, you'll find a quick review of those devices. Once you identify those literary devices, look closely at the way in which they are used. How do they help you interpret a character, a plot, a theme? One way of keeping literary devices straight in your mind is by using logographic (lō·gō·graf′ik) clues. The word *logographic* simply means "a picture that stands for a word." (*Graph* is from a Greek word for "writing," and *logo* is from *logos,* a Greek word for "word.") Logographic clues are little picture clues that you can use to highlight something in a text.

Reading Standard 3.6 Identify significant literary devices (for example, metaphor, symbolism, dialect, irony) that define a writer's style, and use those elements to interpret the work.

A Box of Literary Devices

metaphor: a direct comparison of two unlike things. *The boy was a thorn in my side.*

simile: a comparison of two unlike things using the word *like, as, than,* or resembles. *The boy was* like *a thorn in my side.*

personification: animals or inanimate objects talked about as if they were human or alive. *The wind danced through the branches of the tree.*

(*continued*)

The best logographic clues are the ones you create yourself. A few suggested clues appear below. Use clues like these to mark the literary devices you come across. Many readers draw the little pictures on sticky notes and place the notes next to the places in the text where the literary devices appear. You might want to do that.

Metaphor . . . .

Simile . . . .

Personification . . . .

Symbolism . . . .

Irony . . . .

Dialect . . . .

PRACTICE

Read "Raymond's Run" (page 367), looking for places where Toni Cade Bambara uses **irony** and **dialect** to give you insight into the characters. As you read, use your logographic clues on sticky notes to pinpoint those places where irony and dialect are used. When you've finished reading the story, look back at examples of the dialect you've marked. What does Miss Hazel Elizabeth Deborah Parker's word choice tell you about her? What *tone* of voice do you hear when Squeaky speaks? Now, look at your irony markers. What does the irony tell you about Squeaky and her dreams?

More Literary Devices

symbolism: the use of an object or an event that functions as itself but also stands for something broader than itself. In these lines from an old song, the rainbow is used as a symbol of hope: *God gave Noah the rainbow sign: no more water; the fire next time.*

irony: a contrast between what is expected to happen and what actually happens. *The runner called Speedy lost the race.*

dialect: a way of speaking that is characteristic of a certain region or group of people. Compare *That is like so totally cool* with *I think that is most appropriate.*

Reading Matters

Analyzing Forms of Poetry

Text Reformulation

When the president of the United States invites dignitaries from other countries to dinner, he doesn't send a handwritten note that says "Y'all come." When you invite friends to go out for pizza, you don't send an engraved invitation that requests the honor of their presence. In other words, the form of an invitation matches the situation. In a book on manners, you'll find that different types of invitations even have different names. There's the formal (engraved), the semiformal (printed), the informal (handwritten), and the casual (phone call or e-mail). With each type you'll find that not only does the form change but the language that's used also changes. A formal invitation may request an RSVP (that's an abbreviation for the French term that means "respond if you please"), while your casual phone call might conclude with "Wanna go?"

The Poet's Book of Manners

Poets also have different forms to choose from as they write their poems.

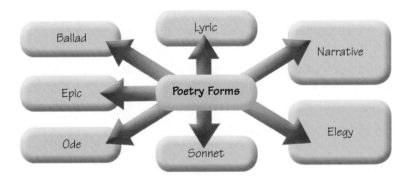

Reading Standard 3.1
Determine and articulate the relationship between the purposes and characteristics of different forms of poetry (for example, ballad, lyric, couplet, epic, elegy, ode, sonnet).

Poets choose a form that best helps them say what they want to say.

Form	Purpose	Example
Ballad	a simple song or songlike poem with a refrain. A ballad tells a story, usually a tragedy or an adventure.	"The Dying Cowboy"
Narrative	a poem that tells a story	"Paul Revere's Ride"
Epic	a very long, complex narrative poem that reflects the values of a whole society and focuses on a hero's quest to win something of great value	Beowulf
Lyric	a poem, usually short, that expresses the feelings of the poet instead of telling a story	"Birdfoot's Grampa"
Sonnet	a fourteen-line lyric poem with a strict form and rhyme scheme	"On the Grasshopper and the Cricket"
Ode	a lyric poem on a serious subject, usually addressed to a person or thing	"Ode to Thanks"
Elegy	a lyric poem that laments the death of someone or the loss of something	"O Captain! My Captain!"

Identifying the form of poetry isn't very hard. If you want to see how form affects the tone or mood of the poem, try a strategy called **text reformulation.** With this strategy you rewrite any text in a different form. You could turn an ode into a sonnet or a ballad into an elegy. You could turn a ballad into a short story or a play. You could turn a news article into a ballad. You could turn a sonnet into a love song.

PRACTICE

Try it out: Find a news story in the newspaper. Reformulate the story as a ballad. You will have to find a gripping story, isolate a few key events, and find at least two characters. Think of a haunting or funny refrain.

A good way to find a story that has ballad potential is to scan the headlines. Look for a story that is tragic or heart-warming—though the old ballad singers preferred the tragic!

7 Ask Questions About the Writer

It Says, I Say, And So

Read this conversation that I once had with a group of eighth-graders. See if you've ever had a reaction like Adam's:

"So, what did you think about the story?" I asked.

"I liked it," some said. Others just nodded. Some just sat.

"Well, what can you tell me about the author from reading this story?" I asked.

Silence for a while and finally Adam said, "I didn't read anything about the author, I just read the story."

Adam was right—he did just read the story—but he was also wrong. When reading a story, you can sometimes make inferences about its writer. Consider these situations:

• You read a story about a boy who goes hunting and shoots a deer and later feels remorse for having killed that animal. You might reach the conclusion that the author doesn't like hunting.

• You read a story about a character who goes through a number of tough experiences, but in the end she is rewarded for all her bravery and feels great happiness. You can guess that this story was written by a writer who believes that the world is fair and rewards good people.

• You read a story about a character who is very religious and finds comfort in his faith. You might determine that the writer holds some religious belief.

Reading Standard 3.7
Analyze a work of literature, showing how it reflects the heritage, tradition, attitudes, and beliefs of its author.

However, you can't always presume that writers have had all the experiences they write about. Consider these examples:

• You can't presume that E. B. White knows what a spider thinks, even though he wrote *Charlotte's Web*. (Remember that Charlotte, the main character, is a spider.)

• You can't presume that J.R.R. Tolkien is a hobbit, even though he wrote *The Hobbit*, a book about an imaginary creature called a hobbit who lives in a made-up setting called Middle Earth.

- You can't presume that Sandra Cisneros is an eleven-year-old girl, even though she wrote the short story titled "Eleven," which is told by an eleven-year-old girl.

You *can* conclude that E. B. White believed that helping people is important and that J.R.R. Tolkien knew a lot about mythology. You *can* conclude that Sandra Cisneros understands what it is *like* to be an eleven-year-old girl—and that she knows that being embarrassed hurts. You can make these assumptions because of the settings the writers have created, the situations their characters face, the ways their characters act and talk.

Your Writing Assignment: "Explain How This Work Might Reflect the Writer's Background"

If you are assigned the above topic to write about or discuss, here is a strategy that can help you dig into the text to find your answer: **It Says, I Say, And So.**

PRACTICE

Write "It Says," "I Say," "And So," in three columns. In the "It Says" column, write down what the story says in a particular passage. Under the "I Say" column, write what you think the passage might reflect about the writer. Under the "And So" column, write your final inference about what the passage reveals. Here's an example from "The Treasure of Lemon Brown" (page 490). Note the assumptions this student makes about Myers's background:

It Says	I Say	And So
Greg lived in Harlem.	I wonder if Myers once lived there.	I think the story's setting is one Myers knew really well. It sounds authentic.
[Add your own notes.]	[Add your own thoughts.]	[Add your own inferences.]

You can't presume
that J.R.R. Tolkien is
a hobbit.

Strategy Lesson 8

Reading for Information

In one basic way, reading technical materials—like the booklet that comes with the thousand-piece starship you plan to build or the directions for assembling a bike—differs from reading stories. Can you figure out what that difference is?

It's not that stories are usually fiction and technical matter is usually nonfiction. With both fiction and nonfiction you still have to

- process information
- think about what the text is saying
- compare and contrast
- predict what will happen next
- summarize what's already happened
- understand the sequence of events
- recognize the writer's point of view
- connect what you already know to what you are reading
- note the relationship of cause and effect
- make inferences
- draw conclusions

Reading Standards 2.5 and 2.6
Understand and explain the use of a complex mechanical device. Use information from a variety of consumer, workplace, and public documents to explain a situation or decision and to solve a problem.

You use those skills whether you're reading fiction or nonfiction, so the truth or non-truth of the selection isn't the difference. It's also not that some readers will say that nonfiction is boring and fiction is exciting or that fiction is boring and nonfiction is exciting. The boring-versus-exciting factor is more about the reader than the text. One reader may think that the article titled "Seventy-five Ways to Care for Your Boa Constrictor" is a wonderful article, while the next reader may think it squeezes the fun out of reading. The most basic difference comes from the fact that almost all fiction follows a narrative structure, and much of nonfiction follows an expository, or explanatory, structure.

A narrative structure uses a narrator to tell you what happens, usually in time order. You generally don't have to wonder where you're going with narrative because a narrator helps you get there. There is no narrator talking to you in an expository text, however. This lack of a guide slows down some readers of expository texts.

Finding a Guide in Informative Texts

When you are reading an expository text, look for some guidelines, such as these:

1. If the text has numbered steps, think of the steps as a character telling you, "First, do this. Next, do that."

2. If the text has subtitles, think of the subtitles as characters telling you, "Look here! This is a new topic we're about to meet."

3. If the text has words or phrases in boldface or italic type, think of these graphic features as a character saying, "This is an important word or definition. Pay attention!"

4. If the text includes a graph or map or chart, think of these graphic features as another character, one who has decided to tell you in another way what the first character was saying. "Listen" carefully to this other character to pick up additional information or to see the information in graphic terms.

5. If the text uses phrases such as *on the other hand* or *by comparison* or *by contrast* or *still others believe,* think of them as a character telling you the other side of what's happened. Read carefully when you see these phrases, because you're about to get information that conflicts with what you've already read.

6. If the text uses phrases such as *as a result* or *consequently* or *this results in* or *therefore,* think of these words as coming from a guide who is explaining the effects of something that has happened.

PART 2

Mastering the California Standards in Writing, Listening, and Speaking

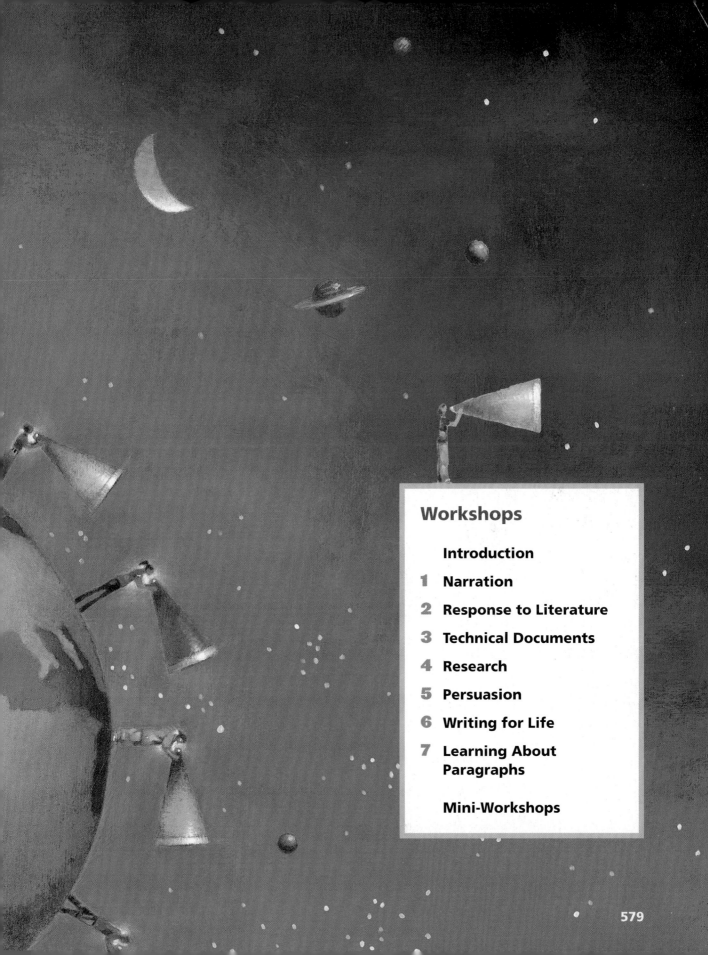

Workshops

Introduction

WHAT'S AHEAD?

In this section you will learn how effective writers

- prewrite
- write
- revise
- publish

L ike many other activities you do every day—from getting ready for school to playing football—writing is a **process** that involves several stages. Each of the following workshops in this section of the book will lead you step-by-step through the process of completing a specific type of writing. This introduction will help get you ready for all the workshops that follow by providing an overview of the writing process. At the same time, you will learn about the following language arts standards.

California Standards

Writing

1.0 Students progress through the stages of the writing process.

1.1 Create compositions that establish a controlling impression.

1.2 Establish coherence within and among paragraphs through effective transitions and parallel structures.

1.4 Plan and conduct multiple-step information searches by using computer networks and modems.

1.6 Revise writing for consistent point of view.

2.0 Student writing demonstrates a command of standard American English and the research, organizational, and drafting strategies outlined in Writing Standard 1.0.

GO TO: go.hrw.com
KEYWORD: HLLA

Writing as a Process

You would probably be dreaming if you thought you could turn out a flawless, well-written paper in just one night. Why? Writing is a process made up of many steps. The chart on the next page summarizes the usual stages of the writing process.

WHAT YOU DO DURING THE WRITING PROCESS

Prewriting	• Choose a manageable **topic** and a **form**. • Identify your **purpose** and **audience**. • Draft a sentence that expresses your **main idea**. • **Gather information** about your topic. • Begin to **organize** your information.
Writing	• Draft an **introduction** that gets your reader's attention, provides background information, and states your main idea. • Follow a **plan** or order. • State your **supporting points** and **elaborate** on them. • Wrap things up with a **conclusion**.
Revising	• **Evaluate** your draft, or ask a peer to evaluate it. • **Revise** to improve content, organization, and style.
Publishing	• **Proofread** your draft to find and correct spelling, punctuation, and grammar errors. • Use the correct **manuscript style.** (See page 583.) • **Publish** your writing. • **Reflect** on your writing experience.

TIP The writing process is not a one-way street. You can always return to an earlier stage if you need to. Suppose you are drafting a report and realize that you need more details about part of your topic. You gather more information (prewriting) and then return to drafting by adding the details to your paper.

Prewriting

Getting Ready

Last-minute writers, like last-minute shoppers, often find themselves settling for second best. No wonder they—and their readers—are often disappointed with the results. To avoid being a last-minute writer, use the following prewriting steps.

1. **Choose and narrow your topic.** Choose a topic that truly interests you. Then, narrow your topic to fit the amount of writing space you have. Huge topics such as "health" have so many parts that they call for books, not brief papers. However, the narrowed topic "health products advertised on infomercials," is more manageable.

2. **Choose a form.** Your teacher may assign the form, but if the choice is yours, you have many options, including letters, editorials, brochures, memoirs, and reviews.

Writing **1.0** Students progress through the stages of the writing process.

COMPUTER TIP

Computer networks and databases are an excellent source of information for many types of writing projects. However, do not forget to evaluate any information you find online to make sure that it is accurate and up-to-date. Also, cite your online sources (see page 678).

3. **Identify your purpose and audience.** First, decide why you are writing. Then, decide who will read what you have written. These decisions will shape your writing. For example, if you were writing a persuasive letter to the school board, you would write differently than if you were writing a personal letter to a friend.

4. **Draft a sentence that expresses your main idea or thesis.** Writing a main idea statement, or thesis statement, will help you focus as you write; you can change it later if you need to.

5. **Gather information about your topic.** You can find information in books and magazines, on the Web, through interviews with knowledgeable people, and, for personal experiences, from your own observations and memories.

6. **Begin to organize your information.** Organize your writing in a way that will help your audience understand your ideas.

Writing

Making a Start

Here are some ways you can help yourself and your readers get the most out of your writing.

Reference Note

For more on **introductions,** see page 763. For more on **transitions** and **parallel structures,** see pages 760 and 717.

- **Draft an introduction.** Make your audience want to read what you have to say by starting with an unusual description, a surprising quote, a remarkable fact, or an intriguing question. Then, state your main idea as clearly as you can.

- **Follow a plan or order.** Develop one major idea per paragraph. In addition, create **coherence** within and among paragraphs by using **transitions,** such as *next* and *finally,* and **parallel structures.** Using parallel structures means using the same kinds of phrases, clauses, and sentences for balance and rhythm. For instance, in a persuasive essay you might issue calls for action in the conclusion, such as: "Write a letter to the school board. Write a letter to your mayor. Write a letter to your state representative."

- **State your supporting points and elaborate on them.** Details can make your ideas clearer to readers. For example, do not just write "Brazilian rain forests should be preserved." Show your readers why you hold that opinion by using facts, statistics, examples, anecdotes, analogies, comparisons, and quotations.

Writing 1.2 Establish coherence within and among paragraphs through effective transitions and parallel structures. **1.4** Plan and conduct multiple-step information searches by using computer networks and modems. **2.0** Student writing demonstrates the research, organizational, and drafting strategies outlined in Writing Standard 1.0.

- **Wrap things up with a conclusion.** End with a sentence or two that restates your overall point in different words or that underscores the main impression you set out to create.

Reference Note

For more on **conclusions**, see page 764.

A little time spent thinking about format as you draft will make it easier to revise and publish your paper later. See the guidelines in the left-hand column below. Before you publish, refer to the guidelines in the right-hand column.

GUIDELINES FOR MANUSCRIPT STYLE

While you draft . . .	Before you publish . . .
use only one side of each sheet of paper and write on a word processor, if available	write your paper neatly in blue or black ink (if you are not using a word processor)
skip lines or double-space so that your paper is easier to edit	indent the first line of every paragraph five spaces or $\frac{1}{2}$ inch
leave one-inch margins at the top, bottom, and sides of your paper	correct any mistakes and make sure your pages look neat and clean
number all pages except the first page in the top right-hand corner	use the heading your teacher prefers, or use a title page

Going Back over Your Draft

The revising stage offers you the opportunity to make your writing better. Follow these suggestions.

- **Evaluate your draft.** Re-read your draft carefully at least twice. First focus on the content and organization; then, focus on style.

- **Revise for content and organization.** Use any or all of the following methods to revise your draft.

  1. **Add.** Flesh out thin writing by adding details, descriptions, or whole paragraphs that make your ideas clearer to readers.

  2. **Delete.** Eliminate unnecessary words, sentences, or paragraphs. Cut ideas that are not consistent with your **point of view,** or way of looking at your topic.

  3. **Replace.** Use strong, precise details in place of weak, vague ones.

  4. **Rearrange.** Move information around to make your message clearer.

- **Revise for style.** Choose language, details, and sentence structures that create a **controlling impression.** For example, if you want your

TIP Peer evaluators may point out problems and suggest ways to clarify your ideas. Specific guidelines for **peer evaluation** appear in the Revising section of each Writing Workshop in this book.

research report to give a scientific impression of tadpoles, choose words that establish a formal tone and provide facts. Avoid informal language, details, and sentence structures that reflect a personal attitude toward tadpoles (such as *They're yucky!*).

When you are revising or proofreading your own work or the work of a peer, use the symbols in the following chart.

SYMBOLS FOR REVISING AND PROOFREADING

Symbol	Example	Meaning of Symbol
≡	at Scott lake	Capitalize a lowercase letter.
/	a gift for my Uncle	Lowercase a capital letter.
∧	Did it cost fifty cents Jane?	Insert a missing word, letter, or punctuation mark.
∧—	Where are you born?	Replace a word, letter, or punctuation mark.
ℐ	What day is is it?	Delete a word, letter, or punctuation mark.
∩	recieved	Change the order of letters.
¶	¶ We said goodbye.	Begin a new paragraph.
⊙	Please be patient	Add a period.
∧	Yes, that's right.	Add comma.
⌒∧	Where is Ghana? Where is Spain? It is in Africa.	Rearrange words or sentences.

Publishing

Going Public

Sharing your writing will bring the process to a satisfying close.

- **Proofread your draft.** Find and correct errors in spelling, capitalization, grammar, usage, and punctuation. You may exchange papers with a partner, but be sure to read your own paper closely, too. Do not rely on computer spellcheckers or grammar checkers for proofreading; these tools may actually introduce errors into your paper if you do not use them carefully.

Writing **1.1** Create compositions that establish a controlling impression. **1.6** Revise writing for consistent point of view.

You can use the following guidelines to proofread your draft. The page numbers in parentheses refer to the *Holt Handbook*.

GUIDELINES FOR PROOFREADING

1. Is every sentence a complete sentence, not a fragment or run-on? (See pages 438–442.)

2. Does every sentence begin with a capital letter and end with the correct punctuation mark? Are punctuation marks used correctly within sentences? (See pages 284–312.)

3. Do plural verbs have plural subjects? Do singular verbs have singular subjects? (See pages 403–404.)

4. Are verbs in the right form? Are verbs in the right tense? (See pages 184–213.)

5. Are pronoun references clear? (See pages 230–231.)

6. Are words spelled correctly? (See pages 368–397.)

- **Publish your writing.** Share your polished piece with the audience you had in mind when you wrote it. You could also submit it to your school newspaper, to a magazine, or to a writing contest.

- **Reflect on your writing experience.** Ask yourself some questions about what you have learned: Did I achieve my purpose for writing? What might I do differently next time I write?

PRACTICE & APPLY **Revise and Proofread**

Use the guidelines that begin on page 583 to revise and proofread the following paragraph. As you revise, remember to make changes that create coherence and establish a controlling impression. Refer to the revision techniques and proofreading guidelines in this workshop, and use the appropriate symbols to indicate any changes.

Last year, my family went to the Yucatán Peninsula of mexico. The best part of our tirp was going to the Chichén Itzá ruins to see the pyramids. When I was little I built a pyramid out of blocks. The biggest pyramid has nine levels and a temple on top. It was built a thousand years ago over a smaller older pyramid. Inside the small pyramid is a Cat carved out of limestone. I have never saw such interesting things before. The cat has jade green eyes.

Writing **2.0** Student writing demonstrates a command of standard American English.

Narration

"**Y**ou had better have a good story," says your exasperated coach when you arrive at practice almost an hour late. "You're probably not going to believe this, but . . . ," you begin. Five minutes into the story of your latest misadventure, you can tell by the look on the coach's face that not only does she believe your story, but she also thinks it's funny. Your **personal narrative,** the story of your experience, has found an appreciative audience. In this workshop you will share a personal experience through writing and speaking. In the process you will practice these language arts standards.

WRITING WORKSHOP

Writing a Personal Narrative Page 588

LISTENING AND SPEAKING WORKSHOP

Telling and Listening to a True Story Page 604

California Standards

Writing

1.0 Students write clear, coherent, and focused essays. The writing exhibits students' awareness of audience and purpose. Essays contain formal introductions, supporting evidence, and conclusions. Students progress through the stages of the writing process as needed.

1.1 Create compositions that establish a controlling impression and end with a clear and well-supported conclusion.

1.2 Establish coherence within and among paragraphs through effective transitions.

1.6 Revise writing for word choice; appropriate organization; consistent point of view; and transitions between paragraphs, passages, and ideas.

2.0 Students write narrative texts of at least 500 to 700 words. Student writing demonstrates a command of standard American English and the organizational and drafting strategies outlined in Writing Standard 1.0.

2.1 Write autobiographies or narratives:

  a. Relate a clear, coherent incident, event, or situation by using well-chosen details.

  b. Reveal the significance of, or the writer's attitude about, the subject.

GO TO: go.hrw.com
KEYWORD: HLLA8 W-1
FOR: Models, Writer's Guides, and Reference Sources

c. Employ narrative and descriptive strategies (e.g., relevant dialogue, specific action, physical description, background description).

Listening and Speaking

1.0 Students deliver focused, coherent presentations that convey ideas clearly and relate to the background and interests of the audience. They evaluate the content of oral communication.

1.3 Organize information to achieve particular purposes by matching the message, vocabulary, voice modulation, expression, and tone to the audience and purpose.

1.4 Prepare a speech outline based upon a chosen pattern of organization.

1.5 Use action verbs, sensory details, and appropriate and colorful modifiers in ways that enliven oral presentations.

1.6 Use appropriate grammar and word choice during formal presentations.

1.7 Use audience feedback (e.g., nonverbal cues).

2.0 Students deliver presentations employing traditional rhetorical strategies (e.g., narration, description). Student speaking demonstrates a command of standard American English and the organizational and delivery strategies outlined in Listening and Speaking Standard 1.0.

2.1 Deliver narrative presentations (e.g., biographical, autobiographical):

a. Relate a clear, coherent incident, event, or situation by using well-chosen details.

b. Reveal the significance of, and the subject's attitude about, the incident, event, or situation.

c. Employ narrative and descriptive strategies (e.g., relevant dialogue, specific action, physical description, background description, comparison or contrast of characters).

WHAT'S AHEAD?

In this workshop you will write a personal narrative. You will also learn how to

- organize ideas in chronological order
- choose relevant details
- choose precise words
- punctuate dialogue correctly

Writing a Personal Narrative

You are lying on your bed listening to your favorite radio station on a lazy Saturday afternoon. The DJ plays a song you remember from the last summer you spent at your grandparents' farm. Suddenly you find yourself reliving an incident from that summer—an incident that changed the way you thought about your grandfather and that taught you something about yourself.

A **personal narrative** is a story about such an experience. In this workshop you will share a meaningful experience from your life by writing a personal narrative.

Professional Model: A Personal Narrative

The personal narrative is a popular form of writing. Personal narratives may appear in books, magazines, and newspapers. In the following personal narrative, first published in the magazine *Voices from the Middle,* the author relates some of his experiences with a sixteen-week-old black bear he adopted. The author begins in the present, describing the bear as a ten-year-old. Then he goes back ten years to tell the story of how the bear gradually became a member of the family.

DO THIS ➤ As you read, create a **think sheet,** asking questions, making connections to your own experiences, and noting important or striking parts of the narrative. To help you create your think sheet, answer the analysis questions that appear next to the narrative.

Writing 2.1 Write autobiographies or narratives.

from Voices from the Middle

Bear in the Family

by Ben Mikaelsen

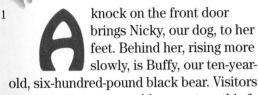

1   A knock on the front door brings Nicky, our dog, to her feet. Behind her, rising more slowly, is Buffy, our ten-year-old, six-hundred-pound black bear. Visitors seldom venture this far up the mountain. Our rustic log cabin, nestled up a winding canyon, is miles from the nearest paved road.

> **1. What details does the writer use to set the scene in the first few paragraphs?**

2   Nicky growls softly, and I praise her for alerting me. Buffy, however, lumbers[1] over to the big arched door and stands up. He wraps a large paw around the elk-antler door handle and swings the thick panel open with an easy tug.

3   Today the visitor is a neighbor wanting to borrow eggs. Towering seven feet tall, Buffy blocks her entrance. As usual, the elderly lady comes armed with a marshmallow. Buffy lips it gently from her hand and moves aside. She tosses another treat to our dog.

4   It's humorous when Buffy opens the door to a stranger. The occasional proselytizer[2] or salesperson can barely remember his or her name with a mountainous unchained bruin[3] looming over them. They do not see Buffy as I do—as a young, innocent child.

> **2. What is the writer's attitude toward his subject?**

5   This child came to us ten years ago. Harboring an insatiable[4] fascination for bears, I jumped at the chance to care for a young cub returned from a research facility. My wife Melanie agreed to help adopt this creature we had never met.

6   Before picking up our baby, we read dozens of books on bears and secured necessary licenses. I built a sturdy chain-link facility around two sides of the house. Our Buffy would have a spring-fed pond, a playground, a den, and plenty of running room. Finally, we were ready—we thought.

7   The twenty-pound, sixteen-week-old rascal who joined our family caught us unprepared. The first night, I lay in bed listening to his haunting cry, a lost, mournful little sound. I crept out and sat near him in his den. After a few minutes he crawled on my lap and sucked the pads on his front feet, voicing his fear with a high-pitched clucking sound. I began to hum and rock him. When he finally fell asleep, I tucked him into the straw.

> **3. What details from this point to the end of the selection make Buffy seem like a child?**

8   The first six months that Buffy lived with us, I rocked him to sleep every night. I spent hours feeding him, playing with him,

---

1. **lumbers:** walks heavily.
2. **proselytizer:** a person seeking to convert others to his or her religion.

3. **bruin:** a bear.
4. **insatiable:** unable to be satisfied.

4. What are some of the words the writer uses to show the passing of time in this and the following two paragraphs?

observing him. At first, every utterance[5] and gesture puzzled me. Because Buffy's muscle structure and coordination resembled that of a human, his play was very humanlike. Emotionally the puzzle was much more complex. One moment he would stand and shake his head playfully at a neighbor's Angus bull. The next moment he cowered[6] behind me at the sight of a small bum lamb.

9   Originally Buffy nursed from a bottle. When I tried to wean him, he refused to switch over to solid foods. Melanie solved the problem by substituting water. Buffy took one suck and angrily threw the bottle across the pen. Then he ran to retrieve it and sucked hopefully. A second time he flung it. By that night he had abandoned his beloved bottle.

10   I often learned things about Buffy the hard way. His long, anteater-like tongue was never fully appreciated until one day during a play session. With a piece of candy in my mouth, I blew gently into Buffy's face to watch his nose twitch. In a blink, Buffy snaked his long tongue to the very back of my throat, licked my tonsils, and stole the candy. While I gagged, my wife howled with amusement.

11   Our friendship with Buffy grew painfully slowly. His distrust made him reclusive.[7] I realized that friendship depended on us somehow joining him in his world. That opportunity came all too soon.

12   On a midsummer's evening, I discovered a wild male black bear tearing at Buffy's pen. He had nearly broken down the gate. I shouted and threw rocks until the bear lumbered off; then I crawled in with little Buffy. The cub's tiny front feet pumped out from under his fuzzy rump as he ran frantically in circles. Fear quivered in every bawl. Finally he slowed and stared at me. Shaking, he clambered[8] onto my lap and hugged me. I found myself crying. What instincts had caused a bruin to almost kill my Buffy?

5. What does the incident described here teach the writer about Buffy and about himself?

13   We cuddled for a long while, Buffy nuzzling and hugging me. When he finally slept, I moved to set him down. He awakened and clung to me. I slept with him that night, cementing our friendship. Overnight we bonded and became family. Overnight I became his guardian, not only his provider.

14   We began treating Buffy as if he were a child. We allowed him in the house. I cradled him in my arms on horse rides. To this day, our horses show no fear of the giant bear. He plays with our dog. The cats rub against his legs. He even accompanies us to town. . . .

15   Although we have become Buffy's parents, my wife and I share different relationships with him. When Melanie visits, she's an oversized toy to Buffy—one which he prefers over . . . his precious feeding dish. On the other hand, my visits are a visit from "Dad." I'm the one who defines the rules and fixes things when they go wrong. . . . I feel very privileged that Buffy has allowed me into his world. I hope never to betray his trust.

---

5. utterance: a sound made by someone; speech.
6. cowered: huddled in fear.

7. reclusive: solitary; shut away from others.
8. clambered: climbed clumsily.

Working with a partner, discuss the following questions and write down your responses.

1. **What is your overall impression of the writer and his subject? What kinds of details create this impression?**

2. **What key details make the bear seem humanlike? List descriptive words the writer uses to relate these key details.**

3. **How does the author reveal what made this experience important to him—directly, by stating what made it important, or indirectly, by sharing his thoughts and feelings about it? Which passages in the narrative include this information?**

4. **Write a brief summary of the model, noting the main incidents in the narrative in the order in which they appear.**

Reference Note

For guidelines and models of **summaries,** see pages 455–456.

Prewriting

Choose and Evaluate an Experience

Memory Lane   A personal narrative is your memory of an important experience. Tap into your personal store of memories by

- looking through old photographs, journals, diaries, or letters
- asking family members or friends for stories about you
- looking at mementos, such as souvenir buttons or play programs
- reading published personal narratives, such as "Bear in the Family" on pages 589–590, looking for connections to your own life

As you review your experiences, be aware of your thoughts and feelings. A strong reaction means that the experience was important to you. One student listed his important memories below.

Mini-Workshop

If you would like to turn an experience you have had or another narrative idea into a **fable,** see the Writing Mini-Workshop on pages 771–772.

my first crush	catching a four-pound bass
working at a snack bar	winning a pepper-eating contest

TIP Be careful not to choose memories that might be too personal to share with your classmates or teacher.

Writing 1.0 Students progress through the stages of the writing process as needed.

Put It to the Test　Now that you have listed some experiences, choose one you might want to explore in writing. Then, use the Thinking It Through steps below to decide whether your favorite choice will work for this assignment.

TIP　Keep in mind that your paper will be 500 to 700 words long, so you should choose an experience that will maintain your readers' interest throughout a paper of that length.

THINKING IT THROUGH　Evaluating an Experience

▶ **STEP 1**　**Summarize what happened.** If you have a hard time **focusing** the experience in a sentence or two, then it is probably too complicated for this paper.

The first time I worked at the snack bar at the citywide garage sale, I thought I would mess everything up, but I did fine and I learned a lot.

▶ **STEP 2**　**Map out what happened.** Make sure you can recall the events clearly and **coherently.** If there are big gaps in your narrative, your readers will have trouble following you.

1. I found out I had to work at the snack bar.

2. I had no experience, so I knew I would make a mess of it.

3. My math teacher helped, and I did a good job.

▶ **STEP 3**　**Explain the significance of your experience.** If you have no clear answer, the experience may not be important enough to choose as a topic.

I learned how important practical math is, and I learned to believe in myself more.

▶ **STEP 4**　**Quiz yourself.** Will you be comfortable sharing your experience with others? What might they learn from you?

I can share this. Reading about my experience might inspire someone else to take on a challenge that looks too difficult.

PRACTICE & APPLY 1　Choose and Evaluate an Experience

Brainstorm a few experiences you might write about and evaluate your favorite experience, using the Thinking It Through steps above. If the experience does not work with all four steps, try another one that matters to you.

Writing　**1.0** Students write focused essays.　**2.0** Students write narrative texts of at least 500 to 700 words.　**2.1b** Reveal the significance of, or the writer's attitude about, the subject.

Think About Purpose and Audience

What's It All About?   In a personal narrative, your main **purpose** is to express yourself. Keep these characteristics of **expressive writing** in mind as you plan your narrative.

- includes vivid details of people, places, events, and things
- includes the writer's thoughts and feelings during the experience
- written in the first person ("I")

The last item above is important to keep in mind. Be sure to maintain a **consistent point of view**—your own—as you write your personal narrative.

Who Wants to Know?   Now that you have identified an experience to share, consider with whom you are comfortable sharing it. If you write about your first crush, will you share that experience in the school newspaper, or would you rather share it with only a close friend? Choose the most appropriate **audience** for your narrative. Keep in mind that your audience could be someone close to you, or it could be readers you have never met. (Remember that your teacher is automatically part of your audience, so be sure you are comfortable sharing this experience with him or her.)

TIP When you write with an expressive purpose, be sure to use your natural voice. Your writing **voice** reveals your attitude about your topic.

> **PRACTICE & APPLY 2** **Think About Purpose and Audience**
>
> Your purpose for writing a personal narrative is to express yourself to others. Use the following steps to identify an appropriate audience.
>
> - First, list several different possible audiences.
> - Then, choose one audience with whom you are comfortable sharing this experience.

Recall and Arrange Details

Make It Real   To involve your readers in your narrative, show them events as you experienced them by providing details. **Details are the heart of an interesting story.** Well-chosen narrative and descriptive details can include the kinds of information listed on the next page.

KEY CONCEPT

Writing 1.0 The writing exhibits students' awareness of audience and purpose. Essays contain supporting evidence. **2.1c** Employ narrative and descriptive strategies (e.g., relevant dialogue, specific action, physical description, and background description).

- smaller events, such as **specific actions** you took, that were part of the experience you are retelling
- what you observed by using your senses (hearing, touch, smell, taste, and sight)—in other words, **sensory details**
- specific information about people involved, including **dialogue,** or what people said, and **physical descriptions**
- **background information,** such as the time and place the experience happened
- your thoughts and feelings during the experience

Walk This Way   Consider how you will arrange the details you recall. Most narratives are written in **chronological order.** That is, events are told in the order in which they happened. Clearly organizing details will make your narrative **coherent,** or logically connected. To plan chronological order, number the events and details in a chart, or make a **time line** like the one below.

Time	Event	Details
8:00	went to set up garage sale	cold, rainy Saturday morning in April, inside a big and empty firehouse, sounds echoed
8:30	was told I had to work the snack bar because a worker was sick	Mom told me to fill in. I argued because I'm bad with money. Mom said, "Nonsense. You can do it."
9:00–12:00	sale started and the snack bar got really busy	Everyone wanted hot food and drinks. I was slow; they were impatient. I was so nervous I spilled a drink. My math teacher showed me how to make change. A girl from my class showed up.
12:00–4:00	I got better at working the snack bar	felt more comfortable; made change quickly; I wished it would stay busy. Mom said she was proud of me.

TIP   Use the *5W-How?* questions (*Who? What? When? Where? Why?* and *How?*) to recall details about an event. Answer questions such as "*Who* was involved?"

PRACTICE & APPLY 3   **Recall and Arrange Details**

Use a time line or chart to list in chronological order as many details as you can recall about your experience. Remember to include:

- specific actions
- sensory details
- dialogue
- physical descriptions
- background information
- your thoughts and feelings

Writing **1.0** Students write coherent essays.   **1.2** Establish coherence within and among paragraphs. **2.0** The writing demonstrates the organizational strategies outlined in Writing Standard 1.0.   **2.1a** Relate a clear, coherent incident, event, or situation by using well-chosen details.

Choosing Relevant Details

On my first day at my new school, I was nervous. The school was at the end of a narrow, winding street. I went to the main office to sign up. It was crazy, with kids running everywhere holding pink permission slips. In comparison, I felt like I was moving in slow motion. "Hurry up, would you?" someone yelled from behind me.

Are all the details in this passage relevant? In other words, do they make the experience clear, or are they simply clutter?

Relevant details create a **controlling impression;** that is, they help readers focus on the main idea: The writer is nervous. The details about the main office, including the line of **dialogue,** show how busy and confusing the school is.

Irrelevant details take readers away from the main idea. The detail about the narrow, winding street does paint a picture, but not the picture the reader should be focusing on—the scene in the office.

THINKING IT THROUGH   **Testing Details for Relevance**

Here is how a writer determined that the details about the school office were relevant to his story.

▶ **STEP 1** Identify the main idea of the narrative. *The main idea is how awkward and nerve-racking the first day of school was.*

▶ **STEP 2** Make sure the details relate to the main idea. *The scene in the office was the first sign that I would be out of step with everybody the whole day.*

▶ **STEP 3** Make sure that the details will help the reader create a mental picture. *The kids running around made me feel like I was in a circus. I want readers to see that.*

PRACTICE

Identify at least five details in the following paragraph. Using the steps above, classify each detail as relevant or irrelevant.

Last Tuesday, my friend Marika's birthday, we went on a field trip to the aquarium. Inside the aquarium it was gloomy. The only light came from the fish tanks, which were like giant, silent TV screens. My grandmother eats fish on Friday. She always says, "Be careful of the bones." Hammerhead sharks soared across the tank in front of us. Our class quietly watched the eerily gliding twenty-foot-long fish.

Writing **1.1** Create compositions that establish a controlling impression. **2.1a** Relate a clear, coherent incident, event, or situation by using well-chosen details. **2.1c** Employ narrative and descriptive strategies (e.g., relevant dialogue).

Writing

A Writer's Framework

Personal Narrative

Introduction
- Attention-grabbing opening
- Details that set the scene

Grab your reader's attention right away with an interesting beginning. Look at professional authors' opening lines for ideas. Also, establish a **first-person point of view,** and keep this point of view consistent throughout your narrative. (For more on writing **introductions,** see page 763.)

Body
- Event 1 of narrative (details about Event 1)
- Event 2 of narrative (details about Event 2)
- Event 3 of narrative (details about Event 3)

  and so on

- Arrange the events of your narrative and their details **in the order in which they occurred.** Start at the beginning and work your way to the end. Create a new paragraph for each major event. Connect the events using **transitional words** such as *first, next, then,* and *finally.*

- Use **details** to **elaborate** on each event in the narrative. Include **sensory details,** details about people who were involved, and **dialogue.** Most important, include just enough details about your feelings at the time to keep your audience in suspense. Save your explanation of the significance of the experience until the very end.

Conclusion
- Significance of the experience for the narrator

Let your readers know the **significance of the experience** for you—how it changed you or what it taught you. (For more on writing **conclusions,** see page 764.)

PRACTICE & APPLY 4 Draft Your Personal Narrative

Now it is your turn to draft a personal narrative. As you write, refer to the framework above and the Writer's Model on the next page.

Writing 1.0 Essays contain formal introductions, supporting evidence, and conclusions. **1.1** Create compositions that end with a clear and well-supported conclusion. **1.2** Establish coherence within and among paragraphs through effective transitions. **2.0** The writing demonstrates the drafting strategies outlined in Writing Standard 1.0.

A Writer's Model

The final draft below closely follows the framework for a personal narrative on the previous page.

A Valuable Lesson

"Two cups of coffee, a bagel with cream cheese, and a hot pretzel." It was a typical order at the snack bar at the citywide garage sale my parents helped run every April. The event was supposed to raise money for the local playground. Every year we made enough money to make some improvement. This was my first year at the snack bar, though, and I was worried that instead of raising money, I would end up owing it.

We got to the firehouse early to set up everything. Usually, people set up tables and sold their "treasures" outside. Because the weather that day was rainy and cold, we moved inside. We set up in the garage where the firetrucks were usually parked. Without them, the room seemed huge, with a sky-high ceiling and a smooth, gray cement floor. Our voices and footsteps echoed off the bare walls and floor and sounded unfamiliar and loud.

I was carrying boxes when my mother told me to fill in at the snack bar because one of the workers had the flu. I protested. I said, "No way. I'll mess it up. You know I'm no good with money, and I'll never remember the orders. Please, Mom, don't make me."

"Nonsense. You can do it. Besides, you won't get much business until lunch," said my mother, "and then I'll help you." I shrugged my shoulders and scraped the sole of my wet sneaker against the cement floor, making a loud squeak. I thought the idea was a bad one, but I went.

My mother was completely wrong. Because the weather was bad, people wanted hot snacks and drinks. I was swamped with orders. At first, I was really slow at taking the orders and making change. The line of people grew, and everybody seemed impatient. I was so nervous that my hands shook, and I spilled orange juice on the floor. What a sticky mess! Then Ms. Muñoz, my math teacher, showed me how to make change by counting up to the total amount I was given. If someone gave me five dollars for something that cost $3.25, I handed over

(continued)

INTRODUCTION
Attention-grabbing opening
Details that set the scene

BODY
Event 1

Details (sensory details)

Event 2

Details (thoughts and feelings)

Details (what others said)

Event 3
Details (smaller events)

(continued)

three quarters and a dollar and said, "Seventy-five cents makes four dollars, plus one dollar makes five." Things went more smoothly after that. In fact, I actually started having fun.

A girl from my class showed up, a girl I had liked since sixth grade. At first I was terrified. What if I made a fool of myself in front of her—giving someone the wrong change or spilling another drink? "Hey, Jimmy," she said when she got to the front of the line, "can I have an orange juice, please?" My hand trembled a little as I poured the orange juice, but then I realized—I can do this! After that, I felt relaxed enough to joke around with her. She flashed me a smile before she left.

By the end of the day, I could pour hot coffee, slice a bagel, add up the bill, and make change quickly with a smile. I was even a little disappointed when the sun came out and dried up business. My mom said that she was proud of me, and when she suggested that I work the snack bar again next year, I did not even shrug. I was too busy imagining the restaurant I would open one day.

Event 4
Details (thoughts and feelings)

Details (what others said)

CONCLUSION
Significance of experience

GO TO: go.hrw.com
KEYWORD: HLLA8 W-1
FOR: A Student Model

TIP If you use dialogue in your narrative, it should reflect the way people really talk. In other words, even though you might normally avoid using contractions (*isn't, it's, we'll*) in your writing, it will sound more natural to use them when you are quoting someone's exact words.

PEANUTS reprinted by permission of United Feature Syndicate, Inc.

Evaluate and Revise Content, Organization, and Style

Checking It Twice   To evaluate a peer's writing or evaluate and revise your own work, you will need to do at least two readings. The first reading will address the content and organization of the writing using the guidelines below. In the second reading you will choose precise words using the Focus on Word Choice on page 601.

▶ **First Reading: Content and Organization**   Use this chart to evaluate and revise your narrative so that it is easy to understand.

Personal Narrative: Content and Organization Guidelines

Evaluation Questions	▶ Tips	▶ Revision Techniques
❶ **Does the introduction grab the reader's attention and set the scene with details?**	▶ **Put stars** next to interesting quotations or surprising statements. **Circle** details that show when and where the experience happened.	▶ **Add** an attention-getting quotation or statement to the introduction. **Add** details about where and when the event took place.
❷ **Is the point of view consistent throughout the narrative?**	▶ **Draw a box** around third-person pronouns such as *they, she,* and *himself.* Check that these pronouns do not refer to the narrator.	▶ If necessary, **revise** to use only first-person pronouns such as *I, we,* and *my* to refer to the narrator.
❸ **Are the events in chronological order?**	▶ **Number** the events as they appear in the paper. Compare the numbered events to the actual order of events.	▶ **Rearrange** the events to put them in the order in which they actually happened, if necessary. **Add** transitions such as *first, next,* and *finally* to link events.
❹ **Does the narrative include details that make the people, places, and events seem real?**	▶ **Highlight** sensory details and dialogue in the paper. In the margin, note to which senses the sensory details appeal.	▶ If necessary, **elaborate** with dialogue or sensory details: sights, sounds, smells, textures, and tastes. **Delete** irrelevant details.
❺ **Does the writer include thoughts and feelings in the narrative?**	▶ **Put a check mark** next to any statement of the writer's feelings or thoughts.	▶ If necessary, **add** specific details about thoughts and feelings.
❻ **In the conclusion, does the writer state why the experience is meaningful?**	▶ **Underline** the writer's statement of why the experience is meaningful.	▶ **Add** a statement that explains why the experience is important, if needed.

Writing 1.6 Revise writing for appropriate organization, consistent point of view, and transitions between passages and ideas.

ONE WRITER'S REVISIONS This revision is an early draft of the narrative on pages 597–598.

> Usually, people set up tables and sold their "treasures" outside. Because the weather that day was rainy and cold, we moved inside. We got to the firehouse early to set up everything. We set up in the garage where the firetrucks were usually parked. ~~The firehouse and the firetrucks reminded me of the days when I was fascinated by firefighting.~~ Without them, the room seemed huge ,*with a sky-high ceiling and a smooth, gray cement floor.* Our voices and footsteps echoed off the bare walls and floor , *and sounded unfamiliar and loud.*

rearrange

delete

add

add

Responding to the Revision Process

1. Why did the writer move a sentence in the paragraph?
2. Why did the writer add phrases to the last two sentences?
3. Why did the writer delete a sentence?

Second Reading: Style In your first reading, you looked at *what* you said and *where* you said it in your narrative. Now, look at *how* you expressed ideas in each sentence. For instance, did you use *precise words*? **Precise words** communicate a specific idea rather than a general one. For example, the precise word *daffodil* creates a specific image, while the vague word *flower* gives only a general idea. Use the following guidelines.

Style Guidelines

Evaluation Question	▶ Tip	▶ Revision Technique
Does the narrative use precise words?	▶ **Draw a wavy line** under precise words that describe specific actions, objects, or ideas.	▶ **Replace** vague or general words with more precise ones if few precise words are used.

Writing 1.6 Revise writing for word choice.

Choosing Precise Words

No two words have exactly the same meaning. Your readers will get a clearer picture of the experience you are describing if you choose your words precisely. Here are two traps to avoid.

- **Trap 1: Choosing vague rather than precise wording.** Readers may picture something very different from what you had in mind if you use vague wording, such as *car*, instead of more precise language, such as *1950s wood-paneled station wagon*.

- **Trap 2: Choosing a precise word that does not fit the situation or feeling of a passage.** For example, *murmur* and *mutter* both refer to a low flow of words or sounds, but *mutter* usually suggests anger. An unhappy customer would probably *mutter* about a bill, but a happy mother would *murmur* (not *mutter*) to her baby.

Word Choice

ONE WRITER'S REVISIONS

> I shrugged my shoulders and scraped the ~~bottom~~ *sole* of my ~~shoe~~ *wet sneaker* against the cement floor, making a loud ~~noise~~ *squeak*.

Responding to the Revision Process

How did the changes the writer made improve this sentence?

PRACTICE & APPLY 5

Evaluate and Revise Your Personal Narrative

Using the guidelines on page 599 and the Focus on Word Choice above,

- evaluate and revise the content and organization of your narrative
- evaluate and revise the style of your narrative
- carefully consider the comments of peer reviewers

COMPUTER TIP

If you are using a computer, format a draft with wide margins and double-spaced lines to allow space for writing comments and corrections during revision.

Writing 1.6 Revise writing for word choice.

Publishing

Proofread Your Personal Narrative

Two Heads Are Better Than One   If you have another person proofread your narrative, you will be more likely to catch mistakes that can distract readers. Have this second reader look for common mistakes, such as spelling, capitalization, and punctuation errors. One common error you might find in personal narratives involves punctuating dialogue.

Grammar Link

Using and Punctuating Dialogue

Punctuating dialogue can be tricky. Here are some rules to help you handle some typical problems with dialogue.

A person's exact words go inside quotation marks, and so do commas and periods. Question marks and exclamation points go inside quotation marks only when what the person said is a question or an exclamation.

"Nonsense!" said my mother.

"What?" I cried.

Can you believe she said "Do it now"?

A sentence in quotation marks is often interrupted to identify who is speaking. The second part of the quotation begins with a lowercase letter.

"You won't get much business until lunch," said my mother, "**a**nd then I'll help you."

When the second part of an interrupted quotation is a complete sentence, it begins with a capital letter.

"Nonsense," said my mother. "**Y**ou can do it."

PRACTICE

On your own paper, revise the following sentences by adding quotation marks and correcting capitalization where necessary.

Example:

1. Let me help you, Ms. Muñoz said. I can teach you an easy way to make change.

1. "Let me help you," Ms. Muñoz said. "I can teach you an easy way to make change."

1. I can do this, I thought.

2. Would you like cream, I asked, or sugar in your coffee?

3. He said, I need a napkin to wipe up this spill.

4. Here is your change, I said. Thank you for coming and enjoy your day.

5. What will I call my future restaurant? I wondered aloud.

Reference Note

For more information and practice on **punctuating dialogue,** see pages 344–348 in the *Holt Handbook.*

Writing 2.0 Student writing demonstrates a command of standard American English.

Publish Your Personal Narrative

Sharing Your Experience   Now is the time to share your personal narrative with the audience you identified in prewriting. Depending on who is in your audience and how comfortable you are with sharing this experience, you may try one of these ways to publish your personal narrative.

- Give a copy to a friend or a trusted adult.

- Share your personal narrative in an oral presentation to your class.

- Turn your personal narrative into a book. Give each event its own page, and add photographs or illustrations.

- Create a "Me" poster to share with your class. Include your personal narrative along with pictures and mementos that show your hobbies, likes and dislikes, and plans for the future.

Reference Note

For information on **presenting an oral narrative,** see pages 604–607.

Reflect on Your Personal Narrative

Building Your Portfolio   Taking time to reflect on your personal narrative will help you improve as a writer. Consider how well you achieved your purpose and reached your audience. Then, answer the following questions about what you wrote and how you wrote it.

- What did you find difficult when writing about yourself? What did you find easy?

- What was the clearest or most exciting detail in your narrative? What makes you think so?

- Which techniques did you use to spur your memory of specific details? (See Recall and Arrange Details, pages 593–594.) How helpful were the techniques? Which would you use again?

PRACTICE & APPLY 6   **Proofread, Publish, and Reflect on Your Narrative**

To wrap up the experience of writing a personal narrative, do the following.

- Correct grammar, usage, and mechanics errors.
- Publish your personal narrative for your target audience.
- Answer the questions from Reflect on Your Personal Narrative above. Record your responses in your portfolio.

Talk **Listen**

WHAT'S AHEAD?

In this workshop you will present an oral narrative. You will also learn how to

- identify differences between oral and written narratives
- select an appropriate story to tell
- create notes and deliver an effective oral presentation

Telling and Listening to a True Story

"**O**nce upon a time" is the way many stories you heard as a child began. When you heard those words, you knew a good story would follow, and you settled down to listen. Now that you are older, you know that a good story does not always begin with those words. Good stories can be true stories about experiences that real people have lived through. In fact, you probably tell such stories all the time—when you tell your friends about the adventure you had over the weekend or about the time you got stuck for hours in a tree you had climbed. In this workshop you will turn a true story, or personal narrative, into an oral presentation.

Choose a Story to Tell

The Story of Your Life Your first step in preparing a presentation of a personal narrative is to choose the story you want to tell. You may tell the story of the experience you wrote about in the Writing Workshop. If you would like, though, you can tell a different true story from your life or even a story from someone else's life. Here are some questions you can ask yourself when choosing a narrative to present.

- **Does the narrative fit my purpose?** First, identify your purpose. What ideas or **message** do you want to express? Tell a story that communicates this idea or message. For instance, if your purpose is to express hope, then your story should have a hopeful message.

Listening and Speaking 1.0 Students deliver focused, coherent presentations that convey ideas clearly and relate to the background and interests of the audience. **1.3** Organize information to achieve particular purposes by matching the message and vocabulary to the audience and purpose.

- **Will the narrative appeal to my audience?** Identify your audience. Will you be telling your story to classmates or to a group of younger students, for example? Once you have identified your listeners, choose a story that they are likely to understand and enjoy. For example, if you are going to tell your story to elementary school students, choose one that *they* might like to hear, such as a story about a person their age.

- **Are the story's grammar and word choice appropriate for the occasion?** For instance, if you are making the presentation as part of a formal occasion such as an awards ceremony, avoid telling a story that depends on using slang and nonstandard English. If, on the other hand, you are telling a story to youngsters, choose a story you can tell using simple **vocabulary** that your audience will understand.

- **Is the narrative the right length?** If you have a time limit for your presentation, can the story be told within that amount of time?

- **Does the narrative have the characteristics of a good story?** Like a written personal narrative, an oral story should include the elements that will make it entertaining to its audience. Choose a story that relates a **coherent incident** about which you can remember plenty of **details** and whose **significance** you can effectively communicate to listeners.

Reference Note

For more on developing the **content of a narrative,** see pages 591–595.

Plan Your Presentation

A Clever Strategy Think about *how* to tell your story so that you will grab your audience. First, organize your ideas in a way that will make sense to listeners. (Most narratives should be told in chronological order to help listeners follow the series of events.) Then, plan to elaborate on those ideas using **narrative and descriptive strategies.** For example, two of the many strategies you may use are *background description* and *comparison or contrast of characters* in your story.

- Use **background description** to give listeners any extra information they might need to understand your story. For example, if you were telling your grandmother a story that features a character from your favorite video game, you would first explain to her the game and character.

- **Comparing or contrasting characters** is useful when you tell a story with characters similar to or different from each other. If you were retelling the story of Cinderella, for example, you could show differences between Cinderella and her stepsisters.

 Listening and Speaking 1.6 Use appropriate grammar and word choice during formal presentations. **2.0** Students deliver presentations employing traditional rhetorical strategies (e.g., narration, description). **2.1a** Relate a clear, coherent incident, event, or situation by using well-chosen details. **2.1b** Reveal the significance of, and the subject's attitude about, the incident, event, or situation.

The following chart lists some additional narrative and descriptive strategies that effective storytellers use. Most of the examples come from the Writer's Model on pages 597–598.

UNDERSTANDING NARRATIVE AND DESCRIPTIVE STRATEGIES

Strategy	Definition	Example
Relevant dialogue	the actual words of the people involved in the events that are important to your story	"I said, 'No way. I'll mess it up. You know I'm no good with money, and I'll never remember the orders. Please, Mom, don't make me.'"
Specific action	events that are a necessary part of the story	"Because the weather that day was rainy and cold, we moved inside."
Physical descriptions	vivid adjectives and precise nouns used to describe people, settings, and things	". . . the room seemed huge, with a sky-high ceiling and a smooth, gray cement floor."
Action verbs	verbs that express either physical or mental activity (as opposed to *be* verbs such as *is, were, am,* and *been*)	"I was so nervous that my hands *shook,* and I *spilled* orange juice on the floor."
Modifiers	a word or group of words that makes the meaning of another word more specific	"*Two* cups of coffee, a bagel with *cream* cheese, and a *hot* pretzel."
Sensory details	words that appeal to one or more of your five senses—sight, hearing, touch, taste, and smell	"I shrugged my shoulders and *scraped* the sole of my *wet* sneaker against the *cement floor,* making a *loud squeak.*"

Act It Out Remember that, in addition to the strategies listed in the chart above, acting out information is an effective way to communicate an idea. For example, instead of telling your audience that a character is angry, you can show them by using **facial expressions,** such as scowling or glaring. You can also raise the **modulation,** or pitch, of your voice to a shrill level and change the **tone** of your voice to sound irritated.

Practice using your body and voice to communicate your message. For example, try telling part of your story several different ways. How does your presentation change if you use a soft voice or a loud voice? a frightened or a child-like voice? a deep or high-pitched voice? Match your voice to the mood you are trying to

Listening and Speaking 1.3 Match voice modulation, expression, and tone to the audience and purpose. **1.5** Use action verbs, sensory details, and appropriate and colorful modifiers in ways that enliven oral presentations. **2.1c** Employ narrative and descriptive strategies (e.g., relevant dialogue, specific action, physical description, background description, comparison or contrast of characters).

create and to the events you are retelling. If your narrative is a happy one, make sure the expression in your voice reflects that happiness.

Much Ado About Noting Have you ever started telling a joke and then realized that you have forgotten the punch line? To avoid finding yourself tongue-tied when you present your personal narrative, jot down some notes. Your notes should be brief and easy to read so that you can glance at them without losing eye contact with your audience. On a note card or piece of paper, jot down key information—an informal **outline** of major events, important details, and delivery notes about gestures or voice modulation. Below is an example of one student's notes on an index card.

—give background

—set scene in firehouse

—Mom's request and me begging: "Please, Mom, don't make me." (whiny voice)

—explain slow start—long line, spilled juice

—Ms. Muñoz helps me

—girl from class

—explain how confident I was at end of day

Rehearse and Deliver Your Presentation

A Twice-told Tale Practice your presentation in front of a mirror. Then, try a rehearsal in front of friends. Listen to their **feedback,** and consider their ideas as you practice and improve your presentation. Here are some ways to make your presentation effective.

■ Speak loudly enough for everyone to hear you. The **volume** of your voice may sound unnaturally loud to you, but the people sitting in the back of the room will appreciate it.

■ Keep an eye on your audience. Notice people's reactions, especially **nonverbal cues.** If they seem bored, it may be because they cannot hear you. If they nod and smile, then you know that you are on the right track.

Listening and Speaking 1.4 Prepare a speech outline based on a chosen pattern of organization. **1.7** Use audience feedback (e.g., nonverbal cues). **2.0** Student speaking demonstrates the organization and delivery strategies outlined in Listening and Speaking Standard 1.0.

Listen to Learn and Evaluate

Just as watching football games can make you a better football player, listening to others tell their stories can make you a better storyteller. Here are some ways to improve your listening skills.

Pick up a Few Pointers Notice what you like about other people's presentations. For instance, you might like the way another speaker uses different voices to suggest different people in dialogue. Use the strategies you like in your own speaking presentations.

It's Elementary It helps to have a list of elements to evaluate as you listen to other presentations. As you listen, jot down answers to the following questions:

- **Clarity and Coherence**—How thoroughly do you understand the events of the story? What does the speaker do to help you follow these events?

- **Narrative and Descriptive Strategies**—How well does the speaker use dialogue, specific action, physical descriptions, action verbs, modifiers, sensory details, and descriptive language?

- **Significance**—What is the significance, or meaning, of the story for the speaker? How does he or she make this meaning clear?

- **Delivery**—Does the speaker maintain eye contact with listeners and respond well to their reactions? How effectively does the speaker use his or her voice, face, and gestures?

Use this list of questions to make notes evaluating your own presentation as you practice and to make notes for a formal evaluation of a classmate's presentation.

> **PRACTICE & APPLY 7** **Tell and Listen to an Oral Personal Narrative**
>
> - Follow the guidelines listed on pages 604–607 to tell a personal narrative to your class or to another group of interested people.
>
> - Then, use the evaluation questions above to take notes as you listen to a classmate's presentation. Discuss the presentation with the speaker, asking questions about his or her content, delivery, and purpose. Write up your evaluation notes and the notes from your discussion in the form of a paragraph evaluating your classmate's presentation.

Listening and Speaking 1.0 They evaluate the content of oral communication.   2.0 Students deliver well-organized formal presentations employing traditional rhetorical strategies (e.g., narration, description).   2.1 Deliver narrative presentations (e.g., biographical, autobiographical).

DIRECTIONS   Read the following draft of a paragraph from a personal narrative. Then, read the questions below and choose the best answer for each question. Write your answers on your own paper.

(1) It was a cool October evening as I stood backstage all dressed up in my black leotard and tights with a gold-sequined belt. (2) My hair was pulled back in a bun, and a strong flowery smell of hair spray wafted around me. (3) My brother had teased me and called my outfit "silly," but I felt beautiful. (4) I was seven years old, and I knew that my first dance performance would be perfect. (5) I had eaten spaghetti, my favorite meal, for dinner. (6) As I pranced proudly onto the stage and into the hot, bright stage lights, I swelled with confidence. (7) Just as I neared my position on stage, my enthusiasm interfered with my footing, and I tripped. (8) On my knees on the stage floor, I could hear my brother's distinctive laugh and feel the heat rushing to my face. (9) I remembered my dance teacher's advice, "If you make a mistake, keep smiling and move on." (10) I held back my tears and jumped up from the floor like a graceful ballerina. (11) I wouldn't let a little fall stop me from enjoying my night in the spotlight.

1. Which of the following strategies would help the writer develop the ideas introduced in this paragraph?
    A   description of the main character's mother
    B   description of the main character's expressions
    C   description of the actions of the other dancers
    D   description of the car ride to the performance

2. Which of the following sentences is least necessary for the paragraph's coherence?
    F   2
    G   3
    H   5
    J   7

3. What should the writer add to this paragraph or to a later passage to make the personal narrative complete?
    A   a reflection on the importance of the event

    B   an explanation of the history of dance recitals
    C   an analysis of dance choreography
    D   a summary of the events leading up to the fall

4. At what point in an oral narrative of this story would the speaker use a shocked expression?
    F   sentence 4
    G   sentence 6
    H   sentence 7
    J   sentence 9

5. If you were delivering an oral narrative of this story, the tone would be a mixture of
    A   embarrassment and sadness
    B   anger and confidence
    C   confusion and sadness
    D   embarrassment and confidence

Response to Literature

Your favorite aunt gave you a gift certificate to a bookstore for your birthday. You know she will question you closely about the book you bought, so you want to buy a good one. How do you know what's good? One way you can find out about books is by reading reviews. Professional reviewers review novels for the sole purpose of telling you whether a novel is worth your time.

In this workshop you will share your own evaluation of a novel in written and oral form. You will also learn how to recite a work of literature and listen to the recitations of others so that you can share not just your responses but the works themselves. By doing so, you will practice these language arts standards.

GO TO: go.hrw.com
KEYWORD: HLLA8 W-2
FOR: Models, Writer's Guides, and Reference Sources

California Standards

Writing

1.0 Students write clear, coherent, and focused essays. The writing exhibits students' awareness of audience and purpose. Essays contain formal introductions, supporting evidence, and conclusions. Students progress through the stages of the writing process as needed.

1.1 Create compositions that have a coherent thesis and end with a clear and well-supported conclusion.

1.2 Establish coherence within and among paragraphs through effective transitions, parallel structures, and similar writing techniques.

1.3 Support theses or conclusions with analogies, paraphrases, quotations, opinions from authorities, comparisons, and similar devices.

1.6 Revise writing for appropriate organization and transitions between paragraphs, passages, and ideas.

2.0 Students write expository essays of at least 500 to 700 words. Student writing demonstrates a command of standard American English and the research, organizational, and drafting strategies outlined in Writing Standard 1.0.

2.2 Write responses to literature:

   a. Exhibit careful reading and insight in their interpretations.

b. Connect the student's own responses to the writer's techniques and to specific textual references.

c. Draw supported inferences about the effects of a literary work on its audience.

d. Support judgments through references to the text, other works, other authors, or to personal knowledge.

Listening and Speaking
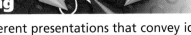

1.0 Students deliver focused, coherent presentations that convey ideas clearly and relate to the background and interests of the audience. They evaluate the content of oral communication.

1.2 Paraphrase a speaker's purpose and point of view and ask relevant questions concerning the speaker's content, delivery, and purpose.

1.3 Organize information to achieve particular purposes by matching the message, vocabulary, voice modulation, expression, and tone to the audience and purpose.

1.4 Prepare a speech outline based upon a chosen pattern of organization, which generally includes an introduction; transitions, previews, and summaries; a logically developed body; and an effective conclusion.

1.6 Use appropriate grammar, word choice, enunciation, and pace during formal presentations.

1.7 Use audience feedback (e.g., nonverbal cues).

2.0 Students deliver well-organized formal presentations employing traditional rhetorical strategies (e.g., exposition). Student speaking demonstrates a command of standard American English and the organizational and delivery strategies outlined in Listening and Speaking Standard 1.0.

2.2 Deliver oral responses to literature:

a. Interpret a reading and provide insight.

b. Connect the students' own responses to the writer's techniques and to specific textual references.

c. Draw supported inferences about the effects of a literary work on its audience.

d. Support judgments through references to the text, other works, other authors, or personal knowledge.

2.5 Recite poems (of four to six stanzas), sections of speeches, or dramatic soliloquies, using voice modulation, tone, and gestures expressively to enhance the meaning.

Writing a Review of a Novel

WHAT'S AHEAD?

In this workshop you will write a review of a novel. You will learn how to

- use criteria to evaluate the elements of a novel
- draw a conclusion in order to make a recommendation
- summarize a novel
- combine sentences using correctly punctuated adjective clauses

You have just finished reading what is now your favorite novel. It has everything—fascinating characters, thrilling adventures, and thought-provoking ideas about life. When you return the novel to the school library, the librarian tells you he is thinking about pulling the book from the shelves because you are the only person who has checked it out in the past four years.

"I'll keep it on the shelves," he says, "if you will write a review and publish it on the library's page of the school intranet. Maybe your review will spark an interest in the book with other students." Without thinking that you don't know how to write a review, you agree to his terms. This workshop will show you how to write a review of a novel.

Professional Model: A Review of a Novel

How do you start planning a review? Begin by reading professional reviews to serve as models. You can find these reviews in many magazines and newspapers, on the Internet, and on the television or radio. On the following page, Kathleen Odean reviews Katherine Paterson's novel, *Lyddie.* As you read the review, use a **think sheet** to make notes about the novel's plot, setting, characters, and theme, and the writer's opinion of the novel. Also, answer in your notes the analysis questions that appear next to the review.

DO THIS ➤

Writing 2.2 Write responses to literature.

from School Library Journal

A Review of
Katherine Paterson's
✿✿✿ ✿✿✿ ✿✿✿ ✿✿✿

Lyddie

by Kathleen Odean

I n this superb novel, Paterson deftly depicts[1] a Lowell, Massachusetts, fabric mill in the 1840s and a factory girl whose life is changed by her experiences there. Readers first meet thirteen-year-old Lyddie Worthen staring down a bear on her family's debt-ridden farm in the Vermont mountains. With her fierce spirit, she stares down a series of metaphorical[2] bears in her year as a servant girl at an inn and then in her months under grueling[3] conditions as a factory worker. Lyddie is far from perfect, "close with her money and her friendships," but she is always trying. She suffers from loneliness, illness, and loss at too early an age, but she survives and grows. An encounter with a runaway slave brings out her generosity and starts her wondering about slavery and inequality. Try as she might to focus on making money to save the farm, Lyddie cannot ignore the issues around her, including the inequality of women. One of her roommates in the company boarding house awakens Lyddie to the wonder of books. This dignity brought by literacy is movingly conveyed[4] as she improves her reading and then helps an Irish fellow worker learn to read. The importance of reading is just one of the threads in this tightly woven story in which each word serves a purpose and each figure of speech, drawn from the farm or the factory, adds to the picture. Paterson has brought a troubling time and place vividly to life, but she has also given readers great hope in the spirited person of Lyddie Worthen.

1. Where and when does this novel take place? How do you know?

2. How would you describe Lyddie's personality?

3. What events trigger changes in Lyddie's life? What greater societal and historical issues are part of the world around her?

4. How does Lyddie improve herself? How does this help her to help others?

---

1. deftly depicts: skillfully represents.
2. metaphorical: symbolic; something different that has a similar characteristic.
3. grueling: extremely difficult; harsh.
4. conveyed: communicated.

In a small group, discuss the following questions. Then, present your group's responses orally to the class.

1. **What does the reviewer think of *Lyddie*? What sentences tell you her opinion?**

2. **What examples does the reviewer use to support her opinion? In other words, what evidence does she give for liking or disliking the book?**

3. **Does Lyddie seem like an interesting character to you? Why or why not?**

4. **Create a summary of the review. Keep the ideas in the same order as they are in the review.**

Reference Note

For guidelines and models of **summaries**, see pages 455–456.

Prewriting

Choose a Novel to Review

TIP Choose a novel that is long enough to require a review of 500–700 words in length.

Pick of the Litter   Choosing a book to review requires careful thought. For this review, you will need to pick a novel, a work of fiction, rather than a factual, or nonfiction, book. Pick a novel you have already read and enjoyed or a new one on a subject that interests you, since you will be spending a lot of time reading and analyzing it.

Read and Record Impressions

First Impressions   Every individual brings his or her unique intelligence and experience to a novel. For this reason, your **interpretation**—your explanation of a novel's meaning—will not be exactly the same as a classmate's. Your insights, however, must be based on careful reading. A careless reading of even a single sentence can lead you to misunderstand an event or a character's motivations, making your overall interpretation of the novel inaccurate.

To make sure that you read carefully, stop reading every so often to write notes about your impressions of the novel. On the next page are some questions to guide your note taking. One student's responses based on the novel *The Outsiders* are given as an example.

Writing **1.0** Students progress through the stages of the writing process as needed.   **2.0** Students write expository essays of at least 500 to 700 words.   **2.2** Write responses to literature.   **2.2a** Exhibit careful reading and insight in their interpretations.

QUESTIONS FOR RECORDING IMPRESSIONS

Questions	Student's impressions
• Who narrates the novel? The main character? An observer?	The narrator is Ponyboy. He's the main character, too. We see everything through him.
• Where does the novel take place? When? Do these factors seem important or unusual?	The novel takes place in a town in Oklahoma in the late 1950s or early 1960s. I don't see anything special about time or place.
• What techniques does the writer use to reveal character? Direct description? Dialogue? Actions?	Sometimes Ponyboy tells us about the characters, but they also reveal themselves through their words and actions. Sometimes we learn about a character from a character other than Ponyboy.
• What conflict causes the events in the novel to happen? Are the events in the story realistic and logically arranged?	The conflict between the Greasers and the Socs leads to everything that happens. The events that make up the story are also realistic. The writer uses a lot of suspense, especially before the big fight.
• What insights into life does the novel give the reader?	Violence doesn't do any good. Also, people aren't as different as they might seem.
• Who is the intended audience for the novel? How will the novel affect that audience?	The novel is meant for young people, teenagers. It should get them emotionally involved because it presents actions and characters teenagers can identify with.

PRACTICE & APPLY 1

Read and Record Your Impressions of a Novel

Carefully read the novel you are reviewing. Record your impressions by jotting down answers to the questions in the list above.

Evaluate Your Novel Based on Criteria

Charting the Elements   When you read a novel just for fun, your personal response is all that really matters. However, when your **purpose** is to write an effective review of a novel, you need to read more thoroughly. You must apply to the novel your knowledge about the general characteristics, or **elements,** of fiction and share that knowledge with an **audience** of readers.

Writing 1.0 The writing exhibits students' awareness of audience and purpose.

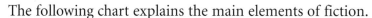
The following chart explains the main elements of fiction.

THE ELEMENTS OF FICTION	
Characters	*Characters* are the individuals in the story. They may be people, animals, or even things. For example, in a folk tale the characters may be animals. In a science fiction fantasy, they may be cyborgs or aliens.
Setting	The *setting* is where and when a story takes place. It may be the streets and sidewalks of Harlem in the 1930s, or it may be the muddy waters of a south Georgia creek in the present day. It may even be an imaginary city in a distant galaxy.
Plot	*Plot* is what happens in the story. It is a series of events that often have a cause-and-effect relationship. A plot is centered around a *conflict,* or problem, that must be resolved (solved or ended) by the end of the story.
Theme	*Theme* is the main idea—the writer's idea or message about the subject of the story. Some stories are meant purely to entertain. In other stories, however, the characters' actions and the way events turn out have some meaning or message for the reader.

The Proof Is in the Pudding (or Product)   When you **evaluate** something, you judge how well it measures up to certain **criteria,** or standards. You can use criteria to evaluate novels in order to determine whether they are worth reading. The following criteria are based on the elements listed in the chart above.

- The **characters** are believable. Even when the characters are animals or fantasy creatures, their actions and motivations should seem natural and real.

- The **setting** is believable. A believable setting adds to the story without distracting readers from the main point.

- The **plot,** or chain of events, seems natural and possible but also includes some surprises.

- The story presents a **theme,** or message, that appeals to the reading audience. A good novel has an **effect** on its readers, giving them an **insight,** or a clearer understanding of some part of life.

TIP   You focused on character analysis in Chapter 2 of Part 1 of this textbook. You may wish to focus on evaluating a character in your review of a novel. If so, be sure to consider the following criteria.
- What do the character's actions and words tell you about him or her?
- What do other characters say about the character you are evaluating?
- Is the author's portrayal of the character realistic?

Drawing a Conclusion

Thumbs Up or Thumbs Down? You know what the conclusion to a story or movie is. It's the ending. However, a *conclusion* can also be a way of thinking. After you evaluate the elements of anything—a car, an article of clothing, a novel—you have to make an overall judgment based on your evaluation. That judgment is called a **conclusion.**

You draw conclusions based on evaluation criteria all the time. You look at a pair of jeans you might buy and ask questions about them. Are they made well? Do they cost too much? Are they the right style for you? After you have finished evaluating a pair of jeans on the basis of your criteria, you draw a conclusion: *I should not buy these jeans because they are not well made,* *and they cost too much.*

You draw conclusions about a novel the same way. You look at the elements and the writer's **techniques,** or methods, of developing them. Next, you decide whether the elements work effectively. Then, you draw a conclusion about whether or not the book is good. Usually, your conclusion will determine whether you recommend the novel to anyone else.

> **TIP** In some cases, you might conclude that a novel has both strong and weak points. You might like the characters and the setting of the book, for example, but think the plot is unbelievable and the theme unclear. In such cases you can recommend the book with reservations or not recommend it at all.

THINKING IT THROUGH **Drawing a Conclusion**

Here are the steps you will use to evaluate a novel. (The questions are based on the criteria for evaluating a novel on page 616; sample responses are based on a student's evaluation of *The Outsiders.*)

▶ **STEP 1** Evaluate the **characters.** Are the characters believable? If so, what techniques does the author use to make them seem natural and real? The characters are very believable. I began to think that I really knew them, especially Ponyboy, his brothers Sodapop and Darrel, and Johnny and Cherry. I felt that way because I know people who are like them. The writer's technique of letting Ponyboy introduce the characters and then letting the characters' words and actions speak for themselves made the characters seem real.

▶ **STEP 2** Evaluate the **setting.** Is the setting believable? Is it important to the plot and the conflict? The setting is very realistic. It could be my hometown, with vacant lots and parks. My town and even my school are divided by social classes the way the town in the novel is. Where the story is set doesn't

(continued)

Writing **2.2b** Connect the student's own responses to the writer's techniques and to specific textual references. **2.2d** Support judgments through references to the text, other works, other authors, or to personal knowledge.

(continued)

seem to play a very important role in the story. The story could have taken place in just about any town in the United States.

▶ **STEP 3** Evaluate the **plot.** Does the plot seem possible? Does it include at least one surprise? What techniques does the writer use to keep you interested as the story develops? The plot definitely seems possible. The whole plot is like a chain of events from the time Johnny and Ponyboy sit down at the drive-in movie with Cherry and Marcia, until Ponyboy starts to write the story. The fire and rescue are a little surprising but not unbelievable. The author uses suspense to build up the fight with the Socs. All in all, the plot is very realistic and exciting.

▶ **STEP 4** Identify the **theme.** What effect or impact do you think the novel will have on its readers? The novel has a couple of important themes, or meanings. First, it shows that violence is totally senseless. Nothing good ever comes of it. Second, it shows that no matter how different people might appear to be, they are much the same on the inside. In the end, the Socs and the Greasers turn out to be a lot more alike than different. I think readers will be very upset by some of the events of the novel, and touched by the novel as a whole. No one who reads it will forget it.

▶ **STEP 5** Draw a **conclusion,** or **judgment,** based on your responses in Steps 1–4. S. E. Hinton's The Outsiders is an unforgettable, touching, and realistic novel about violence and tolerance.

PRACTICE

Movies and television dramas are built from the same basic elements as novels and short stories—character, setting, plot, and theme. Work with a group of classmates to do the following.

- First, make a list of movies or television shows that all of the group members have seen.

- Then, as a group, select one item from the list to review.

- Next, discuss each question in Steps 1–4 above before reaching your conclusion.

- Finally, prepare a short oral presentation explaining whether or not your group would recommend the movie or television show to the rest of your classmates.

- Be prepared to defend your conclusion with details from your evaluation.

Writing 2.2c Draw supported inferences about the effects of a literary work on its audience.

Evaluate a Novel Based on Criteria

Reference Note

For more on **developing details** within paragraphs, see pages 756–757.

To evaluate your novel on the basis of the criteria in the bulleted list on page 616, use the Thinking It Through steps on pages 617–618. Refer to the notes you made earlier or re-read passages of the novel as necessary. When you have finished evaluating the novel, write one sentence stating your conclusion about the novel. Make sure your conclusion is based on all of the evaluation criteria, not just one or two points.

Gather Support for Your Conclusion

Consider the Sources If you list only your evaluations and conclusion, your readers may not accept them. If you say that the plot is surprising, you need to give readers **evidence** that supports that evaluation. Such evidence can come from several sources.

The first source of evidence is the novel itself. Refer to the notes you made earlier and skim the novel, looking for details that will prove your conclusion is sound. The kinds of details that make good evidence are descriptions, actions, and dialogue. The examples in the chart below discuss the character of Ponyboy in *The Outsiders*.

TYPES OF SUPPORTING DETAILS FOR A REVIEW OF A NOVEL

Type of Support	Example
Description: sensory details, often in the form of quotations, about the setting or a character's appearance, or details from a character's thoughts	pages 1–2: "I had a long walk home and no company, but I usually lone it anyway, for no reason except that I like to watch movies undisturbed so I can get into them and live them with the actors." This description shows that Ponyboy is a loner who likes movies and likes to escape his real life.
Actions: details about activities that advance the plot or that demonstrate an important personality trait of a character	page 102: "I was trembling. A pain was growing in my throat and I wanted to cry, but greasers don't cry in front of strangers." This action shows that Ponyboy has feelings, but he hides them behind a tough exterior image.
Dialogue: the words and thoughts of characters (often quoted in reviews)—these also may advance the plot or reveal something important about a character	page 39: "I have quite a rep for being quiet, almost as quiet as Johnny. Two-Bit always said he wondered why Johnny and I were such good buddies. 'You must make such interestin' conversation,' he'd say, cocking one eyebrow, 'you keepin' your mouth shut and Johnny not sayin' anything.' " This dialogue shows that Ponyboy gets along well with Johnny, another quiet boy.

Writing **1.0** Essays contain supporting evidence. **1.3** Support theses or conclusions with quotations. **2.0** The writing demonstrates the research strategies outlined in Writing Standard 1.0. **2.2b** Connect the student's own responses to the writer's techniques and to specific textual references. **2.2d** Support judgments through references to the text.

TIP As you continue your study of the novel, give some thought to the writer's choice of words and the way he or she arranges them into sentences—the writer's **technique,** or style, in other words. For example, when the writer uses dialogue, does his or her style fit the characters who are speaking? Does the style add to or detract from your overall enjoyment of the novel? You may want to include a brief mention of the author's technique in your review.

The text of the novel is not the only source from which you can gather evidence to support your conclusions. You can also use

- **analogies based on your personal knowledge,** such as comparing the character to people you know. (My best friend, Lisa, is a lot like Ponyboy. She's quiet and likes movies, too.)
- **opinions from authorities,** such as another author, a book review, or your librarian. (Our librarian, Mr. Park, said "*The Outsiders* is a very important book. I wish more people would read it.") You can quote or paraphrase these opinions, but if you do, you must give credit to your sources.
- **comparisons to other creative works,** such as books, songs, movies, or television shows. (In some ways, *The Outsiders* is like *Romeo and Juliet.* The characters in both works are torn apart because they belong to different groups.)

PRACTICE & APPLY 3 **Gather Support**

- Skim or re-read your novel, and look at the notes you made earlier. Look for descriptions, actions, or dialogue that support the evaluations you made and the conclusion you reached in Practice and Apply 2. Take notes, and list the page numbers where you find each piece of supporting evidence.
- Consider other sources of support such as analogies based on your personal knowledge, opinions from authorities, and comparisons to other creative works. Include this support in your notes, too.

Write a Summary and State Your Thesis

KEY CONCEPT

The Nutshell Version One important part of any novel review is a *summary* of the book. A **summary** is a brief restatement, in your own words, of the most important ideas of a work. **To summarize a lengthy work like a novel you must compress your insights into the elements of the novel—character, setting, plot, and theme—into a brief interpretation.**

You can use the steps in the following Thinking It Through to help you develop a summary of the novel you are reviewing. In the right-hand column are the notes one student took as she was summarizing *The Outsiders.*

Writing 1.3 Support theses or conclusions with analogies, paraphrases, quotations, opinions from authorities, comparisons, and similar devices. 2.2b Connect the student's own responses to the writer's techniques. 2.2d Support judgments through references to other works, other authors, or to personal knowledge.

Summarizing a Novel

STEP 1 Identify the themes, or messages, of the novel.

Violence and intolerance are senseless. People are not as different as they seem.

STEP 2 Identify the main character or characters, the setting, and the most important parts of the plot.

The main character is Ponyboy, a quiet loner who tries to hide his feelings behind a tough image. The setting is a town in the mid-1960s. The plot is a chain of violent events caused by prejudice that have tragic results.

STEP 3 Write a sentence or two including only the information from Step 1 and Step 2. Avoid adding specific examples or quotes.

Ponyboy, a quiet and sensitive loner with a tough image, deals with violence, prejudice, and tragedy in a mid-1960s town. He finds that people are more alike than different, and that violence and intolerance are senseless.

Making a Statement   To develop a main idea statement—or **thesis**—for your review, add to the conclusion you drew in Practice and Apply 2 a brief explanation of why you came to that conclusion. Mold your conclusion and explanation into a **coherent,** or logically connected, statement that makes your overall opinion of the novel clear. Your thesis statement should appear in the introduction of your review. Here is how one student developed a thesis statement.

Reference Note

For more on developing a **thesis statement,** see page 763.

conclusion: S. E. Hinton's <u>The Outsiders</u> is an unforgettable and realistic novel about violence and tolerance.

reasons for conclusion: The characters are very believable and interesting; the plot is exciting and realistic; the themes are true for people anywhere, any time; the novel stirs up a reader's emotions.

thesis statement: A cast of great characters, an exciting plot, and strong universal themes make S. E. Hinton's <u>The Outsiders</u> an important, touching, and unforgettable novel.

TIP   A good thesis statement helps you produce a **coherent** and **focused** essay and helps your audience understand your purpose.

Writing   **1.0** Students write focused essays. The writing exhibits students' awareness of purpose. Essays contain formal introductions.   **1.1** Create compositions that have a coherent thesis.

Write a Summary and State Your Thesis

- Using the Thinking It Through steps on page 621, write a summary of the novel you read. Your summary should be no more than two sentences long.

- Write a thesis statement based on your conclusion. Include a brief explanation of why you came to that conclusion.

Organize Your Information

Go with the Flow   You can have excellent ideas and plenty of evidence to support them, but if you present them in a muddled manner, your readers may lose interest and stop reading. Make sure that your review has **coherence,** that the ideas are arranged in a way that will make sense to your readers.

Reference Note

For more on **coherence,** see page 760.

To organize your review in an easy-to-follow way, follow these steps:

- First choose the most important elements. Often, these will be the elements about which you have the most notes. A writer reviewing *The Outsiders* might focus on the elements of character, plot, and theme because these elements are the focus of the novel, while other elements such as setting seem less important.

TIP   To get more ideas about organizing your review, read professional reviews, and look back at the review of *Lyddie* on page 613. Take notes on and summarize the review(s) to see how professional reviewers organize their works.

- After you have chosen the two or three most important elements, decide how to arrange those elements in your review. Plan to start with the element your readers will need to understand in order for the rest of your review to make sense. For example, a review of *The Outsiders* might first discuss the characters, because understanding the book's characters will help readers follow its plot and understand its theme.

- Once you choose which element to discuss first in your review, decide on a logical order for the remaining elements. The writer reviewing *The Outsiders* would discuss plot before theme so that she could refer to plot events when explaining the novel's theme.

Reference Note

For more **transitional words and phrases,** see page 760.

Leave a Trail   Once you have organized your ideas, consider how to make your organization obvious for your audience. One way to lead readers is to use **transitional expressions** between and within the paragraphs of your review. Transitional words and phrases show how related details are connected.

Writing   **1.0** Students write clear, coherent essays.   **1.2** Establish coherence within and among paragraphs through effective transitions.

Transitions such as those shown in the following chart will help you guide readers through your body paragraphs, no matter which element of the novel each discusses.

Quick guide!

USING TRANSITIONAL EXPRESSIONS

Type of Order	When to Use	Transitional Expressions		
Chronological Order to Show Time	Discussions or summaries of plot	after before	first later	soon then
Chronological Order to Show Cause and Effect	Discussions or summaries of plot	as a result because	for since	so that therefore
Spatial Order	Physical descriptions of setting, characters, and objects	above across	beneath beside	inside into
Order of Importance	Discussions of the relative importance of characters, themes, or events	furthermore in addition	mainly more important	

Once you choose an order for your review, make an informal outline to guide you in writing your first draft. Here's how one writer outlined the first two body paragraphs of a review of *The Outsiders*.

I. The Characters (first element)
  A. The Greasers
    1. The brothers—Ponyboy, Sodapop, and Darrel
    2. The friends—Johnny, Dally, others
  B. The Socs
    1. The girls—Cherry and Marcia
    2. The boys—Bob and Randy
II. The Plot (second element)
  A. Conflict between Greasers and Socs; Ponyboy meets Cherry
  B. Soc boys attack Ponyboy and Johnny
  C. Conflict becomes much worse; tragic events follow

TIP Another method of achieving coherence is to use **parallel structure** to connect ideas. This means putting related ideas into similar phrases (e.g., infinitive, gerund, or participial phrases). For more on **parallel structure,** see page 459 in the *Holt Handbook.*

PRACTICE & APPLY 5 **Organize Your Information**

Look over your notes from Practice and Apply 4, and decide which elements of fiction are important in your novel. Decide the order in which to present each element. Then, outline your review.

Writing **1.2** Establish coherence within and among paragraphs through effective transitions and parallel structure. **2.0** The writing demonstrates the organizational strategies outlined in Writing Standard 1.0.

Writing

A Writer's Framework

Review of a Novel

Introduction

- Attention-getting opener
- Title, author, summary
- Thesis statement

To grab the interest of readers immediately,

- start with a surprising incident, idea, or quotation from the novel
- relate a theme or event from the novel to a common experience, or
- use a quotation from a review of the novel

(For more on writing **introductions,** see page 763.)

Body

- First element and supporting evidence
- Second element and supporting evidence, and so on

- The first body paragraph should deal with the literary element that readers need to understand in order to understand other parts of the body. The second body paragraph should logically follow the first, and so forth.
- Be sure to use transitional words and phrases to give your paragraphs **coherence.** (For a list of **transitions,** see page 761.)

Conclusion

- Restatement of thesis
- Effect of novel on readers
- Recommendation

Remind your readers of your thesis by restating it in different words. State what effect or impact the novel is likely to have on readers. Make your recommendation clear to readers. (For more on writing **conclusions,** see page 764.)

PRACTICE & APPLY **Write a Book Review**

Now, draft a review of a novel. As you write, refer to the framework above and to the following Writer's Model.

 Writing 1.0 Essays contain formal introductions, supporting evidence and conclusions. **1.1** Create compositions that have a coherent thesis and end with a clear and well-supported conclusion. **1.2** Establish coherence within and among paragraphs through effective transitions. **2.0** The writing demonstrates a command of the drafting strategies outlined in Writing Standard 1.0.

A Writer's Model

The final draft below closely follows the framework for a review of a novel. Transitions used by the writer to connect the ideas in the review have been highlighted.

A Review of S.E. Hinton's The Outsiders

For Ponyboy, life has always been "us against them." Then everything changes. A chance meeting with a girl from across town sets off a chain reaction of events that causes tragic results, and Ponyboy has to reconsider the way things have always been. A cast of great characters, an exciting plot, and strong, universal themes make S.E. Hinton's The Outsiders an important, touching, and unforgettable novel.

Hinton's great cast of characters, tied together by both love and hate, is the strongest element of The Outsiders. Hinton's descriptions, from the mouth of the narrator, Ponyboy, bring them to life. First are the Greasers, who live on the poor side of the town. They are the "outsiders," the focus of the story. Ponyboy, the main character, is a teenager with "quite a rep for being quiet." He likes going to movies by himself so he can "get into them and live them with the actors." Ponyboy lives with his two older brothers, the handsome, happy-go-lucky Sodapop and the hard-working, no-nonsense Darrel. The three brothers are struggling to stay together after their parents are killed in a car wreck. They are surrounded by a close group of friends that includes Johnny, "a little dark puppy . . . kicked too many times," and Dally, a tough older boy with blue eyes "blazing ice, cold with a hatred of the whole world." Next are the Socs, short for "Socials," rich kids from the other side of the town who are in constant conflict with the Greasers. Cherry and Marcia are two Soc girls who seem tolerant and understanding. Bob is the angry leader of the Soc boys. Randy is his gentler friend.

Not only does Hinton create great characters, but she also involves them in an exciting and realistic plot. When Ponyboy and Johnny start a conversation with Cherry and Marcia, the two Soc girls, they innocently start a chain of events that will keep readers turning the pages. After Ponyboy and Johnny

(continued)

INTRODUCTION
Attention-getting opener

Summary
Thesis
Author and title

BODY
First element (characters)

Supporting evidence

Supporting evidence

Supporting evidence

Second element (plot)

Supporting evidence

(continued)

leave Cherry and Marcia, the Soc boys find and confront them for crossing the boundary between groups. The confrontation between the older Soc boys and the youngest and smallest Greasers turns deadly. It is, however, only the first in a series of heartbreaking events—events that seem all the more tragic because of their familiarity. We can picture these events happening in our own communities. Only at the very end of the story—after more loss and grief—is there any sign of hope and understanding between the groups.

Third element (theme)

Finally, The Outsiders offers readers strong themes with which they can almost certainly connect. The world that teaches Ponyboy his "us-against-them" attitude starts to change when Ponyboy makes friends with Cherry, the Soc, and begins to learn that they have much in common. "Maybe the two different worlds we live in weren't so different," Ponyboy says. "We saw the same sunset." Consequently, Ponyboy begins to question what he has always thought about the Socs. He says, "It seemed funny to me that the Socs—if these girls were any example—were just like us." Ponyboy's new understanding of the similarities between the two groups and of the need to end prejudice between them is put to the test by the senseless violence of later events. Finally, though, Ponyboy is saved by the love of his brothers and by the love of his friend, Johnny. The emotional climax of the novel is a scene which is sure to have readers reaching for the tissues. Ponyboy finds the note Johnny left for him. The note tells Ponyboy, "There's still lots of good in the world."

Supporting evidence

Themes

Thesis restated

Effect on audience

CONCLUSION

The Outsiders' strong characters, realistic plot, and worthwhile themes are as relevant today as they were when the novel was first published more than thirty years ago. As readers, we get involved with the characters and are swept along through one tragedy after another until, at last, we see hope for the future. The Outsiders is one novel everyone should read.

Recommendation

GO TO: go.hrw.com
KEYWORD: HLLA8 W-2
FOR: A Student Model

Revising

Evaluate and Revise Content, Organization, and Style

Checking It Twice   As you evaluate and revise the draft of your book review, you should read it at least twice. In the first reading, focus on the content and organization of your draft. In your second reading, focus on sentence style using the guidelines on page 628.

▷ **First Reading: Content and Organization** Use the following chart to evaluate and revise the content and organization of your paper or to review a peer's paper.

Book Review: Content and Organization Guidelines

Evaluation Questions	▶ Tips	▶ Revision Techniques
❶ **Does the introduction grab the attention of readers? Are the title and author of the novel introduced?**	▶ **Star** the sentence or sentences that grab readers' attention. **Bracket** title and author.	▶ **Add** sentences with attention-getting content. **Add** the title and author of the novel.
❷ **Does the thesis draw a conclusion about the novel and explain that conclusion?**	▶ Put a **check mark** at the beginning of the thesis statement.	▶ **Add** a statement that draws a conclusion about the whole novel. **Elaborate** by explaining the conclusion.
❸ **Does each body paragraph discuss only one literary element? Does evidence support statements about each element?**	▶ **Label** each body paragraph with the element of fiction it discusses. Use different colors to **highlight** the evidence for each element.	▶ **Rearrange** ideas so that each body paragraph discusses only one element. **Elaborate** on each element with examples, details, or quotations.
❹ **Is the review organized coherently? Are the ideas connected by transitions?**	▶ **Circle** in each paragraph references to elements discussed in later paragraphs. **Underline** transitions.	▶ **Rearrange** body paragraphs in logical order. **Add** transitional words and phrases where needed.
❺ **Is the thesis restated effectively? Is the recommendation clear?**	▶ Put **parentheses** around the restatement of the thesis. **Draw a wavy line** under the sentence that states or suggests the reviewer's recommendation.	▶ **Revise** the restatement to effectively echo the thesis statement. **Add** a sentence that clearly states the reviewer's recommendation.

Writing 1.6 Revise writing for appropriate organization and transitions between paragraphs, passages, and ideas.

ONE WRITER'S REVISIONS This revision is an early draft of the book review on pages 625–626.

add

For Ponyboy, life has always been ~~the same.~~ A chance *"us against them." Then everything changes.*

meeting with a girl from across town sets off a chain reac-

tion of events that causes tragic results, and Ponyboy has

add

to reconsider the way things have always been. S.E. Hin- *A cast of great characters, an exciting plot, and strong, universal themes make*

ton's <u>The Outsiders</u> ~~is~~ an important, touching, and unfor-

gettable novel.

PEER REVIEW

As you evaluate a peer's book review, ask yourself the following questions.

- Are the writer's recommendation and the reasons for it clear? Why or why not?
- Does the review make me want to read the book? Why or why not?

Responding to the Revision Process

1. Why do you think the writer added to the first sentence of the review's introduction?

2. Why do you think the writer added to the last sentence?

> **Second Reading: Style** In your first reading, you were concerned with the content and organization of your review. Now it is time to look at the sentences you used to present your ideas.

Perhaps you tend to write short, choppy sentences—short simple sentences written one after the other. Readers often find choppy sentences distracting and confusing because they sometimes fail to show the relationships between ideas. One way to improve such sentences is to combine them by using an adjective clause. An adjective clause modifies or describes a noun or pronoun. See the Focus on Sentences on the next page for information on how to use adjective clauses correctly.

Style Guidelines

Evaluation Question	▶ Tip	▶ Revision Technique
Are there two or more short, choppy sentences in a row in the paper?	▶ **Draw a wavy line** under any short sentences. Check to see if there are two or more in a row.	▶ **Revise** one or more of the sentence groups by combining ideas using adjective clauses.

Using Adjective Clauses

A set of two or more very short, similar sentences can be boring enough to distract readers. Look at the following sentences.

> Darrel is Ponyboy's oldest brother. He tries hard to keep the family together.

The sentences above are choppy. Such sentences often disrupt the natural flow of your ideas and sometimes fail to make the connections between ideas clear.

An *adjective clause* can solve the problem. **Adjective clauses** usually follow a noun or a pronoun and tell *which one* or *what kind*. To use an adjective clause, combine the information from one sentence with the ideas in the other sentence and add one of the words in the tip to the right if needed.

> Darrel, **who is Ponyboy's oldest brother,** tries hard to keep the family together.

Rewriting choppy sentences by using adjective clauses will make your writing smoother and more coherent.

TIP Adjective clauses usually start with **relative pronouns** such as *that, which, who, whom,* and *whose.*

ONE WRITER'S REVISIONS

First are the Greasers. ^who ~~They~~ live on the poor side of the town.

Responding to the Revision Process

How did using an adjective clause improve the passage above?

PRACTICE & APPLY 7

Evaluate and Revise Your Book Review

Use the guidelines and tips on page 627 to evaluate and revise the content and organization of your book review. Then, use the Focus on Sentences above to see whether you should use adjective clauses to eliminate choppy sentences from your draft.

Writing 1.2 Establish coherence within and among paragraphs through effective transitions, parallel structures, and similar writing techniques.

Publishing

Proofread Your Review of a Novel

The Final Touch   If you proofread with a partner, you can often catch more mistakes. Others will use your review to decide whether to read the book you reviewed, so edit carefully to make sure your readers are influenced by information, not errors.

Grammar Link

Punctuating Essential and Nonessential Clauses

The adjective clauses you can use to revise choppy sentences come in two types: essential and nonessential. These two types of clauses are punctuated differently.

A **nonessential clause** adds information that is not needed to understand the meaning of a sentence. Use commas to set off a nonessential clause from the rest of the sentence.

Nonessential clause
Darrel, who is Ponyboy's oldest brother, is a hard-working, no-nonsense person.
[The sentence would mean the same thing even without the clause *who is Ponyboy's oldest brother.*]

An **essential clause** tells *which one(s)*, so it cannot be omitted without changing the basic meaning of the sentence. Do not set off an essential clause with commas.

Essential clause
The friend **who is most like Ponyboy** is Johnny.

[The clause explains *which* friend.]

PRACTICE

Use the guidelines to the left to help you identify the essential or nonessential clause in each sentence below. Rewrite the sentences, adding commas where needed.

Example:

1. Ponyboy who is very quiet likes movies and books.

1. *Ponyboy,* **who is very quiet,** *likes movies and books.*

1. *The Outsiders* which is a novel by S. E. Hinton has an important story to tell.

2. The Socs who have nice clothes and flashy cars do not like the Greasers.

3. The Soc whose name is Cherry becomes Ponyboy's friend.

4. The only male Soc who becomes Ponyboy's friend is Randy.

5. Ponyboy who is the smallest Greaser narrates the story.

Reference Note
For more on **essential and nonessential clauses,** see page 321 in the *Holt Handbook.*

Writing 2.0 The writing demonstrates a command of standard American English.

Publish Your Review of a Novel

Spread the News   Your review will not have much effect if the only people who read it are your teacher and your peer editor. Instead, share your evaluation and recommendation with a larger audience. Here's how to let others read your novel evaluation.

- Submit your review to a Web site. Many Internet bookstores allow online visitors to review books that the bookstores sell.

- Collect your class reviews in a notebook, and place it in the school library. Other students may use the notebook as a reference guide to help them decide which books to check out.

- Get together with classmates to develop book review panels of four or five students each. Each panel member should review his or her novel and answer questions from other panel members and from the audience.

Reflect on Your Review of a Novel

Building Your Portfolio   Take some time to reflect on your book review—not just on *what* you wrote, but on *how* you wrote it. Answer the following questions.

- How well did your writing communicate your evaluation of the novel? Do you think your review is convincing?

- What did you learn about using evaluation standards to analyze a book? In what other types of writing might you find evaluation skills useful?

- Did reviewing your novel deepen your understanding and appreciation of it? Explain why or why not.

PRACTICE & APPLY 8 **Proofread, Publish, and Reflect on Your Review**

- First, correct grammar, usage, and mechanics errors.
- Then, publish your review using one of the suggestions from Publish Your Review of a Novel above.
- Finally, answer the questions from Reflect on Your Review of a Novel above. Record your responses, and consider including them in your portfolio.

Talk   Listen

WHAT'S AHEAD?

In this workshop you will give an oral presentation of a response to a work of literature. You will learn how to

- **edit a written response for an oral presentation**
- **make delivery notes**
- **use voice modulation and gestures to emphasize important points**
- **provide feedback on oral responses to literature**

Giving and Listening to a Response to Literature

When you write a response to a work of literature, such as a review of a novel, you do not get immediate feedback. You cannot gauge the audience's understanding and adjust your approach accordingly. When you speak, however, you can use audience feedback to adjust your presentation for maximum impact. You also have more delivery tools available to you. You can use your voice and your face and hands to make your presentation lively and understandable.

In this workshop you will develop a focused and coherent oral presentation of a novel review. Your presentation will be **expository:** you will explain ideas about the novel. You will also listen to and evaluate your classmates' oral reviews and provide feedback.

Adapt Your Written Review

For Starters . . .   As with your written review, your oral response to a novel must accomplish certain goals. An effective oral response to a novel evaluates the novel on the basis of a set of criteria. In the process, the oral review

- presents a well-supported, insightful **interpretation** of the novel

Reference Note

For more on providing **support for a review,** see page 619 in the Writing Workshop.

Listening and Speaking 2.0 Students deliver well-organized formal presentations employing traditional rhetorical strategies (e.g., exposition).   **2.2** Students deliver oral responses to literature. **2.2a** Interpret a reading and provide insight.

- identifies and illustrates the writer's **technique**—how he or she chooses and arranges words in the novel. Your review might show how the writer's technique for description makes characters come alive. You would then quote a passage from the novel for support.

- infers the **effects** of the book on its intended audience and provides support for the inference. Suppose the novel you are reviewing reveals the terrible consequences of an illegal dumping of toxic waste. You might infer that the audience would be upset and support that inference with passages from the novel that show the consequences of the dumping.

Reference Note

For more on inferring a **novel's effect** on its audience, see page 615 in the Writing Workshop.

Making the Cut An effective oral review focuses on fewer main ideas than a written review. Listeners cannot go back over a confusing point as readers can. As you consider what to include in your speech, think about the interests of your **audience.** Would they be most interested in the novel's characters? the plot? the themes? all three?

Making Connections Next, you will need to decide the order in which to present the main ideas from your review. You can adapt—or revise—the outline you produced for your written evaluation. Follow a coherent **pattern of organization,** such as the one illustrated in the chart below.

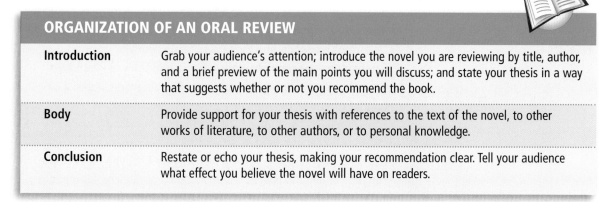

ORGANIZATION OF AN ORAL REVIEW

Introduction	Grab your audience's attention; introduce the novel you are reviewing by title, author, and a brief preview of the main points you will discuss; and state your thesis in a way that suggests whether or not you recommend the book.
Body	Provide support for your thesis with references to the text of the novel, to other works of literature, to other authors, or to personal knowledge.
Conclusion	Restate or echo your thesis, making your recommendation clear. Tell your audience what effect you believe the novel will have on readers.

When you adapt your outline, you may need to delete some items or change the order of the information in the body. For example, in the outline on the next page the writer deleted the sections on characters and themes. She merged her discussion of characters with her discussion of plot. Why? Plot and character are the elements of *The Outsiders* that the writer decided would appeal most to her audience of classmates. The novel's themes are mentioned in the conclusion.

Listening and Speaking 2.2b Connect the students' own responses to the writer's techniques and to specific textual references. **2.2c** Draw supported inferences about the effects of a literary work on its audience. **2.2d** Support judgments through references to the text, other works, other authors, or to personal knowledge.

Since you will be speaking from the final version of your outline, you should add some items that probably were not included in your composition outline. For example, you can write notes to yourself about how to make smooth **transitions** from one point to another. You should also rework your introduction to give the audience a **summary** of the novel and a **preview** of the points you will discuss during your presentation. Previewing your main points will prepare your audience to hear them developed in detail later.

The example below shows one speaker's outline for an oral response to literature. Compare it to the outline for her written review on page 623.

I. Introduction
   A. Attention grabber: Ponyboy, main character and narrator, has an "us-versus-them" attitude.
   B. Preview: The conflict between the Greasers and the Socs. The chance meeting between Ponyboy, a Greaser, and Cherry, a Soc, sets off a chain of events that brings tragedy and, in the end, hope.
   C. Thesis: A great cast of characters, an exciting plot, and strong universal themes make S. E. Hinton's <u>The Outsiders</u> an important and unforgettable reading experience.

II. Body
   A. Hinton's descriptions of the characters bring them to life.
      1. Describe Greasers and Socs and their conflict.
      2. Supporting evidence of good description: Dally is described as a tough older boy with blue eyes "blazing ice, cold with hatred of the whole world."
      3. For transition to B, say, "The conflict turns deadly when . . ."
   B. Plot is both realistic and suspenseful
      1. Describe the meeting between Cherry and Ponyboy and what Ponyboy begins to realize after he talks to Cherry. Connect to episode in my own experience when I discovered someone from another clique was similar to me.
      2. To show how suspenseful the plot is, describe the chain of events set off by the meeting.

III. Conclusion—restate themes, effect on readers, recommendation

Listening and Speaking 1.4 Prepare a speech outline based upon a pattern of organization, which generally includes an introduction; previews, transitions, and summaries; a logically developed body; and an effective conclusion. **2.0** Student speaking demonstrates the organizational strategies outlined in Listening and Speaking Standard 1.0.

Make Delivery Notes

Mark the Spot(s) Once you have decided what to include in your oral presentation, you will need to turn your attention to how you are going to say it. Look over your outline and think about which points will achieve your purpose and have the greatest impact on your audience. Then, decide how and where you can match your **modulation** (the pitch and volume of your voice), **expressions,** and **tone** to match your purpose and audience. Carefully and clearly mark these places on the outline you will use for your oral presentation.

Rehearse and Deliver Your Presentation

Take Aim at the Audience Would your school basketball team play an important game without practicing long and hard beforehand? Would the drama club present a play without first rehearsing? No, and neither should you deliver your oral review of a novel without rehearsing. In fact, you should practice delivering your presentation two or three times. If possible, practice at least once in front of a small group of people—family members or friends—and ask for feedback.

As you rehearse, keep one thing uppermost in your mind—your audience. Ask yourself the following questions, and keep them in mind as you practice.

- Are my **word choices** appropriate to my audience? Are there any technical terms I need to define? Is my vocabulary too simple or too advanced for my listeners? (You do not want to speak to eighth-grade students using a fourth-grade vocabulary, for example.)

- Am I using **standard American English**? (For more information on standard American English, see chapter 17 of the *Holt Handbook.*)

- Am I enunciating clearly so that everyone can understand what I am saying? **Enunciation** refers to the distinctness of the sounds you make when you speak. Good enunciation is clear and precise. Poor enunciation often causes words to be slurred or word endings to be left off.

- Does the **pace** of my delivery sound unhurried, yet not so slow as to lull my listeners to sleep?

> **TIP** As you deliver your oral presentation in class, pay attention to the audience's **nonverbal** responses, or body language. If your audience members seem distracted, pick up the pace or move on to another point. If audience members look puzzled, you may want to go back over a point.

 Listening and Speaking **1.3** Organize information to achieve particular purposes by matching the message, vocabulary, voice modulation, expression, and tone to the audience and purpose. **1.6** Use appropriate grammar, word choice, enunciation, and pace during formal presentations. **1.7** Use audience feedback (e.g., nonverbal cues). **2.0** Student demonstrates a command of standard American English.

Evaluate a Review of a Novel

Reviewing the Reviewer When you evaluate a written review, you can read and re-read passages as necessary. When you evaluate an oral review, however, you have to evaluate the review after listening to it only one time. Moreover, an oral presentation involves more than words on a page—it involves a speaker. Answering the questions in the chart below as you listen to an oral presentation will help you provide valuable feedback.

QUESTIONS FOR EVALUATING AN ORAL REVIEW OF A NOVEL	
Content and Organization	• Is there an effective **introduction**? Summarize the contents of the introduction and explain why it is or is not effective.
	• How is the **body** of the speech developed? Identify one piece of evidence that supports each of the main points of the body. Does the speaker make effective use of transitions between important points? Explain.
	• How does the speaker restate, or echo, the main idea of the review in the **conclusion**? How does the speaker make his or her recommendation clear?
Delivery	• Is the speaker's choice of words appropriate? Explain.
	• Does the speaker use standard American English? If not, provide an example.
	• Does the speaker enunciate words clearly? Explain.
	• Does the speaker maintain a lively but unhurried pace? Elaborate with examples.
	• Do the speaker's gestures and facial expressions add to the meaning of the presentation? Elaborate with examples.
Overall Effect	• What was the speaker's purpose? Did the speaker achieve it? Elaborate.
	• Were you able to visualize characters or events in the novel? Why or why not?
	• Did you agree with the speaker's point of view? That is, did you want to follow the speaker's recommendation to read (or not to read) the novel? Elaborate.

PRACTICE & APPLY 9 ## Present and Evaluate a Response to Literature

■ Follow the steps on pages 632–636 to adapt your written response to a novel for an oral presentation. After your presentation, be prepared to answer questions and receive feedback.

■ Listen carefully to your classmates' oral reviews, and answer the questions in the chart above. Be prepared to provide brief written or oral feedback.

Listening and Speaking 1.0 Students deliver focused, coherent presentations that convey ideas clearly and relate to the background and interests of the audience. Students evaluate the content of oral communication. 1.2 Paraphrase a speaker's purpose and point of view and ask relevant questions concerning the speaker's content, delivery, and purpose.

Reciting and Listening to a Literary Work

When you write and present a review of a novel, you share your interpretation of that novel with an audience. A different way of sharing your interpretation and appreciation of works of literature—poems, plays, speeches, and short stories— is to **recite** them, or expressively read them aloud. Reciting literary works and listening to the recitations of others can deepen your understanding of the works, sharpen your speaking skills, and improve your listening skills. In this workshop you will deliver an oral recitation and analyze the recitations of your classmates.

WHAT'S AHEAD?

In this workshop you will recite a poem, a speech, or a short story. You will also learn how to

■ choose and prepare a selection

■ make delivery notes

■ rehearse a recitation

■ respond appropriately to your classmates' recitations

Choose a Piece to Recite

Half the Battle You should choose a literary work you like and understand. The work you choose should give you the chance to use creative presentation techniques to communicate your interpretation. Oral presentation techniques include the **pace** of your recitation; the **modulations,** or changes, in your voice to emphasize certain words or phrases or to communicate **tone;** and the **facial expressions** and **gestures** you use to enhance the meaning of the work for your audience. You can start getting your piece ready by following these steps.

1. **Study the piece for its meaning.** Learn everything you can about the speaker of the piece—its voice—so that you can find the right tone to take in your reading. For example, should your tone be happy or sad? sincere or sarcastic?

TIP Poems should be four to six stanzas in length. Other literary works, such as sections of speeches or dramatic soliloquies, should be a similar length. Be sure that you can recite the work in the time you are given.

Listening and Speaking 1.3 Organize information to achieve particular purposes by matching voice modulation, expression, and tone to the audience and purpose. **2.5** Recite poems (of four to six stanzas), sections of speeches, or dramatic soliloquies, using voice modulation, tone, and gestures expressively to enhance the meaning.

2. **Decide what impression you want to make on your audience with your recitation.** Then, focus your recitation on the aspect of your piece that will make that impression. For example, if you want your audience to feel compassion for a character in a poem, stress the elements of the poem likely to arouse compassion.

3. **Make a copy of the piece to help you prepare.** You will need to prepare a reading script. On your script, you can write notes to guide you as you memorize and deliver your recitation. A reading script should be typed and at least double-spaced so that you can mark the places where you want to use a certain technique. Clearly mark or write a prompt on the script where you will

   - make **gestures** for emphasis (describe each gesture)
   - **modulate** your voice to emphasize a word or phrase or to change your tone (underline words you want to stress; write a note describing change in tone or other modulations)
   - **pause** briefly or longer (/ for short pause, // for longer pause)
   - increase or decrease the **pace** of your recitation (write notes)

4. **Write down the background material** about your selection and its author that you want your audience to know before they listen to your recitation.

   Here is part of one student's script for a recitation of a poem.

---

from "The Secret Heart" by Robert P. Tristram Coffin

The Poem	Delivery Notes
Across the years / he could recall His father one way / <u>best</u> of all.	Slow, deliberate pace; very slight pauses.
In the stillest hour of night / The boy <u>awakened</u> to a <u>light</u>.	Slow pace; "outloud" whisper for first line; louder voice for second line.
Half in dreams, / he saw his <u>sire</u> With his <u>great</u> <u>hands</u> full of <u>fire</u>.	Dreamy, sleepy voice, both lines. Slow pace.
The <u>man</u> had struck a match to see If his <u>son</u> slept <u>peace</u>fully.	Slow pace. Gentle, caring tone of voice.
He held his palms <u>each</u> side the <u>spark</u> His <u>love</u> had <u>kind</u>led in the dark.	Quiet voice. Continue slow pace.
His two hands were <u>curved</u> <u>apart</u> // In the <u>sem</u>blance of / a <u>heart</u>.	Long first pause. Short second pause. Make heart shape with hands.

Listening and Speaking **1.6** Use appropriate pace during formal presentations. **2.5** Recite poems, sections of speeches, or dramatic soliloquies, using voice modulation, tone, and gestures expressively to enhance the meaning.

Rehearse Your Recitation

Practice for Perfection   To make your recitation as close to perfect as it can be and to give yourself confidence when it is time to perform, you need practice. Use these practice strategies to make your recitation more enjoyable for you and your audience.

- **Get familiar with your selection.** Even if you are not required to memorize your selection, you need to know it so well that you can maintain almost constant **eye contact** with your audience as you deliver your recitation. The better you understand your selection, the easier it will be to memorize it completely or to know it so well that you have to glance at your script only a few times.

- **Make videotapes or audiotapes of your rehearsals, and rehearse before an audience.** Play back the tapes of your rehearsals, and critique yourself. Make notes on the **speaking techniques** in your recitation you need to correct or improve, such as the pronunciation and **enunciation** of certain words, the **modulation** of your voice when you recite an important line or phrase, or the **pace** of your performance. Ask an audience for feedback on your recitation and for specific suggestions to improve it.

Listen to a Recitation

An Appreciative Listener   When you present your recitation, you will no doubt appreciate polite listeners who pay careful attention to you. You will probably appreciate, too, constructive criticism based on thoughtful analysis of your recitation. When you have a chance to listen to your classmates' recitations, be equally attentive and offer useful feedback.

Keep in mind that listening to a recitation of a work of literature is an adventure in appreciative listening. To truly appreciate a recitation, you must **analyze** it, or break it down into its parts to see how it works as a whole. Use the suggestions in the chart on the next page to analyze your classmates' recitations.

When you give feedback to a classmate, remember to be positive. Everyone likes to be praised. If you must point out flaws in the recitation, keep your negative criticisms to a minimum—one or two. Also suggest one or two ways the reciter could improve his or her delivery. Finally, mention one specific thing the reciter did well.

 Listening and Speaking 1.6 Use appropriate enunciation and pace during formal presentations. **2.0** Student speaking demonstrates the delivery strategies outlined in Listening and Speaking Standard 1.0.

Here are the steps you should take to analyze a recitation of a literary work effectively.

ANALYZING A RECITATION

Before you listen

- Think about the background information provided by the speaker. Think about what you know about the selection and its author. What is the selection about? What is the title? Who is the author? What type of literature is it?
- Use what you know to make predictions about what you will hear. Don't worry about whether or not your predictions are correct.

As you listen

- Picture in your mind what you hear as the literature is presented.
- Jot down notes, questions, and ideas you have as you listen.
- Relate what you hear to similar experiences or feelings you have had.

After you listen

- Confirm or adjust your initial predictions. How did your predictions change as you listened?
- Respond to the selection. How did the interpretation of the selection affect you? What did you feel as you listened? What did you like about the selection?
- Identify and analyze literary elements featured in the selection—word choice, imagery, suspense, rhythm. What tone (or tones) did the author's word choices create? What was the theme, or message, of the selection? How did the literary elements contribute to the meaning of the selection?
- Respond to the delivery of the recitation by writing a brief summary of your overall reaction to the presentation. Include within your summary a detailed evaluation of the speaker's effectiveness in using these speaking techniques: pace, enunciation, voice modulation, facial expressions, and gestures.

PRACTICE & APPLY 10 **Deliver and Analyze a Recitation**

- Following the steps on pages 637–639, select a poem of four to six stanzas (or all or part of a famous speech, a speech from a drama, or all or part of a short story), and prepare and deliver your recitation.

- Listen to your classmates deliver their recitations. Analyze the recitations on the basis of the chart above, and be prepared to offer positive feedback to your classmates.

Listening and Speaking 1.0 Students evaluate the content of oral communication. 1.1 Analyze oral interpretations of literature, including word choice and delivery, and the effect of the interpretation on the listener.

DIRECTIONS: Read the following paragraph from a student's response to literature. Then, read the questions below it and choose the best answer for each question. Write your answers on your own paper.

(1) Vivid description makes Ray Bradbury's "The Drummer Boy of Shiloh" one of the best short stories I have read. (2) The story also reminds me of other Civil War stories. (3) Alone and afraid before a battle, fourteen-year-old Joby is awakened by the sound of blossoms falling on his drum. (4) Worried because he only has the drum and no weapons, he begins to cry. (5) Joby considers not joining the battle, thinking "perhaps they might go away, the war with them, and not notice him lying here, no more than a toy himself." (6) The general of the army passes by and convinces him to stay by describing to Joby how he and his drum may be the heart of the army.

1. Which of the following sentences might the writer use in a body paragraph to support her opinion in sentence 1?

  A The story could have been better if only the author had provided more action and used the first-person point of view.

  B Ray Bradbury, who is known for his awesome science fiction, proves by attempting a Civil War story that he is the best short story writer that ever lived.

  C Descriptions, such as "he listened to his own heart ruffle away, away—at last gone from his ears and back in his chest again," gave me a new insight into the Civil War.

  D I have always enjoyed learning about the Civil War, particularly the Battle of Shiloh, so my parents and I are planning a vacation to the battle site.

2. If you were revising this paragraph, which sentence might you delete to improve the consistency of ideas within the paragraph?

  F 2

  G 3

  H 4

  J 6

3. Which of the following transitions could the writer add at the beginning of the sixth sentence?

  A Mainly,

  B Consequently,

  C Later,

  D Therefore,

4. If you were giving an oral review, which sentence in the paragraph above would you deliver in the voice of a character from the story?

  F 2

  G 3

  H 4

  J 5

5. If you were listening to an oral recitation of the short story described in the paragraph above, you would expect the tone to be

  A funny

  B serious

  C happy

  D disrespectful

Technical Documents

Technical documents explain things such as how to operate, assemble, or design something. In this workshop you will develop a technical document explaining the operation of a tool. You will also use software tools to create graphics that illustrate your explanation. By doing so, you will practice the following language arts standards.

WRITING WORKSHOP

Writing Instructions for Operating a Tool

Page 643

MEDIA WORKSHOP

Creating Graphics for Technical Documents

Page 661

GO TO: go.hrw.com
KEYWORD: HLLA8 W-3
FOR: Models, Writer's Guides, and Reference Sources

California Standards

Writing

1.0 Write clear, coherent, and focused essays. The writing exhibits students' awareness of audience and purpose. Essays contain formal introductions, supporting evidence, and conclusions. Students progress through the stages of the writing process as needed.

1.1 Create compositions that have a coherent thesis and end with a clear and well-supported conclusion.

1.2 Establish coherence within and among paragraphs through effective transitions, parallel structures, and similar writing techniques.

1.3 Support theses and conclusions with analogies and comparisons.

1.6 Revise writing for word choice; appropriate organization; and transitions between paragraphs, passages, and ideas.

2.0 Students write expository essays of at least 500 to 700 words. Student writing demonstrates a command of standard American English and the organizational and drafting strategies outlined in Writing Standard 1.0.

2.6 Write technical documents:

   a. Identify the sequence of activities needed to operate a tool.

   b. Include all the factors and variables that need to be considered.

   c. Use formatting techniques (e.g., headings, differing fonts) to aid comprehension.

Listening and Speaking

1.9 Interpret and evaluate the various ways in which image makers (e.g., illustrators) communicate information.

Writing Instructions for Operating a Tool

WHAT'S AHEAD

In this workshop you will write instructions for operating a tool. You will also learn how to

- organize operating instructions
- format a technical document
- use transitional words and phrases
- punctuate introductory words and phrases

A technical document, such as the directions for operating a tool, is a kind of **expository writing** because it explains a process. In this workshop you will have the opportunity to develop a technical document that will fulfill this purpose.

Professional Model: A Technical Document

Instructions and explanations, including those found in technical documents, are written at many levels. For example, a nuclear physicist may read a technical document explaining the design and operation of an experimental reactor. To you and others who are not nuclear physicists, such documents are *highly* technical, written for highly trained specialists.

You, on the other hand, might read instructions such as those on the following pages, originally published in *Boys' Life.* These instructions were designed to teach a young audience how to fix a flat bicycle tire. Although the instructions found in a youth magazine might not be classified as a true technical document, technical writers could learn much from the straightforward, audience-friendly instructions.

As you read the document, create a **think sheet** on which to record notes of your questions, comments, and connections to your own experience. Also, answer the questions that appear next to the article.

DO THIS |

Writing 2.6 Write technical documents.

from Boys' Life

Fix a Flat

by Dennis Coello

Flat tires are part of bicycling. But fixing a flat is easy.

You will need:

- two tire levers (small tools used to pry the tire from the rim)
- a six-inch crescent wrench (if your wheels aren't quick-release)
- a tube repair kit
- an air pump

1. Is this a complete list of materials required to fix a flat according to the directions that follow?

Most flats are in the rear. Removing the rear wheel from the bike is more difficult than removing the front one, but it's easy once you know how.

First, **shift the chain onto the smallest freewheel cog**[1] (see figure 1). Remove the brake cable by pressing both brake pads toward the wheel, giving you enough slack in the cable so you can easily lift the loose end from its housing in the brake lever (not shown).

2. What words are used in this and the following paragraphs to make clear the sequence of activities required to fix a flat?

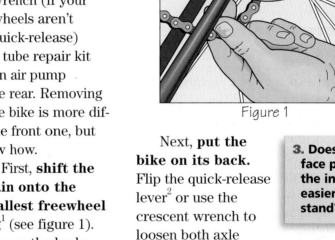

Figure 1

Next, **put the bike on its back.** Flip the quick-release lever[2] or use the crescent wrench to loosen both axle nuts. Take the derailleur body[3] and pull it back toward you. Then, **lift the chain and remove the wheel** (see figure 1).

3. Does the boldface print make the instructions easier to understand? Why?

The front wheel is easy. Remove the brake cable, flip the bike over, and loosen the axle nuts or release lever.

---

1. **freewheel cog:** a ratchet mechanism that lets the rear sprocket or sprockets drive the wheel when the bicycle is pedaled forward but lets the wheel turn freely when the bicycle is coasting.

2. **quick-release lever:** the lever that operates a mechanism that allows for the quick attachment or removal of the bicycle's wheels.

3. **derailleur body:** the mechanism that moves the chain from sprocket to sprocket to change gears on a multispeed bicycle.

Look at a tire lever. One end is slotted to hold a spoke. The other end is bent upward, like a spoon. **Work the spoon-like end of the tire lever under one edge of the tire—** between the tire and the metal rim (see figure 2). Start at a point directly across from the tire valve.[4] Push the lever in about a half inch; then push down on it (toward the spokes). Hook the slotted end onto a spoke.

4. Are the directions for this step given in the correct sequence? How can you tell?

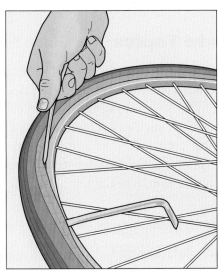

Figure 2

Now use the second lever to pry off more of the tire. Do this on both sides of the first lever. Soon you'll have one side of the tire off the rim.

5. Do the graphics (figures 1–2) make the operation clearer? How?

---

4. tire valve: the device attached to the inner tube of the bicycle tire through which the tire is inflated.

Use your tire levers to pry off the other side; then **remove the tube.**

Find the hole by pumping air into the tube and listening to the *pssss* sound.

Rough up the area around the hole with the sandpaper or metal scraper that comes with your tire repair kit. Do an area slightly larger than your patch. This will help that patch stick better. Cover the area with glue. Wait for it to dry, then **put the patch on the tube.** (That's right. You apply the patch *after* the glue has dried.) Press down the edges with your tire lever.

Look and feel inside the tire for what might have caused the flat. Be sure the "rim tape" (the rubber or cloth strip covering the spoke ends) is in place. Pump a couple of strokes of air into the tube and **put the tube back into the tire.** (The air will keep it from getting twisted.)

Push the valve stem into the valve hole in the rim, and use your fingers to tuck one side of the tire back onto the rim. Use the tire lever when you have about six inches of tire left, and be sure not to pinch the tube.

Now reset the other side of the tire, making sure the valve stem stands straight up when you're through. **Pump up the tire.**

To **replace the wheel,** do the first step in reverse, and reset the brake.

Working with a partner, discuss the following questions and write down your responses.

1. **What was the writer's purpose for writing this article? Do you think he achieved it? Explain.**

2. **What specialized terms did the writer use? How did you figure out the meanings of the terms?**

3. **Did the writer use words or phrases that made clear the sequence of activities required? Should he have used more such words? If so, where and why?**

4. **Write a brief summary of the article, noting steps in the same order in which they appear in the article.**

5. **What would you do to improve the graphics in the article?**

Reference Note
For guidelines and models of **summaries,** see pages 455–456.

Prewriting

Find and Evaluate Topics

Tools of the Trade   Technical documents explain the sequence of activities needed to operate a tool, such as a VCR, or design a system, such as a sound system for an automobile. Even an explanation of the bylaws of an organization, such as a school club, is a technical document. In this workshop your task is to write a clear, coherent, and focused document explaining the step-by-step operation of a tool to accomplish a particular task. Use the list of questions below to help you choose a tool.

Mini-Workshop
See **Writing Bylaws,** page 776.

- Do you use any special tools for a hobby?
- Which common tools (VCR, can opener) do you use?
- Is there one particular tool you feel confident using?

TIP Be sure to pick a topic that will require an explanation of 500–700 words in length.

Judge for Yourself   Once you have considered a few topics, take time to evaluate your choices by answering these questions.
- What is the tool's basic purpose?
- Can the tool be used to accomplish more than one task?
- Does the operation of the tool need explaining?
- Do I know the tool well enough to instruct others in its use?

Writing   **1.0** Students progress through the stages of the writing process. **2.0** Students write expository essays of at least 500 to 700 words.

Here is one student's evaluation of one of the topics on her list.

A possible topic: floor pump with built-in gauge

The basic purpose of the floor pump is to put air into bicycle tires, basketballs, footballs, and other things. Putting air into a bicycle tire requires steps that need to be explained. I have used my floor pump with a built-in gauge to air up the tires on my bicycle so many times that I can tell anyone how to operate it.

PRACTICE & APPLY 1 **Find and Evaluate Topics**

List several topics for a technical document explaining the operation of a tool. Evaluate topics on your list by answering the questions at the bottom of page 646. Choose the topic that you can best explain.

Choose Details and Take Notes

Familiarity Breeds Content Since you chose a tool with which you are familiar, you should not need instruction in its use. Instead, you should concentrate on explaining in detail each step in the operation of the tool based on your own experience. Make notes focusing only on information required for your explanation:

Reference Note

For more on **developing details** within paragraphs, see page 757.

- **essential information,** such as the task the tool was designed to perform and the sequence of activities required to operate it
- **factors** that can affect the result or outcome of the operation, including warnings about things to avoid when operating the tool
- **variables,** or differences in circumstances or equipment, the operator of the tool might face
- **questions** the audience might have about the operation of the tool

PRACTICE & APPLY 2 **Choose Details and Take Notes**

Practice using the tool (or, if necessary, picture yourself using the tool), taking thorough notes on each step in the operation.

Writing **1.0** Students write focused essays. **2.6a** Identify the sequence of activities needed to operate a tool. **2.6b** Include all the factors and variables that need to be considered.

Think About Purpose and Audience

KEY CONCEPT

First Things First   When you have been given the job of writing a technical document, **your purpose is to give readers the benefit of expert knowledge that you have and they need.** Thus, a key factor in developing a successful technical document is identifying and accurately analyzing your audience. Knowing your audience will help you determine what to include in the document besides a full explanation of the steps required to operate the tool. You can see how one writer identified and analyzed her audience by going through the steps in the following Thinking It Through.

TIP   Your audience will appreciate careful **word choice.** Try to eliminate or explain **jargon**—specialized vocabulary used in a particular field. Here are three ways you can help readers understand technical terms.

- Add a definition either right before or right after the term.
- State the idea in simpler words.
- Use graphics, such as photographs, drawings, or diagrams.

THINKING IT THROUGH
Identifying and Analyzing Your Audience

▶ **STEP 1 Decide who would be interested in and benefit from instructions for using the tool.** Most bicycle riders I know are classmates. They often complain about having to push their bikes to a gas station to air up flat tires. They need to know how to use a floor pump.

▶ **STEP 2 Identify questions your audience might have in addition to the basic steps required to operate the tool.** Some of my classmates may not know what a tire valve is or what it looks like. Others might need to know where to look to find the recommended pressure for a bicycle tire.

▶ **STEP 3 Identify factors or variables, including safety concerns, that might cause your audience problems when using the tool.** One factor that causes problems with the pump is not getting the pump head tight on the tire valve. This causes air to escape around the valve instead of going into the tire. One variable that my classmates should be aware of is that narrow tires have higher recommended pressures than wide tires. The only safety factor to mention is the danger of over-inflating a tire.

PRACTICE & APPLY 3
Think About Purpose and Audience

With your purpose and audience in mind, use the steps above to determine what your audience needs to know to operate the tool safely and effectively. Adjust the notes you took for Practice and Apply 2 on page 647 to fit the needs of your audience.

Writing **1.0** The writing exhibits students' awareness of audience and purpose. **1.6** Revise writing for word choice. **2.6b** Include all the factors and variables that need to be considered.

Organize Your Instructions

Stay the Course   To organize your instructions for operating a tool, make notes on the content of the introduction, body, and conclusion. Arrange your ideas in the following way.

1. **Introduction:** Identify the tool, explain the task or tasks the tool was designed to accomplish, and include a **topic sentence:** a sentence that identifies your purpose of explaining the operation of the tool to perform a specific task. Your topic sentence will serve as your **thesis,** focusing readers on the specific aspect of the topic you will discuss. Here is how one student made notes for her introduction.

Reference Note
For more on developing a **thesis statement,** see page 763.

> **Introduction:** Floor pump with built-in gauge, designed to inflate tires, balls, and so on. Use bicycle tire to explain pump's operation.

2. **Body:** To be coherent, **your document must explain clearly the sequence of steps required to operate your chosen tool.** Thoroughly explain each step in the operation of the tool in **chronological order**—the order in which the steps normally occur. In a chart or outline,

   KEY CONCEPT

   - note points at which your audience will need elaboration or further explanation

   - note where **graphics** such as illustrations, diagrams, flowcharts, or graphs might be helpful to readers

   - include variables or other factors that lead to common mistakes or problems, and stress cautions for using the tool safely

   - try to think of **analogies**—comparisons to other activities—that will help your readers picture the step in their minds

Reference Note
For more on **chronological order,** see page 594.

Reference Note
For information on **creating graphics,** see page 778.

   The chart on the following page shows how one student organized the body of her instructions.

3. **Conclusion:** Include a suggestion or tip for using the tool more efficiently or for using it to perform another task. Remind readers why the task you are explaining is important. Finally, restate the tool's usefulness in performing the task or tasks for which it was designed. Here are the student's notes on her conclusion.

> **Conclusion:** Use of floor pump to inflate balls, convenience of built-in gauge, and importance of properly inflated tires and balls

Writing   **1.0** Students write clear, coherent essays. Essays contain formal introductions, supporting evidence, and conclusions.   **1.1** Create compositions that have a coherent thesis and end with a clear and well-supported conclusion.   **1.3** Support theses and conclusions with analogies and comparisons.   **2.6a** Identify the sequence of activities needed to operate a tool.

Here is how one student organized the body of her instructions.

BODY: Sequence of Steps	Elaboration	Cautions, Common Mistakes, and Variables	Graphics
1. Remove dust cap from tire valve.	Two valve types: Schrader and Presta		Show illustration of the two types of valves.
2. If valve is Presta, unscrew the locking barrel.	Only Presta valve has this small nut for adding or releasing air.		Use the same illustration as in Step 1.
3. Press on valve to let air escape.	Use key or thumbnail for Schrader valve.		
4. Place pump head onto valve, and lift lever to lock.	Secure locking important.	Elaborate on not getting tight fit.	
5. Check sidewall for recommended tire pressure.	Pressure is indicated in psi (pounds per square inch).	Narrower tires have higher recommended pressures.	
6. Put both feet on pump footrest, and grasp pump handle. Pull up and push down handle.	Downward motion forces air into tire. Firm footing secures footrest.		
7. Watch gauge, and pump tire to desired pressure.	Pumping will get progressively more difficult.		
8. Unlock pump head lever, and remove it.	Move quickly to avoid letting air escape.		
9. Close locking barrel on Presta valve.	Failure to close will cause loss of air.		
10. Replace dust cap.			

PRACTICE & APPLY 4 **Plan a Technical Document**

Create a chart like the one above to list everything you know about the operation of your chosen tool.

Formatting a Technical Document

A technical document must be formatted in a way that is easy to follow. Notice the formatting in this excerpt.

> **How to Use a Manual Can Opener**
>
> 1. **Position the upper cutting wheel against the lip of the can.** Only the *upper* wheel has a cutting edge.
>
> 2. **Squeeze the handles together until the cutting wheel punctures the can.** You might hear a whooshing sound as the pressurized air is released.
>
> 3. **While holding the handles with one hand, turn the crank with the other.** Crank the opener completely around the top of the can until the lid separates.
>
> *Caution:* The lid and the can have sharp edges, so handle them carefully.

The following suggestions can help you format your technical document.

- Use headings to identify main ideas.
- Use boldface type, different fonts, italics, capital letters, or underlining to call attention to important information.
- Use indented or bulleted lists and numbered steps.
- Insert graphics into your explanation where appropriate.
- To show cautions, use a distinct design, such as *Caution*.
- Use extra white space to set off sections of information and to avoid overwhelming your readers with text.

TIP Be careful not to overformat. Using too many fonts or other unnecessary formatting may only distract readers, not help them learn.

PRACTICE

Using the suggestions above, work with a partner to format the following excerpt from a technical document explaining how to use a pencil.

> Before using the pencil, sharpen it to a point. Caution: A newly sharpened pencil can have a dangerously sharp point. Pick up the pencil, point down, with your thumb and index finger. To hold the pencil for writing, balance it with your middle finger. Press the point to the paper, and move the pencil to make marks. For narrow, distinct lines, use a well-sharpened pencil. For wide, fuzzy-edged lines, use a rounded, worn-down point. To remove unwanted marks from your paper, rub them repeatedly with the eraser end. The eraser is on the end of the pencil opposite the writing point.

 Writing 2.6c Use formatting techniques (e.g., headings, differing fonts) to aid comprehension.

Writing

A Writer's Framework

Instructions for Operating a Tool

Introduction
- Name of tool
- Task (or tasks) of tool
- Clear topic statement

Begin your introduction by naming the tool and describing the task or tasks the tool can perform. Your **topic statement** should identify the tool and task you will explain. (For more information on writing **introductions,** see page 763.)

Body
- First step
- Second step and so on
- Common mistakes and cautions

- Arrange the steps for using the tool in **chronological order** and **elaborate** each step thoroughly.
- Create **coherence** by connecting steps or ideas with **transitions,** such as those on page 657.
- Describe **common mistakes** and include **cautions** for using the tool safely. **Define terms** that readers might not know.
- Include **graphics** to illustrate your instructions.

Conclusion
- Additional suggestions for use
- Restatement of tool's usefulness and task's importance

Keep your conclusion concise. The **additional suggestions** should not require more than three sentences. (For more information on writing **conclusions,** see page 764.)

PRACTICE & APPLY 5

Write Instructions for Operating a Tool

Draft a technical document. As you write, refer to your notes, the framework above, and the Writer's Model on the next page.

1.0 Students write clear, coherent, and focused essays. Essays contain formal introductions, supporting evidence, and conclusions. **1.2** Establish coherence within and among paragraphs through effective transitions. **2.0** Student writing demonstrates a command of organizational and drafting strategies as outlined in Writing Standard 1.0.

The final draft below closely follows the framework for instructions for operating a tool. Transitions used by the writer to connect ideas in the instructions have been highlighted on page 654.

Using a Floor Pump with a Built-in Gauge

The floor pump with a built-in gauge is a handy little tool that was designed to accomplish a single important task—to inflate to the correct pressure bicycle tires, or anything else that can be inflated with a human-powered pump (see Figure 1). The following steps explain the operation of the floor pump with a built-in gauge to inflate a bicycle tire.

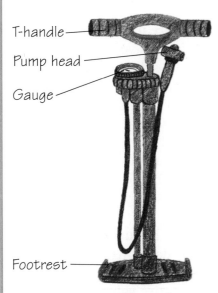

T-handle

Pump head

Gauge

Footrest

Figure 1

1. **Remove the dust cap from your tire valve.** Tires are inflated through valves. There are two types: the Schrader valve and the Presta valve (see Figure 2).

2. **If you have a Presta valve, unscrew the locking barrel (the small nut on the end of the valve) by turning it counterclockwise.** (see Figure 2).

3. **Press on the Presta valve quickly to let a little air escape.** Releasing air will help unstick the valve.

For a Schrader valve, use a key or your thumbnail.

4. **Place the pump head onto the tire valve, and lift the pump head lever to the locked position.** Secure locking is important for efficient pumping. If you hear air releasing around the valve rather than through it as you pump, unlock the lever and try again.

5. **Check the sidewall of your bicycle tire to find the recommended tire pressure.** This number or range of numbers established by the tire manufacturers will be indicated in *psi* (pounds per square inch). Generally, narrower tires call for higher pressures than wider tires.

(continued)

INTRODUCTION

Identification of tool

Task for which tool was designed

Reference to graphic

Topic statement

BODY

Steps with elaboration

Graphic

Common mistake

Term defined

GO TO: go.hrw.com
KEYWORD: HLLA8 W-3
FOR: A Student Model

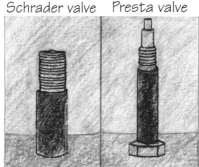

Schrader valve   Presta valve

Figure 2

6. **Now you are ready to inflate the tire. First, place your feet on the pump's footrest and grasp the T-handle of the pump with both hands. Next, pull the handle up as far as it will go to fill the pump with air. Finally, push the handle down to force air into the tire.** Secure footing ensures that the pump will be steady and anchored to the floor on the upward motion.

7. **Watch the gauge, and pump the tire to the desired pressure.** Pumping will get more difficult as you reach the recommended psi printed on your tire's sidewall. *Caution:* Do not pump more air into your tire than is recommended. An over-inflated tire provides a rougher ride, has less traction, and is more prone to blowouts and damage from common road hazards than a properly inflated tire.

8. **Move the pump head lever to the unlocked position, and quickly remove the pump head from the tire valve.** The more quickly you move, the less air you will lose from your tire.

9. **If you have a Presta valve, close it by turning the locking barrel fully clockwise.** If you do not tighten this nut, air will release when pressure is applied to the valve.

10. **Screw the dust cap back onto the tire valve.**

If you want to use your floor pump with a built-in gauge to check and inflate footballs, basketballs, and so on, first insert a needle valve (available at most variety and sporting goods stores) into your ball's valve and follow steps four through seven. Then, quickly pull the needle valve from the ball. Last, remove the pump head from the valve. All inflatables perform better when properly inflated.

The floor pump with a built-in gauge makes the task easy. You can see when you have reached the proper pressure without removing the pump head to check the pressure with a separate gauge.

Eye-catching caution

CONCLUSION
Additional use of tool

Importance of task

Restatement of the tool's usefulness

Evaluate and Revise Content, Organization, and Style

Do a Double Take To evaluate and revise your own writing or a peer's, look over the technical document at least two times. In the first reading, look at content and organization using the guidelines below. In your second reading, concentrate on individual sentences. The Focus on Sentences on page 657 will help you use effective transitions in your writing.

▶ **First Reading: Content and Organization** Use this chart to evaluate and revise your own technical document or a classmate's.

Instructions for Operating a Tool: Content and Organization Guidelines

Evaluation Questions	▶ Tips	▶ Revision Techniques
❶ Does the introduction identify the tool and the task (or tasks) for which it is used and include a topic statement?	▶ **Underline** the name of the tool; **double underline** the task for which it was designed. **Circle** the topic statement.	▶ If needed, **add** a sentence or sentences to identify the tool, its task, and the topic.
❷ Does formatting make the document easy to follow?	▶ **Highlight** all formatting, such as different fonts, boldface type, and numbered steps.	▶ **Delete** unnecessary or confusing formatting. **Add** formatting to improve ease of reading. (See Designing Your Writing on page 658.)
❸ Are the steps in the operation arranged in chronological order?	▶ If numbers are not used in the document, **number** the steps as they appear.	▶ **Rearrange** the steps of the operation so that they are in chronological order.
❹ Do details provide enough elaboration to make each step clear? Are cautions and common mistakes noted?	▶ **Put check marks** next to each detail that elaborates a step, each caution given, and each common mistake noted.	▶ **Elaborate** on unclear steps, and **add** cautions and comments on common mistakes as needed.
❺ Does the conclusion give an additional suggestion for using the tool? Does it restate the tool's usefulness and the task's importance?	▶ **Put brackets** around the final suggestion, the importance of the task, and a restatement of the tool's usefulness.	▶ If necessary, **add** a suggestion, or a restatement of why the task is important and the tool useful.

 Writing 1.6 Revise writing for appropriate organization. **2.6c** Use formatting techniques to aid comprehension.

ONE WRITER'S REVISIONS Here is a revision of an early draft of the technical document on pages 653–654.

rearrange

7. Pump the tire to the desired pressure. Pumping will get more difficult as you reach the recommended psi printed on your tire's sidewall. Watch the gauge., *and*

Caution: Do not pump more air into your tire than is

add

recommended. ∧*An over-inflated tire provides a rougher ride, has less traction, and is more prone to blowouts and damage from common road hazards than a properly inflated tire.*

PEER REVIEW

As you read a peer's essay, ask yourself these questions.

- How easily can I follow the whole process?
- What parts of the process are confusing or unclear? What could the writer do to make the process easier to follow?

Responding to the Revision Process

1. Why do you think the writer moved the third sentence to the beginning of the step?
2. Why did the writer add a sentence to the caution statement?

▷ **Second Reading: Style** Now that you have improved the content and organization of your technical document, it is time to take a look at the style of your technical document. The style of your writing involves the way you express your ideas.

One way to edit the style of your writing is to improve your use of transitional expressions. Transitional words and phrases make the sequence of steps required to operate the tool easy to follow. Use the following guidelines to improve your use of transitions.

Style Guidelines

Evaluation Question	▶ Tip	▶ Revision Technique
Do transitional words and phrases clearly indicate the order within and between the steps of the operation?	▶ **Circle** transitional words and phrases that show the order of the steps.	▶ **Add** transitional words and phrases to clarify the order within and between steps.

Writing 1.6 Revise writing for transitions between paragraphs, passages, and ideas.

Transitional Words and Phrases

You want your audience to be able to follow your instructions. One way to accomplish this goal is to use **transitional words and phrases** to make the order of your document clear. Notice how the boldfaced transitions make the paragraph below easy to understand.

Changing a flat car tire can be quick and easy. **First,** be sure the car is parked on level ground. **Second,** check to see that the car is in park (reverse for manual transmissions) and that the parking, or emergency, brake is set. **Now,** open the car's trunk and remove the spare tire, jack, and lug wrench. . . .

ONE WRITER'S REVISIONS The following revision is from an early draft of the technical document on pages 653–654.

. . . *first* insert a needle valve (available at most variety and

sporting goods stores) into your ball's valve and follow

steps four through seven. *Then,* Quickly pull the needle valve

from the ball. *Last,* Remove the pump head from the valve.

Responding to the Revision Process

Do the transitions added to this explanation make the process clearer? Explain.

Sentences

TIP Some common transitions that show **chronological order** for an operation are *first, next, then, after,* and *last*.

Some common transitions that show **spatial order,** the locations of things in relation to each other, are *above, below, next to, to the right of,* and *inside*.

PRACTICE & APPLY 6

Evaluate and Revise Your Instructions

Evaluate and revise your document using the guidelines on page 655 and the Focus on Sentences above. Also, refer to the following Designing Your Writing feature for formatting suggestions. If peers evaluated your document, think carefully about their comments.

Writing 1.6 Revise writing for transitions between paragraphs, passages, and ideas.

Reference Note

For more on **formatting a technical document,** see page 651.

Formatting a Technical Document To revise the formatting of your technical document, consider how you are using text features such as font styles (including italics, boldface, or all capitals), bulleted lists, and different fonts. Any formatting you use must make your ideas clearer to your readers.

   Font styles should be used sparingly but consistently to emphasize important words or phrases in your technical document.

- If you use *italics* for a technical term you define in the document, all other terms you define should also appear in italics.
- If you use **boldface** for one heading, then all headings must appear in boldface.
- If you use all capitals for the word "caution," then every caution statement should begin with CAUTION.

   Bulleted lists such as the one above should contain only a few items that you want to emphasize. For longer lists (such as all of the steps in using a tool), use a numbered list instead. In either type of list, items must be **parallel**—using the same grammatical forms or structures for all ideas in the list. Look at the two examples below.

Reference Note

For more on **parallelism,** see page 459 in the *Holt Handbook.*

Not parallel	Check the oil and gas in your lawn mower. [imperative]
	You need to adjust the mower blades to the desired height. [not imperative]
Parallel	Check the oil and gas in your lawn mower. [imperative]
	Adjust the mower blades to the desired height. [imperative]

   Different fonts should be used sparingly, if at all. Using a variety of fonts may distract or confuse your readers. Use a different font only if it will make your technical document clearer (for example, to make your caution statements or headings stand out). If you use a font different from the rest of the document for cautions or headings, use it consistently. Look at the examples below of cautions and headings in two fonts that are different from this text's font.

Caution!   *Adjusting the Blades*
Warning!   *Cleaning the Mower*

Writing **1.2** Establish coherence within and among paragraphs through parallel structures. **2.6c** Use formatting techniques (e.g., headings, differing fonts) to aid comprehension.

Proofread Your Instructions

A Fresh Set of Eyes   Errors in your final document will make it harder for your reader to learn how to operate the tool. Try to have another person help you proofread your technical document.

Punctuating Introductory Words and Phrases

When you use chronological order, you will often start sentences with introductory words that show the order in which events occurred or the order of steps in an operation. Here are three rules to help you correctly punctuate introductory words and phrases in your technical document.

1. **Use a comma after introductory words such as *first, second, next,* and *finally.*** A comma lets readers pause where a speaker would.

Example:

First, be sure your VCR's clock is set to the correct time.

2. **Use a comma after an introductory prepositional phrase if the phrase is long or if two or more phrases appear together.**

Example:

On the far right-hand side of your VCR, you will find the eject button.

3. **If the introductory prepositional phrase is short, a comma may or may not be used.** Either is correct as long as the meaning is clear.

Example:

On the tape, you should write the name of the program you recorded.

On the tape you should write the name of the program you recorded.

PRACTICE

Identify the introductory words or phrases in the following sentences. Then, write the sentences on your own paper, adding commas where necessary. Write a *C* next to sentences that are already correct. For each sentence, note which rule you are applying.

1. In every dental-hygiene program brushing your teeth after meals is recommended.

2. In 1938 the first nylon bristle toothbrush was marketed in the United States.

3. First, brush gently to avoid gum damage.

4. In a circular motion on one or two teeth at a time move the toothbrush.

5. Finally rinse your mouth with water.

Reference Note

For more information and practice on **punctuating introductory words and phrases,** see page 326 in the *Holt Handbook.*

Writing 2.0 Student writing demonstrates a command of standard American English.

Publish Your Instructions

Facing the Audience   Now you can share with your audience your technical document for the operation of a tool. Depending upon who that audience is, you might try one of these ideas.

- To your class or to younger students, give a presentation about the safe and effective use of the tool.

- With your class, create a "How It Works" manual with explanations of many different types of tools. Include in the manual polished versions of graphics you and your classmates used to illustrate your instructions. (See the Media Mini-Workshop on page 778.) This manual can be kept in class or in the library for other students to consult.

Reflect on Your Instructions

Building Your Portfolio   Finally, think about what you have learned from writing your technical document. Answer the following questions to build on your writing skills.

- How might you use in other types of writing what you have learned about writing a step-by-step explanation?

- How did you match your explanation to your audience? How well did you achieve your purpose of sharing information with your audience? Do you think your audience fully understood the process of using the tool? Explain.

- How well do you think your instructions measure up to professionally written instructions you have read? Explain.

PRACTICE & APPLY 7   **Proofread, Publish, and Reflect on Your Instructions**

- Correct any errors in grammar, usage, or mechanics.
- Publish your document for your target audience using one of the suggestions above.
- Answer the Reflect on Your Instructions questions above. Include your responses in your portfolio.

Writing 1.0 The writing exhibits students' awareness of audience and purpose.

Creating Graphics for Technical Documents

No matter how clear your technical document is, visuals such as flowcharts and diagrams can make an explanation even clearer to your readers. Providing such graphics helps readers create sharper mental pictures of the information you present.

WHAT'S AHEAD?

In this workshop you will plan and create graphics for a technical document. You will also learn how to
- **evaluate graphics**
- **identify different types of graphics**
- **label graphics**

Evaluating Graphics

An effective graphic in a technical document should be useful, not merely decorative. Here are some things graphics should accomplish.

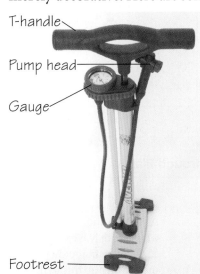

T-handle

Pump head

Gauge

Footrest

Floor Pump with a Built-in Gauge

- **add** to the information in the document or **clarify** something difficult to explain in words
- **focus** on a particularly important or potentially confusing part of an object or a process
- be **simple, clear,** and **uncluttered**

To the left is a graphic the writer of the Writer's Model on page 653 used in a later revision of her document (instead of her orginal drawing).

Listening and Speaking 1.9 Interpret and evaluate the various ways in which visual image makers (e.g., illustrators) communicate information.

Look carefully at the digital photograph on page 661 and evaluate it by answering the following questions.

- In what way, if any, does the graphic add to or clarify written information in the Writer's Model?
- Does the graphic focus on one important or potentially confusing part of the tool or process?
- Is the graphic simple, clear, and uncluttered? Explain.
- Do you prefer the original drawing or the new photograph? Why?

Types and Features of Graphics

Mini-Workshop

See **Creating Charts, Maps, and Graphs,** page 778.

Here are three types of graphics used in technical documents to summarize information, to make complex information clearer, or to emphasize important points.

- **Illustrations,** such as digital photographs and computer drawings, show readers objects or events that are difficult to understand. For example, the computer-generated drawing to the right shows the pattern of a quilt.

- **Diagrams** use symbols, such as arrows, to illustrate how to do something or how something works. The following diagram shows how water moves through a plant.

Water Wheel Variation 2

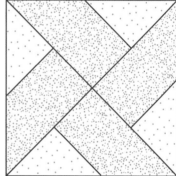

How Water Moves Through Plants

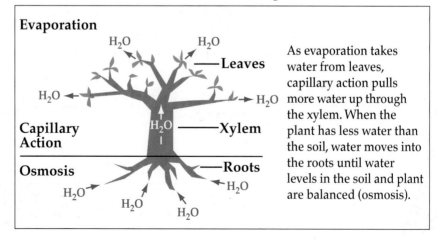

Evaporation

H_2O H_2O

Leaves

H_2O H_2O

Capillary Action

H_2O Xylem

Osmosis   Roots

H_2O H_2O

H_2O H_2O

As evaporation takes water from leaves, capillary action pulls more water up through the xylem. When the plant has less water than the soil, water moves into the roots until water levels in the soil and plant are balanced (osmosis).

- **Charts and graphs** offer a visual way to arrange ideas, showing trends or relationships. **Flowcharts,** such as the one below, show an order of events and can be particularly helpful in summarizing the information in a technical document.

Major Steps in Amending the Constitution

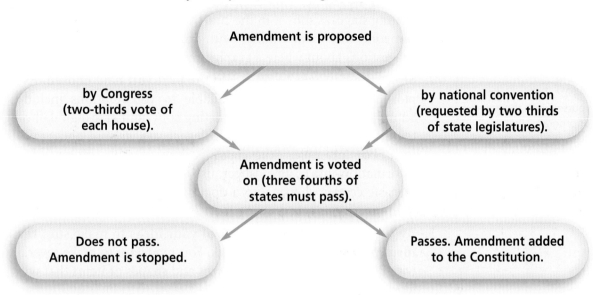

Identification, Please For clarity, graphics need *titles* and often require *captions* and *labels.*

- **Titles** tell in just a few words exactly what the graphic shows.
- **Captions** explain the graphic using sentences placed near it.
- **Labels** briefly identify different parts of the graphic.

Not all graphics will use all of these features. For example, the graphic on page 653 of the Writer's Model uses only an identifying title (*Figure 1*) and labels for the pump's parts. A caption is not needed.

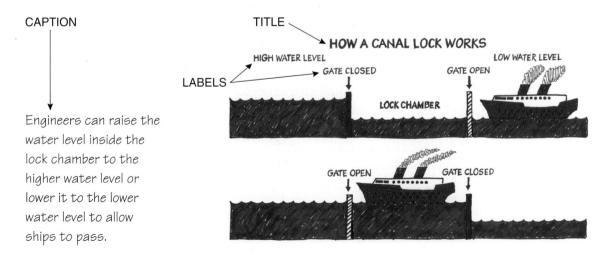

Engineers can raise the water level inside the lock chamber to the higher water level or lower it to the lower water level to allow ships to pass.

Plan and Create Graphics

Use the following steps to create computer-generated graphics for your technical document.

1. **Decide what part of your report could be made clearer with the help of a graphic.** This decision is often made during the prewriting stage, as shown in the chart on page 650. A peer editor—someone who is unfamiliar with your topic—could also offer suggestions about where a graphic might be helpful.

TIP To familiarize yourself with the variety of programs that are available, consult your computer lab instructor or browse the Internet for information.

2. **Select the best way to illustrate the part you have chosen.** Explore the software that is available to you. Options include scanning existing graphics, importing copyright-free digital photographs, or creating original tables, charts, graphs, and drawings. For example, you might create a table by entering information into a spreadsheet, use a word-processing program to paste certain shapes into a document, or use a drawing program to create a line drawing.

3. **By hand, make a rough sketch of your ideas to make sure the form you have chosen will work.** You may have to make several tries before you figure out the sizes and shapes of items that will work best in your graphic.

4. **Use a software tool to create the graphic.** Make your graphics bold and clear, not cluttered with unnecessary information or decorations. Use color only if it will make your message clearer. If you are working with an unfamiliar program, check any available self-tutoring functions or Help menus.

Reference Note

For more on **citing sources,** see page 678.

5. **Add an identifying title, labels, and captions to your graphic where needed.** Also, check the text of your document to be sure you have discussed the graphic. Remember to indicate the source of any information you have borrowed, even if you have created an original graphic using the information.

PRACTICE & APPLY 9 **Create Graphics for a Technical Document**

Use the steps above to create your own graphic for a technical document. Incorporate the graphic into the technical document you wrote for the Writing Workshop.

DIRECTIONS: Read the following passage from a technical document. Then, on your paper answer the questions that follow the passage.

(1) When using a ratchet and a socket to tighten or remove a bolt, you must first determine which socket to use. (2) A basic set of sockets will consist of several sockets measuring from $\frac{1}{4}$-inch to 1-inch in width (the measurement will usually be stamped on the side of the socket). (3) To find the correct socket, use a tape measure to measure the width of the head of the bolt. (4) Find the socket that has the same measurement. (5) Once you have located the correct socket, you will need to attach it to the ratchet, or handle. (6) Place the square opening of the socket on the post that sticks out from the ratchet. (7) On one side of the socket, you will see a square opening. (8) Push hard until the socket snaps in place. (9) Now you can place the socket on the bolt. (10) To tighten a bolt, flip the lever on the back of the ratchet to the right and then turn the ratchet to the right. (11) To loosen a bolt, flip the lever on the ratchet to the left and then turn the ratchet to the left.
Caution: Do not overtighten the bolt.

1. To help readers use a ratchet and a socket, what other factor or variable could the writer add to this passage?

   A You can also use a wrench to tighten or loosen a bolt.

   B Socket and ratchet sets range in size and price from basic and inexpensive to vast and expensive.

   C If you don't have a tape measure, you can place different sockets on the bolt until you find one that fits.

   D A socket and a ratchet set is a helpful tool to know how to use.

2. What information should the writer include in the caution statement?

   F When you are finished using the tools, place them in their container.

   G If you tighten the bolt too much, you may strip the edges from the bolt.

   H A tape measure is a handy tool to have in your tool box.

   J Pliers are another useful tool.

3. How might you format this document to make it easier to understand?

   A by italicizing sentence 7

   B by printing the first word (*when*) in all capital letters

   C by capitalizing all the letters of the word *caution*

   D by using different fonts for each step

4. Which of these transitions best connects the ideas in sentences 3 and 4?

   F Therefore,

   G First,

   H Then,

   J Meanwhile,

5. To put the information in sequential order, which sentence would you move to place right before sentence 6?

   A 3

   B 7

   C 10

   D 11

Research

In this workshop you will research a subject of your choosing and then share the results of your investigation in a written report and oral presentation. In the process you will practice the following language arts standards.

GO TO: go.hrw.com
KEYWORD: HLLA8 W-4
FOR: Models, Writer's Guides, and Reference Sources

 California Standards

Writing

1.0 Students write clear, coherent, and focused essays. The writing exhibits students' awareness of audience and purpose. Essays contain formal introductions, supporting evidence, and conclusions. Students progress through the stages of the writing process.

1.1 Create compositions that have a coherent thesis and end with a clear and well-supported conclusion.

1.2 Establish coherence within and among paragraphs through effective transitions, parallel structures, and similar writing techniques.

1.3 Support theses or conclusions with analogies, paraphrases, quotations, opinions from authorities, comparisons, and similar devices.

1.4 Plan and conduct multiple-step information searches by using computer networks and modems.

1.5 Achieve an effective balance between researched information and original ideas.

1.6 Revise writing for word choice; appropriate organization; and transitions between paragraphs, passages, and ideas.

2.0 Students write expository essays of at least 500 to 700 words. Student writing demonstrates a command of standard American English and the research, organizational, and drafting strategies outlined in Writing Standard 1.0.

2.3 Write research reports:

  a. Define a thesis.

  b. Record important ideas, concepts, and direct quotations from significant information sources and paraphrase and summarize all perspectives on the topic.

  c. Use a variety of primary and secondary sources and distinguish the nature and value of each.

d. Organize and display information on charts, maps, and graphs.

Listening and Speaking

1.0 Students deliver focused, coherent presentations that convey ideas clearly and relate to the background and interests of the audience. They evaluate the content of oral communication.

1.2 Paraphrase a speaker's purpose and point of view and ask relevant questions concerning the speaker's content, delivery, and purpose.

1.3 Organize information to achieve particular purposes by matching the message, vocabulary, voice modulation, expression, and tone to the audience and purpose.

1.4 Prepare a speech outline based upon a chosen pattern of organization, which generally includes an introduction; transitions, previews, and summaries; a logically developed body; and an effective conclusion.

1.5 Use precise language, action verbs, and appropriate and colorful modifiers in ways that enliven oral presentations.

1.6 Use appropriate grammar, word choice, enunciation, and pace during formal presentations.

1.7 Use audience feedback (e.g., verbal and nonverbal cues):

a. Reconsider and modify the organizational structure or plan.

b. Rearrange words and sentences to clarify the meaning.

1.8 Evaluate the credibility of a speaker (e.g., biased material).

2.0 Students deliver well-organized formal presentations employing traditional rhetorical strategies (e.g., exposition). Student speaking demonstrates a command of standard American English and the organizational and delivery strategies outlined in Listening and Speaking Standard 1.0.

2.3 Deliver research presentations:

a. Define a thesis.

b. Record important ideas, concepts, and direct quotations from significant information sources and paraphrase and summarize all relevant perspectives on the topic.

c. Use a variety of primary and secondary sources and distinguish the nature and value of each.

d. Organize and record information on charts, maps, and graphs.

Writing a Research Report

WHAT'S AHEAD?

In this workshop you will write a research report. You will also learn how to

- ask research questions, find sources, and take notes
- paraphrase ideas
- synthesize information and summarize perspectives
- eliminate wordiness
- cite sources correctly

" **I** wonder . . . ." Some of the most interesting discoveries ever made have started with those two words. It is natural to be filled with curiosity about the world around you. As you go through school and on to college or a career, you will frequently encounter subjects that excite your curiosity. When you come across a topic that grabs you, dig in and research! Then, polish your ideas and your findings in a report that documents your discoveries so that you can share them with others.

Professional Model: A Research Report

How can you begin your journey of discovery? You could start by reading a professional model, such as the one on the following pages, for ideas about how you might present your research. The writer, Kathiann Kowalski, explains what two scientists found when they took a closer look at an erupting volcano. What they discovered—the remains of an Inca sacrifice—led them to a rare view into the past.

| DO THIS ➤

As you read, make note of any questions or comments you have. Be on the lookout especially for the questions the scientists had about their discovery and ways in which they found answers to their questions. Also, look for the techniques the writer used to make her findings easy to understand. Answering the analysis questions that appear beside the text will help you create useful notes.

Writing 2.3 Write research reports.

Secrets of the Mummies

by Kathiann M. Kowalski

As a nearby volcano spewed[1] hot ash on Peru's Mount Ampato in September 1995, anthropologist Johan Reinhard and his partner Miguel Zárate made an astounding discovery. They had come to watch the volcano erupt, rather than to search for artifacts, or remains, of the great Inca civilization. But as they peered down a ridge near Ampato's summit 6.3 kilometers above sea level, their plans changed. Curled in a fetal position lay the frozen body of a young girl, surrounded by offerings and the collapsed ceremonial platform where the Incas sacrificed her to their mountain god five hundred years ago. Finding the mummy in a religious context provided a rare opportunity to learn about Inca culture. Reinhard's excitement mounted when he realized that freezing had kept the girl's teeth, hair, skin, organs, and even her body fluids intact. "I knew that it was the first discovery of its kind," recalls Reinhard, "and that it would be like a window into the past."

> **1. What did the scientists think that their discovery would help them learn?**

A Closer Look

Using ice picks, the explorers carefully dug "Juanita" (a catchier name than "the mummy") free from her icy grave and carried her down the summit. Keeping the 36-kilogram body wrapped in foam sleeping pads to prevent melting, they took her by mule to Catholic University in Arequipa, Peru, where she was placed in a freezer for safekeeping. Follow-up expeditions eventually recovered from the mountain two more mummies in 1995 and four more over the next two years. Meanwhile, scientists took a closer look at Juanita.

> **2. Why did the scientists want to keep "Juanita" cold?**

> **3. What might a villager who lived near the site think about these mummies being taken away and studied?**

In May 1996, at Johns Hopkins University in Baltimore, Maryland, Juanita's still-frozen body entered a spiral computerized tomography (CT) scanner.[2] The resulting 3-D images showed her organs and skeleton. Near her right eye was the skull fracture that killed her, a discovery that surprised Reinhard, who believed that she had died by suffocation.

---

1. **spewed:** gushed or threw up.
2. **CT scanner:** a machine that forms a three-dimensional image by combining several X-ray images.

Besides discovering how Juanita died, scientists wanted to know how she had lived. X-rays showed she had the normal bones of a fourteen-year-old. Additional testing showed she had eaten some vegetables several hours before dying. DNA in her cell nuclei had dissolved, indicating that her body did not freeze immediately after she died. But mitochondrial DNA—found outside the nucleus and inherited from the mother—was well-preserved. While scientists at The Institute for Genomic Research in Rockville, Maryland, could not identify Juanita's specific ethnic group, they concluded she was most closely related to the Ngobe people living in modern Panama.

> **4. What information did the scientific tests provide?**

Digging Deeper with Science

Just who were these people who lived so long ago? Mitochondrial DNA analysis won't identify Juanita or any other mummy as your long-lost cousin—only cell nuclei DNA can do that, and hers didn't survive. But it *can* show if mummies were related to each other. And results give scientists information about how groups of people *migrated* (traveled) from one area to another.

Combining medical information with studies of artifacts found near the bodies teaches us a lot about ancient people. "This is all a reconstruction of history where you have no written records," says Marvin Allison, a pathologist[3] at the Medical College of Virginia, who has autopsied[4] South American mummies and studied their ancient cultures since 1969. "You can put together a pretty nice picture on the basis of the individual himself and what you find in the grave."

> **5. What do you think the speaker means by the phrase "nice picture"?**

It's not ghoulish curiosity that spurs scientists to study mummies, but a desire to understand humanity's rich cultural past and to better address health issues in the future. Whether or not Juanita's sacrifice appeased[5] the Inca mountain god five hundred years ago—a practice that makes us shudder today—her mummy and others still present a rich scientific and cultural legacy to us and future generations.

> **6. Why do scientists want to know more about ancient civilizations?**

from Odyssey

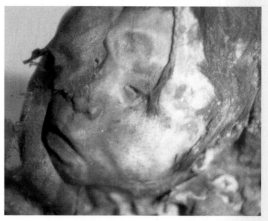

---

3. pathologist: a doctor who studies disease.
4. autopsied: examined to discover the cause of death.
5. appeased: satisfied the demands of.

> **Think About the Model**

In a small group, discuss the following questions. Then, present your group's responses orally to the class.

1. Do you think the author of this report uses original, first-hand information (such as eyewitness accounts); indirect, secondhand information (such as articles written by other people); or both? What makes you think so?

2. Why do you think the author uses the exact words of Johan Reinhard and Marvin Allison in her report?

3. Why do you think the author divides the report into smaller units? How could you tell what information would be found in the smaller units?

4. Write a summary of the report. Keep the order of ideas in your summary the same as it is in the report.

Reference Note

For more guidelines and models of **summaries**, see pages 455–456.

Prewriting

Choose a Subject

Endless Possibilities   What will you research? The possibilities are truly endless. You should pick a subject you will not mind spending quite a bit of time reading, thinking, and writing about. Begin by brainstorming a list of subjects that interest you. If you have trouble making a list, think about topics related to books or stories you have enjoyed. For example, if you loved *Call of the Wild* by Jack London, your list of topics might include dog sledding, the Klondike gold rush of 1897, wolves, and Alaska. You can also read professional models to get ideas for research topics.

Below is one student's list of possible subjects to research. After brainstorming and getting his ideas on paper, he could choose two or three subjects that he wanted to consider in greater depth.

basketball	recording music	Borneo
World War II	martial arts	tropical fish

Writing 1.0 Students progress through the stages of the writing process as needed.   2.3 Write research reports.

Audience As you write a research report, it is important to communicate clearly with your **audience.** For your report, imagine that your readers are about your age and not experts on your topic. You can assume that your readers will know some general information about your topic, but do not make the mistake of thinking that they will know the specifics. Ask yourself these questions.

- What does my audience already know about my topic?
- What does my audience need to know to understand my topic?
- What else will my audience want to know about my topic?

Purpose The main **purpose** of a research report is to share what you have discovered about your topic. You will not just put together a collection of facts, though. **Instead, your research report should be a balanced mixture of information you have found, conclusions you have drawn about your topic, and ideas you have formed about it.**

| KEY CONCEPT

Reference Note
For more on **balancing research and originality,** see page 682.

> **PRACTICE & APPLY ②** **Think About Audience and Purpose**
>
> To help you share with an audience the information you learn, jot down answers to the bulleted questions above.

Develop a Research Question

Funny You Should Ask . . . If the photographer Eadweard Muybridge had never wondered whether a series of movements could be captured on film, we might not be able to watch videos today. One simple question led to an important discovery. **All research begins with a question.** In your own research, a question will give you a purpose for exploring sources. Your research question will guide your research, just as Muybridge's question guided his.

| KEY CONCEPT

I Wonder . . . To develop a broad research question, you might begin with many specific questions. You can start with the *5W-How?* questions (*Who? What? When? Where? Why?* and *How?*). List everything you wonder about your topic, and try to write at least one question for each of the five *W*s and *How.* On the next page are questions the student writing about the 761st Tank Battalion asked.

Writing **1.0** The writing exhibits students' awareness of audience and purpose. **2.0** Student writing demonstrates a command of the research strategies outlined in Writing Standard 1.0.

How did the 761st Tank Battalion form?

Who commanded the 761st?

Where did the soldiers of the 761st train and fight?

How many soldiers fought with the 761st Tank Battalion?

When did they begin fighting battles?

What did the 761st Tank Battalion do during World War II?

What kinds of discrimination did these soldiers face?

The Big Question   Choose one "big picture" question to guide your research. This guiding question will keep you focused and on track. In looking over his list of questions, the student writing about the 761st Tank Battalion realized that researching the question, "What did the 761st Tank Battalion do during World War II?" would probably lead him to answers for most of the other questions on his list. He chose that as his research question.

TIP   You might find that you can turn your "Big Question" into a **thesis statement.** Through his research, the student writing about the 761st Tank Battalion found a broad answer to his research question: "The 761st Tank Battalion proved that African Americans could serve their country with excellence and bravery." That answer might serve as his thesis statement. (For more on developing a **thesis statement,** see page 684.)

PRACTICE & APPLY 3   **Develop a Research Question**

To develop a question to guide your research, first brainstorm several questions using the *5W-How?* technique. It may help to begin by reading general information about your topic. Then, look for a "big picture" question that will lead to answers for many of your other questions. If your list does not contain such a broad question, write one.

Find and Evaluate Sources

Get to the Source   Two types of sources you can use are *primary sources* and *secondary sources.* **Primary sources** are documents and records that contain firsthand knowledge, such as maps, diaries, and letters. **Secondary sources** are interpretations of primary materials produced by others. They include encyclopedia entries, newspaper articles, and documentaries. Secondary sources are good starting places for research since they contain summaries of other sources, but whenever possible you should use primary sources. The first source of information is often the best.

TIP   Another source you may consult is an expert on your topic. You might arrange an interview with that person or plan to listen to a presentation he or she is giving.

Writing 2.3a Define a thesis.   2.3c Use a variety of primary and secondary sources and distinguish the nature and value of each.

Searching the World Wide Web   The World Wide Web is part of the Internet, a huge computer network that you can access using a computer and a modem or other network connection tool. The World Wide Web can be a wonderful research tool, but only if you find trustworthy sources of information. Use a program called a **search engine** to find the sites you need. First, enter a **keyword,** or an important word or phrase, that identifies your topic.

Basic keyword searches often find a large number of sites. Some sites will fit your purpose, but many others will not. To get sources that are **relevant,** or related, to your topic, you can limit your search by using **search operators,** such as *AND, NOT,* and quotation marks. Search operators vary from one search engine to another, but the following chart describes some common operators. It shows how moving from a keyword-only search to a search using one or more search operators can give you fewer, more specific results. If the search engine you choose uses different search operators, check its Web site for more information.

COMPUTER TIP

If you do not find the information you need with the first keyword you try, brainstorm other keywords. For example, if you do not find useful sites for a report about making movies using the keyword *moviemaking,* you might try *filmmaking* or *movie production.*

SEARCH OPERATOR	RESULTS
military segregation (keywords only; no operators)	Some search engines will give you sites that mention one or both of the words in the search term. You may wind up with everything from sites on age segregation in schools to the U.S. Army home page.
military AND segregation	This term will find only sites that include both the words military and segregation. These sites may provide useful information, but the listing will still have off-topic sites, such as an article on military academies admitting female students.
"military segregation"	This term will find only sites that use these two words together in this order. This search will mainly find information on the segregation of women and minorities in the military.
"military segregation" NOT women	This search will find the same sites as the search above, but will leave out those concerning women. This will provide a short list of sites about racial segregation in the military.

Writing 1.4 Plan and conduct multiple-step information searches by using computer networks and modems.

A Closer Look Because some sources may contain out-of-date information or mistakes, you should evaluate each of your sources. For example, even after limiting a World Wide Web search, do not automatically accept all of the information you find. The Internet is a wonderful research tool, but no one checks the accuracy of every site that is posted. To get reliable information, stick to sites created by authoritative sources. Sites with addresses ending in *.org* (nonprofit organizations), *.edu* (educational institutions), and *.gov* (U.S. government agencies) are good places to start.

You can evaluate any source, print or nonprint, by answering the questions in the following Thinking It Through.

THINKING IT THROUGH

Evaluating Sources

STEP 1 Is the source nonfiction? Do not use stories or novels as sources for a factual report.

Yes. The book <u>Black Fighting Men</u> is a nonfiction book. It has facts about African American soldiers.

STEP 2 Is the information current? Topics in rapidly changing fields require up-to-date sources. For historical topics, finding the latest information is not essential.

The book was published in 1994. Since my topic, the 761st Tank Battalion, concerns the 1940s, this information is current enough.

STEP 3 Is the information trustworthy? Whether the source is a primary source or a secondary source, you should be able to verify all of the facts with other sources.

Yes, my source is trustworthy. Another book about the 761st confirms some of the information in the book. The information should be reliable.

Making a List Before you dive into your research, you should list any sources you might use. Formal research reports require a detailed list of sources used called a Works Cited list. You will need to list these sources in alphabetical order, using Modern Language Association, or MLA, style. The chart on the next page gives examples of types of sources you will most likely use, shown in MLA style.

Listing information about your sources now will save you the trouble of going back and finding it later.

MLA GUIDE FOR LISTING SOURCES

Encyclopedia article	Author (if listed). "Title of Article." <u>Name of Encyclopedia</u>. Year or edition.
	Hornsby, Alton, Jr. "African Americans." <u>World Book Encyclopedia</u>. 2000.
Book	Author/Editor. <u>Title</u>. City: Publisher, year.
	Reef, Catherine. <u>Black Fighting Men: A Proud History</u>. New York: Twenty-First Century Books, 1994.
Magazine or newspaper article	Author. "Title of Article." <u>Publication Name</u> Date: page number(s).
	Ringle, Ken. "For Black Soldiers, an Overdue Honor; Seven Cited for Valor in World War II." <u>The Washington Post</u> 14 Jan. 1997: A1.
Interview or guest speaker	Speaker. Personal interview/Telephone interview/Guest speaker. Date.
	McConnell, E. G. Guest speaker. 15 Aug. 2003.
Television or radio program	"Title of Episode." <u>Title of Program</u>. Network. Station Call Letters, City. Date of broadcast.
	"Belated Honor." <u>In Depth</u>. PBS. KUSD, Vermillion. Nov. 2003.
Movie or video recording	<u>Title</u>. Name of Director (Dir.) or Producer (Pro.). Name of Distributor, year released.
	<u>African Americans in WWII: A Legacy of Patriotism and Valor</u>. Pro. Department of Defense. OnDeck Home Entertainment, 1998.
Electronic sources	**Online**
	Author (if known). "Document Title." <u>Web Site or Database Title</u>. Date of electronic publication. Name of Sponsoring Institution. Date information was accessed <URL>.
	Kelly, S. H. "Tanker 'Lets No One Down' in Bloody Fight." <u>ArmyLINK News</u>. January 1997. U. S. Army Public Affairs. 28 Nov. 2003 <http://www.dtic.mil/armylink/news/Jan1997/a19970113761st.html>.
	CD–ROM
	Author's name (if known). "Title of Article." <u>Title of Database</u>. Medium (CD–ROM). City of Electronic Publication: Electronic Publisher, electronic publication date.
	"World War II German Surrender Documents." <u>Multimedia World History</u>. CD–ROM. Parsippany: Bureau of Electronic Publishing, 1994.

You can list information about sources you might use on source cards like those that follow. Number each card, and record the information for each possible source you find.

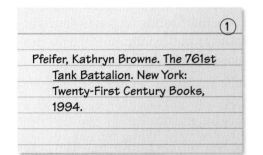

(1)

Pfeifer, Kathryn Browne. The 761st Tank Battalion. New York: Twenty-First Century Books, 1994.

(2)   ——— source number

Kelly, S. H. "Tanker 'Lets No One Down' in Bloody Fight." ArmyLINK News. January 1997. U. S. Army Public Affairs. 28 Nov. 2003 <http://www.dtic.mil/armylink/news/Jan1997/a19970113761st.html>.

PRACTICE & APPLY 4 **Find and Evaluate Sources**

Find a variety of reliable and up-to-date sources. Choose at least three different sources to use for your report, and create a source card for each using the chart on the previous page as a guide.

COMPUTER TIP

If you make your source list on a computer, italicize all items shown underlined in the examples on page 678.

Take Notes

Make a Note of It   Once you have found sources, it is time to take notes. Most of your notes will be **paraphrases** (restatements of all the ideas in your own words) or **summaries** (brief restatements of only the most important points) of information from your sources. If a source states an idea particularly well, you may want to note a **direct quotation**—the writer's exact words inside quotation marks. For all notes, make sure you properly credit your sources. Also include in your notes **opinions from experts** and **analogies** (or **comparisons** to more-familiar topics or situations).

Take notes from a variety of sources, including those with different **perspectives,** or opinions, on your topic. By reading sources with different opinions, you get the most complete picture of your subject. For example, if you are researching a former United States president, make sure that you read articles written by his supporters and his critics to get a balanced view of your subject.

To make your note cards, use the following guidelines.

- **Take thorough notes.** Write down facts, statistics, examples, comparisons, and quotations that help answer your research question.

Reference Note

For more on **paraphrasing and summarizing,** see page 681. For more on other types of **support,** see page 756.

Writing **1.0** Essays contain supporting evidence.   **1.3** Support theses or conclusions with analogies, paraphrases, quotations, opinions from authorities, comparisons, and similar devices.   **2.3b** Record important ideas, concepts, and direct quotations from significant information sources and paraphrase all perspectives on the topic.

Your notes will provide the elaboration you need in each paragraph of your report. Instead of just saying "the 761st Tank Battalion performed admirably in World War II," for example, good notes should provide details about the battalion's accomplishments. How can you decide whether something is important enough to write down? Ask yourself these questions. If you can answer yes to both of them, make a note of the information.

1. Does the information relate to my research question?

2. Will the information interest my audience or give them a clearer understanding of my topic?

■ **Label each note card with its source number.** Also, note the page where you found the information in case you need to find it again.

■ **Label each card with a category that tells the type of information it provides.** When you find other information about the same part of your topic, you will give it the same category label. Your categories will depend on your topic. For example, the student researching the 761st Tank Battalion used these categories: Background, Training, Early Battles, and Later Battles. As you research, you may discover additional categories of information.

Here is a sample note card.

TIP As you find information, you may notice that you have additional questions about your topic. If the questions relate to your guiding research question, it is fine to go back and do more research until these questions are answered.

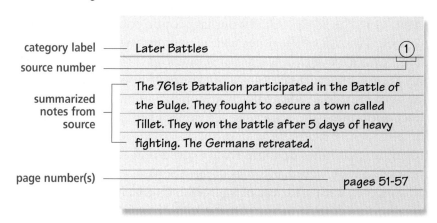

category label	Later Battles ①
source number	
summarized notes from source	The 761st Battalion participated in the Battle of the Bulge. They fought to secure a town called Tillet. They won the battle after 5 days of heavy fighting. The Germans retreated.
page number(s)	pages 51-57

PRACTICE & APPLY 5 Research Your Topic

With your research question in mind, take notes from your sources. Look for facts, statistics, examples, and quotations that will give your readers a complete picture of your topic. Label each note card with its source number and its category of information.

Paraphrasing and Summarizing

When you take notes from your research sources, you may *summarize* or *paraphrase*. A **summary** gives a brief restatement of only the most important points of a source. A **paraphrase,** on the other hand, restates a source's ideas completely and is, therefore, about the same length as the original. When you restate ideas, you must use your own words and sentence structure.

In addition to being helpful in taking notes, paraphrasing and summarizing skills will come in handy when it is time for you to present relevant perspectives, or opinions and ideas, of other writers on your topic. If you want to provide your readers with a detailed report on a particular perspective, you can paraphrase the writer's ideas. Otherwise, you will want to summarize the ideas of other writers.

Read the following passage carefully. Then, take a look at the summary and the paraphrase that follow the passage.

> Helping Hearts is not just any business. This is a candle-making business with a big heart and a big purpose: helping Romanian orphans. Valorie Darling and Arielle Ring of Spokane, Washington, started the business when they were both eleven years old. The two girls started selling handmade beeswax candles that they first made as Christmas presents. During its first year, Helping Hearts donated about $8,000 to charities in Romania.

Summary: Eleven-year-olds Valorie Darling and Arielle Ring use their candle-making business, Helping Hearts, to benefit Romanian orphans.

Paraphrase: Two eleven-year-olds are using their candle-making business to help Romanian orphanages. Valorie Darling and Arielle Ring of Spokane, Washington, were making beeswax candles for holiday gifts when they decided to start selling their home-made candles. They named their business Helping Hearts, and donated about $8,000 to Romanian charities in the first year.

PRACTICE

Write a paraphrase and a summary of the following passage.

> A black hole is a collapsed object, such as a star, that has become invisible. It has such a strong gravitational force that nothing can escape from its surface. Black holes are invisible because they even trap light. They have such strong gravity because they contain a tremendous amount of matter crushed into an incredibly tiny space. If the earth could be squeezed enough to make a black hole, it would be the size of a marble. Most astronomers believe the Milky Way Galaxy contains millions of black holes, though none has definitely been detected.

Writing **1.3** Support theses with paraphrases.   **2.3b** Record important ideas, concepts, and direct quotations from significant information sources and paraphrase and summarize all perspectives on the topic, as appropriate.

Balancing Research and Originality

In research reports, a common weakness that you can avoid is simply stringing together researched information while revealing few (if any) of your own ideas and conclusions about that information. Your research report should also include your perspective on the topic.

To achieve an effective balance between *researched information* and *original ideas,* you must first recognize the difference between them. **Researched information** consists of facts, opinions, statistics, and other ideas that you gather from research sources. **Original ideas** consist of the conclusions you draw, the opinions you form, and the ideas you develop about the researched information.

Take a look at the summary to the right. This passage discusses the famous Tuskegee Airmen, African American fliers of the 99th Squadron of the United States Army Air Corps during World War II. Then, study the Thinking It Through below.

A segregated military aviation program was established at the all-African American Tuskegee Institute in early 1941. The African American trainees at Tuskegee were provided with inferior facilities for their training. Their airfield was incomplete, and their classrooms were inadequate. Nevertheless, they began flight instruction in August 1941. The first class of the 99th Squadron graduated in early March 1942.

By May 1943, they were in North Africa where they were assigned duties escorting bombers. Despite their assignment, they began to establish an impressive record in the air campaigns against the Germans in Italy, both on the island of Sicily and the mainland. In spite of their successes, their every move was watched, and they were the subjects of harsh criticism by those who did not accept them. In October 1943, they integrated with the 79th Fighter Group. No longer escorts, they struck important German targets.

THINKING IT THROUGH **Balancing Research and Originality**

The following steps show how to add originality to researched information. The example responses are those of the student doing research on the Tuskegee Airmen.

▶ **STEP 1 Put together pieces of information that seem important and related.** The men were trained in segregated, inferior facilities. The first class graduated in March 1942. They served with distinction in their first assignments. They were watched very closely and criticized constantly. In October 1943, they were teamed up with another group. Then, they attacked important German targets. They were no longer bomber escorts.

▶ **STEP 2 Draw one or more conclusions from the information.**
The Tuskegee Airmen overcame great obstacles and cruel prejudice to prove their loyalty, courage, and skill as pilots in the United States Army Air Corps.

▶ **STEP 3 Add your own ideas and opinions about the information.** The courage and patriotism of the airmen of the 99th Squadron stand out in clear contrast to the terrible way they were treated.

▶ **STEP 4 Write a coherent paragraph that blends research information with your conclusions, opinions, and ideas.** The Tuskegee Airmen—the 99th Squadron—overcame huge obstacles to prove that they were loyal, patriotic Americans and skilled combat fliers. Despite the fact that they were trained in inferior facilities, their first class graduated less than a year after receiving their first flight instruction. When the 99th Squadron acted as bomber escorts in Sicily and Italy, they developed a fine record. When they served with the 79th Fighter Group to bomb German targets, they continued their impressive service. In everything they did they were watched closely and criticized harshly, but they always proved their worth.

PRACTICE

Read the following passage. Then, use the Thinking It Through steps above to develop original ideas about the information contained in the passage.

> Shortly after the Westward movement began, the Buffalo Soldiers of the U.S. Army played a prominent role in the Wild West. The Buffalo Soldiers were African American soldiers of the 9th and 10th Cavalry Regiments responsible for escorting settlers, railroad crews, and cattle drives on the frontier. They also fought against American Indian tribes in a wide area extending from Montana to Texas. They made up 20 percent of the U.S. Cavalry during the Indian Wars and fought in over 177 battles. The Cheyenne and Comanches nicknamed these African American soldiers "Buffalo Soldiers" both for their courage and for their curly hair. At least eighteen Medals of Honor were awarded to individual Buffalo Soldiers during the Western Campaigns.

 Writing 1.5 Achieve an effective balance between researched information and original ideas.

Write Your Thesis Statement

KEY CONCEPT

Get to the Point The **thesis,** or **main idea statement,** of a report tells readers what the point of the paper will be. The thesis statement is usually located in the introduction to your report. **Your thesis statement should state not only the topic of your paper, but also the most important conclusion you drew from your research.** To write your thesis statement, think about your research question and the answer to it. Here is how one student developed a main idea statement.

Reference Note

For more on developing a **thesis statement,** see page 763.

> Research question: What did the 761st Tank Battalion do during World War II?
>
> What I learned: I learned about their victories and their example of fighting bravely in spite of prejudice against them.
>
> Thesis statement: The 761st Tank Battalion proved that African American soldiers could serve their country with excellence and bravery.

PRACTICE & APPLY ⑥ **Write a Thesis Statement**

Write down your research question. Then, look over your notes and write down the most important conclusion you drew from your research—the answer to your research question. Put these ideas together in one sentence to write the thesis statement for your research report.

TIP Choose an order to arrange your ideas. For example, you may use chronological order if your topic is historical. If you are comparing or classifying two subjects, you may want to use logical order. For other topics, order of importance may be appropriate. For more on **types of order,** see page 760.

Plan Your Report

Place Your Order The category labels on your notes will help you organize the information you have gathered. Begin by sorting your cards into groups based on their labels. Then, create an outline based on these groups, or subtopics, and on the information in your notes. Creating such an outline will help you give your report **coherence.** To turn your organized note cards into a formal outline for your report, follow these steps.

■ Number your subtopics with Roman numerals, and leave several blank lines after each subtopic.

Writing **1.1** Create compositions that have a coherent thesis. **2.0** Student writing demonstrates the organizational strategies outlined in Writing Standard 1.0. **2.3a** Define a thesis. **2.3b** Record important ideas, concepts, and direct quotations from significant information sources and paraphrase and summarize all perspectives on the topic, as appropriate.

- Within each subtopic, you will probably find two or three kinds of information. Give each kind of information a capital letter, and list these items below their Roman numeral. Leave two or three blank lines after each kind of information.
- Finally, list individual facts, examples, and other details from your notes under the appropriate capital letter. Give each of these details a number.

Here is an example of part of a student's outline.

I. Background of African Americans in the military

  A. Limited roles

    1. Served mostly in support units

    2. Segregated from white soldiers

  B. Beginnings of change

    1. Black leaders' pressure on officials

    2. Selective Training and Service Act of 1940

    3. Creation of 761st Tank Battalion

II. Training of the 761st Tank Battalion

  A. Training at Camp Claiborne in Louisiana

TIP When you write your outline, be sure that all the items of each type are parallel. For example, if Roman numeral I is written as a phrase, all Roman numerals should be written as phrases. (For more on **parallel structure,** see page 459 in the *Holt Handbook.*)

Mini-Workshop

You may find it helpful to organize information in a chart, map, or graph. See **Creating Charts, Maps, and Graphs,** page 778.

PRACTICE & APPLY 7   **Create an Outline**

Organize your note cards based on their labels. Then, follow the instructions on pages 684–685 to create an outline for your report.

Designing Your Writing

Creating Headings   Using headings in your research report is an option you can take advantage of to help make your writing clearer and easier to understand. If you use a word processor, you can type your headings in **bold type.** Otherwise, underline headings, or type or write them in all capital letters. The headings will be the major subtopics of information from your notes; these are the items numbered with Roman numerals in your outline.

Writing **1.2** Establish coherence within and among paragraphs through parallel structures.   **2.3d** Organize and display information on charts, maps, and graphs.

Writing

A Writer's Framework

Research Report

Introduction

- Attention-grabbing beginning
- Thesis statement

Hook your readers' attention by contrasting what they already know about the topic with new information or a question. Your **thesis statement** should identify both your topic and the conclusion you have drawn about it.

Body

- Subtopic 1 and elaboration
- Subtopic 2 and elaboration and so on

- Each Roman numeral in your outline will represent a subtopic. Each subtopic will be covered in its own paragraph. However, large subtopics may need more than one paragraph. To create **coherence**, link ideas with logical transitions such as *although, but, still, yet, also, instead, when, after,* and *finally.*

- Provide **supporting evidence** for each subtopic using facts, analogies or comparisons, paraphrases, expert opinions, examples, direct quotations, and your own **original ideas** or **conclusions.**

Conclusion

- Related, unanswered question or final comment

To finish your report, you may want to include a **related** and **interesting question** that your research did not answer. Another way to end is by making a **final statement about why your topic is important.**

Works Cited List

- Alphabetical list of sources used

List the sources you used for your report in a **Works Cited list** or a bibliography (if you used only print sources). Use the correct format for each citation, based on the examples on page 678.

Writing 1.0 Students write clear and coherent essays. Essays contain formal introductions, supporting evidence, and conclusions. **1.1** Create compositions that end with a clear and well-supported conclusion. **1.2** Establish coherence through effective transitions. **2.0** Student writing demonstrates the drafting strategies outlined in Writing Standard1.0.

A Writer's Model

The final draft below closely follows the framework for a research report and the MLA guidelines for correct research paper format.

The Brave Soldiers of the 761st

World War II brings many heroic images to mind. People may think of Rosie the Riveter or the Iwo Jima statue of six Marines. One lesser-known story, though, is the heroism of African American soldiers in World War II. The 761st Tank Battalion proved that African Americans could serve their country with excellence and bravery.

When the war began in the late 1930s, African Americans made up only a small part of the army. The armed forces were segregated, or separated, by race. Black soldiers and white soldiers trained and lived separately. African American leaders began pressuring government officials to change the unfair system. In 1940, the U.S. Congress passed the Selective Training and Service Act. The act included the words, "there shall be no discrimination against any person on account of race or color" (qdt. in Pfeifer 13–14). The act led to the creation of black combat units, including the 761st Tank Battalion (Pfeifer 22).

INTRODUCTION
Attention-grabbing beginning

Thesis statement

BODY
Subtopic 1: Background

Facts

Direct quotation

(continued)

(continued)

TIP The Writer's Model includes examples of **parenthetical citations.** In parentheses following the information, the writer lists the author's last name and the page number where he found the information.

Expert opinion

Subtopic 3: Early battles

Fact

Direct quotation

In 1942, the 761st Tank Battalion was formed at Camp Claiborne, Louisiana (<u>African Americans</u>). The battalion had 27 officers, all of them white, and 313 enlisted men. Within a year a group of black officers, which included the baseball player Jackie Robinson, was assigned to the battalion (Pfeifer 22, 25). Conditions at Camp Claiborne were difficult for the soldiers. Their housing was in a swampy area near the sewage treatment plant (Pfeifer 24). Worst of all, African American soldiers had fewer rights than some German prisoners held at the camp (Pfeifer 30–31). Despite these injustices, the 761st Tank Battalion worked hard to earn a reputation for excellence. In maneuvers, military exercises designed to resemble real combat situations, the soldiers of the 761st proved their readiness for battle (Pfeifer 29).

In October 1944, the battalion joined General George S. Patton's Third Army in Europe. According to writer Catherine Reef, Patton told the soldiers, "I would never have asked for you if you weren't good. I have nothing but the best in my Army" (51). In their first battle, the 761st Tank Battalion had to cut off German escape and supply routes to Metz, France. At the town of

Morville, they encountered heavy gunfire and mines. Although the Germans knocked out seven tanks, the men of the 761st prevented worse losses (Pfeifer 42–45).

Statistic

In December, the 761st Tank Battalion went to Belgium to join the Battle of the Bulge, the largest land battle of the war. The 761st fought a fierce battle for a little town called Tillet. After five days the Germans retreated (Pfeifer 51–57). The battalion pressed on through the Netherlands, France, and Germany, fighting battles along the way. One of their last accomplishments during the war was breaking through the Siegfried Line. This line protected the German border with bunkers and concrete and steel antitank structures. Finally, the 761st Tank Battalion met up with their Russian allies at the Enns River (African Americans). Two days later, the war in Europe was over.

Subtopic 4: Later battles

Facts

The soldiers of the 761st Tank Battalion battled discrimination and inequality to serve their country. In 1978, President Carter awarded them a Presidential Unit Citation for their courageous deeds (Pfeifer 10–11). The 761st Tank Battalion, one of the first African American combat units, set an example of heroism for all Americans.

CONCLUSION
Final comment

(continued)

(continued)

TIP According-
ing to MLA style,
your Works Cited
list should
appear on a sep-
arate sheet of
paper at the end
of your report.

GO TO:
go.hrw.com
KEYWORD:
HLLA8 W-4
FOR:
A Student Model

Works Cited

<u>African Americans in WWII: A Legacy of Patriotism and Valor</u>.

Pro. Department of Defense. OnDeck Home

Entertainment, 1998.

Pfeifer, Kathryn Browne. <u>The 761st Tank Battalion</u>. New York:

Twenty-First Century Books, 1994.

Reef, Catherine. <u>Black Fighting Men: A Proud History</u>. New

York: Twenty-First Century Books, 1994.

PRACTICE & APPLY 8 **Write a First Draft**

Now it is time to write the first draft of your research report. As
you write, refer to the framework and the Writer's Model on
pages 686–690.

Evaluate and Revise Content, Organization, and Style

Take Another Look When you evaluate your own report or a peer's, you should read it at least twice. During the first reading, focus on what is in the report—the content—and how that information is organized. The second time, read each sentence and evaluate its style, using the Focus on Word Choice on page 693.

▷ **First Reading: Content and Organization** Use the chart below to help you evaluate and revise the content and organization of your report.

Research Report: Content and Organization Guidelines

Evaluation Questions	▶ Tips	▶ Revision Techniques
❶ Does the introduction contain a clear thesis statement that identifies both the topic and the writer's most important conclusion?	▶ **Put a star** next to the statement that tells readers the report's topic and thesis.	▶ **Add** a thesis statement or **add** the main point about the topic to the thesis statement.
❷ Does each body paragraph explain no more than one subtopic from your outline?	▶ **Label** the margin of each body paragraph with the subtopic it explains.	▶ If necessary, **delete** unrelated ideas or **rearrange** the information into separate body paragraphs. To create coherence, link ideas with logical **transitions.**
❸ Does each paragraph include facts, statistics, examples, direct quotations, or conclusions that elaborate on the subtopic?	▶ **Highlight** the facts and explanations in each paragraph.	▶ **Elaborate** paragraphs that need support with facts and explanations from research notes.
❹ Is there an unanswered question or final comment in the conclusion?	▶ **Put a check mark** next to the question or final statement.	▶ **Add** a question or final statement or revise the statement or question to make it clearer.
❺ Does the Works Cited list include at least three sources?	▶ **Number** the sources listed in the Works Cited list.	▶ If needed, **add** sources to the Works Cited list, and **add** information from those sources to the report.

 Writing 1.6 Revise writing for appropriate organization and transitions between paragraphs, passages, and ideas.

ONE WRITER'S REVISIONS Here is how the writer revised part of an early draft of the essay on pages 687–690.

delete

add

rearrange

> Within a year a group of black officers, which included the baseball player Jackie Robinson, was assigned to the battalion (Pfeifer 22, 25). ~~After the war, Jackie Robinson became the first African American ballplayer to join a major league team.~~ Conditions at Camp Claiborne were difficult for the soldiers. *Their housing was in a swampy area near the* Worst of all, African American soldiers had *sewage treatment plant (Pfeifer 24).* fewer rights than some German prisoners held at the camp (Pfeifer 30–31).
>
> Despite these injustices, the 761st Tank Battalion worked hard to earn a reputation for excellence.

PEER REVIEW

As you evaluate a peer's research report, ask yourself these questions.

■ What more do I want to know about the topic? Why?

■ Is there information in one part of the report that seems to belong in another part?

Responding to the Revision Process

1. Why do you think the writer deleted a sentence?
2. Why did the writer add a sentence to the paragraph above?
3. Why did the writer move information from a later paragraph back into an earlier paragraph?

> **Second Reading: Style**   During your second reading, you will look at your style, or the way you express your ideas in sentences. One way to revise your sentences is to eliminate wordiness. Use the guidelines below.

Style Guidelines

Evaluation Question	▶ Tip	▶ Revision Technique
Do any sentences use more words than needed to get a point across?	▶ **Put brackets** around unnecessary words or phrases.	▶ **Delete** unnecessary phrases. **Revise** sentences to be more concise.

Writing 1.6 Revise writing for word choice.

Word Choice

Revising to Eliminate Wordiness

When you write a research report, it is easy to fall into the trap of using too many words. Note the difference in the sentences below.

Wordy Sentence It should be pointed out that only with your help can we stop destructive fires from burning down forests.

Concise Sentence Only you can prevent forest fires.

Although research reports are formal papers, avoid using a **voice** that does not sound like you. Cross out unnecessary words or ideas that are repeated in your report. Replace phrases such as "due to the fact that" and "at the present time" with "because" and "now." Straightforward sentences are strong sentences.

ONE WRITER'S REVISIONS

 ~~Due to the fact that~~ ᵀ/the armed forces were segregated,

ᵒʳ/ ~~which means~~ separated by race, ~~the soldiers of different~~

~~colors could not live together.~~ Black soldiers and white

soldiers trained and lived separately.

Responding to the Revision Process

Do you think the passage above has been improved? Why?

PRACTICE & APPLY **9**

Evaluate and Revise Your Report

Evaluate and revise the content and organization of your report using the guidelines on page 691. Then, refer to the Focus on Word Choice above to eliminate wordiness in your report. Finally, if a peer evaluated your paper, carefully consider each of your peer's comments as you revise.

Writing 1.6 Revise writing for word choice.

Publishing

Proofread Your Report

Catching Mistakes After revising for content, organization, and style, you need to **edit** your report one more time. This time, search for errors in grammar and mechanics. Errors in the final draft of your report may make readers doubt the accuracy of your research. Try to have another person help proofread your report.

Grammar Link

Source Citation Format

Most research reports include a Works Cited list. Writers list information about sources in a specific order following certain rules for punctuation. Using a standard format can help your readers find out more about your topic, and it can help your teacher double-check your information.

PRACTICE

Use the formats in the chart on page 678 to write a citation for each source listed. Punctuate each citation carefully, and add underlining or quotation marks as necessary.

Example:

1. An article in Science News magazine called Butterfly May Use Flowery Stepping-Stones, published on April 25, 1998, on page 262. The author is Mari N. Jensen.

1. *Jensen, Mari N. "Butterfly May Use Flowery Stepping-Stones." Science News 25 April 1998: 262.*

1. An article in the newspaper The Washington Post, titled City Ready to Raze Monument. The article was published on July 14, 1998, on page A4.

2. A book by Jeanette Winter called Sebastian: A Book About Bach. It was published in Orlando by Harcourt Brace and Company in 1999.

3. The television show Newstime, hosted by Angel Martinez. The ABC show was broadcast on September 25, 1997, in New Orleans on WGNO.

4. An article in Newsweek magazine called The Power of Big Ideas, published on January 11, 1999, on page 58. The author is Sharon Begley.

5. A Web page called EARTHFORCE on the Franklin Institute Online Web site. The page was published on the Web in 1998, and was accessed on March 22, 2002. The URL is <http://www.fi.edu/earth/earth. html>. No author is given. The site is sponsored and maintained by the Franklin Institute Science Museum.

Reference Note

For more information and practice on using **underlining (italics)** and **punctuation marks** with titles, see pages 342 and 349 in the *Holt Handbook*.

 Writing 2.0 Student writing demonstrates a command of standard American English.

Publish Your Report

Share Your Work   Now it is time to show off your work. Get it in front of your audience by trying one of these ideas.

- Use the Listening and Speaking Workshop on pages 696–702 to turn your report into an informative speech, and share your report with your class.

- Submit your report to an online discussion group that deals with topics similar to yours, and ask for feedback.

- With other students who wrote on topics similar to yours, create a class magazine that includes your group's reports. Your magazine could be about animals, historical figures, or arts, for example.

TIP Your teacher may ask you to create a **title page** for your report. In the middle of a separate sheet of paper, write your name, the date, your teacher's name, and any other information your teacher requests. Attach this page to the front of your report before you publish it.

Reflect on Your Report

Building Your Portfolio   Take a step back and think about your research report. Reflecting on what you wrote and how you wrote it can help you improve on future assignments.

- What was the most interesting part of your report? Why?

- What kinds of sources were the most useful? What sources were easiest to find? What sources could you use in the future?

 Now, consider your research report in the context of your entire portfolio so far. Review the pieces in your portfolio and answer the following questions.

- What writing skills have you improved between earlier pieces in your portfolio and your research report?

- What kinds of writing have you included in your portfolio? What goals can you set for types of writing that you would like to try in future pieces?

PRACTICE & APPLY 10   ## Proofread, Publish, and Reflect on Your Report

- Correct grammar, usage, and mechanics errors using reference materials and resources, such as the proofreading guidelines on page 585, computer grammar and spelling features, or a dictionary.

- Publish your report for your target audience.

- Answer the Reflect on Your Report questions above. Record your responses in your portfolio.

Talk **Listen**

Giving and Listening to a Research Presentation

WHAT'S AHEAD?

In this workshop you will give and listen to a research presentation. You will also learn how to

- adapt a written research report for an oral presentation
- choose appropriate visual resources to organize and display information
- deliver your research presentation
- evaluate the content and delivery of other students' research presentations

An oral **research presentation** presents research results. It may include *visual resources* and allow audience members the opportunity to ask questions. **Visual resources** are materials your audience can see, such as slides, pictures, transparencies, and posters. You can adapt, or make changes to, your research report for a short presentation and support it with visual resources.

Adapt Your Report

Simply reading your research report aloud will not keep your audience interested. You will need to adapt your report in order to use it as a research presentation. The following guidelines will help you.

Save Only the Best   As you prepare your presentation, make notes on the most important points of your report.

- Keep your **thesis statement.**
- If necessary, cut your least important points, and narrow your support to only the strongest evidence, examples, and elaboration.
- Be sure your presentation shares information from a variety of primary and secondary sources.
- Include paraphrases or summaries of various viewpoints, or **perspectives,** on your topic.

Listening and Speaking 2.3 Deliver research presentations.   **2.3a** Define a thesis.   **2.3b** Record important ideas, concepts, and direct quotations from significant information sources and paraphrase and summarize all relevant perspectives on the topic, as appropriate.   **2.3c** Use a variety of primary and secondary sources and distinguish the nature and value of each.

Give Me a Clue Unlike your readers, your listeners will not be able to go back and re-read your report if they do not understand something you said. Therefore, you should organize your information in a way that is easy to follow and that will also hold your audience's attention. The best way to do that is to create an **outline** for your research presentation just as you did for your research report.

Relate It to Your Audience Identify something in your **message** that will relate to your audience's interests, and put that information in the introduction of your presentation. For example, if the student giving the presentation on the 761st Tank Battalion knows that many of his audience members are baseball fans, he might begin by talking about baseball legend Jackie Robinson, even though in his written report the references to Robinson appeared in the body.

A Logical and Comfortable Arrangement As you did in your written research report, clearly separate your presentation into the familiar "introduction, body, conclusion" format. Look back at your prewriting outline and think about details or even whole sections of your report that you may want to rearrange for your presentation audience. For example, if you arranged your report in order of importance from least to most important, you might want to reverse the order for your presentation to be sure that you capture the audience's interest right away with your most important point.

Reference Note
For more information on creating an **outline,** see page 684.

Quick guide!

PRESENTATION FORMAT	
Introduction	Grab your listeners' attention, state your thesis, and then tell listeners what the sections in the body will be so they know what to listen for.
Body	Clearly discuss each section you mentioned in the introduction.
Conclusion	Summarize your ideas about each section and restate your thesis. Make your conclusion memorable by ending with a quotation, a question, or a final thought for the audience to consider after your presentation is over.

TIP Your introduction should not only introduce your topic, but yourself. Tell the audience why you are making a presentation on this topic. If you reveal your **point of view** in the beginning, the audience will be more accepting of your message. For more on **point of view,** see page 702.

Listening and Speaking **1.0** Presentations relate to the background and interests of the audience. **1.3** Organize information to achieve particular purposes by matching the message to the audience and purpose. **1.4** Prepare a speech outline based upon a chosen pattern of organization, which generally includes an introduction; a logically developed body; and an effective conclusion.

Previews At the beginning of each section in the body of your presentation, give a **preview** of the main idea of the section for emphasis. For example, you may begin a section of your body by saying, "I will now discuss the conditions at Camp Claiborne" to let listeners know what will be coming.

Summaries After you have finished discussing that section, you might re-emphasize the main idea with a very brief summary. For example, you might say, "Despite the awful conditions at the camp, these soldiers continued to prove themselves."

Transitions **Transitional words** and **phrases** establish **coherence,** connecting the supporting details in your presentation and guiding your listeners from one idea to another. Use transitional words and phrases such as those below to help make your speech coherent.

Quick guide!

TRANSITIONAL WORDS AND PHRASES	
Showing time or sequence	after, before, eventually, finally, first, later, meanwhile, next, soon, then, while
Showing location	above, across, among, around, behind, beneath, beside, by, down, here, in, near, next to, there, under
Showing importance	first, finally, last, mainly, more important, then, to begin with
Showing comparison and contrast	also, although, and, but, instead, like, on the other hand, similarly, still, too, yet

Credit Where Due In your written research report, parenthetical citations and the Works Cited list told your readers where you found the information. A research presentation, though, does not include these features. For this reason, plan to tell listeners the sources for statistics, quotes, or unusual facts you use within your presentation. If your audience members know where the information comes from, they will consider it more trustworthy. To credit your source, simply say something like, "According to the *World Book Encyclopedia,* the U. S. Armed Forces were segregated until 1948."

Listening and Speaking **1.0** Students deliver focused, coherent presentations. **1.4** Prepare a speech outline based upon a chosen pattern of organization, which generally includes transitions, previews, and summaries.

Choose Visual Resources

Seeing Is Believing Once you have adapted your report, choose visual resources to support your ideas. You may wish to use poster board, individual handouts, slides, or overhead projector transparencies to display **graphics,** such as *maps, charts,* and *graphs.*

Use, but do not overuse, visual resources. Any graphic you choose should reinforce your ideas or help you explain important or hard-to-understand parts of your presentation. Make sure your visual resources meet the following guidelines.

- Graphics should focus on one main image and a few details. Cluttered graphics are hard to understand.

- Lettering and images should be large enough for your audience to see clearly, even from the back of the room.

- Colors must be used for a purpose—to stress important information, to show contrast, or to indicate relationships among ideas.

Mini-Workshop

See **Creating Charts, Maps, and Graphs,** page 778.

Plan Your Delivery

Be Heard Plan to speak loudly, slowly, and clearly. As you plan your delivery, think of your audience.

- Plan to speak more slowly than usual. Be prepared to adjust your **pace,** the speed at which you speak, according to your audience's needs. To make sure a key concept is understood, plan to slow down even further when discussing that concept. Be prepared to speed up if you find audience attention is drifting.

- Plan to **enunciate** each word, clearly distinguishing one word from another. In everyday speech, people may say *prob'ly* for *probably, gimme* for *give me,* or *havin'* for *having.* However, in a formal speaking situation, you should make sure that you do not.

Grab Your Audience You can use the **tone** of your voice and **facial expressions** to indicate appropriate emotions such as excitement, sadness, or happiness and to keep your audience involved. Plan your tone and facial expressions so that they match the content and purpose of your message. Do not undermine an important research presentation by appearing too casual. Also use appropriate **grammar** when giving a speech. Review the section called "Common Usage Problems" in the *Holt Handbook,* page 262.

TIP Vocal modulation, or pitch, is the highness or lowness of your voice. Varying your pitch affects your **expression** and your **tone** and is another effective way of maintaining audience attention.

Listening and Speaking 1.3 Organize information to achieve particular purposes by matching voice modulation, expression and tone to the audience and purpose. **1.6** Use appropriate grammar, enunciation, and pace during formal presentations. **2.3d** Organize and record information on charts, maps, and graphs.

Practice

Dress Rehearsal   Now that you have planned content and delivery, you are ready to practice giving your presentation in front of your parents, classmates, or friends. As you rehearse, focus on your audience. Practice facing them and making eye contact with individuals in all parts of your audience while referring to your visual resources. It may seem natural to turn your back to your audience and face your chart, map, or graph while explaining it, but doing so reduces your listeners' ability to hear you.

Paint a Perfect Picture   Before you rehearse your presentation, ask your audience to pay attention to places where your presentation could use improvement. Have listeners note **vocabulary** problems, such as vague nouns, overused *be* verbs, and dull modifiers. Your audience can provide you with valuable feedback.

Vague Nouns   Replace vague, "fuzzy" nouns with **precise nouns.** Let your listeners know exactly who or what you are discussing.

VAGUE	In 1940, **people** passed a **law** banning discrimination in the military.
PRECISE	In 1940, **Congress** passed the **Selective Training and Service Act** banning discrimination in the military.

Overused *Be* Verbs   Use **action verbs** rather than dull *be* verbs to add a sense of excitement to your presentation. Commonly used *be* verbs include *am, are, is, was,* and *were.*

BE VERB	General Patton **was** the commander of the Third Army in Europe.
ACTION VERB	General Patton **commanded** the Third Army in Europe.

Dull Modifiers   Descriptive words such as adjectives and adverbs are **modifiers.** Replace **dull modifiers** with vivid ones. Commonly used dull modifiers include *very, really, hardly,* and *suddenly* (adverbs); and *pretty, nice, good,* and *bad* (adjectives).

DULL	The soldiers of the 761st Tank Battalion were **very good** fighters.
VIVID	The soldiers of the 761st Tank Battalion were **heroic** fighters.

Listening and Speaking 1.3 Organize information to achieve particular purposes by matching vocabulary to the audience and purpose.   1.5 Use precise language, action verbs, and appropriate and colorful modifiers in ways that enliven oral presentations.   1.6 Use appropriate word choice.

Deliver Your Presentation

Keep Flexible While you are giving your presentation, pay close attention to your audience. **Nonverbal feedback,** such as confused looks, or **verbal feedback,** such as questions, can be a sign that you need to make some quick adjustments to your presentation as you are giving it. Adjustments that you might make successfully on the spot include more-deliberate enunciation (clear and distinct pronunciation of words), slower pace, and more repetition of important ideas and key words and phrases.

Before you give your presentation again, you might change the **organization** of your presentation or **rearrange words and sentences** to clarify ideas, depending upon the verbal and nonverbal cues the audience gives you.

Evaluate a Presentation

Thumbs Up? Or Thumbs Down? As you listen to and view a classmate's research presentation, evaluate the content and delivery by writing down your answers to the following questions. These evaluation notes will be helpful to the speaker the next time he or she prepares to give a presentation.

- **Organization** How well is the presentation organized? Do the ideas flow logically, and are they clearly connected? Do you understand all of the ideas presented?

- **Description** How vivid is description in the presentation? What precise nouns, verbs, and modifiers does the speaker use?

- **Credibility** Is the speaker credible? For example, is the information presented in a balanced way? How does the speaker include other viewpoints?

- **Use of Visuals** How appropriate and effective is the use of visual resources? How do the visual resources relate to the topic and clarify the ideas given in the presentation?

- **Delivery** How was the speaker's delivery? Did he or she speak loudly, slowly, and clearly enough for you to understand the presentation? How well did the presentation keep your attention? What suggestions for improvement can you offer the speaker for the next time he or she delivers a presentation?

 Listening and Speaking **1.7** Use audience feedback (e.g., verbal and nonverbal cues). **1.7a** Reconsider and modify the organizational structure or plan. **1.7b** Rearrange words and sentences to clarify the meaning. **1.8** Evaluate the credibility of a speaker (e.g., biased material).

Clarification, Please   After listening to the speaker, you may have questions. Your teacher may allow time for a question-and-answer session after each presentation, or you may wish to approach the speaker individually following the presentation. When you ask the speaker your questions, consider the following suggestions.

- Begin by restating briefly the speaker's **purpose,** asking yourself, *About what exactly did the speaker inform me?*

- Paraphrase the speaker's **point of view** on the topic. Does the speaker admire the subject, disapprove of it, or appear to be neutral about it? Restating the speaker's viewpoint first can help clear up any wrong assumptions you may have made during the presentation. For example, you might begin a question in this way: "In your talk, you discussed the background and accomplishments of the 761st Tank Battalion, which you clearly admired."

- Make sure your questions are focused on the topic and purpose of the presentation your classmate has delivered. For example, if the topic of the presentation was methods of cleaning up nuclear waste, you should not ask a question about nuclear weapons or highway litter.

- When you prepare your evaluation, consider the speaker's answers to audience questions as part of the presentation. How well did he or she answer audience questions?

PRACTICE & APPLY 11   **Give and Evaluate a Research Presentation**

- Use the information on pages 696–700 to adapt your report, choose appropriate visual resources, and practice your research presentation.

- Pair up with a classmate with whom you can share evaluation notes on each other's presentations. Then, give your research presentation in front of your intended audience.

- Evaluate the presentation of your partner using the guidelines given on page 701. Then, discuss your evaluation notes together and take notes on your partner's comments. Your teacher may wish you to turn in your evaluation notes and discussion notes.

Listening and Speaking 1.0 They evaluate the content of oral communication.   **1.2** Paraphrase a speaker's purpose and point of view and ask relevant questions concerning the speaker's content, delivery, and purpose.   **2.0** Students deliver formal presentations employing traditional rhetorical strategies (e.g., exposition). Student speaking demonstrates organizational and delivery strategies.

DIRECTIONS: Read this passage from a research report and the questions that follow it. Mark the best answer to each question on your own paper.

(1) Some parasites make their hosts behave strangely. (2) A kind of wasp can make a spider build a home for its larva. (3) According to Nature magazine, the wasp stings the spider to paralyze it and then lays an egg on the spider's abdomen. (4) After the larva hatches, it feeds on the living spider's blood. (5) Then, the larva injects a chemical into the spider that makes the spider spin a special kind of web, one very different from its usual web. (6) In a BBC News Online article, Dr. William Eberhard, a scientist who studies these insects, calls it "the ideal web from the wasp-larva point of view" because it provides "a very solid and durable support." (7) When the web is finished, the larva kills and eats the spider, and then builds its cocoon in the spider's last web. (8) As scientist Fritz Vollrath comments in a Discovery.com article, "The irony is that the poor thing that fed this larva builds it a little shelter as its last act. (9) It makes a gruesome fairy tale."

1. Which of the following would be the **best** thesis for this research paper analyzing the effects of parasites on their hosts?

   A There are many types of parasites found all over the world.

   B A parasite is an organism that lives off another species without providing any benefit to that species.

   C After the larva hatches, it feeds on the living spider's blood.

   D While all parasites benefit from their hosts, their effects on those hosts vary from strange to deadly.

2. Which of the following is a **primary source** the writer could consult for more information on this topic?

   F Dr. Eberhard's Web site containing his research notes

   G an encyclopedia article on the effects of parasites on hosts

   H a newspaper article reporting on how wasps benefit gardeners

   J a magazine article analyzing Dr. Eberhard's research results

3. Which transition might be added to the beginning of sentence 2 to show the relationship of ideas in sentences 1 and 2?

   A By the way,

   B On the other hand,

   C For example,

   D As a result,

4. Which visual resource would best support this paragraph?

   F a map showing the habitats of the wasp and spider

   G a chart showing different types of wasps from all over the world

   H a time line showing the stages in the life cycle of the average wasp

   J illustrations showing the two types of webs made by the spider

5. In a research presentation on this topic, the speaker should

   A speak rapidly to keep audience interested

   B give listeners a preview before each section

   C eliminate the introduction and conclusion to focus on important ideas

   D look at notes at all times so as not to leave out important ideas

Persuasion

Thumb through any magazine, and you will find pages of product-selling ads. Glance out the car window, and you will see larger-than-life billboards. **Persuasion,** the art of convincing people to do or believe something, is everywhere. In this workshop you will study persuasion in written, oral, and visual forms. In doing so, you will practice these language arts standards.

GO TO: go.hrw.com
KEYWORD: HLLA8 W-5
FOR: Models, Writer's Guides, and Reference Sources

California Standards

Writing

1.0 Students write clear, coherent, and focused essays. The writing exhibits students' awareness of audience and purpose. Essays contain formal introductions, supporting evidence, and conclusions. Students progress through the stages of the writing process.

1.1 Create compositions that establish a controlling impression, have a coherent thesis, and end with a clear and well-supported conclusion.

1.2 Establish coherence within and among paragraphs through effective transitions, parallel structures, and similar writing techniques.

1.3 Support theses or conclusions with analogies, opinions from authorities, comparisons, and similar devices.

1.6 Revise writing for appropriate organization and consistent point of view.

2.0 Students write persuasive texts of at least 500 to 700 words. Student writing demonstrates a command of standard American English and the research, organizational, and drafting strategies outlined in Writing Standard 1.0.

2.4 Write persuasive compositions:

   a. Include a well-defined thesis (i.e., one that makes a clear and knowledgeable judgment).

   b. Present detailed evidence, examples, and reasoning to support arguments, differentiating between facts and opinion.

   c. Provide details, reasons, and examples, arranging them effectively by anticipating and answering reader concerns and counterarguments.

Listening and Speaking

1.0 Students deliver focused, coherent presentations that convey ideas clearly and relate to the background and interests of the audience. They evaluate the content of oral communication.

1.2 Paraphrase a speaker's purpose and point of view and ask relevant questions concerning the speaker's content, delivery, and purpose.

1.3 Organize information to achieve particular purposes by matching the message, vocabulary, voice modulation, expression, and tone to the audience and purpose.

1.4 Prepare a speech outline based upon a chosen pattern of organization, which generally includes transitions, previews, and summaries; a logically developed body; and an effective conclusion.

1.5 Use precise language, action verbs, sensory details, appropriate and colorful modifiers, and the active rather than the passive voice in ways that enliven oral presentations.

1.6 Use appropriate grammar, word choice, enunciation, and pace during formal presentations.

1.7 Use audience feedback (e.g., verbal and nonverbal cues):

    a. Reconsider and modify the organizational structure or plan.

    b. Rearrange words and sentences to clarify meaning.

1.8 Evaluate the credibility of a speaker (e.g., hidden agendas or bias).

1.9 Interpret and evaluate the various ways in which visual image makers (e.g., graphic artists, illustrators, news photographers) communicate information and affect impressions and opinions.

2.0 Students deliver well-organized formal presentations employing traditional rhetorical strategies (e.g., persuasion). Student speaking demonstrates the organizational and delivery strategies outlined in Listening and Speaking Standard 1.0.

2.4 Deliver persuasive presentations:

    a. Include a well-defined thesis (i.e., one that makes a clear and knowledgeable judgment).

    b. Differentiate fact from opinion and support arguments with detailed evidence, examples, and reasoning.

    c. Anticipate and answer listener concerns and counterarguments effectively through the inclusion and arrangement of details, reasons, examples, and other elements.

    d. Maintain a reasonable tone.

CALIFORNIA STANDARDS

WHAT'S AHEAD?

In this workshop you will write a persuasive essay. You will also learn how to

- **choose and take a stand on an issue**
- **support a thesis statement with reasons and evidence**
- **use parallel structure**
- **add variety to sentence beginnings**
- **revise "There is/It is" constructions**

Writing a Persuasive Essay

Do you feel that CDs should carry warnings about bad language? Do you think school lunch periods should be longer? Do you believe professional athletes have a responsibility to be good role models? You probably have strong opinions about these and many other issues. However, your opinion alone will probably not convince anyone to agree with you. One way to convince others is to use the tools of **persuasion** to show your readers that your point of view is the right one.

In this workshop you will write a persuasive essay that uses reasons and evidence to support an opinion. This is your chance to convince others to see things the way you do.

Professional Model: A Persuasive Essay

There is certainly no shortage of published examples of persuasive writing in your world. Pick up today's newspaper and find the opinions and editorials section, and you will see articles and columns designed to persuade you to act or think the way the writer does. In the following article, originally published in *Newsday,* the writer attempts to persuade her audience that "uniforms would improve the quality of life for students."

DO THIS

As you read the article, create a **think sheet.** Ask yourself questions about the content of the article and the techniques the writer uses to make the article persuasive. Try to make connections between what the article says and your own experiences. To help you create your think sheet, answer the analysis questions that appear next to the essay.

Writing 2.4 Write persuasive compositions.

from Newsday

Should Public School Students Wear Uniforms?

By Charol Shakeshaft

WHEN I WAS a kid in school, we didn't wear uniforms. In junior high, I argued for school uniforms, believing they would save students—especially girls—time and hassle. Thirty-five years later, as a parent of a ten-year-old, I still think uniforms would improve the quality of life for students.

> **1. What is the writer's opinion on the issue? Is it clear?**

Uniforms in public schools are legal, as long as the uniform does not infringe[1] upon students' political speech or impose different standards for males and females. Although the Supreme Court has not addressed the legality of uniforms in schools,

> **2. What audience concern might the writer be addressing in this paragraph?**

lower courts have upheld the right of public schools to require uniforms. California has gone so far as to pass a law explicitly[2] making it legal for public schools to adopt uniform requirements, an action designed to reinforce the legality of this kind of local decision. . . .

From Seattle to Phoenix to Charleston, praise of uniform policies is profuse.[3] One of the most often cited benefits of requiring uniforms is economic. Uniforms generally cost less than do most clothes that students want to wear. For instance, the yearly cost of uniforms in Long Beach, California, is $70 to $90 for a set of three. Compare that to a trip to the mall!

Uniforms also can diminish[4] the display of material wealth among students. If expensive jackets, shoes, and outfits aren't allowed, students are relieved of anxiety over their attire. Wearing uniforms during the school day provides a time when economic privilege seems equalized.

Uniforms promote individuality. Yes, individuality. If students are judged by what they think and how they perform, rather than on how they dress, they are more likely to develop and value diversity[5] of thought. In most school districts, kids already wear uniforms by social category—jocks, . . . preppies . . .—often without

> **3. Are the ideas in this paragraph facts or opinions? How do you know?**

---

1. infringe: to limit; to break a law or agreement.
2. explicitly: clearly stated.
3. profuse: generous; abundant.
4. diminish: lessen.
5. diversity: differences.

articulating what values and lifestyles these uniforms represent.

Long Beach, California, offers impressive evidence that schools where students wear uniforms are safer than those where students don't. Since Long Beach adopted a uniform requirement for its 83,000 students, there have been a third fewer assault and battery cases, student fights have been cut by half, and student suspensions are down by 32 percent.

What compels[6] me to urge school districts to adopt uniforms are the data I've collected during the past three years in nine middle and high schools on Long Island. In those schools, the girls report they spend as much as two-and-a-half hours each day selecting their clothes and "getting ready" for school. These girls describe great anxiety about their appearance, particularly their clothes, and report harassment from both males and females about how they look. I long for a safe space for girls that diminishes such pressure and

decreases their anxiety. Schools that expect all students to wear the same type of dress offer support to girls in their fragile adolescent years.

Studies tell us that nearly all parents welcome uniforms. Students are not so quick to approve of wearing the same dress as their classmates every day. However, many students who first balk at uniforms change their minds once they have tried them.

Uniforms honor the occasion of school. They help students separate what is expected in school from what they do in malls or on beaches or at movie theaters. Uniforms help create a climate that fosters learning and puts it at the center of students' lives.

> **4.** Does the writer support the main idea of this paragraph with facts or opinions? How do you know?

> **5.** To support the main idea of this paragraph, does the writer appeal to readers' minds or hearts or both?

6. **compels:** forces.

Working with a partner, discuss the following questions, and write down your responses.

1. Whether you agree with her or not, do you think the writer provides convincing support for her opinion? Why or why not?

2. Which paragraph or paragraphs do you think the writer includes to address concerns she thinks her audience might have? Why do you think so?

3. Which paragraph appeals most strongly to your mind, or logic? Why? Which paragraph appeals most strongly to your emotions? Why?

4. List the main points the writer makes. Then, based on the strength of support and the space given each point, decide which seems most important. Where in the essay—at the beginning, middle, or end—does she make this point?

Choose and Evaluate Your Issue

First Things First   The final goal, or **purpose,** of persuasive writing is to convince your readers to agree with your opinion on an issue that concerns you. Therefore, the first step you must take in preparing to write a persuasive essay is to choose an issue. **An issue is a subject about which people disagree,** such as whether CDs should carry warnings about potentially offensive language.

When choosing an issue, try to find one that has an impact on your life as well as the lives of others. For example, the issue of year-round school would be a good choice for an essay because it creates strong feelings in you and many others. However, the issue of whether or not your parents should raise your allowance would not be as appropriate because it only affects you and maybe one or two others. An issue such as the need for laws regulating the speed of automobiles through school zones would not be appropriate because virtually everyone agrees on the subject.

KEY CONCEPT

TIP Keep in mind that your persuasive essay will be 500 to 700 words long, so you should choose an interesting issue that will keep your readers' attention throughout a paper of that length.

Writing 1.0 The writing exhibits students' awareness of purpose. Students progress through the stages of the writing process.   2.0 Students write persuasive texts of at least 500 to 700 words.

An excellent way to discover an issue for a persuasive essay is to read persuasive essays such as the professional model on pages 707–708. Look for persuasive essays in magazines or for editorials in the opinion sections of local, state, and national newspapers. If you find a piece expressing an opinion with which you strongly disagree, consider writing your persuasive essay in response to what you have read. To decide if the issue you find is a good one, ask yourself the following questions.

- Is the issue debatable? In other words, will people disagree about it?
- Do I have strong feelings about the issue?
- Would other people have strong feelings about the issue?

Here is one student's list of issues and responses to the evaluation questions above.

Issue	Is the issue debatable?	Do I have strong feelings about the issue?	Would other people have strong feelings about the issue?
banning students from wearing backpacks to class	Yes. Some people think banning them would make school safer, but some think it would cause students to go to class without everything they need.	Not really. I always leave my backpack in my locker.	Yes. When the principal mentioned banning them, many of my classmates complained.
starting a paper-recycling program at our school	Yes. Some people think recycling is too much trouble, but others think it is important.	Yes. I realize that what we do to the planet today affects it—and us—in the future.	Yes. Some of my friends are worried that we are destroying the planet.

PRACTICE & APPLY 1

Choose and Evaluate Your Issue

Brainstorm a list of issues. Then, make a chart like the one above to evaluate the issues. After reviewing the chart, choose a debatable issue that is important to you and that creates strong feelings in others.

State Your Opinion

Choosing Sides   Where do you stand on the issue you have chosen? **In a persuasive essay, your *thesis statement,* or opinion statement, should tell both the issue and your point of view on it.** Your thesis must be well-defined, coherent, and clear so your readers have no question about where you stand. Your thesis should also present a **focused** and **consistent** opinion, rather than appearing to support more than one point of view on the issue. Here is a formula for the thesis statement of a persuasive essay.

KEY CONCEPT

issue: starting a paper-recycling program at our school

+ point of view: We need to start one.

thesis statement: We should start a paper-recycling program at our school.

Reference Note

For more on writing a **thesis statement,** see page 763.

PRACTICE & APPLY 2   **Write Your Thesis Statement**

Keeping your persuasive purpose in mind, write a thesis statement on the issue you have chosen. Make sure that your thesis tells both your issue and your point of view on it.

Identify and Analyze Your Audience

To Whom It May Concern   Would you ever post a note to your best friend on a school bulletin board? Probably not. After all, in a note, you write with a specific person in mind. You use words and ideas that only that person would understand and appreciate. You should also write a persuasive essay with a specific group of people—your **audience**—in mind.

The student writing about starting a paper-recycling program at school answered the following questions to identify his audience.

Which groups of people would find my issue important? My classmates and teachers would find this issue important. Parents and other school employees might also be interested.

Which specific group do I want to convince? I want to convince students because they are the ones who would participate in the program.

 Writing **1.0** Students write focused essays. The writing exhibits students' awareness of audience. **1.1** Create compositions that have a coherent thesis.   **2.4a** Include a well-defined thesis (i.e., one that makes a clear and knowledgeable judgment).

To Know Them Is to Persuade Them Analyzing the audience you have identified is an important part of persuasion. **If you can identify what type of people make up your audience and what they care about, you can use this information to help you write a convincing essay.** The writer of the following example analyzed his audience by answering three simple questions.

Issue: starting a paper-recycling program at our school

Audience: my classmates

What type of people make up my audience? My classmates are all around my age. Many of them are involved in outdoor activities.

How does this group feel about the issue? I'm not sure how they will feel about starting a paper-recycling program, but I do know that most of my classmates care about the future of the environment.

What objections might this group have to my opinion? Students might not think recycling at our school will make a difference because our school is small. Also, some students might think that recycling is too much trouble.

PRACTICE & APPLY 8

Identify and Analyze Your Audience

Identify the audience for your persuasive essay by answering the questions on page 711. Then, analyze your audience by answering the questions in the above example.

Reference Note

For more on **developing support** for a thesis statement, see pages 756–758.

KEY CONCEPT

Evaluate and Support Reasons

The House That Logic Built A good persuasive essay is like a sturdy house: Both rely on strong support to stand. One way to build a strong persuasive essay is to speak to the reader's head, or common sense, by making a **logical appeal. A writer who makes a logical appeal uses reasons and evidence to support an opinion.** Addressing the reader's heart, a technique called **emotional appeal,** is also useful, but only as part of a mainly logical argument. Notice how the author of the article on pages 707–708 uses both kinds of appeals.

Writing 1.0 The writing exhibits students' awareness of audience.

Reasons A **reason** tells *why* a writer has a particular point of view. A writer who provides strong reasons and explanations shows that he or she has made a knowledgeable judgment about the issue. A writer who fails to give good reasons for a point of view will fail to convince the reader. You may have plenty of convincing reasons in mind already. If not, you can research resources such as the following to find reasons.

RESOURCES FOR PERSUASIVE SUPPORT

Resources for National Issues	Resources for Local Issues
major magazines	community leaders, school leaders, or other knowledgeable people
the national section of newspapers, especially the opinion section	local newspapers, especially the opinion section
national news programs	local news programs
general-interest Web sites	local or community Web sites
books and informational videos	books, pamphlets, or videos created by local agencies

To be convincing, each reason you choose must appeal to your audience. Below, one writer, addressing his classmates, listed and evaluated reasons for his school to start a paper-recycling program.

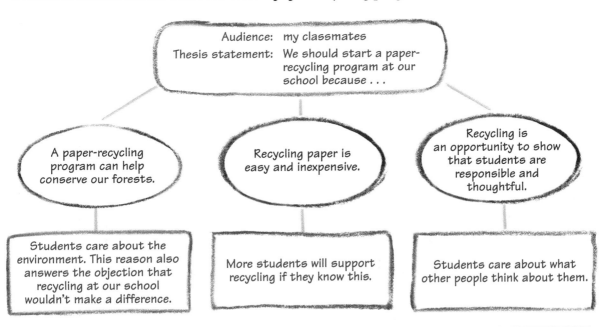

Writing **1.0** Essays contain supporting evidence. **2.4c** Provide details, reasons, and examples, arranging them effectively by anticipating and answering reader concerns and counterarguments.

TIP Answering an objection the audience might raise to your opinion can be very persuasive. As you write your reasons, try to think of these objections, or **counterarguments,** and incorporate answers to them in your essay. For example, a writer who supports a recycling program might expect the counterargument that recycling is too expensive. He or she could respond to that concern by showing that recycling paper is actually inexpensive.

Evidence Your audience will require strong evidence to make a decision. To provide such **evidence,** a persuasive writer uses *facts, statistics, examples, anecdotes, analogies, comparisons,* or *expert opinions* to back up his or her reasons. Giving strong evidence to back up each of your reasons will increase the odds that the reader will be persuaded to accept your point of view. Notice that the evidence (a statistic) in the following example makes the writer's reason more convincing. Also, notice that the writer provides a sentence that **elaborates** on the evidence by explaining how it supports the reason.

TIP The acronym **TREE** (Thesis, Reason, Evidence, Elaboration) can help you remember how to provide effective support for a persuasive essay.

Thesis Statement: We should start a paper-recycling program at our school.

Reason: A paper-recycling program can help conserve our forests.

Evidence: We use about six tons of paper a year at our school.

Elaboration: If we recycled that paper, we could save over one hundred trees a year.

Here are the major types of evidence that writers of persuasive essays typically use.

Reference Note

For more on **facts** and **opinions,** see page 57.

- **Facts** A **fact** is a statement that can be proved true, while an **opinion** is a statement of personal belief. For example, to say "It takes less energy to recycle aluminum than it does to produce it from raw material" is to state a fact. To say "People who do not recycle aluminum should have to pay fines" is to state an opinion.

- **Statistics** A **statistic** is information in number form. "Almost 25 percent of our students are vegetarian" is an example of a statistic.

- **Anecdotes and Examples** An **anecdote** is a brief story from the writer's experience that illustrates a point. An **example** is a specific instance that illustrates a general idea: "Many resources about endangered species are available. For example, the Web has many interesting and informative sites."

Writing 1.0 Essays contain supporting evidence. **2.4b** Present detailed evidence, examples, and reasoning to support arguments, differentiating between facts and opinion. **2.4c** Provide details, reasons, and examples, arranging them effectively by anticipating and answering reader concerns and counterarguments.

- **Analogies and Comparisons** An **analogy** compares two seemingly unlike actions, ideas, or things by pointing out a similarity between them: "Recycling paper is like fighting forest fires: both save trees." A **comparison** is more straightforward: "Recycling paper and using public transportation are effective ways to help the environment."

- **Expert Opinions** An **expert opinion** is the opinion of an authority on the subject. If you were writing about wildlife preservation, you might quote a person from a local wildlife refuge. Be sure that any opinions you use as support are the opinions of experts. Do not use your own opinions as evidence.

To find evidence to back up each of your reasons, you have many options. You can conduct a keyword search on an Internet search engine. Try visiting the library and searching by subject in either the card catalog or the online catalog. Look for books, pamphlets, and informational videos on your issue. You might also search newspapers and magazines for articles about your issue. Finally, draw on your own experience by listing anecdotes and examples relevant to your issue.

Designing Your Writing

Using Graphics to Illustrate Support Persuasive writers often represent evidence in visual form by using charts and graphs. Charts and graphs highlight information and can make it easier to understand. The following line graph supports the opinion that the study hall program at a school should be reinstated.

Mini-Workshop

See **Creating Charts, Maps, and Graphs,** pages 778–779.

When the study hall program was in place, the average grade in my class rose to 90 percent. After a grading period without the study hall, the average fell to 82 percent.

Study Hall Raises Grades

- grade
- study hall in effect

1st 2nd 3rd 4th
grading period

Writing **1.3** Support theses or conclusions with analogies, opinions from authorities, and comparisons. **1.4** Plan and conduct multi-step information searches. **2.0** The writing demonstrates the research strategies outlined in Writing Standard 1.0. **2.4b** Present detailed evidence, examples, and reasoning to support arguments, differentiating between facts and opinion.

PRACTICE & APPLY 4

Evaluate and Support Your Reasons

Brainstorm reasons for your opinion. Then, select the three reasons that would be most convincing to your audience. Finally, for each reason, find at least one piece of evidence from research or your own knowledge. Consider presenting some of this evidence in the form of a chart or graph.

Organize Your Support

Last But Not Least   A persuasive writer works hard to influence, or control, the audience's response. To develop your essay's **controlling impression,** you must organize reasons and evidence effectively. Often, each paragraph in a persuasive essay presents, supports, and elaborates on one reason. Therefore, you will need to consider the order in which to present your reasons.

One effective way to organize reasons in a persuasive essay is by **order of importance.** For instance, you might begin with your second strongest reason, then present your third strongest and so on. Finally, you can present your strongest reason to leave readers with a good final impression. You should create an informal outline to list your reasons and evidence in the order you choose.

Counterarguments   Remember to address counterarguments and work them into your reasons as effectively as possible. For example, begin a paragraph in which you discuss a reason with a statement of the counterargument to that reason. The student writing about paper recycling addressed an audience counterargument in this way: "Although some people believe paper recycling is too much trouble and too expensive, it is actually easy and inexpensive."

PRACTICE & APPLY 5   **Organize Your Support**

Decide on the order in which you will present your reasons, evidence, and elaboration. Then, create an informal outline to refer to when you write your draft. In parentheses, list counterarguments readers might have next to the reasons that answer them.

Writing **1.1** Create compositions that establish a controlling impression.   **2.0** The writing demonstrates a command of the organizational strategies outlined in Writing Standard 1.0.   **2.4c** Provide details, reasons, and examples, arranging them effectively by anticipating and answering reader concerns and counterarguments.

THE WRITER'S LANGUAGE

Using Parallel Structure and Repetition

Mismatched Parts A sentence that expresses related ideas in two different ways lacks *parallel structure*. Using **parallel structure** means that you use the same pattern of words to express closely-related ideas within a sentence. Parallel structure is one way to create **coherence,** or connectedness, within and among paragraphs.

Use parallel structure when you

- link coordinated ideas

> **Not parallel:** Wearing school uniforms can help students to save their money and boosting their self-esteem.
>
> **Parallel:** Wearing school uniforms can help students **to save their money and to boost their self-esteem.**

- compare or contrast ideas

> **Not parallel:** Requiring uniforms on the playing field is fine, but to require them in school seems unfair.
>
> **Parallel: To require uniforms** on the playing field is fine, but **to require them** in school seems unfair.

- link ideas with correlative conjunctions (*both . . . and, either . . . or, not only . . . but also*)

> **Not parallel:** School uniforms not only cost less than regular clothes but also for saving time in dressing.
>
> **Parallel:** School uniforms **not only cost less** than regular clothes **but also save time** in dressing.

Let Me Repeat . . . Another way to create coherence is to use **repetition.** For example, you can repeat a word or words—especially in the same sentence position—to show your reader how all of your ideas are connected to one big idea.

> **Uniforms are** easy on your budget. They will save you money and time. **Uniforms are** the answer to many students' problems.

Take another look at the last paragraph of "Should Public School Students Wear Uniforms?" on page 708. Notice that the writer uses parallel structure to explain the benefits of uniforms.

PRACTICE

Revise the following paragraph, using parallel structure and repetition to create coherence among the ideas. Explain your revisions.

> The benefits of peer-tutoring are clear. Students who work in tutoring sessions with their classmates tend to get better grades, feel more confident in class, and developing lasting friendships. As peer-tutors, students both learn the subject matter well and to discover how much they really know. The point of peer-tutoring is not only to learn a subject but also learning how to study. Acquiring good study habits is the key to lifelong success.

Writing 1.2 Establish coherence within and among paragraphs through parallel structures and similar writing techniques.

Writing

Persuasive Essay

Introduction

- Attention-grabbing beginning
- Thesis statement

Start with an **interesting beginning,** such as a question or a surprising fact, to get your readers' attention. Let your readers know what your issue and point of view are by including a well-defined **thesis statement.** (For more on writing **introductions,** see page 763.)

Body

- Reason #1
  Evidence and elaboration
- Reason #2
  Evidence and elaboration
  and so on

In each paragraph, discuss a different reason.

- Arrange your reasons **in order of importance.**
- Be sure that your reasons and evidence reflect a **consistent point of view** (the one stated in the thesis). Address reader concerns or counterarguments.
- Use **transitional words** and **phrases** to give your essay **coherence** and make clear how evidence supports each reason. (For more on transitional words and phrases, see page 761.)

Conclusion

- Restatement of opinion
- Summary of reasons
- Call to action or closing statement

Restate your opinion in different words, and **summarize your reasons** in one or two sentences. Close your essay with a **call to action** that tells your readers what you want them to do or with a strong **closing statement.** (For more on writing **conclusions,** see page 764.)

 PRACTICE & APPLY 6 **Draft Your Persuasive Essay**

As you write the first draft of your persuasive essay, refer to the framework above and the following Writer's Model.

 Writing 1.0 Essays contain formal introductions, supporting evidence, and conclusions. **1.1** Create compositions that establish a controlling impression, have a coherent thesis, and end with a clear and well-supported conclusion. **1.2** Establish coherence through effective transitions. **2.0** The writing demonstrates the drafting strategies outlined in Writing Standard 1.0.

A Writer's Model

The final draft below closely follows the framework for a persuasive essay.

GO TO: go.hrw.com
KEYWORD: HLLA8 W-5
FOR: A Student Model

One Hundred Trees, Please

As you probably know, the paper we use for our schoolwork and notes to our friends is made from trees. To this, some might say, "So what? Paper must be cheap since it grows on trees." True, paper is inexpensive. However, the environmental cost of making new paper is quite high. We should start a paper-recycling program here at our school if we are truly serious about helping the environment and ourselves.

A paper-recycling program can help conserve our forests—forests filled with vital oxygen-producing trees. By decreasing our demand for trees, we can make a difference right here at our school. A ton of paper made from recycled material saves approximately seventeen trees. We use about six tons of paper each year at our school. If we recycled that paper, we could save over one hundred trees a year.

Although some people believe recycling paper is too much trouble and too expensive, it is actually easy and inexpensive. According to Marjorie Lamb, author of *2 Minutes a Day for a Greener Planet,* "saving paper is one of the easiest and most beneficial contributions we can make to our environment." Across town, North Lake Middle School started a paper-recycling program last year, and it has been a great success. In each classroom the teacher has a box for white paper. All the students have to do is throw white paper into the box and other trash into the regular trash can. The teacher's job is easy, too. At the end of the week, he or she simply sends a student to empty the box into one of the school's fifteen recycling containers. These containers, which are just trash cans marked "white paper only," cost the school only about $150. At the end of the week, the janitors take the recycling cans outside, where the city collects them at no charge. As you can see, for the cost of a few trash cans, we can start our own paper-recycling program.

INTRODUCTION
Attention-grabbing beginning

Counterargument addressed

Thesis statement

BODY
Reason #1

Elaboration

Statistic

Elaboration

Reason #2/Counter-argument addressed

Expert opinion

Anecdote

Elaboration

Fact

Elaboration

(continued)

Reason #3

Statistic

Example

Comparison
CONCLUSION

A student-supported paper-recycling program could also show that we, as students, are responsible and thoughtful. A recent survey that appeared in the school newspaper revealed that 58 percent of adults see teenagers as people who are mostly interested in dating and shopping. We are interested in these things, but we also understand the importance of issues like recycling. We know that what we do now affects the world we live in tomorrow. If we were not concerned about the future, we would not have organized a carnival last year to raise money for endangered whales. Young people are just as capable as adults of caring about serious issues.

Restatement of opinion and call to action

Summary of reasons

Closing statement

Scientists estimate that, in prehistoric times, forests covered about 60 percent of the earth's surface. Today, about 30 percent of the earth is covered with forests. Part of this problem is caused by our demand for new paper. I am not asking everyone to stop using paper. We need to use paper. What I *am* asking is that we do our part to help our environment and ourselves by starting a paper-recycling program. A recycling program is easy and inexpensive. It will not only make a difference, but will also provide a good opportunity for us to show that we care about the future of our planet. We can make a difference but only if we get this program started.

FUNKY WINKERBEAN reprinted with special permission of North America Syndicate, Inc.

Evaluate and Revise Content, Organization, and Style

Take a Second Look   To make your essay a finished piece, read it at least twice. In the first reading, check the content and organization of the essay. When you read it a second time, brush up its style by using the Focus on Sentences on page 723.

First Reading: **Content and Organization**   Use the following chart to edit the organization and content of your essay. Ask yourself the questions in the left-hand column. Then, to answer the questions, follow the suggestions in the middle column. Finally, to make needed revisions, follow the directions in the right-hand column.

Persuasive Essay: Content and Organization Guidelines

Evaluation Questions	▶ Tips	▶ Revision Techniques
❶ Does the introduction have a clear thesis statement?	▶ **Circle** the sentence that states the issue and the writer's point of view on it.	▶ If needed, **add** a thesis statement, or **revise** the thesis statement to make the point of view clearer.
❷ Do the paragraphs progress in order of importance?	▶ **Number** the paragraphs in order of importance.	▶ **Rearrange** the order of paragraphs, if necessary.
❸ Does the writer give reasons and evidence to support his or her opinion?	▶ **Put a star** next to each reason, and **highlight** the evidence for each reason.	▶ **Add** a reason, or **add** a fact, statistic, anecdote, example, analogy, comparison, or expert opinion to support a reason, if needed.
❹ Does all support back up a consistent point of view?	▶ **Draw a wavy line** under any sentence containing support for a different point of view than that expressed in the thesis.	▶ **Cut** any support that does not fit the point of view.
❺ Does the body include elaboration to clarify reasons or evidence? Are counterarguments addressed?	▶ Have a friend **put a box** around anything that does not make sense and **write** any counterarguments not addressed.	▶ **Elaborate** by adding explanations and addressing reader concerns.
❻ Does the conclusion restate the writer's opinion and/or include a call to action? Does it summarize the reasons?	▶ **Underline** the summary of reasons and restatement of opinion and/or call to action.	▶ If necessary, **add** a summary of reasons and a restatement of opinion and/or call to action.

Writing 1.6 Revise writing for appropriate organization and consistent point of view.

ONE WRITER'S REVISIONS The following is an early draft of the essay on pages 719–720.

add

A student-supported paper-recycling program could also show that we, as students, are responsible and thoughtful.
∧ A recent survey that appeared in the school newspaper revealed that 58 percent of adults see teenagers as people who are mostly interested in dating and shopping. We are interested in these things, but we also understand the im-

elaborate

portance of issues like recycling.∧ *We know that what we do now affects the world we live in tomorrow.*

PEER REVIEW

As you evaluate a peer's persuasive essay, ask yourself these questions.

- What is the writer's issue and point of view?
- What is the most convincing reason the writer presents? What makes it convincing?

Responding to the Revision Process

1. Why do you think the writer added a sentence to the beginning of the paragraph?

2. How does adding a sentence to the end of the paragraph improve it?

> **Second Reading: Style** Content and organization have to do with *what* you say and *where* you say it. Style, on the other hand, involves *how* you say it. The content and organization of your persuasive essay may be excellent; however, if your style is boring or lacks variety, you may end up putting the audience to sleep. One way to improve the style of your essay and keep your audience awake is to make sure that your sentences have a variety of beginnings.

Style Guidelines

Evaluation Question	▶ Tip	▶ Revision Technique
Do the sentences in the essay have a variety of beginnings?	▶ **Underline** the first four words of each sentence. Then, read each sentence beginning aloud to identify sentences with similar kinds of beginnings.	▶ **Rearrange** some of the sentences by moving a phrase or clause from the end of the sentence to the beginning.

Revising to Vary Sentence Beginnings

Using a variety of beginnings is one way to keep your audience's interest. When you revise your essay, look for places where you can move a *verbal phrase* or *adverb clause* from the end of a sentence to the beginning. A **verbal phrase** contains a verb but acts as an adjective, noun, or adverb. An **adverb clause** includes both a noun and a verb and modifies a verb, adjective, or adverb.

Focus on Sentences

ORIGINAL SENTENCE	REVISION STRATEGY	REVISED SENTENCE
Many people take showers instead of baths to save water.	Move the *verbal phrase* to the beginning.	To save water, many people take showers instead of baths.
We must change our habits if we want to preserve our natural resources.	Move the *adverb clause* to the beginning.	If we want to preserve our natural resources, we must change our habits.

ONE WRITER'S REVISIONS   The following revision is from an early draft of the essay on pages 719–720.

> We use about six tons of paper each year at our school.
>
> We could save over one hundred trees a year if we recy-
>
> cled that paper.

TIP   A verbal phrase or adverb clause that introduces a sentence is generally followed by a comma.

Responding to the Revision Process

How does this change add variety to this part of the essay?

Reference Note

For more information and practice on **phrases** and **clauses,** see Chapters 5 and 6 in the *Holt Handbook*.

PRACTICE & APPLY 7
Evaluate and Revise Your Persuasive Essay

Evaluate the content and organization of your essay by using the guidelines on page 721. Then, use the Focus on Sentences above to help you add variety to your sentences.

Written and Oral English Language Conventions 1.1 Use correct and varied sentence openings to present a lively and effective personal style.

Publishing

Proofread Your Essay

Reference Note

For more on **proof-reading,** see page 585.

Too Close to See   Have you ever lost something important, such as a key or a homework assignment? You look and look until someone says those words that make you feel silly: "Here it is, right in front of your face." Sometimes you get so close to something—be it a set of keys or an essay—that you cannot see it clearly. That is why it is important to have someone else, such as a friend or classmate, check your essay for mistakes. He or she might be able to find mistakes in grammar, usage, and punctuation that you have overlooked.

Grammar Link

Revising "There is/It is" Constructions

When giving evidence, persuasive writers sometimes use a sentence that begins with "There is," "There are," or "It is." These sentences have *delayed* or *lost subjects*. A **delayed subject** is one that comes too late in the sentence. A **lost subject** is one that is totally missing. Delayed or lost subjects can weaken the evidence in a persuasive essay.

Delayed: *There are* many doctors who say that exercise is important. [The true subject is *doctors.* Beginning the sentence with *There* weakens its focus.]

Better: Many doctors say that exercise is important.

Lost: *It is* believed that the hole in the ozone layer is getting larger. [The subject is lost. *Who* believes the hole in the ozone layer is getting larger?]

Better: *Scientists* believe that the hole in the ozone layer is getting larger.

PRACTICE

The following sentences have lost or delayed subjects. If the sentence has no subject, try to add one that makes sense. Write the revised sentences on your own paper.

1. It is known that it takes light from the sun about eight minutes to reach the earth.

2. It is felt by 32 percent of my classmates that the proposal should be adopted.

3. There are several researchers who credit the new drug with saving lives.

4. It is believed that the world's supply of fossil fuels will not last much longer.

5. There are many people who will vote against Proposition 22.

Reference Note

For more on **identifying subjects,** see pages 7 and 15 in the *Holt Handbook.*

Writing 2.0 The writing demonstrates a command of standard American English.

Publish Your Essay

Extra, Extra, Read All About It   Now that you have brainstormed, researched, written, and revised, it is time for your essay to do what it was meant to do—to persuade. Here are some ideas that will help you get your essay to your audience.

- Make a collection of persuasive essays for your school's library. Ask your classmates to submit their essays. Then, with the help of those who submitted essays, group the essays according to subject. For example, one group might include essays about environmental issues. Then, put the essays into a notebook, and make an index that lists the title, page number, and author of each essay.

- If you participate in a school publication, such as a literary magazine or a newspaper, try to get your essay published as an editorial in that publication.

- If you have a more specialized audience, such as baseball card collectors or Civil War history buffs, post your essay on a Web page that is related to your issue.

Reflect on Your Essay

Building Your Portfolio   Think about what you wrote and how you wrote it by answering the following questions.

- What reason in your essay was the strongest? Why do you think so?

- How did you find supporting evidence for your essay? Do you think finding evidence will be easier the next time you write an essay? Why or why not?

- Do you think your essay could have been more convincing to your audience? Why or why not?

- Did your essay achieve your purpose for writing? In what way?

PRACTICE & APPLY 8   **Proofread, Publish, and Reflect on Your Essay**

- Proofread your essay for grammar, mechanics, and usage mistakes.

- Publish your essay for your audience.

- Answer the Reflect on Your Essay questions. Write your responses, and consider placing them in your portfolio.

COMPUTER TIP

Use a spelling checker to find errors. However, because spelling checkers only show misspellings, you should also read your essay to find words often confused, such as *brake* and *break*. For more information and practice on **words often confused,** see pages 380–391 in the *Holt Handbook.*

Talk **Listen**

Giving and Evaluating a Persuasive Speech

WHAT'S AHEAD?

In this workshop you will give a persuasive speech. You will also learn how to

- adapt a persuasive essay for use as a speech
- practice a good speaking voice
- evaluate a persuasive speech and provide feedback

One way to convince others to accept your opinion is to give a persuasive speech. Since you have already written a persuasive essay, you might be tempted to read your essay out loud directly from the page. However, to give an effective persuasive speech, you will need to do much more than read your essay to your audience; you will need to deliver the most important points of your essay in a solid presentation that will grab your audience.

Adapt Your Persuasive Essay

As you review your essay to find material for your speech, use the following instructions to choose the most persuasive content.

TIP Before an audience can accept your opinion, they must see you as **credible,** or believable. To build credibility, tell the audience why the issue you are sharing is important to you. An honest explanation will help your audience understand your motives for speaking.

What Are You Saying? If your listening **audience** is different from your essay's audience, you will need to reconsider the content of your **message** to make sure that it relates to the listeners' backgrounds and interests. Consider what reasons, examples, and facts would appeal to those who will be listening. For example, if you are giving a speech to convince a group of parents to contribute to the creation of an art gallery in the school's hallways, you can connect with your audience by stressing the fact that the gallery would display the work of students—their children—not professionals. Making the content of your speech match your audience's backgrounds and interests will help you achieve your **purpose**—to persuade listeners that your opinion is the right one. For more information on identifying and analyzing your audience, see pages 711–712.

Listening and Speaking **1.0** Students deliver presentations that convey ideas clearly and relate to the background and interests of the audience. **1.3** Organize information to achieve particular purposes by matching the message to the audience and purpose. **2.4** Deliver persuasive presentations.

Put It in Its Place   Even the best message can get lost in rambling sentences and wandering ideas. To make sure your speech is **coherent**, or easily understood, be certain that all your ideas are clearly related, given in an order that makes sense, and connected with **transitional words** and **phrases.**

Reference Note

For more on **organizing ideas,** see page 716. For more on **transitional words** and **phrases,** see pages 760–761.

Once you have identified which pieces of support from your essay you intend to keep and which need to be changed to fit your listening audience, you can start organizing your speech notes. The first step in organizing is to identify the most important points and write brief sentences and phrases about those points on note cards or in an **outline.** Once you have your points listed on note cards, you can number them in the order you want to present them. The chart below provides you with suggestions on how to organize the different elements of a persuasive speech.

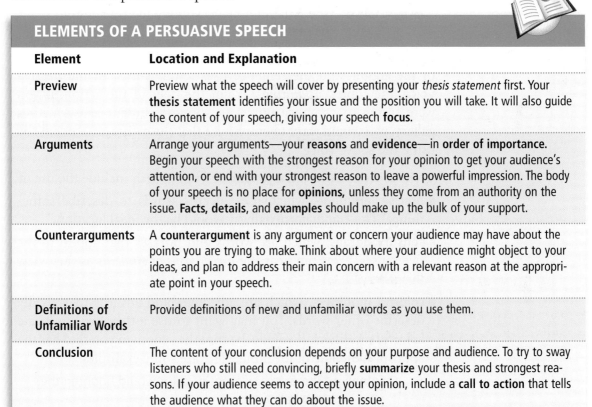

ELEMENTS OF A PERSUASIVE SPEECH	
Element	**Location and Explanation**
Preview	Preview what the speech will cover by presenting your *thesis statement* first. Your **thesis statement** identifies your issue and the position you will take. It will also guide the content of your speech, giving your speech **focus.**
Arguments	Arrange your arguments—your **reasons** and **evidence**—in **order of importance.** Begin your speech with the strongest reason for your opinion to get your audience's attention, or end with your strongest reason to leave a powerful impression. The body of your speech is no place for **opinions,** unless they come from an authority on the issue. **Facts, details**, and **examples** should make up the bulk of your support.
Counterarguments	A **counterargument** is any argument or concern your audience may have about the points you are trying to make. Think about where your audience might object to your ideas, and plan to address their main concern with a relevant reason at the appropriate point in your speech.
Definitions of Unfamiliar Words	Provide definitions of new and unfamiliar words as you use them.
Conclusion	The content of your conclusion depends on your purpose and audience. To try to sway listeners who still need convincing, briefly **summarize** your thesis and strongest reasons. If your audience seems to accept your opinion, include a **call to action** that tells the audience what they can do about the issue.

TIP   The audience's background may be different from yours. Even if you did not explain unfamiliar vocabulary in your essay, define words unfamiliar to your listeners to help them understand your opinion.

Listening and Speaking 1.4 Prepare a speech outline based on the chosen pattern of organization. **2.4a** Include a well-defined thesis.   **2.4b** Differentiate fact from opinion and support arguments with evidence, examples, and reasoning.   **2.4c**. Anticipate and answer listener concerns and counterarguments through details, reasons, examples, and other elements.

Say It and Mean It   Even though you will be speaking from note cards, rather than reading your essay word for word, there are probably some phrases and sentences that you will want to say just so. Make note of these phrases and sentences. As you do so, look for opportunities to replace dull, vague words with lively, precise language. Remember that even though your tone will be conversational, you must still use proper **grammar** and **standard American English** to show your listeners you are serious.

> **TIP**   One way to detect overuse of the passive voice is to look for *be* verbs in your essay. Try to replace most *be* verbs with **action verbs**.

Voice   One of the most important ways to make your speech more forceful is to use the *active voice* rather than the *passive voice*. To understand active and passive voice, read the two sentences below.

Passive Voice: Many beautiful paintings **were created** by our school's students.

Active Voice: Our school's students **created** many beautiful paintings.

In the **active voice,** the subject of the sentence *(students)* is the doer of the action, and the sentence uses fewer words. In the **passive voice,** the subject *(paintings)* is not the doer of the action. If you were trying to convince others to support student artists with a gallery, you would want to emphasize that the artists are students by using the active voice.

Vivid Words   Other ways to enliven your speech include the use of

- **precise language,** which uses specific words to describe something. "The *empty north* hallway would be the ideal location."

- **sensory details,** which are words and phrases that appeal to the five senses. "You can hear the *awed gasps of students* as they view the gallery."

- **colorful modifiers,** which are adjectives and adverbs that vividly describe other words. You may want to use a thesaurus to locate colorful modifiers. If you do, be sure the synonym you find has the appropriate shade of meaning. Here are some examples.

Original: "The *bright* splashes of color would brighten the drab hall."

Inappropriate: "The *lurid* splashes of color would brighten the drab hall." [means "glaring"]

Appropriate: "The *intense* splashes of color would brighten the drab hall." [means "vivid"]

Listening and Speaking **1.3** Organize information to achieve particular purposes by matching the vocabulary to the audience and purpose.   **1.5** Use precise language, action verbs, sensory details, appropriate and colorful modifiers, and the active rather than the passive voice in ways that enliven oral presentations.   **1.6** Use appropriate grammar and word choice during formal presentations.

Deliver Your Persuasive Speech

Since the purpose of your speech is to persuade others, your **delivery,** or *how* you give the speech, is critical. Even a speech with not-so-strong content can be successful if the speaker presents it well.

Be a Smooth Talker   Would you accept someone's opinion if he or she did not look at you, spoke too quietly, and generally did not seem prepared? To ensure that *your* speech runs smoothly, practice giving your speech more than once. Keep the following suggestions in mind when practicing your speech.

- **If possible, practice in front of an audience** so that you can get used to speaking in front of a group.
- **Practice using your note cards** just as you will use them on the day of your speech.
- **Use a timer or watch** to ensure that you stay within a certain time if your teacher has given you a time limit.
- **Review the evaluation guidelines on page 731** before practicing. Knowing what your audience will be evaluating as you present will help you prepare.

Speak Up!   A good speaking voice is another factor that can determine how persuasive your audience finds you. The chart below shows important elements of good delivery and gives guidelines and tips on how to practice using them.

ELEMENTS OF GOOD SPEECH DELIVERY

Element	Guidelines	Practice Tips
Enunciation	Speak clearly and carefully so that your words are easy to understand.	If you practice in front of an audience, ask them if there were words or sentences they could not understand. Remember these trouble spots when you deliver the real speech.
Volume	Speak loudly enough so the people in the back of the room can hear you.	Ask your practice audience if they can hear you. Adjust your volume accordingly.
Eye Contact and Facial Expressions	Make eye contact with the audience rather than looking down at your notes all the time. Make sure your facial expressions match the message you are giving.	If no one is available to watch you rehearse, practice looking at items in the room, such as chairs. Watch your expressions in a mirror, or record your speech on a videotape.

(continued)

Listening and Speaking 1.6 Use appropriate enunciation and pace during formal presentations.

Pace	Speak slowly so your audience can keep up with what you are saying. Pause after a major point to give the audience time to think about what you have said.	On the day of your actual speech, you may tend to speak faster than you expect. Concentrate on speaking at a slow and comfortable pace.
Tone	Match your word choice and the sound of your voice to your audience and purpose. Show the right amount of feeling, but without nagging or whining.	Watch your audience's expressions and gestures. If they are slumped down, looking around, or frowning, you may need to adjust your tone.
Voice Modulation	Emphasize certain words or sentences by **modulating,** or changing, the pitch and volume of your voice—louder or softer, higher or lower—to make your point.	Ask your practice audience if they remember key words or ideas you particularly wanted to emphasize. If not, practice making your vocal expression on those words or ideas more memorable.

Give and Take   **Feedback** from your audience will help you improve your speech. A **verbal cue,** such as a question from an audience member, is an obvious way to receive feedback. However, keep an eye out for **nonverbal cues** as well. As you give your speech, watch for audience members looking around, frowning, or giving quizzical looks. When you notice these types of cues, you will need to adjust your speech to recapture your audience's attention.

■ For example, a distracted audience may respond to a change in your **vocal expression.** Stating an important idea in a loud whisper before repeating it might catch their attention, or you might include a dramatic pause at an important point.

■ Although you may have planned to give your strongest reason last, an audience not already on your side may be convinced if you **modify the organization** of your speech to present a stronger reason earlier.

■ A confused audience may simply need for you to slow down your pace or to **rearrange words and sentences** to make a point clear. Because listeners cannot re-read information they do not at first understand, explain complicated ideas in short, simple sentences and define any terms your audience may not know.

If circumstances such as a time limit keep you from modifying your speech on the spot, be sure you jot down changes you need to make in case you have the opportunity to deliver your speech a second time.

Listening and Speaking **1.3** Organize information to achieve particular purposes by matching the voice modulation, expression, and tone to the audience and purpose. **1.7** Use audience feedback (e.g., verbal and nonverbal cues). **1.7a** Reconsider and modify the organizational structure or plan. **1.7b** Rearrange words or sentences to clarify the meaning. **2.4d** Maintain a reasonable tone.

Listen to and Evaluate a Persuasive Speech

To evaluate a persuasive essay, you have to consider not only the words on the page but also the source. Who is the writer of the essay? What is his or her interest in the topic? You must ask these same questions when evaluating a speech.

What's the Catch?   Before you evaluate a classmate's persuasive speech, keep in mind that most persuasive speakers have a **bias,** or a strong leaning toward a particular point of view. A speaker who reveals the reasons for his or her bias can seem more credible than one who does not. A speaker who does not reveal a bias may have a *hidden agenda.* A **hidden agenda** is a secret reason for speaking. For example, a speaker trying to convince classmates to establish an art gallery in the hallways may not tell his audience that he is really trying to make sure *his* artwork is displayed.

Are You Listening?   To evaluate a speech effectively, you must be a good listener. As you listen, take notes on the speaker's content, delivery, and credibility by answering the questions in the chart below.

QUESTIONS FOR EVALUATING A PERSUASIVE SPEECH	
Content	• What is the **purpose** of the presentation? Paraphrase the speaker's purpose. • What is the topic? Paraphrase the speaker's **point of view** on the topic. Does the speaker clearly state his or her opinion? • Which reasons are convincing and which are not? How are the reasons supported?
Delivery	• Describe the speaker's tone. Is it conversational or does it sound too formal? • Does the speaker speak loudly and slowly enough? • How often does the speaker make eye contact with the audience? • How do the speaker's nonverbal messages (such as gestures and facial expressions) match the verbal message? Are any of the gestures distracting? In what way are they distracting?
Credibility (Believability)	• What is the speaker's bias? How do you know? • What facts has the speaker used to support his or her opinion? • Does the speaker have unsupported opinions? What are they?

Listening and Speaking 1.0 Students evaluate the content of oral communication.   **1.2** Paraphrase a speaker's purpose and point of view.   **1.8** Evaluate the credibility of a speaker (e.g., hidden agendas, slanted or biased material).

An Overwhelming Response To help give the speaker feedback after the speech, ask **relevant questions,** questions that relate to the speaker's topic. Your questions should address the content of the speech, the speaker's delivery, and the overall purpose. A student listening to a speech that supported an art gallery in the hallways asked the following relevant questions.

Content: "Could you explain what you meant when you said all students deserve a place to hang their artwork?"

Delivery: "From your tone, I could tell that the art teacher is also excited about the students' art. Will she support a student gallery?"

Purpose: "I understand your main point to be that the empty hall needs brightening up, and the student gallery is the best use of the space. Am I correct?"

PRACTICE & APPLY 9 **Give and Evaluate a Persuasive Speech**

- Adapt your persuasive essay for use as a persuasive speech, and deliver your speech to your classmates.

- Then, use the chart on page 731 to evaluate a classmate's speech. Provide feedback by asking the speaker relevant questions.

PEANUTS Reprinted with permission of United Feature Syndicate

Listening and Speaking 1.0 Students evaluate the content of oral communication. 1.2 Ask relevant questions concerning the speaker's content, delivery, and purpose. 2.0 Students deliver formal presentations employing traditional rhetorical strategies (e.g., persuasion). Student speaking demonstrates the organizational and delivery strategies in Listening and Speaking Standard 1.0.

Persuasive Images in the Media

People create images for the same reasons they write: to provide information, perhaps in a technical diagram; to express themselves or be creative, as in fine art; or to persuade, as in many media images. Just as you used certain writing techniques to make your Writing Workshop essay more persuasive, people who create media images can use a set of visual techniques to make their images more persuasive. In this workshop you will learn about some of these techniques and evaluate how people who create **still,** or motionless, images use them. Be aware, though, that moving images such as television commercials and movies also use these techniques.

WHAT'S AHEAD

In this workshop you will interpret persuasive media images. You will also learn how to

- **identify techniques used by illustrators, photographers, and graphic artists**
- **explain the ways media images can be used to persuade viewers**

Persuasive Images

When you look at a photograph of yourself, what do you see? You see yourself, right? Actually, the person in the picture is not the *real* you, but a representation of you. In fact, all media images are representations of reality that can shape people's ideas about the world. That is why you need to be a critical viewer of media images. To view images critically, consider these ideas.

- **All images are created by people.** Image makers, from illustrators to photographers to graphic designers, make conscious choices about what an image will show and how it will show it.

- **An image is one person's version of reality.** An image reflects the point of view of the person who created it. When you see an image, consider other points of view people might have about the image's subject.

Listening and Speaking 1.9 Interpret and evaluate the various ways in which visual image makers (e.g., graphic artists, illustrators, news photographers) communicate information and affect impressions and opinions.

People who create all sorts of media images can use *content, color, light and shadow,* and *point of view* to make their images more persuasive.

Content The **content** of an image is what it shows—everything included in the image. The way an image maker chooses to portray a subject is the most important persuasive choice he or she will make. For example, an illustrator may choose to present a subject as comical or serious.

Look at the two images of scientist Albert Einstein shown below. The image on the left is a caricature of Einstein which presents him as a comical figure. The oil painting on the right, on the other hand, portrays Einstein as wise, not humorous. The two images reflect the different purposes of the artists who created them.

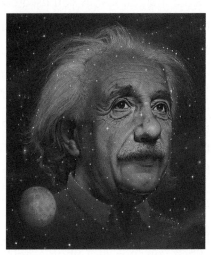

TIP If you had seen only one of the portraits to the right, how would you feel about Einstein? What opinion would you have of this scientist and of his life's work?

You might think a news photographer has little choice about how to present a subject. However, a photographer may choose to capture the subject of a photo during an awkward moment or wait until the subject is prepared. The photographer who photographs the President tripping over an electrical cable will communicate a very different message than the one who shoots a posed portrait of the President.

The other items in an image are also carefully chosen. An image maker may choose to include **persuasive symbols,** such as a bald eagle or an American flag. He or she may also add to a persuasive message by choosing to leave out certain things. For example, although President Franklin Roosevelt used a wheelchair, many portraits depict him from the waist up in order to leave out the wheelchair.

Color   Image makers use **color** to create interest or to establish a mood. To create interest, an illustrator may use color to highlight the most important part of the image—by using a brighter color in that part of the image, for example. A photographer may use a computer, colored pencils, or paints to color one part of a black-and-white photograph to make it stand out.

To create mood, illustrators may use **cool** colors, such as blues and greens, to make viewers feel calm or relaxed, or **warm** colors, such as reds and yellows, to make viewers feel energized. Photographers can choose black-and-white film to create a dramatic or old-fashioned mood or color film for a more realistic mood.

Light and Shadow   Image makers can choose to create areas of **light** and **shadow** in their work. An image maker may carefully place shadows to make a subject look frightening or dramatic or romantic. Using plenty of even light with few or no shadows can make the subject look real and approachable. Sometimes photographers have to work with the light they have.

Point of View, or Angle   The **angle** at which you see the subject of an image can affect your impression of the subject. For example, seeing a subject from a direct angle may not affect your impression of it, but seeing it from above or below a normal angle can change your impression.

Look at the examples below. In the picture on the left, the photographer stood on a ladder and shot the picture looking down at the boy. Do you see how the boy looks small and vunerable? Now, look at the picture on the right taken from a low angle looking up at the same boy. From this angle the boy looks big and powerful, even a little intimidating.

TIP   News photographers may have little control over the light in photos taken at the scene of a news event. At best, they may be able to add light to some subjects using a flash.

News photographers may also have little choice of angle. For example, a photographer in a helicopter can usually get only a high-angle shot of the subject, unless the subject is also up in the air, such as a balloonist or a bird.

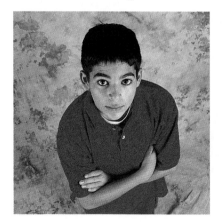

Medium

TIP The plural of *medium* is **media,** a term often applied to television, radio, newspapers, and the Internet.

A **medium** is the means by which an image is created. All image makers use the techniques explained on pages 734–735, but each still medium—illustration and photography—also has its own unique characteristics and techniques.

Illustration An **illustration** is a picture created to explain something or to share a point of view. Drawings, cartoons, paintings, and computer-generated art are examples of illustrations. Each type of illustration lends itself to a different type of persuasive message.

- A **drawing** may create a serious but informal mood, communicating reflectiveness or thoughtfulness.
- A **cartoon** also creates an informal mood, but a more lighthearted, humorous one than a drawing.
- Because **paintings** are more formal than other types of illustrations, they can make their subjects seem more serious.
- **Computer-generated art** may mimic any of the techniques above, or it may create a fun, modern mood.

Which of these types of illustration do you think would work well in an ad for a video arcade? on a health food label? Why?

Photography Photographs are powerful partners to the written and spoken word. In a newspaper, for instance, you might read about an erupting volcano. Only when you see the picture that accompanies the article would you fully understand the massive destruction the volcano caused. Because photographs are so powerful and easy to reproduce, they are a popular medium, especially when they are used with the written word, as in newspapers and magazines.

The persuasive power of photographs is found in our belief that "photographs do not lie"—that they show reality. However, like illustrations, photographs only *resemble* an actual person, place, thing, or event. You should be aware that people can change or influence the information a photograph provides. As a photograph is being taken, a photographer can, under the right circumstances, use camera angle or lighting to alter the reality of a situation to suit his or her persuasive purposes. Even after developing a photo, a photographer can **crop,** or cut out, an unwanted part of a scene to make the image more persuasive.

Look at the following examples. In the image to the right, the photographer cropped in tight around a group of people at a baseball game. By cutting out the context—the empty seats around the group—the photographer created the illusion of a large crowd, even though you can see in the left-hand image that few fans actually attended the game.

Graphic Design

Graphic designers, or graphic artists, may use illustrations, photographs, or both to create a persuasive message. They may design promotional displays and marketing brochures for products or services. They may also develop the overall layout and design of magazines, newspapers, Web sites, and books like this one.

Part of a graphic designer's job is to arrange images and text in a way that grabs viewers' attention and persuades them to buy a product. A designer also selects *type* to add to a persuasive message.

Type   **Type** refers to the characters—letters and other symbols—in a printed text. A **font** is a set of characters of a certain size and design. For example, 12-point Courier is a font. The **font size** is 12 points (about $\frac{1}{6}$ of an inch in height), and the name of the **font design** is Courier. A graphic designer may choose a **font style** such as **boldface** (thick, heavy type) or *italics* (slanted type) to call attention to important information.

Just as color choices can tap into viewers' emotions, fonts and font styles can create a specific mood. Look at the following examples of fonts. Which font do you think would better persuade people to buy the fashion magazine by connecting a feeling of elegance to the magazine's title? Why?

DO THIS

Elegance Magazine   Elegance Magazine

Quick guide

Evaluate Media Images

To interpret and evaluate a media image, either still or moving, consider the following questions.

QUESTIONS FOR EVALUATING MEDIA IMAGES

General Questions	• Who created the image? Do I know of a bias this source has—either positive or negative feelings toward the subject? Does this bias affect the message?
	• For what purpose was this image created?
Questions About Content	• What impression do I get from the image about its subject? Why?
	• How is this version of reality similar to or different from what I know from my own experience?
	• Does the image include any persuasive symbols?
	• What may have been left out of the image?
Questions About Color	• Is the image black-and-white, color, or both? What mood do the color choices create?
	• What parts of the image stand out because of color? Why might these parts be important?
Questions About Light and Shadow	• Is the light in the image even, or are there shadows?
	• What mood do the light and shadows create? Do shadows make the subject seem frightening or dramatic? What message does this send?
Questions About Point of View	• At what angle do you see the subject? a normal, direct angle? an angle above the subject? a low angle?
	• What impression of the subject does the angle give you? Does the subject seem powerful? vulnerable?
Questions About Medium	• What medium carries the image?
	• How do the characteristics of the medium add to the image's persuasive power?

PRACTICE & APPLY 10 **Interpret Persuasive Media Images**

In a small group, look through magazines and newspapers for examples of persuasive media techniques. Find at least one example each of content, color, light and shadow, point of view, and medium. Discuss the images you found. Prepare a short oral presentation sharing the three strongest examples the group found, each of a different technique. Explain how the examples use the three techniques to persuade viewers.

DIRECTIONS: Read the following passage from a draft of a persuasive essay. Then, read the questions that follow the passage. Choose the best answer to each question, and mark your answers on your own paper.

> The train tracks that run through our town have gone unused for years. The rail line could be turned into a protected bikeway through town. Unlike other proposals, including using the tracks for a steam train, this proposal will reduce traffic and pollution. It also will cost much less to create a bikeway than to purchase a steam engine. Most important, a bikeway will give children a safe place to ride their bicycles and will encourage more people who live and work in our town to commute using bicycles rather than cars. The resulting decrease in pollution will improve air quality for all of our citizens, whether they actually use the bikeway or not.

1. Which of these statements would be a clear thesis for the passage?
   A I have an idea I think you will like.
   B The best solution is to turn the rail line into a bikeway.
   C This abandoned rail line is nothing but trouble, and should be removed.
   D Using bicycles to commute can decrease air pollution.

2. Which of the following pieces of evidence would best support the statement that building a bikeway would be less expensive than other options?
   F dollar estimates from city planners of the costs of both options
   G a graph showing how increasing bicycle use can decrease pollution
   H a list of other towns in the region that have created bikeways
   J a comparison of the cost of a bicycle to the cost of a car

3. Which of the following statements is a fact which supports the writer's opinion?
   A Everyone I know thinks the tracks are ugly and need to be removed.
   B A steam train is not as important to our town as a bikeway.

   C Without this bikeway, pollution will continue to increase.
   D Sixty percent of citizens surveyed want a safe place for riding bikes.

4. How might the writer address the concern that maintaining a bikeway will be expensive?
   F by explaining that the beauty of the community outweighs the money
   G by proposing that routine maintenance be done by volunteers
   H by pointing out the high costs of other proposals
   J by telling readers that this concern will be addressed later

5. If you were listening to the passage above during a persuasive speech, you would expect the speaker to
   A show no emotion at all and make no gestures, to appear more reasonable
   B exclude most evidence from his or her written composition, to keep the audience involved
   C back the thesis with opinions, to make a connection with the audience
   D address the audience's concerns based on their backgrounds and interests

Writing for Life

"When are we ever going to use this?" Though you may not realize it, much of what you learn in school will have a direct effect on your life beyond school. This is especially true of writing. Being able to write clearly and correctly will help you achieve many goals, from landing the perfect job to getting a refund for a defective CD player.

You might be surprised to find out how many career fields involve writing. You will even need good writing skills in order to apply for a job in which writing is not essential, such as the position of a store clerk. Beyond the world of work, writing will help you get your point across more effectively. For example, most companies will take your requests for information, complaints about poor service or defective merchandise, and compliments about good employees more seriously if you write your ideas down, rather than simply make a phone call.

In this workshop you will learn to write letters and fill out forms related to career development. In the process you will practice these language arts standards.

GO TO: go.hrw.com
KEYWORD: HLLA8 W-6
FOR: Models, Writer's
Guides, and Reference
Sources

California Standards

Writing

1.2 Establish coherence within and among paragraphs through effective transitions and similar writing techniques.

1.6 Revise for word choice, appropriate organization, and transitions between paragraphs, passages, and ideas.

2.0 Student writing demonstrates a command of standard American English.

2.5 Write documents related to career development, including simple business letters and job applications:

  a. Present information purposefully and succinctly and meet the needs of the intended audience.

  b. Follow the conventional format for the type of document (e.g., letter of inquiry, memorandum).

Business Writing

The world outside of school often involves writing. Here are some examples of writing tasks that you, as a middle or junior-high school student, may encounter.

- writing a letter to your CD club explaining that they sent the wrong disc
- composing an e-mail memo to the pep rally decoration committee, letting them know about a poster-painting session
- filling out an application for employment as a volunteer elementary school tutor

Writing business letters and memos and filling out job applications are part of life, and you will likely use them at some point. You will be much more successful in life if you can do them well.

WHAT'S AHEAD

In this workshop you will write a business letter and a memo and complete a job application. You will also learn how to

- distinguish among types of business letters
- format letters and memos correctly
- present ideas succinctly
- compile information for job applications

Business Letters

Get the Word Out A **business letter** is a formal letter, usually sent to someone you do not know, written for a specific reason. There are several types of business letters.

Letters of Inquiry Letters that request something are called **letters of inquiry.** These letters often ask the recipient to provide answers. You might write a letter of inquiry to ask how to participate in an activity or group, to order a product or service, to inquire about a job or volunteer position, or to request information on a person or topic you are researching.

Job Application Letters When you look for a summer or after-school job, a *job application letter* can give you an edge over the competition. In a **job application letter,** you respond to an advertisement for a job and tell your potential employer why he or she should hire you. For some jobs you may simply need to talk to the employer or

Writing 2.5 Write documents related to career development, including simple business letters and job applications.

fill out an application form. However, writing a letter to apply for a job gives you the opportunity to go into detail about your skills and experience and makes you appear more serious about the position.

Letters of Complaint Suppose you ordered a CD by your favorite group. When the package arrived in the mail, though, you opened it to find an instructional language CD on beginning Hungarian. To make sure you eventually got what you ordered, you could write a *letter of complaint.* A **letter of complaint** explains a problem and requests a response that will solve the problem.

Letters of Commendation A **letter of commendation** is usually written to let an employee's supervisor know how helpful that person was to you. For example, if you were searching for information for a school research report, perhaps the librarian at your community library took extra time to show you how to search the Internet, the *Readers' Guide to Periodical Literature,* and the vertical file. You might return the favor by singing his praises in a letter to the library's director.

Thank-You Letters You have probably written a thank-you note for a gift given to you by a relative. To express your appreciation to someone you do not know well—a volunteer coordinator or an adult who came to speak to your class, for instance—you would write a more formal version of the familiar thank-you note. A **thank-you letter** is written directly to a person who has done something you appreciate.

Getting Down to Business All types of business letters generally include the following parts.

PARTS OF A BUSINESS LETTER

Heading	Your address and the date
Inside Address	Name and address of the person to whom you are writing
Salutation	Your greeting, such as "Dear Mr. Meyers:"
Body	Your message
Closing	A word or phrase that closes your letter, such as "Sincerely," or "Respectfully,"
Signature	Your name signed in your handwriting, followed by your name either typed or printed

Writing 2.5b Follow the conventional format for the type of document (e.g., letter of inquiry).

Body of Information The body of the letter is where you express your message. When writing the body, you must take into account many *variables*. A **variable** is an element that varies, or changes, depending on the situation. In a letter, your *purpose*—for example, whether you are requesting information or expressing thanks—is one variable. The *audience*, the person or people who will read the letter, is another. To achieve your purpose, the body of your letter must have a **logical sequence**, or a predictable order, that helps your audience understand your message.

Purpose The most important variable in a business letter is the **purpose**, or reason, for which you are writing. Each of the types of letters explained on pages 741–742 has a different purpose. The following chart identifies the purposes and provides tips for writing each type of business letter.

PURPOSES OF BUSINESS LETTERS

Type of Letter and Purpose	Tips
Letter of Inquiry—to ask for information or to request a product or service	**Clearly state what you need.** For example, if you want to volunteer at a local animal shelter, your letter of inquiry should request information about available positions and shifts.
Job Application Letter—to provide information	**Include all the important details.** For example, share information that demonstrates that you are dependable and shows why you are interested in the job or volunteer opportunity.
Letter of Complaint—to persuade the reader to take a specific action	**Give specific, relevant information about the problem, and make clear exactly what you expect the reader to do about it.** Writing a brief, polite explanation of the situation will help your reader understand why action is needed.
Letter of Commendation or Thank-You Letter—to express gratitude	**Be specific and sincere.** For example, in a thank-you letter to a person who has spoken to your class, include both the date of the talk and an explanation of why it was important to you.

Audience The second variable in your letter is your **audience,** the person or people to whom you are writing. A letter to the president of the United States would sound quite different from a letter to your favorite music artist. The difference between the letters would be the **tone,** the attitude and feelings that you reveal through your choice of words and the way you handle the subject. All business letters should use **standard American English,** the kind of English used

Writing 2.0 Student writing demonstrates a command of standard American English.

in textbooks and on newscasts. However, your letter may have a formal tone when you write to the president or a less formal tone when you write to a musician. Although both of the following sentences use standard American English to thank someone, notice the difference in tone between the two.

MORE FORMAL   I appreciate the time you are taking to fulfill this request.

LESS FORMAL   Thanks for your help.

Logical Sequence To help your reader understand the ideas in your letter, you must present them in a **logical sequence,** or a predictable order. If you are explaining how your telephone broke a month after you bought it, it is logical to explain the events in **chronological order,** or the order in which they happened in time. If you are sharing your experience and skills in a letter inquiring about a job or volunteer opportunity, a logical sequence would be **order of importance,** moving from the most relevant, or important, information to less important facts about yourself. Notice that even the least important qualification in the following notes for a job application letter still relates directly to the volunteer position for which the student is applying.

Reference Note

For more information on **order,** see page 760.

Qualifications for a volunteer position at an animal shelter

<u>Most important</u>   I have two dogs and a cat of my own.

<u>Somewhat important</u>   I have extra time after school to spend with the animals.

<u>Least important</u>   I need volunteering credits to be eligible for Student Council.

Reference Note

For more on **coherence,** see page 760.

Using a logical sequence will help give your letter *coherence.* **Coherence** is a clear connection among all of the ideas in your writing. The sequence of ideas in your letter and the way you move from one thought to the next will determine how well your reader understands your message. If your thoughts jump from one idea to another, the reader will get lost and your letter will not get the results

Writing 1.2 Establish coherence within and among paragraphs.

you want. To keep your readers on track, use appropriate **transitional words** and **phrases,** such as *for instance, however,* and *mainly,* to connect one paragraph to another, one idea to another.

All Together   The Thinking It Through steps below will guide you through the process of writing a well-organized body of a business letter.

THINKING IT THROUGH

Preparing the Body of a Business Letter

STEP 1   **Determine the purpose of your letter.**
I want to request information about volunteering opportunities at the animal shelter.

STEP 2   **Jot down notes about the relevant information you will include in your letter.**
I can work after school. I enjoy working with both dogs and cats. I need to get official credit for my hours for Student Council.

STEP 3   **Determine the audience of your letter and decide how formal the tone should be.**
The audience is the director of the animal shelter. I want her to see that I'm mature enough to work responsibly with animals, so the tone of the letter should be formal.

STEP 4   **Organize the information into a logical sequence by writing down the information in order of importance or in chronological order.**
I'll use order of importance. First, I will explain my love of cats and dogs to show that I will be an enthusiastic volunteer. Then, I will tell the hours I can work to help the director decide where I will fit in at the shelter. Finally, I'll tell her about the credit, which will let her know that I plan to work all of my assigned hours.

STEP 5   **Write the body, creating complete sentences from your notes in the order that you chose.**

STEP 6   **Revise your letter. Make sure the transitions between paragraphs and ideas are clear, creating a logical sequence. Also, ensure that the words you have chosen match your audience and tone.**

Writing   **1.2** Establish coherence within and among paragraphs through effective transitions.
1.6 Revise for word choice, appropriate organization, and transitions between paragraphs, passages, and ideas.

Read the following letter of request, and answer the questions at the top of page 747.

Heading

4804 Homestead Drive
Rancho Dominguez, CA 90220
September 6, 2003

Inside Address

Amelia Worthy
A Friend Indeed Animal Shelter
5602 Main Street
Rancho Dominguez, CA 90220

Salutation

Dear Ms. Worthy:

Body

I have loved animals all my life. My dogs Daisy and Jake and my cat Hugo are my favorite companions, and all of them came from unwanted litters. Because of my desire to help animals that do not have homes, I would like to request information about volunteer positions at your animal shelter.

I could work at the shelter any time after school from 3:30 to 6:00 P.M. and occasionally on weekends. A bonus of helping at the shelter would be that I could earn the volunteer credits I need to join my school's Student Council next year. With this incentive, you know I will be prompt and reliable.

Please send me information about any positions or opportunities you have available. I have included a self-addressed, stamped envelope, or you can call me at 555-0118 after 3:30 P.M. Thank you.

Closing

Sincerely,

Signature

Leticia Redmond

Leticia Redmond

In a small group, discuss the following questions. Then, present your group's responses orally to the class.

1. How did the information in the body of the letter fulfill the writer's purpose?

2. How did the sequence of the letter help the reader understand the information?

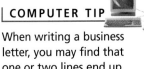

COMPUTER TIP

When writing a business letter, you may find that one or two lines end up on a second page. You can use the margins feature to adjust your margins until the entire letter fits on one page. This feature can sometimes be found in the format menu under the heading *page setup* or *document layout.* Remember, though, that you should maintain a minimum margin of one inch on all sides of the paper.

Designing Your Writing

Business Letter Formats   Formatting your letter in a standard way will add to your credibility with your reader. The two most common formats for business letters are *block style* and *modified block style*. In a **block style** letter, all information starts at the left margin of the page and paragraphs are not indented. In a **modified block style** letter, the heading, closing, and signature align with an imaginary line just right of the center. Look at the examples below. Whichever format you choose for your letters, be sure to use it consistently.

Block Style

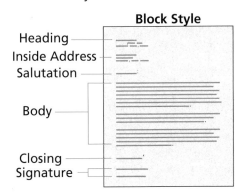

Heading
Inside Address
Salutation

Body

Closing
Signature

Modified Block Style

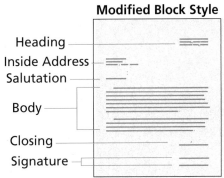

Heading
Inside Address
Salutation

Body

Closing
Signature

You should also follow these guidelines for all formal letters.

- Use only one side of unlined, full-size (8-1/2" x 11") paper.
- Type or word process your letter, or use your best handwriting, using blue or black ink.
- Single-space your letter. If the body contains more than one paragraph, leave a blank line between paragraphs.

Writing   2.5b Follow the conventional format for the type of document.

Look for volunteer opportunities in your area. Look in the Yellow Pages (under headings such as *Social Services*), in the newspaper, or on the Internet for your specific areas of interest, such as nursing homes or parks and recreation programs. Identify an audience, and write a letter of inquiry to request information about volunteering. (You may need to call the organization for the name of the person you should contact.) Include specific information, such as the amount of time you can spend and why you are interested in this position.

Memos

Keep It Simple   A **memo,** short for memorandum, is a brief, informal letter sent to members of an organization or business. Unlike business letters, which require addresses, greetings, and closings, memos are simpler and are usually sent to people who work with the writer.

Bare Necessities   Memos are quick and simple. The parts of a memo are shown in the chart that follows.

PARTS OF A MEMO	
Heading	Date: To: From: Subject:
Body	Your message

TIP To check your writing for clarity, ask others to read it and explain what it says in their own words. If their explanation does not match what you meant, add precise, specific words.

Short and Sweet   To communicate your point effectively, the body of a memo must be *clear* and *succinct.* You can make sure your writing is **clear** by carefully choosing precise, specific words.

UNCLEAR   Several people from the company down the street are coming to talk. [How many people? What company? To talk about what?]

CLEAR   Four people from Abbott Computers are coming to present information about how to get a job at their company.

Writing   2.5b Follow the conventional format for the type of document (e.g., memorandum).

Succinct writing states information in a short, direct way. Weeding out unnecessary and repeated words will make your writing more precise and easier to read.

WORDY What I'm trying to say is that we need to provide thirty minutes of class time in order to give the group of students time to present their information.

SUCCINCT We need to provide thirty minutes of class time for the group presentation.

THINKING IT THROUGH

Clarity and Succinctness

Reference Note

For more information on using **precise words**, see page 601. For more on revising **wordy sentences**, see page 693.

Follow these steps to check your writing for clarity and succinctness.

STEP 1 Read the sentences in your memo.

Remember to bring all the stuff you need to make posters to the gym next week. We need a lot of people to help with the decorations because we have to make twelve giant, wall-sized posters.

STEP 2 Note any sentences that might not be precise or specific enough.

In the first sentence, "stuff" and "next week" aren't very clear.

STEP 3 Rewrite those sentences, adding or changing the information to make the meaning more clear.

Remember to bring poster board, paint, brushes, and old rags to the gym on Thursday, September 18.

STEP 4 Look for repeated information and cross out unnecessary words or sentences.

We need a lot of people to help ~~with the decorations because we have to~~ make twelve ~~giant~~, wall-sized posters.

TIP Be careful not to cut information that not everyone in your audience may know. Think about the organization or business for which you are writing the memo. Are there any new members who might not know where the group regularly meets or whom to contact for more information? Include that necessary information, but keep it brief if most members already know it.

Writing 2.5a Present information purposefully and succinctly and meet the needs of the intended audience.

Read the following memo, and answer these questions.

- Why do you think the writer wrote a memo rather than a letter?
- How did the writer make sure the information was clear for new members of the Decoration Committee?

A Writer's Model

Memo

Heading

Date: September 4, 2003

To: Pep Rally Decoration Committee

From: Brian Nguyen, Decoration Committee Leader

Subject: Pep Rally Posters

Body

The first football game is almost here! The pep rally decoration committee will be holding its first poster-painting session to get ready for the big day. Remember to bring poster board, paint, brushes, and old rags to the gym on Thursday, September 18. We need a lot of people to help make twelve wall-sized posters.

If you know any other students who would like to join our committee, please tell Mrs. Casey, our sponsor.

PRACTICE & APPLY 2 Write a Memo

Write a memo to a committee of your classmates asking them to help you kick off a fund-raiser or activity you have created. Remember to do the following.

- Use a standard memo format including all of the parts listed on page 748.
- Keep the body of your memo clear and succinct using the Thinking It Through steps on page 749.
- Include any necessary information that not all of the members of your committee might know.

Job Applications

The Right Start   A *job application* is the first link between you and a future employer. In most cases a **job application** is a form on which you must list information about yourself and your work experience. Getting the job may depend on how neatly you fill out the application and the words and information you choose.

Be Prepared   When an employer is hiring quickly, you may be asked to fill out a job application and turn it in immediately. To make sure you are prepared when you are looking for a job, always bring with you a sheet of paper containing the following information.

INFORMATION FOR A JOB APPLICATION

Personal	Your name, address, and phone number
Education	Names of schools you have attended and your grade average
Experience	Information about each job you have held, including • the job title • the name of your supervisor • a phone number someone can call to check your employment information • the dates when you began and ended your employment • a description of your job responsibilities
Activities	Organizations, sports, volunteering, or other activities
References	Names, addresses, and phone numbers of people who will say what a good job you have done as their employee, or personal references (such as neighbors or teachers) who will say you are a reliable, hardworking person

Neatness Counts   When you go to a potential employer, always bring your sheet of information and a blue or black pen. Print everything but your signature (if you are asked for it). Work slowly and neatly, taking care not to smear your writing or to fill out a section incorrectly.

Pay attention to the instructions. For example, you may be asked to put your job information in chronological order, starting with your most recent job. If you see a question you do not understand, ask about it. Do not skip a question if it does not apply to you. Instead of leaving the space blank, write *N/A* or *not applicable.*

Writing   2.5 Write documents related to career development, including job applications.

Read the following completed job application, and answer these questions.

- How did the writer use his family and school life to create employment experience?
- How might the writer's list of activities help him get the job?

A Writer's Model

Application for Arroyo Elementary School Tutors			
Personal:	Name	Address	Phone
	Khalil Smith	4702 Shady Lane San Diego, CA 92108	(619) 555-0127
Education:	Last Grade Completed	School Name	City and State
	7th Grade	Blanco Middle School	San Diego, CA
Experience:	Dates of Employment	Name and Phone of Supervisor	Description of Duties
	April 2001– present	Cara Smith (619) 555-0127	Helped younger sister with school work
	Summer 2002	Juan Gonzalez (619) 555-0178	Assisted teacher with elementary school summer math camp activities
Activities:	Member of Blanco Middle School Soccer and Math Teams		
References:	Name	Relationship	Address and Phone
	Carla Peña	Teacher	5316 Nimitz Blvd. San Diego, CA 92106 (619) 555-0109
	Preya Patel	Soccer Coach	8705 Rose St. San Diego, CA 92108 (619) 555-0151

PRACTICE & APPLY 3 **Fill Out an Application**

Copy the tutoring application above onto a piece of paper, leaving the white spaces blank. Then, fill out the application with information from your own life. Remember that neatness is important.

DIRECTIONS: Read the following paragraph from a student's business letter. Then, read the questions below it. Choose the correct answer, and mark your answers on your own paper.

> Most important, I have the experience necessary to be an excellent part-time daycare worker. My references, listed on the attached résumé, are happy people I have baby-sat for. I have taken a CPR course through the local YMCA. My parents, who after all know me better than anyone, trusted me to take care of my five-year-old sister this summer while they were at work. For these reasons, you can trust me to take excellent care of the children in your daycare center after school each day.

1. Where in the letter should the paragraph above appear?
   A salutation
   B first paragraph of the body
   C last paragraph of the body
   D closing

2. Which transitional phrase connects the ideas in this paragraph to the ideas in another paragraph of the letter?
   F Most important
   G after all
   H For these reasons
   J after school each day

3. Which of the following steps would the student who wrote this letter take in order to complete an application form for the same job?
   A bring with her a telephone book for contacting references
   B skip items that do not apply to her
   C write neatly in ink
   D complete the form quickly without reading the instructions

4. Which of the following might **clearly** and **succinctly** replace the phrase, "happy people I have baby-sat for" in the letter?
   F people
   G parents satisfied with all of my baby-sitting abilities, talents, and skills
   H pleased and delighted neighbors and family members who have children
   J satisfied baby-sitting customers

5. Where in a correctly formatted business letter should the date appear?
   A under the writer's signature at the end of the letter
   B in the heading on the line below the writer's address
   C in the body of the letter as part of the writer's message
   D below the inside address and above the salutation

Learning About Paragraphs

A **paragraph** is a group of sentences that relates one main idea. Usually, a paragraph is part of a longer piece of writing; however, to write an effective multiparagraph essay, you must understand the characteristics of individual paragraphs.

In this workshop you will learn to develop clear, coherent, and focused paragraphs. In the process you will practice the following language arts standards.

California Standards

Writing

1.0 Students write clear, coherent, and focused essays. Essays contain formal introductions, supporting evidence, and conclusions.

1.1 Create compositions that establish a controlling impression, have a coherent thesis, and end with a clear and well-supported conclusion.

1.2 Establish coherence within paragraphs through effective transitions.

1.3 Support theses or conclusions with analogies, paraphrases, quotations, opinions from authorities, comparisons, and similar devices.

1.6 Revise writing for appropriate organization; consistent point of view; and transitions between passages and ideas.

GO TO: go.hrw.com
KEYWORD: HLLA

What would happen if cars were not equipped with turn signals? Obviously, more accidents would occur. Turn signals are designed to inform one driver when another driver plans to turn or change lanes. In the same way, paragraphs also serve as signals: They tell the reader when the writer is switching to a new main idea. Without paragraphs, main ideas would run into each other, confusing the reader. So remember, as a writer, you are in the driver's seat—be courteous and signal when you switch to a new main idea by creating a new paragraph.

The Paragraph

The Parts of a Paragraph

Paragraphs usually contain a *main idea,* a *topic sentence,* and *supporting sentences.* In addition, some paragraphs end with a *clincher sentence.*

The Main Idea   Most paragraphs have a main idea. The **main idea** is the topic on which the entire paragraph focuses. Look back at the paragraph at the bottom of page 754. What is the main idea? It is that paragraphs are similar to turn signals. The other sentences in the paragraph give specific details about the characteristics that make turn signals and paragraphs similar.

The Topic Sentence   The **topic sentence** clearly states the main idea of the paragraph. It can occur anywhere in the paragraph, but it is usually the first or second sentence. However, a topic sentence can come later in the paragraph, or even at the end. A topic sentence that comes later in a paragraph can often pull the ideas together and help the reader see how they are related. Sometimes the topic sentence summarizes, as in the following paragraph.

> The first skateboard was probably constructed in the 1930s. This skateboard was a homemade contraption consisting of a two-by-four and the metal wheels from a roller skate. Eventually in 1958, Bill Richards and his son Mark made a deal with the Chicago Roller Skate Company to produce skateboards, and the modern skateboard was born. Today, skateboarding is a sport enjoyed across the country. From garage hobby to national sport, skateboarding has certainly come a long way.

WHAT'S AHEAD

In this workshop you will develop focused, coherent paragraphs. You will also learn how to

- **choose supporting details that elaborate on a main idea**
- **choose an appropriate organizational structure**
- **use transitional words and phrases**
- **write introductions and conclusions**

TIP A sentence at the end of a paragraph that pulls together the ideas in the paragraph is also called a **clincher sentence.** The last sentence of the model paragraph to the left serves as a clincher. Not every paragraph needs a clincher; consider using them sparingly in your own writing to emphasize certain main ideas.

Writing **1.0** Students write clear, focused essays.

Many paragraphs have no topic sentence. This is especially true of narrative paragraphs that tell about a series of events. The reader has to add the details together to figure out what the main idea is. Look at the following paragraph. What is the main idea?

> When the coyote had finished drinking, it trotted a few paces, to above the steppingstones, and began to eat something. All at once it looked up, directly at me. For a moment it stood still. Then it had turned and almost instantly vanished, back into the shadows that underlay the trees. From behind the trees, a big black hawklike bird with a red head flapped out and away. Up in the lake, the herons took wing. They, too, circled away from me, angled upriver.
>
> Colin Fletcher, *The Secret Worlds of Colin Fletcher*

Each sentence in the previous paragraph describes a separate action. However, if you put them all together, they suggest an **implied,** or unstated, main idea: Colin Fletcher disturbed the animals and they fled.

PRACTICE & APPLY 1

Identify a Main Idea and Topic Sentence

Identify the main idea in the following paragraph. If the paragraph has a topic sentence, tell what it is. If there is not a topic sentence, summarize the main idea in your own words.

> In the sun's family of planets, the earth is unique in its possession of oceans. Indeed, it is remarkable that oceans exist at all. They do only because the largest part of the earth has a surface temperature in the small range within which water remains a liquid: in short, between 32° F (below which, under ordinary conditions, water freezes) and 212° F (when it boils and becomes a gas).
>
> Leonard Engel, *The Sea*

Supporting Sentences In addition to a main idea and a topic sentence, effective paragraphs also have *supporting sentences.* **Supporting sentences** give specific details that explain, elaborate on, or prove the main idea. These details may include sensory details, facts, examples, analogies or comparisons, and paraphrases, quotations, or opinions from authorities.

Sensory Details When you use words that appeal to one or more of the five senses—sight, hearing, touch, taste, and smell—you are using **sensory details.** Vivid sensory details help your reader form a clear image of the subject. The following sensory details elaborate on a description of an apple.

Sight	The deep red, shiny apple was streaked with green near the stem.
Hearing	It crunched loudly and crisply as Zach took his first bite.
Touch	One velvety leaf still hung from the stem against the apple's smooth skin.
Taste	Zach devoured the sweet, but slightly tart apple.
Smell	A squirrel sniffed at the sweet, fresh-smelling core.

Facts A **fact** is a statement that can be proved true by direct observation or by checking a reliable reference source. For example, if you say that Washington, D.C., is the capital of the United States, you state a fact that can be proved. However, if you say that Washington, D.C., is the best city in the world, you state an *opinion.* **Opinions** are statements that cannot be proved.

Examples **Examples** are specific instances or illustrations of a general idea. In the following paragraph the author gives examples of how people in Japan make use of limited space.

> If anyone on earth knows how to get the most out of cramped quarters, it is the Japanese. . . . A typical Japanese washing machine is so light and small it can be moved easily with one hand from one room to another. Many Japanese sleep on quilted mattresses called futons . . . [which] can be rolled up after use. . . . Aisles in many shops are so narrow that a visitor needs a shoehorn to move around in them. . . . Pizzas are the size of apple pies; coffee isn't served in mugs but in delicate cups; [and] newspapers have only between four and a dozen pages.
>
> John Langone, *In the Shogun's Shadow*

Writing **1.0** Essays contain supporting evidence. **1.3** Support theses or conclusions.

Comparisons and Analogies A **comparison** explains similarities between two things, often to explain an idea new to readers in terms they will understand. An **analogy** is a type of comparison that explains one specific similarity found in both a familiar and an unfamiliar thing. The following examples explain the structure of atoms.

Comparison   Models of an atom and our solar system both have a center (a nucleus or the sun) and bodies that circle that center (electrons or planets).

Analogy   Like planets around the sun, electrons were once thought to follow an exact orbit around the nucleus. (Scientists have different theories now.)

Paraphrases, Quotations, and Expert Opinions   Support for ideas may come from outside sources, such as books and articles, television programs, and interviews or speeches. To include this information, you can **paraphrase,** explaining the ideas in your own words, or use a direct **quotation,** putting the words of the source inside quotation marks.

Information from other sources may include factual information on a topic, or it may represent the **opinion** of an authority on the subject. Here is how a writer might quote or paraphrase a supporting opinion from an authority about the explorer Meriwether Lewis.

Quotation   In his book, *Undaunted Courage,* Stephen Ambrose calls Lewis's journals "a priceless gift to the American people."

Paraphrase   Historian Stephen Ambrose considers Lewis's journals a valuable contribution to our history.

PRACTICE & APPLY 2   **Collect Supporting Details**

Think of at least two details to support and elaborate on each of the following main ideas. Use a variety of types of details—sensory details, facts, examples, analogies or comparisons, and ideas from outside sources.

1. Staying healthy is partly under your control.
2. When I walk around my neighborhood (or city), there is always something going on.
3. No one in my class is just like me.

Writing 1.0 Essays contain supporting evidence. 1.3 Support theses or conclusions with analogies, paraphrases, quotations, opinions from authorities, comparisons, and similar devices.

The Makings of a Good Paragraph

Although a paragraph may have a main idea, a topic sentence, and supporting sentences, the reader may still not understand it fully. What may be missing is *unity* or *coherence*.

Unity   When a paragraph has **unity,** all the sentences relate to the main idea. For example, in a paragraph explaining the origin of baseball, every sentence should give information about baseball's beginnings. Including a sentence that describes your own batting skill would ruin the paragraph's unity. That sentence is not about the paragraph's main idea—how baseball began.

A unified paragraph should also reflect a **consistent point of view.** The way you discuss the subject should not change within the paragraph. For example, the paragraph about the origin of baseball should most likely show an **objective,** or neutral, point of view. You would destroy the unity of the paragraph if you were to include a sentence that expresses your opinion about history's greatest team. That sentence would shift the point of view from providing objective information to sharing an opinion.

TIP A paragraph with irrelvant details or a shifting point of view will fail to create a **controlling impression.** To avoid this problem, include a strong thesis statement to guide your paragraph development. For information on **thesis statements,** see pages 763–764.

PRACTICE & APPLY 3 **Identify a Sentence That Destroys Unity**

In the following paragraph, one sentence should make you say, "What is *that* doing there?" Find the sentence that destroys the unity of the paragraph.

> The disappearance of Amelia Earhart remains a mystery. Earhart, who was the first woman pilot to fly across the Atlantic Ocean, crashed into the Pacific Ocean while attempting to fly around the world. She was born in Atchison, Kansas, in 1897. Some searchers believe that she survived the crash into the Pacific, because radio distress calls were received. An intensive search for the source of the signals was made. Searchers were not able to find her, however. Finally, the distress signals ceased. In spite of continued searches by airplane and ship, no clue about what became of Amelia Earhart has yet been found.

Writing 1.6 Revise writing for consistent point of view.

Coherence In addition to having unity, a paragraph also needs to be coherent. A coherent paragraph is one in which all of the sentences logically fit together. When a paragraph has **coherence,** the reader can easily see how all of the details are connected. You can use two methods to create coherence in your writing. First, you can organize details in an *organizational pattern* that makes sense to the reader. Second, you can show how the details are connected by using appropriate *transitional words* and *phrases.*

Organizational Patterns Organizing your details in a specific order is one way to be sure your paragraph is clear and coherent. Use one of the four patterns listed below. To choose the most appropriate pattern for your paragraph, consider the suggestions in the right-hand column.

HOW TO CHOOSE AN ORGANIZATIONAL PATTERN

Pattern	Explanation	Uses
Chronological Order	presents details in the order in which they occur	▪ to tell a fictional story or a true narrative ▪ to explain a process ▪ to explain causes and effects
Spatial Order	presents details according to their location in space—nearest to farthest, left to right, or any other reasonable arrangement	▪ to describe a person, a scene, or an object
Order of Importance	arranges details from the least to most important, or the reverse	▪ to provide persuasive reasons to support a position or thesis
Logical Order	groups related details together	▪ to divide a topic into categories according to its characteristics ▪ to compare and contrast two subjects

Transitional Words and Phrases The second way to create coherence is to use transitional words and phrases. **Transitional words** and **phrases** can help create coherence by showing how related details are connected. The chart on the next page lists some common transitions and identifies the types of writing in which you might use them.

Writing **1.0** Students write coherent essays. **1.2** Establish coherence within paragraphs through effective transitions. **1.6** Revise writing for appropriate organization and transitions between passages and ideas.

Chronological Order

Showing Time

after	before	first	next	thereafter
at last	eventually	later	soon	when
at once	finally	meanwhile	then	while

Showing Cause-and-Effect Relationships

as a result	consequently	for this reason	so	therefore
because	for	since	so that	

Spatial Order

above	before	beyond	inside	there
across	behind	by	into	through
along	below	down	near	to the left
among	beneath	here	next to	to the right
around	beside	in	over	under

Order of Importance

first	last	mainly	more important	to begin with

Logical Order

Comparing Ideas

also	another	like	moreover	too
and	just as	likewise	similarly	

Contrasting Ideas

although	however	instead	on the other hand	yet
but	in spite of	nevertheless	still	

Writing 1.2 Establish coherence within paragraphs through effective transitions.

In the following paragraph, notice how the underlined transitions help create coherence by showing how ideas are related.

TIP Think about what kind of connection each transitional word or phrase in this paragraph makes between ideas. What do the transitions tell you about how the piece is organized? In your own writing, try to use transitions that will give readers clues about the pattern of organization you have chosen.

In ancient times, it was a very expensive process to dye cloth or any other material. With no chemical dyes or synthetic products, artisans had to make dyes from products found in nature. <u>For this reason</u>, explorers in the Americas must have been quite excited <u>when</u> they discovered that the natives knew how to make a dye extract . . . from a common tree, known as the *brasil*. European merchants <u>soon</u> developed a great trade in brasil wood. The Portuguese, who, <u>as a result</u> of the treaty of Tordesillas, laid claim to the land where these trees grew, named the area *Terra de Brasil* or "Land of Red-dye-wood." <u>Soon</u> cartographers and others began to refer to the land as *Brasil*. Speakers of English <u>later</u> adopted the name and the way it was pronounced. <u>However</u>, <u>because</u> an s between two vowels sounds like a *z* in Portuguese, English changed the spelling of *Brasil* to *Brazil*.

"Word Stories: Brazil," *Calliope*

PRACTICE & APPLY 4 **Identify Transitional Words and Phrases**

List the transitional words and phrases in this paragraph about bartering.

Kino, a fisherman living in ancient times, realizes he needs a new coat to keep him warm at sea. How does he get it? First, he takes twenty fish from his basket so that he can trade for the coat. Then, he makes the day's journey to the coatmaker's shop. When he arrives, he learns that the coatmaker hates fish but loves carrots. As a result, the coatmaker will supply Kino with a coat for ten bushels of carrots. Consequently, Kino walks about the region and finally finds a carrot farmer willing to take the fish. Kino at last returns to the coatmaker and trades the carrots for the coat. However, after all of this, the long journey has completely worn out Kino's shoes, and, unfortunately, the shoe-maker likes neither fish nor carrots.

Types of Paragraphs

By now, you know that a paragraph is a group of sentences that communicates one distinct main idea. There are four main kinds of paragraphs.

- **Narrative** paragraphs tell a story or relate a sequence of events.
- **Descriptive** paragraphs describe a scene or object.
- **Expository** paragraphs reveal information about a subject.
- **Persuasive** paragraphs convince others to agree with the writer.

Most paragraphs do not stand on their own. Instead, most writing is composed of several paragraphs that relate to one topic. Two types of paragraphs are used to tie together several paragraphs that discuss a single topic—*introductions* and *conclusions*.

Introductions   The **introduction** to a composition has two functions: It must catch the attention of readers and present the main idea, or **thesis,** of the composition.

First, to catch readers' attention, try one of these techniques.

HOW TO CATCH READERS' ATTENTION

Ask a question.	Do you like to exercise and have fun? Do you like having people cheer for you? If so, why not participate in a team sport?
Tell an anecdote.	I remember how nervous I was when I came up to bat in my first game. My knees trembled as I stood at the plate. The pitch came in fast and low, but somehow I managed to hit it. Although I only got to first base, this was one of my most exciting moments.
State an interesting or surprising fact.	Experts say that approximately forty million school-age boys and girls participate in organized sports.

Once you have the attention of readers, present your main idea. A **main idea statement,** or **thesis statement,** sums up in one or two sentences the main idea of a composition. Every detail in each paragraph of a composition should be connected with the thesis statement and create a **controlling impression** about the topic. (A composition that does not create a controlling impression may lack **unity.** For more information on unity, see page 759.) Including your thesis in the introduction will keep both you and your readers on track. To develop a thesis statement, use the steps on the following page.

Writing   1.0 Essays contain formal introductions. 1.1 Create compositions that establish a controlling impression and have a coherent thesis.

Writing a Thesis Statement

▶ **STEP 1** **Identify the topic of your composition.** *My topic is playing organized team sports.*

▶ **STEP 2** **Look at your prewriting notes.** What do the facts and details suggest might be the main idea about your topic? *Playing organized team sports is more than just an opportunity to have fun.*

▶ **STEP 3** **Sharpen your focus and present a clear thesis.** Be specific but concise. *Playing organized team sports is fun, but it also gives boys and girls the opportunity to learn responsibility and sportsmanship.*

Conclusions The **conclusion** of a composition should wrap up the ideas in a piece rather than simply stopping. Try one of these strategies to develop your own conclusions.

HOW TO WRITE A CONCLUSION	
Refer to your introduction.	*If you enjoy having fun while getting exercise, consider joining a school sports team or a local summer league.*
Restate the main idea.	*Fun, fairness, and a sense of responsibility are three of the many benefits of playing organized team sports.*
Close with a final idea or comment.	*Video games may be fun, but they are no match for an afternoon game of baseball.*

PRACTICE & APPLY **5** ## Write Original Paragraphs

Choose a topic, and write two different kinds of paragraphs about it. For example, on the topic of kites, you might write one paragraph about the first time you flew a kite (narrative) and another about what a kite looks like (descriptive). For each paragraph you write, do the following.

- Express your main idea in a topic sentence. (See page 755.)
- Choose details to support your main idea. (See pages 756–758.)
- Choose an appropriate organizational pattern and connect ideas using transitions. (See pages 760–761.)

Writing **1.0** Essays contain supporting evidence and conclusions. **1.1** Create compositions that end with a clear and well-supported conclusion. **1.2** Establish coherence within paragraphs through effective transitions. **1.3** Support theses with analogies, paraphrases, quotations, opinions from authorities, comparisons, and similar devices.

DIRECTIONS: Read the following paragraph. Then, read the questions below it. Mark the best answer for each question on your own paper.

> (1) People often mistake dolphins and porpoises for one another because they have many similarities, but some important distinctions separate them. (2) Dolphins and porpoises are both toothed whales with torpedo-shaped bodies. (3) They both breathe through blowholes on the tops of their heads. (4) Dolphins have a beaked head and sharp, pointed teeth, but porpoises have a rounded head with no beak and flat teeth. (5) Both eat fish, squid, and shrimp, and both hunt using echolocation, which means they bounce sounds off objects to find food. (6) Dolphins live in all the oceans of the world, usually in coastal areas. (7) Porpoises are found only in temperate coastal waters.

1. Which of the following transitions should be added to the beginning of sentence 7 to connect it to sentence 6?

   A Therefore,

   B Additionally,

   C Next,

   D However,

2. Which of the following comparisons would support the point that it is not difficult to tell dolphins and porpoises apart?

   F In a way, using echolocation the way dolphins and porpoises do is like seeing with your ears.

   G Porpoises and dolphins are much more similar than they are different.

   H Just as you can tell two friends apart at a glance, certain features distinguish dolphins from porpoises.

   J Like porpoises and dolphins, most species of bats use echolocation to search for their food.

3. What is the **best** location in the paragraph for the following sentence? *Because the usually playful, sociable dolphins are found in more areas, people encounter them more often than porpoises, which tend to avoid human contact.*

   A before sentence 1

   B between sentences 1 and 2

   C between sentences 3 and 4

   D after sentence 7

4. Where should the writer add this elaboration? *A blowhole is like one big nostril that a dolphin or porpoise can inhale and exhale through when it is at the surface of the water.*

   F after sentence 1

   G after sentence 3

   H after sentence 5

   J after sentence 7

5. Which of the following sentences would best connect the ideas in this paragraph to those in a paragraph comparing frogs and toads?

   A Like dolphins and porpoises, frogs and toads are often mistaken for one another, but they have differences.

   B At a glance, you might mistake a frog for a toad, or a toad for a frog.

   C While porpoises and dolphins are similar, they are different enough that you can easily tell them apart.

   D Some pairs of different animal species are alike enough to make them difficult to tell apart.

Mini-Workshops

How often has something like this happened to you? You ask a friend or family member for help getting from home or school to someplace you have never been. Instead of clear, concise directions, that person gives you vague, general directions such as "take a left by the tree" or "I don't remember the street, but the library used to be there." All you really wanted was something quick and easy, so you could hop on your bike and head out. This section of the book attempts to do what a good set of directions does—to take you step by step through tasks, in this case, writing and media tasks.

This section of the textbook contains several short writing and media workshops on a variety of topics. The mini-workshops in this section will help you learn to

- write a descriptive essay
- write a fable
- write a response to a poem
- write bylaws
- create charts, maps, and graphs

As you work through each of these mini-workshops, you will practice the following language arts standards.

California Standards

Writing a Descriptive Essay, pages 768–770

Writing

1.1 Create compositions that establish a controlling impression and end with a clear and well-supported conclusion.

1.3 Support theses or conclusions with comparisons and similar devices.

1.6 Revise writing for word choice.

2.0 Students write descriptive essays of at least 500 to 700 words. Student writing demonstrates the organizational and drafting strategies outlined in Writing Standard 1.0.

Writing a Fable, pages 771–772

Writing

2.0 Students write narratives.

2.1 Write short stories or narratives:

    a. Relate a clear, coherent incident, event, or situation.

    b. Reveal the significance of, or the writer's attitude about, the subject.

    c. Employ narrative and descriptive strategies (e.g., specific action).

Writing a Response to a Poem, pages 773–775

Writing

1.1 Create compositions that have a coherent thesis and end with a well-supported conclusion.

1.3 Support theses or conclusions with quotations and comparisons.

2.2 Write reponses to literature:

    a. Exhibit careful reading and insight in their interpretations.

    b. Connect the student's own responses to specific textual references.

    c. Draw supported inferences about the effects of a literary work on its audience.

    d. Support judgments through references to the text.

Writing Bylaws, pages 776–777

Writing

2.6 Write technical documents:

    a. Identify the sequence of activities needed to explain the bylaws of an organization.

    b. Include all the factors and variables that need to be considered.

    c. Use formatting techniques (e.g., headings) to aid comprehension.

Creating Charts, Maps, and Graphs, pages 778–779

Writing

2.3 d. Organize and display information on charts, maps, and graphs.

Listening and Speaking

2.3 d. Organize and record information on charts, maps, and graphs.

CALIFORNIA STANDARDS

Writing a Descriptive Essay

Think about a *place* that matters to you. Maybe that place is your own room with the stereo blasting or a quiet corner of the public library. Wherever your important place is, you will have a chance to describe it in detail by writing a *descriptive essay*. The purpose of a **descriptive essay** is to magnify a single subject by revealing many sensory details and describing the writer's feelings about the subject.

Details, Details The key to a good descriptive essay is the details. The chart below explains descriptive techniques.

The **audience** for a descriptive essay might be yourself and your teacher, your classmates, or another group. As you develop details, think about similes, metaphors, and sensory description that will appeal to your audience.

Show Me By going to the place, you can identify details. If you are unable to go there, close your eyes and picture it. Answer these questions: *What do you see? What do you hear? What do you smell? Can you taste anything? What can you touch? What are your feelings about this place?*

DESCRIPTIVE TECHNIQUES

Technique	Definitions and Examples
FIGURE OF SPEECH	makes vivid comparisons
Simile	compares two things using *like* or *as* *The terrible news hit us like a tidal wave.*
Metaphor	compares two things by saying that something is something else *The dog's wagging tail was a welcoming smile.*
Personification	gives human characteristics to nonhuman things *The sun smiled down on our soccer game.*
SENSORY DESCRIPTION	describes with words that appeals to the five senses ▪ sights — *the blinding lightning* ▪ sounds — *the crack of the baseball bat* ▪ smells — *the sweet perfume of roses* ▪ tastes — *fiery jalapeños* ▪ sensations — *gritty sandpaper*
MEASUREMENT	estimates size to give the reader some perspective *The grass snake was no bigger than a pencil.*

Writing 1.0 Students write clear, coherent, and focused essays. The writing exhibits students' awareness of audience and purpose. **1.3** Support theses or conclusions with comparisons and similar devices.

Order in the Court You can organize the details you gather in one of these ways.

- **Spatial order** Share details in the order that you see them.
- **Chronological order** Describe the details of an event that occurred at the place in time order.
- **Order of importance** Organize details by beginning with the least important and ending with the most important detail.

Whatever the overall order, you will use the **introduction** to tell your audience what your subject is. In the **conclusion,** you will reveal your feelings about the subject.

Pen to Paper In your first draft, organize your details in a way that makes sense.

Then, have a classmate read your essay and answer these questions to help you revise your essay.

- Does the writer create a **controlling impression?** In other words, do the details work together to create a vivid picture in my mind, or do some details distract from the overall picture?
- Does the writer's **word choice** bring figures of speech and sensory details to life?
- Is it clear why this place is **significant** to the writer?

Look at the following description of a creek. What kinds of details are used? What is the organizational structure?

Writer's Model

INTRODUCTION

The summer after our seventh-grade year, Kelly, Millicent, Karuna, and I hiked down the long, dusty trail to the creek almost every day. The trail started at the end of a dead-end street, then twisted down a hillside through brush and short, scrubby trees. As we walked, loose rocks and gravel tumbled down the hill, lizards shot under larger rocks, and small brown birds rose into the sky. Toward the bottom, we could hear the rush of the creek that spring rains had filled with water.

Sensory description

BODY

Sweaty and coated with dust, we waded, then let our entire bodies slip into the water. When we dove below the surface, the summer sun's harsh glare dissolved into blues and greens. The creek was cool and quiet.

Simile

The creek was also fun. We dove in and out of the water like dolphins; we did the crawl, the backstroke, and the butterfly. We kept going until we reached the farthest of the tall cottonwoods. From one of the tree's branches hung the rope swing.

(continued)

Writing **1.0** Essays contain introductions, supporting evidence, and conclusions. **1.1** Create compositions that establish a controlling impression and end with a clear and well-supported conclusion. **1.6** Revise writing for word choice. **2.0** Student writing demonstrates the organizational and drafting strategies outlined in Writing Standard 1.0.

(continued)

Sensory description

In order to understand what it was like to fly through the air at the end of this knotted, yellow rope, close your eyes and imagine the tallest swing you have ever seen. Now imagine that instead of swinging back and forth, you fly to the farthest point and then let go. You fall. You fall for a full second until . . . splash! You plunge into the water. Then, you scramble up the muddy bank and do it all over again.

Metaphor

Sensory description

Most important, the creek was a place to relax with friends. After we had hiked and swum and swung off the rope swing until we had had our fill of flying, we would just float. We were leaves floating on the current all the way along the creek to where we'd started. By that time dusk would be falling, and we would sit on the flat, warm rocks at the creek's edge and dangle our feet in the water. Small fish nibbled our toes while we talked. Every evening, thick clouds gathered. We hoped for rain that would keep the creek full. Sometimes, we even saw lightning in the distance, but it never rained.

CONCLUSION

Measurement

Day after day we went down to the creek, and each time it had gone farther down. By the end of June we could no longer go off the rope swing—the water was too shallow. By the end of July, we could only wade. By August the creek bed was dry. In two weeks we would start school. Karuna's family was moving back to India, and Kelly would be going to another district.

Writer's feelings

We sat and threw rocks at the dry creek bed. Although we knew that the water would be back the following spring, it seemed as if the creek was gone forever.

PRACTICE & APPLY   Write a Descriptive Essay

Use the instructions on pages 768–769 and the model above to help you write and revise a 500- to 700-word descriptive essay about a place. Then, make a clean copy of your essay, and share it with your audience.

Writing 2.0 Students write descriptive essays of at least 500 to 700 words.

Writing a Fable

Although pigs cannot write, they can be very persuasive—at least when they are characters in a *fable*. **Fables** are short stories or narratives that teach lessons about life.

A Fabulous Recipe Fables generally follow a formula. Using this formula helps a writer make a point in just a few paragraphs. The main ingredients of a fable are shown below.

ELEMENTS OF FABLES

Element	Definition	Example
Characters	usually animals that talk and act like humans	an ant who saves food all summer and a grasshopper who relaxes all summer
Conflict	the problem the characters face illustrated in a single, clear incident	In winter, the ant has food because he prepared, but the grasshopper has none.
Moral	the lesson	Be prepared.

A Lesson for Us All The most important part of a fable is its *moral*. The **moral**, or lesson, is like the theme of a short story. It tells readers the **significance** of the fable.

Read the following fable by Aesop, retold by Anne Terry White.

Professional Model

The Dog and His Shadow

Curly the Dog was happily trotting home. It wasn't every day that the butcher gave him a juicy bone with meat on it! The Dog was carrying it very carefully in his mouth.

On the way he had to cross a little stream. He looked down from the footbridge into the clear water. And, to his surprise, he saw another dog under the water. Yes, and that other dog also had a bone in his mouth! It seemed to Curly that it was a bigger bone than his own.

With a growl he dropped his bone in order to grab the other dog's bone too. But he had no sooner done that than the dog under the water also dropped his bone.

For a moment Curly stood looking angrily down at his shadow. He couldn't understand it. All he knew was that he had lost his bone and must now trot home without it.

MORAL: Grasp for all and lose all.

Aesop's character is a dog named Curly. The conflict is that Curly wants more than he has. The moral is that greed causes unhappiness.

The steps on the next page will show you how to write a fable of your own.

Writing **2.0** Students write narratives. **2.1** Write short stories or narratives. **2.1b** Reveal the significance of, or the writer's attitude about, the subject.

THINKING IT THROUGH **Planning a Fable**

▶ **STEP 1** Decide what lesson you want readers to learn from your fable, and write your moral. *I want people to learn that they should always try to help others. The moral could be "Those who help others will be helped when they need it."*

▶ **STEP 2** Choose a conflict that will lead to your moral, and choose a setting. *Two characters will get in a bad situation. The one who has helped others will get help and the other will not. I'll set my fable in an airport.*

▶ **STEP 3** Decide what part each character will play in the lesson. *I'll use a dog and a cat. The dog will be helpful to others. The cat will always ignore people who need help.*

▶ **STEP 4** Map out the plot events that will show the lesson in action. *Before getting on the plane, a passenger asks the cat for some money to use the phone, but the cat ignores him. The dog loans money to the needy passenger. The cat and the dog get off the plane, but neither has enough money to get a taxi home. Since the needy passenger is a taxi driver, he gives the dog a ride home in his taxi to thank him. The cat has to walk five miles home in the rain with his luggage.*

Room for Improvement After you draft your fable, use these suggestions to improve it.

- **Explain *why* your characters do what they do.** Provide **action details** that give your readers an understanding of the reasons for the actions of your characters.

- **Rewrite your moral to fit the ending of the story better.** You may find that your story idea changed as you wrote. If your moral no longer fits the story well, it will lose some of its punch.

- **Change your characters to better fit the roles they play.** Fable writers choose characters that represent certain personality traits. A greedy character might be a vulture, or a clever character might be a fox. Choosing traditional characters or ones well known to your audience will help your readers understand your lesson.

PRACTICE & APPLY **Write a Fable**

Follow the Thinking It Through steps above to plan a fable. Then, write and revise your fable using the suggestions above.

Writing **1.0** The writing exhibits students' awareness of audience and purpose. **2.1a** Relate a clear, coherent incident, event, or situation. **2.1c** Employ narrative and descriptive strategies (e.g., specific action).

Writing a Response to a Poem

The **purpose** of a written response to a poem is to explain to your **audience** (usually your teacher and classmates) your understanding of a poem and why you did or did not like the poem. This mini-workshop will show you how to write a response.

Understanding a Poem Poetry can pack a lot of ideas into just a few words. To respond to a poem, you need to make sense of it first. Read the following poem and consider your personal response to it.

Growing Up
by Harry Behn

When I was seven
We went for a picnic
Up to a magic
Foresty place.
I knew there were tigers   5
Behind every boulder,
Though I didn't meet one
Face to face.
When I was older
We went for a picnic   10
Up to the very same
Place as before,
And all of the trees
And the rocks were so little
They couldn't hide tigers   15
Or *me* any more.

You can use the following questions to help you understand a poem.

- Who are the characters in the poem?
- What are the characters doing?
- Where does the poem take place?
- What does the poem describe?

Here is how one student answered these questions about "Growing Up."

> - The character is the speaker, who talks about two visits to a picnic spot.
> - As a child, the speaker imagines tigers behind boulders. As an adult, he describes the place as ordinary—the boulders are just rocks.
> - The poem takes place in a picnic area with trees and rocks.
> - The poem describes the speaker's different views of a picnic area.

Take a Message Once you have made sense of the poem, think about its message or **theme,** usually an idea about life. Your **interpretation** of the poem's message will serve as your essay's **thesis.** Below are one student's thoughts.

> The poem made me think about how different things are when you are a child. Grown-ups wouldn't imagine tigers behind boulders like the seven-year-old did. I think the message about life is that our viewpoints become less magical and more ordinary as we grow up.

Writing **1.0** Students write clear, coherent, and focused essays. The writing exhibits students' awareness of audience and purpose. **2.2** Write responses to literature. **2.2a** Exhibit careful reading and insight in their interpretations.

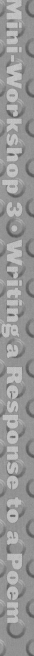

Getting Personal Reading a poem is like peeling an orange; it can take some work to get to the good parts. A poem that you did not like at first may become your favorite. Answer these questions to determine your personal response to a poem.

- What words, phrases, or ideas from the poem stick in your mind?

- What about the poem's message could you really understand? Can you make a **comparison** between something expressed in the poem and your own experience? What effects do you think this poem might have on other readers?

- Did you like the poem? Why or why not?

Here are one student's answers.

> One thing that sticks out is how the speaker believed that tigers were hiding behind the boulders. I remember feeling scared about monsters when I was little.
>
> I can see how visiting a special childhood place later in life would change your view of it. I think most people could relate to the feelings of missing some of the magic of childhood the narrator describes.
>
> I liked the poem. Even though I am not a "grown-up," I can see that I have changed since I was little. For example, I am no longer afraid of monsters.

Get Graphic Graphic organizers can help you get your information and ideas in order. Before writing an essay, it is helpful to make a graphic organizer like the following one to get your ideas on paper.

Introduction
- Introduce the poem by title and author.
- Describe what the poem is about.
- In your thesis, interpret the poem's message.

↓

Body
Give support for your interpretation with examples from the text of the poem.

↓

Conclusion
Describe your personal response to the poem. Explain your response through a comparison to your own experience.

Crafting the Draft Finally, turn the ideas in your graphic organizer into a short essay. Refer directly to the text of the poem as often as possible. Place direct quotations in quotation marks, as shown in the example below.

> I could understand how the seven-year-old felt when he thought there were "tigers behind every boulder."

The model on the next page shows the short essay that the student wrote based on information in the graphic organizer.

Writing **1.0** Essays contain formal introductions, supporting evidence, and conclusions. **1.3** Support theses or conclusions with quotations and comparisons. **2.2b** Connect the student's own responses to specific textual references. **2.2c** Draw supported inferences about the effects of a literary work on its audience. **2.2d** Support judgments through references to the text.

Writer's Model

A Poet Grows Up

INTRODUCTION

In the poem "Growing Up," by Harry Behn, the speaker describes two visits to the same picnic spot. In the first stanza, the speaker is only seven and thinks the place is "a magic foresty place." In the second stanza, however, the speaker is older and everything about the place seems small and ordinary.

Thesis

The poem's message is that when you grow up, you lose childhood's fears but you also give up childhood's magic.

BODY

The tigers are the key to the poem's message. The tigers stand for a child's fear. They also stand for magic, because only by magic could a tiger show up in a park. When the grown-up speaker returns and says "And all of the trees/ And rocks were so little/ They couldn't hide tigers/ Or *me* any more," the poet is saying that childhood fears look small from a grown-up's point of view, but it is also harder to see the magic in things.

Example from text

CONCLUSION

I liked this poem. I could understand how the seven-year-old felt when he thought there were "tigers behind every boulder." I remember being afraid of monsters under my bed. I have also grown up some, and I now know those monsters are not real—just like the tigers in this poem.

Comparison

PRACTICE & APPLY **Write a Response to a Poem**

- Find a poem you like. Use the questions on pages 773 and 774 to help you understand the poem and form a personal response.

- Create a graphic organizer like the one on page 774 to organize your ideas about the poem. Then, write a first draft of your response. Include at least one quote from the poem in your essay.

- Revise your draft, watching for punctuation and grammar errors. Make sure you explain your feelings about the poem and its message.

- Make a clean copy of your response, or deliver your response orally to your class.

Writing **1.1** Create compositions that have a coherent thesis and end with a well-supported conclusion. **2.0** Students write expository essays. Student writing demonstrates the organizational and drafting strategies outlined in Writing Standard 1.0.

Writing Bylaws

Bylaws are technical documents that outline the rules for governing a group, club, or organization. In this mini-workshop you will learn how to write the bylaws for a group, club, or organization.

Rules Rule!   Think of a group, club, or organization that needs rules. This group might already exist, or it could be one you would like to start. Then, consider what requirements the group needs.

The chart below lists requirements commonly found in bylaws. Be sure to consider any **variables** that might apply to your group. For example, if the group collects dues, your bylaws should state what the dues are, when they will be collected, and how they will be used.

The Look of the Law   Once you know the rules needed, write them so that they are easy to understand.

To start, create a heading for each requirement. These headings for different sections of the bylaws are called **articles.**

Articles should be numbered. For example, the fifth requirement in the chart below, setting a club's meetings, can become the heading *ARTICLE V: Meetings.*

Under each article, write the specific rules. Each rule is called a **section,** and each section is also numbered. For example, to tell when and where meetings will take place, the rule would read *Section 1. The Spanish Club will meet the first Tuesday of every month after school in the cafeteria.*

TIP   Formatting bylaws makes them easier to read. You may want to use boldface type or capital letters to make the articles and sections stand out as shown in the bylaws on the next page. For more on **formatting,** see page 651.

See How It's Done   On the next page are bylaws one student wrote for a club that exists at his school.

GENERAL REQUIREMENTS FOUND IN BYLAWS
the name of the group, club, or organization
the objectives the group, club, or organization would like to accomplish
the steps to becoming a member
the titles, responsibilities, eligibility requirements, and procedures for election of officers
the location and times of meetings
the steps to amend or revise the bylaws once they are written

Writing 2.6 Write technical documents. **2.6a** Identify the sequence of activities needed to explain the bylaws of an organization. **2.6b** Include all the variables that need to be considered. **2.6c** Use formatting techniques (e.g., headings) to aid comprehension.

Writer's Model

ARTICLE I: NAME
Section 1. The name of the organization shall be the Buenos Amigos Club.

ARTICLE II: OBJECTIVES
Section 1. The primary club objective will be to provide volunteer services to the community and to the school.

Section 2. Other objectives are to develop leadership and teamwork skills.

ARTICLE III: MEMBERSHIP
Section 1. Students in grades seven and eight may apply for membership.

Section 2. Applications will be reviewed and members will be selected by the club's officers and faculty advisor.

ARTICLE IV: OFFICERS
Section 1. Officers will be president, vice-president, secretary, and reporter.

Section 2. Duties of Officers:
- President—to run meetings, represent the club, and call special meetings
- Vice-President—to stand in for and assist the president as needed
- Secretary—to record and file meeting minutes and club records
- Reporter—to submit the club's plans and achievements to newspapers

Section 3. Eligibility:
- Officer candidates must maintain a B average, display satisfactory conduct, and have no unexcused absences.
- Officers may be re-elected to office.

Section 4. Elections and term of office:
- New officers shall be elected by majority vote at the last spring meeting.
- Officers will serve for one year.

ARTICLE V: MEETINGS
Section 1. The club will meet Tuesdays at 3:15 P.M. in the auditorium.

ARTICLE VI: AMENDMENTS
Section 1. Two thirds of the members present must vote to change, or amend, these bylaws.

Section 2. Members must be notified before a vote to amend bylaws.

PRACTICE & APPLY　**Writing Bylaws**

Use the instructions on page 776 and the model above to write the bylaws for a new or existing group, club, or organization.

Creating Charts, Maps, and Graphs

Graphics, such as charts, maps, and graphs, can help you clarify and support the ideas in your writing and speeches. Graphics support your ideas by helping your readers visualize information that may be difficult for them to understand.

Listeners will also better remember information that they both hear and see represented in a graphic.

Here are some useful types of graphics and the types of information they can present.

CHOOSING THE BEST GRAPHIC

Type of Information and Examples	Best Graphic to Use and Example
pieces of information that relate to each other such as parts of a whole **Examples:** ▪ percentages of votes cast for each candidate in the 1860 Presidential election ▪ **water usage in the United States**	**pie chart** Water Usage in the United States 9% 44% 47% ■ AGRICULTURE ■ RESIDENCES ■ INDUSTRY
an area's physical features, political divisions, or other geography-related topics **Examples:** ▪ mountains, valleys, lakes, and rivers of California ▪ **the location of Death Valley National Park**	**map**
information that changes over time **Examples:** ▪ student/teacher ratios over the past ten years ▪ **skateboarding accidents in Central City, May–August 2001**	**graph** Skateboarding Accidents in Central City May–August 2001 (Number of Accidents vs. Month: May, June, July, August)

Writing 2.3d Organize and display information on charts, maps, and graphs. **Listening and Speaking** 2.3d Organize and record information on charts, maps, and graphs.

Time to Choose If you tried to demonstrate every detail from a speech or composition with a graphic, your audience would be overwhelmed. Choose only the most important subtopic or detail to illustrate. To determine which of your ideas most needs a supporting graphic, ask yourself these two questions.

- Is one section of this piece more difficult to understand than the others?
- Is one section essential to understanding the rest of the piece?

Once you choose which information to support visually, you need to choose the most appropriate way to represent it. Use the chart on page 778 to help you decide.

Making It Happen When you have decided which type of graphic to use, you need to choose how to create it. Try one of the methods listed below.

- **Use a spreadsheet or computer drawing program** to create attractive graphics.
- **Draw your graphics by hand.** Use a ruler or graph paper to draw to scale.

Tracing paper can help you copy the outlines of maps.

- **Reproduce others' graphics.** Photocopy graphics from books, magazines, or newspapers, or download them from Internet sites. If you publish your writing outside of your classroom—in your school newspaper or on the Internet, for example—you must get permission to reproduce the graphic from its publisher. In any case, give credit to the graphic's creator or publisher, just as you would if you were using a direct quotation.

Reference Note

For more on **using software tools to create graphics,** see pages 661–664.

TIP Give every graphic you create or use a title that tells your audience exactly what the graphic shows. Also, label the parts of your graphic, and draw lines to clearly connect those labels to the appropriate parts of the graphic. Plan to explain briefly what your graphic shows in the speech or piece of writing it supports.

PRACTICE & APPLY **Create Charts, Maps, and Graphs**

Follow these steps to create graphics to support your presentations or writing.

- Choose the most important subtopic or detail in your writing or speech that you want to support with a graphic.
- Decide whether a chart, map, or graph can best represent your information.
- Create your graphic using the method of your choosing.

Resource Center

Test Smarts

Handbook of Reading and Informational Terms

Handbook of Literary Terms

Glossary

Index of Skills

Index of Authors and Titles

Test Smarts *by* **Flo Ota De Lange and Sheri Henderson**

Strategies for Taking Multiple-Choice Tests

If you have ever watched a quiz show on TV, you know how multiple-choice tests work. You get a question and (usually) four choices. Your job is to pick the correct one. Easy! (Don't you wish?) Taking multiple-choice tests will get a whole lot easier when you apply these Test Smarts:

T rack your time.

E xpect success.

S tudy the directions.

T ake it all in.

S pot those numbers.

M aster the questions.

A nticipate the answers.

R ely on 50/50.

T ry. Try. Try.

S earch for skips and smudges.

Track Your Time

You race through a test for fear you won't finish, and then you sit watching your hair grow because you finished early, or you realize you have only five minutes left to complete eleven zillion questions. Sound familiar? You can avoid both problems if you take a few minutes before you start to estimate how much time you have for each question. Using all the time you are given can help you avoid making errors. Follow these tips to set **checkpoints:**

- How many questions should be completed when one quarter of the time is gone? when half the time is gone?

- What should the clock read when you are halfway through the questions?

- If you find yourself behind your checkpoints, you can speed up.

- If you are ahead, you can—and should— slow down.

Expect Success

Top athletes know that attitude affects performance. They learn to deal with their negative thoughts, to get on top of their mental game. So can you! But how? Do you compare yourself with others? Most top athletes will tell you that they compete against only one person: themselves. They know they cannot change another person's performance. Instead, they study their own performance and find ways to improve it. That makes sense for you too. You are older and more experienced than you were the day you took your last big test, right? So review your last scores. Figure out just what you need to do to top that "kid" you used to be. You can!

What if you get anxious? It's OK if you do. A little nervousness will help you focus. Of course, if you're so nervous that you think you might get sick or faint, take time to relax for a few minutes. Calm bodies breathe slowly. You can fool yours into feeling calmer and thinking more clearly by taking a few deep breaths—five slow counts in, five out. Take charge, take five, and then take the test.

Study the Directions

You're ready to go, go, go, but first it's wait, wait, wait. Pencils. Paper. Answer sheets. Lots of directions. Listen! In order to follow directions, you have to know them. Read all test directions as if they contained the key to lifetime happiness and several years' allowance. Then, read them again. Study the answer sheet. How is it laid out? Is it

1

2

3

4

or

1   2   3   4 ?

What about answer choices? Are they arranged

A   B   C   D

or

A   B

C   D ?

Directions count. Be very, very sure you know exactly what to do and how to do it before you make your first mark.

Take It All In

When you finally hear the words "You may begin," briefly **preview the test** to get a mental map of your tasks:

- Know how many questions you have to complete.
- Know where to stop.
- Set your time checkpoints.
- Do the easy sections first; easy questions are worth just as many points as hard ones.

Spot Those Numbers

"I got off by one and spent all my time trying to fix my answer sheet." *Oops.* Make it a habit to

- match the number of each question to the numbered space on the answer sheet every time
- leave the answer space blank if you skip a question
- keep a list of your blank spaces on scratch paper or somewhere else—but *not* on your answer sheet. The less you have to erase on your answer sheet, the better.

Master the Questions

"I knew that answer, but I thought the question asked something else." Be sure—very sure—that you **know what a question is asking you.** Read the question at least twice before reading the answer choices. Approach it as you would a mystery story or a riddle. Look for clues. Watch especially for words like *not* and *except*—they tell you to look for the choice that is false or different from the other choices or opposite in some way. If you are taking a reading-comprehension test, read the selection, master all the questions, and then re-read the selection. The answers will be likely to pop out the second time around. Remember: A test isn't trying to trick you; it's trying to test your knowledge and your ability to think clearly.

Anticipate the Answers

All right, you now understand the question. Before you read the answer choices, **answer** the question yourself. Then, read the choices. If the answer you gave is among the choices listed, it is probably correct.

Rely on 50/50

"I . . . have . . . no . . . clue." You understand the question. You have an answer, but your answer is not listed, or perhaps you drew a complete blank. It happens. Time to **make an educated guess**—not a *wild* guess, but an *educated* guess. Think about quiz shows again, and you'll know the value of the 50/50 play. When two answers are eliminated, the contestant has a 50/50 chance of choosing the correct one. You can use elimination too.

Always read every choice carefully. **Watch out for distracters**—choices that may be true but are too broad, too narrow, or not relevant to the question. Eliminate the least likely choice. Then, eliminate the next, and so on until you find the best one. If two choices seem equally correct, look to see if "All of the above" is an option. If it is, that might be your choice. If no choice seems correct, look for "None of the above."

Try. Try. Try.

Keep at it. **Don't give up.** This sounds obvious, so why say it? You might be surprised by how many students do give up. Think of tests as a kind of marathon. Just as in any marathon, people get bored, tired, hungry, thirsty, hot, discouraged. They may begin to feel sick or develop aches and pains. They decide the test doesn't matter that much. They decide they don't care if it does—there'll always be next time; whose idea was this, anyway? They lose focus. Don't do it.

Remember: The last question is worth just as much as the first question, and the questions on a test don't get harder as you go. If the question you just finished was really hard, an easier one is probably coming up soon. Take a deep breath, and keep on slogging. Give it your all, all the way to the finish.

Search for Skips and Smudges

"Hey! I got that one right, and the machine marked it wrong!" If you have ever—ever—had this experience, pay attention! When this happens in class, your teacher can give you the extra point. On a machine-scored test, however, you would lose the point and never know why. So, listen up: All machine-scored answer sheets have a series of lines marching down the side. The machine stops at the first line and scans across it for your answer, stops at the second line, scans, stops at the third line, scans, and so on, all the way to the end. The machine is looking for a dark, heavy mark. If it finds one where it should be, you get the point. What if you left that question blank? A lost point. What if you changed an answer and didn't quite get the first mark erased? The machine sees two answers instead of one. A lost point. What if you made a mark to help yourself remember where you skipped an answer? You filled in the answer later but forgot to erase the mark. The machine again sees two marks. Another lost point. What if your marks are not very dark? The machine sees blank spaces. More lost points.

To avoid losing points, take time at the end of the test to make sure you

- did not skip any answers
- gave one answer for each question
- made the marks heavy and dark and within the lines

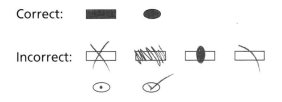

Get rid of smudges. Make sure there are no stray pencil marks on your answer sheet. Cleanly erase those places where you changed your mind. Check for little stray marks from pencil tapping. Check everything. You are the only person who can.

Reading Comprehension

Many tests have a section called **reading comprehension.** The good news is that you do not have to study for this part of the test. Taking a reading-comprehension test is a bit like playing ball. You don't know where the ball will land, so you have to stay alert to all possibilities. However, just as the ball can come at you in only a few ways, there are only a few kinds of questions that can be used on reading-comprehension tests. This discussion will help you identify the most common ones.

The main goal of the reading comprehension section is to test your understanding of a reading passage. Be sure to keep these suggestions in mind when you read a selection on a test:

- **Read the passage once** to get a general overview of the topic.

- If you don't understand the passage at first, keep reading. **Try to find the main idea.**

- Then, **read the questions** so that you'll know what information to look for when you **re-read the passage.**

Two kinds of texts are used here. The first one is an informational text. The second is an updated fairy tale.

DIRECTIONS: Read the following selection. Then, choose the best answer for each question. Mark each answer on your answer sheet in the square provided.

Stars and Stripes Forever

The U.S. flag defended by Barbara Frietchie during the Civil War had only thirty-four stars. Those stars stood for the thirty-four states that had been admitted to the Union by 1862. (Although the Southern states had <u>seceded</u> from the Union, President Abraham Lincoln refused to have their stars removed from the flag.)

Since 1960, the year after Hawaii became the fiftieth state, the U.S. flag has had fifty stars. Congress decided in 1818 that the number of stripes would be kept at thirteen, representing the original thirteen colonies. Known as the Stars and Stripes, the red, white, and blue flag has represented the United States at home, around the world, and even on the moon, where it was planted by astronauts in 1969.

ITEM 1 asks for vocabulary knowledge.

1. In the first paragraph, the word <u>seceded</u> means —

   A yielded

   B benefited

   C withdrawn

   D banished

Answer: Look at the surrounding sentences, or **context,** to see which definition fits.

A is incorrect. *Yield* means "to give in" and does not fit the context.

B is incorrect. If the Southern states had benefited, or helped, the Union, removing their stars would probably not have been an issue.

C is the best answer. Since the Southern states had withdrawn from the Union, some might have called for the removal of their stars from the flag.

D is incorrect. It doesn't fit the context.

ITEM 2 asks for close reading. Read carefully to see if the answer is stated directly in the text.

2. According to the passage, how many stars were on the U.S. flag in 1862?

   F Thirteen

   G Fifty

   H Twenty

   J Thirty-four

Answer: Read the passage carefully to see if the answer is directly stated.

J is the correct answer. The last sentence of the first paragraph of the passage indicates that there were thirty-four stars on the flag in 1862.

ITEM 3 asks for close reading. Read carefully to see if the answer is stated directly in the text.

3. In which year did Hawaii become a state?

   A 1818

   B 1862

   C 1959

   D 1960

Answer: Read the passage carefully to find the answer.

C is the correct answer. The first sentence of the second paragraph of the passage tells the year in which Hawaii became a state.

ITEM 4 asks for an inference.

4. What is this passage mainly about?

   F How the U.S. flag has changed over time

   G Why the Civil War was fought

   H How a territory becomes a state

   J When U.S. astronauts first reached the moon

Answer: Think about which statement covers the passage as a whole.

F is the best answer. It covers most of the details in the passage.

G is incorrect. The passage does not provide an explanation of why the war was fought.

H is incorrect. The passage does not tell how a territory becomes a state.

J is incorrect. It is only one detail in the passage.

ITEM 5 asks for a prediction.

5. What would happen if a U.S. territory or commonwealth, such as Puerto Rico, became a state?

   A Another star would be added to the flag.

   B Another red stripe would be added to the flag.

   C Another white stripe would be added to the flag.

   D Neither a star nor a stripe would be added to the flag.

Answer: Find the information in the passage that supports a probable future outcome.

A is the best answer. Since a new star is added for each new state, if Puerto Rico or some other territory becomes a state, Congress will add a fifty-first star.

B is incorrect. Since the passage indicates that the number of stripes is fixed at thirteen, there is no reason to think that another red stripe will be added.

C is incorrect. Since the passage indicates that the number of stripes is fixed at thirteen, there is no reason to think that another white stripe will be added.

D is incorrect. Although stripes are not added for new states, stars are.

ITEM 6 asks for a summary.

6. Which is the *best* summary of this passage?

F The U.S. flag is known as the Stars and Stripes.

G The U.S. flag has a unique design.

H The U.S. flag has changed over the years but continues to represent the United States.

J The fifty stars on the U.S. flag represent the fifty states in the Union.

Answer: Think about the answer that best sums up the passage as a whole.

F is incorrect. It states a fact and does not cover the passage as a whole.

G is incorrect. This statement simply describes the flag.

H is the best answer. This answer best sums up the content of the paragraph.

J is incorrect. This answer states a fact about the flag.

DIRECTIONS: Read the following selection. Then, choose the *best* answer for each question. Mark each answer on your answer sheet in the space provided.

Goldilocks and the Cyberbears

There was once a family of cyberbears who lived in a cozy cottage in the cyberwoods. There was gigasized Papa Bear, megasized Mama Bear, and byte-sized Baby Bear.

These three bears were notables be-cause a wolf at their door had sold them a webcam which had turned them into media stars. Each morning, people all over the world went to their Web site to watch Mama Bear preparing the family's breakfast porridge. Each morning she, of course, served it so hot the entire family had to go for a walk in the woods until the steam cleared.

One morning when the steam did clear, what did people see but Goldilocks doing her famous routine of "This porridge is too hot; this porridge is too cold; this porridge is just right" and eating it all up.

The fact that Goldilocks was a tres-passer on private property prompted two hundred people to sign on to the Bears' chat room immediately. They protested the fact that this girl had broken into the Bears' cottage. The president of the Cyberwoods Conservancy also signed on. He warned that it was wise not to feed the humans.

Goldilocks, unaware of the webcam that was tracking her every movement, next went into the Bears' study. . . .

ITEM 1 is a vocabulary question. To identify the best definition of the underlined word as it is used in the context, consider the surrounding words and phrases.

1. In the fairy tale the underlined word notables means —

A unknowns

B typical folk

C contestants

D celebrities

A is incorrect. The Bears' star status makes choice A the opposite of *notables*.

B is incorrect. These are anything but ordinary, run-of-the-mill bears.

C is incorrect. Nothing in the text says they are on a quiz show.

D is the best answer. Celebrities have the star status of these fine bears.

ITEM 2 is another vocabulary question.

2. In the fairy tale the word <u>trespasser</u> means —

F a person with a pass

G an intruder

H an unexpected guest

J a building inspector

G is the best answer. Two hundred people wouldn't protest the presence of F, H, or J in the Bears' cottage. None of the other people would have "broken into" the cottage.

ITEM 3 is a factual question. Re-read the fairy tale to find the correct answer.

3. Where do the three Bears live?

A In the forest

B In a clearing

C In the cyberwoods

D In town

A is incorrect. It is close but not quite right. Read on.

B is incorrect. Nothing is said in the fairy tale about a clearing.

C is the best answer. This is what the story says.

D is incorrect. This is *way* off base.

ITEM 4 is another factual question.

4. What can viewers from around the world watch each morning?

F Mama Bear preparing the family's breakfast porridge

G The story of Goldilocks and the three bears

H Goldilocks doing her famous song-and-dance routine

J Goldilocks breaking Baby Bear's chair

F is the best answer. G, H, and J are incorrect for several reasons, including the fact that Goldilocks shows up at the Bears' house only once, not every morning.

ITEM 5 asks you to make a judgment based on details in the story.

5. The Bears could be described as leading which kind of life?

A Hard

B Wild

C Exciting

D Comfortable

A is incorrect. The only hard thing about the Bears' life was too-hot porridge.

B is incorrect. Life in the Bears' cottage was more tame than wild.

C is incorrect. The Bears followed a pretty ordinary daily routine.

D is the best answer. The Bears had all the comforts of home, plus a webcam.

ITEM 6 asks you to place events in chronological order, the order in which they occur.

6. Which event belongs in the blank?

Goldilocks arrives at the cottage.

_____ .

Two hundred people sign on to the Bears' chat room in protest.

F The Bears go for a walk.

G The wolf sells the Bears a webcam.

H Goldilocks tastes the porridge.

J The Bears get a lesson in pet care.

H is the answer. F and G happen before Goldilocks arrives, and J never happens.

Writing a Response to an Expository Passage

On a writing test, you may be asked to respond to an **expository,** or informative, reading selection. Such tests often give you both a selection and a writing prompt.

The steps and student responses below will help you respond to a prompt like the one to the right. "Secrets of the Mummies" can be found on pages 669–670.

Prompt

"Secrets of the Mummies" by Kathiann M. Kowalski tells about the discovery of a mummy named "Juanita." Write an essay in which you explain what can be learned from studying a mummy. Include details from the article to support your ideas.

THINKING IT THROUGH

Writing a Response to an Expository Passage

▶ **STEP 1 Read the prompt carefully, noting key words and phrases.**
The key words and phrases are "explain" and "include details."

▶ **STEP 2 Read the selection at least twice.** Read first for the overall meaning of the work. Then, read the selection a second time, keeping the key words and phrases from the prompt in mind.

▶ **STEP 3 Write a main idea statement.** Your main idea statement should give the title and author of the work and should directly address the task described in the prompt.
In "Secrets of the Mummies," Kathiann M. Kowalski identifies several interesting things that can be learned from studying a mummy.

▶ **STEP 4 Find specific details from the selection to support your main idea.** If you include quotations, remember to enclose them in quotation marks.
Scientists used a CT scanner to determine the girl died from a skull fracture. Further testing showed that she was fourteen when she died and that she was related to the Ngobe people. "Additional testing showed she had eaten some vegetables several hours before dying." Artifacts found near her body told about the culture of the Inca people.

▶ **STEP 5 Draft, revise, and proofread your response.** Be sure to organize your essay effectively, including a formal introduction, body, and conclusion. When you are finished writing, proofread to correct mistakes in spelling, punctuation, and capitalization.

Writing an Expository Essay

When you take a writing test, you may be asked to **explain** how to do something. Because you cannot do research during a test, you will already know all of the information you need to answer the prompt. How might you handle a prompt such as the one to the right?

THINKING IT THROUGH

Writing an Expository Essay

▶ **STEP 1 Identify the writing task.** The prompt gives you clues about the audience, purpose, and format of your answer.

Audience: a child in elementary school
Purpose: to explain how to do something
Format: a letter

▶ **STEP 2 Choose a topic, and write a thesis statement** that identifies your purpose—to explain how to perform the task you have chosen.

Topic: finishing homework on time

Thesis: Finishing homework on time is important for success in school and only requires a few simple steps.

▶ **STEP 3 Organize your ideas** by jotting down the steps you want to explain. A time line can help you put your ideas in chronological order.

Time line for finishing homework on time

| 1. Write due date. | 2. Put work in notebook. | 3. Do work before watching TV. | 4. Bring work on due date. |

▶ **STEP 4 Write your response.** Keeping your audience and purpose in mind, list the steps in chronological order, and elaborate on each step. Be sure to include specific details that will be helpful to your audience.

Possible elaborations:

Step 1: Tell students to do this so they will not forget when assignments are due.

Step 2: Explain that they should do this to keep from losing assignments.

Step 3: Tell them that doing homework right away will be easier than trying to do it late at night when they are sleepy.

Step 4: Explain that this will keep them from losing points for late work.

Using the M.E.E.T.S. Strategy to Develop a Persuasive Essay

In a writing test, you may be asked to write a **persuasive essay.** To generate reasons and evidence to support your position, use the M.E.E.T.S. strategy explained in the steps below. The student responses are based on the prompt to the right.

Prompt

Your principal has decided that students should complete twenty hours of community service during the school year. The two plans under consideration are assigning students a job during school hours or allowing students to choose a job and complete the hours on their own time. Decide which plan you prefer. Then, write an essay in which you defend your position.

THINKING IT THROUGH

Using the M.E.E.T.S. Strategy to Develop a Persuasive Essay

▶ **STEP 1** **Identify your position on the topic given in the prompt.**
I think students should choose a job and complete the hours on their own time.

▶ **STEP 2** **Use the memory device M.E.E.T.S. (Money, Effort, Education, Time, Safety) to list the benefits of your position.**
M = The school may have to pay someone to find jobs for students.
E = Teachers will not have to make the effort to find jobs for students.
E = I'll learn more since I get to do the work I enjoy.
T = I can complete the hours when I want.
S = Students may leave school, saying they have work to do when they don't. Allowing students to complete the hours on their own time reduces the chances of students getting into trouble for lying.

▶ **STEP 3** **Identify the three strongest reasons you developed using M.E.E.T.S.** Your strongest reasons will be those for which you have the most evidence and those that address readers' concerns about the topic.
My three strongest reasons: Teachers will not have to find jobs for students. I'll learn more from a job I choose. I can complete the hours when it is convenient for me.
I think these are the issues my readers are most concerned about.

▶ **STEP 4** **Draft, revise, and proofread your essay.** Make sure you present your ideas in a logical order. Afterward, correct mistakes in spelling, punctuation, and capitalization.

Handbook of Reading and Informational Terms

For more information about a topic, turn to the page(s) in this book indicated on a separate line at the end of the entries. To learn more about *Cause and Effect,* for example, turn to page 100.

On another line there are cross-references to entries in this Handbook that provide closely related information. For instance, *Chronological Order* contains a cross-reference to *Structural Patterns.*

ANALOGY An **analogy** (ə·nal′ə·jē) compares one thing with another thing to show, point by point, how they are alike. Writers often use analogies to show how something unfamiliar is like something well-known. Writers of scientific and technical texts often use analogies to explain difficult concepts.

Another kind of analogy is a **word analogy.** This kind of analogy is often used in tests. It asks you to compare two words and figure out how they are related to each other. To complete a word analogy,

1. figure out the relationship between the two words; then,

2. identify another pair of words that are related to each other in the same way.

In a word analogy, the symbol : means "is to." The symbol : : means "as." Once you get the hang of it, completing analogies is fun. Here's an example:

> Select the pair of words that best completes the analogy.

> STANZA : POEM : : _____
>
> **A** metaphor : simile
>
> **B** chapter : book
>
> **C** fiction : nonfiction
>
> **D** words : music
>
> The correct answer is B. The completed analogy should read: Stanza is to poem as chapter is to book. The relationship between stanza and poem is one of *part* to *whole.* Just as a stanza is part of a poem, a chapter is part of a book.

In another kind of verbal analogy, the words might be opposites:

> DRY : WET : : cold : hot
>
> Dry is to wet as cold is to hot.

See pages 176, 377.

CAUSE AND EFFECT The **cause-effect pattern** is a text structure that writers use to explain how or why one thing leads to another. The **cause** is the reason that an action or reaction takes place. The **effect** is the result or consequence of the cause. A cause can have more than one effect, and an effect may have several causes. Writers may explain causes only or effects only. Sometimes a text is organized in a cause-and-effect chain. One cause leads to an effect, which causes another effect, and so on. Notice the cause-and-effect chain in the following paragraph from an interview with John Lewis in *The Power of Nonviolence.* (another excerpt of which appears on page 339):

In April, unknown people bombed the house of our attorney. It shook the whole area, and it shook us. How could we respond to the bombing and do something that would channel the frustration of the students in a nonviolent manner? We decided to have a march, and we sent the mayor a telegram letting him know that by noon we would march on city hall. And the next day, more than five thousand of us marched in twos in an orderly line to the city hall.

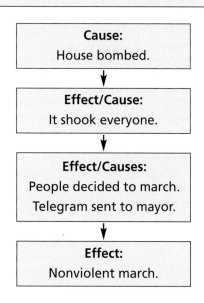

Writers use the cause-effect pattern in both narrative and informational texts. In many stories, events in the plot are connected in a cause-and-effect chain. Some words and phrases that are clues to the cause-effect pattern are *because, depended on, inspired, produced, resulting in, led to,* and *outcome.* Never assume, either in your reading or in real life, that one event causes another just because it happens before it.

See pages 100, 191.
See also *Coherence, Organizational Patterns, Structural Patterns.*

CHRONOLOGICAL ORDER Writers use **chronological order,** or time order, when they put events in the sequence in which they happened, one after the other. Chronological order is a common text structure in narratives, both fictional and nonfictional. Chronological order is very important in history texts and in science texts. You will also find chronological order in directions, from directions for a simple process, such as making hot chocolate, to technical directions for using a complex mechanical device, such as an electric generator. Some words and phrases that signal the chronological-order pattern are *first, after, finally, in the meantime, as soon as,* and *at this point.*

See pages 100, 167.
See also *Coherence, Organizational Patterns, Structural Patterns.*

COHERENCE The word *cohere* means "stick together." A text has **coherence** (kō·hir'əns) when ideas stick together because they're arranged in an order that makes sense to the reader. To aid in coherence, writers often help you follow a text by using **transitions,** words and phrases that show how ideas are connected.

Common Transitional Words and Phrases	
Comparing Ideas also, and, moreover, too, similarly, another	**Contrasting Ideas** although, still, yet, but, on the other hand
Showing Cause-Effect for, since, as a result, therefore, so that	**Showing Importance** first, last, to begin with, mainly, more important
Showing Location above, across, over, there, inside, behind	**Showing Time** before, at last, when, eventually, at once

See pages 502–503.
See also *Cause and Effect, Chronological Order, Comparison and Contrast, Order of Importance, Spatial Order.*

COMPARISON AND CONTRAST When you **compare,** you look at how two or more things are similar, that is, alike. When you **contrast,** you look at how things are different. Comparison and contrast is a text structure that discusses similarities and differences. There are two basic ways to organize a comparison-and-contrast text.

1. **Block method.** Discuss all the features (sometimes called **points of comparison**) of Subject 1 first; then, all the features of Subject 2. For each subject, discuss the same features in the same order. A block comparison and contrast of the two subjects Earth and Mars (see page 180) would be organized by subject.

Subject	Features
Earth	• planet surface • weather • length of day and year
Mars	• planet surface • weather • length of day and year

2. **Point-by-point method.** Discuss one feature at a time. First, talk about a feature in Subject 1; then, discuss the same feature in Subject 2.

Features	Subject
planet surface	• Earth • Mars
weather	• Earth • Mars
length of day and year	• Earth • Mars

Expect to see transitions that help you follow the ideas in both block structure and point-by-point structure. The transitions *both* and *neither* help you find similarities.

Transitions such as *but* and *however* help you pinpoint differences.

A graphic organizer such as a Venn diagram, which uses overlapping circles to show relationships, can help you keep track of similarities and differences. See page 163 for an example of a Venn diagram.

See pages 100, 163, 286, 290. See also *Coherence, Organizational Patterns, Structural Patterns.*

CONCLUSION A **conclusion** is a final idea or judgment that you draw, or come to, after you've considered all the evidence. In "In Trouble," from his memoir *Woodsong* (page 153), Gary Paulsen tells how he observed his dog Columbia playing a joke on another dog. That observation leads him to a chain of reasoning based on what he knows about other animals. After he considers the evidence, he draws a conclusion.

> If Columbia could do that, I thought, if a dog could do that, then a wolf could do that. If a wolf could do that, then a deer could do that. If a deer could do that, then a beaver, and a squirrel, and a bird, and, and, and . . .
> And I quit trapping then.
> It was wrong for me to kill.

As you read, you draw conclusions based on information in the text combined with what you already know. You may or may not agree with Paulsen's reasoning and the conclusion it leads him to. Your own experiences with animals may tell you that a dog and a wolf may have a sense of humor—but that other animals might not. In that case, you might conclude that Paulsen's conclusion is valid (true and logical) for him, but not for you.

See page 196.

CONSISTENCY A text is **consistent** when its details focus on the main idea and are in agreement with it. Consistency is important because details that have little or nothing to do with the main idea of the text distract and confuse the reader. Why is the second sentence in the following passage inconsistent with the point of the passage?

> In the winter of 1866–1867 blizzards gripped the Sierra Nevada. Spring came early, and the weather was unusually warm on the East Coast. Dwellings were buried in blowing, shifting, drifting, driving snow.

See pages 502–503.

CONTEXT CLUE If you don't know the meaning of a word, **context clues,** the words and sentences surrounding it, can sometimes help you guess its meaning. The following chart gives you four types of context clues. In the examples the unfamiliar word appears in boldface (dark type). The context clue is underlined.

Definition: Look for words that define the unfamiliar word, often by giving a **synonym** for it.

> She peeled onions and grated potatoes for the **latkes,** the potato pancakes.

Restatement: Find words that restate the unfamiliar word's meaning.

> Ballet dancers perform on the **pointe** of their toeshoes—a platform about the size of a silver dollar.

Example: Look for examples that reveal the meaning of the unfamiliar word.

> Street vendors offered their **wares:** goods of all kinds were piled in their stalls.

Contrast: Find words that contrast the unfamiliar word with a word or phrase you already know.

> The land was **arid,** in contrast to the rich, fertile land we had left behind.

See pages 22, 136, 166, 199, 317, 488.

DETAIL The details that are most important in a text are called **critical details.** If you e-mail a faraway friend about a film you've seen, you have to make decisions about which details to include and which to leave out. A critical detail is one that you must include for the text to make sense. Being able to separate critical details from minor ones is especially important in writing a summary.

See pages 137, 338, 434.
See also *Summarizing.*

ENUMERATION Enumeration (ē·nōō′mər·ā′shən) is a kind of text structure that organizes information into a list. The facts or events on the list may be cited in the order of size, location, importance, or any other order that will make sense to the reader. Some of the words and phrases that signal the enumeration text pattern are *to begin with, secondly, most important, for instance, another, for example,* and *in fact.* Social studies textbooks and science textbooks often use the enumeration text pattern. For an example of the enumeration pattern, see "The Fugitive Slave Acts of 1793 and 1850" (page 101).

See page 100.
See also *Coherence, Logic.*

FACT A **fact** is something that can be verified, or proved. It can be proved by direct observation or by checking a reliable reference source. The following statement is a fact:

> In 1860, Abraham Lincoln was elected president despite winning only 40 percent of the popular vote.

You can verify this fact by looking it up in a history book or in an encyclopedia. In fields where discoveries are still being made, you need to check facts in a recently published source. A Web site on the Internet may be current, but it may not be reliable. Remember that anybody can post a statement on the Internet. If you suspect that a statement given as a fact is not true, try to find the same fact in another source.

See page 57.
See also *Opinion.*

FALLACIOUS REASONING Statements that seem reasonable at first may, if examined closely, prove to be based on **fallacious** (fə · lā′shəs) **reasoning,** faulty reasoning, or mistakes in logic. (The word *fallacious* comes from a Latin word meaning "deceptive" or "tricky." The word *false* comes from the same root, as does the word *fallacy.*) Fallacious reasoning leads to false or incorrect conclusions. Here are some types of fallacious reasoning:

1. **Begging the question,** also called **circular reasoning,** assumes the truth of a statement before it has been proved. You appear to be giving a reason to support your opinion, but all you're doing is restating the same thing in different words.

> Everyone should be required to attend school sports events because mandatory attendance at such events is important.
>
> We can't control worldwide air pollution because every country in the world is guilty of polluting the air.

2. **Name-calling** uses labels to attack the person on the other side of the argument, instead of giving reasons or evidence to support the opposing point of view. This fallacy includes attacking the person's character, situation, or background.

> You're not seriously considering Latisha's childish ideas for the school dance, are you?
>
> Of course, Allen's not going to say that doctors make too much money. His mother's a doctor.

3. **Stereotyping** gives all members of a group the same (usually undesirable) characteristics. It assumes that everyone (or everything) in that group is alike. (The word *stereotype* comes from the word for a metal plate that was used to print the same image over and over.) Stereotypes are often based on misconceptions about racial, social, religious, gender, or ethnic groups.

> Smart kids are poor athletes.
>
> Actors are conceited.
>
> Big cities are dirty and dangerous.

4. **Hasty generalization** is a broad, general statement or conclusion that is made without sufficient evidence to back it up. A hasty generalization is often made on the basis of one or two experiences or observations.

> My brother is left-handed, and he's an artist. My aunt is left-handed, and she writes songs. I'm right-handed, and I have no artistic or musical talent at all.
>
> **Hasty generalization:** Left-handed people are more creative than right-handed people.

If any exceptions to the conclusion can be found, the generalization is not true.

5. **Either/or fallacy** assumes that there is only one correct choice or one solution, even though there may be many.

> Either we have free trade, or we return to the cold war.
>
> If you don't get good grades this year, you're not college material.

6. **False cause and effect** occurs when one event is said to be the cause of another event just because the two events happened in sequence. You cannot assume that an event caused whatever happened afterward.

> We got new uniforms, and our team won four straight games. The uniforms helped us win.
>
> Our mayor should be reelected. During her first term the crime rate in our city fell almost 10 percent.

See page 363.

GENERALIZATION A **generalization** is a broad statement that applies to many individuals, experiences, situations, or observations. A generalization is a type of conclusion that is drawn after considering as many of the facts as possible. A valid generalization is based on evidence, specific data, or facts. Here are some specific facts and a generalization based on them. Notice that each fact is one piece of evidence. The generalization then states what the evidence adds up to, drawing a conclusion that applies to all members of the group.

> **Specific Facts:** My dog wags her tail when she's happy. Kathy's dog, Soot, wags his tail when he is happy.
>
> **Generalization:** All dogs I've seen wag their tails when they're happy.

A generalization jumps from your own specific experiences and observations to a larger, general understanding. To be **valid,** or true, a generalization must apply to every specific individual or instance within the group—including the millions in the group that are not mentioned or listed in arriving at the generalization.

See pages 196, 318.

IDIOM An **idiom** (id'ē · əm) is an expression peculiar to a particular language that means something different from the literal (dictionary) meaning of the words. If your brother tells you he's fallen for Angela, you know that he means he likes her a lot. Despite what the words say, you know he hasn't fallen down. Every language has its own idioms. When you grow up speaking a language, you understand its idioms without even thinking about them. When you're learning a new language, it's hard to figure out what its idioms mean, and it's even harder to use them correctly.

See pages 506, 507, 512.

INFERENCE An **inference** is a guess based on clues. When you read, you make inferences based on clues that the writer provides. For example, you guess what will happen next in a story based on what the writer has already told you. You change your inferences as the writer gives you more information. Sometimes a writer will deliberately drop a clue that leads you, for a short time, to an incorrect inference about what is going to happen next. That's part of the fun of reading. Until you get to the end of a suspenseful story, you can never be sure about what will happen next.

When you're writing about a story or an informational text, you must be sure your inferences are supported by details in the text.

Supported inferences are based directly on evidence in the writer's text that you can point to and on reasonable prior knowledge. Some interpretation of the evidence is possible, but you cannot ignore or contradict facts in the text that the writer has given you.

Unsupported inferences are conclusions that are not logical. They ignore the facts in the text, or misinterpret them. Whenever you're asked to write an essay about a text, it's a good idea to re-read the text before and after you write your essay. Check each inference you make against the text to make sure you can find evidence for it. For example, if you write an analysis of a character in a story and you say that the character is self-centered, you should cite details from the text to support your inference.

See pages 86, 182, 196, 378.

INFORMATIVE TEXTS When you're reading for your own enjoyment, a mystery story, for instance, you can read at your own pace. You can speed up to see what happens next. If you get bored, you can move on to another story. When you're **reading for information,** you need to read slowly, looking for main ideas and important details. Slow and careful reading is especially important when you're trying to get meaning from consumer, workplace, and public documents. These documents are often not written by professional writers, so they may be difficult to read. **Consumer documents** are texts like warranties, contracts, product information, and instructional manuals. Here are some points to keep in mind when you read consumer documents:

1. Try to read the consumer document before you buy the product. Then you can ask the clerk to explain anything you don't understand.

2. Read all of the pages in whatever language comes most easily to you. (Many documents are printed in two or three languages.) You will often find important information where you least expect it, such as at the very end of the document.

3. Read the fine print; *fine,* here, means "tiny and barely readable." Some fine-print statements in documents are required by law. They are designed to protect you, the consumer, not the company that makes the product, so the company may not be interested in emphasizing these points.

4. Don't expect the document to be interesting or easy to read. If you don't understand a statement and you can't ask someone at the store that sold you the product, send an e-mail to the company that made it. It's OK to complain to the company if you find their consumer document confusing.

5. Before you sign anything, read everything on the page and be sure you understand what you're agreeing to. Ask to take the document home, and have your parent or guardian read it. If you are not of legal age in your state, an adult may be responsible for whatever you've signed. Make a copy of any document that you've put your signature to—and keep it in a place where you can find it.

Workplace documents include items like job applications, memos, instructional manuals, and employee handbooks. In addition to the points about reading consumer documents, you might want to keep these points in mind:

1. Take all the time you need to read and understand the document. Don't let anyone rush you or tell you that a document is not important, that it's just a formality.

2. Read technical directions carefully, even if they're just posted on the side of a device you're supposed to operate. Read all of the directions before you

start. Ask questions if you're not sure how to proceed. Don't try anything out before you know what will happen next.

3. An employee handbook contains the "rules of the game" at a particular business. It tells you about holidays, work hours, break times, and vacations, as well as other important company policies. Read an employee handbook from cover to cover. Pay special attention to information about health benefits, probationary periods, and policies on sexual harassment.

Public documents are texts put out by public agencies and not-for-profit groups such as community-action organizations and church groups. They might inform readers about matters like health concerns, schedules, and records. As you get older, this type of document will become increasingly important to you. Practice reading public documents now, and talk about your understanding of them with your family.

Question Sheet for Informational Texts

1. What is the topic? _____

2. Do I understand what I'm reading? _____

3. What parts should I re-read? _____
_____

4. What are the main ideas and details?

   Main idea: _____ Main idea: _____

   Details: _____ Details: _____

   Main idea: _____ Main idea: _____

   Details: _____ Details: _____

5. Summary of what I learned:
_____
_____

See pages 528–530, 531.

JUDGMENT When you make **judgments,** you form opinions. As you read a text or watch TV, you're constantly making judgments about what you read and see. When you express your opinions in writing, it's important to support your judgments with evidence. If you're writing about a story's plot or characters, you should support your judgments with references to the text, to other works, or to your own experiences. Before you make judgments about a TV show or a movie, here are some points to keep in mind:

1. Identify the purpose of the program or film. You need to know the writer's goal before you say to what extent the goal was reached. If the writer's purpose was humor, you should judge it for its humor, not for the credibility of its characters and plot.

2. Think about the beliefs and assumptions that the work represents. For example, is violence considered funny? tragic? ordinary? Does the program attack or ignore stereotypes?

3. Evaluate the information presented, especially in a nonfiction TV program. What are the program's sources? How reliable are they? What biases or prejudices do you notice? Be sure to distinguish between provable facts and someone's opinions.

4. Make your own judgment. After you've observed the work critically, draw your own conclusions and support them with references to the work itself, to other works of the same type and purpose, and to your personal knowledge.

See page 366.
See also *Fallacious Reasoning, Opinion, Purposes of Texts.*

KWL CHART Before you start reading a text, it's a good idea to review what you already know about the subject. As you think about

---

the subject, you'll come up with questions that the text may answer. Making a **KWL chart** can help you focus on a text. The following chart is based on the text from *Harriet Tubman: Conductor on the Underground Railroad* (page 87):

- In the **K** column, jot down what you already know about Harriet Tubman.

- In the **W** column, write any questions you have that the text might answer. Glancing through the text, looking at the pictures, if any, and reading subtitles and captions will help you come up with questions.

- As you read, note in the **L** column what you learn that supplements, answers, or contradicts what you wrote in the other two columns.

K	W	L
What I Know	What I Want to Know	What I Learned
She was African American.	What underground railroad?	

See page 294.

LOGIC is correct reasoning. A **logical text** supports statements with reasons and evidence. A text is illogical when it does not provide reasons backed by evidence (facts and examples). Notice how each sentence in the following text, from "Blasting Through Bedrock: The Central Pacific Railroad Workers" (page 520), gives evidence that supports the sentence before it:

In the winter of 1866–1867, blizzards gripped the Sierra Nevada. Dwellings were buried in blowing, shifting, drifting, driving snow. Men who were building the western portion of the country's first transcontinental railroad had to tunnel from their camp to the mountainside, where they spent long, cold days digging out rock so tracks could be laid. The Central Pacific Railroad was building east from California to meet the Union Pacific Railroad, which was working west from Omaha, Nebraska.

See page 363.
See also *Logical Order.*

LOGICAL ORDER is a method of organization used in informational texts. In **logical order,** details are classified into related groups. Writers who use this order may use the **comparison-and-contrast** pattern to show similarities and differences among various groups. For an example of logical order, see "Fast, Strong, and Friendly Too" (page 163), an article about dogs.

See page 484.
See also *Comparison and Contrast.*

MAGAZINE A **magazine** is a publication, usually in paperback, that comes out at regular intervals, such as weekly, monthly, or even annually. There are all kinds of magazines that appeal to general or special interests—from groups that love dogs (the magazine *Bark*) to people who enjoy reading about celebrities (the magazine *People*). A growing number of magazines are written especially for teenagers. Magazines may seek to entertain, to inform, or to persuade readers. Most have certain structural features in common:

- An attractive cover gives you the title, price, and date of the magazine and usually some idea of what's inside. A brightly colored illustration is usually included on the cover to grab your attention.

- The table of contents page appears close to the beginning of the magazine.

Handbook of Reading and Informational Terms **803**

You may also find a list of contributors and letters to the editor in the opening pages.

- Most magazines contain photographs and other kinds of illustrations. Many include cartoons. Graphic features such as color and headings and subheadings in different sizes and fonts (printing styles), along with charts and maps, organize the text visually and often highlight information. You'll often find stories and articles printed in columns, but each page is designed for maximum appeal to the reader. Sidebars, short articles set off within the article, develop a topic related in some way to the main story.

- Many magazines are supported financially not by the price of the publication but by advertising revenues. Advertisers choose to sell their products in magazines that appeal to the kind of buyer they are looking for. Some readers think the splashy ads in some magazines are almost as entertaining as the magazine's features.

See page 177.
See also *Purposes of Texts.*

MAIN IDEA The **main idea** of a nonfiction text is the writer's most important point, opinion, or message. The main idea may be stated directly, or it may be only suggested or implied. If the idea is not stated directly, it's up to you to look at the details and decide on the idea they all seem to support. Try to restate the writer's main idea in your own words.

In a **persuasive text,** the writer's main idea, or thesis, is called a **proposition.** It is usually presented as a positive statement of opinion.

Middle-school students should be required to wear uniforms.

The sale of junk food should be prohibited in public schools.

Every kid should get an allowance.

A proposition should be supported by reasons that explain the writer's opinion. Each reason should be supported, in turn, by details and evidence. The evidence may include **facts** and **figures (statistics), examples, anecdotes** (especially those that tell about personal experiences), and statements or direct **quotations by experts** on the subject.

See pages 19, 129, 312, 338.
See also *Note Taking, Outlining, Summarizing.*

MAPS Maps show the natural landscape of an area. Shading may be used to show physical features, such as mountains and valleys. Colors are often used to show elevation (height above or below sea level). **Political maps** show political units, such as states and nations. The map of Europe before World War II on page 214 is a political map. **Special-purpose maps** present information that is related to geography, such as the route of the Underground Railroad (page 95).

How to Read a Map

1. **Identify the map's focus.** The map's title and labels tell you its focus—its subject and the geographical area it covers.

2. **Study the legend.** The **legend,** or key, explains the symbols, lines, colors, and shading used in the map.

3. **Check directions and distances.** Maps often include a **compass rose,** a diagram that shows north, south, east, and west. If you're looking at a map that doesn't have one, assume that north is at the top, west is to the left, and so on. Many maps also include a **scale** to help you relate distances on the map to actual

distances. One inch on a map may equal one, ten, or fifty miles or more.

4. **Look at the larger context.** The **absolute location** of any place on earth is given by its **latitude** (the number of degrees north or south of the equator) and **longitude** (the number of degrees east or west of the **prime meridian,** or zero degrees longitude). Some maps also include **locator maps,** which show the area depicted in relation to a larger area. Notice the locator map in the upper right corner of the map shown here:

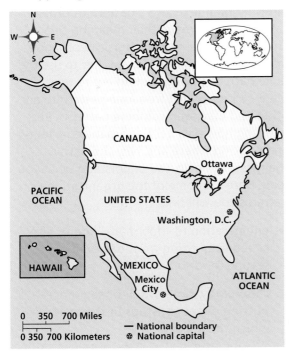

See page 214.

MEANING The most important idea or message of an informational text is called its **underlying meaning.** When you're reading or summarizing a text, to find the underlying meaning, you need to ask yourself the following questions:

- What is the writer's point? What is his or her reason for writing this text?

- What idea do all the critical details add up to?

- What connection can I make between the meaning of this text and the meaning of other texts I have read?

- What connection can I make between this text and my own life? What special meaning does this text have for me? How do I feel about what the writer is saying? Do I agree or disagree? What reasons can I give for my opinion?

NOTE TAKING Taking notes is a good way to remember a writer's major ideas and interesting details. Notes are especially useful when you read an informational text such as a history or science assignment. You can jot down notes in a notebook such as the kind you might use for a reading log. Many students like to use three-by-five-inch note cards, which can be clipped together or filed in a small file box.

Tips for Taking Notes

1. **Your own words.** Notes don't have to be written in complete sentences. Put them in your own words, using phrases that will help you recall the text. When you take notes, it's a good idea to use either of the following techniques:

   - **Summarize** the information by writing only the important ideas.

   - **Paraphrase** by writing all the ideas in your own words.

   Taking notes in either of these ways will help you avoid using another writer's words. Copying information word for word and presenting it as your own is called **plagiarism** (plā′jə·riz′əm). When you want to copy another writer's words, you need to put quotation marks around the passage you copy and be sure to identify the writer.

2. **Main ideas.** Jot down each main idea at the top of its own page or note card. As

you keep reading, add details that relate to that idea page or to the note card.

3. **Write clearly.** Even though no one but you may ever see your notes (unless you become famous), try to write clearly for your own sake. You'll want to read your notes later, and decoding your own mysterious handwriting can take a lot of time. When you finish taking notes for the day, review them to make sure they make sense to you.

See page 338.
See also *Main Idea*.

OPINION An **opinion** is a belief or an attitude. An opinion cannot be proved to be true or false. The following statement is an opinion:

> Lincoln was the best president the United States has ever had.

People have different opinions about who was the best president.

A **valid opinion** is an opinion that is supported by facts. The following opinion is valid. It is supported by two verifiable facts.

> Lincoln was a great president because he freed the slaves and led our country through the Civil War.

When you read a persuasive text, remember that statements of opinion can't be proved, but they can and should be supported by facts.

See page 57.
See also *Fact*.

ORDER OF IMPORTANCE is a method of organization often used in informational texts. Writers of persuasive texts have to decide whether to give the strongest reason first or to present the weakest reason first and end with the strongest point. News articles always begin with the most important details because they want to grab the readers' attention immediately. The structure of a news article looks like an upside-down triangle, with the least important details at the bottom.

See also *Details*.

ORGANIZATIONAL PATTERNS Writers of informational texts use a pattern of organization that will make their meaning clear. There are several ways writers can organize information. Don't expect a writer to use the same pattern throughout an entire text. Many writers switch from one pattern to another and may even combine patterns. Recognizing how a writer has organized a text—and noticing where and why the pattern changes—will help you understand what you read. Here are some of the organizational patterns you will find:

- **enumeration** (ē · nōō'mər · ā'shən), also called **list**—citing a list of details: first, second, and so on

- **chronology,** time order, or sequence—putting events or steps in the order in which they occur

- **comparison-contrast**—pointing out and explaining similarities and differences

- **cause and effect**—showing how events happen as a result of other events

- **problem-solution**—explaining how a problem may be solved

- **question-answer**—asking questions, then giving the answers

See pages 100, 484.
See also *Cause and Effect, Chronological Order, Comparison and Contrast, Enumeration*.

OUTLINING If you've taken notes on a text, you may want to organize your notes into an outline. Outlining puts main ideas and details in a form that you can review quickly. An **informal outline,** sometimes called a working outline, should have at least three main ideas. You put supporting details under each main idea, like this:

Informal Outline

First main idea

Detail supporting first main idea

Another detail supporting first main idea

Third detail supporting first main idea

Second main idea

[etc.]

A **formal outline** is especially useful if you're writing a research paper. You might start with a working outline and then revise it into a formal one. Your teacher may ask you to submit a formal outline with your completed research paper, so you have to be sure that it has the correct form. When you create a formal outline, you revise it, making changes as you revise your paper.

Formal outlines use Roman numerals (I, II, III), capital letters (A, B, C), and Arabic numerals (1, 2, 3) to show order, relationship, and relative importance of ideas. The headings in a formal outline should have the same grammatical structure, and you must be consistent in your use of either phrases or sentences (you can't move back and forth between them). There are always at least two divisions under each heading or none at all.

Here is the beginning of a formal outline of "Memory a Matter of Brains and Brawn" (page 58):

Formal Outline

I. Importance of exercise in protecting brain function

A. Mental exercise

1. Reading

2. Learning a foreign language

B. Physical exercise

II. Preventing Alzheimer's disease

See page 338.
See also *Main Idea.*

PARAPHRASING Paraphrasing is usually used to restate a poem. In a **paraphrase,** you restate every line in your own words. A paraphrase is longer than a summary. In some cases, it may even be longer than the original text! A paraphrase can help you understand a difficult text. Here is a paraphrase of the poem "A word is dead" by Emily Dickinson (page 390):

> In the first three-line stanza, the speaker says that some people claim that a word is "dead," that is, it no longer has meaning or importance, after it is spoken. In the second three-line stanza the speaker states an opposing opinion, that a word only begins to "live" after it is spoken. This means that a word, especially a loving or hateful word, is like a living thing—it can hurt or bring hope or happiness to people.

PREDICTIONS As you read a story, you may keep guessing about what will happen next. That means you're already using a reading strategy called **making predictions.** To make predictions, look for clues that the writer gives you. Try to connect those clues with other stories you've read and with experiences in your own life. As you continue to read and more information comes in from the writer, you'll change, or adjust, your guesses. Making predictions as you read helps you become involved with the story and its characters and their conflicts.

See page 61.

PREVIEWING When you **preview** a text, you look over the material to see what lies ahead. **Scan** (look specifically for) chapter titles, headings, subheadings, and terms printed in boldface or italics. Glance at the illustrations and graphics (such as charts, maps, and time lines), and **skim** (read quickly) a paragraph or two to check the vocabulary level and writing style.

See page 353.

PRIOR KNOWLEDGE The knowledge you already have about a topic before you read a text is called your **prior knowledge.** (Prior means "before.")

See pages 293–294.

PURPOSES OF TEXTS Texts are written for different purposes. The writer may want to

- provide information
- influence the way you think or act
- express personal feelings
- entertain you

Readers also have different purposes: You read to get information, to enjoy a good story, to share an experience. Being aware of why you are reading helps you to **establish a purpose for reading,** which helps you to decide how you will read the text. If you are reading a science fiction novel just for fun, you might read quickly and eagerly to find out what happens next. If you decide to read that same novel for a book report, however, you would read more slowly and carefully.

You might even re-read some parts of the book to decide how you will evaluate it. Sometimes you read to find an answer to a particular question, such as "Where do penguins live?" To find the answer, you may need to use an index or table of contents first and then skim a text (read quickly) to locate the information you want.

See pages 19, 57, 122.
See also *Magazine.*

QUESTIONS One way to monitor your understanding is to ask **questions** as you read. Get in the habit of carrying on a dialogue (in your head or in a reading notebook) with the writer. Make comments, ask questions, and note what puzzles you. Jot down facts that you might want to look up and verify. Experiment with ways of noting questions, such as using sticky notes that you place by paragraphs. If you find yourself confused by a passage, try one of the following strategies:

- Re-read the passage more slowly.
- Read the passage aloud.
- Put the ideas into your own words.
- Look for context clues that might help you figure out the meaning of an unfamiliar word.
- Use a graphic organizer to jot down the text's ideas.

See page 470.
See also *Detail, Fallacious Reasoning.*

RETELLING A reading strategy called **retelling** helps you understand and recall what you read. As you're reading a text, stop often to retell the important events that have happened up to that point. You might want to tell a partner what has happened, or you can jot down notes in a reading note-book or journal. Retelling can be used in reading fiction and in reading historical and scientific texts.

See page 489.
See also *Detail*.

SOMEBODY WANTED BUT SO Stories are built on conflict. A good way to summarize a story's plot is to reduce it to the following formula:

Somebody (name the main character):

_____

Wanted (tell what the main character wants):

_____

But (tell what complications develop that get between the main character and what he or she wants):

_____

So (tell how it all comes out in the end):

_____

_____

See page 6.

SPATIAL ORDER Spatial (spā′shəl) order is one of the patterns writers use to organize their texts. **Spatial order** shows where things are located. (The word *spatial* is related to the word *space*. Spatial order shows where things are located in space.) Spatial order is often used in descriptive writing. Here is an example from "Camp Harmony" (page 319):

> Our home was one room, about eighteen by twenty feet, the size of a living room. There was one small window in the wall opposite the one door. It was bare except for a small, tinny wood-burning stove crouching in the center.

STORY MAP A graphic organizer like the following one can help you map the plot structure of a story:

Characters	What they want
Conflict (what keeps them from getting it):	
Complications 1. 2. 3.	
Climax (moments when conflicts are resolved):	

Resolution (how it all turns out):

See page 6.

STRUCTURAL PATTERNS All texts have a structure. Without structure a piece of writing would fall apart—just as a house would fall down if its basic structure were faulty. The structure that holds a story together is called its **plot**. The structures that support the details in informative texts can be **chronology, order of importance, comparison and contrast,** or **cause and effect.**

See pages 100, 163, 167, 191, 484.

SUMMARIZING When you **summarize,** you mention and explain only the most important ideas of a work. Because a summary is much shorter than the original text, you have to decide which ideas to include and which ones to leave out. To summarize an informational text, start by naming the title, the author, and the subject. Then, go on to state the main ideas and the **key details,** those that support the main idea or underlying meaning. Follow the same order that the writer used. If you quote any of the writer's words, be sure to put quotation marks around them.

> "Picking Strawberries: Could You Do It?" by Flo Ota De Lange gives information about picking strawberries for a living. The writer explains that strawberries are "easily bruised," but a worker has to pick about 840 strawberries every hour, or ten thousand strawberries in twelve hours to provide the worker's family "with the basics." To give readers some idea of how difficult it is to pick that many strawberries without damaging them, the writer describes a knot-tying experiment. She shows that picking strawberries is a difficult, repetitive job requiring a great deal of speed and coordination.

If you are summarizing a short story, you cite the story's title and author and the main events of the plot. You should mention the story's main characters, the conflict, and, of course, the resolution of the conflict.

See pages 6, 106, 113, 434, 455.
See also *Main Idea.*

TIME LINE Use a **time line** to find out when events happened.

A time line may show a vast span of time, such as thousands or millions of years.

Events on a time line are arranged in chronological order, with long-ago events at one end and more recent events at the other. The approximate date (year or century) of each event appears above, below, or beside the line.

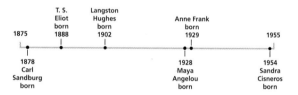

See pages 215–216.

Handbook of Literary Terms

For more information about a topic, turn to the page(s) in this book indicated on a separate line at the end of the entries. To learn more about *Alliteration*, for example, turn to pages 403 and 450 in this book.

On another line are cross-references to entries in the handbook that provide closely related information. For instance, at the end of *Autobiography* are cross-references to *Biography* and *Nonfiction*.

ALLITERATION The repetition of consonant sounds in words that are close together. Alliteration occurs mostly in poetry, though prose writers use it from time to time. Although alliteration usually occurs at the beginning of words, it can also occur within or at the end of words. In the following stanza, notice the repeated *s*, *m*, and *b* sounds:

> The sun was shining on the sea,
>   Shining with all his might:
> He did his very best to make
>   The billows smooth and bright—
> And this was odd, because it was
>   The middle of the night.
>
> —Lewis Carroll, from "The Walrus
> and the Carpenter"

The repetition of vowel sounds in words that are close together is called **assonance**.

See pages 403, 450.
See also *Poetry*.

ALLUSION A reference to a statement, a person, a place, or an event from literature, the arts, history, religion, mythology, politics, sports, or science. Allusions enrich the reading experience. Writers expect readers to recognize allusions and to think about the literary work and the allusions contained in it almost at the same time. For example, "I Have a Dream" (page 333) alludes to the song "My Country, 'Tis of Thee." A reader who is not familiar with that song will miss some of the speech's intended meaning.

See pages 332, 366.
See also *Literary Devices*.

ANALOGY A comparison made between two things to show how they are alike. Writers often make analogies to show how something unfamiliar is like something well known or widely experienced. Analogies are often used by scientific writers to explain difficult concepts.

See pages 176, 337.
See also *Literary Devices*, *Metaphor*, *Simile*.

ANECDOTE A brief story told to illustrate a point. Anecdotes are frequently found in memoirs, biographies, and autobiographies. In "In Trouble" (page 153), for example, Gary Paulsen uses two anecdotes about his huskies to illustrate their intelligence.

ANTAGONIST *See Protagonist.*

ASSONANCE *See Alliteration.*

ATMOSPHERE The overall mood or feeling of a work of literature. A work's atmosphere, or mood, can often be described in one or two adjectives, such as *scary, happy, sad,* or *nostalgic.* A writer produces atmosphere by creating images and using sounds that convey a particular feeling. "The Tell-Tale Heart" (page 354) is noted for its eerie atmosphere. The setting of a story can also contribute to its atmosphere. For example, the hot sun beating down on the farmworkers in "The Circuit" (page 183) contributes to a mood of oppression.

See pages 150–151, 152.

AUTHOR **The writer of a literary work or document.** Toni Cade Bambara is the author of "Raymond's Run" (page 367); Abraham Lincoln is the author of the Gettysburg Address (page 330).

See page 489.

AUTOBIOGRAPHY **A person's account of his or her own life or of part of it.** "Camp Harmony" (page 319) is an example of autobiographical writing.

See page 129.
See also *Biography, Nonfiction.*

BALLAD **A song or songlike poem that tells a story.** Ballads usually tell stories of tragedy, love, or adventure, using simple language and a great deal of repetition. They generally have regular rhythm and rhyme patterns that make them easy to memorize. "The Dying Cowboy" (page 423) and "The Cremation of Sam McGee" (page 417) are both ballads.

See pages 404, 416.
See also *Narrative Poem, Poetry.*

BIOGRAPHY **An account of a person's life or of part of it, written or told by another person.** The excerpt from *Harriet Tubman* (page 87) is part of a longer biography.

See page 86.
See also *Autobiography, Nonfiction.*

CHARACTER **A person or an animal in a story, a play, or another literary work.** Characters can be classified according to the changes they undergo. A **static character** does not change much in the course of a work. Billy Weaver in "The Landlady" (page 62) is a static character. In contrast, a **dynamic character** changes as a result of a story's events. Squeaky in "Raymond's Run" (page 367) is a dynamic character.

A character's **motivation** is any force (such as love or fear or jealousy) that drives the character to behave in a particular way.

See pages 84–85, 86, 106, 129, 167, 211.
See also *Characterization,
Motivation, Protagonist.*

CHARACTERIZATION **The way a writer reveals the personality of a character.** A writer may simply tell readers that a character is amusing or evil or dull or brave. This method is called **direct characterization**. Most often, though, writers use **indirect characterization**, revealing personality in one or more of the following ways:

1. through the words of the character

2. through description of the character's looks and clothing

3. through description of the character's thoughts and feelings

4. through comments made about the character by other characters in the story

5. through the character's behavior

When a writer uses indirect characterization, we must use our own judgment and the evidence the writer gives to infer the character's **traits**.

See pages 84–85, 286.

CHRONOLOGICAL ORDER **The arrangement of events in the order in which they occurred.** Most stories are told in chronological order. Sometimes, however, a writer interrupts the chronological order to flash back to a past event or to flash forward to a future event. *The Diary of Anne Frank* (page 217), for example, begins in 1945, when Mr. Frank arrives at the hiding place. The main story, however, takes place from 1942 to 1944.

See page 484.
See also *Flashback*.

CLIMAX The point in a story that creates the greatest suspense or interest. At the climax something happens that reveals how the conflict will turn out.

See pages 4–5.
See also *Drama, Plot, Short Story*.

COMEDY In general, a story that ends happily for its main characters. The hero or heroine usually overcomes a series of obstacles to get what he or she wants. (In contrast, the main character in a **tragedy** comes to an unhappy end.) The word *comedy* is not always a synonym for *humor*. Some comedies are humorous; others are not.

See also *Tragedy*.

CONFLICT A struggle between opposing characters or opposing forces. In an **external conflict** a character struggles with an outside force, which may be another character, society as a whole, or a natural force. In contrast, an **internal conflict** takes place within a character's own mind. It is a struggle between opposing needs, desires, or emotions. Alfonso in "Broken Chain" (page 7) has an external conflict with his brother over borrowing his bike and an internal conflict over his fears of facing his date without a bike.

See pages 4–5, 6, 150.
See also *Plot*.

CONNOTATION A meaning, association, or emotion suggested by a word, in addition to its dictionary definition, or denotation. Words that have similar denotations may have different connotations. For example, suppose you wanted to describe someone who rarely changes plans in the face of opposition. You could use either *determined* or *pigheaded* to describe the person. The two words have similar denotations, but *determined* has positive connotations and *pigheaded* has negative connotations.

See page 311.
See also *Diction, Style, Tone*.

COUPLET Two consecutive lines of poetry that rhyme. Couplets are often used in humorous poems because they pack a quick punch. "Casey at the Bat" (page 430), "The Cremation of Sam McGee" (page 417), "Maiden-Savin' Sam" (page 424), and "Ode to a Toad" (page 439) are all written in four-line stanzas consisting of two couplets in each stanza. Shakespeare uses couplets in many of his plays, often for a more serious purpose, to give closure to a speech or an act.

See pages 403, 442.
See also *Poetry, Rhyme, Stanza*.

DENOTATION See *Connotation*.

DESCRIPTION Writing intended to re-create a person, a place, a thing, an event, or an experience. Description uses images that appeal to the senses of sight, smell, taste, hearing, or touch. It is often used to create a mood or emotion. Writers use description in all forms of fiction, nonfiction, and poetry. This description of the effect of extreme cold on a dog and its owner may make you feel cold, too:

> The frozen moisture of its breathing had settled on its fur in a fine powder of frost, and especially were its jowls, muzzle, and eyelashes whitened by its crystaled breath. The man's red beard and moustache were likewise frosted, but more

solidly, the deposit taking the form of ice and increasing with every warm, moist breath he exhaled. Also, the man was chewing tobacco, and the muzzle of ice held his lips so rigidly that he was unable to clear his chin when he expelled the juice. The result was that a crystal beard of the color and solidity of amber was increasing its length on his chin. If he fell down, it would shatter itself, like glass, into brittle fragments.

—Jack London, from "To Build a Fire"

See pages 152, 167, 182, 353, 470.
See also *Imagery.*

DIALECT A way of speaking that is characteristic of a certain geographical area or a certain group of people. A dialect may have a distinct vocabulary, pronunciation system, and grammar. In a sense, we all speak a dialect. One dialect usually becomes dominant in a country or culture, however, and is accepted as the standard way of speaking and writing. In the United States, for example, the formal language is known as **standard English.** (It's the kind of English taught in schools, used in national newspapers and magazines, and spoken by newscasters on television.)

Writers often reproduce regional dialects or speech to bring a character to life and to give a story color. For example, the dialect Squeaky speaks in "Raymond's Run" (page 367) helps us see and hear her as a real person.

See pages 352, 366.
See also *Literary Devices.*

DIALOGUE Conversation between two or more characters. Most stage dramas consist entirely of dialogue together with stage directions. The dialogue in a drama must move the plot along and reveal character. Dialogue is also an important element in most stories and novels, as well as in some poems and nonfiction. By using dialogue, a writer can show what a character is like.

In the written form of a play, dialogue appears without quotation marks. In prose or poetry, however, dialogue is usually enclosed in quotation marks.

A **monologue,** or **soliloquy,** is a part of a drama in which one character who is alone on stage speaks aloud his or her thoughts and feelings.

See also *Drama.*

DICTION A writer's or speaker's choice of words. People use different types of words, depending on the audience they are addressing, the subject they are discussing, and the effect they are trying to produce. For example, slang words that would be suitable for a humorous piece like "Casey at the Bat" (page 430) would not be appropriate for a serious essay like "A Tragedy Revealed: A Heroine's Last Days" (page 295). Diction is an essential element of a writer's style and has a major effect on the tone of a piece of writing.

See also *Connotation, Style, Tone.*

DRAMA A work of literature meant to be performed for an audience by actors. (A drama, or **play,** can also be enjoyed in its written form.) The actors work from the **playwright's** script, which includes dialogue and stage directions. The script of a drama written for the screen is called a **screenplay** (if it's for TV, it's a **teleplay**), and it also includes camera directions.

The action of a drama is usually driven by a character who wants something and takes steps to get it. The main stages of a drama are often described as **exposition, complications, climax,** and **resolution.** Most dramas are divided into **acts** and **scenes.**

See page 212.

ELEGY **A poem of mourning, usually about someone who has died.** "O Captain! My Captain!" (page 447) is an elegy on the death of President Abraham Lincoln.

See pages 402, 446.
See also *Poetry*.

EPIC **A long narrative poem that is written in heightened language and tells stories of the deeds of a heroic character who embodies the values of a society.** One of the oldest surviving epics is *Gilgamesh,* which was written down around 2000 B.C. in ancient Mesopotamia. Homer's *Iliad* and *Odyssey,* dating from around 500 B.C. in Greece, are two of the best-known Western epics. *Beowulf* (page 428), from around A.D. 700, is the oldest surviving Anglo-Saxon epic. A mock epic, such as "Casey at the Bat" (page 430), imitates the epic style in a comical way in order to poke fun at its topic.

See pages 404, 427.
See also *Poetry*.

EPILOGUE **A brief closing section to a piece of literature.** Shakespeare's plays often have an epilogue spoken by an actor directly to the audience (see page 819, under *Meter,* for an example). In this textbook, "Saying Yes" (page 514) is an epilogue that sums up the selections in Chapter 7.

See page 513.

ESSAY **A short piece of nonfiction prose that examines a single subject.** Most essays can be categorized as either personal or formal.

The **personal essay** generally reveals a great deal about the writer's personality and tastes. Its tone is often conversational, sometimes even humorous, and there may be no attempt to be objective. In fact, in a personal essay the focus is the writer's feelings and response to an experience. Personal essays are also called **informal** or **familiar** essays.

The **formal essay** is usually serious, objective, and impersonal in tone. Its purpose is to inform readers about a topic or to persuade them to accept the writer's views. The statements in a formal essay should be supported by facts and logic.

See pages 19, 290, 363.
See also *Nonfiction, Objective Writing*.

EXAGGERATION **Overstating something, usually for the purpose of creating a comic effect.** *He's so thin that if he turned sideways, he'd disappear* is an example of exaggeration. Much of the humor in "The Cremation of Sam McGee" (page 417) comes from exaggeration.

See page 416.
See also *Literary Devices, Understatement*.

EXPOSITION **The kind of writing that explains or gives information.** You'll find exposition in newspaper and magazine articles, encyclopedias and dictionaries, and textbooks and other nonfiction books. In fact, what you're reading right now is exposition.

In fiction and drama, **exposition** refers to the part of a plot that gives information about the characters and their problems or conflicts.

See pages 4–5, 6, 353, 507.
See also *Drama, Nonfiction, Plot, Short Story*.

FABLE **A brief story told in prose or poetry that contains a moral, a practical lesson about how to get along in life.** The characters of most fables are animals that speak and behave like people. Some of the most popular fables, such as "The Dog and The Wolf" (page 342), are attributed to Aesop, a storyteller of ancient Greece. Often a moral is stated at the end of a fable.

FICTION A prose account that is made up rather than true. The term *fiction* usually refers to **novels** and **short stories.** Fiction is often based on a writer's experiences or on historical events, but a writer may add or alter characters, events, and other details to create a desired effect. "The Landlady" (page 62) is entirely made up. "The Circuit" (page 183), on the other hand, is based to some extent on the writer's experiences.

> See also *Historical Fiction, Nonfiction.*

FIGURE OF SPEECH A word or phrase that describes one thing in terms of another and is not meant to be understood as literally true. Figures of speech always involve some sort of imaginative comparison between seemingly unlike things.

The most common figures of speech are the **simile** (*The sun was shining like a new penny*), the **metaphor** (*The sun was a huge, unblinking eye*), and **personification** (*The sun smiled down on the bathers*).

> See pages 350–352, 450.
> See also *Literary Devices, Metaphor, Personification, Simile.*

FLASHBACK Interruption in the present action of a plot to show events that happened at an earlier time. A flashback breaks the normal forward movement of a narrative. Although flashbacks often appear in the middle of a work, they can also be placed at the beginning. They usually give background information the audience needs in order to understand the present action. The first scene of *The Diary of Anne Frank* (page 217) takes place about one year after the main action of the play. Almost the entire play, then, is a flashback to an earlier time. Flashbacks are common in stories, novels, and movies and sometimes appear in stage plays and poems as well.

> See also *Plot.*

FOLK TALE A story that has no known author and was originally passed on from one generation to another by word of mouth. Unlike myths, which are about gods and heroes, folk tales are usually about ordinary people—or animals that act like people. Folk tales tend to travel, and you'll often find the same **motifs**—elements such as characters, images, or story lines—in the tales of different cultures. Cinderella, for example, appears as Aschenputtel in Germany, Yeh-Shen in China, Cam in Vietnam, and Little Burned Face among the Algonquin people of North America.

> See also *Fable, Legend, Myth, Tall Tale.*

FORESHADOWING The use of clues or hints to suggest events that will occur later in the plot. Foreshadowing is used to build suspense or anxiety in the reader or viewer. A gun found in a bureau drawer in Act One of a drama may foreshadow violence later in the play. In the early part of "The Landlady" (page 62), details that hint at mystery and danger suggest what later happens to the main character, Billy.

> See page 61.
> See also *Suspense.*

FREE VERSE Poetry without a regular meter or rhyme scheme. Poets writing in free verse try to capture the natural rhythms of ordinary conversation—or, as in this free-verse poem, a very unusual conversation:

Love in the Middle of the Air

CATCH ME!
  I love you, I trust you,
  I love you
CATCH ME!
  catch my left foot, my right
  foot, my hand!
  here I am hanging by my teeth
  300 feet up in the air and

> CATCH ME!
>   here I come, flying without wings,
>   no parachute, doing a double triple
>   super flip-flop somersault
> RIGHT UP HERE WITHOUT A
> SAFETY NET AND
> CATCH ME!
>   you caught me!
>   I love you!
>
>   now it's *your* turn
>
> —Lenore Kandel, from "Circus"

Poets writing in free verse may use **internal rhyme, repetition, alliteration, onomatopoeia,** and other sound effects. They also frequently use vivid imagery and striking metaphors and similes. "I Hear America Singing" by Walt Whitman (page 451) is a famous poem written in free verse.

See pages 403, 450.
See also *Meter, Poetry, Rhyme.*

HISTORICAL FICTION A novel, story, or play set during a real historical era. Historical events (such as battles that really happened) and historically accurate details give us an idea of what life was like during a particular period and in a specific setting.

See also *Fiction.*

IAMBIC PENTAMETER A line of poetry that contains five beats consisting of an unstressed syllable followed by a stressed syllable. The iambic pentameter line is the most common in English poetry. Shakespeare's plays are written in iambic pentameter, and so is "On the Grasshopper and the Cricket" (page 443), as can be seen in the first line:

The poetry of earth is never dead

See page 442.
See also *Meter, Poetry, Sonnet.*

IDIOM An expression peculiar to a particular language that means something different from the literal meaning of the words. *Hold your tongue* (Don't speak) and *Bury your head in the sand* (Ignore a difficult situation) are idioms of American English, as is the title "A Smart Cookie" (page 508).

See pages 506, 512.

IMAGERY Language that appeals to the senses. Most images are visual—that is, they create pictures in the reader's mind by appealing to the sense of sight. In "Mrs. Flowers" (page 130), Maya Angelou uses words to paint a picture of a smile: "A slow widening of her thin black lips to show even, small white teeth, then the slow effortless closing."

Images can also appeal to the senses of hearing, touch, taste, and smell, or even to several senses at once.

See pages 352, 450.
See also *Description.*

INVERSION The reversal of the normal word order of a sentence. For example, a writer might change *Her hair was long* to *Long was her hair,* inverting the sentence to emphasize the word *long* or to fit a poem's rhyme scheme (*Long was her hair—she had plenty to spare*).

IRONY A contrast between expectation and reality. Irony can create powerful effects, ranging from humor to strong emotion. The following terms refer to three common types of irony:

1. **Verbal irony** involves a contrast between what is said or written and what is really meant. If you were to call a baseball player who has just struck out "slugger," you would be using verbal irony.

2. **Situational irony** occurs when what happens is very different from what we expected would happen. When Casey

Handbook of Literary Terms   817

strikes out after we've been lead to believe he will save the day in "Casey at the Bat" (page 430), the poet is using situational irony.

3. **Dramatic irony** occurs when the audience or the reader knows something a character does not know. *The Diary of Anne Frank* (page 217) is filled with dramatic irony. We know about the tragic fate of the people in the Secret Annex, but they do not. Note the irony in the following words spoken by Mr. Frank to Mr. Van Daan. "Didn't you hear what Miep said? The invasion has come! We're going to be liberated! This is a time to celebrate!" (Act Two, Scene 3)

See pages 352, 353.

LEGEND A story of extraordinary deeds that is handed down from one generation to the next. Legends are based to some extent on fact. For example, George Washington did exist, but he did not chop down his father's cherry tree when he was a boy.

See also *Fable, Folk Tale, Myth, Tall Tale.*

LIMERICK A very short humorous or nonsensical poem. A limerick has five lines, a definite rhythm, and an *aabba* **rhyme scheme.** It tells a brief story. President Woodrow Wilson is said to have written this limerick:

> I sat next to the Duchess at tea;
> It was just as I feared it would be;
>   Her rumblings abdominal
>   Were truly phenomenal,
> And everyone thought it was me!

See also *Poetry, Rhyme.*

LITERARY DEVICES The devices a writer uses to develop style and convey meaning. Literary devices are a writer's tricks of the trade. They include allusion, analogy, dialect, exaggeration, figures of speech, imagery, irony, repetition, symbolism, and understatement. Literary devices that are used mostly in poetry include alliteration, assonance, meter, onomatopoeia, rhyme, and rhythm.

See pages 350–352, 353, 366, 382, 389.

LYRIC POEM A poem that expresses the feelings or thoughts of a speaker rather than telling a story. Lyric poems can express a wide range of feelings or thoughts. Both "A word is dead" and "The Word" (page 390) explore the speaker's feelings about words. Lyric poems are usually short and imply, rather than directly state, a single strong emotion or idea.

See pages 404, 405.
See also *Poetry.*

METAMORPHOSIS A miraculous change from one shape or form to another one. In myths and other stories, the change is usually from human or god to animal, from animal to human, or from human to plant. Greek and Roman myths contain many examples of metamorphosis. The myth of Narcissus, for example, tells how the vain youth Narcissus pines away for love of his own reflection and is finally changed into a flower.

METAPHOR An imaginative comparison between two unlike things in which one thing is said to be another thing. The metaphor is an important type of figure of speech. Metaphors are used in all forms of writing and are common in ordinary speech. When you say someone has a heart of stone, you do not mean that the person's heart is made of rock. You mean that the person is cold and uncaring.

Metaphors differ from **similes,** which use words such as *like, as, than,* and *resembles* to make comparisons. William Wordsworth's famous comparison "I wandered lonely as a cloud" is a simile because it uses *as*. If Wordsworth had written "I was a lonely, wandering cloud," he would have been using a metaphor.

Sometimes a writer hints at a connection instead of stating it directly. T. S. Eliot uses an **implied metaphor** in one of his poems when he describes fog as rubbing its back on windows, making a sudden leap, and curling around a house to fall asleep. By using words that we associate with a cat's behavior, Eliot implies a comparison without stating "The fog is a cat."

"I'm running a loose ship."

Drawing by Victoria Roberts; © 1992 The New Yorker Magazine, Inc.

An **extended metaphor** is a metaphor that is extended, or developed, over several lines of writing or even throughout an entire work. "O Captain! My Captain!" (page 447) contains an extended metaphor in which the United States is compared to a ship and President Abraham Lincoln is compared to the captain of the ship.

See pages 351, 388, 389, 393, 405.
See also *Figure of Speech, Simile.*

METER A pattern of stressed and unstressed syllables in poetry. It is common practice to show this pattern in writing by using two symbols. The symbol ´ indicates a stressed syllable. The symbol ˘ indicates an unstressed syllable. Indicating the metrical pattern of a poem in this way is called **scanning** the poem. The following lines by William Shakespeare have been scanned in part. (The lines make up the speech of the mischief-maker Puck, or Robin Goodfellow, at the end of the comedy *A Midsummer Night's Dream. Reprehend* means "criticize"; *serpent's tongue* means "hissing"; *Give me your hands* means "Clap.")

If we shadows have offended,
Think but this, and all is mended,
That you have but slumbered here
While these visions did appear,
And this weak and idle theme,
No more yielding but a dream,
Gentles, do not reprehend.
If you pardon, we will mend.
And, as I am an honest Puck,
If we have unearned luck
Now to scape the serpent's tongue,
We will make amends ere long,
Else the Puck a liar call.
So, good night unto you all.
Give me your hands, if we be friends,
And Robin shall restore amends.

—William Shakespeare,
from *A Midsummer Night's Dream*

See page 402.
See also *Poetry, Rhythm.*

MOOD See *Atmosphere.*

MOTIF See *Folk Tale.*

MOTIVATION The reasons a character behaves in a certain way. Among the many reasons for a person's behavior are feelings, experiences, and commands by others. In

"Too Soon a Woman" (page 114), Mary does not let the children eat the mushroom until she learns by eating it herself that it is not poisonous. Her motivation is her concern for their well-being.

See pages 85, 86, 113.
See also *Character*.

MYTH **A story that explains something about the world and typically involves gods or other supernatural forces.** Myths reflect the traditions and beliefs of the culture that produced them. Almost every culture has **creation myths,** stories that explain how the world came to exist or how human beings were created. Other myths explain different aspects of life and the natural world. One of the ancient Greek myths, for instance, tells how Prometheus gave humans the gift of fire. Most myths are very old and were handed down orally before being put in written form. The exact origin of most myths is not known.

See also *Fable, Folk Tale, Legend, Tall Tale.*

NARRATION **The kind of writing that tells a story.** Narration is the main tool of writers of fiction. It is also used in any piece of nonfiction that relates a series of events in the order in which they happened (for example, in historical writing and science articles).

See page 353.
See also *Exposition, Fiction, Nonfiction.*

NARRATIVE POEM **A poem that tells a story.** "Paul Revere's Ride" (page 410) and "Casey at the Bat" (page 430) are narrative poems.

See pages 404, 409.
See also *Poetry.*

NONFICTION **Prose writing that deals with real people, things, events, and places.** Popu-lar forms of nonfiction are the autobiogra-phy, the biography, and the essay. "Mrs. Flowers" (page 130) is an excerpt from Maya Angelou's autobiography. Other examples of nonfiction are newspaper stories, magazine articles, historical writing, science reports, and even diaries and letters.

See also *Autobiography, Biography, Essay, Fiction.*

NOVEL **A long fictional story, usually longer than one hundred book pages.** A novel uses all the elements of storytelling—plot, charac-ter, setting, theme, and point of view. It usually has more characters, settings, and themes and a more complex plot than a short story. A **novella** is a fictional story that is shorter than a novel and longer than a short story.

See also *Plot, Short Story.*

OBJECTIVE WRITING **Writing that presents facts without revealing the writer's feelings and opinions.** Most news reports in news-papers are objective writing.

See also *Essay, Subjective Writing.*

ODE **A lyric poem, rhymed or unrhymed, on a serious subject.** Odes are usually addressed to one person or thing. In "Oda a las gracias / Ode to Thanks" (pages 437–438), Pablo Neruda praises the word *thanks.*

See pages 404, 437.
See also *Poetry.*

ONOMATOPOEIA The use of words whose sounds imitate or suggest their meaning. *Buzz, rustle, boom, ticktock, tweet,* and *bark* are all onomatopoeic words. In the following lines the poet suggests the sound of sleigh bells in the cold night air by using onomatopoeia:

> Hear the sledges with the bells—
> Silver bells!

> What a world of merriment their melody
> foretells!
> How they tinkle, tinkle, tinkle,
> In the icy air of night!
> While the stars that oversprinkle
> All the Heavens, seem to twinkle
> With a crystalline delight.
> —Edgar Allan Poe,
> from "The Bells"

See pages 404, 450.

PARALLEL EPISODES Repeated elements of the plot. Three times the Big Bad Wolf goes to a little pig's house and says, "I'll huff and I'll puff and I'll blow your house in." Each time this happens, we have a parallel episode. Each of Melinda Alice's wishes in "Those Three Wishes" (page 73) is a parallel episode.

See pages 5, 22.
See also *Plot*.

PERSONIFICATION A figure of speech in which an object or animal is spoken of as if it had human feelings, thoughts, or attitudes. This poet writes about the moon as if it were a woman wearing silver shoes ("shoon"):

> Slowly, silently, now the moon
> Walks the night in her silver shoon;
> This way, and that, she peers and sees
> Silver fruit upon silver trees.
> —Walter de la Mare, from "Silver"

See pages 351, 389, 392, 393.
See also *Figure of Speech*.

PERSUASION A kind of writing intended to convince a reader to think or act in a certain way. Examples of persuasive writing are found in newspaper editorials, in speeches, and in many essays and articles. The techniques of persuasion are widely used in ad-

vertising. Persuasion can use language that appeals to the emotions, or it can use logic to appeal to reason. When persuasive writing appeals to reason and not to the emotions, it is called **argument.** The Gettysburg Address (page 330) and "I Have a Dream" (page 333) are examples of persuasive writing.

PLAYWRIGHT The author of a play, or drama. Playwrights Frances Goodrich and Albert Hackett wrote *The Diary of Anne Frank* (page 217), which they based on Anne Frank's diary and life story.

See also *Author, Drama*.

PLOT The series of related events that make up a story. Plot is what happens in a short story, novel, play, or narrative poem. Most plots are built from these basic elements: An **introduction,** or **exposition,** tells us who the characters are and usually what their conflict is. **Complications** arise when the characters take steps to resolve the conflict. Eventually the plot reaches a **climax,** the most exciting moment in the story, when the outcome is decided one way or another. The final part of the story is the **resolution,** in which the conflict is resolved and the story is brought to a close.

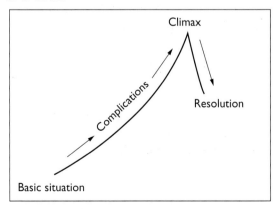

Not all works of fiction or drama have a traditional plot structure. Modern writers often experiment with plot. At times they eliminate some or almost all of the parts of a

syllables or by the repetition of certain other sound patterns. Rhythm occurs in all forms of language, both written and spoken, but is particularly important in poetry.

The most obvious kind of rhythm is the regular repetition of stressed and unstressed syllables found in some poetry. In the following lines, which describe a cavalry charge, the rhythm echoes the galloping of the attackers' horses:

> The Assyrian came down like the wolf on the
>   fold,
> And his cohorts were gleaming in purple and
>   gold;
> And the sheen of their spears was like stars on
>   the sea,
> When the blue wave rolls nightly on deep
>   Galilee.
>
> —George Gordon, Lord Byron, from
> "The Destruction of Sennacherib"

Writers also create rhythm by repeating words and phrases or even by repeating whole lines and sentences. The following passage by Walt Whitman is written in free verse and does not have a regular pattern of rhythm or rhyme. Yet the lines are rhythmical because of Whitman's use of repetition.

> I hear the sound I love, the sound of the
>   human voice,
> I hear all sounds running together, combined,
>   fused, or following,
> Sounds of the city and sounds out of the city,
>   sounds of the day and night,
> Talkative young ones to those that like them,
>   the loud laugh of work-people at their
>   meals . . .
>
> —Walt Whitman, from "Song of Myself"

See pages 329, 402–404, 409, 450.
See also *Meter.*

SATIRE Writing that ridicules something, often in order to bring about change. Satire may poke fun at a person, a group of people, an attitude, a social institution, even all of humanity. Writers use satire to convince us of a point of view or to persuade us to follow a course of action.

SETTING The time and place of a story, play, or narrative poem. Most often the setting is described early in the story. For example, the story "Too Soon a Woman" (page 114) begins, "We left the home place behind, mile by slow mile, heading for the mountains, across the prairie where the wind blew forever." Setting often contributes to a work's emotional effect. It may also play an important role in the plot, especially in stories involving a conflict between a character and nature such as "In Trouble" (page 153).

See pages 150–151, 152, 167.

SHORT STORY A short fictional prose narrative. The first short stories were written in the nineteenth century. Early short story writers include Sir Walter Scott and Edgar Allan Poe. A short story's plot usually consists of these basic elements: the **introduction (basic situation** or **exposition), complications, climax,** and **resolution.** Short stories are more limited than novels. They usually have only one or two major characters and one important setting.

See pages 4–5, 6.
See also *Fiction, Novel, Plot.*

SIMILE A comparison between two unlike things, using a word such as *like, as, than,* or *resembles.* *Her face was as round as a pumpkin* and *This steak is tougher than an old shoe* are similes.

See pages 351, 389, 393, 405.
See also *Figure of Speech, Metaphor.*

SONNET A fourteen-line poem, usually written in iambic pentameter. There are two kinds of sonnets: The **English,** or **Shakespearean, sonnet** has three four-line units and ends with a couplet. The **Italian,** or **Petrarchan, sonnet** (named after the fourteenth-century Italian poet Petrarch) poses a question or makes a point in the first eight lines. The last six lines respond to that question or point. "On the Grasshopper and the Cricket" (page 443) is in the form of an Italian sonnet.

> See pages 404, 442.
> See also *Iambic Pentameter, Poetry.*

SPEAKER The voice talking to us in a poem. The speaker is sometimes, but not always, the poet. It is best to think of the voice in the poem as belonging to a character the poet has created. The character may be a child, a woman, a man, an animal, or even an object.

> See page 470.

STANZA A group of consecutive lines in a poem that form a single unit. A stanza in a poem is something like a paragraph in prose: It often expresses a unit of thought. A stanza may consist of any number of lines; it may even consist of a single line. The word *stanza* is an Italian word for "stopping place" or "place to rest." In some poems, such as "Casey at the Bat" (page 430), each stanza has the same rhyme scheme.

STEREOTYPE A fixed idea about the members of a particular group of people that does not allow for any individuality. Stereotypes are often based on misconceptions about racial, social, religious, gender, or ethnic groups. Some common stereotypes are the ideas that all football players are stupid, that all New Yorkers are rude, and that all politicians are dishonest.

STYLE The way a writer uses language. Style results from **diction** (word choice), sentence structure, and tone. One writer may use many figures of speech, for example; another writer may prefer straightforward language with few figures of speech.

> See pages 350–352, 366.
> See also *Diction, Literary Devices, Tone.*

SUBJECTIVE WRITING Writing in which the feelings and opinions of the writer are revealed. Editorials, personal essays, and autobiographies are examples of subjective writing, as are many poems.

> See also *Objective Writing.*

SUBPLOT A minor plot that relates in some way to the main story. In "Broken Chain" (page 7), Alfonso's problems with his brother are a subplot of the major story of his date with Sandra. In "Flowers for Algernon" (page 23), Charlie's relationship with Miss Kinnian and his problems at his job are subplots of the main plot, involving the surgery to make Charlie more intelligent.

> See pages 4–5, 22.
> See also *Plot.*

SUSPENSE The uncertainty or anxiety that a reader feels about what will happen next in a story, novel, or drama. In "The Tell-Tale Heart" (page 354), the suspense builds as the insane narrator describes his long vigil at his victim's door.

> See page 61.
> See also *Plot.*

SYMBOL A person, a place, a thing, or an event that has meaning in itself and stands for something beyond itself as well. Some symbols are so well known that we sometimes forget they are symbols. The bald eagle, for example, is a symbol of the United

States; the Star of David is a symbol of Judaism; and the cross is a symbol of Christianity. In literature, symbols are often personal and surprising. In "Suéter / Sweater" (page 385), for example, a sweater symbolizes the grandmother's love and caring.

See pages 351, 382.

TALL TALE **An exaggerated, far-fetched story that is obviously untrue but is told as though it should be believed.** Almost all tall tales are humorous. "The Cremation of Sam McGee" (page 417) is a tall tale told in the form of a poem.

See page 416.
See also *Exaggeration, Folk Tale.*

THEME **The general idea or insight about life that a work of literature reveals.** A theme is not the same as a subject. The subject of a work can usually be expressed in a word or two: *love, childhood, death.* A theme is an idea or message that the writer wishes to convey *about* that subject. For example, one theme of "Camp Harmony" (page 319) might be stated as *Innocent people often suffer in times of conflict.* The same themes, such as *Good will triumph over evil,* often recur in works from different cultures and times.

"If you were to boil your book down to a few words, what would be its message?"

Drawing by Koren; © 1986 The New Yorker Magazine, Inc.

A work's themes (there may be more than one) are usually not stated directly. Most often the reader has to think about all the elements of the work and use them to make an **inference,** or educated guess, about what the themes are.

See pages 210–211, 212, 318, 507.

TONE **The attitude a writer takes toward his or her subject, characters, and audience.** For example, a writer's tone might be humorous, as in "Ode to a Toad" (page 439), or passionate and sincere, as in "I Have a Dream" (page 333). When people speak, their tone of voice gives added meaning to what they say. Writers use written language to create effects similar to those that people create with their voices.

See pages 151, 182.
See also *Connotation, Diction, Style.*

TRAGEDY **A play, novel, or other narrative in which the main character comes to an unhappy end.** A tragedy depicts serious and important events. Its hero achieves wisdom or self-knowledge but suffers a great deal—perhaps even dies. A tragic hero is usually dignified and courageous and often high ranking. The hero's downfall may be caused by a **tragic flaw** (a serious character weakness) or by external forces beyond his or her control. *The Diary of Anne Frank* and Shakespeare's *Hamlet* are tragedies.

See also *Comedy, Drama.*

UNDERSTATEMENT **A statement that says less than what is meant.** Understatement is the opposite of exaggeration. It is usually used for comic effect. If you were to say that the Grand Canyon is a nice little hole in the ground, you would be using understatement.

See also *Exaggeration, Literary Devices.*

Glossary

The glossary below is an alphabetical list of vocabulary words found in the selections in this book. Use this glossary just as you use a dictionary—to find out the meanings of unfamiliar words. (Some technical, foreign, and more obscure words in this book are not listed here but instead are defined for you in the footnotes that accompany many of the selections.)

Many words in the English language have more than one meaning. This glossary gives the meanings that apply to the words as they are used in the selections in this book. Words closely related in form and meaning are usually listed together in one entry (for instance, *compassion* and *compassionate*), and the definition is given for the first form.

The following abbreviations are used:

adj.	adjective
adv.	adverb
n.	noun
pl.	plural
v.	verb

Each word's pronunciation is given in parentheses. A guide to the pronunciation symbols appears at the bottom of this page. For more information about the words in this glossary or for information about words not listed here, consult a dictionary.

A

acute (ə·kyōōt′) *adj.*: sharp.
alleviate (ə·lē′vē·āt′) *v.*: relieve.
animation (an′i·mā′shen) *n.*: liveliness.
annihilation (ə·nī′ə·lā′shən) *n.*: complete destruction.
appall (ə·pôl′) *v.*: horrify. —**appalled** *v.* used as *adj.*
apparent (ə·per′ənt) *adj.*: visible.
audacity (ô·das′ə·tē) *n.*: boldness.

B

benign (bi·nīn′) *adj.*: kind.
breach (brēch) *n.*: opening.
brittle (brit″l) *adj.*: having a sharp, hard quality; ready to break.

C

cavort (kə·vôrt′) *v.*: leap about.
chagrin (shə·grin′) *n.*: embarrassment.
circuit (sʉr′kit) *n.*: regular route of a person doing a certain job.
clamorous (klam′ər·əs) *adj.*: loud and demanding.
cognitive (käg′nə·tiv) *adj.*: having to do with the process of knowing and being able to remember.
conspicuous (kən·spik′yōō·əs) *adj.*: noticeable.
contention (kən·ten′shen) *n.*: conflict.
creed (krēd) *n.*: statement of belief or principles.
crucial (krōō′shəl) *adj.*: highly important.

---

at, āte, cär; ten, ēve; is, īce; gō, hôrn, look, tōōl; oil, out; up, fʉr; ə *for unstressed vowels, as* a *in* ago, u *in* focus; ′ *as in* Latin (lat′'n); chin; she; zh *as in* azure (azh′ər); thin; *the*; ŋ *as in* ring (riŋ)

D

derision (de·rizh′ən) *n.:* ridicule.

detect (dē·tekt′) *v.:* discover; notice.

deterioration (dē·tir′ē·ə·rā′shən) *n.:* worsening; decline.

discord (dis′kôrd′) *n.:* conflict.

disgruntle (dis·grunt′′l) *v.:* displease, annoy. —**disgruntled** *v.* used as *adj.*

dispel (di·spel′) *v.:* scatter; drive away.

dispirit (di·spir′it) *v.:* make sad; discourage. —**dispirited** *v.* used as *adj.*

drone (drōn) *n.:* continuous buzzing sound.

E

eloquence (el′ə·kwəns) *n.:* ability to write or speak gracefully and convincingly.

emaciate (ē·mā′shē·āt) *v.:* make extremely thin, as from starvation or illness. —**emaciated** *v.* used as *adj.*

emerge (ē·mūrj′) *v.:* come out.

exaltation (eg′zôl·tā′shen) *n.:* great joy.

exalt (eg·zôlt′) *v.:* lift up.

exertion (eg·zʉr′shən) *n.:* hard work or effort.

exile (ek′sīl′) *n.:* living away from one's country or community. Exile is usually forced.

exotic (eg·zät′ik) *adj.:* foreign; strange in a fascinating way.

F

forlorn (fôr·lôrn′) *adj.:* abandoned and lonely.

fortify (fôrt′ə·fī′) *v.:* strengthen.

fugitive (fyo͞o′ji·tiv) *n.:* person fleeing danger.

G

gaunt (gônt) *adj.:* very thin and bony.

gesticulation (jes·tik′yo͞o·lā′shən) *n.:* energetic gesture.

gingerly (jin′jər′lē) *adv.:* cautiously.

grudge (gruj) *v.:* give reluctantly or unwilling. —**grudging** *v.* used as *adj.*

H

harass (har′əs) *v.:* trouble; bother. —**harrassed** *v.* used as *adj.*

host (hōst) *n.:* army.

hypothesis (hī·päth′ə·sis) *n.:* theory to be proved.

I

illiteracy (i·lit′ər·ə·sē) *n.:* inability to read or write.

impromptu (im·prämp′to͞o′) *adj.:* unplanned.

impulse (im′puls′) *n.:* urge.

inarticulate (in′är·tik′yo͞o·lit) *adj.:* unable to speak.

incentive (in·sent′iv) *n.:* reason to do something; motivation.

incomprehensible (in·käm′prē·hen′sə·bəl) *adj.:* impossible to understand.

indignant (in·dig′nənt) *adj.:* feeling anger because of something thought to be unjust. —**indignantly** *adv.*

indomitable (in·däm′i·tə·bəl) *adj.:* cannot be conquered.

inevitable (in·ev′i·tə·bəl) *adj.:* unavoidable.

inexplicable (in·eks′pli·kə·bəl) *adj.:* incapable of being explained.

infuse (in·fyo͞oz′) *v.:* fill.

instinctive (in·stiŋk′tiv) *adj.:* automatic. —**instinctively** *adv.*

intent (in·tent′) *adj.:* paying close attention. —**intently** *adv.*

intolerant (in·täl′ər·ənt) *adj.:* unwilling to put up with.

introspective (in′trə·spec′tiv) *adj.:* looking inward.

invariable (in·ver′ē·ə·bəl) *adj.:* not changing. —**invariably** *adv.*

irrevocable (i·rev′ə·kə·bəl) *adj.:* unable to be undone or changed. —**irrevocably** *adv.*

L

laborious (lə·bôr′ē·əs) *adj.:* hard; difficult.

laconic (lə·kän′ik) *adj.:* using few words. —**laconically** *adv.*

loathe (lō*th*) *v.:* hate.

M

mislead (mis·lēd′) *v.:* fool; lead to believe something that is incorrect.

O

oasis (ō·ā′sis) *n.:* place or thing offering relief.

oblivious (ə·bliv′ē·əs) *adj.:* unaware.

obscure (əb·skyoor′) *v.:* hide.

ominous (äm′ə·nəs) *adj.:* threatening.

ostentatious (äs′tən·tā′shəs) *adj.:* showy. —**ostentatiously** *adv.*

P

paranoia (par′ə·noi′ə) *n.:* mental disorder that causes people to feel unreasonable distrust and suspicion.

populate (päp′yə·lāt′) *v.:* live in. —**populated** *v.* used as *adj.*

premonition (prem′ə·nish′ən) *n.:* feeling that something bad will happen.

prodigious (prō·dij′əs) *adj.:* huge; amazing.

provocative (prə·väk′ə·tiv) *adj.:* stirring up thoughts or feelings.

R

raucous (rô′kəs) *adj.:* loud and rough.

reconciliation (rek′ən·sil′ē·ā′shən) *n.:* act of making up after arguments.

refrain (ri·frān′) *v.:* hold back.

refuge (ref′yoōj) *n.:* place of safety.

refute (ri·fyoot′) *v.:* prove wrong using evidence.

regression (ri·gresh′ən) *n.:* return to an earlier or less advanced condition.

remorse (ri·môrs′) *n.:* deep feeling of guilt.

rend (rend) *v.:* tear. —**rent**

retrieve (ri·trēv′) *v.:* get back.

rivet (riv′it) *v.:* fasten, hold firmly.

rummage (rum′ij) *v.:* search through the contents of a box, a drawer, and so on.

S

sagacity (sə·gas′ə·tē) *n.:* intelligence and good judgment.

savor (sā′vər) *v.:* enjoy with great delight.

skimpy (skim′pē) *adj.:* less than enough.

staff (staf) *n.:* pole.

steep (stēp) *v.:* fill with. —**steeped** *v.* used as *adj.*

stir (stʉr) *v.:* wake up.

suavity (swäv′ə·tē) *n.:* smooth manner.

sublime (sə·blīm′) *adj.:* majestic; grand.

sullen (sul′ən) *adj.:* grumpy; resentful.

T

tangible (tan′jə·bəl) *adj.:* seen and felt.

taut (tôt) *adj.:* tightly stretched.

tentative (ten′tə·tiv) *adj.:* uncertain or hesitant. —**tentatively** *adv.*

terse (tʉrs) *adj.:* brief and clear. —**tersely** *adv.*

tread (tred) *n.:* step.

tremulous (trem′yoō·ləs) *adj.:* trembling.

tyranny (tir′ə·nē) *n.:* cruel and unjust use of power.

U

unabashed (un′ə·basht′) *adj.:* unembarrassed.

V

vehement (vē′ə·mənt) *adj.:* forceful. —**vehemently** *adv.*

verify (ver′ə·fī′) *v.:* confirm.

vex (veks) *v.:* disturb.

vigil (vij′əl) *n.:* watch.

W

wary (wer′ē) *adj.:* cautious.

Z

zeal (zēl) *n.:* great enthusiasm; devotion to a cause.

Acknowledgments

For permission to reprint copyrighted material, grateful acknowledgment is made to the following sources:

Agencia Literaria Carmen Balcells on behalf of Fundación Pablo Neruda: From "Oda a las gracias" from *Odas Elementales* by Pablo Neruda. Copyright © 1954, 1995 by Pablo Neruda and Fundación Pablo Neruda.

American Library Association: From "Starred Reviews: Books for Youth: *Parallel Journeys* by Eleanor H. Ayers" by Hazel Rochman from *Booklist,* vol. 91, no. 18, May 15, 1995. Copyright © 1995 by American Library Association.

The Associated Press: "Memory a Matter of Brains and Brawn" by Lauran Neergaard from *San Francisco Chronicle,* July 25, 2000. Copyright © 2000 by The Associated Press.

Susan Bergholz Literary Services, New York: From "Redwing Sonnets" from *Homecoming: New and Collected Poems* by Julia Alvarez. Copyright © 1984, 1996 by Julia Alvarez. Published by Plume, an imprint of Dutton Signet, a division of Penguin USA; originally published by Grove Press. Autobiographical comment by Sandra Cisneros. Copyright © 1987 by Sandra Cisneros. First published in *The Texas Observer,* September 1987. All rights reserved. "A Smart Cookie" and "Gil's Furniture Bought and Sold" from *The House on Mango Street* by Sandra Cisneros. Copyright © 1984 by Sandra Cisneros. Published by Vintage Books, a division of Random House, Inc., and in hardcover by Alfred A. Knopf in 1994. All rights reserved. "Bien águila" from *La casa en Mango Street* by Sandra Cisneros, translated by Elena Poniatowska. Copyright © 1984 by Sandra Cisneros; translation copyright © 1994 by Elena Poniatowska. Published by Vintage Español, a division of Random House, Inc. All rights reserved.

Boa Editions, Ltd: "Valentine for Ernest Mann" from *Red Suitcase* by Naomi Shihab Nye. Copyright © 1994 by Naomi Shihab Nye.

Curtis Brown Agency: "The Panther" from *Verses from 1929 On* by Ogden Nash. Copyright © 1933, 1936, 1940, 1942, 1950 by Ogden Nash; copyright renewed © 1977 by Frances Nash, Isabel Nash Eberstadt, and Linnell Nash Smith. "The Panther" first appeared in *The Saturday Evening Post.*

Diana Chang: "Saying Yes" by Diana Chang. Copyright © 2000 by Diana Chang.

Chronicle Books: "Oranges" from *New and Selected Poems* by Gary Soto. Copyright © 1995 by Gary Soto.

Jennifer Sibley Clement: "The Word" by Manuel Ulacia, translated by Jennifer Clement. Translation copyright © 1995 by Jennifer Clement.

Cobblestone Publishing Company, 30 Grove Street, Suite C, Peterborough, NH 03458: From "Word Stories: Brazil" from "Fun With Words" from *Calliope: 1494: Portugal and Spain Divide the World,* vol. 8, no. 8, April 1998. Copyright © 1998 by Cobblestone Publishing Company. "Secrets of the Mummies" by Kathiann M. Kowalski from *Odyssey: Tales from the Crypt,* October 1998. Copyright © 1998 by Cobblestone Publishing Company. All rights reserved.

Dennis Coello and Boy's Life magazine: From "Fix a Flat" by Dennis Coello from *Boy's Life,* April 2000. Copyright © 2000 by Dennis Coello. Published by the Boy Scouts of America.

Don Congdon Associates, Inc.: From "Drunk, and in Charge of a Bicycle" from *The Stories of Ray Bradbury.* Copyright © 1980 by Ray Bradbury. "There Will Come Soft Rains" by Ray Bradbury. Copyright © 1950 by the Crowell-Collier Publishing Co.; copyright renewed © 1977 by Ray Bradbury. From "Ray Bradbury," an interview by Frank Filosa from *On Being a Writer,* edited by Bill Strickland. Copyright © 1967 by Frank Filosa.

Doubleday, a division of Random House, Inc.: From "Salvation Is the Issue" by Toni Cade Bambara from *Black Women Writers (1950–1980),* edited by Mari Evans. Copyright © 1984 by Mari Evans. From *Anne Frank: The Diary of a Young Girl, the Definitive Edition* by Anne Frank, edited by Otto H. Frank and Mirjam Pressler. Copyright © 1995 by Doubleday, a division of Bantam Doubleday Dell Publishing Group, Inc. From *The Cay* by Theodore Taylor. Copyright © 1969 by Theodore Taylor.

Dutton Signet, a division of Penguin Putnam Inc.: From *Beowulf,* translated by Burton Raffel. Translation copyright © 1963 by Burton Raffel; afterword copyright © 1963 by New American Library.

Mary Jennifer Ellison, Webb School of Knoxville, Knoxville, Tennessee: "Maiden-Savin' Sam" (ballad) by Jenny Ellison from *Webb of Words, 1992–93.* Copyright © 1992 by Mary Jennifer Ellison. Published by the students of the Middle School of Webb School of Knoxville, TN.

Farrar, Straus & Giroux, LLC: "The Puppy" from *Stories and Prose Poems* by Alexander Solzhenitsyn, translated by Michael Glenny. Translation copyright © 1971 by Michael Glenny.

Alberto Forcada: "Suéter" from *Despertar* by Alberto Forcada. Copyright © 1992 by Alberto Forcada. Published by Centro de Información y Desarrollo de la Comunicación y la Literatura Infantiles (CIDCLI).

The Gale Group: From "Walter Dean Myers" from *Something About the Author,* vol. 41, edited by Anne Commire. Copyright © 1985 by Gale Research Company Inc. From "Gary Paulsen" from *Something About the Author,* vol. 54, edited by Anne Commire. Copyright © 1989 by Gale Research Company Inc. From "Ann Petry" from *Contemporary Authors: Autobiography Series,* vol. 6, edited by Adele Sarkissian. Copyright © 1988 by Gale Research Company Inc.

Marcia Ann Gillespie: From "Maya Angelou," an interview by Marcia Ann Gillespie from *Essence,* December 1992. Copyright © 1992 by Marcia Ann Gillespie.

GRM Associates, Inc., for The Estate of Ida Cullen: "For My Grandmother" from *Color* by Countee Cullen. Copyright © 1925 by Harper & Brothers; copyright renewed © 1953 by Ida M. Cullen.

Judith Gorog: "Those Three Wishes" from *A Taste for Quiet and Other Disquieting Tales* by Judith Gorog. Copyright © 1982 by Judith Gorog.

Harcourt Inc.: "Broken Chain" from *Baseball in April and Other Stories* by Gary Soto. Copyright © 1990 by Gary Soto.

HarperCollins Publishers: From *No Pretty Pictures: A Child of War* by Anita Lobel. Copyright © 1998 by Anita Lobel. From "In Her Own Words" by Naomi Shihab Nye from HarperChildrens' Web site accessed on October 5, 2000 at http://www.harperchildrens.com/hech/authorpage/index .asp?authorID=15255. Copyright © 2000 by Naomi Shihab Nye.

Harvard University Press and the Trustees of Amherst College: "Fame is a bee" and "A word is dead" from *The Poems of Emily Dickinson*, edited by Thomas H. Johnson. Copyright © 1951, 1955, 1979 by the President and Fellows of Harvard College. Published by The Belknap Press of Harvard University Press, Cambridge, MA.

Hill and Wang, a division of Farrar, Straus and Giroux, LLC: From "I've Known Rivers" from *The Big Sea* by Langston Hughes. © 1940 by Langston Hughes; copyright renewed © 1968 by Arna Bontemps and George Houston Bass.

Judith Infante: "Sweater" by Alberto Forcada, translated by Judith Infante. Copyright © 1995 by Judith Infante.

Francisco Jiménez: Comment on "The Circuit" by Francisco Jiménez. Copyright © 1997 by Francisco Jiménez.

Daniel Keyes: "Flowers for Algernon" (short story version) by Daniel Keyes from *The Magazine of Fantasy & Science Fiction*. Copyright © 1959, 1987 by Daniel Keyes. Book-length paperback version published by Bantam Books. Companion book, *Algernon, Charlie and I: A Writer's Journey*, published by Challenge Press, Challcrest Books, Boca Raton, FL. Quote by Daniel Keyes.

The Heirs to the Estate of Martin Luther King, Jr., c/o Writers House, Inc. as agent for the proprietor: "I Have a Dream" by Martin Luther King, Jr. Copyright © 1963 by Martin Luther King, Jr.; copyright renewed © 1991 by Coretta Scott King.

Alfred A. Knopf, Inc.: "The Landlady" from *Kiss, Kiss* by Roald Dahl. Copyright © 1959 by Roald Dahl. From "Lucky Break" from *The Wonderful Story of Henry Sugar and Six More* by Roald Dahl. Copyright © 1945, 1947, 1952, 1977 by Roald Dahl. From "Along the Colorado" from *The Secret Worlds of Colin Fletcher* by Colin Fletcher. Copyright © 1989 by Colin Fletcher. "I, Too" from *The Collected Poems of Langston Hughes*. Copyright © 1994 by the Estate of Langston Hughes.

Barbara S. Kouts on behalf of Joseph Bruchac: "Birdfoot's Grampa" by Joseph Bruchac. Copyright © 1978 by Joseph Bruchac.

Little, Brown and Company: "Ode to Thanks" from *Odes to Opposites* by Pablo Neruda. Copyright © 1995 by Pablo Neruda and Fundacion Pablo Neruda; English translation copyright © 1995 by Ken Krabbenhoft.

Liveright Publishing Corporation: "who are you,little i" from *Complete Poems: 1904–1962* by E. E. Cummings, edited by George J. Firmage. Copyright © 1963, 1991 by the Trustees for the E. E. Cummings Trust.

McIntosh and Otis, Inc.: "Too Soon a Woman" by Dorothy M. Johnson from *Cosmopolitan*, March 1953. Copyright © 1953 and renewed © 1981 by Dorothy M. Johnson.

Merlyn's Pen, Inc.: "Walking with Living Feet" by Dara Horn from *Merlyn's Pen*, October–November 1993. Copyright © 1993 by Merlyn's Pen, Inc. First appeared in *Merlyn's Pen: The National Magazines of Student Writing*. All rights reserved. "Ode to a Toad" by Anne-Marie Wulfsberg from *Merlyn's Pen*, April–May 1991. Copyright © 1991 by Anne-Marie Wulfsberg. First appeared in *Merlyn's Pen: The National Magazines of Student Writing*. All rights reserved.

Walter Dean Myers: "The Treasure of Lemon Brown" by Walter Dean Myers from *Face to Face: A Collection of Stories by Celebrated Soviet and American Writers,* edited by Thomas Pettepiece and Anatoly Aleksin. Copyright © 1990 by Walter Dean Myers. From "Walter Dean Myers" by Walter Dean Myers from *Speaking for Ourselves*, edited by Donald R. Gallo. Copyright © 1990 by Walter Dean Myers.

National Council of Teachers of English: From "Bear in the Family" by Ben Mikaelsen from *Voices from the Middle,* vol. 5, no. 2, April 1998. Copyright © 1998 by Ben Mikaelsen.

National Geographic Society: From "Destination Mars" from *National Geographic World,* January 2000. Copyright © 2000 by National Geographic Society.

NEA Today: From "Making Intellect Cool," an interview with Walter Dean Myers by Nancy Needham from *NEA Today,* December 1991. Published by the National Education Association.

Dwight Okita: "In Response to Executive Order 9066" from *Crossing with the Light* by Dwight Okita. Copyright © 1992 by Dwight Okita. Published by Tia Chucha Press, Chicago.

Teresa Palomo Acosta: "My Mother Pieced Quilts" by Teresa Palomo Acosta from *Festival de Flor y Canto: An Anthology of Chicano Literature,* edited by Alurista et al. Copyright © 1976 by El Centro Chicano, University of Southern California.

Random House Children's Books, a division of Random House, Inc.: From *Green Eggs and Ham* by Dr. Seuss. TM and copyright © 1960 and renewed © 1988 by Dr. Seuss Enterprises, L.P. From "The Dog and His Shadow" from *Aesop's Fables,* retold by Anne Terry White. Copyright © 1964 by Anne Terry White.

Random House, Inc.: Excerpts (retitled "Mrs. Flowers") from *I Know Why the Caged Bird Sings* by Maya Angelou. Copyright © 1969 and renewed © 1997 by Maya Angelou. "Raymond's Run" and "A Sort of Preface" from *Gorilla, My Love* by Toni Cade Bambara. Copyright © 1971 by Toni Cade Bambara. *The Diary of Anne Frank* by Albert Hackett and Frances Goodrich Hackett. Copyright © 1954, 1956 as an unpublished work by Albert Hackett and Frances Goodrich Hackett.

Marian Reiner: "Growing Up" from *The Little Hill: Poems and Pictures* by Harry Behn. Copyright © 1949 by Harry Behn; copyright renewed © 1977 by Alice L. Behn.

Russell & Volkening as agents for Ann Petry: "Go On or Die" and "The Railroad Runs to Canada" from *Harriet Tubman: Conductor on the Underground Railroad* by Ann Petry. Copyright © 1955 and renewed © 1983 by Ann Petry.

School Library Journal: From a book review of Katherine Paterson's *Lyddie* in *School Library Journal,* vol. 37, no. 2, February 1991. Copyright © 1991 by Cahners Business Information, a division of Reed Elsevier Inc.

Estate of Robert Service: From *Ploughman of the Moon* by Robert Service.

Charol Shakeshaft: From "Should Public School Students Wear Uniforms?" by Charol Shakeshaft from *Newsday,* March 10, 1996, page A 45. Copyright © 1996 by Charol Shakeshaft.

Simon & Schuster Books for Young Readers, an imprint of Simon & Schuster Children's Publishing Division: Excerpt (retitled "In Trouble") from *Woodsong* by Gary Paulsen. Copyright © 1990 by Gary Paulsen.

Monica Sone: Comment on "Camp Harmony" by Monica Sone. Copyright © 1997 by Monica Sone.

Sources Cited

From "The Mysteries of the Watery Depths" from *Young Readers Edition: The Sea* by Leonard Engel and the Editors of Time-Life Books. Published by Time-Life Books, Alexandria, VA, 1967.

From "Black Hole" by Jeffrey E. McClintock from *The World Book Multimedia Encyclopedia*™. Published by World Book, Inc., Chicago, IL, 1995.

Picture Credits

The illustrations and/or photographs on the Contents pages are picked up from pages in the textbook. Credits for those can be found either on the textook page on which they appear or in the listing below.

Illustrations

Index of Skills

The boldface page numbers indicate an extensive treatment of the topic.

LITERARY RESPONSE AND ANALYSIS (INCLUDING READING SKILLS AND STRATEGIES)

Guess, **196**
  educated, 785
Hasty generalization, **363**, 365, 800
Illustration, **177**
Inference, 68, 70, **86**, 89, 90, 91, 94,
    98, 110, 175, **182**, 184, 185, 186,
    187, **196**, 198, 202, 243, 289, 355,
    378, 387, 800–801, 826
  supported, **378**, 381, 800–801
  unsupported, **378**, 381, 801
Informative texts, 801–802
  question sheet for, 802
Instruction
  on Internet, 547
  in workplace documents, 528
Instructional manual, **529, 530,**
    543–544, 547
  elements of, 544
  features of, 544
  purpose of, 544
Internal consistency, **502**, 505, 521
Internet, 555
  advertisements on, **546–548**
  downloading, instructions for, 549
Key passages, **293**
Key statements, **293**
Legend, 804
Licenses, software user's agreement
    and, 548
Limited scope, 122
Loaded words, 127
Logic, 363, **502–503**, 505, 803
Logical order, **484**, 487, 803
Logical text, 803
Magazines, 177, 803–804
  advertisement, 804
  caption, 177
  cover, **177, 804**
  illustration, **177, 804**
  sidebar, **177**, 181
  subtitle, **177**, 181
  table of contents, **177**, 804
  title, **177**
Main characters, 434
Main events, 434
Main idea, 79, **129**, 135, 141, 143,
    292, **293**, 310, **312**, 316, **338**, 341,
    455, 459, 461, 487, 521, 804,
    805–806, 807
Main point, 127
Maps, 212, 804–805
  for words, 60
Master the questions, 784
Meaning, 210, 805
Memorandum, 532
Name-calling, **363**, 799
Newspaper article, 533
Note cards, **338**
Note taking, **338**, 805–806
  details and, **338**
  main ideas and, **338**, 806
  note cards for, **338**
  tips for, 806
Objective treatment, 122
Opinion, **57**, 77, 292, 327, 806
  expert, 57, 59
  valid, 806
Order of events, 434, 455

Order of importance, **484**, 502, 806,
    809
Organizational patterns, 806
  cause and effect, **100, 191**, 194,
    434, 484, 796, 806
  chronological order, **100**, 310, **484,
    502**, 796, 806
  compare-and-contrast, **100**, 163,
    286, **290**, 797, 806
  enumeration, **100**, 798, 806
  problem-solution, 806
  question-answer, 806
Organizing ideas, **100**, 103
Outline, **338**, 341, 487, 807
  formal, **338**, 807
  informal, **338**, 807
Paraphrasing, 805, 807–808
Persuasion, 804, 821
Plagiarism, 805
Point-by-point pattern of
    organization, **290**, 797
Points of comparison, 797
Previewing the test, 784
Problem, 434
  solving, **531**
Product information, **529**, 541
  advertisement, 541
Propositions, **19**, 21, **57**, 59, 77, 804
Public documents, **528**, 531, 536, 802
  agency report, 534–535
  newspaper article, 533
  Web site, 536, 538
Purpose, 21, 77, 127, 310, 316,
    808–809
  of informational texts, 808
  of instructional manuals, 544
Questioning, **470**, 808
Quotation marks, 457, 461
Quotations by experts, 804
Reading carefully, 137
Reading comprehension test, 786–790
Reading comprehension (Reading
    Check), 21, 59, 103, 127, 165,
    181, 194, 198, 292, 316, 341, 381,
    436, 457, 487, 505, 539, 549, 556
Reading comprehension (Test
    Practice), 21, 59, 76–77, 103, 127,
    142–143, 165, 181, 194, 198, 292,
    316, 341, 365, 381, 436, 457,
    460–461, 487, 505, 520–521, 539,
    549, 556
Reading for information, **528,
    576–577**, 801–802
Reasoning, fallacious, **363**
Reasons, 19, 57
Rely on 50/50, 785
Resolution, 434
Scope of ideas, **122**
  broad, 122
  limited, 122
Search for skips and smudges, 785
Service agreement, 542
Sidebar, **177**, 181
Similarities, 127
Software user's agreement, 545, **548**
  license, 548
  title, 548
  use, 548

Spatial connections, 502
Spatial order, 502, 809
Speeches, 142
Spot those numbers, 784
Statistics (number facts), 57, 363, 804
Stereotyping, **363**, 799, 825
Strategies for taking a multiple-
    choice test, 783–785
Structural patterns, **484**, 809
  cause-and-effect relationships, 484,
    809
  chronological order, **484**, 809
  comparison and contrast, 809
  logical order, **484**, 487
  order of importance, **484**, 809
Study the directions, 784
Subjects, 143
Subtitles, in magazines, **177**, 181
Summary, 327, **434, 455**, 461,
    809–810
  author, 434, 455
  cause-and-effect relationships, 434
  checklist for, 434, 455
  conflict, 434
  critical details, **434**, 436, 457, 461,
    810
  main characters, 434
  main events, 434
  main ideas and, 455, 461
  note taking and, 805
  order of events, 434, 455
  problems and, 434
  quotation marks, 457
  resolution, 434
  supporting details, 455
  theme, 434, 436
  title, 434, 455
  topic, 455
  underlying meanings and, 436, 461
Support, **19, 57**, 77
  anecdotes as, 57
  definitions as, 57
  details as, 455, 807–808
  examples as, 19, 57
  facts as, **57**
  opinions from experts as, 57
  reasons, 19, 57
  statistics as, 57
Supported inferences, **378**, 381,
    800–801
Symbol, 316. *See also* Literary
    Response and Analysis: Symbol.
Table of contents, in magazines, **177**,
    803
Take it all in, 784
Taking notes. *See* Note taking.
Technical directions, **529, 530, 550**
  for basic functions, 550
  for central processing unit, 551
  for computer, **550–555**
  following, 550
  for hardware, 551–552
  for input devices, 551
  for internal modems, 555
  for Internet, 553
  for memory, 552
  for modem, 552
  for monitor interface cable, 554

of inquiry, 741, **743**
inside address in, 557, 742
for job application, **741–742, 743**
purpose of, 743
salutations in, 557, 742
signature on, 557, 742
as thank-you, **742, 743**
variables in, 743
writer's model of, 746
Bylaws, 205, **776–777**
Characters, 616
analysis of, 119
compare and contrast, 284
evaluation of, 145
evaluation of changes in, 145
evaluation of motivation in, 145
evaluation of problem in, 145
evaluation of resolution in, 145
in fables, 771, 772
word as, 392
Charts, creation of, **778–779**
Children's story, 392, 500
Chronological order
in paragraphs, 760
in personal narrative, 594
in technical documents, 649, 652
transitional words and phrases
and, 761
Clarity
in graphics, 661
in memos, 748–749
in persuasive essays, 711
Class poll or survey, 22, 129, 353
Clincher sentences, in paragraphs,
755
Coherence
in business letter, **744–745**
and drafting, 582
in paragraphs, **760**
in personal narrative, 594
in persuasive essay, 711
in research report, **684**
in review of a novel, 621, 622, 624
in technical document, 652
Colors
cool, 735
in persuasive images, 734, 735
warm, 735
Common mistakes, in technical
documents, 652
Comparing two childhoods, 482
Comparison and contrast
of characters, 284
of personal experiences, 345
of texts, 135
Comparisons
in response to a poem, 774
as supporting evidence, 620, **715,**
758
Computer-generated art, in
persuasive images, 736
Computer networks and databases,
in prewriting, 582
Conclusion
of descriptive essay, 770
drafting, 583
drawing, **617–618**
paragraphs of, **764**

of personal narrative, 596
of persuasive essay, 718
of research report, 686
of response to a poem, 775
of review of a novel, 624
support for, 619
of technical document, 649, 652
Conflict, in fables, 771
Consistency, of point of view, 593,
599, 711, 721, **759**
Content, of persuasive images, 734
Controlling impression, 583–584
in descriptive essay, **769**
in personal narrative, **595**
in persuasive essay, 716
Counterargument, **714, 716,** 721
Definitions, in technical document,
652
Delayed subject, 724
Description, 161, 619
Descriptive essay, 70, 161, 397, 523,
768–770
writer's model of, 769–770
Descriptive paragraphs, 763
Descriptive writing
factual details and, 397
figures of speech and, 397
sensory details and, 152, 161, 387,
397, 450, 454
Designing your writing. *See* Formatting, Word-processing/desktop-
publishing skills.
Details
action, **772**
of actions, 619
of descriptions, 619
in descriptive essays, **768**
of dialogue, 619
in fables, 772
facts as, 397
irrelevant, 595
in personal narrative, 593–594, 596
relevant, 595
sensory, 397, 596
in technical document, 647
Dialogue, 595
in personal narrative, 596
punctuation of, 602
Diary entry, 54, 145
Direct quotations, 679, 686
Dramatic readings, 110
Drawing conclusions, **617–618**
Editor in Charge: Content and
Organization
for personal narrative, 599
for persuasive essay, 721
for research report, 691
for review of a novel, 627
for technical document, 655
See also Organization.
Editor in Charge: Style
for personal narrative, 600
for persuasive essay, 722
for research report, 692
for review of a novel, 628
for technical document, 656
Elaboration
and drafting, 582

in personal narrative, 596
in technical document, 652
Elegy poems, 449
Ending, writing an, 70
Essay
descriptive, 161, 482, 523, **768–770**
persuasive, 79, 523
Essential clauses, 630
Eulogy, 336, 449
Evaluation
of graphics, 661–662
in persuasive essay, **712–716**
of persuasive images, 738
of review of a novel, **615–616**
of sources, **675–677**
of style, 361
and writing process, 583
See also Editor in Charge: Content
and Organization, Editor in
Charge: Style.
Evidence
analogies as, 620, 686, 715
anecdotes as, **714**
comparisons as, 620, **715**
direct quotations as, 686
elaboration of, **714**
examples as, 686, **714**
expert opinions as, 686, **715**
facts as, 686, **714**
opinions as, 620
paraphrases of, 686
in research report, 686
statistics as, **714**
supporting, **619–620,** 686, **714**
See also Details, Support.
Exaggeration, 425
Examples
as evidence, 686, 714
as support, 757
Expert opinions, 679
as evidence, 686, 715
as support, 758
Explanation, of labor-saving device,
175
Expository essay, 793
Expository paragraphs, 763
Expository writing, technical
documents as, 643. *See also*
Research report, Response to
literature, Review of a novel.
Fable, 771–772
professional model of, 771
Factors, in technical document,
647
Facts
versus opinions, **714**
as supporting evidence, 686, 714,
757
False impression, in personal
narrative, 376
Fiction, elements of, 616
Fictional narratives. *See* Fable.
Figures of speech, 397
in descriptive essay, **768**
metaphors, **768**
personification, **768**
similes, **768**
Final statements, 686

INDEPENDENT READING

Index of Authors and Titles